AF576545

A Gallery of Modern Art at Washington University in St. Louis

A Gallery of Modern Art

at Washington University
in St. Louis

Joseph D. Ketner
Director

Jane E. Neidhardt
Editor

With essays by contributing authors

The publication of this catalog was made possible by the generous assistance of the National Endowment for the Arts and the Institute of Museum Services, federal agencies. In addition, the Hortense Lewin Art Fund, the James Yeatman Fund, the Charles Parsons Fund, the Feldman Art Fund, and the St. Louis Printmarket Fund of Washington University provided matching funds for the publication.

Editor: Jane E. Neidhardt
Designer: Nathan Garland, New Haven, Connecticut
Printer: Amilcare Pizzi, S.p.A., Milan, Italy

ISBN: 0-936316-16-0
Library of Congress Catalog Card Number: 93-60307

Contents

Chancellor's Statement

I should like to express my deepest gratitude to those who have donated works of art, contributed time and resources to the Gallery of Art, and combined their efforts for nearly 150 years in support of the arts at Washington University. The legacy of their contributions has made possible one of the finest university art collections in the United States.

The visual arts are important to Washington University and our academic mission. We offer degree programs in Architecture and Fine Arts and maintain a department of Art History and Archaeology within the Faculty of Arts and Sciences. By preserving and exhibiting the cultural heritage of many peoples, the art collections serve these departments and the larger community by challenging the viewer to examine and understand cultural history. Through the University art collections we encourage appreciation for and understanding of the visual arts.

William H. Danforth
Chancellor

Foreword

In its second century of collecting art, Washington University has assembled one of the finest university art collections in the United States. Unfortunately, only a limited audience beyond the privileged circles of scholars and the art community is aware of the outstanding collection and collecting tradition at the University. The Washington University Gallery of Art is committed to its mission to share the University's artworks with the academic community and the broader public. *A Gallery of Modern Art* realizes this mission by introducing the University's distinguished collection to a larger audience. This is the first publication to survey the achievements of nearly 150 years of collecting art at Washington University, focusing on 85 of Washington University's finest artworks with interpretive essays by 53 leading scholars.

The "treasures" format of this publication is a time-honored forum for presenting an institution's "masterpieces." But it is a weary format that reflects an outmoded art historical methodology, emphasizing an individual's artistic achievement outside of the historical and cultural context. This publication is more than simply a "treasures" book; it serves as a useful tool fulfilling several important functions. *A Gallery of Modern Art* not only features some of the University's "masterpieces," it also provides the scholarly foundation for future collection interpretation. In addition, this publication relates the history of collecting and patronage in the St. Louis region.

The artworks highlighted in this publication reflect the artistic tastes of the cultural and civic leaders (until recently almost exclusively men) of this midwestern art community who, over the past two centuries, have molded and shaped the Washington University art collections. By outlining the collecting tastes and patronage in this region, these artworks illuminate the dominant culture's artistic history. It is through these artworks that our audience can better understand their cultural heritage and the changing generational conceptions of art, culture, and education. Furthermore, these 85 artworks epitomize Washington University's consistent approach to collecting the art of its time. Beginning with its founders, Washington University's administrators, directors, and curators over the past two centuries have demonstrated a commitment to acquiring contemporary art, exercising their remarkable prescience that has resulted in an excellent art collection.

The artworks selected for this publication represent my curatorial choices, with all of its inherent biases, and offer only a glimpse of the larger University art collections. I decided to focus on the primary concentrations and strengths of the University collection—nineteenth- and twentieth-century European and American paintings and sculpture—in order to narrow the scope of this project. Additional important collections maintained by the University include the tremendous John Max Wulfing Numismatics collection, Egyptian, Greek, and Roman antiquities, and the comprehensive print collection, each of which merits a publication in its own right.

The 85 artworks in this book represent acquisitions made by the University and its benefactors from the 1850s through the 1980s. In the mid-1980s the Gallery of Art initiated an ambitious acquisition program, reviving the century-old tradition of acquiring modern art. These acquisitions have introduced the art of the 1980s to the University collection, including conceptual art and post-modern works that deal with social, ecological, ethnic, and gender issues. However, to avoid the self-indulgence of preserving in print the current administration's acquisitions, I leave these artworks for posterity to judge.

A Gallery of Modern Art builds upon over a century of research and publications on various sections of the collection, principally for exhibition catalogs. The scholarship of many directors, curators, faculty, and students has culminated in this project; I am indebted to these people for their work. Yet, no publication in the history of the University has focused on a scholarly assessment of the University's most important artworks as the foundation for understanding and appreciating the collections. For this publication I invited 53 of the leading authorities in their fields to research and interpret the artworks in relation to their inherent significance—aesthetic quality, historical importance, or rarity—and to place them in the context of the artist's oeuvre and artistic milieu. I extend my sincere appreciation to the authors for their conscientious efforts, insightful contributions, and dedication to this project.

I appreciate the contributions of each Gallery staff member toward the realization of this publication. Especially, Jane E. Neidhardt, Administrative Assistant, handled the daunting task of meticulously editing the manuscripts for the book. I credit the consistency and quality of the text to her considerable editorial skills. Gallery registrar, Marie Nordmann, and her student assistants Ken Stuckenschneider and Margarita Tschomakoff, compiled the archival documentary information on the artworks for the authors. Instrumental to the project and the Gallery's educational mission was a team of bright and talented student interns and assistants who managed correspondence, conducted research, and computerized the essays. These included John Butler-Ludwig, Esther H. Chao, Cynthia Green, Emily Gutheinz, Elizabeth Kerr, and Anna Vemer.

The design of this publication testifies to the creative abilities of Nathan Garland. Nathan, B.F.A. School of Fine Arts 1967, enthusiastically responded to my proposal to design a catalog of the collection that nurtured his artistic sensibilities during his undergraduate days at Washington University. The high quality of the photography in this publication was principally the work of Robert Kolbrener.

Over the course of the University art museum's history literally hundreds of munificent patrons have donated artworks to the collections; it is not possible to mention all of them in this text. Their contributions to the cultural history of the University and the St. Louis region are significant and are acknowledged in the addendum at the conclusion of this publication.

The production of this publication would not have been possible without the generous sponsorship of granting agencies and individuals. The Institute of Museum Services, a federal agency, funded a significant portion of the research and essays by the scholarly consultants to the project. Printing was funded, in part, by a grant from the National Endowment for the Arts. A number of munificent St. Louisans and friends of the Gallery over the past century contributed to this publication through funds established at Washington University: the Ronald and Frayda Feldman Art Fund, the Hortense Lewin Art Fund, the Charles Parsons Fund, the St. Louis Printmarket Fund, and the James E. Yeatman Fund.

In its selection, creation, and sponsorship, *A Gallery of Modern Art* reflects the mission of the University museum and the vision of its benefactors, directors, and public. I offer this publication to these individuals, institutions, and the Gallery's audience for their education and enjoyment.

Joseph D. Ketner, Director
Washington University Gallery of Art

Fig. 1. Anonymous
The Museum of Fine Arts, St. Louis, Missouri, 1881
Wood engraving, 7¾ x 10¾"
Published in *Harper's Weekly* (June 25, 1881): 414
Washington University Gallery of Art, St. Louis
Gift of Gerald D. Bolas, 1986

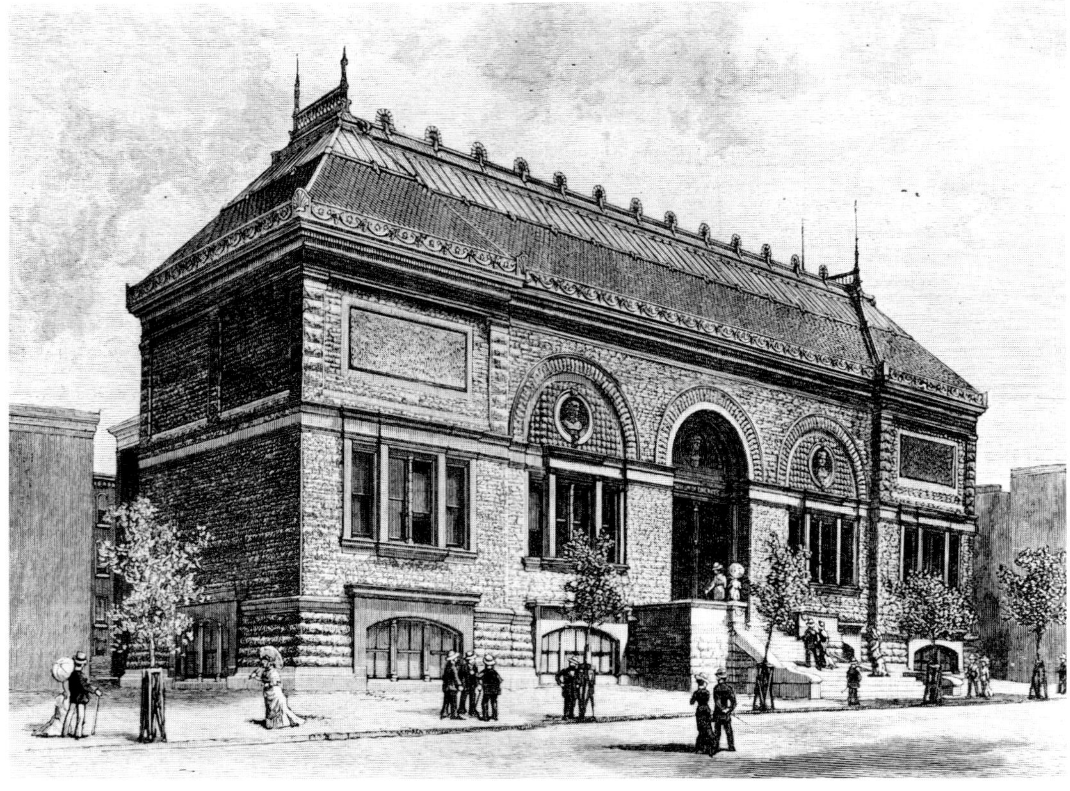

Fig. 2. Entrance hall of the St. Louis School and Museum of Fine Arts with Harriet Hosmer's *Oenone* (c. 1854–55) in 1881.
Archives of The Saint Louis Art Museum

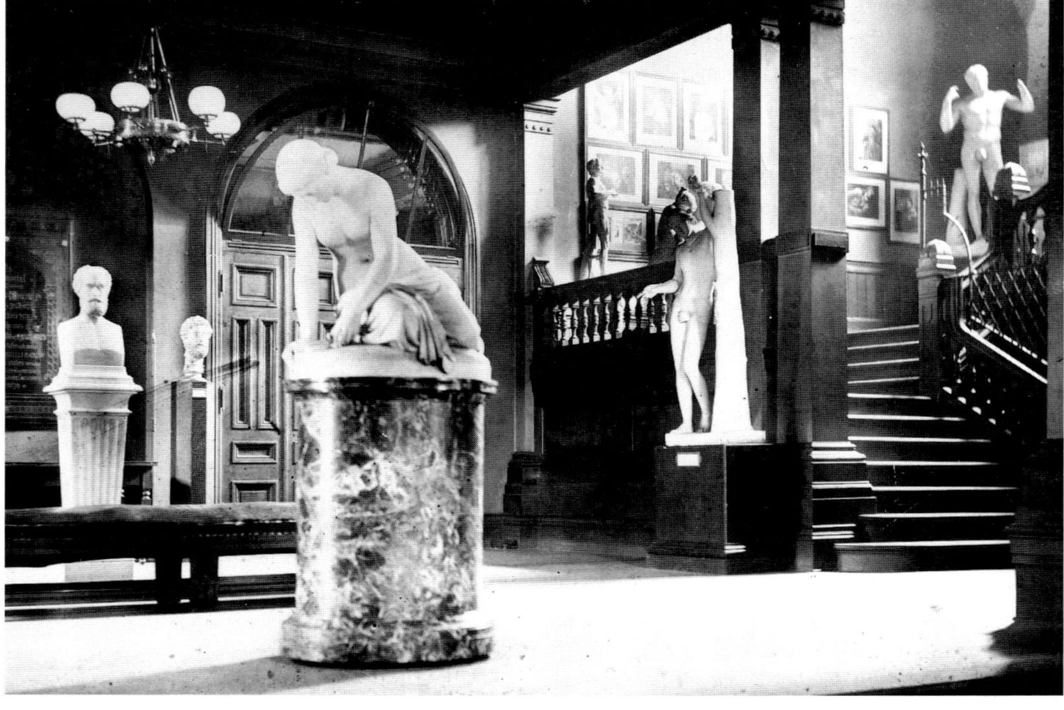

A Gallery of Modern Art at Washington University in St. Louis

At the inauguration of Washington University's "new gallery of modern art" in 1946, curator Horst W. Janson unveiled his purchases and proudly announced the "finest collection of contemporary art assembled on any American campus." During the previous year, Janson had acquired 38 artworks that embodied his conception of modern art, introducing twentieth-century artistic trends to the central United States. Janson believed that his "duty" as an art educator was to fulfill his role of "intellectual leadership" in assembling an art collection that would serve the educational needs of both the academic and regional communities. Despite the fact that the University Chancellor, Nobel Prize-winning physicist Arthur Holly Compton, confessed in his opening remarks that he could not understand modern art, Janson believed that his acquisitions "represent a new and important step in the growth of the Washington University Art Collection."[1]

Indeed, Janson's bold statement on modern art did "represent a new and important step" introducing the advances of Cubism, German Expressionism, and Surrealism to this region and helping to motivate a generation of collectors and collections. From an historical perspective, Janson's seminal acquisitions marked a climactic mid-point in the evolution of Washington University's art collections. Nevertheless, his desire "to reshape [the art collection's] character . . . in accordance with the educational needs of today" conformed to the University's educational mission and collecting tradition from its founding in 1853, through the establishment of its first museum in 1881, and continuing beyond the rededication of the University museum as the Gallery of Art in 1960.[2] The curatorial vision to acquire and exhibit the art of the time characterizes the nearly 150 years of collecting art at Washington University.

In the first decades after the State of Missouri chartered the Eliot Seminary (later Washington University) in 1853, the University's founders actively patronized living artists whose work realized the University's educational mission. For example, Wayman Crow (fig. 3), author of Washington University's charter, founding board member, and benefactor, sponsored the neoclassical sculptor Harriet Hosmer. As a token of her appreciation the sculptor offered Crow, as a "love gift," her first original marble from Rome, *Daphne* (1854). Crow enthusiastically responded by commissioning Hosmer's first monumental marble, *Oenone* (1854–5).[3] These marbles formally entered the University collections over the subsequent decades, beginning in 1868. By thus patronizing the work of a promising local sculptor, Crow evinced his civic philanthropy and demonstrated remarkable enlightenment in sponsoring a woman artist during the antebellum era in the traditionally male field of marble sculpting.

Founding chancellor William Greenleaf Eliot (fig. 4) demonstrated his leadership in art patronage through his role in commissioning Thomas Ball's *Freedom's Memorial* (1875) in commemoration of Lincoln's emancipation proclamation. Eliot visited Thomas Ball's Florentine studio during a tour of Europe in the summer of 1869, where he saw the sculptor's plaster model of the memorial. As a member of the Western Sanitary Commission charged with erecting the monument on behalf of African-Americans, Eliot recommended the commission of Ball's figure group for a bronze, which was subsequently dedicated in Lincoln Park, Washington, D.C. in 1876. At the same time he commissioned a marble copy of the original plaster for Washington University.[4]

Chancellor Eliot's and Wayman Crow's prescience in the visual arts culminated in the creation of the first public art museum west of the Mississippi River, the St. Louis School and Museum of Fine Arts, a department of Washington University, dedicated on May 10, 1881. Crow sponsored the Italian villa-styled building (fig. 1), designed by the Boston architectural firm Peabody and Stearns, as a memorial to his recently deceased son, Wayman, Jr. In his inaugural remarks Crow articulated his ambitions for the new museum "to educate the public taste, instil [sic] sound principles of aesthetic culture and foster a distinctively American type of art." In its architecture, collections, and programs the institution embodied what Chancellor Eliot envisioned for the University's first art museum—"a conservatory of art, a treasure-house of beauty, the historical record of all that the past has accomplished; promoter and creator of greater things to come." The national and international press as well as the St. Louis public recognized the significance of this new western cultural institution as launching "one of the most important epochs in the history of St. Louis."[5]

To fulfill its ambitious aims the University selected the dynamic young designer, Halsey C. Ives, to direct the School and Museum. Ives' vision of art education, formulated during his years of study at the South Kensington Museum (now the Victoria and Albert Museum), London, shaped the school's program of instruction and the museum's collections. Ives intended to integrate art education into society to improve the quality of the crafts, trades, and industry in the region. His program focused on the interrelationship of fine arts, design, and crafts through rigorous technical instruction and by exhibiting examples of great art and design throughout western history.

For the inauguration of the St. Louis School and Museum of Fine Arts in the Crow Memorial building, Ives mounted the most ambitious art exhibition to date in the west, embodying the educational mission of the University and the collecting tastes of the regional arts patrons. Ives exhibited his purchases of some 300 plaster casts and bronze replicas of the great art historical monuments of near eastern and western civilization, a collection described as "superior to any in America"[6] (fig. 2). In addition, an extensive loan exhibition from prominent local private collections filled the upper galleries, testifying to the prevailing interest in contemporary European and American art. Of the 143 paintings on exhibit, almost three-quarters were created by living artists, principally from France and Germany. A number of lenders to this exhibition eventually donated their paintings, including Gustave Brion's *Invasion* (1867) and Frederic E. Church's *Twilight* (1865), to the University. Recognizing this rare opportunity to see modern art, the press reported that the new museum's exhibition presented works by "artists of high repute, [which] together afford the means of study of much of the best of modern art."[7]

For three decades Ives was the central cultural figure in the region, and catalyzed the movement toward acquiring modern art. Ives dedicated his summers to touring the galleries and salons of Europe, purchasing artworks and becoming intimately familiar with the artistic milieu in Paris and London. On these tours, Ives befriended numerous European artists, including Jules Breton, Julien Dupré, and Leon Lhermitte, and purchased or commissioned their artworks directly for the museum as well as encouraging purchases by such patrons as Charles Parsons. His friendship with Julien Dupré resulted in the commission for *Haying Scene* (1882, fig. 5), perhaps the most popular painting in the museum at this time, and the purchase, by popular subscription in 1886, of *In Pasture* (1882). Ives also promoted such American artists as William M. Chase, acquiring his largest European painting, *Courtyard of a Dutch Orphan Asylum* (c. 1884), again by popular subscription in 1885.[8]

Ives' regional preeminence in cultural affairs resulted in his selection as chairman of the Art Department for the Chicago World's Columbian Exposition of 1893. While organizing the international exhibition Ives included objects which he coveted for the St. Louis School and Museum. In March 1894 the St. Louis Museum exhibited 183 artworks that he acquired from the Columbian Exposition, featuring the first place medal-winning painting, *¡Otra Margarita!* (1892) by Joaquin Sorolla, and 143 plaster casts, bronze replicas, and Danish book bindings that exemplified his art education philosophy.[9] In the brief span of a decade, the St. Louis School and Museum of Fine Arts, under the leadership of Ives, had established a position of "intellectual leadership" in art and education that influenced the entire region.

By the last decade of the century both the University and the museum had outgrown their downtown St. Louis campus. The University purchased land on the edge of the city, next to Forest Park, in 1894 and devised a masterplan to build a new, expanded campus. At the same time, the progressive City Council endorsed the creation of the Louisiana Purchase Exposition Company to organize a world's fair for St. Louis and erect a new building in Forest Park to house the St. Louis School and Museum of Fine Arts. Naturally, the Exposition Company selected Ives as Chief of the Art Department to orchestrate an international art exhibition in the newly constructed Palace of Fine Arts, designed by Cass Gilbert (fig. 6). Perhaps the single most significant event in the cultural history of St. Louis, the World's Fair motivated a tremendous resurgence in the arts in St. Louis.

Following the highly successful 1904 Louisiana Purchase Exposition, the University moved its collections into the Palace of Fine Arts, rededicated as the St. Louis Museum of Fine Arts. A populace institution from its founding, the St. Louis Museum of Fine Arts opened on August 13, 1906 with an overwhelming public response. Within months the museum reported a remarkable record attendance of 6,000 on a sunny October afternoon. Both the working and wealthy classes of the city rallied behind their new museum with their attendance and generous gifts. In 1905, after the fair, local banker, art collector, and Museum benefactor Charles Parsons died and bequeathed to the Museum his entire collection. Parsons had amassed a substantial collection of Oriental porcelains, applied arts, and Victorian bric-a-brac during his world travels. Yet, Parsons' acute artistic sensibilities are best preserved in his collection of paintings. Over forty years Parsons had acquired a significant group of British portraits, French Barbizon and academic paintings, and American landscapes—a collection that represents the artistic tastes of the principal patrons in St. Louis and across the nation during the late nineteenth century. Through his acquisitions and a fund established in his name, Charles Parsons provided the foundation of the University's painting collections, including numerous pieces selected for this catalog—Honoré Daumier's *Le Dessinateur;* Jules Breton's *Wine Shop-Monday;* Jean Baptiste Camille Corot's *Le Chemin des Vieux;* and Frederic E. Church's *Sierra Nevada de Santa Marta.*[10]

Commencing with its opening, the St. Louis Museum of Fine Arts organized a continuous series of exhibitions featuring contemporary German, French, Norwegian, and American artists. From these exhibitions Ives purchased artworks for the collection, including modern European paintings by Leon Lhermitte (*La Moisson,* 1883) and Puvis de Chavannes (*Charité,* 1904). In realization of Crow's inaugural dream to "foster a distinctively American type of art" and Ives' ambition to create an "American art museum," local arts patron William K. Bixby endowed the museum in 1906 with a fund for the purchase of American paintings. Ives utilized the Bixby Fund to acquire a number of important modern American paintings, including Thomas W. Dewing's *Brocart de Venise* (c. 1905), Frederick Childe Hassam's *Diamond Cove, Isles of Shoals* (1908), George Inness' *Storm on the Delaware* (1891), and Dwight Tryon's *Sunrise* (1906–07), which introduced St. Louis to the recent developments of Tonalist and Impressionist painting.[11]

Due to the tremendous public response, the new University museum could proudly proclaim, "The importance of the Museum as a civic attraction in the new St. Louis may be regarded as established." After its first successful season, Ives and the Board of Control of the Museum launched a campaign to pass a tax proposition in support of the Museum. In its massive lobbying effort the Museum appealed to the public's nationalist sentiments by articulating its mission to serve "all branches of constructive effort" and to "aid in implanting a national artistic consciousness—a national motive or inspiration in art and an American art message for the world." The proposition passed convincingly in 1907, resulting in the establishment of the first municipally supported art museum in the United States. However, the city refused to release the tax levy to Washington University which, as a private institution, could not, according to the state constitution, administer public funds. After two years of negotiation between University and municipal officials, the St. Louis Museum of Fine Arts dissolved as a department of Washington University and became, in 1909, the City Art Museum, with Ives as its director. The University agreed to lend its collections to the city and the two institutions co-existed for over fifty years in a unique cooperative relationship.[12]

Over the next twenty years the City Art Museum expanded exponentially, building a major art collection held in the public trust. During this period the University continued to acquire artworks,

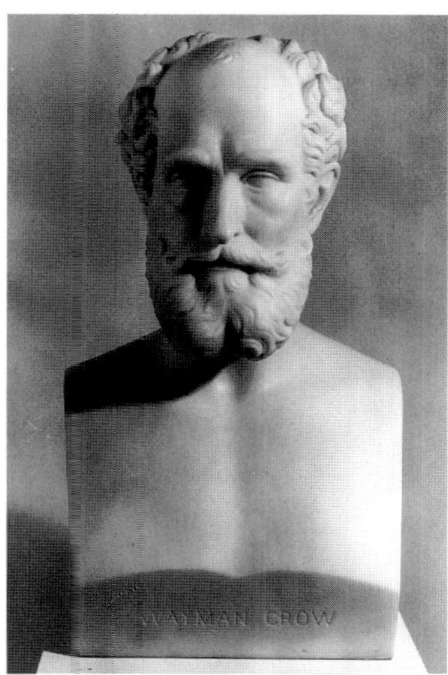

Fig. 3. Harriet Hosmer
Portrait of Wayman Crow, Sr., 1866
Carrara marble, 24 x 13½ x 10¾"
Washington University Gallery of Art, St. Louis
Gift of the heirs of Wayman Crow, Sr., 1868

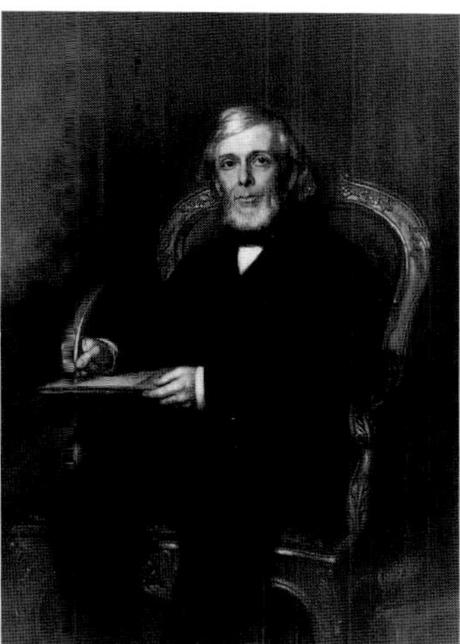

Fig. 4. George Peter Alexander Healy
Portrait of William Greenleaf Eliot, c. 1869–70
Oil on canvas, 59¼ x 39¾"
Washington University Gallery of Art, St. Louis
Gift in honor of William Eliot Smith by his family

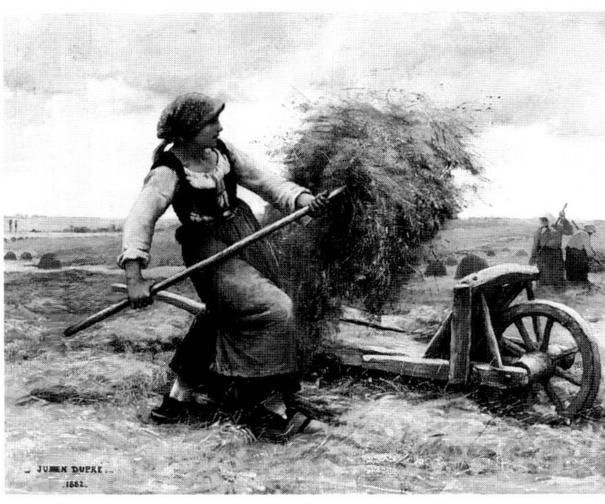

Fig. 5. Julien Dupré
Haying Scene, 1882
Oil on canvas, 21¼ x 18⅛"
Washington University Gallery of Art, St. Louis
Gift of Mr. Charles Parsons, 1905

including John Max Wulfing's bequest of a major numismatics collection in 1925, Dr. Malvern B. Clopton's gift of masterprints by such artists as Dürer, Rembrandt, and Whistler in 1930, and the purchase of two paintings, Thomas C. Eakins' *Portrait of Professor W. D. Marks* (1886) and John Henry Twachtman's *House in Landscape* (c. 1890s) in 1936, to fill historical gaps in the collection.[13]

However, the tremendous growth in the City Art Museum gradually displaced the University's collections, which became relegated to storage and inaccessible for faculty and students. Responding to the loss of the collection for academic purposes, the University unveiled a plan in 1929 for "A Washington University Art Center," revolving around the construction of a Museum of Art, Architecture, and Archaeology (fig. 7) and a School of Architecture to join the existing William K. Bixby Hall for the School of Fine Arts. The University proceeded with its ambitions "to become the leading center for the study and teaching of the arts in the middle west" and constructed Givens Hall in 1932. Unfortunately, the great depression followed by World War II suspended the completion of the University's planned art center and the "university's art collection had disappeared from public consciousness altogether."[14] Not until after the cessation of hostilities in the mid-1940s did Horst W. Janson resurrect the plans and continue the tradition of the University art museum.

During his centennial celebration lecture in 1981, Janson recounted that after the war "I became aware of the existence of the Washington University Art Collection." Labels on certain artworks displayed at the City Art Museum triggered his curiosity about the University art collections. Stirred by the "rediscovery" of a major cultural resource, Janson and a group of concerned faculty petitioned Chancellor Arthur Holly Compton to form an Art Collections Committee "to survey the material and to make recommendations as to its future use." As the curator, Janson inventoried the collection in storage at the City Art Museum and found hordes of material, including beer steins, book bindings, and applied arts, that did not fit his conception of art. The committee deaccessioned approximately 750 objects, nearly one-sixth of the entire University collection, and sold the art at auction in 1945. Motivated by the need for "contemporary works in connection with our training in the schools of art and architecture," Janson spent the $40,000 in income, assembling a collection of 38 paintings, sculptures, prints, and drawings that represented his vision of twentieth-century art.[15]

Simultaneously, the Art Collections Committee worked toward the realization of the University's 1929 masterplan to build an art museum on campus. Recognizing the economic hardships of the postwar recovery, the committee renovated a classroom in Givens Hall into a gallery "to attract the attention of those who might be in a position to donate such a building." Indeed, St. Louis' leading cultural figures attended the unveiling of Janson's "gallery of modern art" on April 14, 1946, and within ten years the University secured funds for a new museum building. Janson's purchases also captured national attention: *Artnews* reported that "the University has obtained the wherewithal to assemble one of the finest collections of modern art to be found in the Midwest."[16]

The legacy of Janson's "gallery of modern art" survives in his "intellectual leadership" that introduced to the Midwest the aesthetic advances of the twentieth-century European avant-garde. Assessing the quality of his purchases, Janson was "proudest" of the Picasso collage *Glass and Bottle of Suze* (1912) and Gris' *Still Life with Playing Cards* (1916) "because they are classic works of cubism."[17] Janson also recognized the contributions of modern American artists and acquired works by William Baziotes, Philip Guston, and Joseph Stella, initiating what his successor, Frederick Hartt, would later expand into a significant part of the collection.[18]

After Janson departed for New York University in the late 1940s, the Art Collections Committee appointed Frederick Hartt, professor of Art History, as curator of the University collections. Hartt and the Art Collections Committee focused on the Bixby Fund for the purchase of American paintings to supplement Janson's acquisitions in order "to make the University collection represent the movements we consider the most powerful and most creative in contemporary art." In his first two years Hartt judiciously acquired important early modern American paintings by Arthur Dove, Lionel Feininger, and Marsden Hartley to supplement Janson's acquisitions in this area. He then acquired an impressive collection of the radical new Abstract Expressionists, buying paintings by Arshile Gorky, Philip Guston, Willem de Kooning, and Jackson Pollock. Local art critics reacted to these purchases with some skepticism, describing de Kooning's work as "a phantasmagoria in contrasting colors" and Pollock's as "controversial."[19] Despite this critical response, Hartt's acquisitions during this heroic age of American painting resulted in one of the finest university collections of Abstract Expressionist art in the United States.

Within months after the purchase of de Kooning's *Saturday Night* (1956), the University announced that the Visual Arts Center first proposed in 1929 was "closer to reality than many are aware." The University had been negotiating with Mrs. Etta Steinberg to secure funds to build a new museum on campus, to create the University's center of art education and to sustain its role of "cultural leadership." The Steinberg family enthusiastically endorsed the plans for a distinctive modern structure by the young Japanese architect-in-residence, Fumihiko Maki. Maki designed Steinberg Hall to house the University art collections, the Department of Art and Archaeology, and the Art and Architecture Library. Dedicated on May 15, 1960 in memory of Mark C. Steinberg, Steinberg Hall physically linked the visual arts departments on campus with the University's art museum, renamed the Washington University Gallery of Art, as its centerpiece. Maki's dynamic folded-plate design of the building's roof-line metaphorically established the modern tone of the Gallery of Art (fig. 8), which would become recognized by the end of the decade as "a St. Louis Museum of Modern Art."[20]

William N. Eisendrath, Jr., the first director of the Gallery of Art, announced his aim "to create interest in art through our exhibi-

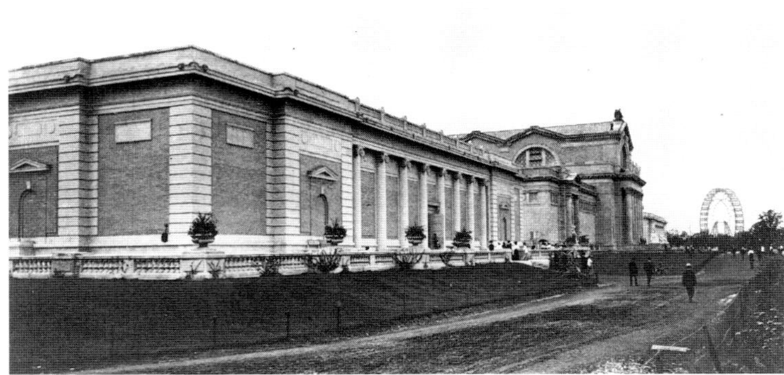

Fig. 6. The Palace of Fine Arts, designed by Cass Gilbert during the 1904 Louisiana Purchase Exposition.
The Missouri Historical Society, St. Louis

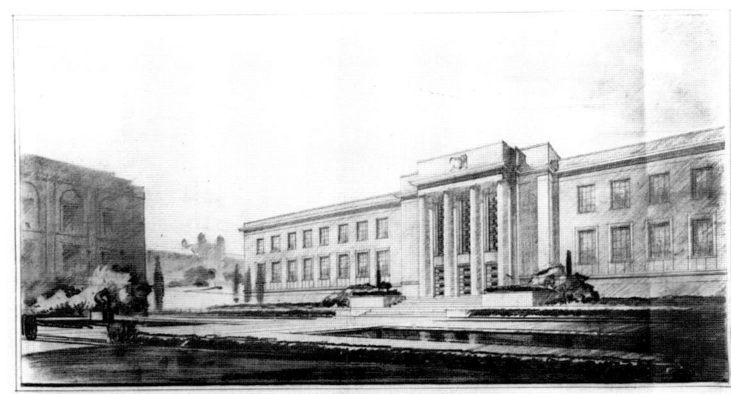

Fig. 7. "An Art Museum for Washington University" Elevation from brochure, *A Washington University Art Center* (St. Louis: Washington University, 1929)
Art and Architecture Library, Washington University, St. Louis

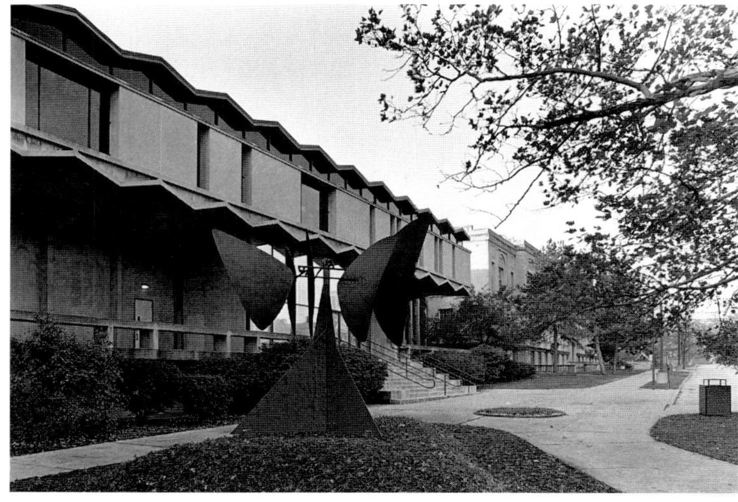

Fig. 8. Steinberg Hall with Alexander Calder's *Five Rudders* (1964)

tions and lectures, making Steinberg a university museum and also a center for those in the community as a whole who are interested in art."[21] Eisendrath's vital exhibition program and charismatic personality molded the Gallery of Art into one of the most dynamic modern art centers in the country and the center of cultural life in the region. Eisendrath's outstanding exhibitions and acquisitions encouraged a dramatic resurgence in the growth of the University collections during the 1960s.

Over the eight years of his directorship Eisendrath worked to bring a remarkable series of exhibitions to St. Louis, including *New Spanish Paintings and Sculpture* from the Museum of Modern Art in 1961 and retrospectives of Dubuffet and Ernst in 1962, Kandinsky in 1963, Calder in 1965, and Klee in 1967. These exhibitions stimulated great interest among local collectors and resulted in a series of major gifts of art to the University. In commemoration of the dedication of Steinberg Hall Mrs. Etta Steinberg donated funds for Eisendrath to purchase Picasso's late painting *Les Femmes d'Alger* (1955). Mrs. Steinberg's interest in the Calder retrospective encouraged her to purchase Calder's monumental outdoor stabile *Five Rudders* (1964) that now signals the entrance to Steinberg Hall. Enthusiasm for Eisendrath's program snowballed and led to donations from many of the major collectors in the region—Morton J. May, Joseph Pulitzer, Jr., Sidney M. Shoenberg, Jr., and Charles Yalem. The gifts from these patrons indicated the prevailing regional collecting taste for modern European art. Largely due to the efforts of Eisendrath and these benefactors, *Time* magazine identified Washington University, in its 1967 survey of the recent university art museum boom, as having "built its collection into one unmatched by any school in the Midwest."[22]

Robert T. Buck succeeded Eisendrath as director in 1968, continuing his predecessor's successful exhibition programs. Conforming to the original mission for the University's art museum, Buck expanded the contemporary art programs further to "serve both the university and our community in a common educational endeavor." Buck reached out to the regional art community and formed the Steinberg Art Gallery Associates (SAGA), headed by Joseph Helman, a local art collector, "to keep abreast of what's best and latest on the American art scene. Whatever it is they will bring it to Steinberg Hall to exhibit." In a brief two year period Buck and SAGA produced several landmark exhibitions that introduced the region to 1960s avant-garde art. In addition, Buck continued the tradition of collecting modern art, acquiring Stuart Davis' *Max #2* (1949), Gene Davis' *Equinox* (1965), and Tom Wesselmann's *Bedroom Painting #2* (1968). These acquisitions completed the collection of early American moderns and brought the contemporary Washington Color Field School and Pop Art to the University collection.[23]

During the three decades after the dedication of Steinberg Hall Mr. and Mrs. Richard K. and Florence Steinberg Weil, direct descendants of the Steinbergs, made the most significant impact upon the University art collections. Their remarkable acumen in collecting post-war European art resulted in the University possessing an extremely significant, and rare, collection of works by Karel Appel, Alberto Burri, Eduardo Chillida, Pietro Consagra, Jean Dubuffet, Nicolas de Staël, Pierre Soulages, and Antoni Tápies. Furthermore, the Weil's contribution of paintings by Sam Francis and Robert Rauschenberg filled significant gaps in the modern American painting collection.[24] The generous gifts of the Steinbergs, Weils, and other St. Louis collectors continued the tradition of collecting modern art at Washington University through the 1980s.

A century earlier Washington University participated in a national movement for public art and education when it established the St. Louis School and Museum of Fine Arts in 1881. In the 1870s and '80s the United States witnessed an expansion of the public school system and a museum building boom that produced the Metropolitan Museum of Art (1870), the Museum of Fine Arts—Boston (1870), the Philadelphia Museum of Art (1876), and the Art Institute of Chicago (1879). Washington University pursued its role of intellectual and cultural leadership at the gateway to the frontier by founding an art museum dedicated "to educate the public taste" and "instil [sic] sound principles of aesthetic culture."[25]

Now well into its second century, the Gallery continues to realize the University's role of cultural leadership by acquiring and exhibiting contemporary and historical art for both academic and public education. The benefactors, directors, and curators over the past century serve as beacons for current and future Gallery administrators. In the mid-1980s the Gallery revived the University's collecting tradition, embarking on an acquisition program to fill important historical gaps, such as Thomas Cole's *Aqueducts Near Rome* (1832), and contemporary art since the 1970s. Under this program, the Gallery purchased the artwork of Arakawa, John Baldessari, Josef Beuys, Jenny Holzer, Barbara Kruger, Annette Lemieux, and Tim Rollins, introducing conceptual and post-modern art to our audience. These artworks respond to the changing art and culture since the 1960s and address gender, ethnic, social, and ecological issues central to the art of the 1980s. Although the University and society have experienced fundamental changes over the past two centuries, the Gallery of Art continues to maintain "a gallery of modern art" in fulfillment of founding Chancellor Eliot's vision of the University art museum as a "promoter and creator of greater things to come."[26]

Joseph D. Ketner, Director
Washington University Gallery of Art

A Gallery of Modern Art

1. Honoré Daumier (France, 1808–1879)

Le Dessinateur (The Artist), 1853

Oil on panel, 10 x 13¼"

University purchase, Parsons Fund, 1962

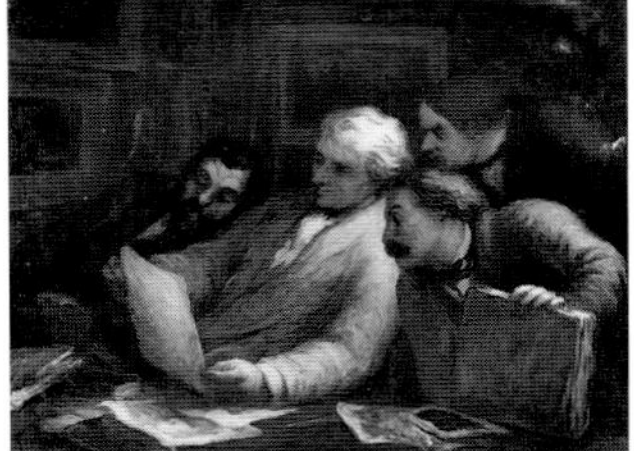

Honoré Daumier
The Print Collectors
Oil on panel, 12⁹⁄₁₆ x 15¹⁵⁄₁₆"
Sterling and Francine Clark Art Institute
Williamstown, Massachusetts

Honoré Daumier launched his prolific artistic career in the tumultuous years following the Revolution of 1830. Through much of the July Monarchy (1830–1848), he worked in the media of sculpture and lithography, making scathing satires of Bourbon politics as well as pungent social caricatures of the Parisian bourgeoisie. Sometime during the 1840s he began to paint scenes of modern urban life, but it was not until after the Revolution of 1848 that he began to regularly produce large-scale oils, mostly of religious, mythological and literary themes. His increased interest in this medium is in some ways an extension of his love of draftsmanship to the expanded potential of color offered by oil paint and watercolor. But the differences here are social as well as material: paintings, as objects, occupy a different social space than caricatures published in daily journals, and Daumier's serious venture into painting seems connected to his increased desire around 1848 to participate in the reformed Salon exhibition system and to compete for public commissions offered in the newly democratic atmosphere of the Second Republic.[1] After the fall of that government in 1851, and the general suspension of the Republican and populist ideology Daumier so whole-heartedly endorsed, he continued to work in paint as well as the graphic arts. During the Second Empire (1852–1870), he painted not only large canvases (many with literary themes may have been intended initially for submission to the Salon), but also smaller, more intimate oils on panel and watercolors of quotidian themes drawn from modern Parisian life. While his success as a Salon artist was limited, he sold numerous small oils and watercolors to fellow artists and to collectors linked to the Barbizon circle. The first major exhibition of his paintings was held in 1878, the year before his death. The show at the Galerie Durand-Ruel included some two hundred paintings and drawings, among them *Le Dessinateur.*

This panel, painted in the opening years of the Second Empire, is a fine example of his nearly forty oil compositions which explore the life of the artist and *amateur.* These are themes he first explored in the July Monarchy in caricatures published in the journals *La Caricature* and *Le Charivari*; in the later paintings, which are far less satirical in tone and intent, he examined the process of artistic creation and appreciation. These works include such scenes as the painter pausing in contemplation in front of his easel, the draftsman earnestly bent over his paper, the collector admiring his own collection, the print *amateur* leafing through a portfolio of works, and a group of critics gathered around in judgement of a canvas or sketch.[2]

The two men depicted in *Le Dessinateur* are probably in an artist's studio. Their massive bodies are firmly anchored in a shallow pictorial space between the broad flat plane of the table top and a rectangular patchwork created by the numerous works of art that crowd the wall behind them. Using a dark palette typical of his interior scenes, Daumier separates the bulky figures from their murky background by means of a dramatic shaft of light from the right that selectively illuminates heads, shoulders, and hands—key elements of physical expression. In the measured weight of the artist's arm and in the pensiveness suggested by his shadowed visage, Daumier inscribes the habits of the artist's life; in the keen interest of the younger man, Daumier registers both an attitude of sharp curiosity and of polite respect. Such is an archetypal exchange between the generations, and between a master and his audience—a dialogue so sensitively expressed by Daumier in this simple scene that we may understand why the poet and critic Charles Baudelaire would find in Daumier's art a moving balance between elements of the transitory and the eternal.[3]

The subject of the older male artist sharing his craft or expertise with a younger man is one explored by Daumier in other works, such as *Advice to a Young Artist* (National Gallery of Art, Washington, D.C.). But the figure on the right of *Le Dessinateur* may be either fellow artist or *amateur*; a variation of the same male figure, with similar posture, face, and flowing moustache, appears in Daumier's panel *The Print Collectors* (Clark Art Institute, Williamstown), in which the figure leans eagerly toward the center in order to inspect a print. These themes of artists and their admirers or students in the studio are hardly unique to Daumier, or to the art of realism in Paris at this time. In the Salons of the first half of the century, Ingres and his followers had frequently portrayed anecdotal episodes from the lives of famous Renaissance artists; such themes still appeared, with less frequency, in the Salons of the Second Empire.[4] Moreover, in this age which had not quite yet dispensed with history, eighteenth-century genre scenes became popular in a wave of nostalgia for the *ancien régime* that swept over Paris after 1852. Daumier may well have known the aristocratic scenes by Ernest Meissonier that celebrated the French tradition of discerning collecting and patronage.[5]

However, Daumier's taste ran more to the contemporary than the historical, and more to the humble than the pretentious. His focus on the modern artist was shared by only a few of the Salon painters who exhibited pictures of *amateurs* and studio interiors in Salons of 1852, 1853, and 1855.[6] It is undoubtedly less in the Salon and more among the members of the realist circle, including the notorious Courbet and the more mild-mannered Corot and Millet, and Daumier's friends, where he found shared belief in the nobility of painting scenes from artistic life. His close friend Corot (who purchased from Daumier the painting *Advice to a Young Artist*) painted numerous small-scaled atelier scenes that share the quiet intimacy and nostalgic reverie of many of Daumier's studio pictures. Yet Corot never exhibited his atelier pictures at the Salon either; they were, for him, private meditations on an interior world. Indeed, it was outside the official sanctions of the Salon that the most important studio picture of the mid-nineteenth century made its public debut, when Courbet first exhibited his modernist manifesto *The Studio, or an allegory of seven years of my life* (Musée d'Orsay, Paris) at an independent exhibition of 1855. While the present work by Daumier has neither the panoramic ambition nor the allegorical subtext of the massive Courbet painting, Daumier's scenes of artists and *amateurs* are very much a part of the same modernist project. Courbet, Millet, and Baudelaire all shared an urgent aesthetic of contemporaneity, one summed up in Daumier's often-quoted axiom, "Il faut être de son temps" (One must be of one's own time).

Elizabeth C. Childs

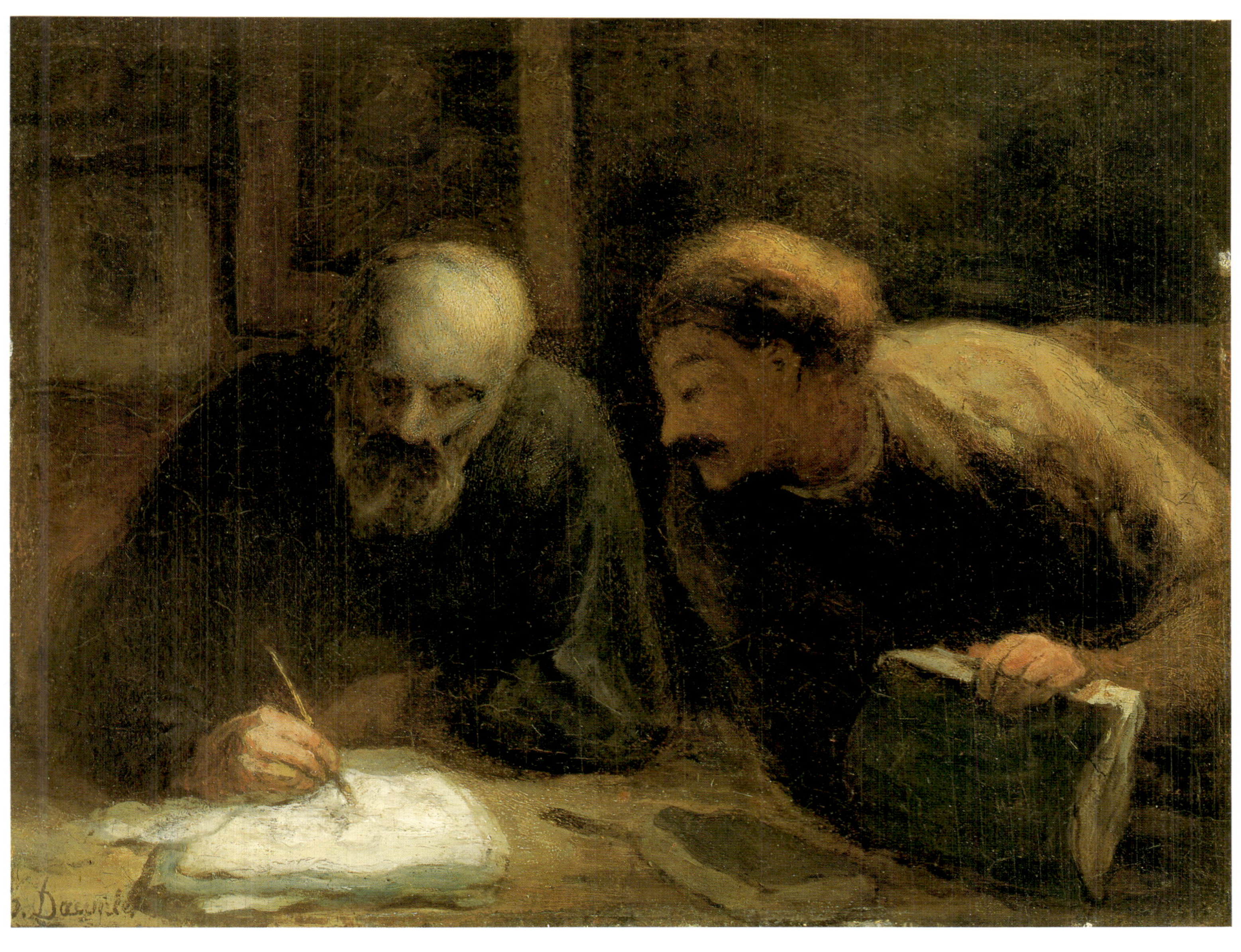

2. Jules Breton (France, 1827–1906)

Wine Shop-Monday (Le Lundi), 1858

Oil on canvas mounted on masonite, 29¾ x 43⅜"

Gift of Mr. Charles Parsons, 1905

Although Jules Breton exhibited four paintings at the 1859 Paris Salon—*Recall of the Gleaners* (1859, Musée des Beaux-Arts, Arras), *Dedication of a Calvary* (1858, Musée des Beaux-Arts, Lille), *Seamstress* (1860, private collection, Paris), and *Wine Shop-Monday*—this painting from the series has remained the least known and commented upon.[1] *Recall of the Gleaners* is now recognized as one of Breton's principal canvases; it was also a work that was well-known in the nineteenth century when any number of young painters had an opportunity to copy the whole composition (or sections of it) when the work was put on public exhibition.[2] By contrast, *Wine Shop-Monday,* which represents an aspect of rural life which people probably did not care to emphasize, was little appreciated or commented upon. In 1859, it disappeared from view after it was purchased by English dealer Ernest Gambart—a patron and enthusiast for modern art who was much taken with Jules Breton in the 1850s.[3]

It is now clear that in exhibiting these works at the 1859 Salon, Breton had in mind the completion of a symbolic cycle of images drawn from rural life in his native village of Courrières. *Recall of the Gleaners* emphasized the return from the fields at the close of a work day; *Dedication of a Calvary* drew on the piety, humility and ritualistic religious traditions of Courrières; and *Seamstress* shifted focus toward life inside the home and the ritual of daily work. Only *Wine Shop-Monday* focused on a more problematic theme: the effect of drink on local types and especially on those individuals who spent considerable time in the local tavern.

In the construction of the painting Breton used actual models from Courrières. His brother Louis is situated at the left, smoking his pipe; the woman in the center, gesticulating for the drunken ragpicker to leave, was the actual proprietess of the tavern; and the figure at the right of the table, lost in a stupor, was the actual *garde champêtre* who worked the fields around Courrières and called in the gleaners at the close of the day.[4] In providing this degree of specificity to his models—where a coarse humor and crudeness of presentation dominated the interior—Breton capitalized on the use of the town drunk for the central figure at the table. This figure, wearing a top-hat, might also have provided a symbolic reference to a ragpicker gleaning the droppings of society in order to indulge his addiction to alcohol. By setting his painting in the interior of this particular inn, and demonstrating that the narrative content was all important, Breton also emphasized two other aspects. First, he wanted his painting to document reality, and he did so by selecting live models from among the group of people who frequented the tavern. Second, by focusing on the daily drama and interconnections between the players in the drama, Breton was able to link his image with the tradition of Dutch and Flemish genre painting of the seventeenth century, especially the small compositions of Adrien Brouwer, who stressed the rambunctiousness of his drunkards in scenes set within Flemish taverns.

Aside from Breton's native inclination to maintain a strong realist tradition in some of his works, the response of the critics to his painting was negative. Many of the critics of the 1859 Salon entries neglected to mention the painting at all; a wall of silence was constructed around *Wine Shop-Monday,* suggesting that both the style and theme were too difficult for most to grasp and understand. Those who did mention the work found it too coarse, prefering the more idealized representations of labor in the fields or religious devotion. Five years later, Jules-Antoine Castagnary, then at the height of his influence as an advocate of realism in painting, commended the strong attributes of the composition. He noted that the painting was a "study of vigorous reality," although he believed that the artist was unable to maintain the true path of a vigorous realism because he had been corrupted by the popular success he had received for his more idealized picture, *Recall of the Gleaners.*[5] In essence, Castagnary was pointing to a basic conflict apparent in the early works of Breton, and an issue which crystallized in the works Breton exhibited in 1859: the artist shied away from a type of realism that focused on the coarseness of daily life, knowing that such scenes would not sell. The more idealized visions of reality provided the direction that the painter was to follow. Breton seldom again, aside from a few preparatory studies and some of his late detailed charcoal drawings, created works of such visual truthfulness as in *Wine Shop-Monday.*

One remaining issue also needs to be examined with regard to this work: the nature of Breton's type of realism and what it signified in 1859. *Wine Shop-Monday* must be placed within the context of the strong sense of social realism found in two early, destroyed paintings by Breton: *Misère et désespoir* (1849 Salon) and *La Faim* (1850–51 Salon). Both works were inspired by social distress related to political events of 1848, the struggles of the urban poor to make ends meet, and Breton's willingness to depict very difficult themes with little obvious support from potential clients. While *Wine Shop-Monday* is not as graphically charged as these earlier images, it maintains some of the truthfulness and interest in social types functioning as potential outcasts from society. At the same time, the earlier pictorial precedents for this work remain clear: Breton was using the Dutch and Flemish masters as mentors for a tavern theme. But there was one difficulty that critics also identified: Breton did not fully grasp the sense of objectified reality significant to Gustave Courbet, then the emerging leader of realism and a dominant, provocative painter. Instead he emphasized what was anecdotal in the earlier masters, a tendency that had the impact of weakening his statement drawn from daily life. Because of this, Breton has not received recognition—despite a few contemporary advocates of his early work—as a primary figure in the early phases of realism.[6] Ties with major early realists have been neglected in light of his creation of a popular style that sweetened reality. *Wine Shop-Monday* clearly reminds us of the other direction to Breton's imagery and a path he decided not to follow.

Gabriel P. Weisberg

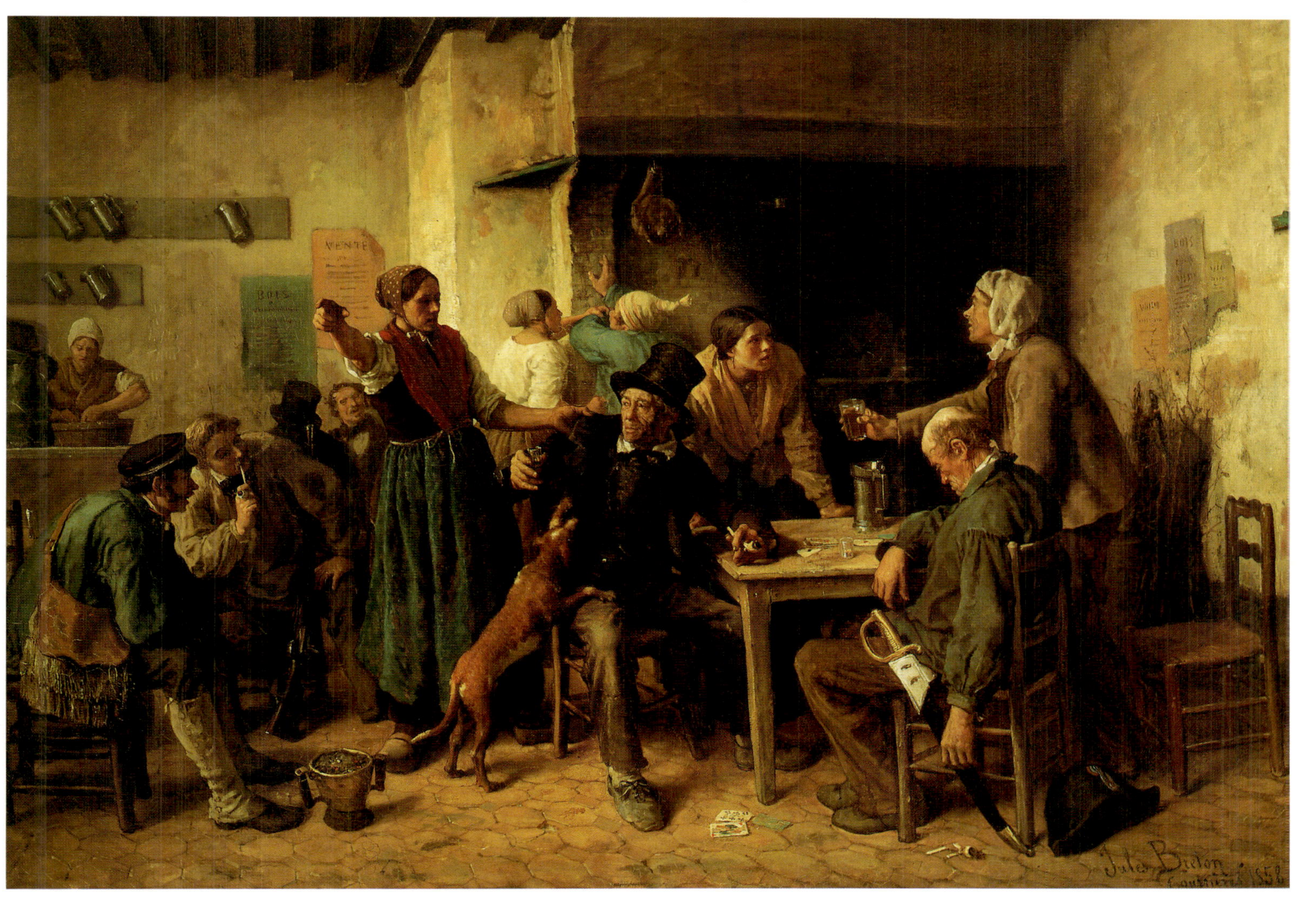
VENTE
BOIS
Jules Breton

3. Gustave Brion (France, 1824–1877)

Vosges Peasants Fleeing before the Invasion, 1867

Oil on canvas, 43⅜ x 68$\frac{5}{16}$"

Bequest of Charles Parsons, 1905

By the late 1860s Gustave Brion had become one of the principal painters of the Alsatian school active in Paris. His paintings had grown increasingly popular, he had been awarded a first-class medal at the 1863 Salon, and in 1867, when he showed *The Invasion,* Brion received a second-class award.[1] In the following year, he won a medal of honor, most likely based on the reception for this canvas, further assuring him of a continuing public appreciation and a stream of potential clients for his compositions.

The type of paintings that Brion did, however, were unusual for the decade of the 1860s as they were based on a historical reconstruction of earlier episodes in the Alsace region. These scenes were often recast to underscore a folklore tradition or to stress a deeply symbolic resonance that was appropriate to his native region. In effect, Brion could be considered a historical genre painter, an artist determined to expand this category of creativity destined for popular consumption. *The Invasion,* exhibited at the 1867 Exposition Universelle, was in keeping with Brion's defined purpose. Brion actively recasts a historical episode from the last days of Napoleon I's Empire to comment on contemporary conditions with an eye to the increasingly destabilizing atmosphere in the Empire of Napoleon III.

Brion's scene of villagers, fleeing after being turned out of their homes by invading Prussians, commemorates the strength of the people of Alsace. Although completed in his studio, Brion reconstructed attitudes and costumes of individuals with the meticulousness of an archaeologist of the recent past. The young couple at the head of the contingent carry their children on their backs and in wicker baskets (along with household possessions), emphasizing the urgency of their flight and the growing danger that they were under. Smoke from their burning village and homes hangs in the air. Moving stoically forward, in rhythms and cadences that suggest a classical frieze, Brion's figures exude an atmosphere of somber nobility akin to the compositions of Jules Breton.

Although one could make the case that Brion was not a fully political painter, his paintings by the late 1860s had relinquished an overt social agenda. Brion did not produce works which commented on the problems of peasant life, but chose to show the exterior trappings of such an existence. Since Brion was displaying his works in open exhibitions and winning public awards with historical reconstructions, he did not want to attract the anger of the officials who were nurturing his career with statements of unrest. As a result, Brion emphasized the authenticity of costume; the general documentary impact of the composition appealed to similar tendencies which were also found in the works of such Salon favorites as Jean-Leon Gérôme or Ernest Meissonier. However, given the fact that events in Alsace were anything but settled during the reign of Napoleon III, and that there were undercurrents of revolt and unrest in the region long before the smoldering eruption of the Franco-Prussian War in 1870, Brion's selection of theme seems prophetic and couched with intrinsic deeper significance.

Inasmuch as such latent realists as Brion were trying to redirect the category and strength of historical genre painting, this work must take on added resonance.[2] The fact that Brion selected a moment when peasants had been forced on the roads, when they were being stripped of possessions and land, undoubtedly struck a subliminal note in the late years of the Second Empire. Brion is not supporting an image of opulent wealth and social entertainment; this historical theme centers attention on those who were oppressed, those who were outcasts from society, and on a region that remained in the public consciousness. Brion emphasized the traditions of Alsatians peasants, and the darker tones of the theme were either missed or bypassed by those in power. The painting was commented on in the press and eventually seen as one of his principal compositions.

Needless to say, Brion's painting could be read in several ways. Attention was focused on Alsace due to Napoleon III's program to stimulate awareness of Alsatian customs, culture and history, including an 1864 exhibition in Paris (later shown in Strasbourg) that displayed a broad range of works by Alsatian artists. During the 1860s, there was a definite propagandizing effort made to educate Parisians about the nature of provincial life, and the customs and dress of the people. This was similar to what had been happening in the regions of Britanny and of the Limousin. What is unusual in *The Invasion* is that Brion selected a Napoleonic theme—ostensibly because Alsace was a region where the Napoleonic cult still flourished. During the First Empire, Alsace had contributed many soldiers to the Emperor's army and an exceptional number of generals to the military staff. Alsatian loyalty to France remained strong and Napoleon III counted on this tradition at a time when his own policies were being challenged at home and abroad.

In a sense, then, *The Invasion* would have been seen as a propagandistic canvas, completed in cinematic terms to appeal to the public audience. But the canvas does not glorify either Napoleon I or Napoleon III—it remains closest to the facts and stresses the common sense, dedication and perspicacity of the French peasant. Brion's conditioned interest in the Second Empire strikes a chord of ambivalence as this historical group becomes prophetic of what would befall the country from another invasion within a few years' time.

After the debacle of the Franco-Prussian War, Brion became despondent. He was unable to overcome the loss of Alsace-Lorraine to Prussia; he could no longer paint scenes based on activity from his lost homeland. The tenor of this work increases the probability that *The Invasion* contains notes of prefigurement both for France in general and for Brion as a creator. It remains one of his last potent images inspired by social and historical implications from the past and present—a symbolic reminder that decoding historical genre paintings is a complicated exercise.

Gabriel P. Weisberg

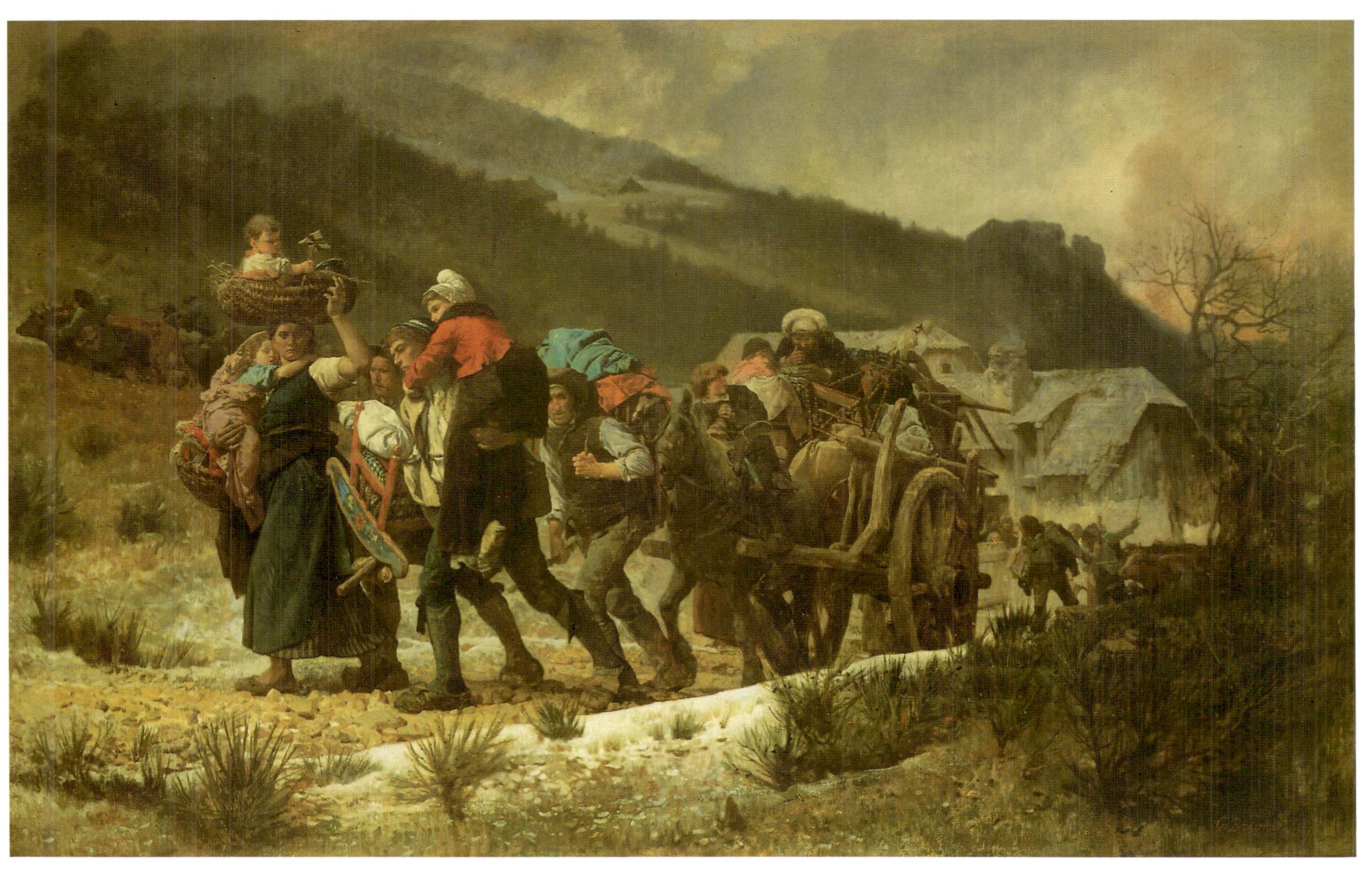

4. Narcisse-Virgile Diaz de la Peña (France, 1808–1876) *Wood Interior,* 1867

Oil on canvas, 33⅛ x 41⅝"
Bequest of Charles Parsons, 1905

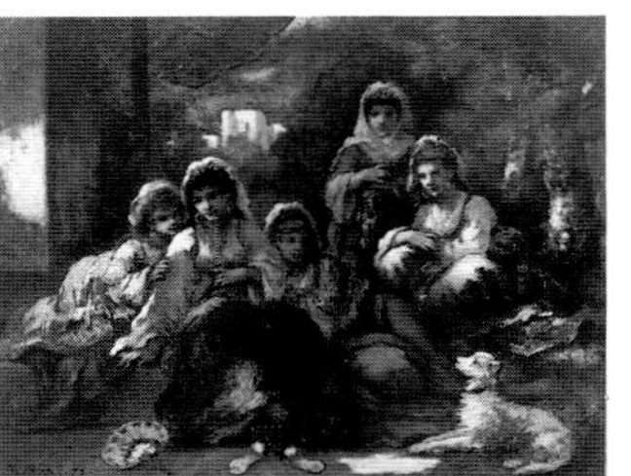

Narcisse-Virgile Diaz de la Peña
The Smyrna Girls, 1875
Oil on board, 12 x 15⅜"
Washington University Gallery of Art, St. Louis
Gift of Charles Parsons, 1905

The sparkling, sunstruck forest clearings so often celebrated by Narcisse-Virgile Diaz[1]—framed by twisted oaks and storm-shattered birches and flashing with sunlight splintered through a web of treelimbs and fluttering leaves—have gained the status of an icon defining the Barbizon movement, a particularly telling symbol for the group of landscape artists who led the development of naturalistic painting in France. *Wood Interior,* one of the largest and most intricate of Diaz's *sous-bois* (forest undergrowth) pictures, was painted in 1867, just as these long-denied masters were finally achieving international fame and passing along to the next generation, the Impressionist painters, their admiration for the native landscape of France, for natural light effects, and for boldly individualized techniques of paint handling.

Diaz was a central figure among the painters of rural life and landscape associated with the tiny village of Barbizon where they often worked. One of the first to exhibit landscapes of the great Forest of Fontainebleau at the prestigious Salon exhibitions in Paris, Diaz found that his open personal manner and generally accessible paintings made him an important mediator between the more reclusive Barbizon masters and the Parisian art world; he proved a supportive friend to those in the group whose success came more slowly than his.

Born in Bordeaux in 1808, he was largely self-taught (as were most of his closest colleagues), for the conservative art academies of the 1820s and 1830s had little enthusiasm for the natural landscapes and realistic subject matter that attracted Diaz and his friends. In any event, as the orphaned son of Spanish refugees, Diaz could not afford the years of studio training required of an ambitious painter of religious or historical subjects and at an early age he entered an apprenticeship as a painter of decorative porcelain, training that emphasized the use of bright, clear colors and a sophisticated, facile execution. Living in Paris during the 1830s, he gravitated to the circle of rebellious young writers and artists who rejected the classical subject matter and refined formality of the established academic masters in favor of a more personalized, spontaneous self-expression. Diaz admired both his contemporary Delacroix and such seventeenth- and eighteenth-century masters of the nude as Correggio and Prudhon (whose work he studied in the Louvre). Diaz quickly made a name for himself with colorful, confidently painted scenes of Turkish harems, forest nymphs, and exotically-costumed young women in parklike settings. Throughout his long career, such charming figure scenes brought Diaz popular success, while the pure landscapes that he took up late in the 1830s (in response to the example of Théodore Rousseau) bound him to the most advanced circles of artistic creation. By the 1860s, the range of his skills, his artistic contacts, and his personal charm had made Diaz an important influence for such younger artists as Renoir, Fantin-Latour, and Monet, who passed through the Forest of Fontainebleau in their search for artistic identity.

Diaz frequently spent the summer months in Barbizon working on the nearby Chailly plain or deep in the Fontainebleau woodlands, and *Wood Interior* probably depicts the heavily wooded, old growth section of the forest known as the Bas Bréau, famous for its ancient oaks and fern-choked depths. In thirty years of painting in the forest, Diaz developed a favored format for his Fontainebleau scenes, shaping an arched ceiling of foliage to close off the upper reaches of his canvas and casting the foreground in deep shadow to suggest the experience of moving through the gloomy darkness into brilliant sunlight. For *Wood Interior,* he limited the sky to an irregular glimpse of blues and lavenders that gives definition to the central treetops and helps the viewer interpret the few well-defined tree trunks and individual branches that shape the clearing. Over this simple skeleton, Diaz built up a dense web of varied paint touches that mimic the colors and textures of leaves and ferns, broken tree bark, sandy soil and mossy rocks in a lush and exuberant pattern that rejects the constraints of silhouetting lines and precise botanical descriptions. As if to emphasize the variety and disorderliness of the forest's attractions, Diaz scattered his strongest highlights without regard to a structured fall of light and he worked touches of a deep sky blue well into the depths of the foliage, creating the illusion of a distant space beyond the wall of trees.

The simplicity of the structure Diaz created for *Wood Interior* belies the daring it took to reject such traditional notions of landscape illustration as the recession of space in orderly rhythms and the placement of objects distinctly in front, beside, or behind one another. For logical perspectival organization, he substituted a more sensual exploration of the forest, one that employed painterly shifts in color, texture, and light and dark values to suggest the unpictorial qualities of movement, humidity, and changing temperatures. In the process of unleashing color and texture from line's constraints, Diaz took one of the most important steps toward the purer painting that would dominate the art of the next century.

Alexandra R. Murphy

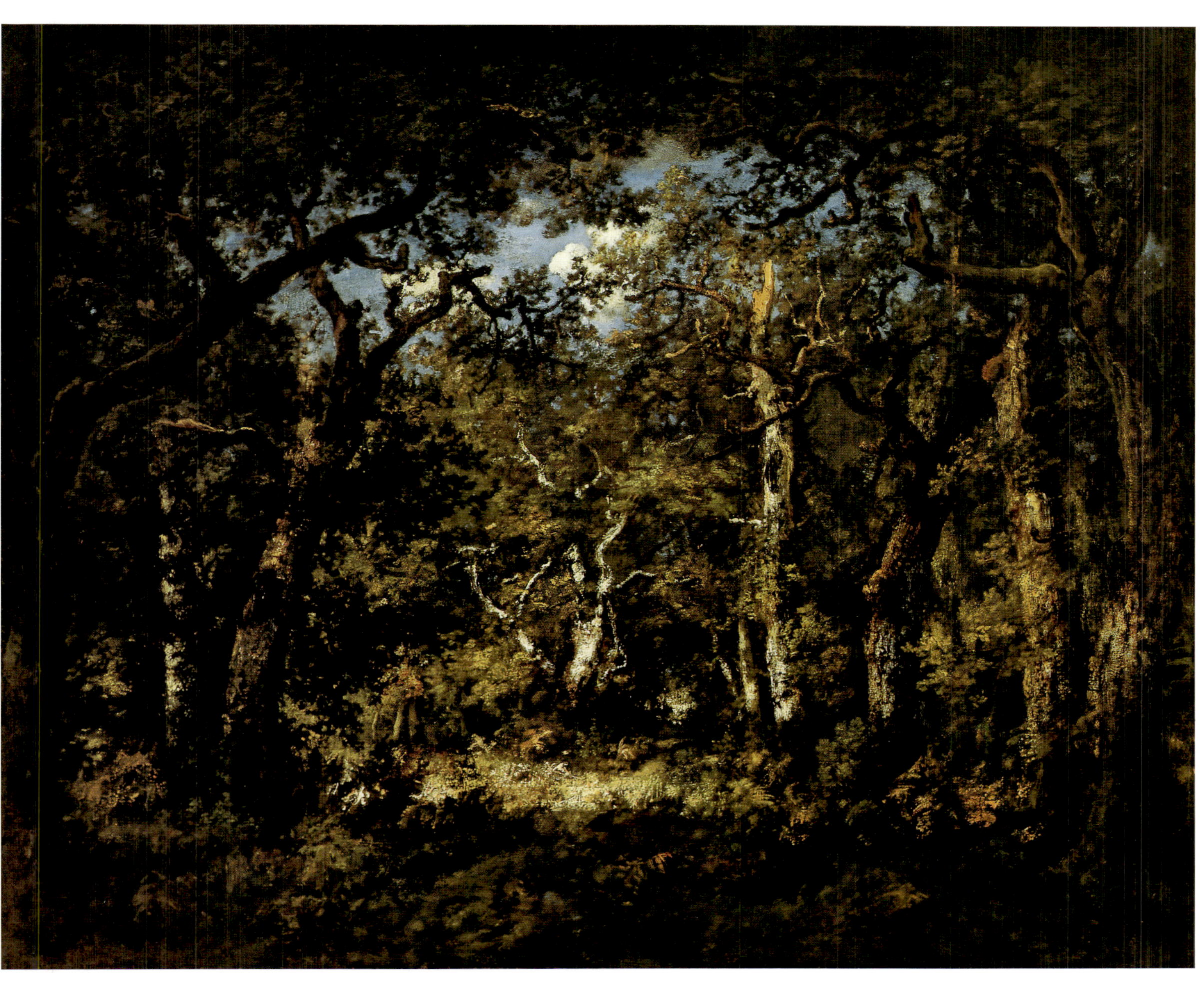

5. Jean-Baptiste-Camille Corot (France, 1796–1875)
Le Chemin des Vieux, Luzancy, Seine-et-Marne (The Path of the Old People), 1871-72

Oil on canvas on Masonite, 12¾ x 22"
Bequest of Charles Parsons, 1905

Corot was one of the most successful landscape painters of the nineteenth century coming to prominence as a leader of the new school of landscape painting in the 1830s.[1] After a late start and a number of years painting works for public exhibition at the annual Salons based on seventeenth-century prototypes, around 1850 he developed his signature style, typified by softened, even indeterminate, forms and muted color harmonies. By limiting his palette to silvery greens or tawny golds—colors associated with the fugitive effects of dawn and dusk—and establishing the correct relationship of values between light and dark areas, he created paintings that evoke the feeling of a place without describing it.

In *Le Chemin des Vieux*, a small copse in the middle ground is cut by a rutted road, along which two country people, a man and a woman, have just passed each other. Branches of the trees reach out overhead and intersect, forming an arch of foliage. To the left are a few houses and a stretch of water. This composition, like many others Corot painted in the last decade of his life, inspired a slightly smaller variant (location unknown, Robaut 2084), which was included in the memorial exhibition held in the artist's honor after his death in 1875.[2]

Le Chemin des Vieux differs in an important way from its variant. Corot's chronicler, Alfred Robaut, who was the first owner of the St. Louis painting and who gave it its title,[3] asked Corot to repaint the left side of the picture, replacing a clump of bushes—as documented in the variant—with water stretching to the horizon, suggesting the sea. This change is significant, for the picture now no longer depicts Luzancy, where it was painted. Luzancy, a small town about seventy-five miles east and a little south of Paris, lies on the Marne river, far from the English Channel or any other large body of water. Robaut's request for the change, and Corot's acquiescence, points out what a small role topographical accuracy played in Corot's late works; the formal construction of the picture and the mood it created were far more important than the delineation of a specific locale.

By opening the composition to include a horizon to the left, Corot made the painting stronger, balancing the darkened arch of trees with the greater expanse of pearly sky and contrasting the tremulous edge of the trees with the regularity of the horizon. White flecks dance through the foreground. Initially apprehended as reflections off foliage, they draw the eye across the scene and at the same time keep it on the surface, an effect that visually flattens the picture space. Yet this device is at odds with the plunging perspective created by the rutted road in the middle. The combination of the two devices lends the painting an animation that the motifs of trees and path alone would not provide.

Robaut did not keep the painting very long; in 1880 it was in the hands of Louis Tedesco, a Paris art dealer who handled many works by Corot. That same year the St. Louis collector Charles Parsons bought it, and it has been in St. Louis ever since. Collectors in late-nineteenth-century America, such as William T. Walters of Baltimore,[4] avidly sought out pictures from late in Corot's career. They saw in them an escape from their everyday routine. The lack of definite form and detail, saturated color, narrative, and identifiable locale gave such works as *Le Chemin des Vieux* a universal appeal. Jules-Antoine Castagnary, a nineteenth-century critic who was not sympathetic to Corot's landscapes, nonetheless accurately described the features of Corot's works, almost as if he were looking at this very picture.

> *He sees but one hour in the day. . . . It is an uncertain, colourless hour, devoid of light and depth of shade, drowned in half-tints, but full of soft languor and morbid sentiment.*
>
> *. . . He has looked only at forest glades, solitary nooks, covert bowers, the edge of a wood, the shade of a copse, a sunk and covered lane. . . .*
>
> *. . . If he has found endless themes, it has only been to decompose them in his studio, and to recompose them from his personal point of view, producing them at last as set in the key of his own idyllic mood.*[5]

Collectors such as Parsons found Corot's personal point of view—the sophistication of the pictorial structure and the emotional resonance of the paintings—to their liking. Quiet, contemplative, and serene, Corot's paintings are not immediately apprehended. Corot explained, "To understand my landscapes, you must have patience at least until the mist has lifted: you can get into them only by degrees, but once there they ought to please you."[6]

Fronia E. Wissman

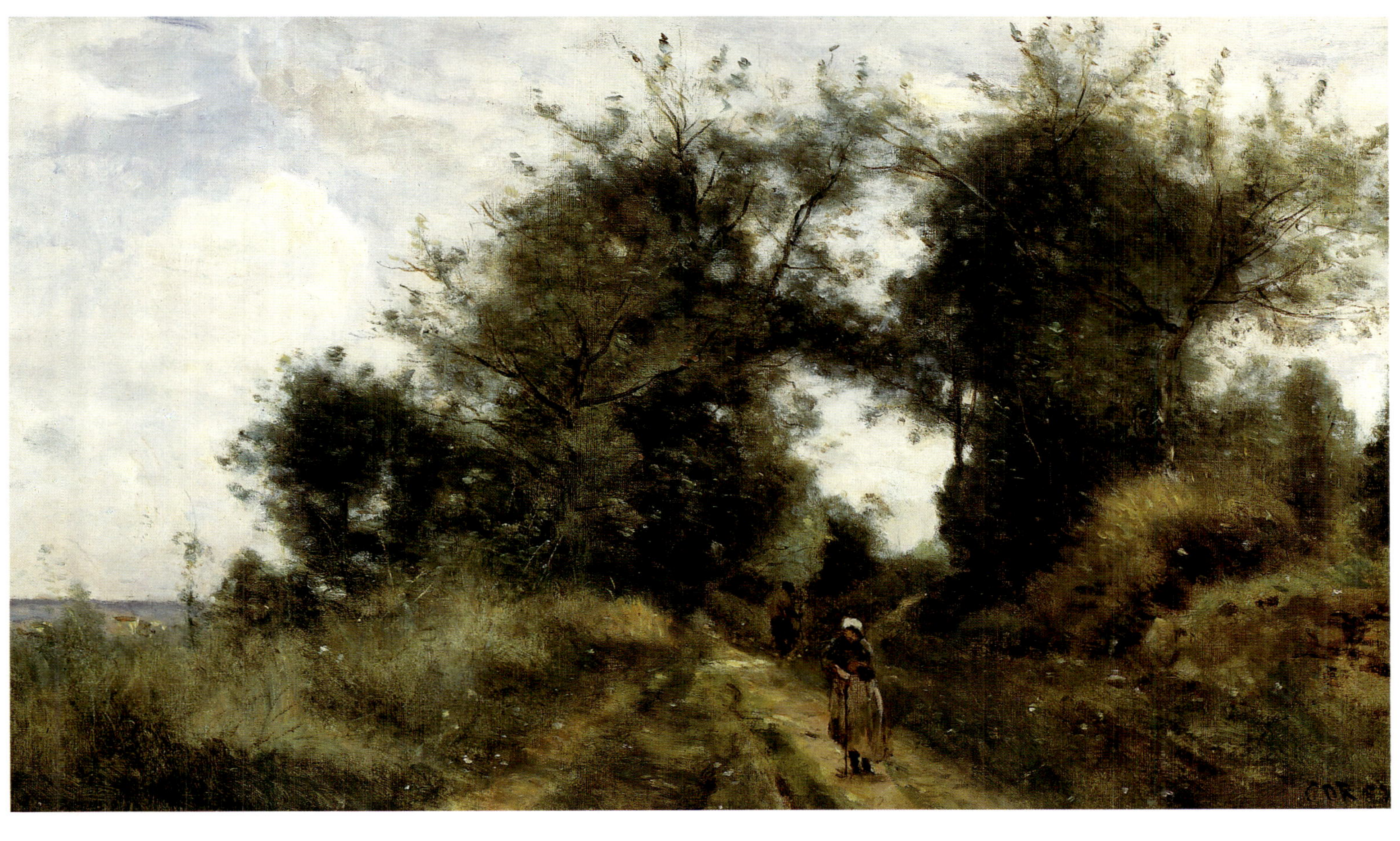

6. Julien Dupré (France, 1851–1910)

In Pasture, 1882
Oil on canvas, 54 x 78¾"
Purchase by subscription, 1886

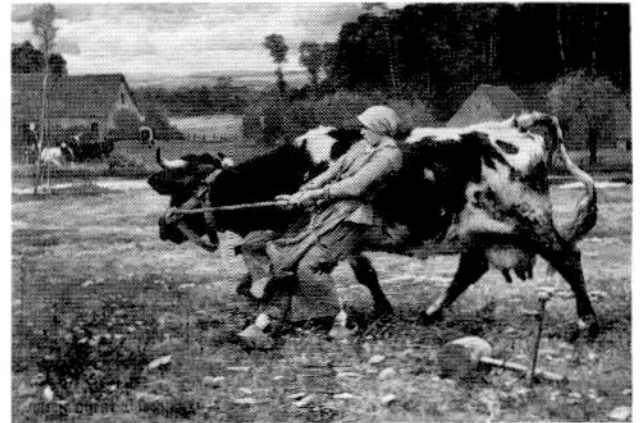

Julien Dupré
In the Pasture, 1883
Oil on canvas, 53 x 78"
University of Kentucky Art Museum, Lexington
Gift of Mr. and Mrs. Henry H. Knight

The tradition of animalier painting, well-established during the period of early realism, remained a constant during the Salons of the Third Republic with the works of Julien Dupré. Trained in the traditional studios of such powerful academic painters as Isidore Pils, Georges Laugée and Henri Lehmann, Dupré developed an impeccable draughtsmanship combined with a bravura application of paint that made his large compositions appear modern when they were exhibited at the annual Salons.[1] Dupré first exhibited an oil painting (*La Moisson en Picardie*) at the 1876 Salon; a version of this early painting, of a single figure working in the field, is most likely in the collection of the Huntington Art Museum.[2] Dupré graduated from scenes of single figures toiling in the fields to more complex arrangements that allowed him to display his technical abilities of interrelating figures with animals. These themes Dupré continued to exhibit at the Salons until his death. They received considerable support from French public and private collections and they also found, via the promotion of art dealers, an active clientele in the United States.

At the beginning of the 1880s Dupré was at the height of his popularity. In 1880 he received a third-class medal at the Salon for his large-scale *Faucheurs de Luzerne* (now in a private office in the Sénat, Paris), and in 1881 he received a second-class award for his *La Récolte des foins* (1881, Paris, Private Collection).[3] At the close of the decade, with French painting of the century extensively reconsidered at the Exposition Universelle, Dupré was awarded a prestigious gold medal for his themes of rustic life and field labor. Many of these paintings were, by then, gracing public buildings throughout France. Dupré had become a prime supporter of an idealized vision of rustic life that was essential to the well-being of a country moving toward massive industrialization. In almost all of these compositions, Dupré followed a type of formulaic expression: pleasant peasants went about their ritualistic chores in the field, along private lanes, and in the gardens of farms. Frequently his pretty girls were larger than life, further extolling the virtues of milking cows, feeding chickens or geese, and guarding flocks of sheep. As guardian of the earlier Barbizon heritage established by Charles Jacque, Jean-François Millet or Rosa Bonheur, Dupré went far in popularizing these rustic themes for an audience that often had the means to purchase smaller versions of Dupré's large-scale Salon machines.

In Pasture was exhibited at the Paris Salon of 1882 where it attracted attention from both a Parisian and an international audience. A variant of the Salon painting was prepared (1883, University of Kentucky Art Museum), attesting to the way in which successful academically-trained Salon painters worked.[4] When there was interest in a Salon painting from more than one potential client, the painter often agreed to do one or more variants of that painting to satisfy prospective collectors. At the same time, Dupré employed assistants to complete some of these commissions or orders which he as the master painter oversaw to completion.

In this painting, a recalcitrant cow, restrained by a single struggling figure, is trying to join a herd in the distant pasture. Dupré provides a narrative that involves the viewer who has to decide whether the cow can be successfully contained and secured by the powerful peg dug into the ground. With cinematic gusto Dupré has produced a work that appealed to the modern tendencies of the Salon, including a vibrant application of paint that resembled some of the more successful paintings of Jules Bastien-Lepage, clearly the reigning favorite in 1882. It was Bastien-Lepage who ultimately influenced Dupré in the enlargement of close-up detail and in the rich handling of pigment in the foreground.

In Pasture proved to be one of Dupré's enduring themes. It was widely reproduced through the firm of Goupil and Company, and appreciated by critics. A small study for the composition was also included at the end of the biography on Dupré published as part of a series under the general rubric of *Figures contemporaines.* Its purchase, through subscription in 1886, further documents the ways in which Dupré's best works appealed to collecting taste in the United States at the close of the last century.

Gabriel P. Weisberg

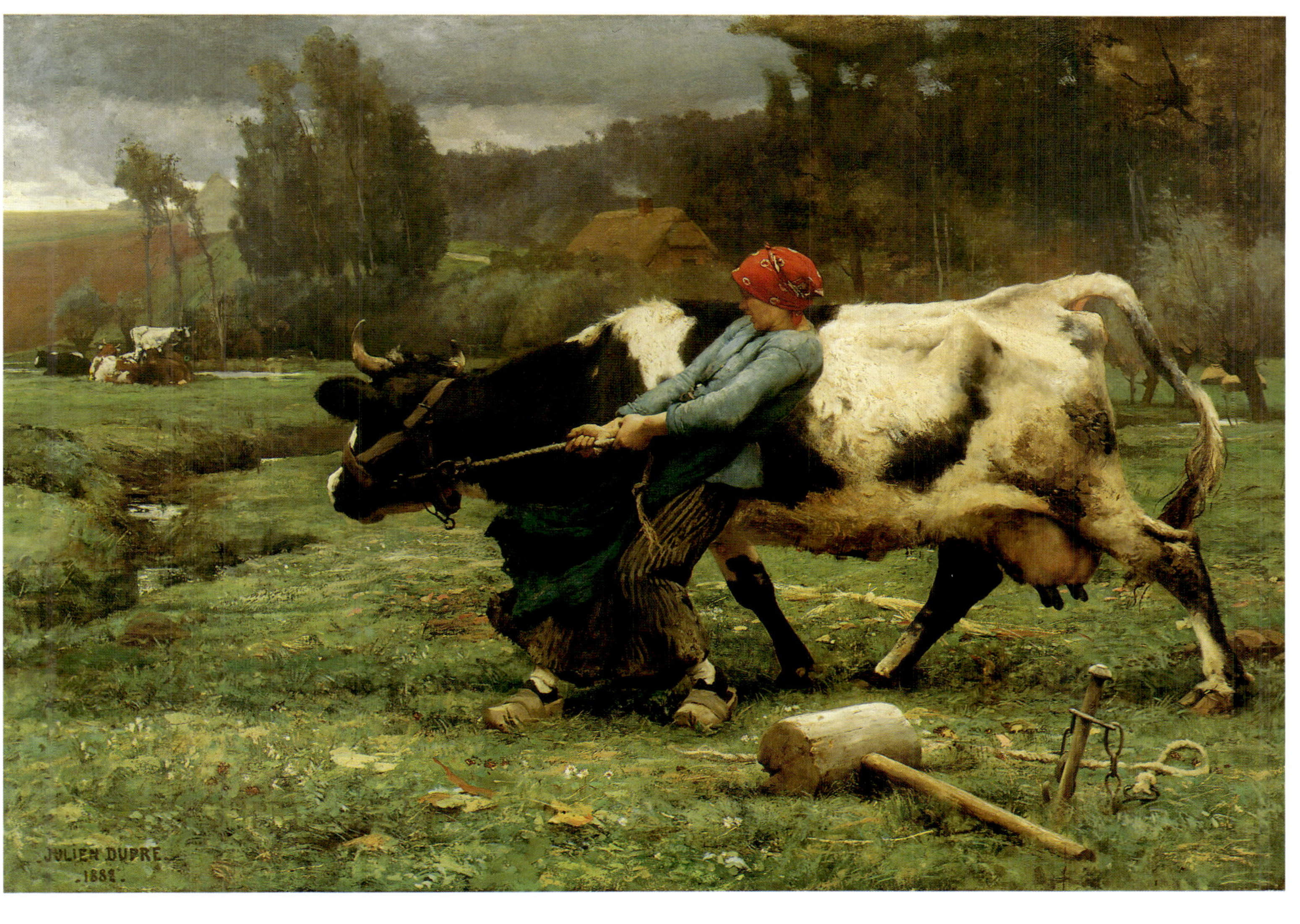
JULIEN DUPRE

7. Léon Lhermitte (France, 1844–1925)

La Moisson (The Harvest), 1883

Oil on canvas, 92½ x 104"
University purchase, Parsons Fund, 1912

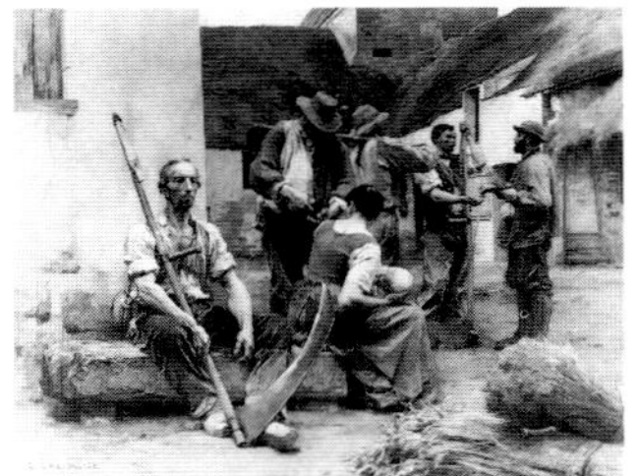

Léon Lhermitte
La Paye des Moissonneurs
(The Payment of the Harvesters), 1882
Oil on canvas, 84½ x 107"
Musée d'Orsay, Paris

La Moisson of 1883 is one of the most famous, characteristic, and didactic paintings of rustic life by the 19th-century second-generation French peasant painter, Léon Lhermitte. It was seen by thousands when Lhermitte sent it to the 1883 Salon and the Paris World's Fair in 1889. The mass public saw it reproduced dozens of times in newspapers, journals and catalogues. Moreover, it was noteworthy as the third oil in a cycle of six ambitious "grand manner" canvases depicting a group of solemn, heroic, agricultural workers in daily activities.[1] With the conviction of an able portraitist, Lhermitte rendered this life-size, tangible vision to recall rural customs of his birthplace, Mont-Saint-Père (Aisne).

In his "grand manner" paintings such as *La Moisson*, Lhermitte insistently emphasized objects of material culture as historical context. The Washington University painting painstakingly illustrates a team of harvesters laboring in a ripe wheat field with a veritable wealth of meticulous, ethnographic detail and diagrammatic information: the proper clothing and its simple assembly, the tools used with the correct handling and their optimum condition, the division of labor and coordination of the specific duties of each member. The setting suggests a stage-space, like a *tableau vivant* observed from a studio ladder either in Mont-Saint-Père, or located in the artist's primary *Rue de Buci* residence in Paris. Central to the action is an older man between a pair of assistants; two other mowers work further away. All wear the usual blue/white/brown of the practical, everyday peasant "uniform." The half-kneeling woman, a comb ornamenting her hair, wears a plain white blouse with short sleeves and a deep, scooped neckline, and a serviceable blue vest. A long, dun-colored apron covers most of her patterned, red skirt. She is a binder, deftly manipulating a sheaf, ready to tie it with stalks. The gatherer wears a similar blouse, and separate pull-over sleeves to protect the forearms. Her coarse, red-plaid head scarf, navy skirt, and dark blue apron present a fierce, incongruent appearance in the hot, golden surroundings. Two separated bundles lie gathered on the stubble; she holds a third bundle with her hand sickle.

The central figure—le père Casimir Dehan—was by now familiar to the astute viewer.[2] Seated with his scythe he was the keynote of Lhermitte's grandiose composition entitled *La Paye des Moissonneurs (The Payment of the Harvesters)* of 1882 which was quickly acquired by the French state for display in Paris and is now in the Musée d'Orsay. *La Moisson* is important as the sequel to the renowned *La Paye.* In *La Moisson,* Casimir is still distinctively bareheaded and balding, with a strong, athletic body. He wears open the same rolled-sleeve, three-button shirt, and similar baggy, brown trousers. His suntanned face, bony chest and arms are unmercifully weathered and creased like his garments. Out of mowing position, Casimir stops to wipe his brow. He dominates the composition, the sole figure neither overlapped nor obscured. His scythe is prominent and individualized, resting on the heel of its broad, razor-sharp, hammered blade. It shines from peening, showing curvature in every dimension for cutting efficiency. Parts are rendered lucidly enough to virtually reconstruct the scythe's technology. For instance, it is easy to determine how the continental-styled, offset handle is mortised into the straight, pole snath and held together with a wooden reinforcing pin. The whetstone holder with its rectangular, protruding stone hangs on a leather belt around his waist, and his rough sabots are much thicker than the lighter clogs worn by the binder. Through these details, *La Moisson* succeeds as a life-size demonstration piece on the human side of history. Its immediacy is striking and unequivocal—a story told with scientific precision. Yet the sunny canvas is simultaneously archaic and modern. It is more a romantic reverie about a disappearing rural world than about reality.[3]

La Moisson has firm roots in traditional academic art. Its primary wellspring is the academic biblical homily on gleaning, the painting *Ruth and Boaz* by Charles Gleyre, now lost but known from prints.[4] Beside similar subjects, settings, and designs, there are many common attitudes and details shared by the three principal figures in each painting. Clearly, Lhermitte derived much from Gleyre's example. Another source for *La Moisson* was a sculpted piece by Rodin. Around 1880, Lhermitte had developed his two-dimensional mature style which recalls the effects of Rodin's actual sculpture contours, broken surfaces, and the exaggerated contrasts of light and shadow raking over facial features and objects. It should not be overlooked that Rodin's *Age of Bronze* of 1876 provides direct precedent for the appearance and gesture of the aged mower in Lhermitte's *La Moisson.* The ambiguous, somnambulant posture and remarkable naturalism of Rodin's nude is transformed into the vulgar, agricultural worker wiping his brow.[5] Risking the mundane, Lhermitte recreated his own promised land in Mont-Saint-Père, where the harvests were bountiful and the workers were strong and willing.

Mary Hamel-Schwulst

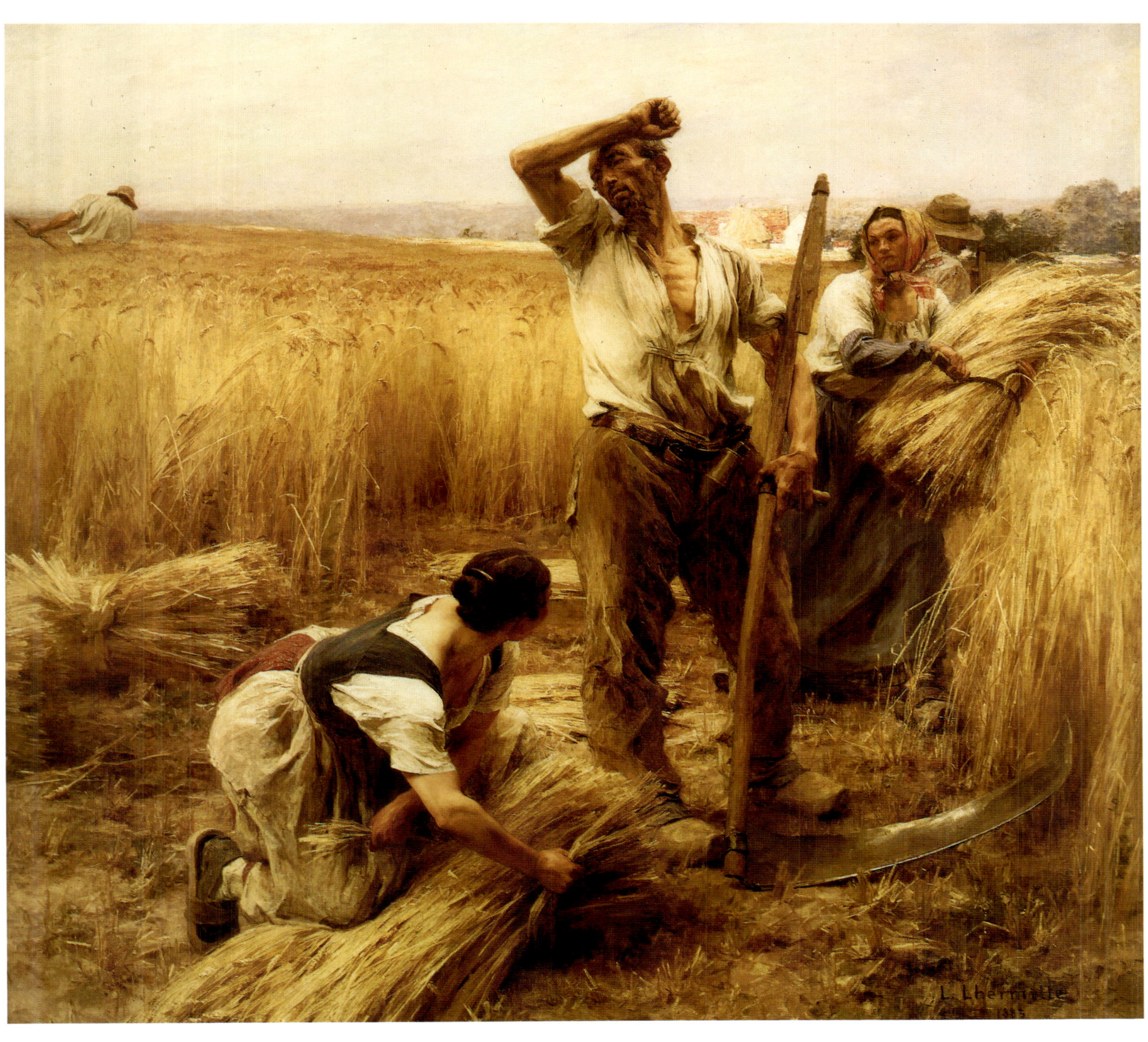
L. Lhermitte

8. Léon Joseph Florentin Bonnat (France, 1833–1922)

Peasant Girl, 1891

Oil on canvas, 54¾ x 36½"

Gift of Charles Parsons, 1905

Peasant Girl illustrates some of the problems in the contemporary and posthumous reception and interpretation of the art of Léon Bonnat.[1] Wealthy and honored during his lifetime, Bonnat was posthumously ignored or villainized by proponents of modernism who condemned him for his official success and academic associations. In the last third of this century, he has gradually re-emerged in revisionist scholarship to be classified as an "academic Realist" or a "Third Republic *juste milieu*" artist, categorization which his complex art and career defy. Despite an enduring label as a portraitist, Bonnat painted both large, controversial history pictures and modest-sized, popular Italian and Orientalist genre scenes; he both advocated the 1863 reforms in the French arts administration[2] and was an admirer and collector of Ingres; he was both a reform-minded *patron* of an independent *atelier* and a teacher at the Ecole des Beaux-Arts. In 1881, he was elected to the Académie des Beaux-Arts, the highest honorary body of artists in France, but not until 1892 did the Musée du Luxembourg, the State-sponsored museum of contemporary art, purchase a picture from him,[3] an honor given to many less acclaimed artists.

The Washington University painting depicts a young peasant girl in the native dress of nineteenth-century Rome or Naples.[4] Part of the nineteenth-century tradition of painting Italian folk in rustic attire, this costume piece followed the precedent set by such earlier artists as Léopold Robert and Bonnat's own teacher Léon Cogniet. At the 1861 Salon, Bonnat's first Italian genre work, *La Mariuccia* (location unknown), was a popular and critical success, and paralleled Edouard Manet's *Spanish Singer* (1861, Metropolitan Museum of Art, New York), another large genre picture of an "exotic" European in picturesque costume at the same Salon. Painting lowly genre subjects life-size and exhibiting them at the Salon still constituted an affront to academic principles, which held that genre painting demanded less intellect, imagination, and skill from the artist than did history, religious, mythological, and portrait painting, and consequently deserved smaller-sized canvases. Moderate and liberal critics saw Bonnat and Manet as promising young painters who could invigorate French painting.[5] By 1891, however, Bonnat's Italian genre painting had lost all of its progressive aesthetics and represented a popular but dated formula.

In *Peasant Girl,* Bonnat has slightly turned the figure of the young girl away from the viewer, both to suggest movement, which a completely frontal figure would deny, and coyness, since her eyes directly engage the viewer's. The figure's placing of hands on hips signified a masculine gesture to a nineteenth-century audience. Along with this gesture, the female figure assumed the masculine role of sexual aggressor, becoming simultaneously the seeker-initiator and site-provider of sexual pleasure. This pose assigned a saucy, provocative intention to the female figure, here made all the more piquant, or perhaps masked, by her youthful guise. Countless nineteenth-century constructions of the female in both high- and low-art forms use this pose of hands on hip to make lower-class ethnic women, especially from colonial and otherwise politically-oppressed lands, readily available for aesthetic and sexual consumption.

Although Bonnat worked in a variety of modes, for *Peasant Girl* he chose a looser handling of paint which relied on the *ébauche* technique that he learned in Cogniet's atelier. The *ébauche* was the preliminary stage of painting in which the artist sketched in the principal masses and voids with large areas of light and dark tones, adding scumbled layers of brighter pigments to help define forms. Increasingly more painters, even history painters like Bonnat, retained aspects of the *ébauche* in their finished works to achieve effects of relief and luminosity in less time and with less effort than that demanded by an academic technique.[6] Bonnat originally initialed this work "LnB," still visible in the lower right-hand corner. At a later date, after reworking the canvas, he signed "Ln Bonnat" just underneath. Bonnat often pledged pictures of Italian genre subjects to charity and benefit auctions, and he sometimes provided a sketch with the promise to complete the work.[7] If this were the case with *Peasant Girl,* the sketchy handling, particularly in the right forearm and the gauzy white scarf wrapped around the bodice, may owe to the fact that Bonnat had already "sold" the *ébauche* and, therefore, had less incentive to invest much time and effort in finishing the painting.

Bonnat executed Italian and other ethnic genre pictures throughout his career, and obviously painted specific Italian sites from memory and imagination. Explicitly made for the private market and usually without a commission, many of these works have remained in private hands, and recent appearances on the French art market suggest that they make up a more significant portion of Bonnat's oeuvre than once thought. He frequently exhibited them at the Salon or other public venues and paired them with didactic religious paintings in order to enhance their non-narrative and picturesque qualities. Lest one presume that Bonnat's Italian scenes appealed mainly to the middle class, aristocratic purchasers included the Imperial couple, Princesse Mathilde, and the Marquise de Carcano-Landolfo.[8]

Bonnat created *Peasant Girl* in the final phase of his career. Though he painted until his death in 1922, Bonnat had less energy and fewer occasions to paint due to poor health and increasing demands upon his time by his administrative duties and his art collecting, including the museum he bequeathed to his hometown Bayonne. If Bonnat began to lose significance as a painter in France in the 1890s, his reputation survived in the United States due to his American students, including Thomas Eakins, William Sartain, Edward Weeks, Edwin H. Blashfield, and Walter Gay. Charles Parsons, who gave *Peasant Girl* to Washington University, participated in mainstream American art collecting with his purchase of a work by Bonnat, but he did not have his portrait painted by the famous French artist, as did dozens of prominent Americans, including his fellow St. Louisan Henry Pulitzer in 1891, the same year that *Peasant Girl* was completed.[9]

Alisa Luxenberg

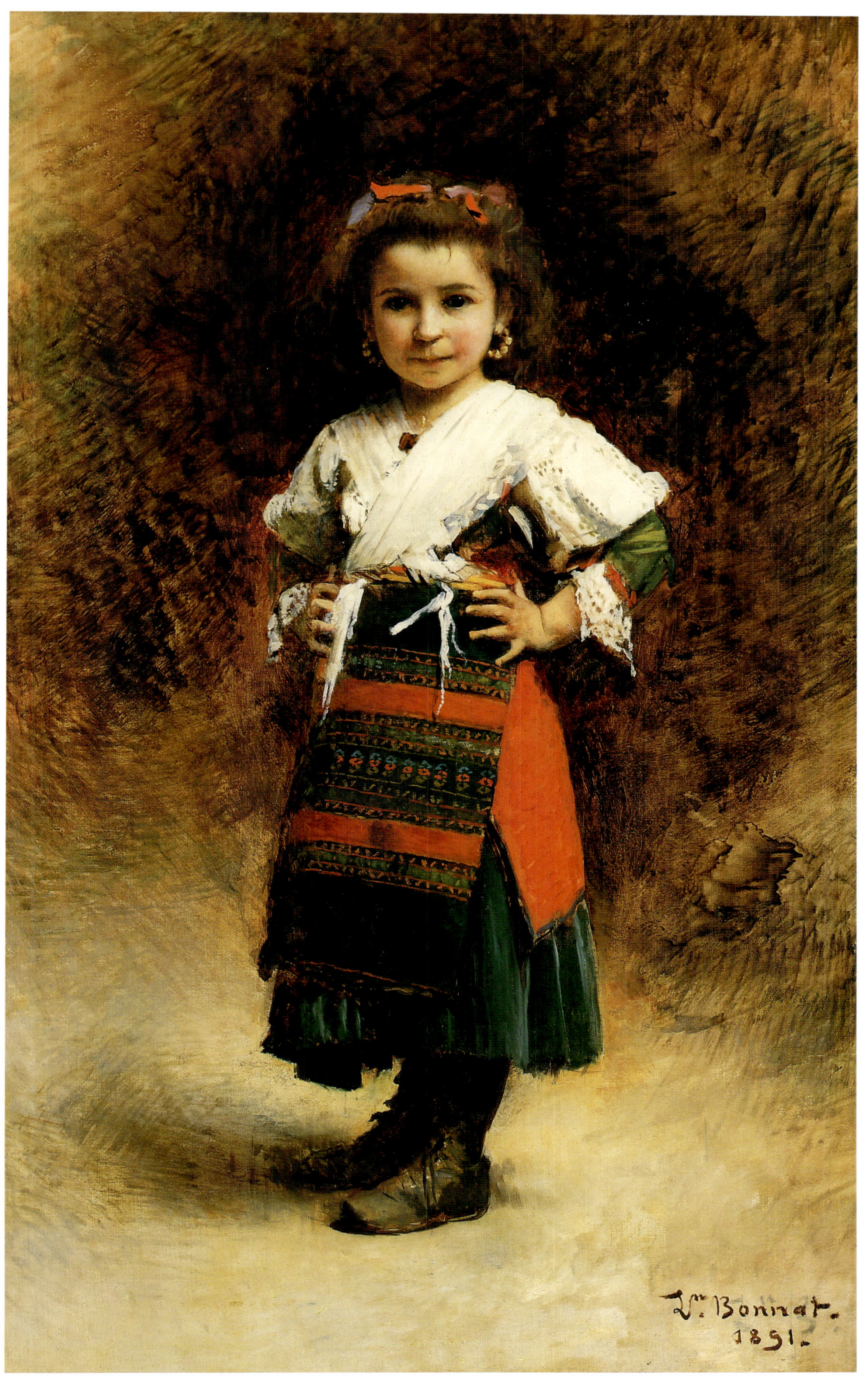
Ln. Bonnat.
1891.

9. Joaquín Sorolla y Bastida (Spain, 1863–1923)
¡Otra Margarita! (Another Marguerite!), 1892

Oil on canvas, 51¼ x 78¾"
Gift of Charles N. Nagel, Sr., 1894

Best known for his paintings of a sun-drenched Spain, Sorolla believed that with this tranquil yet tragic scene, *¡Otra Margarita!*, he had at last defined his pictorial objectives. Painted when he was twenty-nine following twenty years of study, *¡Otra Margarita!* brought him both self-assurance and recognition, despite lingering hesitations and apprehensions that he experienced when producing it. This key painting which was awarded a gold, first class medal in Madrid's International Exhibition of 1892 and praised in Spain's periodicals, represented the conclusion of a period of artistic struggle for Sorolla. Following the Madrid exhibition, *¡Otra Margarita!* joined other pictures bound for the International Columbian Exposition in Chicago, where it again won a first place medal, as well as the plaudits of an American public. Reportedly, this sombre scene attracted crowds, who were moved to tears by the painting, and established a reputation for the young Valencian in the United States.[1]

By 1900, just when artists in Paris recognized Sorolla and admired his painting as original, independent and audacious, Sorolla abandoned all that was sorrowful or conscience-invoking in his art.[2] He turned instead to a joyous interpretation of color and light. The hot Spanish sun as it played upon the people and beaches of Mediterranean Spain became his principal subject and continued his successes in European exhibitions. Then, in February 1909, he at last "brought the sun," as he put it, to Americans chilled by wintry snows. Record-breaking attendances at exhibitions of his paintings in The Hispanic Society of America, New York, and then in Buffalo and Boston—and return engagements in 1911 in New York, Chicago and St. Louis—testify to the appeal of his exhilarating views of a Spain saturated with warmth, color and sunlight, which Sorolla presented with spontaneity and bravura brushwork. As a portraitist rivalling John Singer Sargent, Sorolla filled many commissions while in the States, among them the portrayal of President Taft (Taft Museum, Cincinnati). On a larger scale, Sorolla commemorated his land and its people in huge wallcovering canvases of *The Provinces of Spain*, painted from 1911 to 1919 for the Hispanic Society, where they remain as part of the largest collection of his works outside Spain.[3]

With *¡Otra Margarita!*, Sorolla in 1892 clearly succeeded in satisfying his artistic aspirations for realistic painting that would convey the essence of everyday life.[4] His aesthetic concerns represent Spanish thought on art then shared by some critics. Assaying the period's conflicting schools of naturalism in 1894, Madrid artist and critic Pedro de Madrazo saw one school as consisting of false and ephemeral interpretations of nature, resulting in overly familiar genre, costume and landscape pictures, while the other affected a more universal "art for art's sake" approach.[5] Two years earlier, Madrazo had defined the two dominant trends in Spanish art as "modern academicism," based upon early nineteenth-century Spanish academic teachings focusing on the study of "the natural," and an opposing realist style that recalled seventeenth-century Spanish realism while tending toward the *fin-de-siècle* realism of Barcelona's "modernismo" artists. Placing Sorolla among those artists practicing his preferred "modern academicism," Madrazo praised Sorolla's entries in that year's Madrid International Exhibition—including *¡Otra Margarita!*—as works created by one of the few exhibitors who knew how to draw. He was also aware, however, of an "explosion" of democratic ideals introduced in sentimental paintings of everyday people, and argued that the "sad grayness" of such pictures by "modernismo" artists must cede to a Latin, Spanish taste for vivid, harmonious color.[6] *¡Otra Margarita!* straddled such convictions, Sorolla here embracing contemporary concerns without dismissing his academic training. Another critic, A. Garciá Llansó, felt that art should be based in social philosophy and psychology, and that it should penetrate the social spirit and new dramas stirring contemporary society.[7] When these critiques were published in a Barcelona journal carrying a reproduction of *¡Otra Margarita!* in February 1893, Sorolla's prize-winning painting was critically approved as a moving scene.[8]

Just as realist artists must often "invent" their painted realities, Sorolla, for the creation of *¡Otra Margarita!*, recomposed, with models he placed within a railway car, a scene he observed while traveling from Valencia to Madrid.[9] The metaphorical significance of the central subject of the painting, who he identified in his title, *¡Otra Margarita!*, but called simply "Pobra Margarita" (Poor Margarita) in a preparatory study, has passed unnoticed by critics. Clearly Sorolla's solitary seated female prisoner recalls the young Marguerite of Goethe's *Faust*, by 1892 a well-established figure in European artists' pictorial repertoires. Many portrayals of this "most beautiful creature of Goethe's genius"—whose temptation by Mephistopheles led to her fall—were recognized in Spanish journals during the 1880s and 1890s.[10] German artists, well represented in Madrid's 1892 International Exhibition, especially favored this attractive subject that evoked the audience's sympathies. Though most artists interpreted her as a beautiful but sad and contemplative female whose tragedy stirred the emotions, her imprisonment was also pictured, as in a painting of 1870 by Felon.

Thus, Sorolla's title parallels his plain, forlorn *¡Otra Margarita!* with the familiar Goethe-inspired image which arouses pity and empathy for this pathetic woman in chains, eyes downcast, who is a victim, perhaps unjustly so, of her own time. However, the painterly touches of sunlight that penetrate the dismal railway cabin—Sorolla's first attempt to render sunshine—provide a ray of hope for this disconsolate prisoner.

¡Otra Margarita! therefore involves not only social commentary as has been thought,[11] but offers Sorolla's response to a popular and often over-sentimentalized pictorial theme. It was Sorolla's youthful rebelliousness, which he later acknowledged, that compelled him to recast this theme to reflect the realities he knew. Not Goethe's fallen woman, Sorolla's *¡Otra Margarita!* is yet another Marguerite—a pathetic creature, a helpless young Spanish Margarita ruined by misfortune and reduced to shame.

Priscilla E. Muller

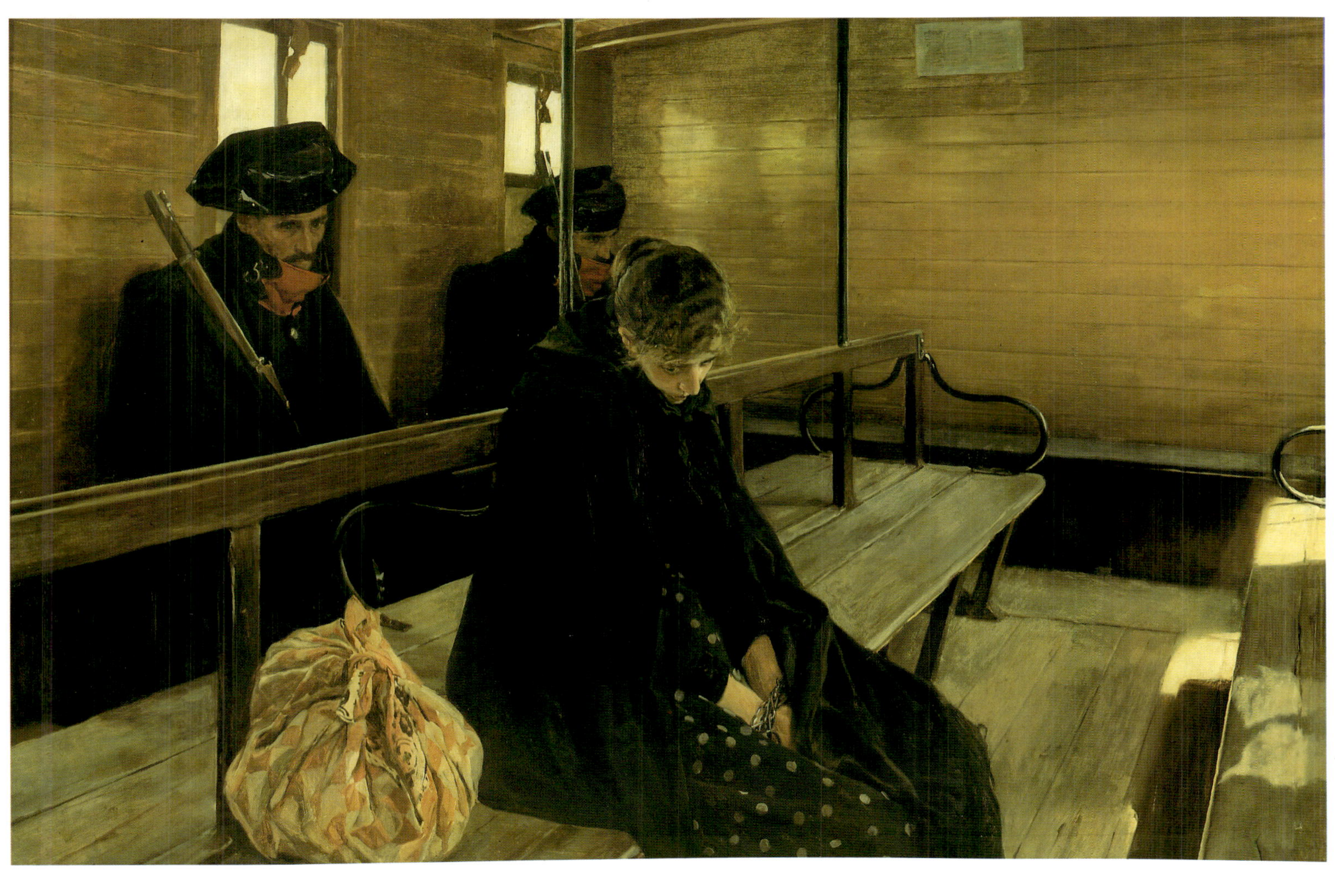

10. Pierre Puvis de Chavannes (France, 1824–1898) *La Charité (Charity)*, 1894

Oil on canvas, 36¼ x 29¼"
University purchase, Bixby Fund, 1908

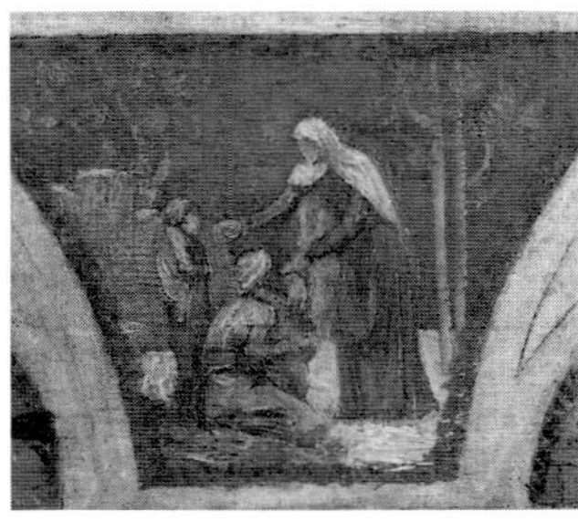

Pierre Puvis de Chavannes
La Charité, 1892–94
Tempera mural
L'Hotel d'Ville, Paris

La Charité is a compelling canvas that exemplifies Puvis de Chavannes' introduction of a new, simplified aesthetic into late nineteenth-century imagery.[1] It presents a very modern idea about giving, by picturing an individual act of charity without reference to a theological virtue. A standing, simply gowned woman in a white mantle with a protective gesture ministers to a woman seated huddled with a child on the ground. Another child nearby hugs himself against the cold of the white blanketed wintry landscape. Bare-armed, in ragged clothing, the destitute trio are enframed but scarcely sheltered by a stone outcropping and tree, a bower of branches at the top. Characteristic of the artist's mature idiom is the carefully constructed composition: simple forms subtly engineered to rhyme with one another, flat areas of whitened, opaque colors of some delicacy, and a roughly scumbled surface enlivened with small, patterned elements, such as sprigs of leaves. The generalized figurations, limited range of chalky colors and flatness sharply curtail verism and yield an oddly removed, poetic and emblematic image. The brilliant invention of a white landscape, pink sky, and strip of blue sea, and sparse, silhouetted gold leaves, hay, and children's hair serve through their aesthetic appeal to lighten the composition visually, emotionally and ideologically despite the grueling nature of the imagery.

La Charité is a variant of an image Puvis devised for mural decorations he executed in 1892–1894 for the recently reconstructed Paris Hôtel de Ville. As the most important muralist for civic buildings throughout France in the last third of the nineteenth century, Puvis developed a special aesthetic of highly simplified, legible and powerful, flat imagery of fresco-like matte finish and relatively unmodulated color chords that would embellish without piercing the two-dimensional walls and architecturally-shaped areas that were his theater of operation. At a time when mural decorations and easel paintings were considered very different kinds of endeavors, he brought this mural aesthetic to his independent paintings.

La Charité was formulated as one of Puvis' series of *Parisian Virtues* for the newly rebuilt center of municipal government, the former building having been destroyed in the 1871 Commune. *La Charité* is part of his complex on the theme of *The Glorification of Paris.* A companion to *Patriotism, Artistic Ardour,* and *Study* (or *Paris, Home of the Intellect*), it occupies one of the trapezoidal sections of the coving that surrounds the central ceiling mural, *Victor Hugo's Homage to Paris,* above the great ceremonial staircase. Tympana and hemicycles— *Wit, Beauty, Urbanity, Fearlessness, Nostalgia, Fantasy,* and *Generosity*—complete the series; *Enthusiasm* and *Industry, Lutetia* (the ancient name of the city) and *Modern Paris* complete the complex. The entire scheme needs to be closely examined, as the structure, composition, rhythms and colors of individual areas were worked out in conjunction with the whole. Indeed, even such elements as the gold leaves of the St. Louis painting derive from those in the decorations.

Since the late 1860s Puvis had been interested in modernizing and secularizing allegorical themes to make them more germane to his time. Charity (with faith and hope) had long been considered an important theological virtue. Much of the institutionalized public charity in Paris had traditionally been carried out by the Church. But in the late nineteenth century city government increasingly appropriated this function, and the question of whether administrative authority over aid to the poor should be under the auspices of church or state was the subject of intense debate.[2] Appropriate to a mural decoration for the center of municipal government with a Public Assistance program under its jurisdiction, the act of giving is promoted as a secular, humanitarian virtue. The poor are pictured as helpless innocents at a time when their worthiness was controversial: many disagreed about the causes of their plight, whether they themselves were not responsible for it, what kind of charity they should receive and their relationship to those better off.

The theme and pictorial idea for *La Charité* seems to have originated with Puvis' important large pastel *Pity* (*La Pitié,* 1887, Pushkin Museum, Mosow), which includes a similar setting and ministering figure of similar pose, a secularized *Pietà.* There are a number of versions of *La Charité*: preliminary drawings, oil studies and sketches relating to the mural composition, as well as drawings and a preliminary oil study of the independent St. Louis painting. Moreover, a related motif and setting appears in Puvis' *Winter* (1892), elsewhere (the Zodiac Salon) at the Hôtel de Ville, Paris. The St. Louis version is more detailed and not as stark as the mural variants. The standing figure has a tender expression, the garments are worked out in several colors, and framing devices, even to a modified cape, bracket and soften the composition. Gestures and structure create a system of parallels that lock the composition in place. In a Cézannesque manner, certain spatial elements are purposefully ambiguous. The tree and diagonal branch cannot firmly be located and may be read within the interior image and on the pictorial surface within a system of formal geometries.

With its gaunt, angular figures, rudimentary setting along a shore, theme of poverty and opaque colors with an overriding tonal cast (compare particularly the bleak, bluish Gifu Museum, Japan, version), *La Charité* is the kind of painting by Puvis to which Picasso, painting his wretched, meager outcasts in equally restrained colors during his Blue Period, less than a decade later, would owe so much.

Aimée Brown Price

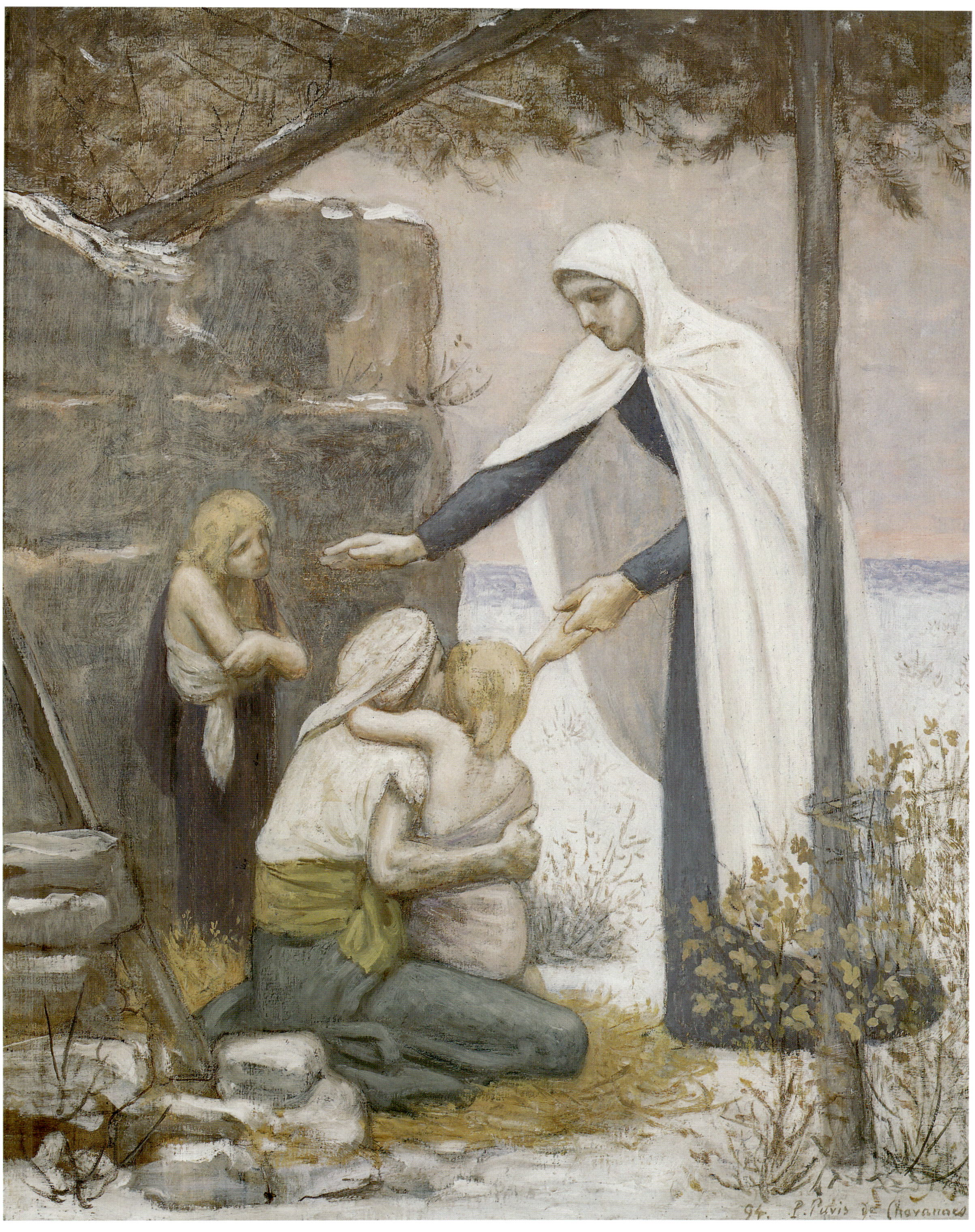
94. P. Puvis de Chavannes

11. Thomas Cole (United States, 1801–1848)

Aqueduct near Rome, 1832

Oil on canvas, 44½ x 67⁵⁄₁₆"
University purchase, Bixby Fund, by exchange, 1987

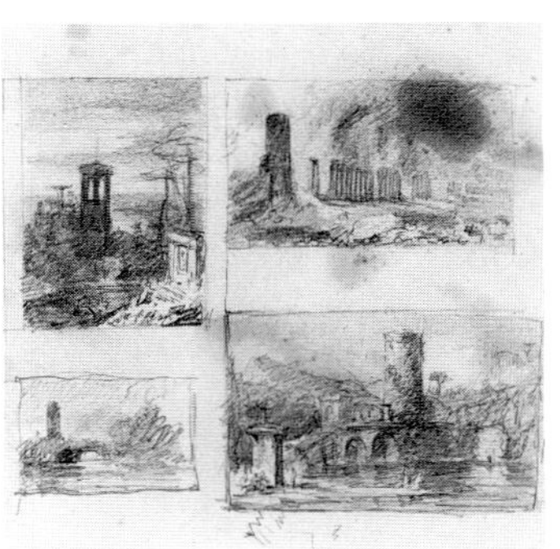

Thomas Cole
Compositional Studies for Italian Landscapes (detail), 1832
Pencil on paper, 8¹⁵⁄₁₆ x 13⅝"
The Detroit Institute of Arts
Founders Society Purchase,
William H. Murphy Fund

Since the "discovery" of his artwork in a New York shop window by American history painter John Trumbull in 1825, Thomas Cole has been recognized as the founder of the American landscape painting school.[1] In 1829 self-taught Cole decided to complete his art education by embarking on the traditional "grand tour" of Europe. Fearing that the cultured society and historical associations of Europe would tarnish Cole's distinctive wilderness vision of North America, William Cullen Bryant, a friend and romantic nature poet, penned a sonnet on the occasion of his departure foreshadowing that "Thine eyes shall see the light of distant skies," yet beseeching Cole to "keep that earlier, wilder vision bright."[2] Of course, Cole's conception of landscape painting was irrevocably altered by his European sojourn, particularly by the Italian landscape.

Aqueducts near Rome occupies an important place in Cole's oeuvre as his most ambitious painting of Italians ruins from his first "grand tour." In this painting he orchestrated a romantic statement on ancient ruins as a metaphor for the omnipotent forces of God and nature over the greatest accomplishments of mankind. With this painting he introduced the themes of English romantic ruins painting to the United States and established the compositional and iconographical prototype for American landscape paintings of ruins scenery for several generations.

Aqueducts near Rome records the stretch of aqueducts on the Roman Campagna where the aqueducts of Marcia cross the Claudian aqueducts as one looks to the southeast toward Rome. The scene is anchored on the left by a watchtower, the Tor Fiscale, and the water channel flows out of the picture space to the right into infinity with the noble Sabine Hills and Mount Albano on the horizon.[3] The artist set the austere scene with a bleating goat greeting the sunrise and a waning crescent moon disappearing over the summit of Mt. Albano. The new day sun shines full face on the ancient stones and highlights a bleached skull thats rests among the architectural fragments in the lower left.

After spending nearly two years in England and a year in Florence, Cole traveled to Rome in February 1832. There he rented a room that was reputed to have been formerly occupied by the seventeenth-century classical landscape master Claude Lorrain. While in Rome he received several commissions for Italianate subjects from Americans on their "grand tour," including a commission from Mr. Charles Lyman of Boston that resulted in *Aqueducts near Rome.*

The drama of the vast expanse of aqueducts first appears late in an Italian sketchbook begun March 10, 1832 (Detroit Institute of Arts, 39.565) occupying two full-page spreads and two detailed studies. Later, in May, while touring Sicily, Cole drew his first compositional sketch for the finished painting along with three other works which were to be among his most important Italian paintings from this journey.[4] In June Cole returned to Florence where, in July, he commenced work on "a view of the Campagna of Rome."[5] Horatio Greenough, an American sculptor in residence in Florence, remarked that Cole "has painted several things of high merit, and a 'Campagna di Roma,' which is a masterpiece."[6] This period proved an especially productive one for Cole. Reflecting on his summer of 1832 in Florence Cole fondly recalled this inspirational period: "I painted more pictures in three months than I have ever done in twice the time before or since. I was in the spirit of it. . . . Oh that I was there again and in the same spirit."[7]

Ruminations on the course of civilization weighed heavily on Cole's mind during this phase of his career. Since 1827, he had been considering a series of paintings on the cycle of civilizations from a primitive state to an arcadian existence, culminating in an empire which was doomed to destruction and desolation. Before leaving on his inspiring trip to Rome and the Campagna, Cole had been working on a large canvas embodying the idea of the primitive state of civilization, *A Wild Scene* (1831–32, Baltimore Museum of Art). Confronted by the abundant ruins of antiquity in Rome, Cole's thoughts thrust forward to the concluding theme of his projected series. Of all the ruins around Rome, the aqueducts on the Campagna held the greatest fascination for him. Tightly integrated with the surrounding landscape the aqueducts conveyed for him the qualities of "silence and solitude" that he sought for the concluding picture of his *Course of Empire* series, *Desolation.*[8]

The choice of ancient Roman ruins was significant to Cole's theme of the cycle of civilizations. Like many Americans, Cole held a millenialist theory of history which, briefly summarized, proposed that Americans could avoid the traditional cycle of growth, empire, and destruction of nations by pursuing a society firmly based in Protestant Christian moral precepts. For Cole and others the decline of the decadent Romans most clearly demonstrated the demise of "pagan" cultures. By depicting Roman ruins, Cole was offering not only a pastoral view of the storied past, but also a warning to Americans that their young nation could suffer the same fate. In an article on "Sicilian Scenery" Cole prophesied the importance of ruins scenery to Americans: "Our only means of judging the future is the past. We see that nations have sprung from obscurity, risen to glory, and decayed. Their rise has in general been marked by virtue; their decadence by vice, vanity, and licentiousness. Let us beware."[9]

Upon his return to the United States in the fall of 1832 Cole publicly exhibited his Italian paintings in his New York studio to universal praise. Cole's friend and author Nathaniel Parker Willis proclaimed that "Cole's picture of the Roman Campagna . . . is, I think, one of the finest landscapes ever painted."[10] Because of its great appeal Henry Tuckerman commissioned an engraving of the painting by James Smillie as the frontispiece for his *Italian Sketch Book* (New York, 1835). *Aqueducts near Rome* was a seminal painting to both Cole, who produced a variation of this painting following his second "grand tour" of Europe, *Roman Campagna* (1843, Wadsworth Atheneum), and the next generation of landscape painters, who turned to Cole's *Aqueducts near Rome* as their compositional and iconographical precedent for ruins scenery.

Joseph D. Ketner

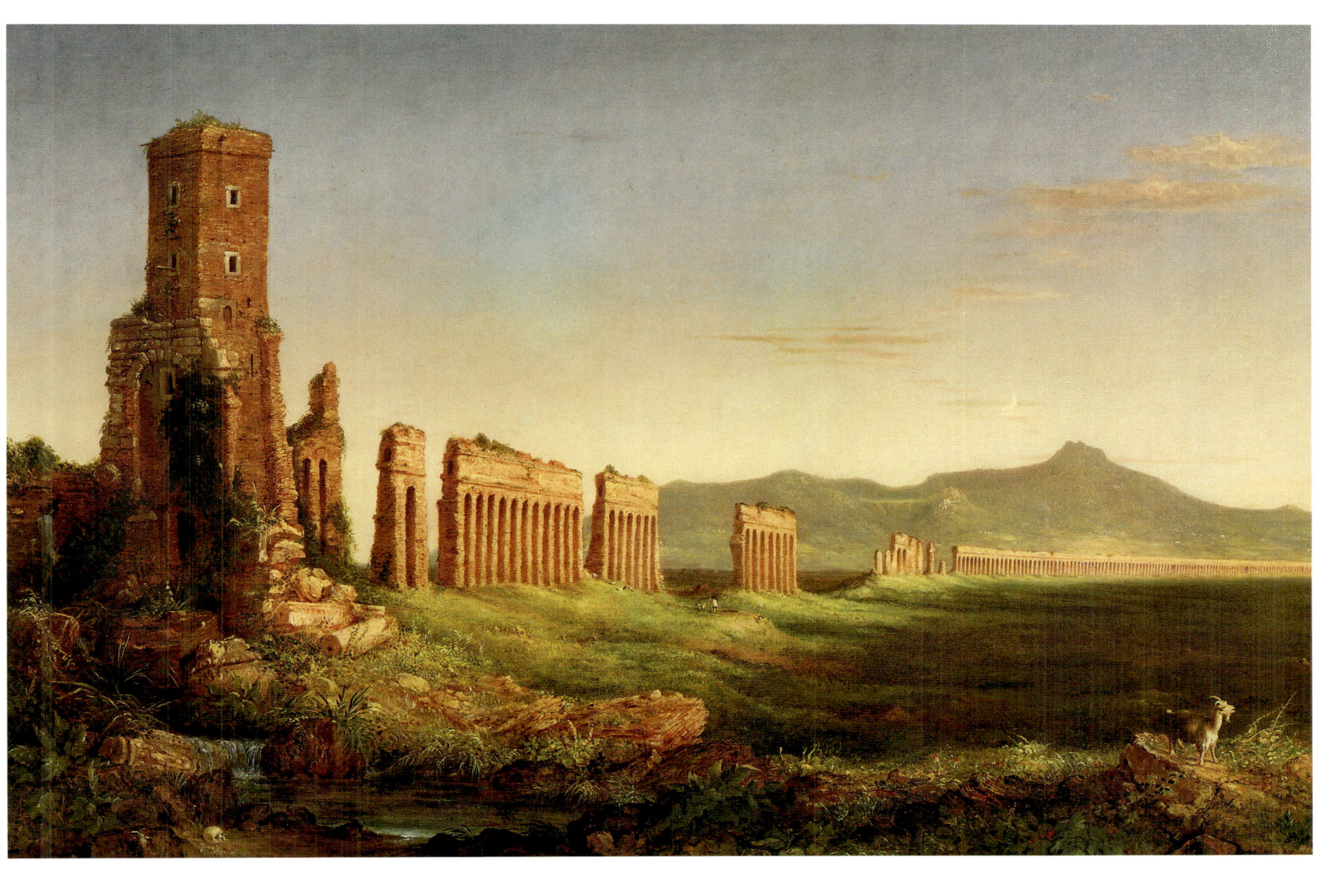

12. Asher B. Durand
(United States, 1796–1886)
A New England Landscape, 1870

Oil on canvas, 14¼ x 24⅛"
Bequest of Charles Parsons, 1905

In 1870, Asher Brown Durand, at the age of seventy-four and nearing the end of his long and distinguished career as one of America's leading landscape painters, presented a small exhibition of recent work at Goupil's Gallery in New York. One of the pictures he showed was *A New England Landscape.* In April of the previous year, after living fifty-two years in New York, Durand had retired to a newly built house and studio in the rural environs of Maplewood, New Jersey, near the present city of South Orange. This had been the place of his birth in 1796. According to John Durand's biography of his father, "The few works executed by him during this final period of his career sum up the labour of his life."[1] Although Durand began his career as an engraver and portraitist, by the 1850s he had gained notice as a landscape painter and was often considered, along with his friend Thomas Cole, as a founder of the Hudson River School. From the late 1830s on Durand was increasingly identified as a landscape painter, a position that was cemented in 1855 with the publication in *The Crayon* of his "Letters on Landscape Painting."[2] Durand's *A New England Landscape* perfectly summarizes the sentiments of the pastoral mode of landscape painting that he had advocated in his letters and practice.

In a lengthy review of Durand's exhibition at Goupil's Gallery in 1870 the New York *Evening Post* described the picture, interpreting the image in terms that Durand's audience would have understood, and providing valuable access to its meaning for viewers in the period following the national trauma of the Civil War:

> *The scene is a "New England Landscape," showing in the foreground a roadway leading up a hill, by a farm cottage, and onward until lost in the distance. . . . The picture is tenderly painted, exquisite in sentiment and poetry of feeling, and admirably expresses the quiet and repose which associate around the country home, and are the twin attractions of a pastoral landscape.*[3]

In a recent study entitled *Pastoral Inventions: Rural Life in Nineteenth-Century American Art and Culture* scholar Sarah Burns clarified the importance of landscapes imbued with the type of pastoral sentiments such as are expressed in Durand's *A New England Landscape.*[4] As Burns and other scholars have observed for Americans of the nineteenth century the illusion of a blissful life in the country held special appeal. The desire to counterpoint the alleged harmonies of rural life with the increasing alienation of large-scale urban life and the ruthlessness of industrial capitalism made images of the farm and the simple dignity of agrarian labor a perennially popular subject for many artists and writers. The Jeffersonian vision of America as an agrarian utopia populated by self-reliant farmers who were incorruptible because of their ownership of the land they tilled was a fiction that fueled political and social controversies in the nineteenth century, many of which have survived into the twentieth century.

The appeal of images of pastoral life for an urban middle class peaked in the decades around and particularly following the Civil War. Although artists and members of the literary elite often extolled the virtue of the wilderness, they understood that wild places would inexorably yield to the progress of the nation. For artists and patrons of Durand's period the middle landscape of the pastoral symbolized a passing moment of welcome equilibrium. The rural landscape such as glimpsed in an "ideal" or composite image like *A New England Landscape* represented the progress the nation welcomed, yet maintained the illusion of an environment unspoiled by the excesses of the urban and industrial landscape. As Durand's friend and mentor Thomas Cole put it in his "Lecture on American Scenery":

> *I have alluded to wild and uncultivated scenery; but the cultivated must not be forgotten, for it is still more important to man in his social capacity; it encompasses our homes, and though devoid of the stern sublimity of the wild, its quieter spirit steals tenderly into our bosoms, mingling with a thousand domestic affections and heart-touching associations—human hands have wrought and human deeds have hallowed all around.*[5]

It was to just such a landscape that Durand had retired a year previous to painting *A New England Landscape.*

Durand himself recognized the usefulness of images of pastoral harmony and repose. In a long passage in his "Letters on Landscape Painting" he explained how such paintings as *A New England Landscape* were intended to function in perpetuating the fiction of the bliss of rural life.

> *To the rich merchant and capitalist. . . [who have] a little time to rest and reflect in, Landscape Art especially appeals. . . . [He sees] the beautiful country-seat suddenly rising among green trees that were young with himself, and almost regarded as playmates. He returns to end his days where they began, and loves to embellish the consecrated spot with filial tenderness. . . .*
>
> *Suppose such a [person], on his return home, after the completion of his daily task of drudgery—his dinner partaken, and himself disposed of in his favorite arm chair, with one or more of faithful landscapes before him, and making no greater effort to look into the picture instead of on it, so as to perceive what it represents . . . many a fair vision of forgotten days will animate the canvas, and lead him through the scene, pleasant reminiscences and grateful emotions will spring up at every step, and care and anxiety will retire far behind him. If he possess aught of imaginative tissue . . . he becomes absorbed in the picture . . . and stretching fields and green meadows meet his hay; by the road-side stands the school-house, and merry children scatter from its door—such was the place where he first imbibed the knowledge that the world was large and round, while ambition whispered that the village grounds were too narrow for him,—and with the last rays of the setting sun, the pictures fade away.*[6]

Such commentary enables viewers at the end of the twentieth century to comprehend how images represented the imaginative fiction of America as an agrarian paradise, and better enables us to understand its continuing appeal, even today.

J. Gray Sweeney

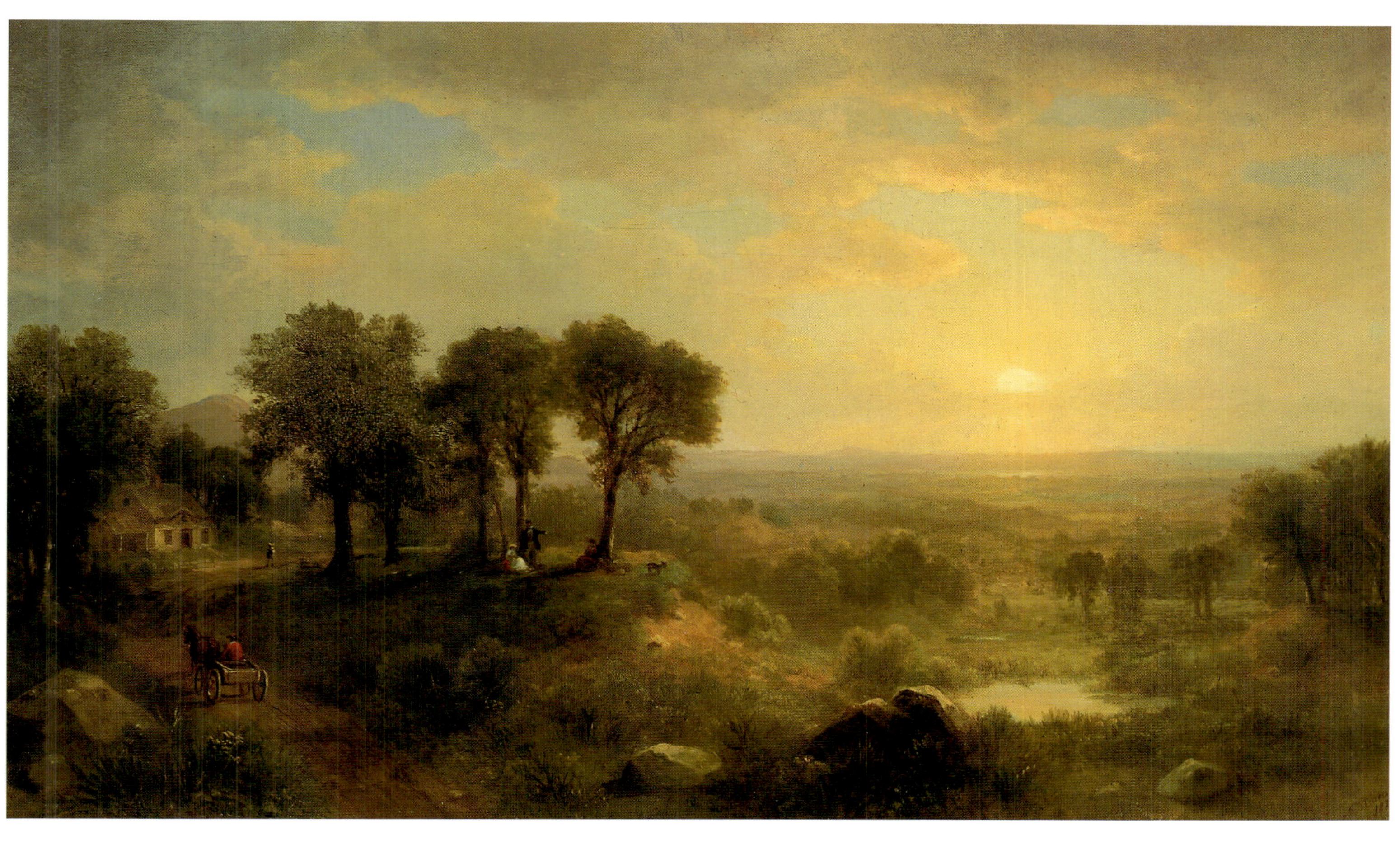

13. Frederic Edwin Church (United States, 1826–1900) *Twilight: Mount Desert Island, Maine,* 1865

Oil on canvas, 31¼ x 48½"
Gift of Charles Parsons, 1905

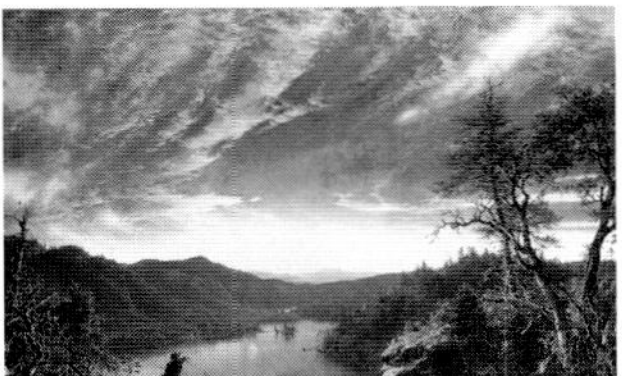
Frederic Edwin Church
Twilight in the Wilderness, 1860
Oil on canvas, 40 x 64"
The Cleveland Museum of Art
Mr. and Mrs. William H. Marlatt Fund, 65.223

In April 1865, with the Civil War drawing to a close and himself confronting a personal tragedy, Frederic Edwin Church completed a picture of Mount Desert Island, Maine, he called *Twilight.* Unlike the apocalyptic sunset he had painted only five years earlier at the beginning of the war, *Twilight in the Wilderness* (1860, Cleveland Museum of Art), his painting of 1865 evokes a mood of deep exhaustion that resonates with the psychic wounds of the nation and with the devastating loss of his two children. Church's son and daughter had died of diphtheria less than eight days apart in March 1865. The artist finished his picture the next month, just before the end of the Civil War on May 26. Art critic William M. Bryant, reviewing the picture in 1881, sensed these concerns: "It is the very picture of a world in which all differences are on the point of vanishing. A devout Buddhist might accept it as a solemn and sublime hymn to Nirvana! . . . The light is not focused: it is radiated, diffused. Here, there has been a struggle; but it is ended. The storm-cloud has spent its strength."[1]

The somber mood of malaise was first noticed when the picture was exhibited at the National Academy of Design. An unidentified reviewer for *The Albion* observed:

> *Mr. Church has become so great a man, that one wonders, perhaps unreasonably, that every work from his easel is not a masterpiece. Certainly, his Twilight, no. 310, cannot be so called. It is a landscape made up of broken foreground, a lake, and distant hills, over which a thunderstorm impends. The hues of the setting sun are nearly absorbed by the lurid clouds, save in the upper sky, where cloudlets of orange—that ought to float, but don't—are brilliantly tinted. These latter tints, to our eye, are so laid in, that they resemble chalk more than oil-color, and thereby produce a want of harmony throughout.*[2]

In contrast to *Twilight in the Wilderness* with its sharply defined clouds and brilliant sky that one critic thought represented "the Father of Lights," Church's 1865 painting has a diffuse sky that appears vague and undefined, producing "a want of harmony throughout." The powerful optimism of the earlier work gives way to the solemn darkness of an impending thunderstorm. In the foreground a large flat rock is highlighted in the cheerless glow, like some ancient sacrificial altar. At the left, a small deer comes down to drink. It is an image that recalls the drinking deer in Thomas Cole's *Desolation,* the last picture in the series *The Course of Empire.* In that series, the drinking deer symbolizes the renewal of life after a devastating holocaust. In light of Church's admiration for Cole's work, in particular *Desolation,* it is evident the deer performs a similar symbolic function in *Twilight.* In the distance a small white sail on the water of the bay suggests another of Cole's series, *The Voyage of Life.* The metaphor of a ship nearing the end of its voyage after a storm carried strong associations with the idea of the end of life's voyage. To the right, large rocky pinnacles seem formed in paint as emblematic symbols of nature's enduring anthropomorphic presences, inscrutable witnesses to the mystery of life.[3] *Twilight* is constructed by Church to represent not the turbulent ecstasy and optimism of his great picture of 1860, but the melancholy of personal and national exhaustion. It is for these reasons that the work attracted little positive attention when it was shown at the National Academy of Design in the fall of 1865.[4]

The inception of *Twilight* is recorded in a letter of 7 July 1864 to Church's friend William H. Osborn, the railroad entrepreneur. In it Church seems to express a hesitancy about the work and a pressing need for funds:

> *I have commenced a picture, four feet long, which includes a fine twilight effect which I made a sketch of from nature some weeks ago. I intend the picture for England according to your kindly expressed desire. I hope to make a good thing of it—certainly I shall try. . . . It would be of great service to me if I could [sic] a fair price for it. For my expenses are greatly increased and my engagements for the next season are of the greenback-ache kind. . . .*"[5]

The desire to own a painting like *Twilight in the Wilderness* may even help explain the patronage of the 1865 picture. *Twilight* was begun by Church toward the middle of 1864, without a buyer-in-advance. Fairly early on, the collector J. Strickler Jenkins of Baltimore wrote to Church in a letter dated 11 January 1865 that he had wanted to own one of Church's works "for a long time." Jenkins had heard apparently that a new painting of the twilight theme was in the formative stages on the artist's easel and asked if he might purchase it. Evidently Jenkins received a quick reply from Church, because on 25 February 1865 Jenkins again wrote to thank the painter for a reply of 23 January. In this letter Jenkins said, "I feel assured that you will complete the twilight in your best manner and that it will give me entire satisfaction and pleasure."[6]

It is easy to surmise that Mr. Jenkins of Baltimore might have become interested in Church's twilight paintings because W. T. Walters of Baltimore had commissioned the famous *Twilight in the Wilderness* and had owned it in that city until 1864. Whether Jenkins actually was pleased with his *Twilight* of 1865 is not recorded, although by 1880 it was owned by Charles Parsons of St. Louis who later presented his collection to Washington University.[7] Parsons wrote to Church on 24 November 1880 to say that he owned a "sundown effect at Mt. Desert. . . . I am under the impression that it formerly belonged to Mr. Walters of Baltimore." Parsons asked Church if this were so, and requested the artist to paint for him a tropical scene of the same size. Church's reply to Parsons is lost, but it is evident that he had to disabuse the St. Louis collector that the picture he had acquired was not the *Twilight in the Wilderness* once owned by Mr. Walters, although Church evidently did not dispute Parsons attribution of the scene as "Mt. Desert." The title had been changed to "Twilight Mount Desert" by the time the picture appeared at the original exhibition of the St. Louis School and Museum a year later.

J. Gray Sweeney

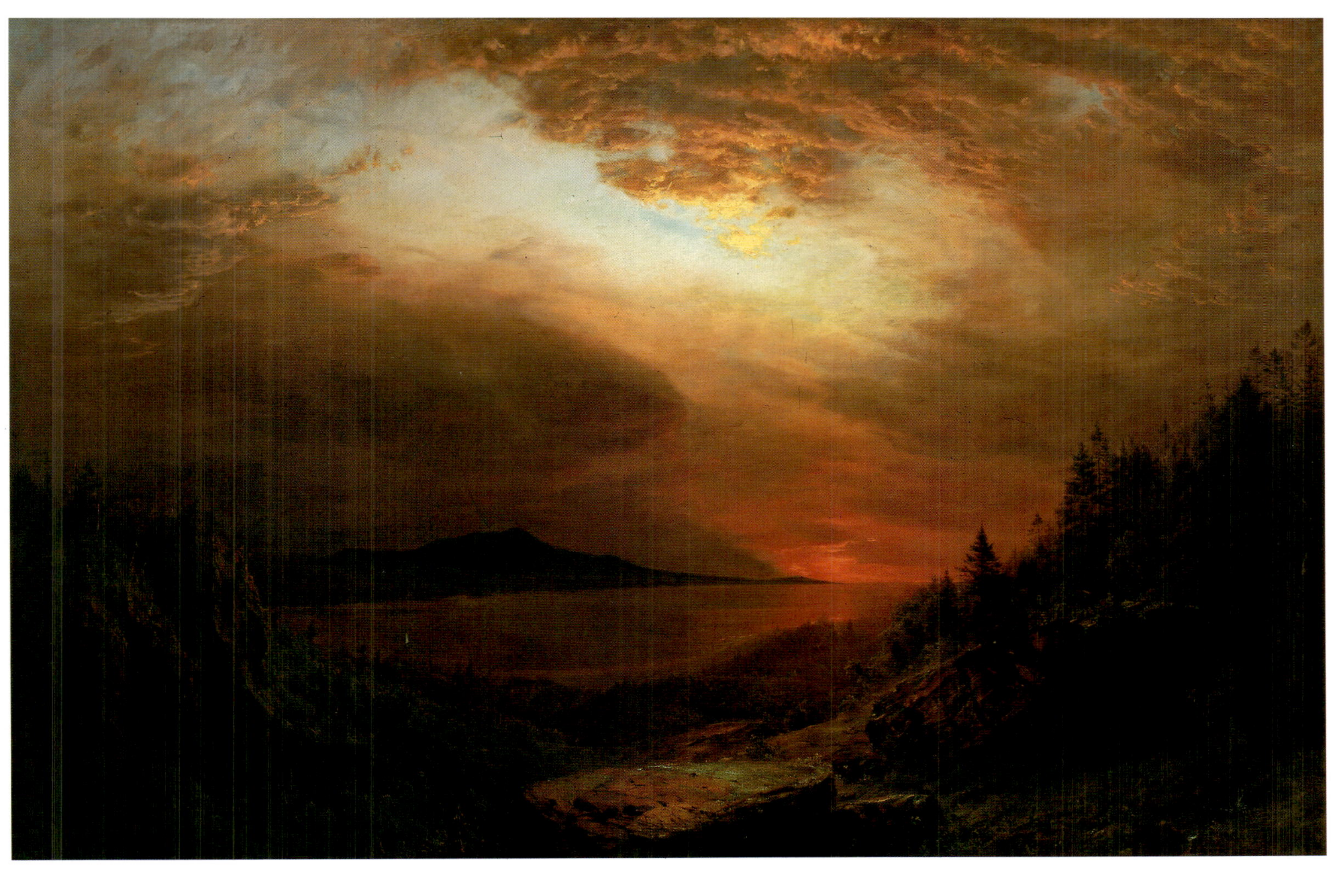

14. Frederic Edwin Church (United States, 1826–1900) *Sierra Nevada de Santa Marta,* 1883

Oil on canvas, 40 x 60½"
Gift of Charles Parsons, 1905

In November 1880 Frederic Edwin Church received a letter from the St. Louis collector Charles Parsons, who had already purchased his painting *Twilight: Mount Desert Island, Maine* of 1865, inquiring "for how much will you paint me a piece of the same size giving a full day effect either one of your tropical subjects or other as you think best—I am inclined to a tropical scene—."[1] Past the prime of his career and suffering from incurable rheumatoid arthritis that had crippled his painting hand, forcing him to use his left hand, Church agreed to provide Parsons with a work identical in size to his earlier picture. The purchase price agreed upon was $3500. The painting was based on an experience Church had thirty years earlier in 1853 when he first traveled to South America in search of volcanoes. In a letter to a friend written in 1895 Church nostalgically recalled the moment:

> *[Santa Marta] was the first snow peak I ever witnessed and [it] made a profound impression which my memory has perhaps exaggerated. . . . I saw it from the sea level at Barragnuilla, [Ecuador] looking across the Magdalena River where it is several miles wide and a low horizon. . . . I noticed a peculiar light high up in the sky which a single glance revealed to be 'Sta Marta'—Little else than the great pyramid of snow was visible but it was wonderfully grand.*[2]

In the spring of 1883, around the 30th anniversary of that memorable voyage, Church completed his picture of the South American volcano and presented it to Parsons. The subject was one that had gained Church fame in the mid-nineteenth century.[3] South America and its verdant equatorial landscapes and sublime volcanoes held considerable interest for Americans during the expansive era of Manifest Destiny. Yet Church's painting for Parsons was an image of recollection and of nostalgia for his earlier successes with such paintings as *Heart of the Andes* (1859, Metropolitan Museum of Art, New York) and *Cotopaxi* (1862, Detroit Institute of the Arts). In what is possibly the most substantial exchange of letters with a patron, Church explained his intentions to Parsons. Writing on 11 April 1883, Church stated:

> *As I developed the picture I introduced a more verdant country than exists in that part of New Granada where I first saw the great snowy mountain—But it is reasonable to believe—indeed it is more than probable that the country in the interior is well watered and all the conditions I have presented may be found there—So we may regard it as a Title consistent with the subject.*[4]

In his letter of 11 April Church also seemed concerned that Parsons would like the work. "I hope that the picture will please not only you and Mrs. Parsons at first sight but what is more important that it will grow in favor the more it is studied."[5] His concern was undoubtedly precipitated by the difficulty he had in painting—a fact he referred to explicitly in a letter of 3 June 1883. "I do not know when I shall undertake so large a picture again . . . unless I can get rid of the rheumatism which has got me in its grip as a vise."[6]

In his letters to Parsons Church touched on a number of issues concerning the "seasoning" of the painting and its frame. For example, on 11 April 1883 Church wrote: "The frame is effective and I think suits the picture. . . . This frame will look better in a few years than it does now so the picture softens and grows more harmonious by time so the frame will appear less harsh and more in keeping."[7]

A few days later Church again wrote to Parsons:

> *The last days work on the picture improved it greatly. I felt some confidence in sending it to you feeling that if you and Mrs. Parsons were pleased with my former work you will certainly like this one which has cost me so much time and study. After 4 or 5 years it will begin to assume those delicate and harmonious tones which time only can give and will continue to improve thereafter. I hope it will long prove a cheerful and pleasant friend.*[8]

By late April Parsons had received his long awaited picture and wrote to Church with some disappointment. Church responded in a fascinating letter of 23 April 1883 that disclosed his defensiveness about his abilities, his notions about the "seasoning" of the picture, his intentions in the image, and the relationship of his traditional Hudson River School aesthetics to the Impressionists.

> *Although I confess to being much disappointed that it did not impress you with the decided favor I hoped and expected it would—yet I feel confident that as you study and contemplate it more and more you will be more impressed with certain features and effects which cost me much study and effort to attain—. . . .*
>
> *With regard to the strength of it I aimed mainly for the luminosity—As the picture has not yet been varnished . . . —The picture will grow richer and deeper especially in the foreground as time goes on—That always follows the use of earth colors—It was so in the "Andes of Equador" and others—*
>
> *I hope that you have not been much impressed by the "Impressionists"—that sort of art is really but one Phase of decoration and so easily acquired. . . . It is really very superficial all in the surface which accounts for the sudden springing up of a crowd of young geniuses fully armed. I forgot to state that the time in your picture is near the sunset—I assumed that the foreground is about 5000 or 6000 feet above the sea. The snowy mountain is upwards of 20,000 feet high—and of course very distant.*[9]

The last letter to Parsons from Church is dated 28 April 1883. In it Parsons evidently accepted the picture with more enthusiasm, much to Church's relief.

> *I was much gratified to learn by your last letter that the picture—after being well placed in your gallery impresses you all favorably. I feel sure it will continue to grow in favor and I hope will prove a source of pleasure to yourself and Mrs. Parsons for many years to come.*[10]

This exchange of letters, albeit one-sided as only Church's are preserved, provides important evidence of the relationship between artist and patron as the taste for Hudson River School landscapes was waning. They illuminate the meaning and importance that such works as *Sierra Nevada de Santa Marta* were once thought to possess.

J. Gray Sweeney

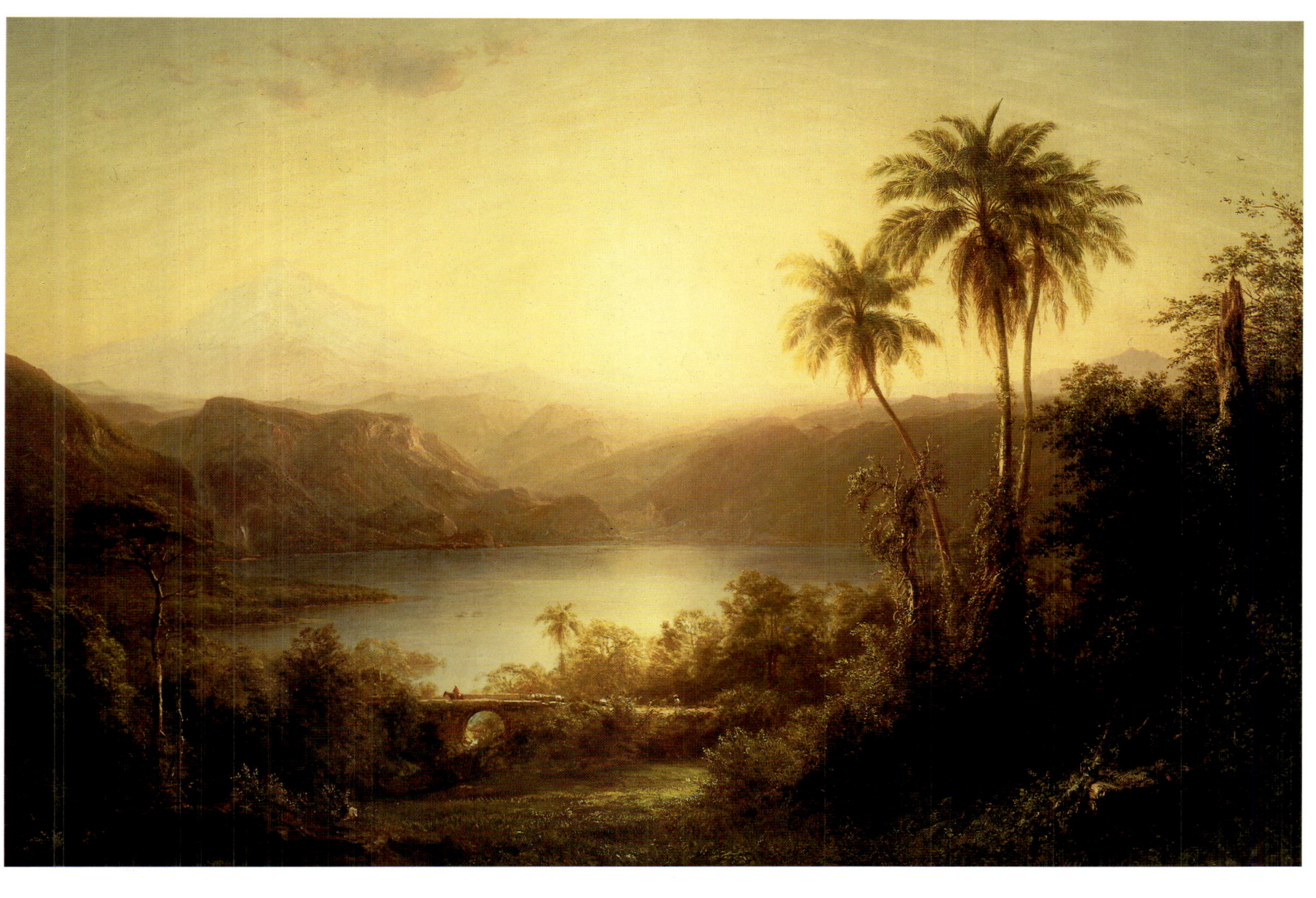

15. Sanford R. Gifford (United States, 1823–1880)
Early October in the White Mountains, 1860

Oil on canvas, 14⅛ x 24"
Gift of Charles Parsons, 1905

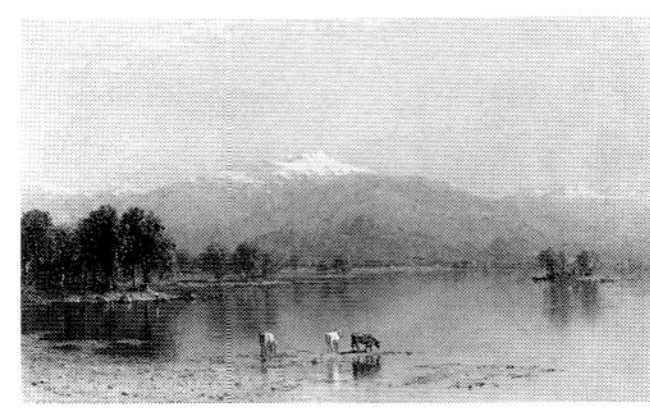

Sanford R. Gifford
Early October in the White Mountains, c. 1859
Oil on canvas, 9 x 14½"
New Britian Museum of American Art, Connecticut
Stephen B. Lawrence Fund
Photo, E. Irving Blomstrann

In paintings like *Early October in the White Mountains* Sanford Robinson Gifford—properly considered among the most intellectual of the Hudson River School painters—created works of such startling simplicity that early efforts to understand his art focused mainly upon its stylistic and topographic aspects. Gifford's own colleagues and the best critics of his time considered him to be an artist of exquisite emotional and intellectual subtlety. "His best pictures can not be merely seen but *contemplated* with entire satisfaction," wrote Henry T. Tuckerman (the "American Vasari") in his definitive accounting of mid-nineteenth-century artists.[1] According to Tuckerman, Gifford's best works are "the reverse of sensational; their subjects are often destitute of exceptional picturesqueness, but selected simply because they include average and suggestive traits, normal aspects, recognized and familiar charms." Gifford's power with his contemporaries lay in his mastery of the elusive aesthetic mode of "beauty" in repose. His works "do not dazzle, they win; they appeal to our calm and thoughtful appreciations; they minister to our most gentile and gracious sympathies, to our most tranquil and congenial observations."[2] These aspects of Gifford's achievement are effectively revealed in *Early October in the White Mountains.*

A critic writing in *The Home Journal* the same year Gifford painted *Early October in the White Mountains* framed the reception of the artist's landscapes by his contemporaries in this way:

> *It does one good to sit an hour with Gifford; to muse over the warm, glowing atmosphere, the rich mellow foliage which gives such a dream-like charm to his landscapes. You see at once that he has the eye of a true poet; and a heart in sympathy with nature writes its longings in the delicacy and naturalness of his touches. There is something so soft, so balmy, and yet so bewitching, in the leafy vestments of Gifford's hills and dales, that you overlook an attempt to enrich nature at times, and think only of sharing the treasures of a mind capable of spreading such rich a feast of delicacies out on canvas.*[3]

In his address at the Gifford Memorial Meeting at the Century Club in New York in 1880 the artist John F. Weir observed, "Gifford's art was poetic and reminiscent. It was not realistic, in the formal sense. It was nature passed through the alembic of a finely organized sensibility."[4]

What sets Gifford apart in the estimation of art historians and curators today was his evocation of light—a light which has often been linked with the effects of what some modern scholars writing in the early 1960s named "luminism"—a term that neither Gifford or his associates in the Hudson River School ever used or would have likely appreciated because of its derivation from "Impressionism." Yet the artists assembled at the memorial clearly recognized that "Gifford loved the light," as Weir put it. For Weir and Gifford's contemporaries, as for admirers of the artist today, the distinguishing feature of his work was its ability to elicit impressions "derived from the landscape when air is charged with a effulgence of irruptive and glowing light." Yet these poetic qualities had little, as recent studies have shown, to do with mere representations of glowing light, planar arrangements of space and a pervasive sense of quiet—attributes associated by scholars promoting the ahistorical idea of luminism with the Emersonian "transparent eyeball." Gifford's contemporaries understood that Gifford's art "stands apart as the sincere outcome of a serious and steadfast aim, directed by firm intelligence." Weir grasped that Gifford was "unerringly profound in his insight into that which was most truly nature; of those potent truths that underlie the superficial aspects that engage the common mind or attract the common eye." Weir believed that Gifford's "motives were deep-seated; they were not of the idle surface-rippling kind that would make of art a mere reflection in lieu of expression." Weir and others discerned that "Gifford was the artist rather than the painter."[5]

What meaning is expressed by the glowing sentiments of light in Gifford's image of *Early October in the White Mountains*? The aesthetic ideal of beauty in the unity of repose was certainly a major element in the work. The minute detailing of foreground rocks and trees, the contentment of grazing cattle, the comfortable farmer's home at left, and the light enveloping the distant mountains all reinforced the sentiment of nature in a soothing, comforting moment. Such images were designed to fulfill the pre-Raphaelite demands for "truth to nature," and could readily satisfy middle-class patrons who longed for an armchair trip to the country, which it was believed could refresh and console the fatigued city dweller. *The Crayon,* a leading art magazine of the mid-nineteenth-century, expressed this sentiment:

> *Gifford's works are characterized by a happy choice of subjects—subjects that suggest a poetic grasp of the scene selected. His pictures are generally chaste, and unpretending in color, and are remarkable for a luminous atmosphere. Their poetic quality is recognizable in a fine sense of the picturesque, a feeling of repose, and that subordination of minor truths to important truths, the artistic combination of which is intelligible in the term unity.*[6]

The Crayon's comment could easily be a review of Gifford's *Early October in the White Mountains.* In fact, a review of 1881 by William Bryant singled out these qualities in Gifford's picture for praise: "The whole scene is expressive of the utmost peacefulness. The smooth lake, the fine mountains, and the motionless trees, all give the impression of perfect repose; while the rich harmonious tone of color is like a tranquil breath of satisfied completeness."[7]

According to Weir, "[Gifford's] life was a quiet one, uneventful—in a spectacular sense—and absorbed in the practice of his art."[8] He was born in 1823 and raised at Hudson, New York, in sight of the Catskill Mountains and Thomas Cole's studio. His early work was deeply influenced by the example of Cole. He began painting around 1847, and by 1855 he made a "pilgrimage" to Europe. Upon his return he settled in the 10th Street Studio Building in New York, and he exhibited regularly at the National Academy of Design. In the summer of 1870 he journeyed to the Colorado Rockies with Worthington Whittredge and John F. Kensett. Gifford died in New York in 1880.

J. Gray Sweeney

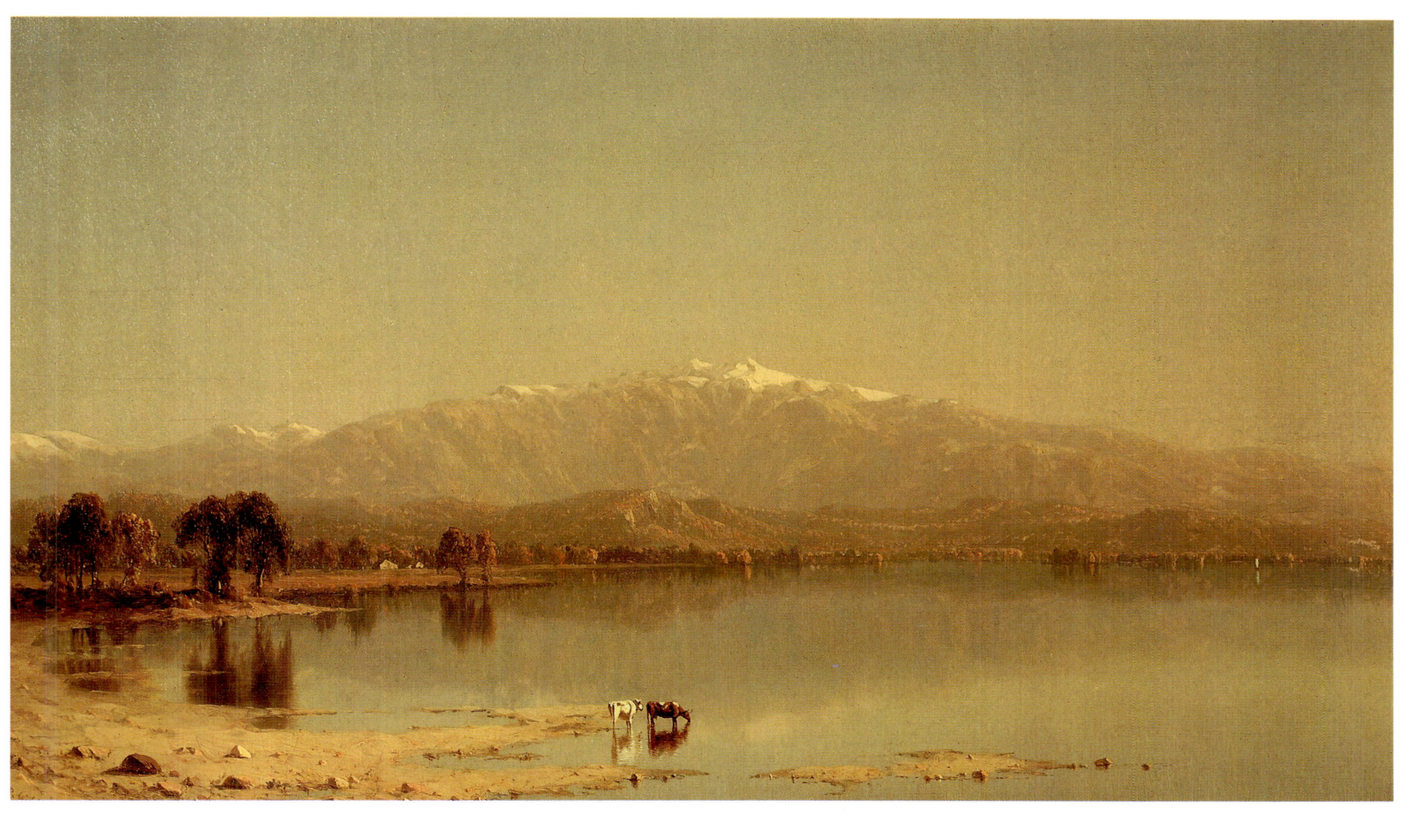

16. Sanford R. Gifford (United States, 1823–1880) *Rheinstein,* 1872–74

Oil on canvas, 31¼ x 27⅜"
Bequest of Charles Parsons, 1905

In 1873 at a reception in his studio in New York's famous Tenth Street Studio Building, American landscape painter Sanford R. Gifford exhibited his dramatic painting of the historic German castle Rheinstein perched high above the Rhine river. A writer for the *New York Evening Post* described *Rheinstein* as "elaborately finished" with "a glowing sunlight effect."[1] Gifford had first visited Rheinstein in June 1856. He painted another version of the same subject that he exhibited at the National Academy of Design in 1860, but that picture remains unlocated.[2] More than a decade later the image of a picturesque castle purchased on a rocky promontory high above the entrance to a legendary stretch of the Rhine leading to the Lorelei continued to exert a strong romantic attraction on the American artist's imagination. Gifford revisited the site during his second European trip in August of 1869, and composed a small 10¼ x 9" sketch of the castle that he sold in 1872 (private collection).[3]

The image of a perfectly restored gothic castle bathed in the golden light of the setting sun, while on the horizon a silver-orbed full moon rises, exemplified the mystery of and a poetic nostalgia for the great events of Germany's fabled Rhine region—an essential part of the approved experience of medieval history that American tourists frequently sought. Although Gifford's *Rheinstein* is a more naturalistic image, the sentiment of nostalgia for the fabled middle ages that Americans had come to appreciate in the poetry of Sir Walter Scott and Lord Byron is ultimately related to the historical reconstructions found in Thomas Cole's series *The Departure* and *The Return* (1837, Corcoran Gallery of Art) and *The Past* and *The Present* (1838, Amherst College) that Gifford had greatly admired as a young artist. Gifford's admiration of the castle also resonates with the mid-nineteenth-century fascination with the architectural styles of the Gothic Revival, which was particularly strong in England, America, and Germany.

During his first visit to Rheinstein in 1856 Gifford had commented in his diary on the accuracy of the restoration of the castle, which had been a ruin, by Frederick of Prussia.[4] The Prince had gone to great lengths between 1825 and 1829 to not only restore the exterior appearance of the castle to an early nineteenth-century Romantic estimation of what a medieval structure should have looked like, but he had extensively furnished it with period furnishings and decorative objects. Gifford may have also been influenced by the tales he had read of in guide books of the Emperor Rudolph of Hapsburg, who built the nearby Clemens-Capelle to insure the repose of the soul of robber barons he had hanged. Gifford's image accentuates the reflection from the gothic windows of the chapel at Rheinstein, as an allusion to these legendary events of German history.

The artist was also careful to record such important details as the large iron basket used for lighting signal fires hanging from the lower tower that had been restored by Prince Frederick, and the Hohenzollern banner flying from the upper tower. These details, along with the solitary figure of the wanderer silhouetted on the road below and the tiny figures glimpsed on the parapets above, add to the associations of a place completely removed from the hurly-burly industrial world of nineteenth-century Europe. The presence of a distant sailboat, its sails reflected on the calm surface of the Rhine, instead of a modern steamboat, functions to complete Gifford's sentiment-filled fantasy of a poetic return to an earlier, more harmonious medieval world.

The name of Rheinstein itself may have also played a role in the construction of Gifford's image. It means literally "Rhine rock," referring to the towering rocky promontory on which the castle had been constructed in the eleventh century and which for many decades, until it became obsolete and was abandoned in the early seventeenth century, had made the castle virtually impregnable to siege.[5] The name may have also suggested to Gifford an allusion to the power of nature, and to the emblematic means familiar to artists such as Gifford for its visual personification. I have argued elsewhere that Gifford, like many artists of his period, remained committed to the romantic belief in the "pathetic fallacy," the attribution of human emotions, even the human countenance, to such inanimate objects as rocks, trees and clouds.[6] Directly below the castle parapet, etched in the living rock, is the profile of a human visage gazing serenely outward towards the Rhine River and the rising moon. Such anthropomorphic emblems were also a feature of Cole's work that Gifford had absorbed as a young artist, and which he had returned to frequently in the 1860s, most notably in the personification the "nude" of mother earth in his renown painting of 1866, *Twilight on Hunter Mountain* (Terra Museum of American Art).

The subject of the Rhine River and its history was one that held special meaning to Gifford's American contemporaries. Early art historian S. G. W. Benjamin, writing in 1875, opened his sketch of Sanford R. Gifford by noting:

> *There are two rivers, which above all others, have become famous for the beauty of their scenery, the Rhine and the Hudson. The former has the charm of romantic castles and legends to add to the loveliness of its shores. But if the Hudson lacks these attractions, it has no less natural beauty, and, in some places, more grandeur than its rival.*[7]

Gifford's youth was spent near the Hudson, and his later attraction to the scenery of the Rhine combined his love of nature with his contemporaries' fascination with medieval pageantry and history. His colleague artist John Ferguson Weir, reviewing Gifford's work two years later, observed that his style "is thoroughly matured, rich, elegant in the manipulation of the materials of his art, and free from all effort or straining after effect." Weir thought that Gifford's art "interpret[s] that which is most poetic and profound in the aspects of nature. . . . His pictures are not the mere collective statement of facts, they are something more; they are the free expression of the highest and most poetic qualities of the landscape; and thus his art is enduring, sympathetic and profound."[8]

J. Gray Sweeney

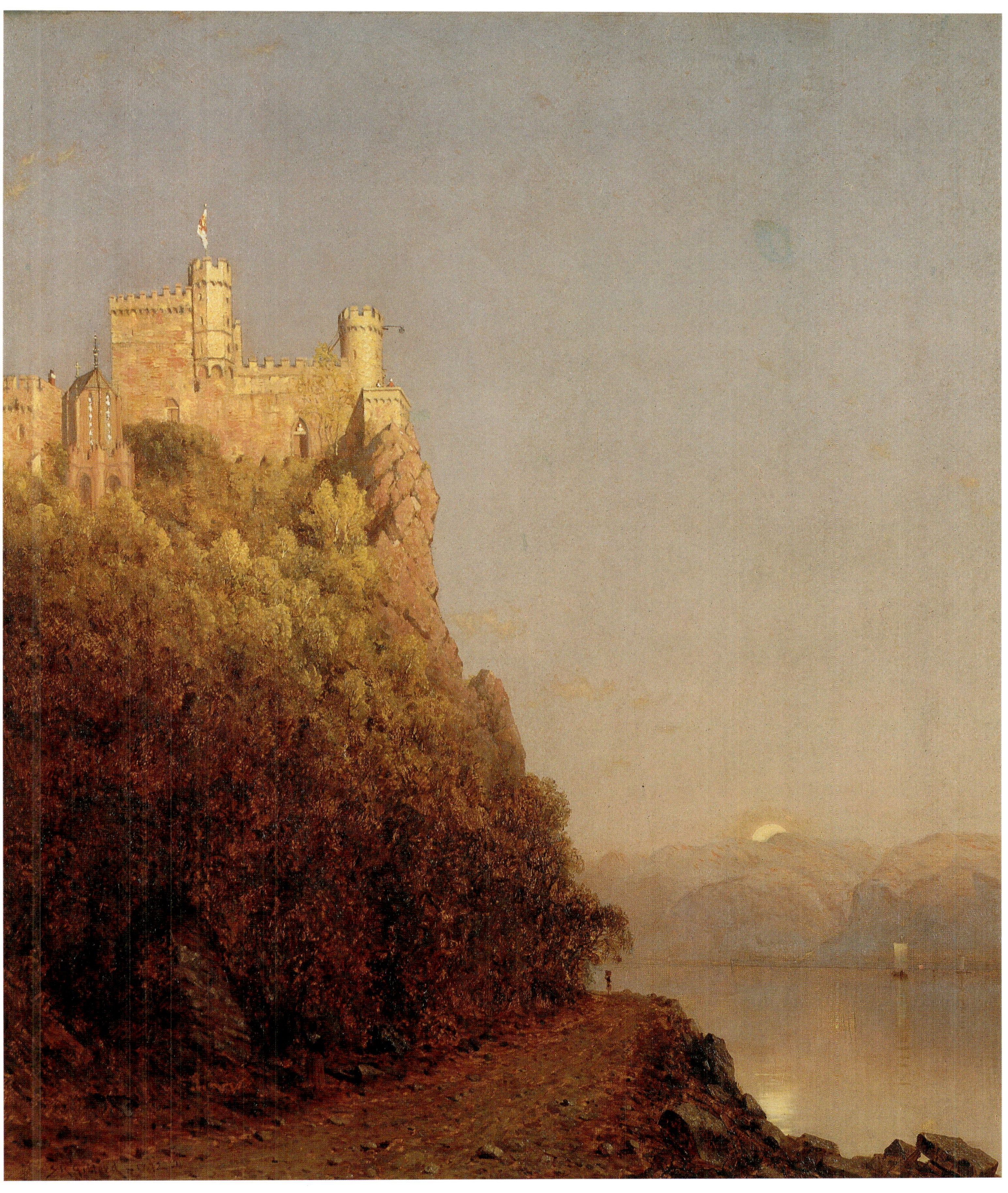

17. George Caleb Bingham (United States, 1811–1879) *Daniel Boone Escorting Settlers through the Cumberland Gap,* 1851–52

Oil on canvas, 36½ x 50¼"
Gift of Mr. Nathaniel Phillips, 1890

Claude Regnier (after George C. Bingham)
The Emigration of Daniel Boone, 1852
Lithograph, 18⁵⁄₁₆ x 23¾"
The Missouri Historical Society, St. Louis

Daniel Boone was a quintessential symbol of western expansion in mid-nineteenth-century America. No single work of art has contributed more to establishing Boone's mythic status for nineteenth- and twentieth-century Americans than George Caleb Bingham's *The Emigration of Daniel Boone* or *Daniel Boone Escorting Settlers through the Cumberland Gap.* Only a few years ago Bingham's paintings were celebrated as little more than charming, naive images of an "heroic age" of American history.[1] Today, however, this view has radically shifted, and the meaning of Bingham's image of Daniel Boone is now understood as representing many of the complex social, political and intellectual issues that faced the young nation in the turbulent decade of the 1850s, just before the Civil War.[2]

The subject of Daniel Boone fascinated the Missouri artist from his youth. Around the age of ten Bingham witnessed portraitist Chester Harding making finished paintings from his 1820 life sketch of Boone, which was drawn the same year the pioneer died.[3] Boone continued to absorb Bingham's attention for over two decades, leading to his 1851–52 painting of the pioneer, and also to one of the greatest frustrations of his career. As early as 1830, and in several lost works of the 1840s, Bingham represented Boone in political banners that he hoped "would take with the multitude, and . . . might be emblematical [sic] of the early state of the west."[4] In 1851, while working in New York, Bingham began painting the picture now at Washington University's Gallery of Art. He had expectations of selling the work to the American Art-Union, and of profiting from an engraving of the image. "The subject is a popular one in the west," he wrote, "and one which had never been painted."[5]

In constructing the complex meaning of his image Bingham relied on several texts, and used both Christian and classical allusions in formulating the picture's symbolism. The picture represents a conflation of two major events in Boone's penetration of the Indian Territories of Kentucky in 1773 and 1775. The first was unsuccessful, while the second led to Boone's later fame as the first settler in Kentucky. In the image Bingham showed Boone marching frontally toward the spectator on his successful march into Indian territory. Bingham asserted that he used Humphrey Marshall's book, *History of Kentucky* (1824), but more importantly it is now clear that he also relied on John M. Peck's *Life of Daniel Boone* (1847). The latter contains passages that are reflected almost verbatim in the picture. Bingham's awareness of classical art as a source for the designs of his figures has long been recognized. The pose of the striding figure of Boone is modeled on the Greek sculpture of the *Doryphorus,* although the position of the legs are reversed, and Boone's companion, the guide at left, ties his shoes in the manner of *Jason* or *Cincinnatus.*[6]

Bingham's ambition to sell his picture to the Art-Union was disappointed because in the spring of 1851 it was rejected. He then sent it to be engraved in Paris by Goupil & Co. However, shortly after, Bingham extensively reworked the image. Comparing the Goupil lithograph with the painting as it looks today reveals important evidence of how Bingham reconceived the meaning of his image. He further idealized the faces of his figures, moving some of them in the background, and he extensively reworked the landscape. The clear serene light seen in the lithograph was replaced with dark storm clouds, and the broad, light-filled valley in the early version was replaced by a sublime valley with menacing cliffs. Bingham's treatment of the sky, beetling cliffs, and dramatic tree at left were all additions that reveal the influence of Thomas Cole. The dramatic expression of anthropomorphic rocks in the background contributes impressively to the foreboding valley seething with unseen dangers, through which the pioneers emerge into the dramatic light of the foreground. This mountain valley also evokes associations with the 23rd Psalm for Bingham's audience.

In reworking his picture Bingham softened the physiognomy of his figures, especially that of Boone and his scout. Ennobling these lead figures with a more youthful, idealized facial characterization allowed the artist to replace symbolically the scoundrels and exploiters who had gone west with an image proclaiming the nobility of the nation's westward expansion. Bingham's pioneers are families of farmers, not squatters, moving their entire communities to build a permanent agrarian civilization on the western frontier.

Furthermore, Bingham relied on the popular idea of typology to cast Boone into an American type of a biblical hero. In this case the figure of Boone is represented as Moses confidently leading his chosen people into the promised lands of the west. At his feet a curiously exaggerated horizontal root intersects another upright branch to create a deliberate cruciform. This subtle but important detail reminded spectators that, unlike the Hebrew prophet Moses, Daniel Boone and his party of chosen people are specifically Christian.

Boone's wife, Rebecca Boone, likewise resonates with dual meanings and associations. Sitting behind her husband atop a white horse, a shawl draped around her, she forms the highest point in the triangular composition and acts as a powerful reminder of the Virgin Mary. She also symbolizes all courageous pioneering women, just as Boone becomes an archetype for the heroic pioneering male in the guise of Moses.

Bingham's pictorial strategy was to control the point of view from which the spectator encounters Boone and his company. A careful mixture of conservative and progressive political values are expressed in the figures of Boone's party.[7] These were combined with their resonances to biblical prophecy, and their implicit endorsement of nationalistic views on westward migration, to visually identify the Christian future of the nation with the claiming of the west by a few "good" white men and their families.

Bingham remained preoccupied with the subject of Daniel Boone through the 1850s. During that period he repeatedly proposed but was completely frustrated in his ambition to paint a large painting of the pathfinder for the Capitol in Washington. After the Civil War Bingham became increasingly absorbed by political issues and never again returned to the subject of Daniel Boone.

J. Gray Sweeney

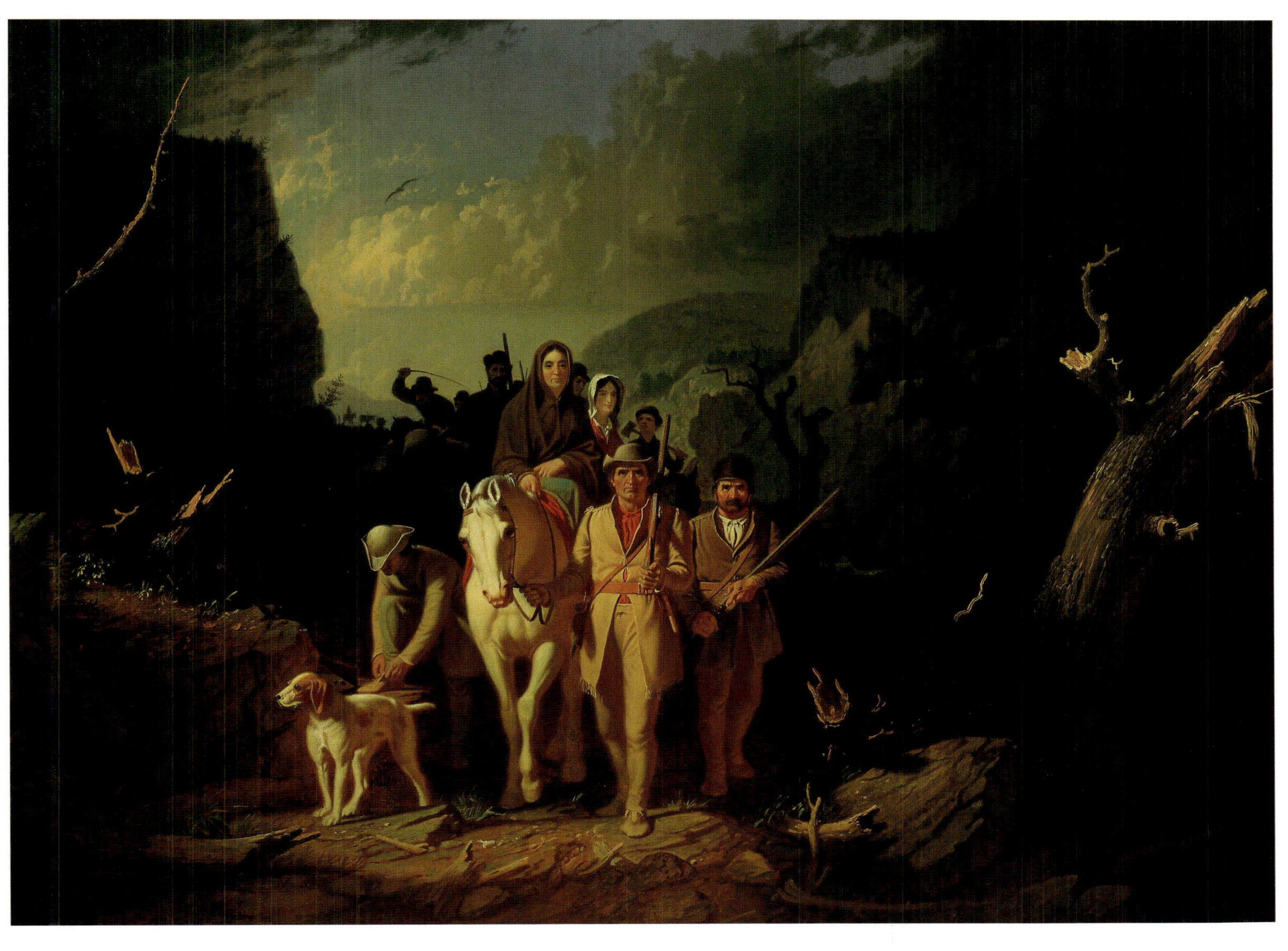

18. Carl F. Wimar
(United States, b. Germany, 1828–1862)
The Abduction of Daniel Boone's Daughter by the Indians, 1853
Oil on canvas, 40 x 50"
Gift of Mr. John T. Davis, Jr.

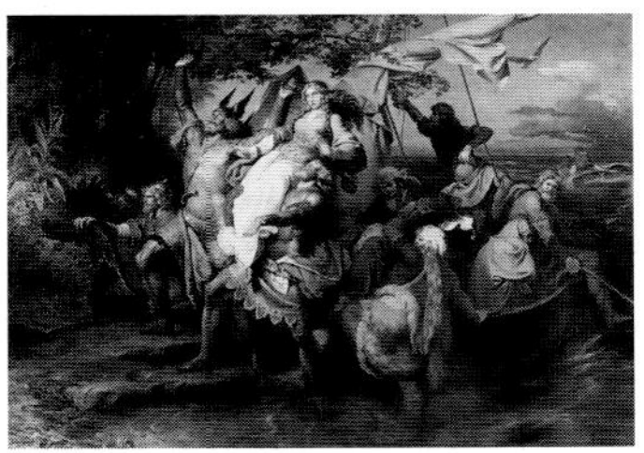

Emanuel Leutze
The Vikings' First Landings in America, 1845
Oil on canvas
Kunstmuseum Düsseldorf im Ehrenhof
Loan from the collection Volmer, Wuppertal

In *The Abduction of Daniel Boone's Daughter by the Indians* Carl F. Wimar created one of the most compelling captivity paintings in the history of American art that reflects, through its complex symbolism, contemporary social preconceptions concerning women, Native Americans, and the "West." Wimar orchestrated a captivity narrative into a mythical image of heroic American pioneers in their struggle to settle the west.

Wimar immigrated to the United States in 1843 with his family as a youth of 15 years full of German romantic ideas concerning the American west. After a brief apprenticeship with a local painter and decorator, Wimar was motivated by Emanuel Leutze's *Washington Crossing the Delaware* (1851, Metropolitan Museum of Art) to return to his homeland to study under the German-American master of history painting in Düsseldorf. While in Düsseldorf Wimar earned the appelation, "the Indian painter," both because of his appearance, and because he was the only artist in Europe painting the popular subject of Native Americans. *The Abduction of Daniel Boone's Daughter by the Indians* was Wimar's first ambitious painting and established the style, subjects, and iconography of his Düsseldorf works. During his four years in Düsseldorf (1852–1856), he painted approximately twenty Indian subjects, including four versions of *The Abduction,* all of which focused on the confrontation and conflict between the Native Americans and the encroaching European settlers.[1] In these paintings Wimar depicted the Natives as pagan savages abducting and attacking the pioneers, who are portrayed as saints or martyrs historically and morally justified in their Manifest Destiny to occupy the continent.

Completed at the end of Wimar's first year in Düsseldorf, *The Abduction* illustrates the moment Jemima Boone is abducted from her canoe while picking flowers on the banks of the Kentucky river. She kneels in her boat with her hands folded, pleading for mercy from her captors while two of them search anxiously for signs of Boone's presence. The third Indian gazes up in rapture at the beautiful white woman whose dress has fallen from her shoulder. This abduction was originally recorded in John Filson's book *The Discovery, Settlement and Present State of Kentucky* (Wilmington, DE: James Adams, 1784), but Wimar appears to have been inspired by the more expansive account of this abduction in Daniel Bryan's epic poem *The Mountain Muse* (Harrisonburg, VA: Davidson and Bourne, 1813), which devoted a significant section of the poem to a dramatic description of this subject.

The abduction of Boone's and Callaway's daughters appeared frequently in the literature on Daniel Boone; however, the first illustration of the subject was not printed until almost seventy years after the event was first recorded in Filson's book. Karl Bodmer and Jean-François Millet jointly created the lithograph, *The Capture of the Daughters of Boone and Callaway* (1852, Washington University Gallery of Art), that established the prototype for future book illustrations of this subject. Wimar could have seen Bodmer's print in his Cologne studio, which he may have visited in 1852; however, Wimar looked to his mentor Emanuel Leutze for his interpretation of the subject, borrowing from Leutze's *The Vikings First Landing in America* (1845, private collection, Düsseldorf). The landscape setting, the angle of the boat to the shore, the triangulation of the figures and the luminous vista off to the right are all borrowed from Leutze's precedent.

After the Bodmer and Millet print numerous illustrations of this story appeared in the literature on Boone[2]; however, no other artist besides Wimar created a captivity painting of this subject. Expanding on the popularity of the Boone myth at mid-century, Wimar made a significant contribution to the important American tradition of the captivity narrative. Captivity narratives were extremely popular throughout the eighteenth and nineteenth centuries, serving as moral treatises focusing on the trials of a captive woman, the embodiment of civilizing virtues in European society, to dramatize the conflict between "civilized" Christian European settlers and "savage" pagan Natives. Often these books use the moral imperative implicit in the Christian religion to justify the domination and annihilation of the Native American.

Wimar deftly conveyed the moral dichotomy central to captivity narratives by departing from the traditional abduction figure type established by John Vanderlyn's *Murder of Jane McCrea* (1804, Wadsworth Atheneum), which depicts the captive kneeling with her arms spread to repel her attackers. Vanderlyn's figure type for the captive maiden was ultimately derived from the European tradition of rapes and abductions portraying women protesting their abduction with open arms, a pose that suggests their sexual vulnerability. By contrast, Wimar portrayed "the high-soul'd Jemima" (Bryan) in the pose of a Christian martyr or saint kneeling in prayer. Jemima's pose recalls that of Mary Magdalen at the base of the cross found in crucifixion imagery since the Renaissance. The parallel between Jemima Boone and Mary Magdalen implies several levels of potential meaning. On a superficial level, Jemima Boone is pleading for mercy from her captors, and, secondarily, praying for rescue or salvation from the Indians. Metaphorically, she may be seeking redemption from the moral compromise that she may suffer at the hands of the Indians.

One scholar surmised that Carl Wimar's *The Abduction of Daniel Boone's Daughter by the Indians* "is a rather unimaginative picture rooted in an overworked tradition."[2] However, an interpretation based upon the iconography of European history painting reveals that Wimar created a painting that reflects essential beliefs and myths of the American cultural identity in the era of Manifest Destiny through the tales of Daniel Boone and the captivity narrative.

Joseph D. Ketner

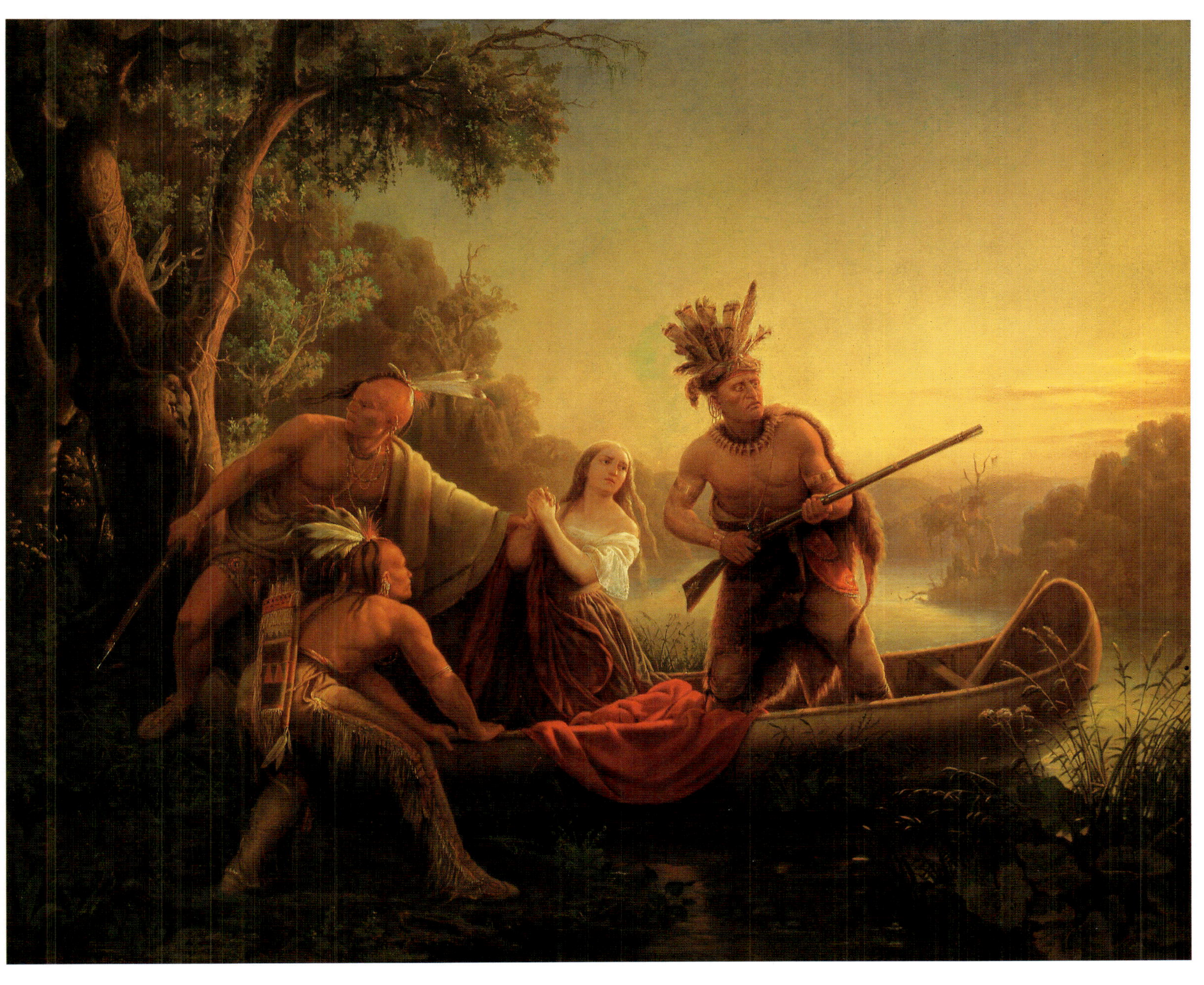

19. Carl F. Wimar
(United States, b. Germany, 1828–1862)
The Buffalo Hunt, 1860

Oil on canvas, 35¼ x 60"
Gift of Dr. William Van Zandt, 1886

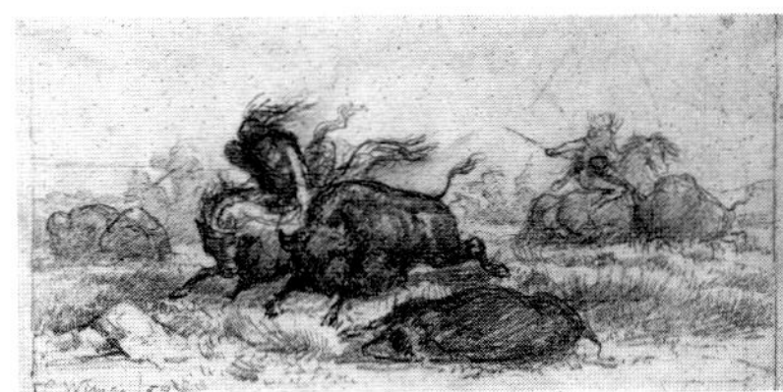

Carl F. Wimar
Buffalo Hunt, 1859
Pencil and charcoal on paper, 4½ x 8⅛"
The Missouri Historical Society, St. Louis

Wimar's dramatic paintings of frontier conflicts were imaginary compositions derived largely from European history painting and literature. Well-trained in the Düsseldorf academic method, Wimar was taught to sketch from nature for the subjects and details of his finished paintings. Dedicated in his pursuit of academic ideals, Wimar became determined to explore the frontier and its inhabitants for the subjects of his future western paintings. At the conclusion of his Düsseldorf studies under the guidance of Leutze in 1856, he traveled "to America, not to remain there, rather to gather studies, and then spend several more years [in Düsseldorf]."[1] Unfortunately, he was never to return to Germany. In 1862, at the youthful age of thirty-four, he succumbed to consumption (tuberculosis). However, by the time of his unfortunate demise, he had realized his ambition to explore the frontier. In the summers of 1858 and 1859, Wimar took two steamboat expeditions up the Missouri River on which he gathered artifacts and made drawings, oil sketches, and even ambrotypes of the plains, the Indians, and the buffalo. Back in his St. Louis studio these provided the sources for his most enduring contributions to American art, his panoramic landscapes of the Upper Missouri River.[2]

The Buffalo Hunt (1860) is the signature image of Wimar's career and perhaps his most important painting. It is accurate in its depiction of a Sioux buffalo hunt, but, more importantly, its romantic metaphors on the demise of the Native Americans established the iconography for future interpretations of this subject. In *The Buffalo Hunt* Sioux Indians aggressively pursue a buffalo bull on the small horses that were typical of the plains tribes. The bowman approaches the buffalo in the traditional manner, from the right, while a warrior with a lance rode on the left to direct the buffalo toward the bowman. The bowman would position himself to shoot the buffalo directly in the heart behind the right fore-quarter.[3] Wimar saw many herds of buffalo and participated in buffalo hunts during his Missouri River expeditions; however, it is unlikely that he witnessed the Sioux, who were hostile to Europeans at this time because of a treaty dispute, in a buffalo hunt. The pictorial sources for this painting were probably the prints after works by George Catlin and, particularly, Karl Bodmer. Two of Wimar's three preliminary drawings for this painting (c. 1859–60, Missouri Historical Society) bear a close formal relationship to Bodmer's *Indians Hunting Bison* (1843–44, *Travels in the Interior of North America,* v. 2, pl. 31) where a single Indian bowman rides behind a buffalo with the action moving to the left. In the final sketch for his painting (1859, The Saint Louis Art Museum) Wimar reversed the action, correctly oriented the bowman and the lancer, and added the other Indians and buffaloes. Utilizing his experience of the frontier and the printed resources available to him, Wimar imaginatively orchestrated his sketches of Indians and buffaloes to create one of the great images of the American west.

Although Wimar took great pains to assure the ethnographic accuracy of *The Buffalo Hunt,* his primary intention was to comment on the passage of the buffalo and, therefore, also the plains Indian culture. In Wimar's era it was widely recognized that the fate of the plains Indian was directly linked to the prevalence of the buffalo. Due to the massive hunts by settlers, herds of buffalo were being massacred and the remaining herds were forced further west. As early as 1840 Catlin had written that it is an "irresistible conclusion that the buffalo is soon to be extinguished and with it the peace and happiness (if not the actual existence) of the tribes of Indians who are joint tenants with them in the occupancy of these vast and idle plains."[4] The earliest images of the buffalo hunt by Catlin and Bodmer established the compositional formulas that were followed by such subsequent artists as Alfred Jacob Miller, Peter Rindisbacher, and John Mix Stanley.

Wimar, however, was the first to fully exploit motifs that symbolized the eventual fate of both the Natives and the buffalo. In *The Buffalo Hunt* Wimar placed a rock shaped like a gravestone in the foreground below the central hunting group, thus foreshadowing the ultimate fate of these two inhabitants of the great plains.[5] The significance of this detail becomes more explicit in Wimar's 1861 version of *The Buffalo Hunt* (Missouri Historical Society) in which the artist has replaced the gravestone with a buffalo skull, a traditional symbol of death, clarifying the significance of the gravestone-rock in the Washington University painting. These motifs made a significant contribution to western art and established the iconographical prototype that reappeared in many later interpretations of the buffalo hunt. This metaphorical treatment of the buffalo hunt reached its culmination in Albert Bierstadt's *The Last of the Buffalo* (c. 1889, Corcoran Gallery of Art), where the noble Indian drives his spear into the last buffalo on a plain littered with skulls.

Wimar's *The Buffalo Hunt* was a centerpiece at the inaugural exhibition of the Western Art Academy (St. Louis) in 1860. The first art academy west of the Mississippi River, this organization was founded by local arts patrons to provide instruction and exhibition opportunities for western artists. Because of his prestigious position in the local arts community, Wimar was nominated to be the Academy Librarian. For the grand opening the academy organized a tremendous exhibition that was the most important cultural event in the west up to that time. The royal appearance of the Duke of Wales, the future Edward VII, added great prestige to the occasion. After their trip to Canada for the dedication of the Victoria Bridge in Montreal, the Duke of Wales and his entourage toured the western United States and attended the grand opening of the Western Academy of Art. Lord Lyons, in the Duke's party, was attracted to Wimar's large *The Buffalo Hunt* (1860), already in the collection of a local patron, and commissioned a copy (Thomas Gilcrease Museum in Tulsa, Oklahoma). This commission marked the ultimate recognition of Wimar's art and his ascension to commercial success, only two short years before his premature death.

Joseph D. Ketner

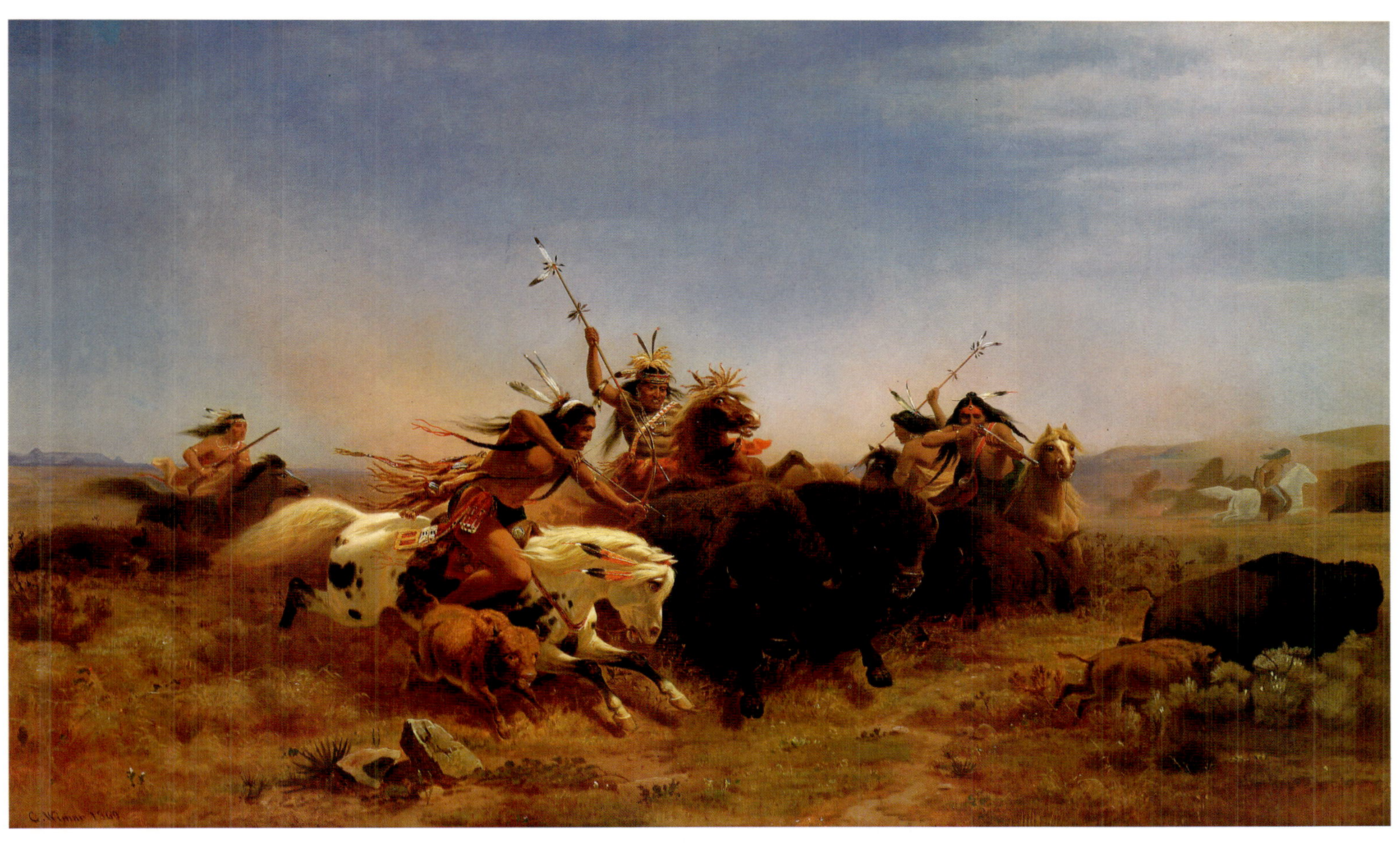

20. Harriet Goodhue Hosmer (United States, 1830–1908)

Oenone, 1854–55

Marble, 34 x 43½ x 27½"
Gift of Wayman Crow, Sr., 1855

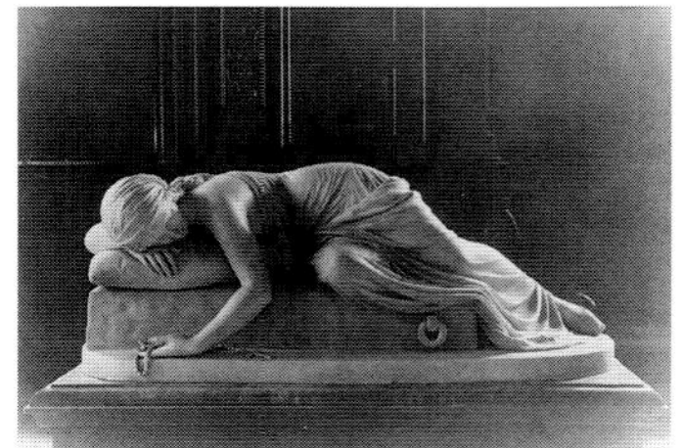

Harriet Goodhue Hosmer
Beatrice Cenci, 1856
Marble, 24 x 60 x 24"
The St. Louis Mercantile Library

An important American sculptor in the neoclassical tradition, Harriet Hosmer produced some of her most significant works for St. Louisans, of which *Oenone* is one. Daughter of a Watertown, Massachusetts doctor, Hiram Hosmer, she was encouraged early to pursue her own interests and thus developed an independence unusual for women of her time.[1] As a young woman Hosmer attended Mrs. Charles Sedgwick's School in Lenox, Massachusetts. There she met Cornelia Crow, daughter of prominent dry-goods merchant and early patron of the arts in St. Louis, Wayman Crow, with whom she was to maintain a lifelong friendship.[2] Upon graduation she returned briefly to Watertown and studied modeling and drawing with Boston sculptor Peter Stephenson. Frustrated with her inability to learn anatomy in New England because she was excluded from the all-male medical classes (despite her father's considerable influence), she traveled to St. Louis in 1850, lived with the Crow family and for a year attended the Missouri Medical College (also sometimes called McDowell Medical College) which had already established the precedent of admitting a woman to the chemistry program.[3] Hosmer, however, was the first woman to study anatomy at what later became the Washington University School of Medicine.

Shortly after receiving her certificate, she traveled to Rome to study with the English neoclassical sculptor John Gibson, who had himself studied with Antonio Canova and Bertel Thorwaldsen. Her first attempt at original work while in Rome was her *Daphne* (1854, Washington University Gallery of Art), which she presented as a "love gift" to the Crow family.[4] In addition, Mr. Crow commissioned her first large-scale figural work, *Oenone*. Completed under Gibson's tutelage, this was her most ambitious effort to date. The marble was so favorably received that Crow arranged for a third sculpture from her, in association with the Mercantile Library, *Beatrice Cenci* (1857, Mercantile Library Association, St. Louis), about which Hosmer later wrote to her friend, "I am not afraid to say that it beats the Oenone which I wish were better for your sake."[5] Hosmer's St. Louis reputation culminated with her monumental bronze of Missouri Senator Thomas Hart Benton in 1868, which Crow also helped commission. This sculpture's unveiling was attended, amid much fanfare, by nearly 30,000 people and the work remains today in Lafayette Park.[6]

Daughter of the river-god Oeneus, Oenone was a mythical naiad of Mount Ida (a nymph of fountains and streams). She was married to Paris (son of Priam, the king of Troy), but he deserted her in favor of Helen, the Spartan queen whom he carried off to Troy in the famous episode that began the Trojan War. After the fall of Troy the wounded Paris returned to a resentful Oenone who refused to help him. She relented too late, and wept over his body before committing suicide in remorse.[7] In Hosmer's sculpture we see the grieving Oenone without the accompanying Paris, leaving open for speculation whether she is mourning his abandonment or his death.[8] Her only identifying feature is her shepherdess' crook and Hosmer's inscription on the base. In typical neoclassical fashion, Oenone's emotions are restrained, her form highly idealized, and her face serene, with the crystalline marble adding a heightened sense of purity to the subject.

Hosmer's rarified treatment of overtly sentimental subjects was extremely popular with St. Louis audiences, who were in the mid-1850s envisioning their city as an important art center. The story of Oenone was recounted in various reviews and notices and the work was exhibited at the Mercantile Library, where it received favorable comment, and at the galleries of the St. Louis School and Museum of Fine Arts (forerunner of the Washington University Gallery of Art).[9] The theme, which is recounted in a number of ancient sources, was certainly made more prominent by Alfred Lord Tennyson's poem, "Oenone" (1832, revised in 1842), a mournful ode that Hosmer probably knew.[10]

Hosmer never married and her choice of subjects, many of which are suffering females, invites speculation as to their personal significance for the artist.[11] She was deeply committed to her career, but in a letter to Wayman Crow she admitted that it entailed sacrifice:

> *Even if so inclined, an artist has no business to marry. For a man, it may be well enough, but not for a woman, on whom matrimonial duties and cares weigh more heavily, it is a moral wrong, I think, for she must either neglect her profession or her family, becoming neither a good wife and mother nor a good artist. My ambition is to become the latter, so I wage eternal feud with the consolidating knot.*[12]

Hosmer's comment that she waged "eternal feud" with the prospect of marriage suggests that she was hardly oblivious to the difficulties of being a single woman with a career. On the other hand, she hardly presented herself as a suffering female; she seemed to thrive on her work and had many intimate friends. In Rome she regularly wore trousers while working, kept her hair short for convenience, and was, as Elizabeth Browning noted, "a perfectly emancipated female . . . she lives here [in Rome] all alone (at twenty-two); dines and breakfasts at the cafes, precisely as a young man would, works from six o'clock in the morning till night, as a great artist must. . . ."[13] In 1861 Hosmer wrote:

> *I don't approve of bloomerism and that view of woman's rights, but every woman should have the opportunity of cultivating her talents to the fullest extent, for they were not given her for nothing, and the domestic circle would not suffer thereby, because in proportion to the few who would prefer fighting their own way through the world, the number would be great who would choose a partner to fight it for them; but give those few a chance, say I. And those chances will be given first in America. What fun it would be to come back to this earth after having been a wandering ghost for a hundred years or so and see what has been going on in flesh while have been going on in spirit!*[14]

In her letters Hosmer continually referred to her sculptures as her children and seemed content with marble as her progeny.[15] She did seem to identify with her work, if not literally in its subject matter, then in the sense that it was an extension of her chosen work.[16] In *Oenone*, therefore, we encounter both the tragic story of the ancient naiad and the triumphant one of Hosmer herself.

Joni L. Kinsey

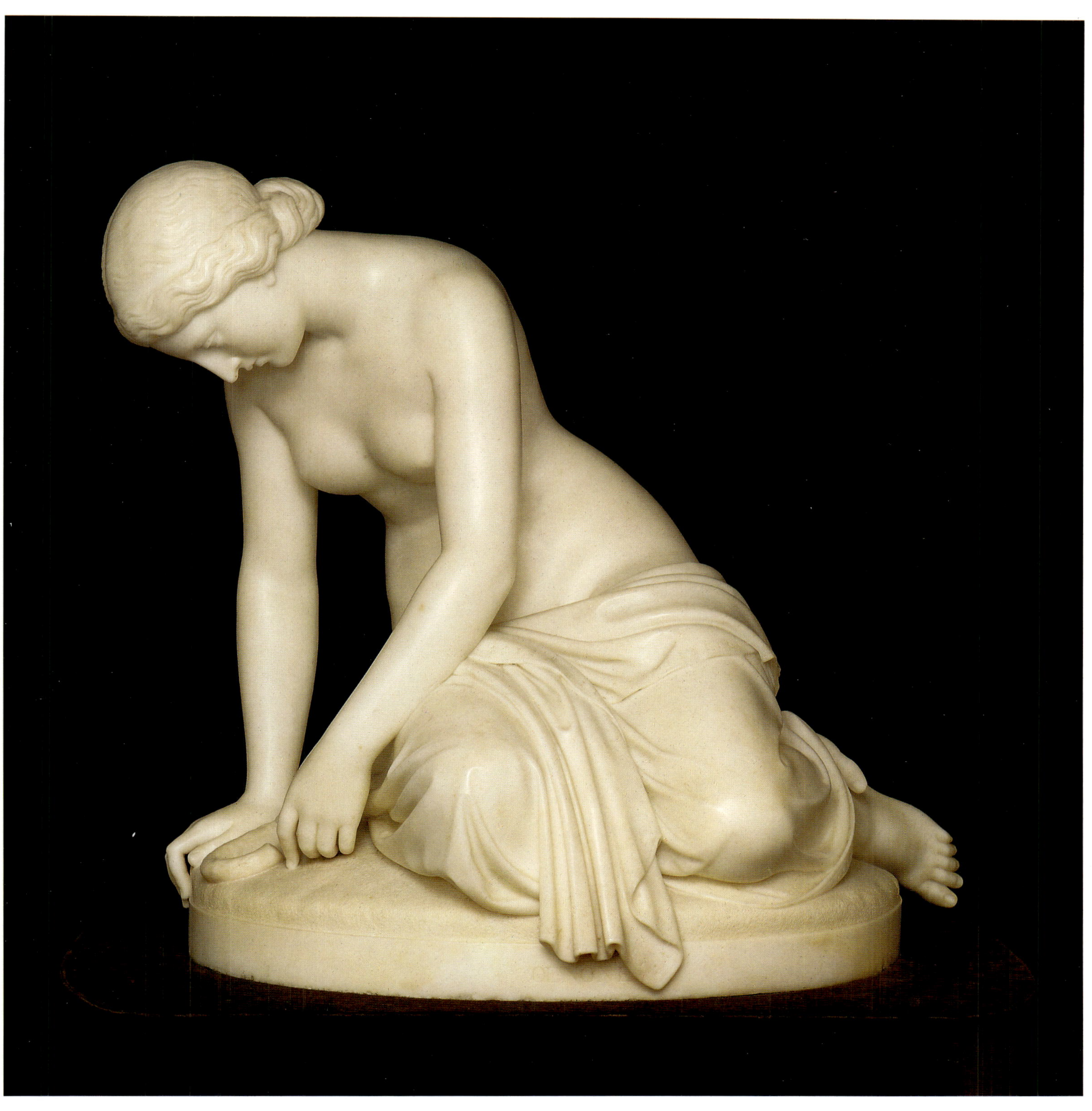

21. Thomas Ball (United States, 1819–1911) *Freedom's Memorial,* 1875

Marble, 44¾ x 28 x 17½"
Gift of Reverend William Greenleaf Eliot

Thomas Ball, a native of Boston, was one of many American sculptors who lived and worked primarily in Italy, the mecca for the neoclassical movement that dominated sculpture throughout much of the nineteenth century. Best known, perhaps, for his equestrian statue of George Washington which still stands in the Boston Public Gardens, Ball also sculpted many of the leading figures of his day, including Daniel Webster, Charles Sumner, and Josiah Quincy.

Ball began his *Freedom's Memorial,* also known as *The Emancipation Group,* in Florence shortly after receiving the news of Lincoln's assassination in 1865. He produced the design on his own initiative, as he said, "partly as a duty I felt I owed to the memory of so great and good a man and partly from the conviction that it would be required for some city in our union. . . ."[1] From the original model a number of finished sculptures were subsequently commissioned: two small bronzes (Houghton Library at Harvard and Montclair Art Museum, Montclair, New Jersey), two small marbles (Elvehjem Art Center, University of Wisconsin, Madison, 1873, and Washington University, 1875), and two heroic scale bronzes, one in Washington, D.C. (1875) and one in Boston (1877). These works vary in some details.

Of the commissioned works, both the Washington University marble and the heroic bronze in the nation's capital have important St. Louis connections, as do more indirectly all of the post-1870 versions. In 1865, shortly after Lincoln's assassination, a former slave, Charlotte Scott of Marietta, Ohio, offered five dollars, her "first earning in freedom," toward the erection of a monument of "the colored people['s] . . . best friend on earth." Her gift was received by St. Louisian James Yeatman, president of the Western Sanitary Commission, a Union relief organization, and in the course of several months over $16,000 was raised, mostly from black infantry regiments and former slaves. The amount was not sufficient at the time to commission a large original sculpture, but the fund appreciated to about $21,000 by 1873, allowing Yeatman and his committee to approach Ball with the order for a larger than life-sized bronze version of *Freedom's Memorial.* This is the sculpture today in Lincoln's Park in Washington, D.C.[2]

Apparently Harriet Hosmer, who was well known in St. Louis and whose monumental bronze of *Thomas Hart Benton* had been unveiled in Lafayette Park there in 1868, was the first choice for the job, but her price was too high.[3] Reverend William Greenleaf Eliot, founder and chancellor of Washington University, prominent St. Louis Unitarian minister and member of the Sanitary Committee, had seen the plaster original of Ball's sculpture in Florence several years before and suggested it as an alternative.[4] Ball had already failed to place the work in Philadelphia and, anxious to have it reproduced, agreed to execute the bronze for the cost of the casting and shipping.[5]

Along with the heroic bronze, the small marble version now at Washington University was simultaneously commissioned by the Western Sanitary Commission for a "public building in St. Louis."[6] The use of white Carrara marble was in keeping, of course, with the neoclassical style popular at the time, and Lincoln's pose and gesture refer simultaneously to ancient heroic monuments and the Christian prototypes. Other aspects of the work, however, are obviously contemporary and specific to the subject. For the president's portrait Ball presumably used photographs of Lincoln which were readily available. The figure holds the Emancipation Proclamation of 1862 in his right hand which rests on a pedestal composed of *fasces,* or bound reeds, ancient symbol of authority, justice, and strength in unity.[7] The other hand reaches out benevolently to the rising freedman at his feet.[8]

After searching unsuccessfully for a suitable model Ball patterned the slave's figure from his own body. "I decided to constitute myself both model and modeler. By lowering the clay so that I could work upon it while in a kneeling position (that of the slave), and placing a looking glass on each side of me, I brought everything quite conveniently before me. As I did not require an Apollo for a model, but one who could appreciate exactly the position I required; and could not only see but feel the action of each muscle, I could not have had a better one–certainly, for the money."[9] In both the original plaster version and in the Washington University marble the face of the slave is idealized and he wears a Phrygian cap, an ancient symbol of liberty. His hands are shackled, but the chain is broken. Below the figures on the base is inscribed one of the concluding phrases of the Emancipation Proclamation: "On this act I invoke the considerate judgment of mankind, and the gracious favor of Almighty God."

Upon seeing photographs of Ball's prototype, the St. Louis committee suggested that, in order to provide a greater sense of literal history for the heroic Lincoln Park bronze, an actual freedman's likeness be substituted for the idealized face of the slave. For this purpose Eliot himself contributed photographs of his own employee, a former slave he had befriended named Archer Alexander who was the last slave in Missouri to be captured under the Fugitive Slave Law and about whom Eliot later wrote an informative biography.[10] Ball agreed to the changes, removed the Phrygian cap and altered the facial features to resemble those of Alexander. Interestingly, the Washington University marble, which was donated to the museum by Reverend Eliot, does not contain the changes, but is in fact a copy of the earlier, more idealized model.[11]

Freedom's Memorial, in all of its versions, stands as a testament to the efforts, in the wake of the Civil War, to recognize the slain president's achievements and offer reconciliation and reparation for past injustices. The St. Louis example remains a memento of local citizens' commitment to the principles embodied by its design during a most difficult period in American history.

Joni L. Kinsey

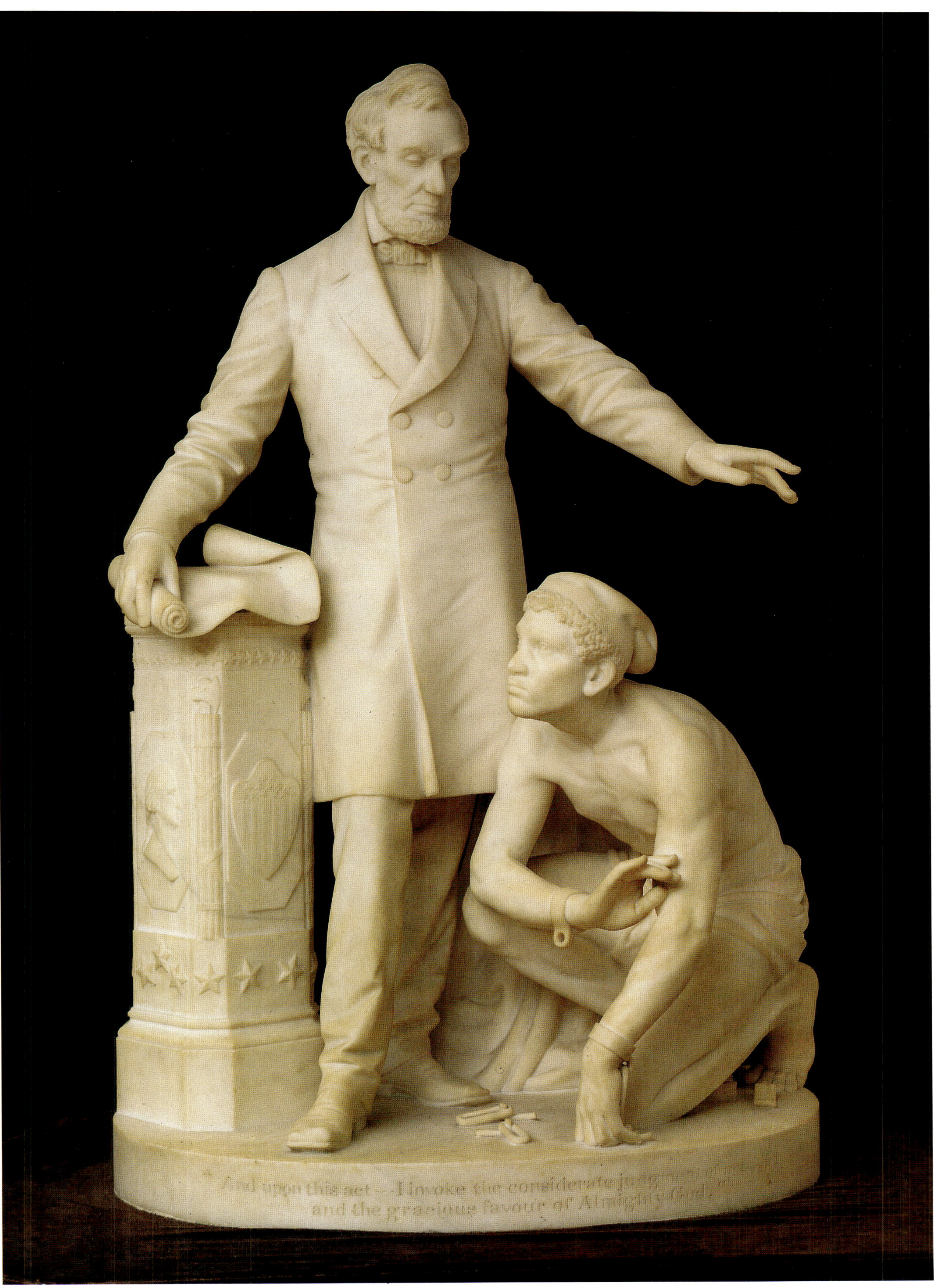
"And upon this act---I invoke the considerate judgment of
and the gracious favour of Almighty God."

22. William Merritt Chase
(United States, 1849–1916)
Courtyard of a Dutch Orphan Asylum, c. 1884

Oil on canvas on board, 66⅞ x 78⅛"
University purchase, Subscription Fund, 1885

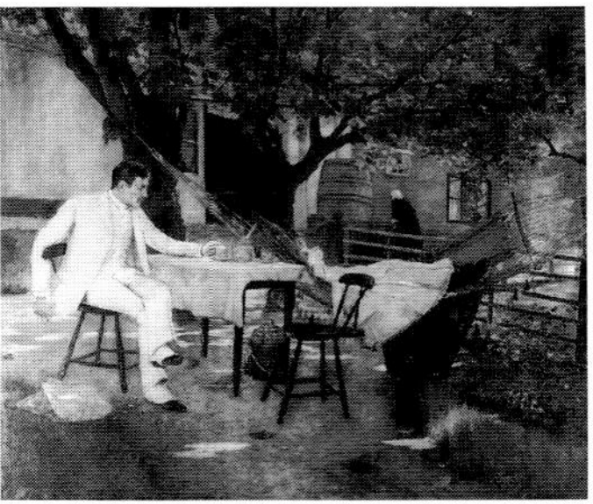

William Merritt Chase
Sunlight and Shadow, 1884
Oil on canvas, 65¼ x 76½"
The Joslyn Art Museum, Omaha, Nebraska
Gift of the Friends of the Art Collection

Courtyard of a Dutch Orphan Asylum is one of William Merritt Chase's most ambitious pictures from a period of stylistic transition in his career. It represents a major shift from his early work that was patterned on the example of old master European art and the "dark manner" of the contemporary Munich school, to a lighter, more pastel palette of the Impressionists, an influence that was to dominate much of the rest of Chase's art.[1]

The presence of *Courtyard of a Dutch Orphan Asylum* at Washington University reflects Chase's long association with St. Louis. One of the most prominent artists in America by the end of the late nineteenth century, Chase owed much of his early success to the city's residents. He was already working in New York as a still life painter when his family moved to Missouri in 1869, but spent 1871 in St. Louis where he shared a studio with James William Pattison and became friendly with James Mulvaney, an artist who had recently returned from studying in Europe. Through them Chase learned of the progressive approach of the Royal Academy in Munich which offered an appealing alternative to the classically-oriented Ecole des Beaux Arts in Paris. He lacked the means to finance his study himself, but his situation attracted the attention of several philanthropic St. Louis businessmen who raised $2,100 in 1872 to send him to study in Munich.[2] This opportunity launched Chase into the international art world, introducing him to emerging artistic trends and to many artists at the vanguard, including Frank Duveneck, Walter Shirlaw, and John Twachtman.

Upon his return to the U.S. in 1878 Chase ingratiated himself into New York society through his professorship at the Art Students League, by his flamboyant appearance and personality, and with his lavish atelier/salon in the Tenth Street Studio Building which he filled with exotic furniture, paintings, and objects acquired in the markets of Europe. The spacious accommodations that had previously belonged to the landscapist Albert Bierstadt became famous for their new erudite, bohemian ambience and were considered by many to be the "sanctum sanctorum of the artistic fraternity."[3] Chase cultivated his central position in the New York scene as well through membership in a variety of clubs and artistic societies, including the Society of American Artists, the Tile Club, the Society of Painters in Pastel, and the Ten, which were among the most innovative associations of the period.[4] His prominence made him one of the most influential artists of the time.

Through the mid-1880s Chase spent nearly every summer in Europe, traveling between Spain, Paris, and Holland which he visited in 1882, 1884, and 1885. These years were a time of artistic growth for the artist; he studied the work of Velazquez and Manet and gained new appreciation for the innovations of *plein air* painting, moving away from his affinity with the old masters as he had been advised by the Belgian painter Alfred Stevens.[5] The Washington University picture, *Courtyard of a Dutch Orphan Asylum,* reveals many of these developments. Although it retains an historical connection with seventeenth-century Dutch art through the figures' traditional costumes and the intimate, enclosed setting, the brushwork, coloration, and lightened tonality all reflect Chase's newer style that he would develop further in subsequent years.

Compositionally and chronologically the work is allied with *Sunlight and Shadow* (1884, Joslyn Art Museum, Omaha) which depicts Chase's close friend, artist Robert Blume (1857-1903), and a companion in the garden of Blume's summer house in Zandvoort, Holland.[6] Chase travelled with his friend in Europe in the early 1880s and spent the summer at Blume's home in 1884; the orphan asylum was probably one of the many sites the two visited. The similarities of setting in the two paintings, especially in the arrangement of the arching trees and the sunlit lawns, indicate Chase's concentration on the interplay of light and foliage as he attempted to modify his style from his darker earlier pictures. The swag hammock form is also found in both works, although in *Sunlight and Shadow* it is an actual support for repose and in *Dutch Orphan Asylum* this is merely suggested as two girls standing by two trees hold a long cloth between them.

The most striking dissimilarity in the two paintings is the obvious contemporaneity of *Sunlight and Shadow.* Depicting a languorous teatime for two well-dressed, thoroughly modern individuals, it provides a marked contrast to *Dutch Orphan Asylum's* traditionally-dressed figures that recall Dutch art of the seventeenth century or mid-nineteenth-century representations of laborers by such artists as Jean Millet or Jules Breton.

To repay the St. Louis benefactors who financed his early European study, Chase painted pictures for each major contributor and acted as an agent, purchasing art for their private collections. He may, as well, have offered *Courtyard of a Dutch Orphan Asylum* to the citizens of the city in return for their support. The work was purchased by the public subscription for the St. Louis School and Museum of Fine Arts collection, the forerunner of the Washington University Gallery of Art.

Joni L. Kinsey

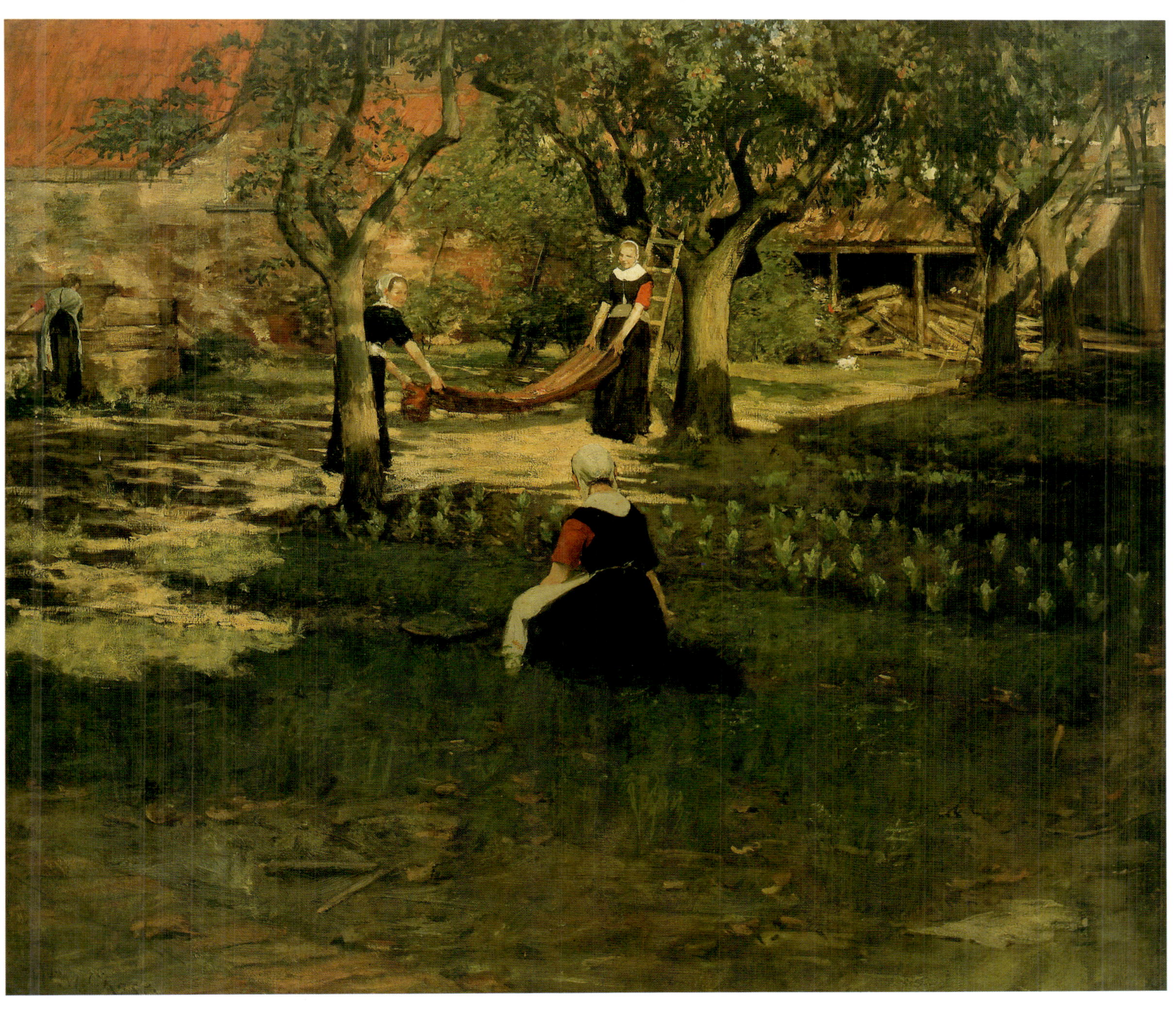

23. Thomas Cowperthwaite Eakins (United States, 1844–1916) *Portrait of Professor W.D. Marks,* 1886

Oil on canvas, 76⅜ x 54⅛"
University purchase, Yeatman Fund, 1936

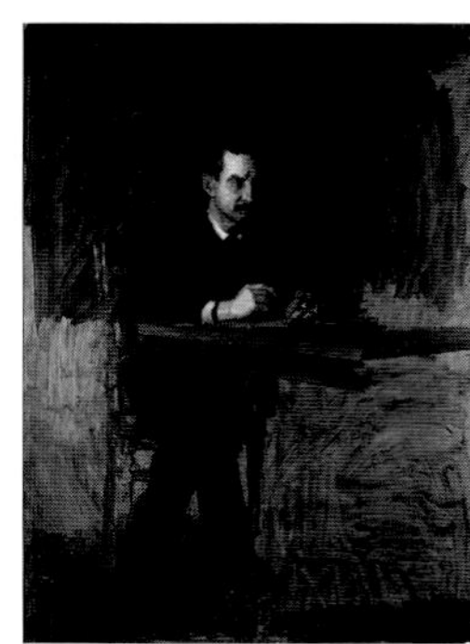

Thomas Eakins
Portrait of Professor W.D. Marks, c. 1886
Oil on canvas, 76½ x 54¼"
Private collection
Courtesy Sotheby's

Thomas Eakins' portrait of W.D. Marks provides a revealing glimpse into the penetrating style that has made Eakins one of the most respected portraitists in American art. Through it we may perceive something of the artist's own relationship to Marks and his activities, and to his perception of portraiture more generally.

Blessed with the advantage of financial independence, Eakins avoided commissioned work and chose his subjects according to his own ideals. Committed to studying the human figure in its varied activities, his choices were most often portraits of people he knew and respected, individuals who had distinguished themselves through their work, talents, or personality, and who, as Eakins scholar Elizabeth Johns has said, were "definitive of the best of . . . [their] times."[1]

William Dennis Marks (1849–1914) certainly fit these specifications. A St. Louis native, he had studied at Washington University and Yale, and by the 1880s was a prominent Philadelphia engineer who headed the department of Dynamic Engineering at the University of Pennsylvania.[2] In 1884, about the time he began working with Eakins, he was appointed General Superintendent of the Franklin Institute's International Electrical Exposition. The success of the exposition resulted in the formation of the Edison Electric Light Company, the forerunner to the Philadelphia Electric Company, with Marks as its supervisor.[3] In the late 1890s Marks resigned from the University to pursue the job full time. As a result of his efforts, Philadelphia was the first city in the country to install electric street lights, and by the turn of the century it could boast being the best lighted community in the United States with the most economical service.[4]

During this period, from 1884–1885, Marks was also engaged in engineering developments of other sorts. He was a member of the committee that awarded photographer Eadweard Muybridge a grant to study the photography of motion. As a mechanical/electrical engineer, Marks became involved with the project, as did Thomas Eakins, who had been interested in photography since at least the early 1870s.[5]

Eakins' portrait of Marks, painted shortly after their cooperative experiments, depicts the professor at his desk, lost in thought amid his books, instruments, and inventions. Engaged in his work, he may thus be compared to other men of science whom Eakins portrayed, such as Dr. Samuel D. Gross (*The Gross Clinic,* 1875, Jefferson Medical College, Philadelphia), or Dr. B. Howard Rand (*Portrait of Dr. Rand,* 1874, Jefferson Medical College). Unique to Marks' portrait, however, is the distinctive instrument on the desk in front of the sitter, an electrical/mechanical device variously called a chronograph, chronometer, or galvanometer, which Marks invented especially for Muybridge's and Eakins' photographic motion studies. Not a camera, the device measured the timing and duration of photographic exposures and facilitated the precise measurements required in tripping the multiple camera shutters that recorded human and animal movement.[6] The instrument under the desk at Marks' feet is less well understood, but may be the battery connection or the electro-magnet contact motor that powered the chronograph.[7]

Eakins produced a full-scale oil sketch for his portrait of Marks (private collection) which contains little more than the figure of the inventor seated at his desk. None of the details that distinguished Marks as a man of science—the books, tools, and machines—was included in this version. Although his face and hands are well-developed, most of the composition is simply a thin layer of paint, presumably a chromatic ground from which Eakins could key his overall tonality. The purpose of this painting is unclear; it has consistently been referred to in past literature as a sketch, but its size makes it unusual in this regard. Eakins gave the finished portrait, now at Washington University, to the sitter, as was his practice with such works, but the "sketch" remained in the artist's studio until his death. This leaves open the possibility that Eakins may have planned a replica of the portrait, perhaps for Marks' company or for the University of Pennsylvania, a supposition which would suggest that the unfinished painting was created after rather than before the finished work.[8] Whatever its chronology, the painting provides insight into Eakins' process, both compositionally and conceptually. It is clear that he concentrated first on Marks' most distinctive personal attributes, his face and hands, but it is not coincidental that these are also the elements that unify the sitter with his surroundings in the finished image.

Eakins' rendering of the machines and of Marks' face and hands in the completed work are scrupulous and exacting, allowing precise analysis of the apparatus and a strong sense of identification with the inventor.[9] The rest of the composition is less distinct, however, and much darker than these focal points, indicating the artist's desire to draw attention to them as the most important elements in the portrait. Eakins' emphasis on these areas and the sensitivity with which he painted them is comparable to many of his other works, such as Gross' hand holding the scalpel in *The Gross Clinic,* but equally importantly, they reveal his desire to portray the fundamental relationship between Marks and his machines. The placement of the chronograph, directly across the table from the sitter and vertically positioned between the scientist's hands and head, suggests the process by which the machine was contrived. This recognition is further accentuated by Marks' gaze toward the device, but beyond it, and the delicate way he holds the instruments with which he designed the apparatus. The interplay between mind and hand, tools and invention, and man and machine underlies this apparently pragmatic painting, a subtext that renders it more philosophically and psychologically probing than it might first appear. The painting stands as a testament both to Eakins' relationship with the scientist and to the intellectual process with which they were engaged.

Joni L. Kinsey

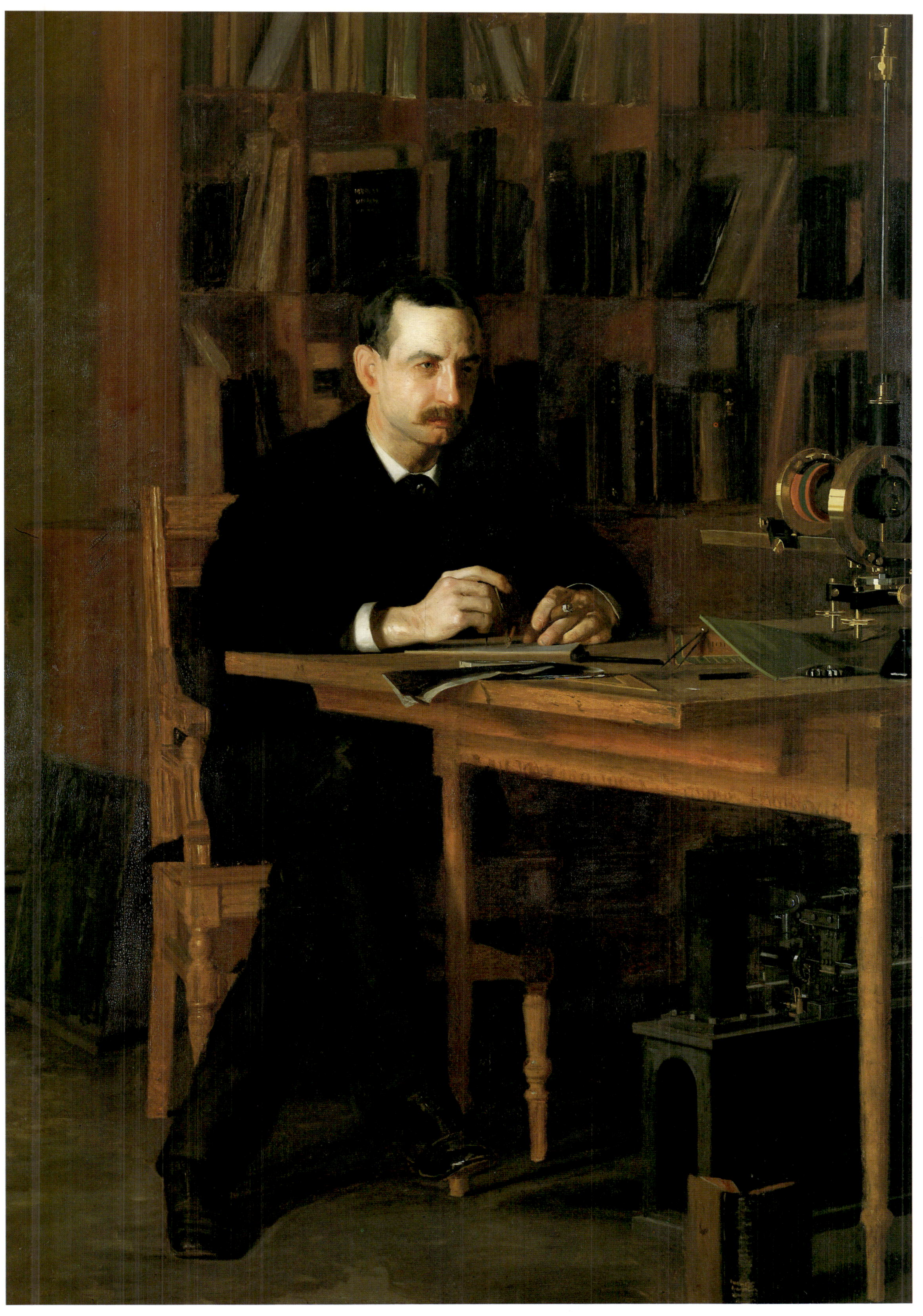

24. George Inness (United States, 1825–1894) *Storm on the Delaware*, 1891

Oil on canvas, 29¾ x 44¾ "
University purchase, Bixby Fund, 1910

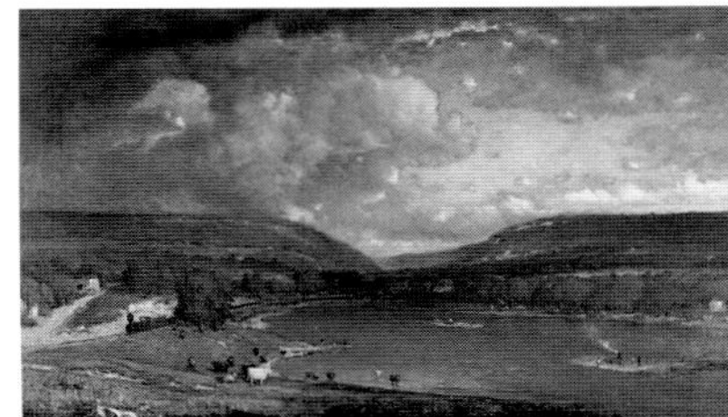

George Inness
On the Delaware River, 1861–63
Oil on canvas, 28³⁄₁₆ x 48⅛"
The Brooklyn Museum
Special Subscription Fund

Storm on the Delaware is a revealing and beautiful example of George Inness' late style.[1] His career spanned the shift from the art of the Hudson River School to American Impressionism, but his late works, those of his "signature years" of the 1880s and early 1890s, are perhaps the most indicative of his philosophy of art.[2] As the artist himself said in the late 1870s, the job of a painter is:

> *simply to reproduce in other minds the impression which a scene has made upon him. A work of art does not appeal to the intellect. It does not appeal to the moral sense. Its aim is not to instruct, not to edify, but to awaken an emotion. . . if the work has unity, as every such work should have, the true beauty of the work consists in the beauty of the sentiment or emotion which it inspires.*[3]

While such ideas were not unique to Inness, they exemplify the late nineteenth-century trend toward art that emphasized mood and effect over didactic narrative or topographical documentation.

Storm on the Delaware embodies such aspirations in its combination of softened focus and intensified chromatic and tonal relationships. The subject itself, the valley of the Delaware River, seems common enough, but Inness' treatment elevates it to a spiritual realm that seems at once familiar and other worldly. Here the contrasts of the greens is heightened, the infusion of complementary oranges striking, and the juxtaposition between storm and sunshine almost surreal.

The moodiness of the image is characteristic of the style known as American Tonalism, a turn-of-the-century poetic modification of Impressionism practiced by Thomas Wilmer Dewing, Dwight Tryon and Alexander Wyant, to mention only a few.[4] These artists were not organized nor unified as were many other artistic movements; each artist practiced on his own distilling visual subjects, usually landscapes, through a dreamy veil of personal reverie. This lack of cohesion, as well as the murkiness of some of the basic tenets of the style, such as "tone," have led to differences in discussing both the artists and their works.[5] On the other hand, the very individualism of artists considered Tonalists befits their approach to subject matter; both conceptually and stylistically these artists were seeking a highly personal response to nature.

Of all the Tonalists Inness is one of the most difficult to characterize, in part because his career was so long and stylistically varied. His early landscapes, highly influenced by the French Barbizon school after he toured Europe in the early 1850s, are traditional in composition and detail; his works from the 1860s–80s are frequently linked to the problematic concept of Luminism; and his more elegiac works from the 1890s are often seen as the musings of an old man at the end of his career. In the case of the latter period, to which *Storm on the Delaware* belongs, Inness' progress toward a greater subjectivity may be connected as well to the late nineteenth-century movement away from the Hudson River School's glorification of observed reality, and Inness' own conversion in the mid-1860s to Swedenborgianism—a transcendentalist religion that holds that the universe is a vital being united by a spiritual life force.

In all of its variety and complications, Inness' ultimate achievement may lie in the fact that he successfully adapted to changing concepts of landscape painting. Other landscapists of the same generation, most notably Frederic E. Church and Albert Bierstadt, who altered their basic style and subject matter very little throughout their careers, fell from favor in the late 1880s and died in virtual obscurity. Inness, by contrast, was celebrated after his death as "not only the greatest landscape painter that America has produced, but . . . one of the greatest artists of the modern world, fit to rank with the best of all nations."[6] Instead of being seen in his last years as an anachronism, he was considered to be at the forefront of new developments and understandings of American painting.

Storm on the Delaware, painted three years before his death, is one of the last paintings Inness produced of the Delaware Water Gap, his most frequent subject. As Nicolai Cikofsky has written:

> *He may have painted it so often [first in* 1857 *and last in* 1891*] because it was beautiful, because the water gap (where the Delaware River penetrates the Kittantinny Mountains in eastern Pennsylvania) had a certain fame as a picturesque subject, or because he was familiar with it from traveling to visit his brother James in Pottsville, Pennsylvania.*[7]

Indeed, the Delaware Water Gap is an important and historic place, both geologically and socially. A natural opening in the mountains, it has, since the earliest westward migrations, been a throughway for a variety of transportation.

When *Storm on the Delaware* is compared with *On the Delaware* (c. 1861–63, Brooklyn Museum), the differences in Inness' mid-career and his late style are clearly evident. Instead of the relatively clear details that characterize the earlier painting—the cows, the railroad, and the rafts—a hazy, misty netherworld emerges in the later. The elements are almost the same, but the differences are not merely due to a change in atmospheric conditions. A fundamental shift of emphasis has replaced the clarity and the palpability of the earlier work with an amorphous, evocative suggestion of a spiritual realm in the later.

The surface of Washington University's *Storm on the Delaware* appears to have been sanded, perhaps in preparation for painting over it (a practice common to Inness). The work is, however, clearly signed twice, once before the sanding and then once afterwards. While the overly smooth surface may obscure the original splendor of the image, the presence of the second signature suggests that Inness liked the altered effect and considered the work worthy of a second signing. It is interesting that the picture has thus undergone several transformations and transmutations; not only has it been softened with the brush, but it has also been physically muted through the sanding process. It is as if by physically moving farther from the image as originally seen, Inness was suggesting that, just as in memory, certain spiritual aspects stand out with greater clarity.

Joni L. Kinsey

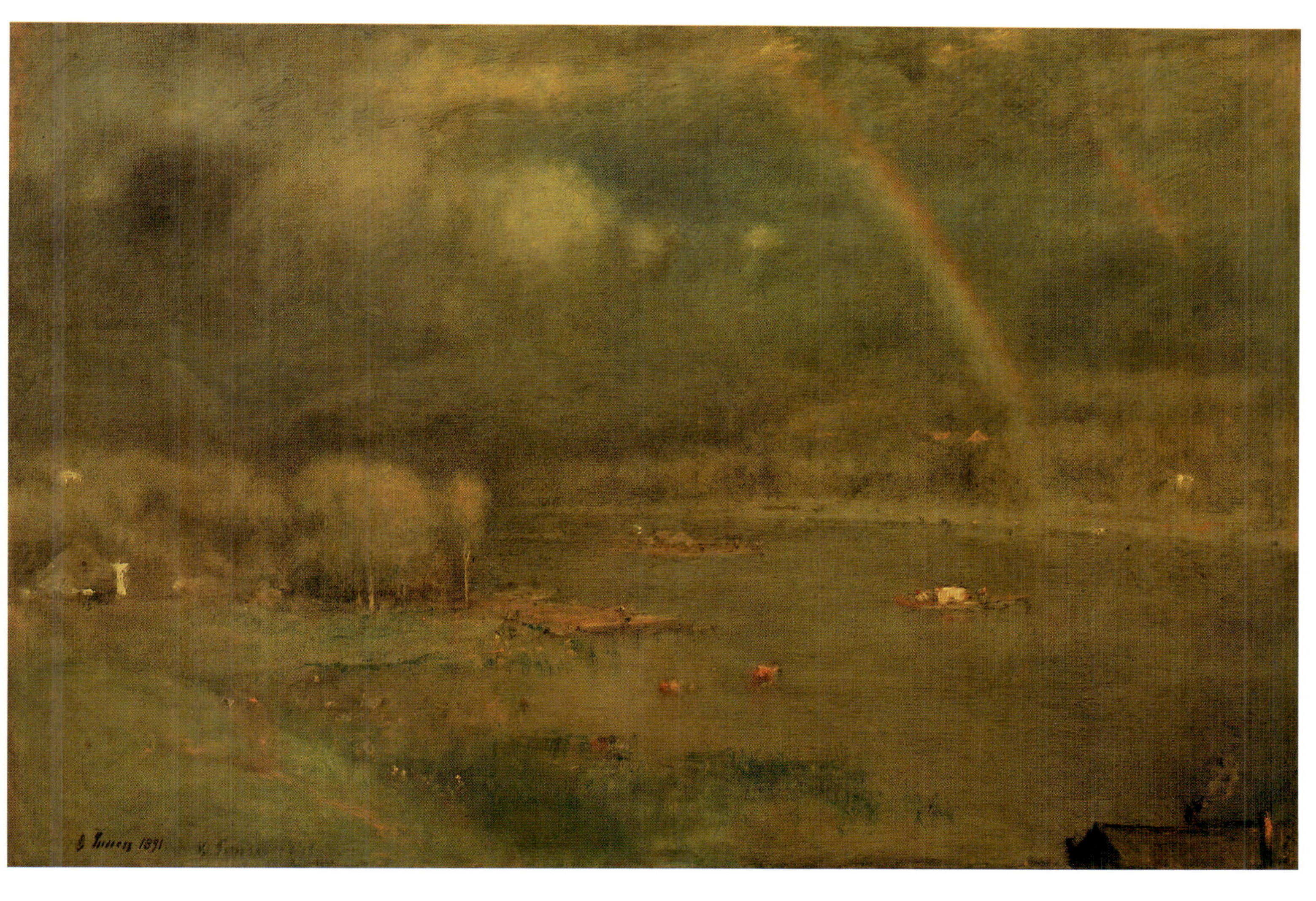

25. Thomas Wilmer Dewing (United States, 1851–1938)

Brocart de Venise (Venetian Brocade), c. 1905

Oil on board, 19⅜ x 25⅜"
University purchase, Bixby Fund, 1906

Some paintings compel a viewer to return to them again and again, despite the difficulty inherent in an interpretation, or perhaps even because of it. Thomas Wilmer Dewing's *Brocart de Venise* is such a painting.[1] In *Brocart de Venise,* Dewing painted a view of a room in which the furniture and the women who occupy it are pushed to the outer edges of the painted space. While the room and the elements contained within are clearly defined, the meaning of the arrangement of objects and figures is enigmatic. The women are isolated from one another and the space between them seems vast, with only the unheard music of the spinet uniting them. Even the decorative animal heads of the occupied chair in the foreground turn away from one another.

Dewing often painted women playing musical instruments, reading to one another, or gossiping. Indeed many of the accoutrements of the room were standard objects from Dewing's studio and they appear in a number of paintings. The sense that this painting is about the leisured world of late-nineteenth-century women is emphasized by the casual placement of a yellow paper-covered book on the background table between the two women. French, English, and American fiction was published in yellow paper-backed editions which the owner could, if they so chose, send out to be properly bound.[2] Otherwise the atmosphere of the painting is one of exquisite elegance. A contemporary art critic, Royal Cortissoz, wrote of Dewing's women, "these gracious figures move in a world which he seems to have created for them, a world in which it suffices that they should nonchalantly pause seated or standing, and allow us to admire them, their grace and their exquisite robes."[3] The soft hazy quality of the picture is indicative of much of Dewing's painting. As early as the 1890s, the tonal quality of work became a concern to artists. Dewing and other painters and photographers used effects of light and atmosphere to veil the image, helping to transform painted reality into a timeless mist. This style of presentation has since been called Tonalism by the art historian Wanda Corn.[4]

Brocart de Venise is a delicate rendering of a suggestive interior space, a recurring theme for which Dewing was well-known. One of the most beautiful paintings of this type, it escaped the avid grasp of Detroit collector Charles Lang Freer because of his tendency to not purchase a painting if he thought that he already had a similar example in his collection. Instead he would encourage sympathetic friends to purchase works from his favorite artists. Consequently, *Brocart de Venise* came to St. Louis through the efforts of St. Louisian William H. Bixby, one of Freer's partners and a fellow connoisseur.

As it was not a commissioned piece, *Brocart de Venise* had been placed in the Montross Gallery in New York by Dewing. In 1905, it was sent to the Detroit Institute of Arts for consideration by their Picture Purchase Fund Committee, headed by Freer. After they declined, it traveled to St. Louis for consideration by the St. Louis School and Museum of Fine Arts, where it was acquired by Washington University in April of 1906.

Typical of Dewing's paintings, *Brocart de Venise* came with a frame designed by the noted architect Stanford White. White began designing frames for his artist friends in the early 1880s. These ranged from custom frames for specific paintings, to more standardized style frames. The frame surrounding *Brocart de Venise* is from this second type. As was typical for many of the White frames, it was designed to be highest in profile closest to the picture and to angle back toward the wall at its outer edge, causing the painting to be thrust forward from the wall. Additionally, the largest portion of the edge molding was patterned with a separate screen of plaster-covered wire coated in gilding, creating a shadowy dappled pattern which enhanced the picture. "[Because] of the suggestion of gray made by its design, it sets off a painting better (in the opinion of Dewing) than any other frame ever designed."[5]

The title *Brocart de Venise* refers to the patterned wall covering which extends across the rear wall of the visible space of the painting. Its delicate patterning is echoed in the arabesque design on the short end of the spinet and also in the sinuous forms of the furniture. The dark expanse of the waxed and polished floor and the plain edge of the large mirror behind the spinet provide a hushed counter-balance to the liveliness of the wallpaper. Altogether the various elements of this painting capture a still image of a musical interlude, a moment of upper-class domestic leisure in which the furniture and the women are in equal part decorative objects which fill the space.

Joyce K. Schiller

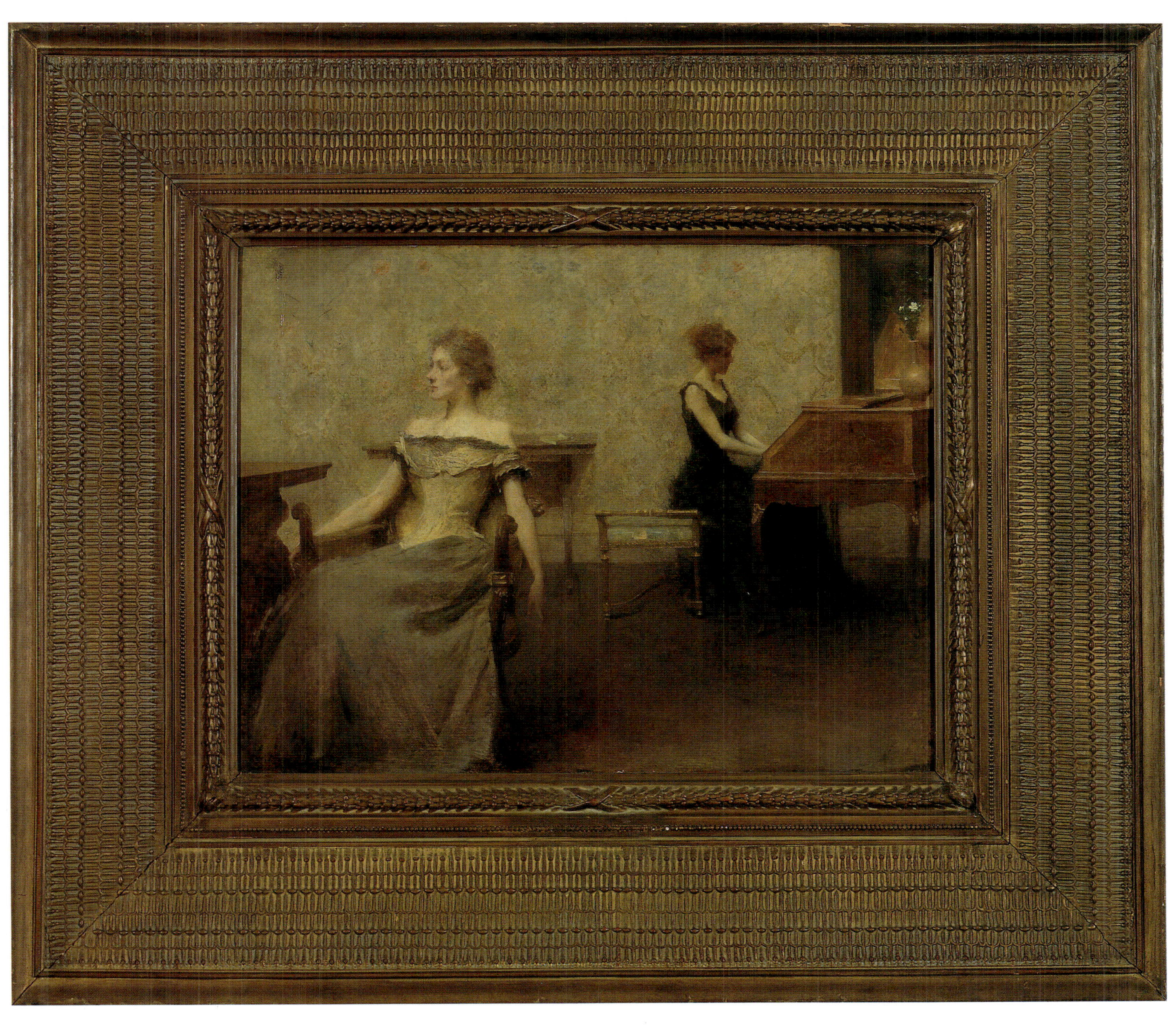

26. Dwight William Tryon (United States, 1849–1925) *Before Sunrise (Morning Twilight, At Daybreak)*, 1906–7

Oil on canvas, 20 x 30"
University purchase, Bixby Fund, 1910

Dwight Tryon's *Before Sunrise* is an excellent example of the artist's style and subject matter from the early years of the twentieth century, a period during which Tryon distilled and personalized the influences of Impressionism into his own version of American Tonalism. This movement is associated as well with the turn-of-the-century work of George Inness, Thomas Wilmer Dewing, and James McNeill Whistler, and is characterized by highly poetic expressive canvases that convey their subjects through a tightly controlled range of values and colors, a softened focus, and a suggestive evocation of moods.[1] Equally important, *Before Sunrise* is the only work from a large group of Tryon's paintings to remain at Washington University out of a total of seventeen that belonged to St. Louis businessman and art collector William Bixby.[2] The relationship of the two men, Bixby and Tryon, reveals much about the tastes that helped form the University's collection of American art, as well as about the painting, *Before Sunrise.*

Bixby was introduced to Tryon's work through Charles Lang Freer, the Detroit industrialist known for his important collection of Asian art and as the founder of the Freer Gallery of Art in Washington, D.C. Freer also, however, collected American Tonalist paintings, particularly those by Whistler, Dewing and Tryon, because he understood their work to have important affinities with art of the Far East.[3] Both collectors were associates in the transportation business, and Bixby valued Freer's advice on art. After his first purchase of a Tryon, which Freer arranged for him in 1900, Bixby established a close relationship with the artist that would continue for at least twelve years.[4] Freer negotiated several other transactions between the two men, but it is Tryon and Bixby's direct correspondence that provide the greatest insight into their shared interests.[5]

Bixby bought Tryon's works both for his home and for the St. Louis School and Museum of Fine Arts (now the Washington University Gallery of Art) and it seems clear that from the beginning he envisioned *Before Sunrise* in the school's collection.[6] The work has several titles in Tryon's letter, *Morning Twilight, At Daybreak,* and *Before Sunrise,* and it is clear he regarded it as one of his most significant pictures:

> *I want very much to have you see a large "Morning Twilight" which I have just finished. I have been at work on it for over three years and it is one of my most important works. I am anxious to have it go into a collection of my work of importance or else into a central museum. The last picture of this size and general character was bought about three years ago by Freer and is illustrated in an article on the Freer coll'n [sic] in Jan 07 Century [Century Magazine]. I consider and all who have seen it consider it one of my strongest works. . . .*[7]

Tryon shipped the painting in early April 1907 and wrote again of the work: "It is not perhaps the most delicate picture of this phase, but I think you will find it by far the most powerful and lasting in its qualities of any of my works. . . . I think you will find the picture responds to long and careful study. It is subtle and powerful at the same time, more so than perhaps any other work of mine."[8]

Without detracting from *Before Sunrise's* significance, it should be recognized that the artist's flattery of his patron's judgment and taste and of his own accomplishment, which he repeatedly emphasized with "I feel it is one of my most important works . . .," was typical of Tryon. Almost invariably he told Bixby each painting was one of his "best."[9] Such consistency, however, is less a salesman's hyperbole than it is an indication of the esteem with which Tryon regarded his St. Louis patron. The most important insight the artist's letters provide is that he regarded Bixby's collection of his works as second only to Freer's and he worked closely with the collector to coordinate a grouping which would be of the very highest quality.

Tryon kept close track of Bixby's pictures and he painted and reserved complementary works especially for him. Early in 1906 Tryon wrote, "As, next to Freer, you have the most complete collection of my work in existence I take much interest in it and will do all in my power to enable you to add to it such examples as I feel will best supplement and round out your group."[10] A few months later he continued,

> *As I said, I am very desirous that only very representative works of mine be added to your present collection of my work which is the second in importance in the country. Of course where one has so many works by one painter as you have of mine it is difficult to add new notes. Every painter must repeat his thoughts more or less but I try as far as possible to touch new realms in my work and this is what I shall endeavor to put in your way from time to time as they occur.*[11]

When he sent Bixby a new picture he frequently remarked which paintings of the existing collection it would look best close to, and recommended lighting and spatial considerations for viewing it to best effect.

Before Sunrise beautifully portrays Tryon's mature style. Its focus on a single row of trees seen through a poetic haze was a favorite motif for the artist. He rarely painted out-of-doors, but preferred distilling his memories from the vantage of his studio. The repetitiousness of his work—*Before Sunrise* is one of many paintings with essentially the same composition and palette—was less a lack of originality than it was a seeking of subtle nuance.[12] Unfortunately, much of the subtlety Tryon and Bixby worked so hard to convey is lost to us today because the group of paintings is no longer together. It is clear that Tryon regarded his works as interdependent and understanding them required a sustained experience which could only be successfully achieved when they were seen together. His efforts in coordinating Bixby's paintings certainly aspired to such an effect. Although the pictures have long since been dispersed, such recognition provides new significance to *Before Sunrise.* It is the only remaining work in the university museum out of what had been a carefully crafted collection of national stature. Had it remained intact this grouping of Tryons would have been, like the Freer paintings in Washington which are still together, a remarkable representation of American artistic taste in the early years of the twentieth century.

Joni L. Kinsey

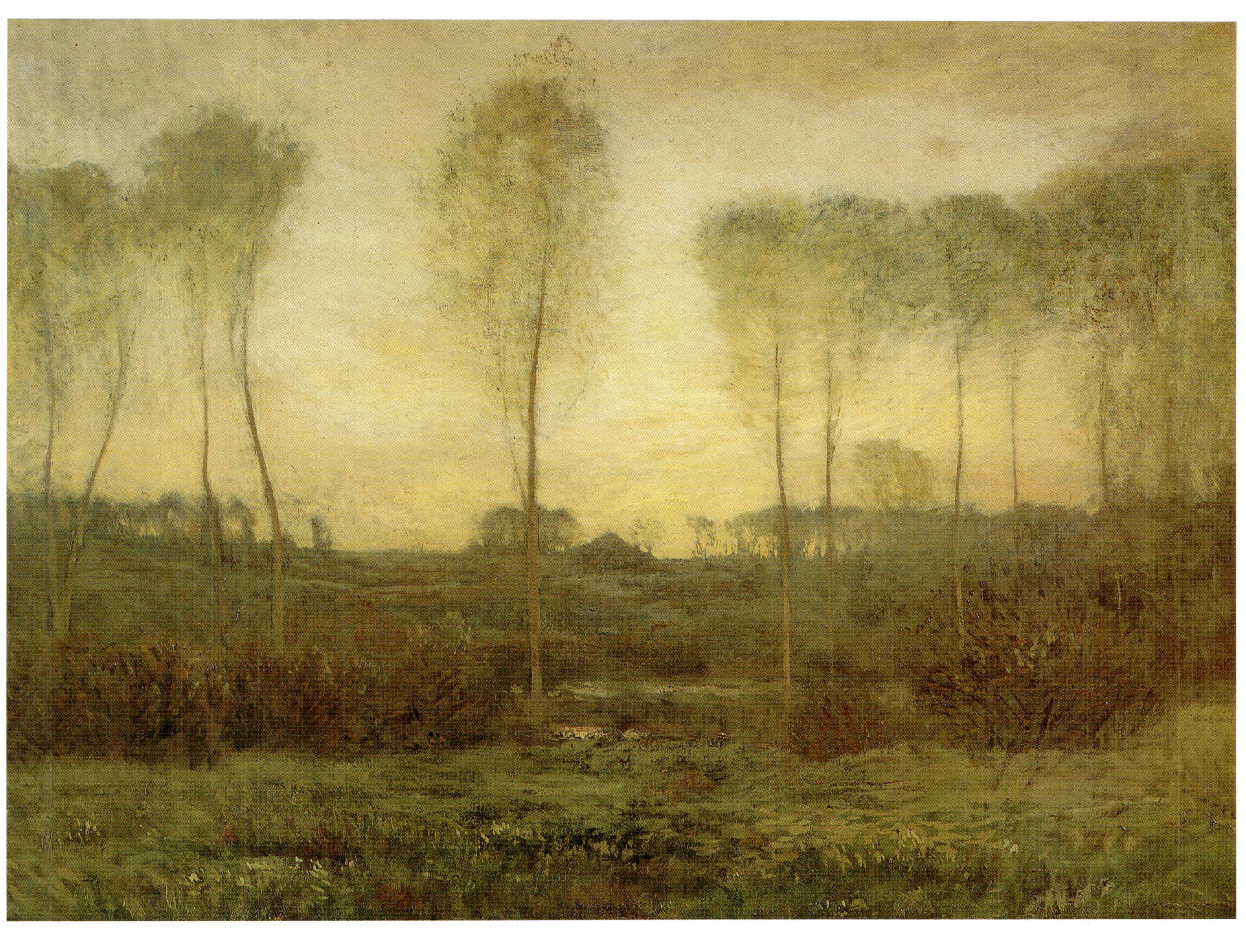

27. John Henry Twachtman (United States, 1853–1902) *House in Landscape,* c. 1890s

Oil on canvas, 22 x 24"
University purchase, Yeatman Fund, 1936

John Twachtman's devotion to the Connecticut landscape is revealed in the many paintings he produced of it, shimmering in an evanescent veil of atmosphere and color, as in *House in Landscape.* His attention to mood and effect, as well as to chromatic harmony, elements of design, and the passage of time and seasons, reveals his debt to French Impressionism, Japanese design, and the emerging trends that were the foundation of the modernist movements of the early twentieth century. His willingness to push the boundaries of painting beyond conventions was an inspiration to his contemporaries, and in retrospect stands as a testament to his independent spirit.

While *House in Landscape* is enigmatic in many ways, it is an excellent example of the artist's late style, revealing those qualities which made him an important artistic figure at the turn of the century. Twachtman's own career paralleled sweeping changes in the visual arts, and his paintings, particularly those from the last decade of his life, reflect those wider influences as well as specific circumstances of the artist's own life.

The son of German immigrants who settled in Cincinnati, Twachtman got his start in the visual arts from his father who was, among other things, a designer of painted window coverings. Young Twachtman also worked there for a time, starting in 1867, while he attended the Ohio Mechanics Institute, but he aspired to be an artist and by 1871 had persuaded his parents to allow him to attend the new McMicken School of Design in Cincinnati. There he met Frank Duveneck (1848–1919) who was to have an important influence on his career.[1]

Duveneck had recently returned from the Royal Academy in Munich, bringing with him a style characterized by free-flowing brush strokes and a Courbet-like realism that was markedly different from the effects of the prevailing Hudson River School. Twachtman studied with him, both at the McMicken School and privately, and in 1875 he accompanied Duveneck to Europe. There Twachtman worked with Ludwig Loefftz, who later became director of the Munich academy, staying for two years before traveling to Venice with Duveneck and William Merritt Chase.[2]

After his return to the United States in 1878 because of his father's death, Twachtman lived briefly in New York and became active in the progressive art community, exhibiting with the Society of American Artists and attending meetings of the Tile Club. It was about that time he met Julien Alden Weir, who became a close friend and colleague. During the 1880s Twachtman traveled frequently between Cincinnati, Chicago, New York, Italy, and Paris where he studied at the Academie Julian, and his style began to move away from the dark Munich manner toward a lighter French-inspired palette with Whistlerian overtones. In the fall of 1889 he moved to Greenwich, Connecticut and, during the first year, with the proceeds from a number of sales of paintings and the promise of a teaching position at the Art Students League in New York, he bought a seventeen-acre farm. Much of his subsequent work was inspired by this place, which still exists in much the same condition as in Twachtman's day. Frequent visitors to the farm on Round Hill Road included Weir, who lived at nearby Branchville, Connecticut, and such other American Impressionists as Theodore Robinson, Childe Hassam, and Robert Reid.[3]

In 1897 these and five other artists resigned from the Society of American Artists, which they believed had become too conservative, and formed their own informal organization that became known as "The Ten." Twachtman was one of the primary initiators of the group and he contributed paintings to their joint exhibitions until his early death only a few years later.[4] Although disgruntled with the SAA, the artists of The Ten did not envision themselves as a "rival society" or as especially radical, but rather a group of like-minded artists whose work would harmonize better in smaller exhibitions than at the more disparate displays sponsored by the larger art associations. This premise was challenged by many who were threatened by the dissention, but like the French Impressionists' earlier efforts at self-determination, The Ten's cohesion was based on the ideal of conveying each artist's work to the public more intimately and directly.[5] The group's action, whether truly revolutionary or not, did pave the way for subsequent dissentions from large art organizations. In conjunction with such dissenters as those known as "The Eight" in the early years of the twentieth century, The Ten ultimately contributed to an eventual breakdown of the artistic stronghold of the leading art associations.

While the Washington University painting probably predates The Ten, it deals with issues that preoccupied Twachtman in the 1890s. The theme of the house in the landscape was a favorite of his throughout the decade, inspired to a great extent by his own Connecticut farm and by those he visited.[6] While the exact location of this work's subject is uncertain, comparison with other paintings the artist produced during this period suggests that this is a scene either of or near Round Hill.[7] The picture's delicate color relationships, softened focus, and the house's placement in the middle background are also characteristic of Twachtman's style of the 1890s, a decade during which he pushed his experimentation with subtle effects to their most harmonious and abstract point.[8]

As several scholars have noted, however, the chronology and exact subject matter of the artist's late works is difficult to determine. Twachtman rarely dated his pictures or included objects that might locate their subjects, and archival material that could provide details of their creation is brief. Similarly, little is known of the "Willcox" to whom Twachtman inscribed Washington University's picture. An Arthur V. Willcox is listed in the 1900 *American Art Annual* as a member of the Art Club of Philadelphia and residing at Glendalough House, Galway County, Ireland, but the relationship between the two men remains unclear.[9]

Even with its lingering questions, *House in Landscape* clearly reveals Twachtman's commitment to the principles of landscape painting and Impressionism, coupled with an independence that made him a leading artist of his time.

Joni L. Kinsey

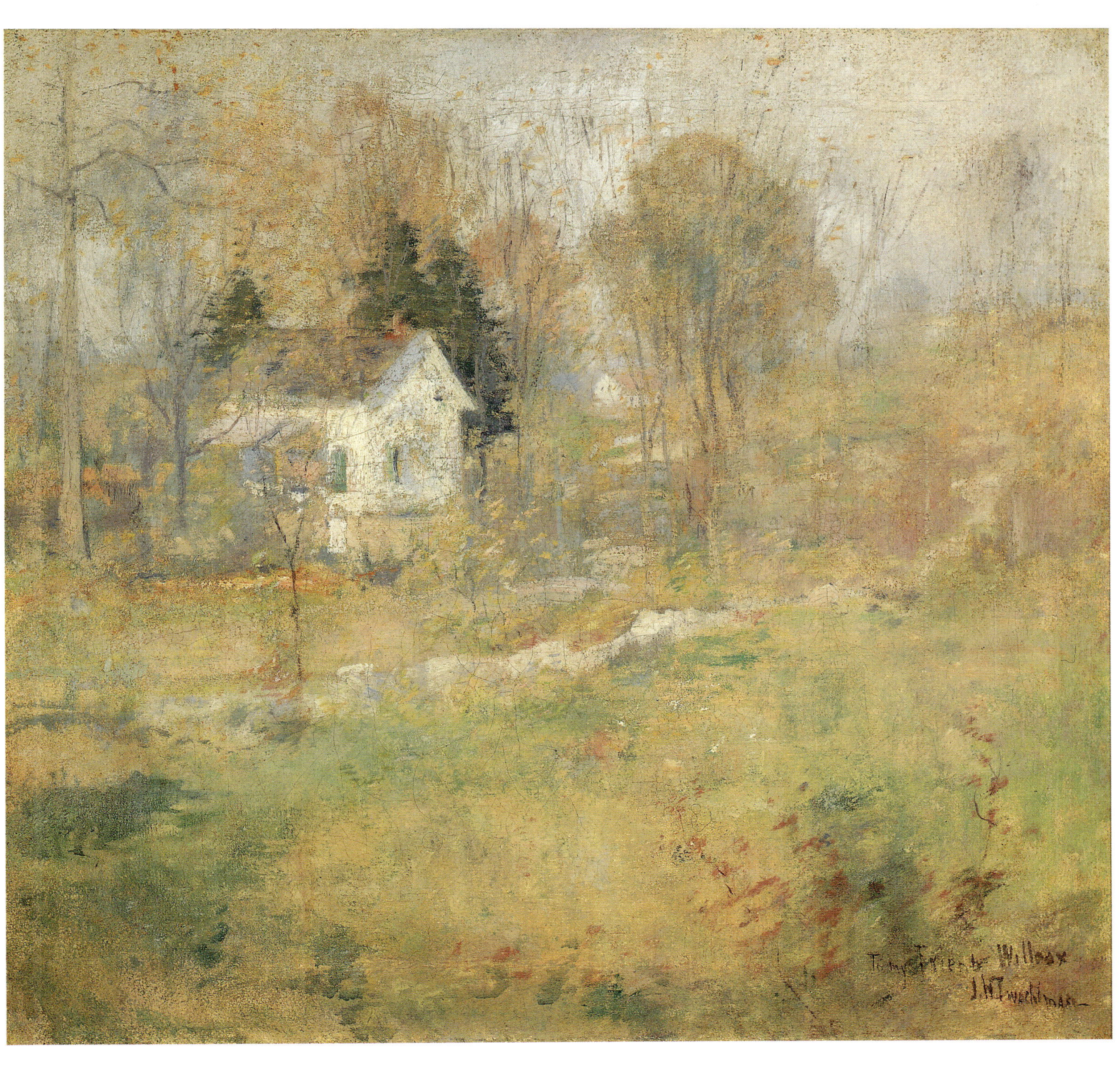

28. Frederick Childe Hassam (United States, 1849–1935)

Diamond Cove, Isles of Shoals, 1908

Oil on board, 25 x 30"

University purchase, Bixby Fund, 1914

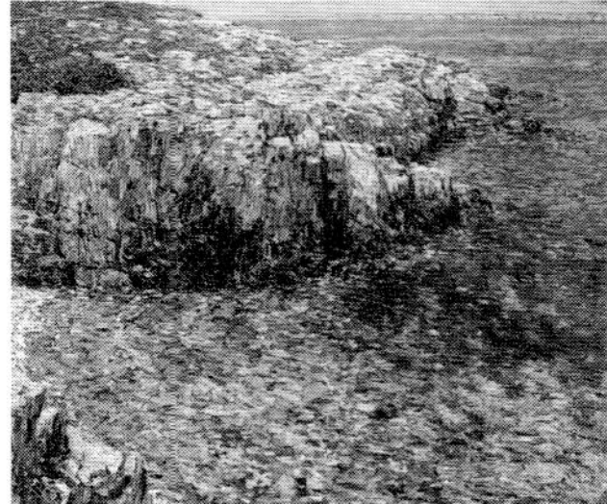

Frederick Childe Hassam
Isle of Shoals, 1907
Oil on canvas, 26 x 31"
The Portland Art Museum, Oregon Art Institute
Gift in Memory of William Maxwell Wood IV, 1982

Washington University's *Diamond Cove, Isles of Shoals* by Childe Hassam is a distinguished example from a series the artist produced of a group of granite cliffs at Appledore Island, ten miles off the New Hampshire coast, near Portsmouth. Hassam began visiting the cluster of rocky islands in the mid-1880s, drawn, as were many artists, writers, and musicians, to the celebrated circle of poet and journalist Celia Laighton Thaxter (1835–1894), a long-time resident.[1] Thaxter's influence on Hassam's art was considerable; in addition to her hospitality, which provided him opportunities for artistic inspiration, it was she who persuaded the artist to drop his first name in favor of the more romantic "Childe Hassam."[2]

Thaxter's father, Thomas Laighton, had purchased four of the islands in 1839. He moved his family there and served as a lighthouse keeper for several years before establishing a resort hotel on Appledore with a partner, Levi Thaxter, a well-connected Harvard graduate who married Celia in 1851.[3] Their hotel, and another on nearby Star Island, attracted well-to-do city dwellers until the first burned in 1914.[4] The Thaxter's nearby home was an important adjunct to the complex, becoming famous for its "parlor," a flower and art-filled room that was the gathering place for dozens of well-known creative people, including John Greenleaf Whittier, Sarah Orne Jewett, William Dean Howells, Harriet Beecher Stowe, William Morris Hunt, William Trost Richards, and Alfred Thompson Bricher, to name only a few.[5] Celia Thaxter was herself a visual artist in addition to her career as a writer; her delicate floral designs painted on china and the watercolor sketches that adorned her writings were in great demand.[6]

Over the course of his visits to the island, Hassam painted nearly 400 images of its varied offerings, comprising approximately ten percent of his sizable oeuvre. These range from an early watercolor series of lighthouses from 1886, a group of flower and interior images from 1889–1894 which culminated in the watercolor illustrations he produced for Thaxter's book, *An Island Garden* (1894), and a number of landscapes that he began around 1900.[7] The Washington University picture belongs to this last series.

Hassam was, along with John Twachtman, a leading member of The Ten, the group of American artists who broke away from the Society of American Artists in 1897 to form their own exhibition society. Although each member had his own unique style, all were engaged with Impressionism to some degree. Hassam remained an active and outspoken member of the group from its conception to its conclusion, exhibiting with it throughout the period that he frequented the Isles of Shoals and frequently speaking out against the prevailing prejudice against American art.[8]

Although the similarity of Hassam's work to that of Claude Monet has been noted by many, the American painter never met his French contemporary and never visited his garden at Giverny. The connection, however, was recognized early and the frequent comparisons apparently irritated Hassam, who identified more strongly with other artistic influences, including the work of British landscapist J.M.W. Turner, the aesthetic criticism of John Ruskin, and more generally, the so-called "Aesthetic Movement" that pervaded painting in New England in the late nineteenth century.[9] Hassam did, however, have ample opportunity to see Monet's works, which were regularly exhibited in the United States and during his stay in Paris in the late 1880s.[10] Despite the artist's annoyance at such pairings, an analysis of his *Diamond Cove, Isles of Shoals* benefits from a comparison to the French Impressionist's *Etretat of Belle Ile* series from the 1880s. In both artists' works we see a sustained interest in a distinctive coastal landscape, an emphasis on muted tones, and the characteristic tendency toward prominent brushstrokes. The differences, however, may be more compelling than the similarities; Hassam's work consistently displays a greater emphasis on chromatic contrast than does Monet's, as well as a stronger sense of linear relationships.

In *Diamond Cove, Isles of Shoals,* the painting's surface is suffused with a scintillating interplay of rock and water. The large gray cliffs projecting into the sea from the upper left are in some ways overshadowed by the shimmering pebbles seen through the shallow in the foreground. The colors range widely over the canvas, dispelling any preconception of a simplistic composition, simultaneously projecting and receding between liquid and granite.

Other works in Hassam's series are instructive for understanding this painting. A 1907 drawing entitled *Diamond Cove* (Rhode Island School of Design) compares closely in composition, but his work contains suggestions of foliage growing on the rocks in the upper left. This creeping covering is also found in a 1907 oil of the same subject in the Portland Art Museum. The cliffs in the St. Louis canvas are barren and the foreground outcroppings that distinguish both the sketch and the Portland painting are noticeably absent. The lack of this feature, which provides a semblance of secure footing in the earlier images, gives Washington University's version a more threatening quality, a characteristic heightened by its less verdant shoal. Nevertheless, the chromatic richness of the painting softens the effect, and even in its starkness the scene echoes the beautifully variegated gardens that Celia Thaxter so carefully cultivated.

When coupled with Hassam's paintings of Thaxter's parlor and garden which are overwhelmed with flowers and greenery, the coastal scenes provide a unique view of a special place and time. The rocky outcroppings echo the isolation of the islands, the harshness of nature, and even the creative struggles of the artist, and the flowers reflect the warmth and abundance that Thaxter's salon brought to the barren shores. For Hassam the two were inseparable; at the Isles of Shoals he could both confront isolation and enjoy the benefits of companionship. It was such a confluence that enabled the creation of paintings like *Isles of Shoals.*

Joni L. Kinsey

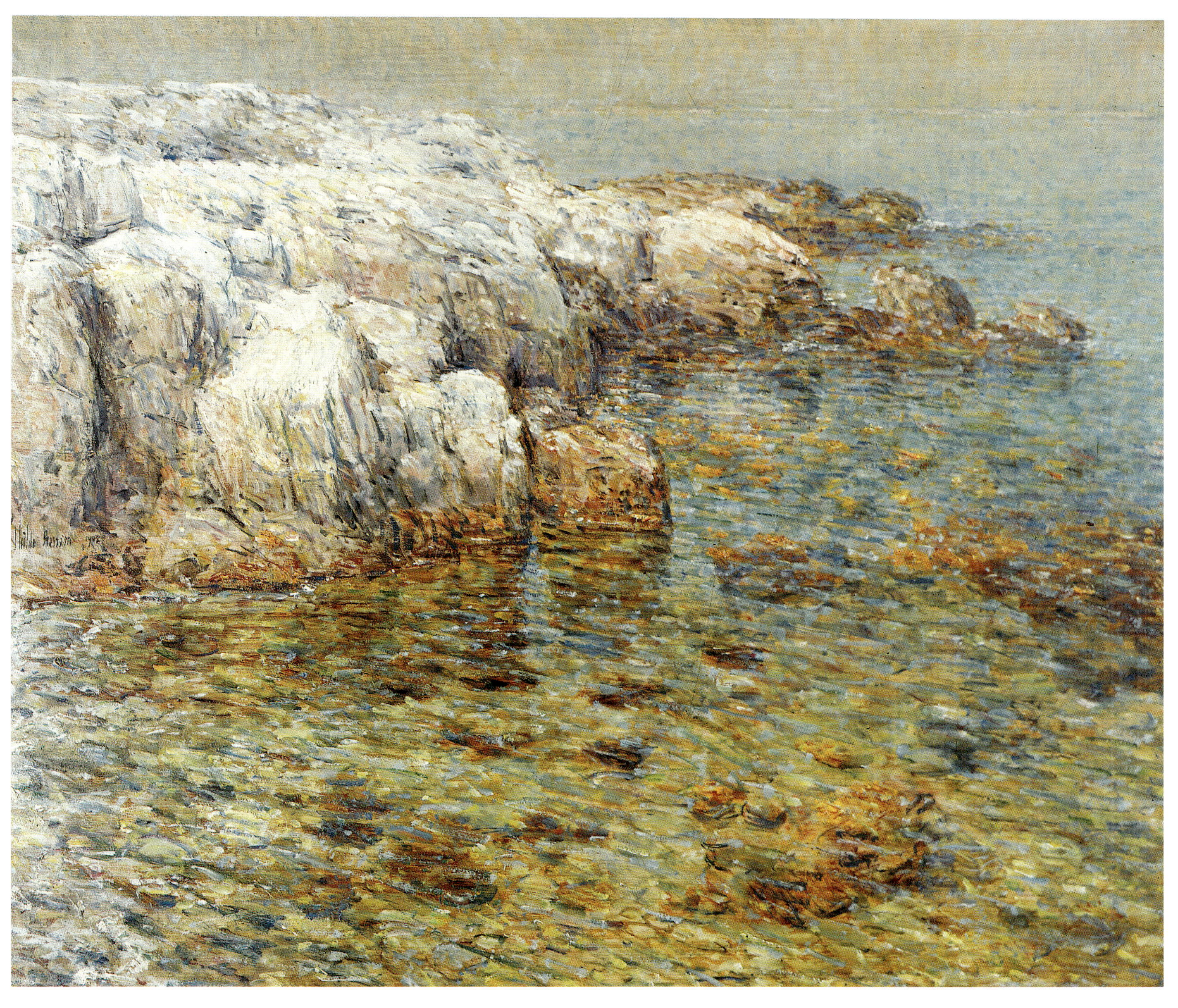

29. Henri Matisse (France, 1869–1954)
Still Life with Oranges (II), c. 1899

Oil on canvas, 18⅜ x 21¾"
Gift of Mr. and Mrs. Sydney M. Shoenberg, Jr., 1962

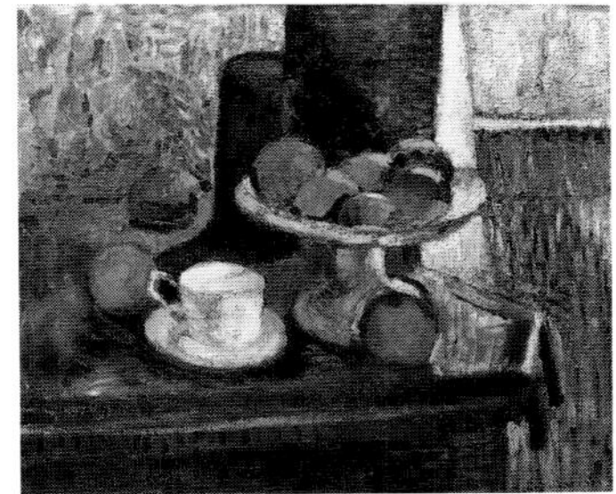

Henri Matisse
Still Life with Oranges (I), 1899
Oil on canvas, 18½ x 22"
The Baltimore Museum of Art
The Cone Collection

Still Life with Oranges (II) is one of a pair of still lifes that Matisse painted from the same motif early in 1899, probably while he was visiting his wife's family in Toulouse. This picture reflects Matisse's experimental state of mind around the turn of the century, when he worked in a wide range of different styles and found still life painting to be particularly congenial for working out the pictorial problems that preoccupied him.

This is an especially luminous painting, in which brilliant yellows and oranges are played off against resonant violets and blues to create a splendidly radiant effect. It also employs a boldly musical composition, in which the rhythmic circular forms are set in counterpoint to the angular geometry of the table and window. A complex dialogue is established between the strong surface design and the illusion of deep space, and between the materiality of the paint surface and the effulgence that emanates from it. The translucent glass pitcher plays an especially important role in this regard, acting as a kind of paradigm for the alternating passages of opacity and transparency that characterize the painting as a whole.

This painting is virtually the same size as *Still Life with Oranges (I)* (1899, The Baltimore Museum of Art), in which the same motif is rendered in greater detail with stippled, probing strokes and more mellow color.[1] In *Still Life with Oranges (II)* the picture space is flatter and more highly patterned than in the Baltimore version; the color is brighter and the description of the objects is more condensed and summary. These two pictures seem to comprise the earliest instance in which Matisse deliberately painted two different versions of the same motif—the first usually more plastic and modeled, the second flatter and more graphic. This practice of "theme and variation" would be continued in such celebrated pairs as the two versions of *The Young Sailor* (1906, private collection; Jacques and Natasha Gelman collection), of *Le Luxe* (1907, Musée National d'Art Moderne, Centre Pompidou, Paris; Statens Museum for Kunst, Copenhagen), and of *View of Notre Dame* (1914, Kunstmuseum, Solothurn; The Museum of Modern Art, New York).

In some of his later paired pictures, Matisse rendered the second canvas from the first rather than directly from nature, and it is possible that he also employed this procedure for *Still Life with Oranges (II)*. But one cannot be certain about this.[2] It is similarly difficult to ascertain whether the two versions of *Still Life with Oranges* were done before or after Matisse completed the large *Sideboard and Table* (1899, private collection), his earliest essay in neo-Impressionist technique, in which the same combination of objects is seen from a different viewpoint at the left.[3] But it is worth noting that Marguerite Duthuit, the artist's daughter who worked on the catalogue raisonné of her father's work, clearly described the Washington University picture as the last of the three paintings he did of the motif, asserting that they were all done directly from nature: "This painting is the third canvas done after nature from the same subject, but all three treated in a different way."[4] Indeed it seems quite likely that after Matisse painted *Sideboard and Table*, he did the Baltimore painting as a freer rendering of part of the still life, then undertook the Washington University picture, which he blocked in quite boldly, probably in preparation for a more elaborately developed picture.

It is impossible to ascertain whether Matisse considered this painting finished when he stopped working on it in 1899. As with other unfinished-looking paintings of this period, the signature appears to have been added later. And given the fact that in paintings like *Sideboard and Table* he appears to have set down his general areas of color in simplified flat forms before he rendered them in a modified version of neo-Impressionist divided touch and color, it is quite possible that this painting was originally conceived as a kind of underpainting. It was probably left unfinished because Matisse, unable to carry its implications to their logical conclusion and fix the whole picture space within flat and intensely colored shapes, realized that he had gone as far with it as he could.[5] For in this picture Matisse seems quite literally to have gotten ahead of himself. As Lawrence Gowing has remarked, the radiance of the picture must have appeared quite strange in 1899, and "Matisse himself could not pursue for some ten years the possibility that opened before him; indeed he did not realize it fully until the last years of his life."[6]

In fact, this is such a forward-looking painting that some writers have insisted on a later date for it.[7] The apparent lack of finish and the cultivation of the chance possibilities generated by the process of painting itself anticipate characteristics of Matisse's later works—as do its flattened space, decorative composition, and bright colors. The intensely abstracted view through the window also foreshadows some of Matisse's most radical later imagery, such as the highly synthetic window views he painted between 1914 and 1916.

The color in *Still Life with Oranges* represents an especially radical departure from Matisse's earlier procedure. As Gowing has remarked, this is one of the earliest instances in which Matisse appears to have realized that "for him the function of colour was not to imitate light but to create it."[8] This is one of the first pictures in which Matisse used high-key color as a structural rather than descriptive element—a practice that would have enormous repercussions not only for his own future work but for modern painting in general.

Jack Flam

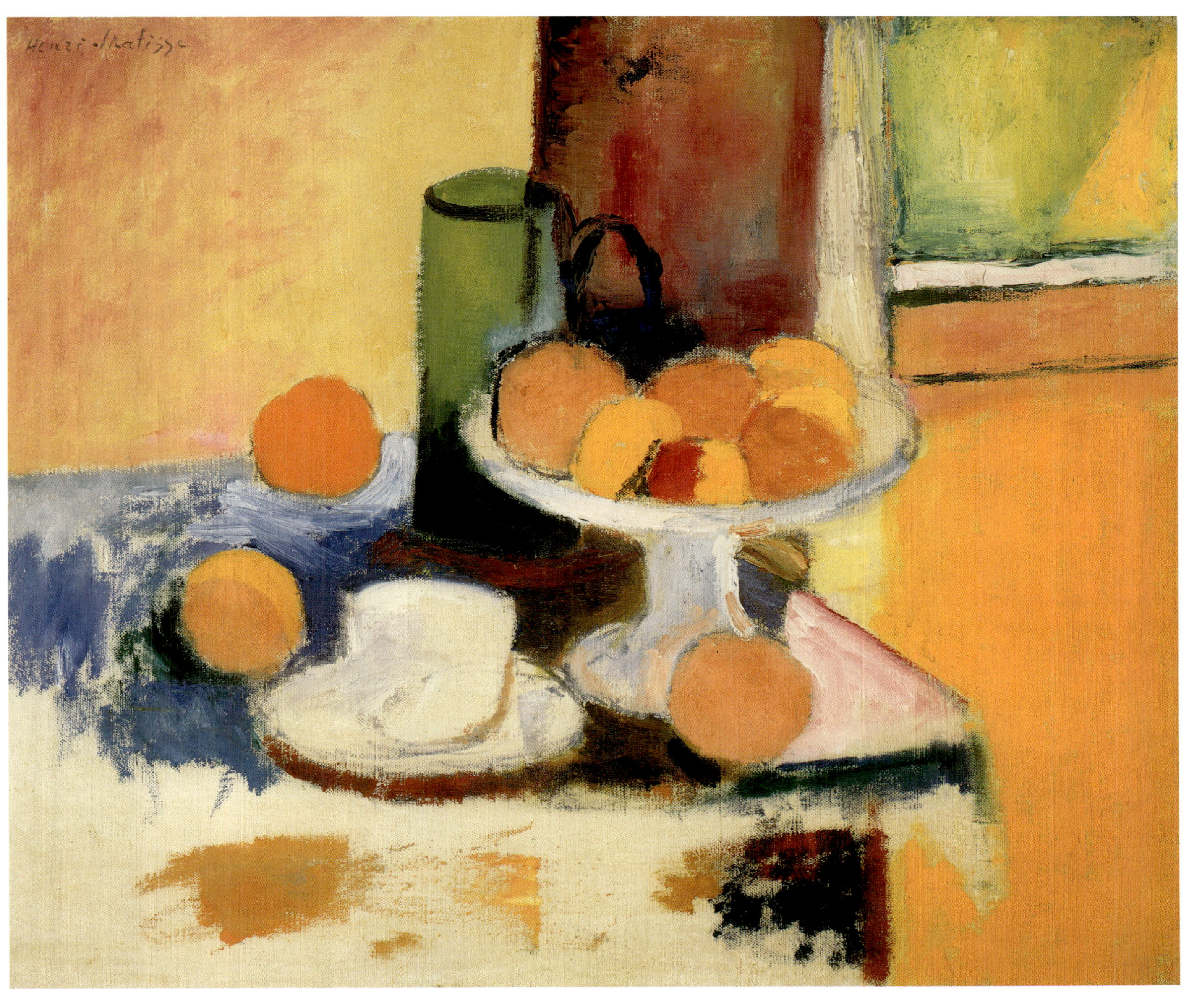

30. Pablo Picasso (Spain, 1881–1973)

Glass and Bottle of Suze, 1912

Pasted paper with gouache and charcoal, 25¾ x 19¾"
University purchase, Kende Sale Fund, 1946

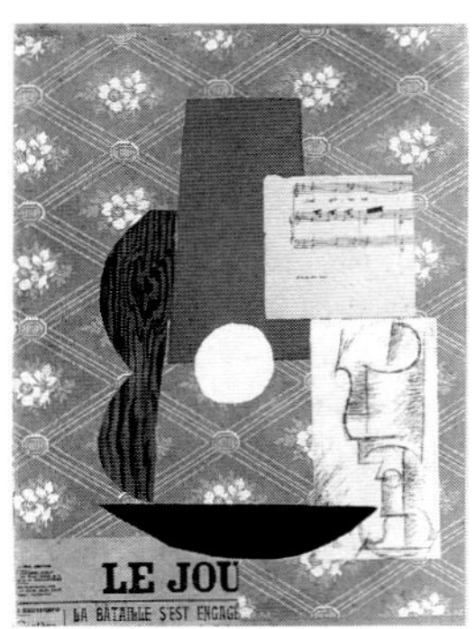

Pablo Picasso
Guitar, Sheet Music, and Glass, 1912
Pasted paper with gouache and charcoal, 19⅞ x 14¾"
Marion Koogler McNay Art Museum, San Antonio, Texas
Bequest of Marion Koogler McNay, 1950

In 1912 when Spanish artist Pablo Picasso made the *papier collé, Glass and Bottle of Suze,* he was thirty-one, had visited Paris for the first time in 1900 and had lived there fairly continuously since 1904. By 1912 he had achieved a certain reputation, even internationally, and had a supportive dealer, D. H. Kahnweiler. Even more significant is the fact that Picasso was at the apogee of his close relationship with the French painter Georges Braque. It was in May of that year that Picasso had made the "first" collage, the famous horizontal oval, *Still Life with Chair Caning* (1912, Musée Picasso, Paris), with its pasted oilcloth and frame of rope. In September of that year Braque limited a collage to pasted papers and produced the first *papier collé.* Picasso soon followed Braque, even using the decorator's tricks of combing paint to give the effect of wood graining and of using decorators' materials like wallpaper, devices Braque had learned from his father. Picasso also ventured forth into another more daring (and less durable) form of paper—newsprint. Often, as in Washington University's *Glass and Bottle of Suze,* the newspaper came from the sensational Parisian daily, *Le Journal,* which he seems to have read voraciously, here using the issue of 18 November 1912.

Critics first viewed the use of newsprint as a formal element, adding a variation in texture to the works. This seemed confirmed by the large drawings with newsprint, which almost immediately followed in December, and which Picasso photographed proudly pinned up together in his boulevard Raspail studio. Critics may have been surprised that Picasso would use a material which would darken quickly and then inevitably disintegrate, but they probably saw this as almost a proto-Dadaist gesture of daring.[1] It was not until 1971 that Robert Rosenblum suggested that the newsprint should be read, if only for puns and other witticisms.[2] Daix and Rosselet in their catalogue raisonné of the artist's cubist works in 1979 identified the issues of newspapers and the events described as a way of providing termini after which the works must have been made, but with the reasonable assumption that Picasso used the clippings very shortly after their publication.[3] It was, however, only in the 1980s that Patricia Leighten read the newspaper clippings for their political significance.[4]

Three of the clippings in the Washington University's *Glass and Bottle of Suze* refer to incidents during the First Balkan War in which Turkey was trying to defend the Ottoman Empire against Bulgaria, Serbia, and Greece. As Leighten has pointed out, the dispatches (two here by Pal Erio) are vivid and make the horrors of war, with winter and the wounded and dying, particularly harrowing. Finally Leighten found even more significance in the fact that the newsprint that forms a left-hand column, as observed by Daix and Rosselet, records the meeting of 40,000 socialists at Pré-Saint-Gervais to protest any involvement in war. These blocks of newsprint, now very much browner than they would have been but nevertheless shadowed by Picasso with touches of charcoal, cut or torn carelessly, pasted somewhat unevenly and certainly placed apparently haphazardly so that some have to be read upside down, do remind us of a world that is murky, disturbing and, in fact, disintegrating. This is one level of meaning in *Glass and Bottle of Suze.* Leighten ignores the fact that there are other pieces of newsprint which come from serialized fiction in *Le Journal,* a novel by Abel Hermant (1862–1950) about some of the most snobbish and frivolous aspects of Parisian life. In their very silliness they represent an antidote to the Balkan Wars and socialism, or at least an expression of the absurdity of contrasts in the society in which Picasso was living.

The excerpts from the serialized novel are not the only elements that lighten the effect of this *papier collé.* The two pieces of wallpaper he cut and pasted crudely—and upside down—have a certain domestic charm that Picasso also employed in two contemporary works. One is an expansive and almost square *papier collé* called *Guitar and Sheet Music* (1912, private collection), the other the simpler, more classic and resolved *Guitar, Sheet Music, and Glass* (1912, Marion Koogler McNay Art Museum, San Antonio), which does contain a small piece of *Le Journal* with a heading "La Bataille s'est engagé" (The Battle has Begun). In neither, although the wallpaper is identical in all three, is there evidence of the same concern for social and political matters as in Washington University's *papier collé.*

Where are we with the seeming ambiguities of the *Glass and Bottle of Suze* in the contrasts between the serious if obscured images of war and demands for social reform suggested by the newspaper clippings, and the clarity and decisiveness of the world of frivolous fiction and the bottle of Suze? Did Picasso ever expect that someone would read those newspaper clippings which he pasted together almost illegibly and which only can be read with photographs or by taking the *papier collé* down from a wall and putting it on a table? Perhaps he enjoyed the knowledge that certain secrets had to be unravelled before the work could be understood. Over thirty years later his young companion Françoise Gilot asked him about his *papiers collés,* which she herself then believed was "a kind of by-product or perhaps even the fading-out of Cubist painting." Picasso denied this and said,

> *We tried to get rid of "trompe l'oeil" to find a "trompe l'esprit." We didn't any longer want to fool the eye; we wanted to fool the mind. The sheet of newspaper was never used in order to make a newspaper. . . . This displaced object has entered a universe for which it was not made and where it retains, in a measure, its strangeness. And this strangeness was what we wanted to make people think about because we were quite aware that our world was becoming very strange and not exactly reassuring.*[5]

We are still left uncertain that we have unravelled all the mysteries of this provocative work. As we look at it we can even discover that its more frivolous parts form the image of a man, the table his torso, the light brown gouache vertical at the left a leg with a foot standing on the bottom of the sheet of paper, the black zigzag the other leg, the cork a head undeniably small and modestly bowed, and a spiral of black charcoal around the stem of the glass a hand holding it toward us in a toast. The *Glass and Bottle of Suze* may reveal other secrets still.

Jean Sutherland Boggs

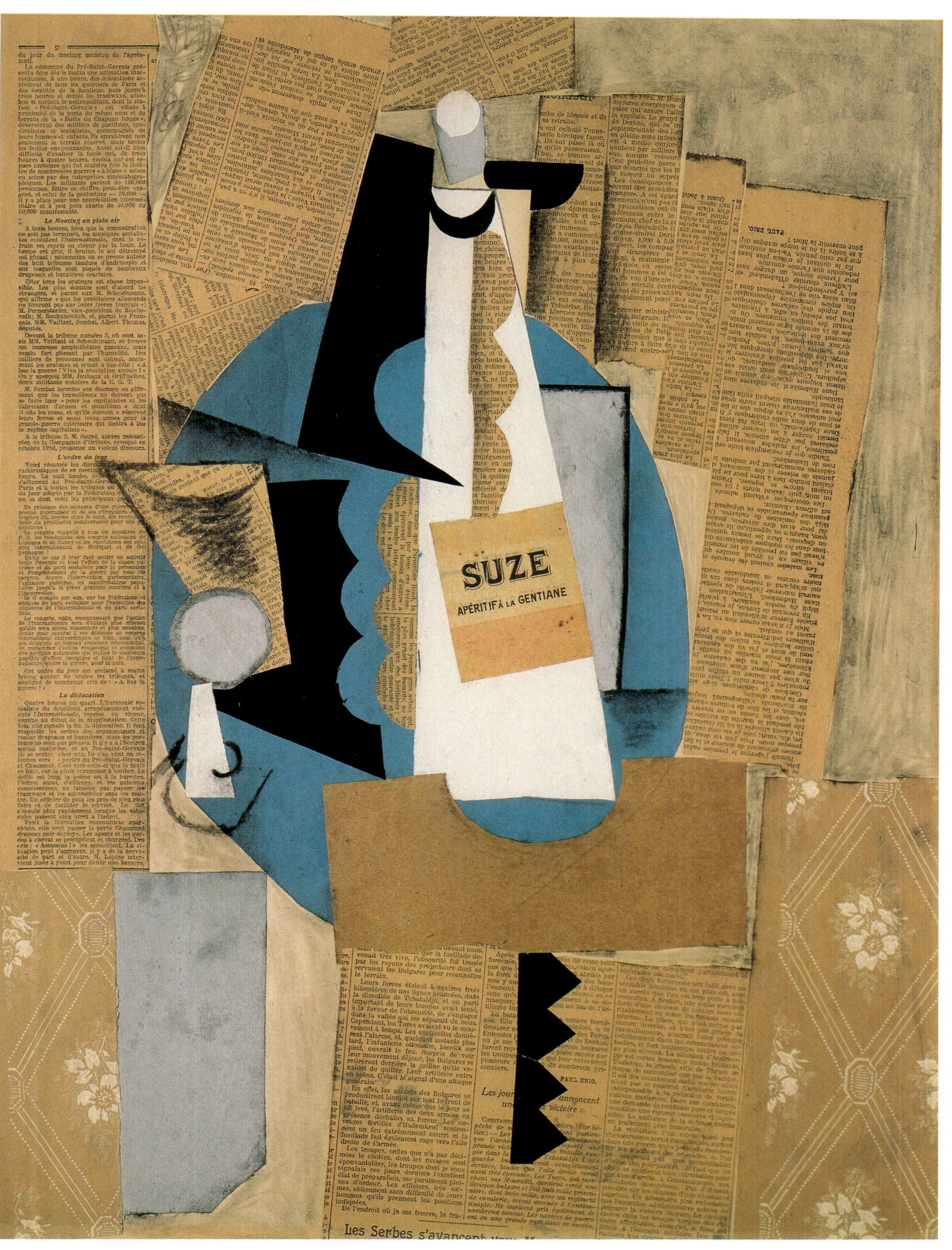
SUZE
APÉRITIF À LA GENTIANE
Le Meeting en plein air
La dislocation
Les Serbes s'avancent

31. Pablo Picasso (Spain, 1881–1973)
Les Femmes d'Alger (Women of Algiers), 1955

Oil on canvas, 44½ x 57⅜"
University purchase, Steinberg Fund, 1960

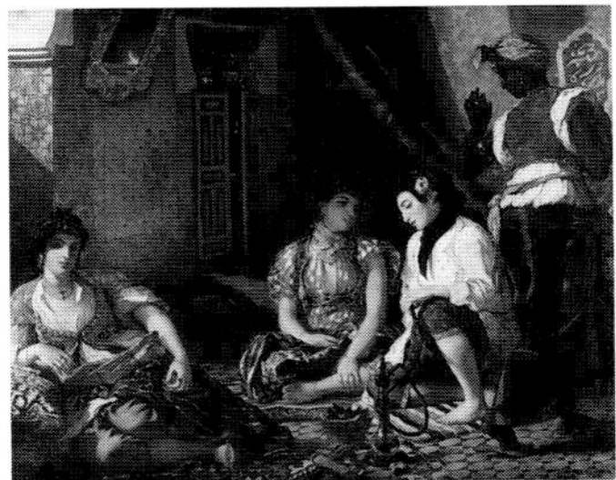

Eugéne Delacroix
Les Femmes d'Alger, 1834
Oil on canvas, 70⅞ x 90⅛"
Musée du Louvre, Paris

Picasso had always been interested in, and often challenged by, the works of earlier artists. In the 1950s, when he was in his seventies, he was obsessed with painting variations of famous masterpieces. It was, however, only in 1954–55 with *Les Femmes d'Alger* after the French Romantic painter, Eugène Delacroix, that he began to produce a series on a single work. With Delacroix he actually combined the other artist's two versions of *Les Femmes d'Alger*, the more famous in the Louvre (1834), the other in the Musée Fabre, Montpellier (1849). Upon these two works he based fifteen paintings (lettered in chronological sequence from A–O), two lithographs, and innumerable drawings (the Musée Picasso, Paris, has seventy).[1] Picasso's affection for Delacroix and the Louvre's painting is well-established, but we are told by his English friend, Roland Penrose, that he "had not seen it for years, though he had only to cross the Seine and enter the Louvre to do so."[2] In any case, since he was working with the subject and the composition alone, consultation with the original was not essential.

The Louvre's version of *Les Femmes d'Alger* had an attraction for Picasso that was more than artistic. The crouching figure, second from the right, very much resembled Jacqueline Roque, whom he would eventually marry. He was also undoubtedly seduced by the wonderfully indolent atmosphere of an oriental harem. Indeed, Hélène Parmelin, who has recorded Picasso's life in these later years, has stated that when the women of the Picasso household would sit around on a lazy Sunday they would call it behaving like *Les Femmes d'Alger*.[3] His free translations of the two paintings by Delacroix also gave him an opportunity to make use of the style of his friend Henri Matisse, who he claimed had "left his odalisques to me as a legacy" when he had died the previous November.[4] Françoise Gilot, who had been Picasso's companion before Jacqueline Roque and has reason to be bitter about Picasso as a man, which she rarely reveals in her writings on the artist, points out that *Les Femmes d'Alger* "displayed [Picasso's] usual ferocity toward women as well as a nihilistic despair over [Matisse's] demise."[5]

Although the relationships of all the paintings in Picasso's series to the two paintings by Delacroix remain surprisingly constant, each departed daringly from its source and each was very different from the next. When Picasso had finished the last, Roland Penrose visited his Paris apartment. Penrose describes the artist showing him all his *Les Femmes d'Alger*:

> *The stacked canvases left little space, but in the center of the room he stood there friendly and smiling. Bringing them out one after another he showed me the rich variety of style and fantasy to which the "Women of Algiers" had been subjected. . . . As he continued to bring out more canvases I remarked upon the variations between the representational and cubist styles. I could discover no direct sequence leading in either direction. With an enigmatic smile he told me that he himself never knew what was coming next, nor did he try to interpret what he had done. "That is for others to do if they wish," he said.*[6]

The reactions of Hélène Parmelin on seeing the completed series were similar.[7] In addition, Parmelin speculated about the news that a single collector, Victor W. Ganz of New York, who was passionately devoted to Picasso's late work, had bought the whole series. The Picasso household wondered about the "whole harem in one American's house. It was too many—canvases—for one man. . . . We wagered he would not keep the lot."[8] And indeed he did not, but he kept, however, the very different versions C and O as well as version M, a *grisaille*.

In the many variations Picasso worked upon the paintings by Delacroix, he was directing himself toward the final version which is closest to the style of the Romantic artist. In that last painting in the series, the figure at the left with a golden turban and large, woeful eyes is undoubtedly Jacqueline. The colors are more varied, broken and decorative, as if in a calligraphic fashion Picasso, in a manner comparable to Matisse, could create something of the exoticism of the original works by Delacroix. But as Penrose has pointed out, "The discreet eroticism of Delacroix's harem has vanished."[9]

Washington University's version, letter N, is the penultimate, painted on 13 February 1955, only the day before the last canvas. It establishes the locations and the positions of the four figures with greater boldness than in the later work. In the angularity of the planes that define the room or tent there are reminiscences of Cubism of over forty years before. The essential departure from Cubism is that it is the bodies in their positions and movements that essentially describe the space in an athletic and energetic manner. Four figures have survived although, throughout the thirteen earlier paintings in the series, their number was sometimes reduced to three and twice to one. The remotest in this version is in the background, the figure of a servant, fully clad in olive drab with an outstretched arm. She seems a harbinger, pointing to the world beyond the harem. In a mirrored reflection beside her is a crouching blue nude holding her arms above her head as if she were admiring her reflection in the same mirror. The bather in the foreground both reclines and stretches upward through her strong legs and gigantic foot. But the actions of all three are set off by, and resolved in, the large seated figure at the left which is partly covered by a dress of red. She is quiet, solemn and totemic, her inflated breasts making it clear that she is an object of desire. We know from the final version in the series that she is Jacqueline, which we might also guess from her long neck and black ringlets. But with the blank white circle for a face, she remains almost complacently enigmatic and aloof.

The whole composition, in spite of its abstraction, is sexually highly charged. As Penrose points out, the scenes have become "more orgiastic" as Picasso developed them through the series. He adds, "In Picasso's summary treatment of anatomy, the seduction of the female form is no longer veiled and segregated, it floods the whole picture."[10] And it seems choreographed in space here like a highly formalized dance. Such inanimate objects as the servant's vessel, the hookah, or the plate with three figs seem inconsequential and hardly tangible against the forces of nature the bodies represent. All are dominated finally by the self-controlled figure of Jacqueline, who presides like some still and exotic goddess.

Jean Sutherland Boggs

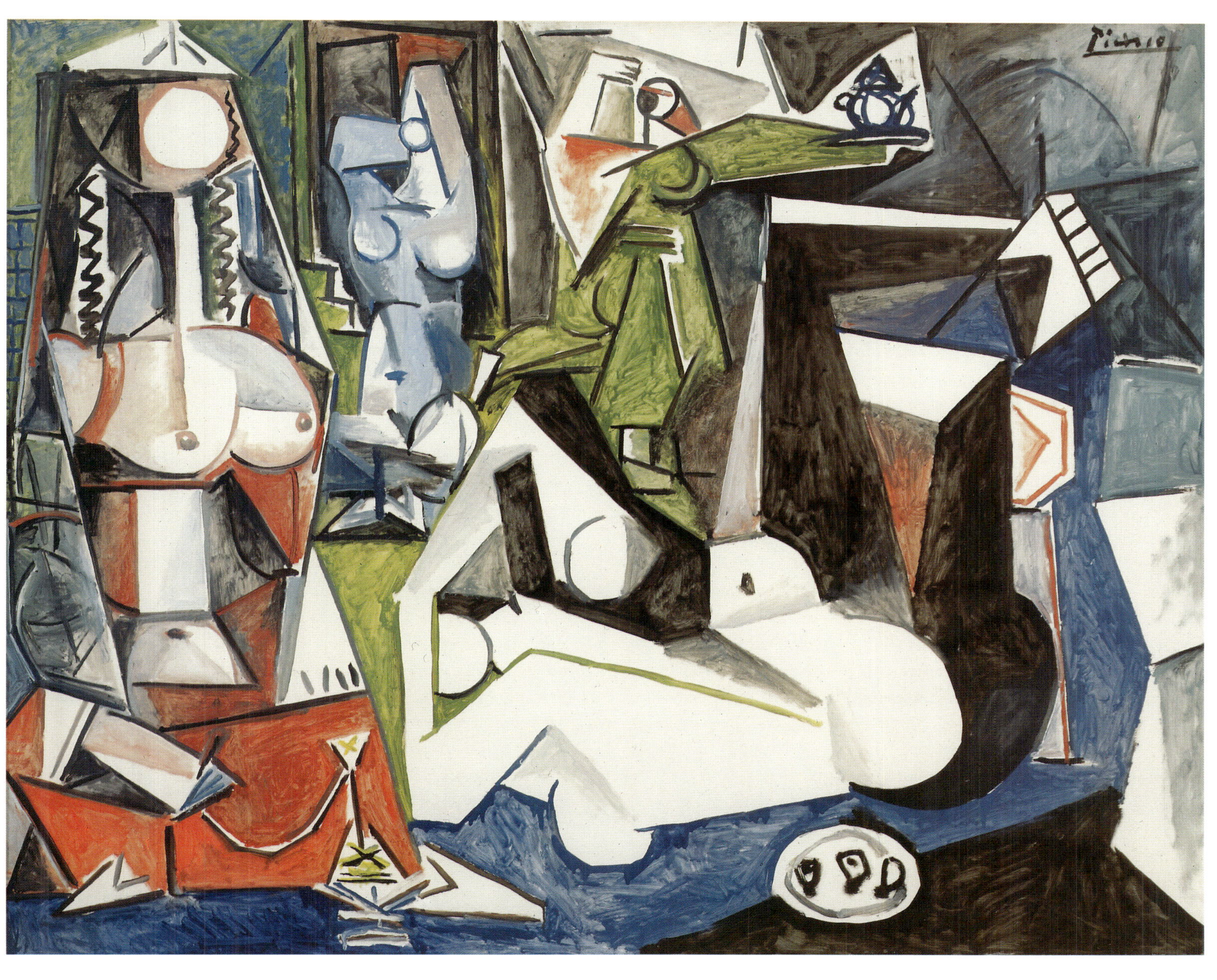

32. Georges Braque (France, 1882–1963)

Still Life with Glass, 1930

Oil on canvas, 20 x 25½"
University purchase, Kende Sale Fund, 1946

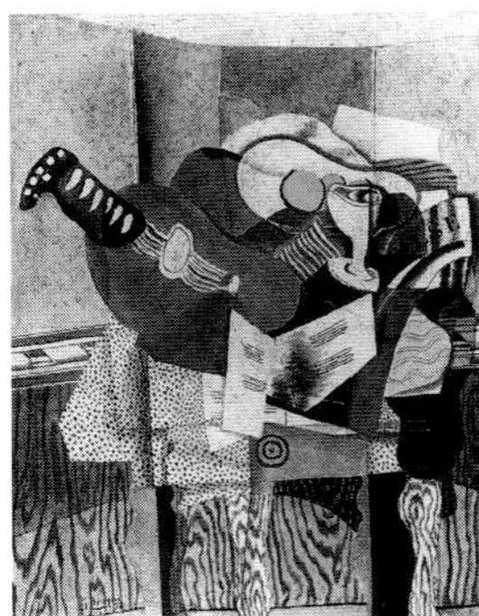

Georges Braque
The Blue Mandolin (The Blue Guitar), 1930
Oil and sand on canvas, 45½ x 35"
The Saint Louis Art Museum
Purchase

The relatively modest dimensions of *Still Life with Glass* are belied by its presence; in reproduction it invariably appears to be larger than it is. The picture's gravity and weightiness undoubtedly owe much to the fact that it occupies a significant position in Braque's stylistic evolution: on the one hand it looks back over past achievements, on the other it anticipates important new developments.[1]

In 1928 there was a marked change in the outward appearance of Braque's art when he adopted a lighter, blonder palette and executed a series of works on absorbent grounds of gesso, often mixed with sand. Many of the paintings of 1928–30 have dry, fresco-like surfaces which contrast with the darker velvety tonalities and surfaces that had preceded them. If Braque was above all a painter of still life, the exploration of space had always been his major pictorial concern and in these works he enlarges his spatial repertoire, extending and exploring the space behind and around his familiar subject matter, often folding or accordion-pleating it in screen-like effects that are new to his art. All these features are very much in evidence in, for example, the *Large Blue Guitar* of 1930 now in the St. Louis Art Museum.

The space in *Still Life with Glass* is more restricted and the table appears to be pressed back against the wainscoted wall behind it. In this respect it relates to many of the "cabinet" pictures (small easel paintings) executed between 1918 and 1929, a period when, in keeping with one of the major currents in advanced French art, Braque's art had become once again more naturalistic and accessible. The palette employed in *Still Life with Glass,* which is limited to blacks, greys, creamy off-whites and warm rich earth colors (siennas, ochers and umbers), is even more reminiscent of Braque's pre-war Cubism; one senses that in this picture he is reappraising some of its implications.

In 1912–13 Braque evolved a new "synthetic" Cubist manner, largely as a result of his experiments with *papier collé.* Rather than beginning with a specific subject and analyzing and abstracting it in the light of a Cubist multi-viewpoint perspective, Braque worked from abstraction towards representation, laying in a spatial complex of interacting planes onto which a subject was superimposed, or out of which it emerged. With these new working methods the identities of individual objects in Braque's paintings and their relationship to each other became increasingly conditioned by the way each separate painting evolved; a configuration of shapes or planes could suggest a fruit bowl or a carafe or bottle. Occasionally the identity of an object is not easy to discern or is ambiguous, so that at times objects seem to be themselves and yet simultaneously not themselves. In these respects certain canvases of 1913–14 look forward to the profoundly questioning and philosophical works of Braque's later years.

In *Still Life with Glass* the reflective, metaphysical properties hinted at in certain synthetic Cubist works come once more to the fore. The glass and the pipe are immediately recognizable, and the pipe, the smallest of the still life components, is the more insistent; hard and brittle, it seems to invite the spectator to pick it up. The compotier or fruit bowl which dominates the left hand side of the composition is harder to assimilate visually and has become almost pulpy and evanescent (although the grapes it contains are enclosed in shapes that are angular and cube-like); one senses that the compotier might at some point have been metamorphosed into something else, a mandolin for example. The severe, almost geometric pictorial architecture provided by the wall skirting, the drawer and the legs of the table is played off against the curvilinear, wavy patterns of the tablecloth which deliberately destabilize the still life and put it, as it were, out to sea. The pattern acts, moreover, not simply as a decorative device, but seems to read also like a hermetic pictorial script, like the hieroglyphs of some new language that is in the course of invention. The letters JO suggest the presence of a newspaper (*Le Jour*), and O becomes a "rhyming" shape for the circular handle of the drawer below, a device of which Braque was to make increasing use.

In all these respects *Still Life with Glass* is a forerunner of the great, sumptuous and richly patterned still lifes of the mid-1930s which mark one of the summits of Braque's career. These paintings often derive their titles from the colors of the tablecloths on which the still lifes are placed (*Red Tablecloth* and *Blue Tablecloth,* both of 1938 and both in private collections in New York, are examples). The sensuous, decorative appeal of these canvases can perhaps only be rivalled in twentieth-century French painting by certain works of Bonnard and Matisse. And yet it is in these works (which reach a climax in, for example, *Still Life with Mandoline* of 1935, in the Norton Gallery of Art, West Palm Beach, Florida) that the metamorphic, metaphysical properties implicit in *Still Life with Glass* achieve for the first time full expression. Hard, unyielding forms become soft and pliable; napkins and tablecloths assume a sculptural, almost mineral existence. Some objects cast no shadows, while others project shadows more palpable than themselves. Sometimes what Braque himself called "rhyming" forms, divorced from objects, are more insistent than the objects themselves. Shafts of light are crystallized into immobility while the objects around them throb insistently.

Still Life with Glass was almost certainly painted in Paris in one of the two top-floor studios in the house built for Braque by the architect Auguste Péret at 6 rue du Douanier, now rue Georges Braque.

John Golding

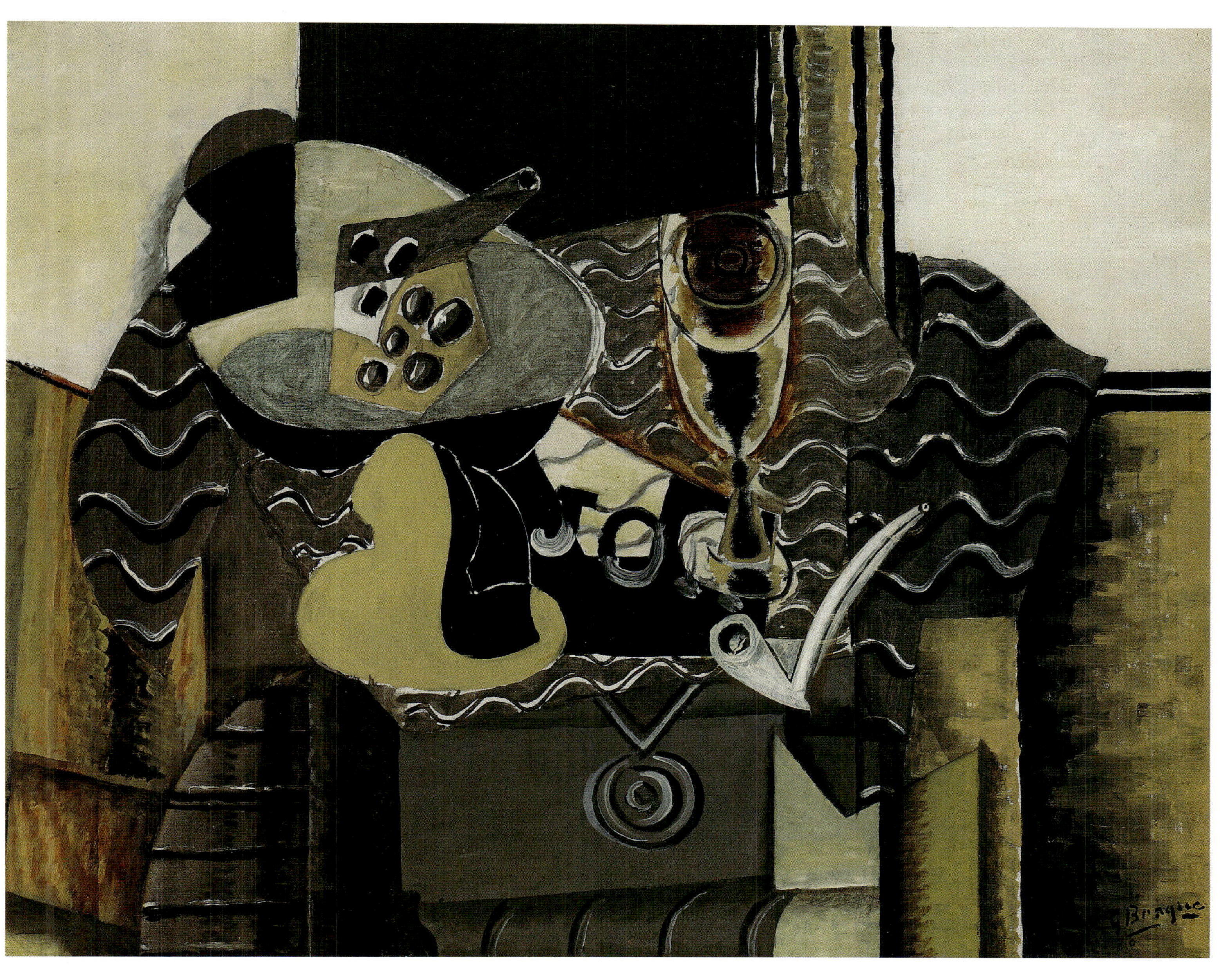

33. Georges Braque (France, 1882–1963)
Still Life with Oysters, 1937

Oil on canvas, 20 x 25½"
University purchase, Kende Sale Fund, 1946

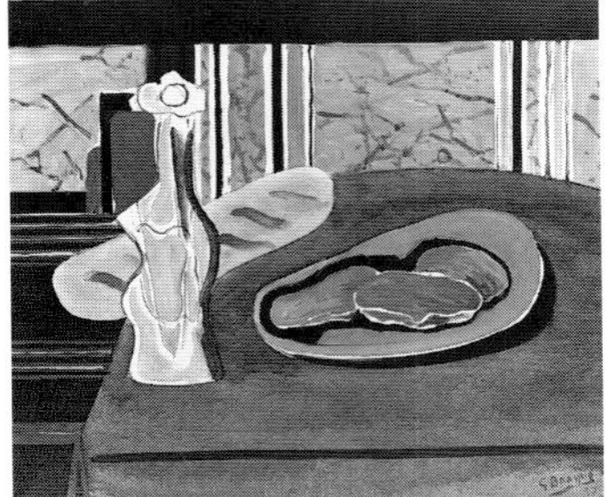

Georges Braque
Still Life with Oysters, 1937
Oil on canvas, 21¼ x 25⅝"
Kunsthalle, Hamburg

Braque's major achievements in the 1930s lay in his large, commanding and often elaborately colored canvases which simultaneously embodied his increasingly metaphysical approach to the painting of still life, and, at the end of the decade, introduced the first of his monumental studio interiors. Throughout his career, however, Braque continued to pour out a steady succession of smaller, more intimate canvases, domestic in scale and feeling. *Still Life with Oysters* is one of a group of paintings that in their restraint and simplicity complement the contemporary, more ambitious and celebrated canvases.

Still Life with Oysters is a conflation of two other works of 1937, and the three pictures were clearly painted within a very short space of time, possibly during the course of a few consecutive days. Both related works are reproduced in the Braque catalogue raisonné, published by Maeght in Paris in 1962 but still in process of revision.[1] It has not been possible to trace the whereabouts of the smallest of these pictures, *Oysters, Lemon and Serviette*; *Bread, Oysters and Carafe,* which is of similar dimensions to *Still Life with Oysters* but of a squarer format, is now in the collection of the Kunsthalle, Hamburg.

The light key and blond tonalities of these paintings and other related works remind one of Braque's lifelong admiration for the work of Chardin and of certain small still lifes by Manet (who also painted oysters); the paintings are also in certain respects reminiscent of a persistent strain of silvery high-key seventeenth-century Dutch still lifes, exemplified by such artists as Willem Kalf, Juniaen van Streek and A. S. Coorte. However, although Braque admired much Dutch art, more than any other of the great French painters of his generation he remained firmly within a national context and seldom sought inspiration from abroad or from afar. Cézanne was a constant mentor and his presence can be felt, at a distance, in *Still Life with Oysters.*

In their accessibility these small, light paintings of the latter part of the 1930s are the counterparts of the "black" cabinet paintings of the 1920s; the pronounced horizontal format of *Still Life with Oysters* was one that Braque favored between 1920 and 1928. The element of naturalism which had characterized much of the work of the 1920s (and which perhaps helps to explain the great popularity of these works) is here even more marked: the bread, serviette, lemon and oysters are economically but almost realistically rendered; only the carafe or pitcher retains traces of Braque's more convoluted, curvilinear manner and conveys, although to a lesser degree, some of the "metamorphic confusion" (the term is Braque's own) of the compotier in *Still Life with Glass.* The woodgraining and the patterned cloth in the earlier work have been rendered in a bold, almost cursory manner. Here the false marbling of the wallpaper behind the table is rendered with sensitivity and skill and reminds us that Braque, like his father and grandfather, had been trained as a house painter.[2] The presence of oysters would suggest that the picture was painted in the house Braque had had built for him in 1931 at Varengeville on the Normandy coast.

The smaller comparable still lifes painted during the Second World War, during which Braque was in Paris, are, like their larger counterparts, even more restrained in manner, and many of them reflect a mood of anxiety and sometimes even a feeling of deprivation. Subsequently, and as Braque's preoccupations increasingly centered on the studio there (the eight late *Ateliers* were painted between 1949 and 1956), the smaller still lifes take on a more relaxed, occasionally even casual appearance. In *Still Life with Oysters,* on the other hand, the effect is one of elegant, restrained simplicity.

John Golding

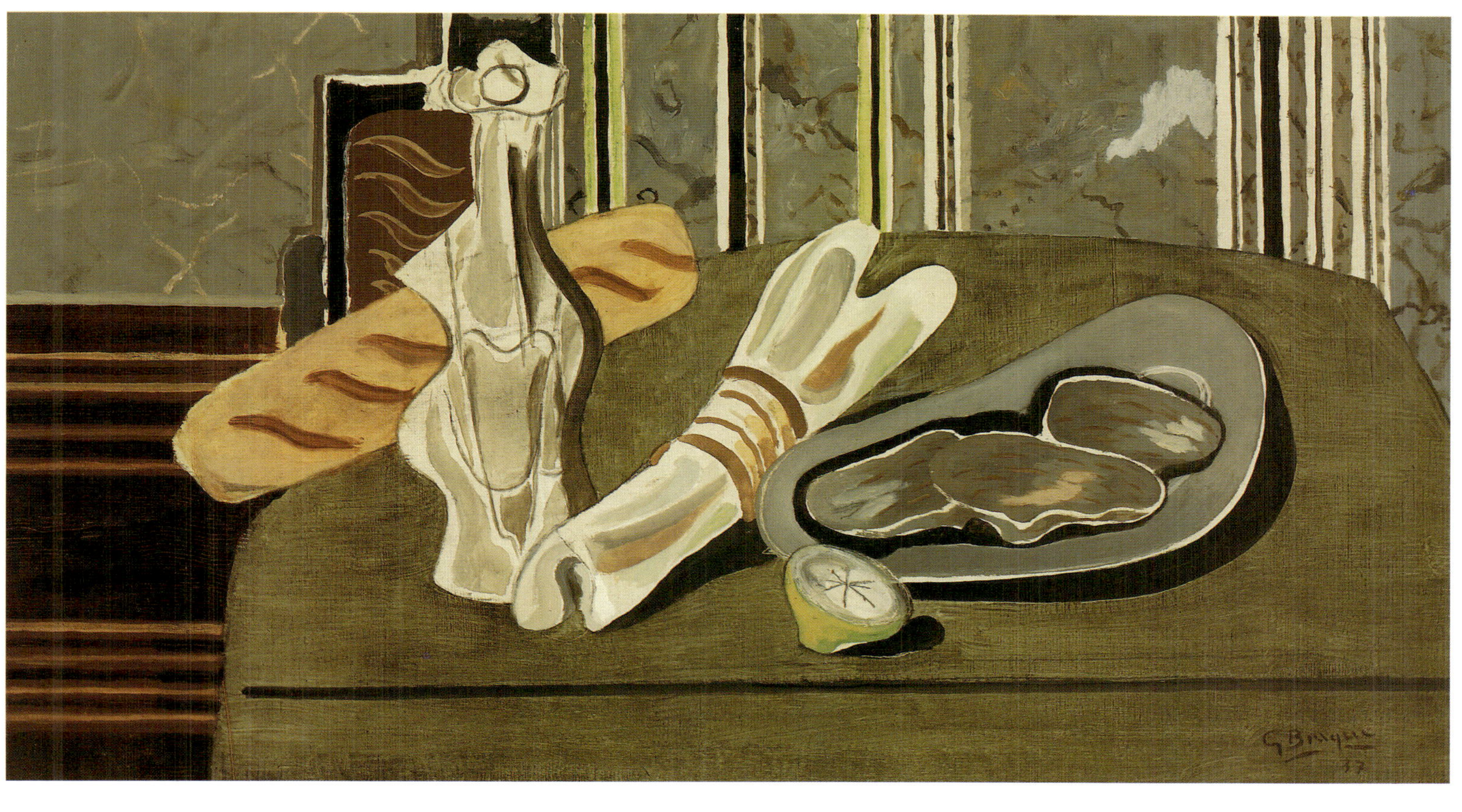

34. Juan Gris (Spain, 1887–1927)
Still Life with Playing Cards (Draughts Board and Playing Cards), 1916

Oil on canvas, 28¾ x 23⅝"
University purchase, Kende Sale Fund, 1946

Each still life by Juan Gris is a tour-de-force in which objects on a tipped tabletop are depicted as a mass of flat, colored planes that closely overlap or are adjacent. From the mid-teens, he began such compositions with an "architecture,"[1] by which he meant an arrangement of arbitrarily determined color planes, after which references to objects would be introduced. In *Still Life with Playing Cards* the architecture is indicated by the arrangement of black rectangles signifying shadow sections, which were then amplified with the glass, checkerboard and playing cards. Notwithstanding his consistent pictorial approach, Gris' work fluctuated in the period of 1915 through 1917 between moody, shallow, black and brown interiors and airy, high-key still lifes before open windows. Even within 1916 alone, the fluctuation can be observed. Early in the year, he made a series of sunny, pointillist paintings, but, as if influenced by the changing fortunes of contemporary life, these were succeeded by the series to which *Still Life with Playing Cards* belongs. This painting is signed and dated August 1916, a time when Gris' letters were filled with news of injuries sustained by friends in the war.[2]

Although distinct in mood, the two strains of work in 1916 show a singular concern for light, a concern that had barely existed earlier among Gris' fellow Cubist painters. At times Gris added to the normally hermetic interiors of Cubism a natural bright light. On other occasions, his apparently nighttime interiors, though still self-contained, have evidence of an obscure light source within. In effect, that illumination resulted in the white areas of a painting, each of which should be read as a kind of objectified light, an area of light made tangible and plastic within the whole composition.

Nearly all light in *Still Life with Playing Cards* is focused on the playing cards at the lower center of the painting, making that area the principal focus of the composition. A second shaft of light plays on the top and side of the checker box, giving it a strikingly plastic identity within the arrangement of flat surfaces. At the top, the box is not just flat but transparent. Indeed, the identity and location of surfaces is in question: if the grid is the top of the box, is a separate checkerboard laid over it? *Still Life with Playing Cards* is a medley of objects, each of which is partly solid and partly transparent, partly seen in shadow and partly in light. Adding to this hallucinatory air are the misleading displacements of objects, as with the playing cards and mouth(s) of the glass.

Gris' choice of objects, as was so typical among the Cubist painters, depicted leisure pursuits in a cafe, where drinks were consumed and games of chance were engaged in. During the teens, Gris often painted cards and checkerboards; here he related the two by the light emphasis, and the parallel fanning and overlapping of the aspects. The checkerboard pattern was usually a visual pun for Gris, who utilized it variously as a tablecloth, floor covering, and harlequin costume, in addition to a board game. The playing cards involve a more complex and personal analogy. First, as the signifier for the sense of sight, playing cards are similar to painting which also engages that sense organ.[3] Second, for Cubists and card sharks alike, sleights-of-hand are an expected trait. Hence, the ambiguous disposition of the cards in Gris' painting is likened to the Cubistic rendering of the glass and checkerboard: all equally challenge, if not bewilder, the observer's eyes.

Mark Rosenthal

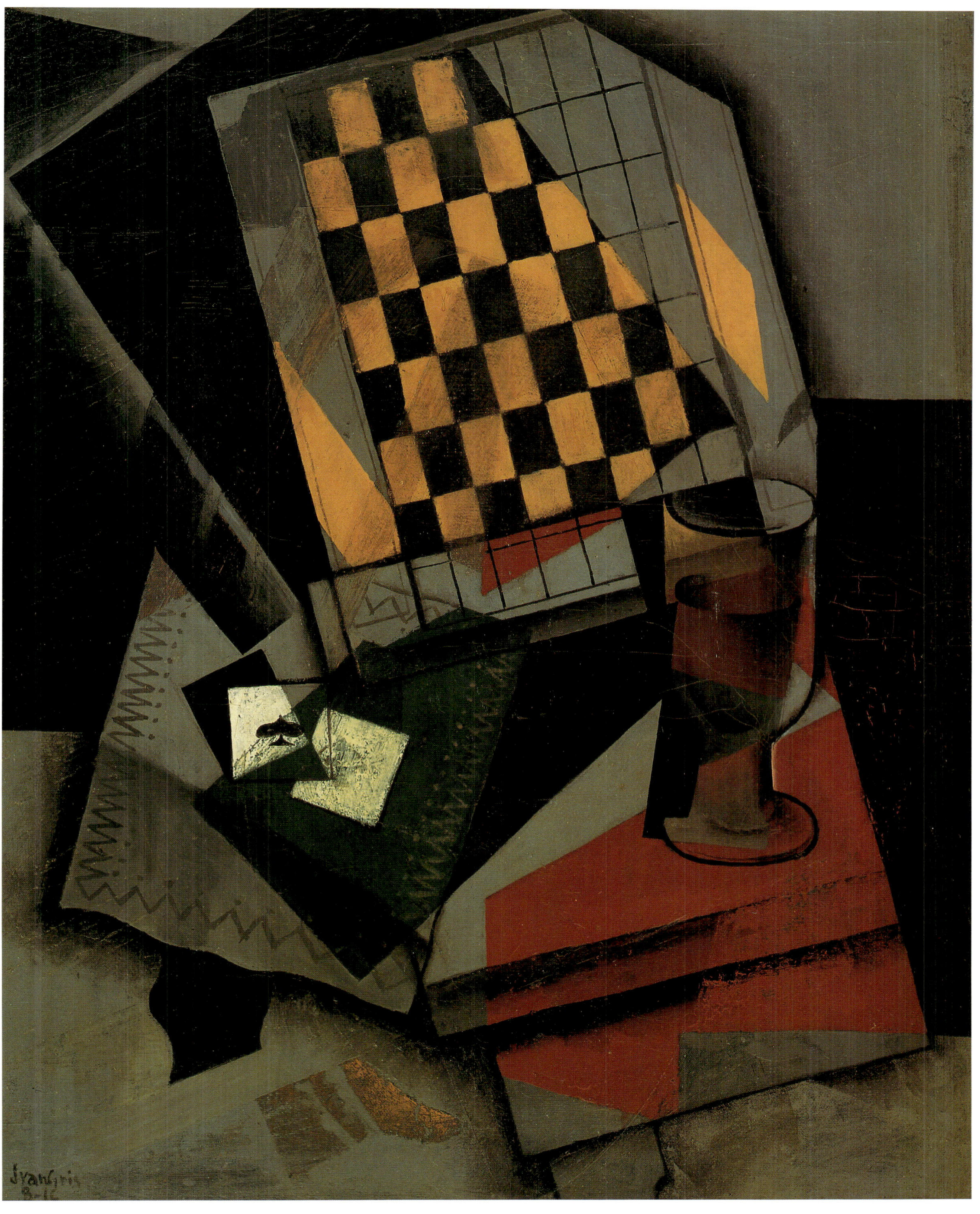
Juan Gris
8-16

35. Juan Gris (Spain, 1887–1927)

Still Life: Table with Red Cloth, 1926

Oil on canvas, 36¼ x 23⅝"
Gift of Mr. Charles H. Yalem, 1963

In November of 1926, the probable date when *Still Life: Table with Red Cloth* was painted,[1] Gris had just moved to Hyères. This move was one of a number he made in his last years (1920–27) as he sought more healthful climactic conditions. Near the end of his life he was only able to paint sporadically, and then with considerable physical pain. 1926 was especially difficult, and Gris was often reduced to the life of an "invalid," rarely leaving his room. He further described his lifestyle at this time as "sober,"[2] a characterization that is apt for *Still Life: Table with Red Cloth.*

The subject of a still life before an open window had played a major role in Gris' repertoire since 1915, probably inspired in part by Henri Matisse. For Gris the subject seemed to have had a specifically personal and poetic significance to do with the manner in which an artist relates his activities (the still life) to nature (what is seen through the window). Art and nature, of course, each possess distinct characteristics. Nature is lush, sensuous, and seemingly boundless, while the artist's sphere—that is, a Cubist's—is hermetic, interior, and perhaps overly intellectual. As Gris continued to explore this theme in the early 1920s he was not only interested in these distinctions, but also in the overlaps. A specific, iconographic aspect became the hallmark of Gris' renderings: a guitar was usually placed in front of the window. In this context the guitar symbolized the attribute and perhaps even the soul of a (musical) artist.[3] Variations included depictions of a woman with a guitar before a window (recalling his earlier interpretation of Corot's *Woman with Mandolin*) and sad-eyed, melancholic pierrots and harlequins, all surrogate artists. Late in Gris' life, the natural world seen through the window was observed as if from the opening of a cell or hospital room, and usually curtains were parted to show simple planes of blue.

At first Gris may have had in mind a kind of peaked window for *Still Life: Table with Red Cloth,* as that shape is still evident in the paint layer of the canvas. But the device of the parted curtain in others of his contemporaneous paintings must have inspired the invention of the architectural fenestration that encloses the objects in *Still Life: Table with Red Cloth.* This profile imparts an eloquent monumentality to the composition, reinforcing the archetypal character of the theme for Gris. The severity of the depiction allows nature a merely schematic existence within the whole, its sensuosity reduced to a colored emblem. The exaggerated play of darks and lights is equally diagrammatic and mirrors the distinction between the sensuous, clear world of nature and the shadowy interior. The tools of the artist do, however, conjoin the two spheres, as if Gris meant to suggest that art might somehow partake of the eternality of nature, in contrast to the transitory character of the fruit and wine.

Coincident with Gris' illness, the period of the 1920s was particularly difficult for Cubism, which was under attack from many quarters. Surrealist manifestations were taking center stage in the Parisian art world, and Cubism seemed to be in a state of demise. The influence of Cubism on Surrealism was not yet recognized. Only later would it become evident that the marvelous fold of red drapery in *Still Life: Table with Red Cloth* predicts the bent clock in Salvador Dali's *Persistence of Memory* (1931, The Museum of Modern Art, New York) and that Gris' appreciation for the literary associations of objects, and his careful juxtaposition of these for their poetic effect, also foreshadowed Surrealist practice. Indeed, in 1916, in a collaboration with the Chilean poet Vincent Huidobro, Gris wrote: "on ouvre la tête/comme une fenettre (sic)" (one opens the mind/like a window).[4]

Mark Rosenthal

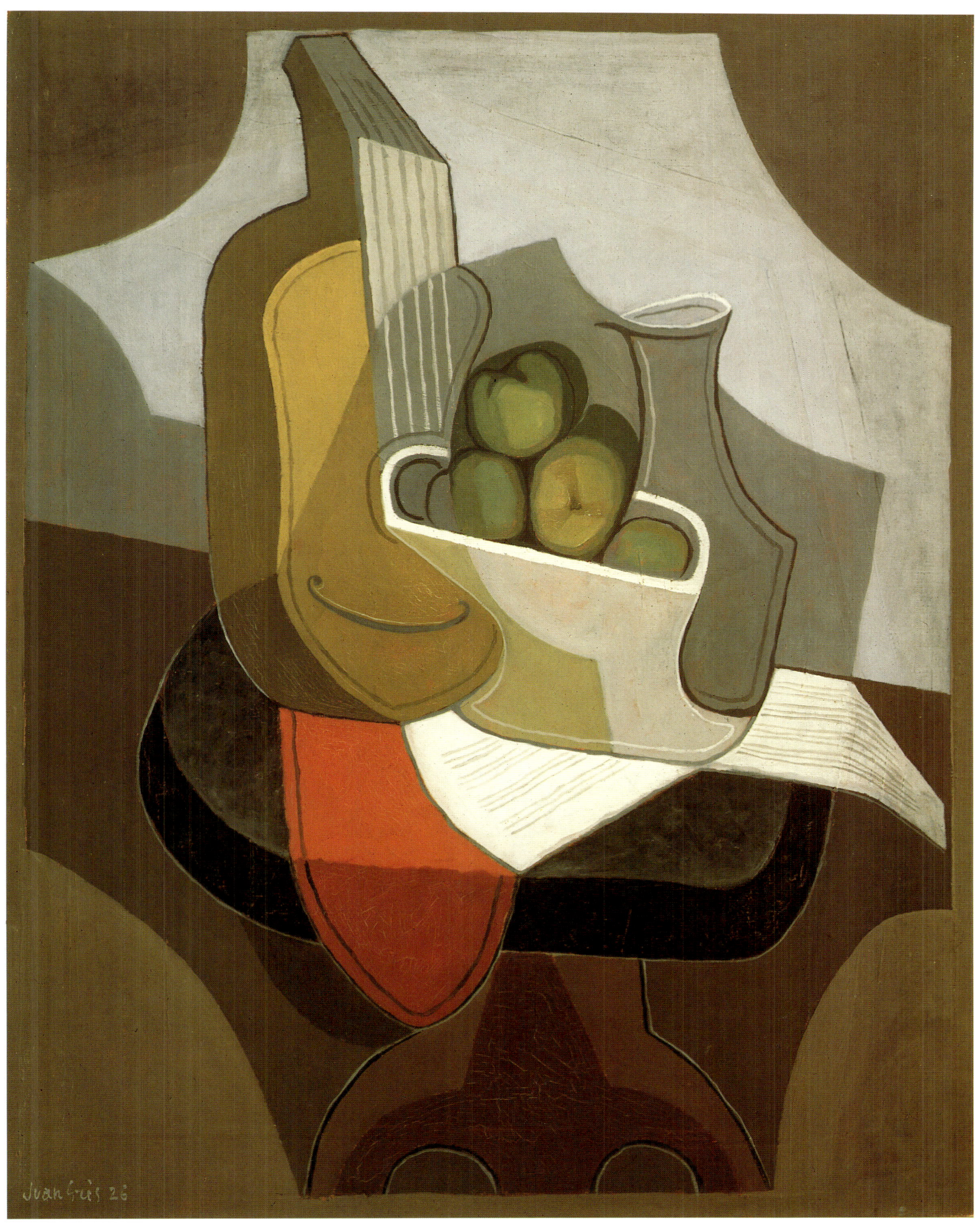
Juan Gris 26

36. Raymond Duchamp-Villon (France, 1876–1918)

Le Cheval (The Horse), 1914, cast 1954–56

Bronze, 17¼ x 18 x 11¾"
Gift of Mr. and Mrs. Richard K. Weil, 1977

Le Cheval is recognized as the most important work of French sculptor Raymond Duchamp-Villon. By equating animal and machine, he created an enduring icon of the Machine Age.

Pierre-Maurice Raymond Duchamp was born in 1876 in Damville near Rouen. He was the second of six children in a talented family that included older brother Jacques Villon (né Gaston Duchamp) and younger brother Marcel Duchamp. When he abandoned a medical career to become an artist, Raymond, like his older brother, adopted a professional pseudonym, Duchamp-Villon. In 1907, he established a studio in the suburb of Puteaux, where members of the pre-war French vanguard congregated. In August 1914, he enlisted as a medical officer and served at the front during World War I. He contracted typhoid fever in 1916, and died in October 1918 after a prolonged illness.

In his brief career, Duchamp-Villon surpassed the limits of academic sculpture and Rodinesque naturalism. In his mature work (from the years 1910 to 1914) he abandoned expressive modelling, emphasizing instead simplified, sculptural mass. He developed a distinctive style of modern sculpture marked by planar forms and an almost classical simplicity. Duchamp-Villon advocated the synthesis of sculpture and modern technology. In 1913, he wrote in a letter to a friend: "The power of the machine imposes itself upon us, and we can scarcely conceive of living beings without it. . . ."[1]

Le Cheval embodied Duchamp-Villon's ideal of machine imagery and marked the culmination of his efforts at radical abstraction. The sculpture evolved over a two-year period from 1912 to 1914. Duchamp-Villon created numerous drawings and clay studies of a horse and rider before he focussed on the figure of the horse alone. In his initial choice of subject matter, he may have been inspired by his observation of polo matches.[2] In several ink drawings (now in the artist's estate), Duchamp-Villon simplified elements of equine anatomy into mechanical parts resembling gears and fly-wheels. During the late nineteenth century, researchers—notably E. J. Marey and the photographer Eadweard Muybridge—had proposed analogies between animal locomotion and mechanical movement. Duchamp-Villon may have been aware of such theories.[3] In any case, the original idea for *Le Cheval* may be traced to a sketch of an equestrian monument within Duchamp-Villon's preliminary drawing for the now lost model of the *Cubist House* (c. 1912, estate of the artist).[4] In a group of small plaster and clay studies, Duchamp-Villon developed the dynamic, pyramidal form of the sculpture, while he began to transform the horse's body into mechanical elements. In the final sculpture, Duchamp-Villon balanced the graceful arc of the horse's head and mane with the thrusting lines of its mechanized body. The resulting tension between organic and geometric forms endowed *Le Cheval* with its compelling power.

In 1914, when he joined the French army, Duchamp-Villon left behind in his studio one seventeen-inch-high plaster cast of *Le Cheval* and an armature for its enlargement to one meter. After his death, his family and friends sought to preserve the fragile sculpture by arranging for a series of bronze editions. In 1921, New York attorney and art collector John Quinn acquired the original plaster cast of *Le Cheval* (now lost) from the sculptor's widow and commissioned Roman Bronze Works to cast the first bronze of the sculpture (now in a private collection). In 1930, Jacques Villon supervised an enlargement of *Le Cheval* to the height of one meter, and in 1966, Marcel Duchamp authorized another edition enlarged to the scale of one and a half meters. The cast in the Washington University collection is number five in an edition of eight produced between 1954 and the early 1960s by Louis Carré of Paris. Unlike the 1930 and 1966 enlarged editions, this posthumous cast preserves the scale of Duchamp-Villon's original plaster sculpture.

Although *Le Cheval* was never exhibited or cast in permanent media during his lifetime, Duchamp-Villon's reputation as a vanguard sculptor rests on his daring achievement in this one work. On a visit to the sculptor's Puteaux studio shortly before the outbreak of World War I, the French painter Henri Matisse viewed *Le Cheval* and proclaimed Duchamp-Villon's metaphoric fusion of animal and machine "a projectile."[5] Many years later, Marcel Duchamp called his brother's last major work "a classic piece of Cubist sculpture."[6]

Judith Zilczer

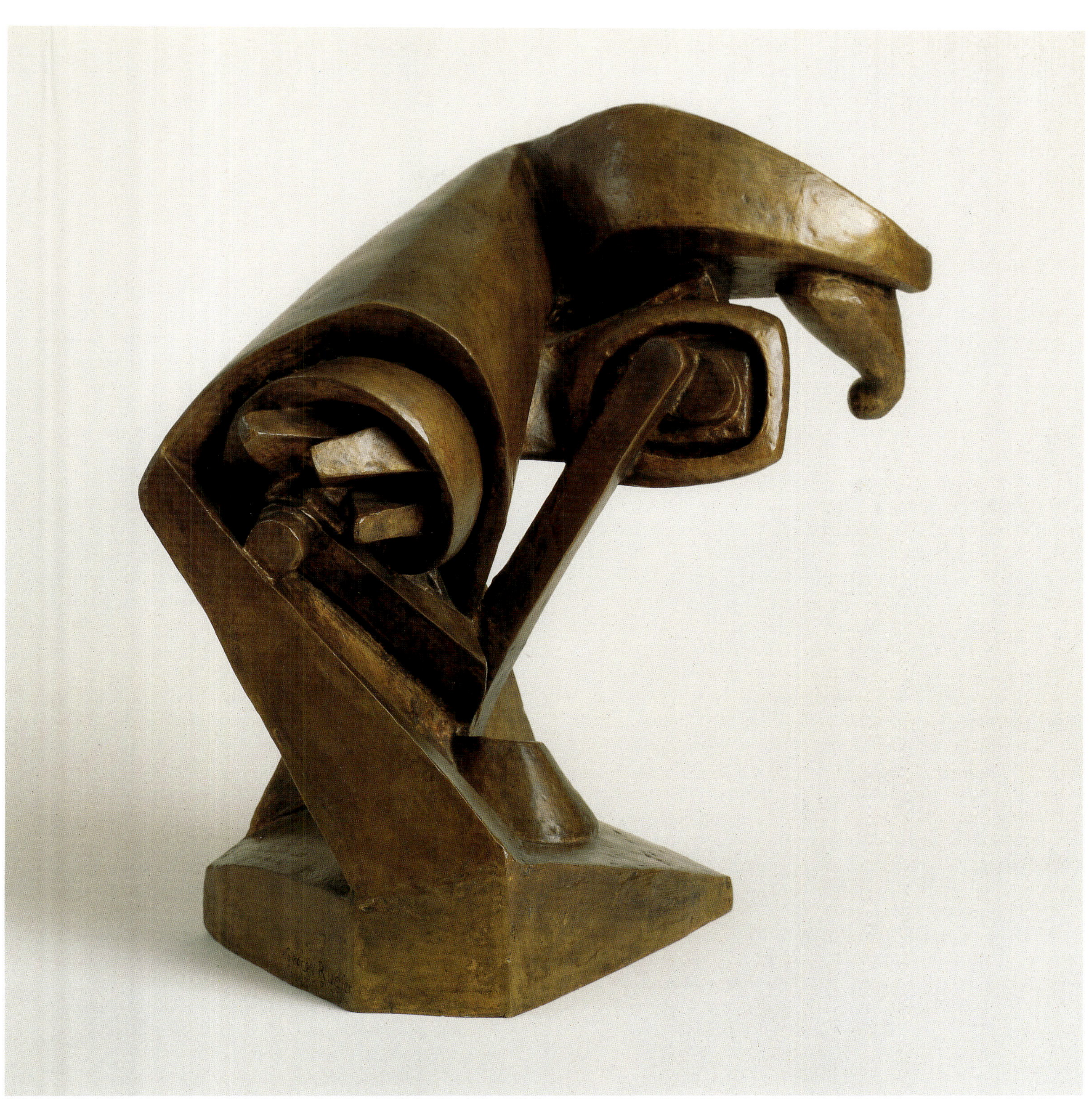

37. Jacques Lipchitz
(United States, b. Lithuania, 1891–1973)
Pierrot with Clarinet, 1919

Bronze, 7/7, 29½ x 10 x 11¾"
Gift of Mr. and Mrs. Richard K. Weil, 1978

Lipchitz's reputation as one of the masters of modern sculpture has for many years been based almost exclusively on his great Cubist carvings and bronzes of 1915–25. Since 1916, when his works joined those of Picasso, Braque, Léger, Gris and Laurens at the Galerie de l'Effort Moderne in Paris, the originality and importance of his contribution to the evolution of early Cubist sculpture in France has been fully recognized.[1] *Pierrot with Clarinet* belongs to this seminal Cubist phase.

Chaim Jacob (Jacques) Lipchitz, born on 22 August 1891 in Druskieniki, Lithuania, was the son of a successful building contractor who wanted his son to qualify as an architect or engineer and join the family business. He had little sympathy for his son's ambition to become a sculptor. During high school, Lipchitz became determined to study art in Paris, arriving in the French capital in October 1909, at the age of eighteen.

Lipchitz's formative training was purely academic, but by 1912 he became aware of the work of a number of avant-garde artists working in Paris. That year, *La Section d'Or,* the most important Cubist exhibition to date, was held in Paris and included sculptures by Duchamp-Villon and Archipenko. The sculpture of the Italian Futurist Umberto Boccioni was also first shown in Paris in 1912, providing Lipchitz with a convincing example of how two-dimensional, pictorial Cubist concepts could successfully translate into three dimensions.

By 1913–14 Lipchitz was working on the fringes of the Parisian avant-garde. He had moved to a studio at 54 rue Montparnasse next door to Brancusi. Lipchitz also developed a close friendship with Mexican painter Diego Rivera, who introduced him to Picasso, probably in the spring of 1914. Picasso, the "father" of Cubist sculpture, saw the sculptural implications of his Analytic Cubist paintings three or four years before Archipenko, Boccioni and Lipchitz created their first proto-Cubist sculptures. On Lipchitz's visits to Picasso's studio he certainly saw the sheet metal and wire *Guitar* (1912, The Museum of Modern Art, New York), the first constructed sculpture to make the revolutionary break with the time-honored techniques of modelling and carving. Seeing this work, Lipchitz realized that the creation of sculpture had changed forever.

Cubist sculpture was from the outset inexorably linked to its two-dimensional counterpart. No other period and style of sculpture in the history of European art had been so completely dependent on the iconographic and formal characteristics of its pictorial equivalent. Within an amazingly short time Lipchitz was, by 1914, grappling with the challenge that confronted all Cubist sculptors: how to adapt and translate the elusive, spatial ambiguities of pictorial Cubism into a convincing yet independent three-dimensional language.

The development of Lipchitz's Cubist sculpture followed the evolution of Cubist painting—that is, progressing from an analytic to a synthetic approach, from simplifying and geometricizing a realistic figure, to building it up from abstract forms. *Sailor with Guitar* (1914, Musée National d'Art Moderne, Paris) marked a radical departure in Lipchitz's working method, which he described as "the final step towards Cubism."[2] In 1915 Lipchitz created his first constructed sculptures, the "detachable figures," as he called them, that reflect his short-lived interest in the machine aesthetic. Following the detachable sculptures, Lipchitz embarked in the latter part of 1915 on a group of works in which abstract, sculptural forms dominate, with only the most tenuous links to the human figure. Abstract architectural forms became metaphors for the human figure, as in *Standing Personage* (1916, Solomon R. Guggenheim Museum, New York), which Lipchitz compared to "a cluster of skyscraper towers, something like those in Rockefeller Center, New York."[3]

During 1916 and 1917 Lipchitz made a series of bathers and seated figures which reflect his attempt to find a balance between abstract and figurative elements in his work. By 1919, in the charming series of Harlequins and Pierrots, the balance had swung in favor of readily legible, figurative sculptures. Washington University's *Pierrot with Clarinet* is rich in associations past and present. It reflects Lipchitz's interest in musical instruments, an interest shared by other Cubists, and also reveals Lipchitz's admiration for eighteenth-century painting, particularly the work of Watteau. As he wrote: "The Pierrots and harlequins were part of our general vocabulary, characters taken from the *commedia dell'arte,* particularly popular in the eighteenth century."[4]

Stylistically, *Pierrot with Clarinet* is closely related to the paintings of Spanish Cubist Juan Gris, whom Lipchitz met in 1916. They soon became good friends and during the next six years enjoyed a close working relationship. Lipchitz helped Gris execute his first sculpture, *Harlequin* (1917, Philadelphia Museum of Art). Harlequins and Pierrots dominated Gris's figurative work between 1918 and 1922, and Lipchitz's sculpture in 1919. *Pierrot with Clarinet* relates to several of Gris's paintings, such as *Seated Peasant Woman* (1918, private collection) and *Pierrot* (1919, Kunstmuseum, Winterthur). In Lipchitz's bronze certain features, such as the curved form behind the small, circular face, the dominantly flat planes of the arms and legs, and the crisp, angular contours of the body, are remarkably close to Gris' figurative paintings of 1918 and 1919, suggesting that *Pierrot with Clarinet* was, in part, a three-dimensional response and homage to them.

In his Pierrots and Harlequins, Lipchitz's art connects on the one hand with the French tradition represented by Watteau and Cézanne, and on the other with current interpretations, found in the work of his Cubist colleagues Picasso and Gris. Within a few years, the classical flavor of Lipchitz's work and the rigid syntax of Cubism would be replaced by a more lyrical, expressionist style, more suited to expressing the joys and sorrows of his personal life, but also his reactions to political events, to war, and to the past and present history of the Jewish people.

Alan G. Wilkinson

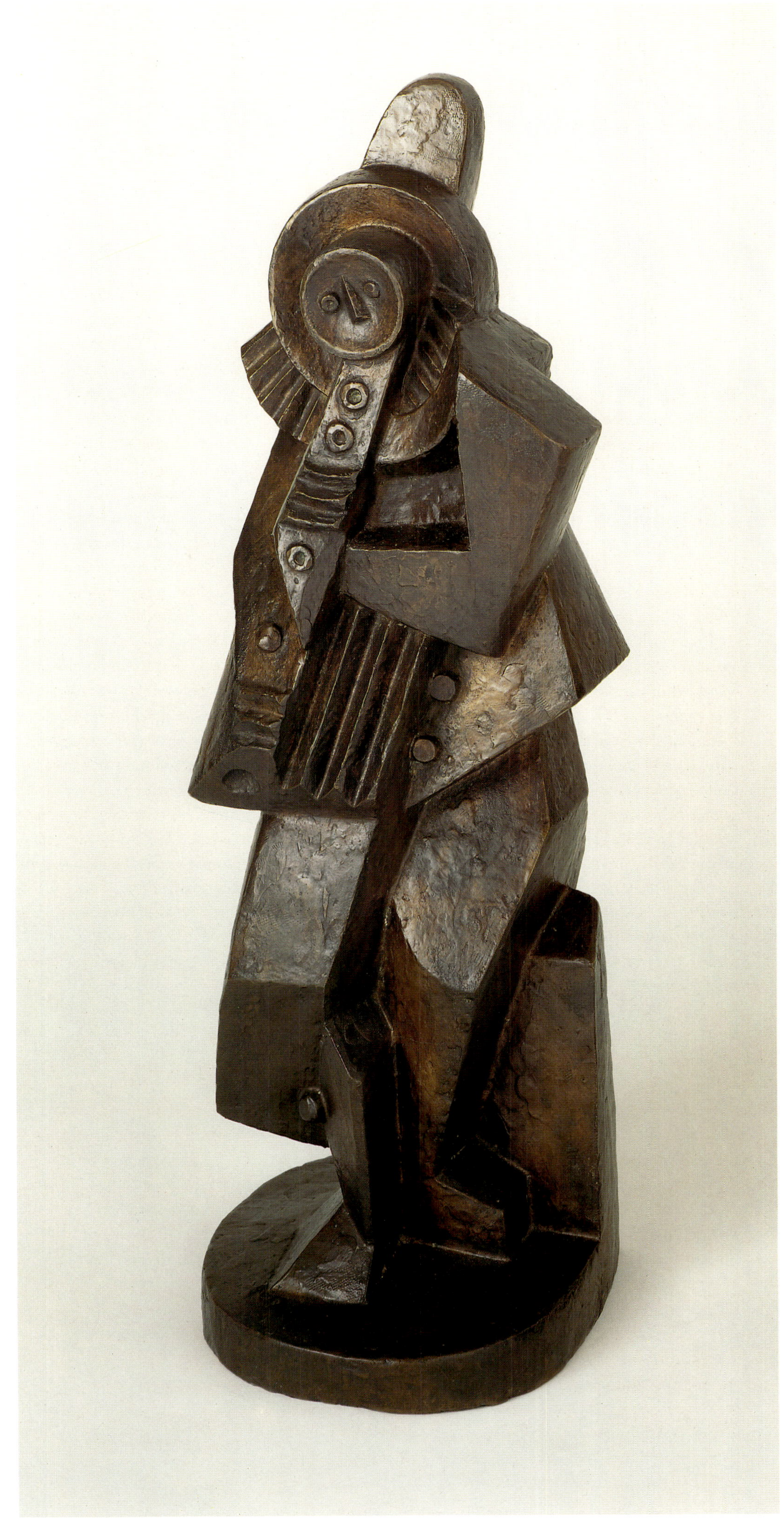

38. Jacques Lipchitz (United States, b. Lithuania, 1891–1973) *Mother and Child*, 1949

Bronze, 48 x 32⅛ x 30⅜"
Gift of Mr. and Mrs. Richard K. Weil, 1964

The mother and child theme haunted Lipchitz throughout his life. Among his earliest sculptures are the pre-Cubist 1913 *Mother and Child* (private collection) and the 1914–15 *Mother and Children* (private collection), which reflect diverse influences, from Russian Byzantine icons to African sculpture and the work of his contemporaries Modigliani and Brancusi. From the outset, Lipchitz's representations of the mother and child motif are closely related to the joys and sorrows of his personal life. The 1914–15 *Mother and Children* derived, he wrote, simply "from my feeling for my own mother. . . . " The small *Mother and Child* maquette of 1930 (private collection) is one of the most anguished representations of the mother and child theme in twentieth-century art. It was made, Lipchitz wrote, during "a very difficult time for me, with the death of my father and my sister, and I was questioning many things. 'For what am I born? For what did I come on this earth?'"[1] The 1941–45 *Mother and Child II* (The Museum of Modern Art, New York) was begun soon after Lipchitz arrived in New York. Again, the sculpture was based on Lipchitz's personal experience:

> *In 1935 while visiting a sister in Russia, we had come out of a theatre late at night in the rain, and hearing the voice of a woman singing in a loud, hoarse voice, traced it through the darkness until suddenly she appeared under a street lamp, a legless cripple in a little cart, with both arms raised. . . .*[2]

Washington University's 1949 *Mother and Child* was also rooted in a specific event in Lipchitz's life, in this case, his joy at the birth of his daughter Lolya in 1948.

> *It was a fantastic experience at the age of fifty-nine [sic] finally to have my own child, particularly a daughter, which is what I wanted, partially because I wanted her to have my mother's name. The result in my sculpture was a series of extremely lyrical works on the theme of the mother and child. These have the curvilinear movement in-the-round of the dancers of the 1940s, but the mood is now much more tender and obviously maternal.*[3]

Hagar I of 1948 (Art Gallery of Ontario, Toronto) anticipates Washington University's sculpture both in style and subject matter. *Hagar I* embodies two concepts that preoccupied Lipchitz at the time the work was created: his feelings as a father (or father-to-be) for the mother and child theme, and his deep concerns about the birth of Israel and the conflict between Jews and Arabs. Lipchitz identified with a story from the Old Testament and used it to symbolize contemporary events. On a purely formal level, *Hagar I* is a tender representation of the mother and child theme, showing Ishmael lying face down against his mother's body. Stylistically, *Hagar I,* with the massive, curved forms of the limbs and drapery, is the first in the series of powerful "baroque" sculptures of the late 1940s, culminating in the 1949 *Mother and Child.*

Probably the first sculpture to celebrate the birth of Lolya was the 1948–49 *Mother and Child* (private collection). The almost unbearable pain and anguish of several of Lipchitz's earlier depictions of this theme, such as *Mother and Child II* (1941–45), have been replaced by an image of maternal love and protection, as the seated mother envelops the child, cradled in her arms.

The original study for Washington University's *Mother and Child* is the 19" high *Mother and Child I* (1949) of which there is a plaster in the Tate Gallery, London. Here the basic composition has been established, with the right hand touching the head, while the curved left arm cradles the child. The surface of the figure is relatively smooth, with the exception of incised lines on the drapery below the left arm. In Washington University's 48" high version, the small child nursing at the mother's breast is totally integrated with and almost indistinguishable from the swollen, curvilinear forms and deeply incised folds of the drapery. (In the larger, closely related 57" high *Mother and Child* [1949, private collection] the flow of drapery is even more pronounced.) The mother's head reflects the influence of Cubism, with the eyes on different planes, and the lower section of the head hollowed out. The surface of the sculpture is dominated by the massive flow of drapery, like lava erupting from a volcano. This image of maternal love, very "baroque" in feeling, could be seen as a homage to Bernini, a sculptor whom Lipchitz greatly admired.

Alan G. Wilkinson

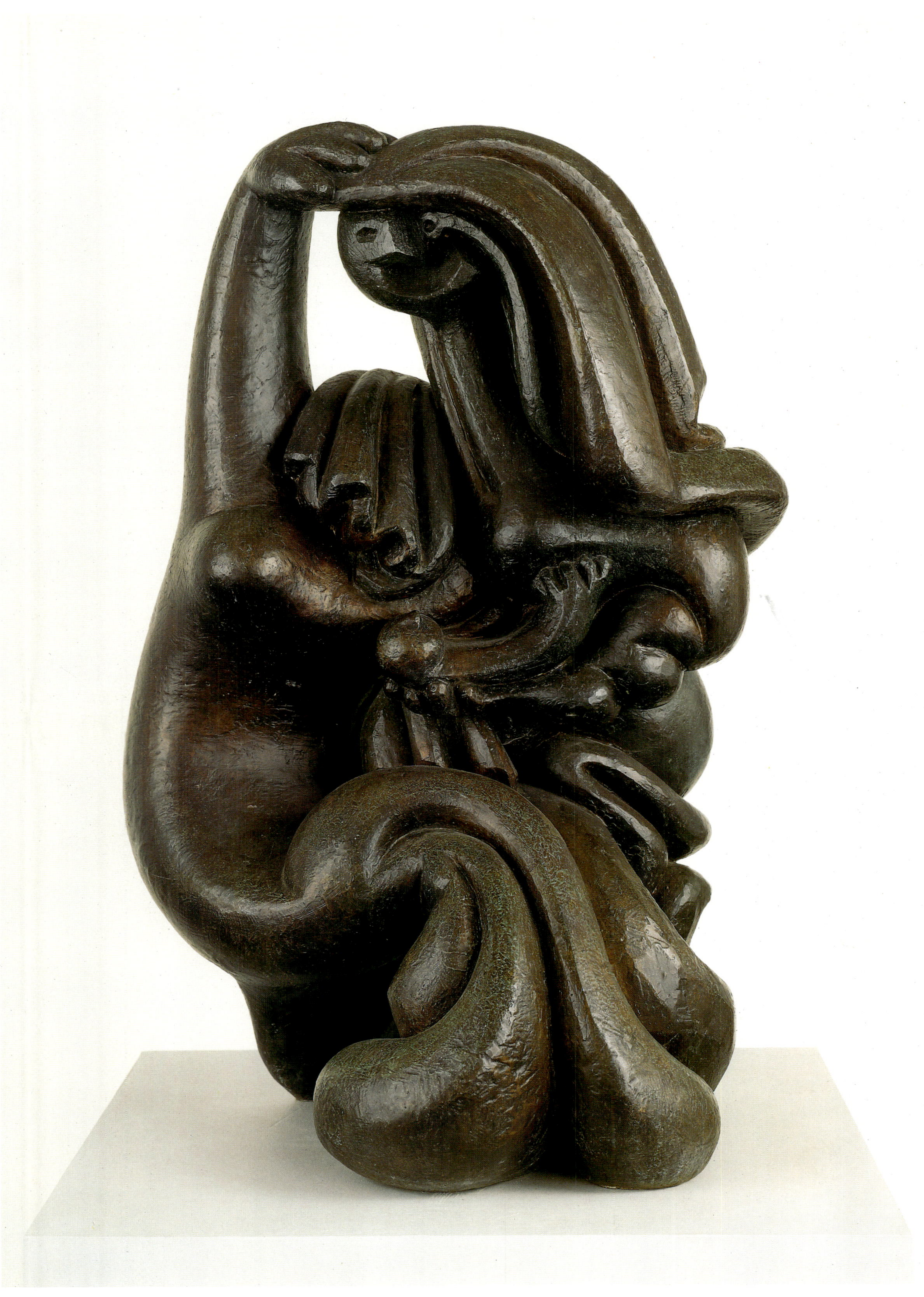

39. James Ensor (Belgium, 1860–1949)

Le Christ Tourmente (Christ Tormented), 1887

Oil on linen, 23¾ x 27⅝"

Bequest of Morton J. May, 1968

Despite the frequent publications devoted to him over his long career and since, James Ensor's varied and enigmatic work still remains both strange and disturbing. Because Ensor does not fit easily into familiar art historical categories it has been difficult for scholarship to consider him as part of some established current in art. Ensor was an individualist and so to a great extent must be appreciated on his own terms and merits. He is frequently adduced as a prime example of one of the prescient forerunners of such movements as Surrealism and Expressionism. Ensor's principal connections with these artistic manifestations are the fertile fantasy of his imagination and the intensely personal feeling with which his most memorable images are imbued.[1]

In a profound way, Ensor's principal subjects are his own temperament and emotional concerns: not surprisingly, he was a prolific and forceful self-portraitist. But the full range of Ensor's emotional concerns extends beyond what was possible (at least for him) in self-portraits. He frequently saw the emotional conflicts, personal involvements, and artistic rivalries with which he was concerned in terms of familiar symbols of spiritual trial; among these, Christological themes prove the most telling and intense.

While Ensor was subject to neither religious delusions nor irrational identifications with Christ or other sacred figures, he seems to have been fascinated by those aspects of Christ's life in which His assumption of the human condition resulted in revilings, humiliations, and rejection. For Ensor medicine, the law, literary and artistic criticism, the military, and the state had all treated him with rejection, misunderstanding, cruelty, and injustice. These issues had begun to fester in Ensor's imagination probably by 1885, when he produced some large drawings which led to his greatest work, the huge *Entry of Christ into Brussels in 1889* (1888, Getty Museum, Malibu, California), and the Christological themes also emerge powerfully in the first mature etchings which Ensor began to produce in 1886.

The climax of Christ's human history is of course the Crucifixion—Christ enduring the fullest measure of what it is to be human—the experience of death. But for Ensor the torments and tortures just previous to Christ's death are also of great significance. In these events even Christ's divinity avails Him naught and His suffering is extreme. It is clear that after some initially favorable critical and commercial success in the first half of the 1880s the shift in artistic taste and fashion which took place between 1885 and 1890 left Ensor feeling injured and frustrated despite his faith in the authenticity of his own artistic nature and vision.

Washington University's painting of *Le Christ Tourmente* should be considered as an important example of Ensor's personal Christological works from his prime early period. While the crucified figure in the painting is not obviously a self-portrait, its appearance among the masks and demonic figures which belong to the artist's idiosyncratically personal imagery establish the significance of the scene as a parallel to the artist's own state of mind. A circumstance which enhances this interpretation is the death of Ensor's father the same year. Ensor felt much closer to his father than to other members of his family and his death profoundly affected the artist: in this connection it should be recalled that Christ's words in the penultimate moments of human life are the agonized cry, "Father, why has Thou forsaken me?"

In the execution of this painting Ensor employs a loose and bold handling of relatively thick paint. The sketchy handling and the intimate scale of both the picture and its imagery suggest a work done privately, out of personal motives and not primarily intended for public consumption. Ensor's painting style here is very much in the grand manner painterly tradition of Rubens and Goya. This is a tradition which Ensor felt to be an indigenous feature of the greatest Northern masters, such as Rubens and Rembrandt, whom he still at this period admired greatly. The brushy vigor of their technique and the freedom and mastery of their effects of light as an emotional vehicle are qualities to which Ensor himself remained devoted. Ensor's color here is an odd mix which produces a scalding luminescence: pearly glows are set off by vivid scarlets and touches of green and blue. The effect is a peculiar blend of the fascinating and the horrific—perfectly suited to Ensor's visionary image which is personal, general, scriptural, and cosmic all at once.

In its quality and intensity *Le Christ Tourmente* is associated with two other visionary masterpieces by Ensor done in 1887: *The Tribulations of St. Anthony* (Museum of Modern Art, New York) and the cataclysmic *Fireworks* (Albright-Knox Gallery, Buffalo). All three paintings seem adumbrations of the mordant explosiveness Ensor was to unleash the next year in his prophetically titled *The Entry of Christ into Brussels in 1889*. This imagining of what would happen if the Messiah returned to (then) present-day Belgium seems to have been at least in part stimulated by Balzac's 1848 tale, *Jesus-Christ en Flandre,* included in his *Côntes Drôlatiques.* What is irony in Balzac's story Ensor has transformed (in all his Christological subjects which can be related to it) into a searing visualization pervaded by the frenzied anguish of the painter. It is this remarkable spirit which gives Washington University's painting its special and unforgettable power.

Dennis Adrian

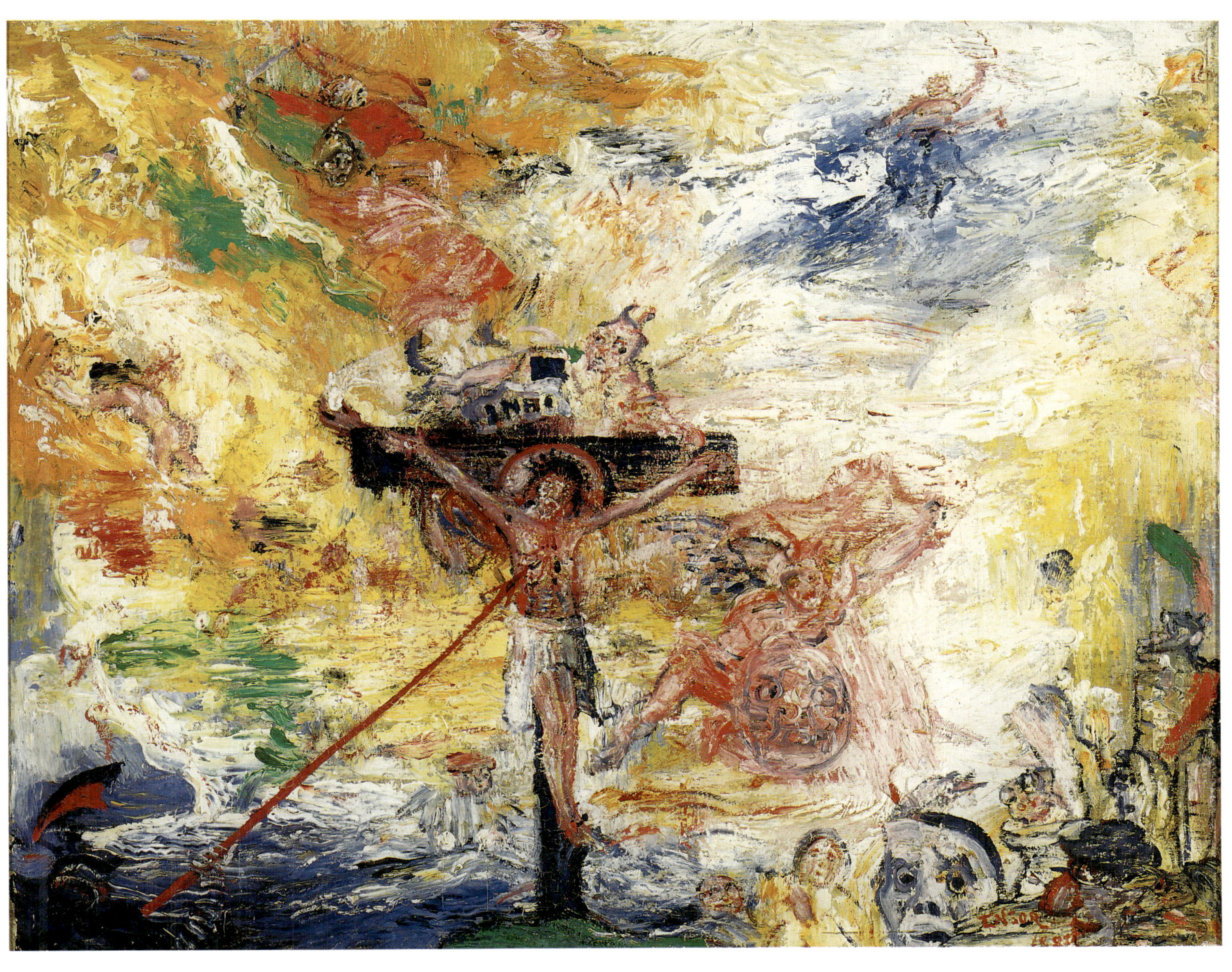

40. Edvard Munch (Norway, 1863–1944)

Portrait of Irmgard Steinbart, 1913

Oil on canvas, 69⅜ x 34½"

Gift of Morton J. May, 1968

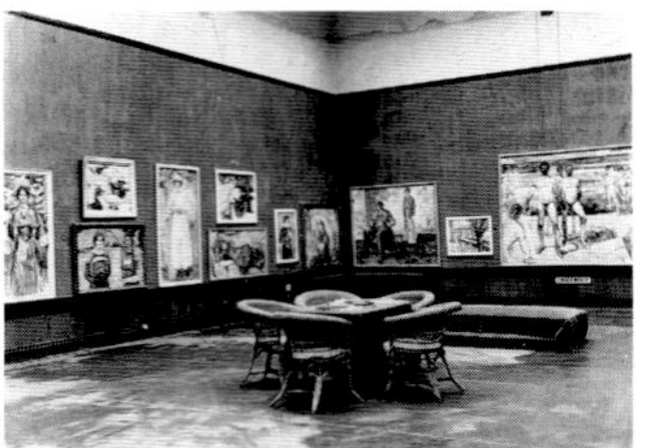

Munch's exhibition at Blomqvist's Art Gallery, 1915, Kristiania, Norway
Photograph courtesy Munch Museum, Oslo

This life-sized portrait, long identified as an image of Edvard Munch's sister Inger,[1] is in fact a commissioned portrait of Irmgard Steinbart, the daughter of a representative of the Mendelssohn banking house in Berlin. According to a letter from the end of 1913 that Munch wrote to his Hamburg collector and biographer Gustav Schiefler, the artist executed the painting at his home in Norway: "I shall travel now to Kragerø to work for around three weeks, in part to carry out a large commission for Herr Steinbart. . . ."[2]

Munch is best known for his paintings and prints from the 1890s, such as *The Scream* (1893, Nasjonalgalleriet, Oslo), which display the technical audacity and psychological extremity that established the artist as a modern European master. Less known is Munch's long, distinguished, and lucrative career as a portraitist.[3] In the years just after the turn of the century, Munch became active as a portrait painter, first in Germany, where he lived through 1908, and then in Norway. In 1909, following a decade of immense productivity and frequent travel, Munch settled permanently in Norway, purchasing property first in the town of Kragerø, then in Hvitsten, both south of Kristiania (present-day Oslo) on the Oslofjord. There, after some effort, Munch secured the commission to decorate the University of Oslo Festival Hall, the most important public art project in newly independent Norway (the paintings were installed in 1916). At the same time, Munch arranged exhibitions of his paintings and prints throughout Europe, and worked prodigiously. A photograph documenting Munch's October 1915 exhibition at Blomqvist's Gallery in Kristiania illustrates the range of the motifs that preoccupied him during these years—landscapes, robust nudes, and portraits, including the portrait of Irmgard Steinbart (at the center) and, at the left, that of his model Ingeborg Kaurin Onsager (1912, Munch Museum; a version is in the Museum of Fine Arts, Boston).

The portrait of Irmgard Steinbart was painted during Munch's most fruitful period as a portraitist, between his return to Norway and the outbreak of the Great War. Its loose handling and glowing palette are characteristic of Munch's Expressionist work of the 1910–20s. Munch frequently varied the viscosity of his paint, at times thinning his pigments with turpentine to achieve a glowing transparency, seen here in the background greenery, and at others, laying on thick layers of paint, used here to define the volume of the figure's dress. The figure's solid white mass stands in stark contrast to the diaphanous green surround, its separation from the background reinforced by the short, spontaneous-looking parallel brush strokes that run horizontally across the figure's skirt, and vertically throughout the background. These articulated brush strokes, which, in the words of Reinhold Heller, "preserve visible tracks of the picture's formation,"[4] suspend traces of the artist's presence in the surface of the painting.

The scale and perspective of the composition are also characteristic of Munch's portraiture of this period. The depiction of a full figure viewed from waist level, in which the head is depicted slightly from below and the feet from above, is a convention that Munch initiated in his 1885 portrait of the painter Karl Gustav Jensen-Hjell (private collection), reinvestigated in a self-portrait of 1904 (Munch Museum), and employed in his life-sized portraits throughout his career. This perspective elongates and enlarges the figure as a presence that commands the pictorial space and dominates the spectator.

Little is known about either Irmgard Steinbart or her father.[5] Steinbart, who collected the works of Lovis Corinth, expressed a desire to amass the largest existing Munch collection. The writer Hugo Perls, who met Steinbart in Norway, judged him harshly: "He was the type who collected indiscriminately and thought everything could be achieved by throwing the name of Corinth around. He continually referred to his age without realizing that an old fool is no better than a young fool."[6] Such a reaction may in part be explained by the fact that Steinbart apparently returned the portrait of his daughter to Munch because he found no likeness in it.[7] Munch admitted that he did not flatter his sitters: "Every time I paint people, I always find that the sitter's enemies regard it as a good likeness. The sitter himself says that all my portraits are good, except the one I painted of him."[8]

Munch frequently painted second versions of his commissioned paintings, or of paintings that he sold, for his private collection. A second version of the portrait of Irmgard Steinbart, now in the collection of the Munch Museum in Oslo, was exhibited throughout the 1910–20s, and at Munch's vast retrospective exhibition at the Oslo National Gallery in 1927. Washington University's version of the Steinbart painting was exhi-bited frequently between 1914 and 1917, suggesting that both this portrait and the version that Munch painted for himself were regarded by the artist as strong examples of his work, and as magnets to attract other commissions.

Patricia Berman

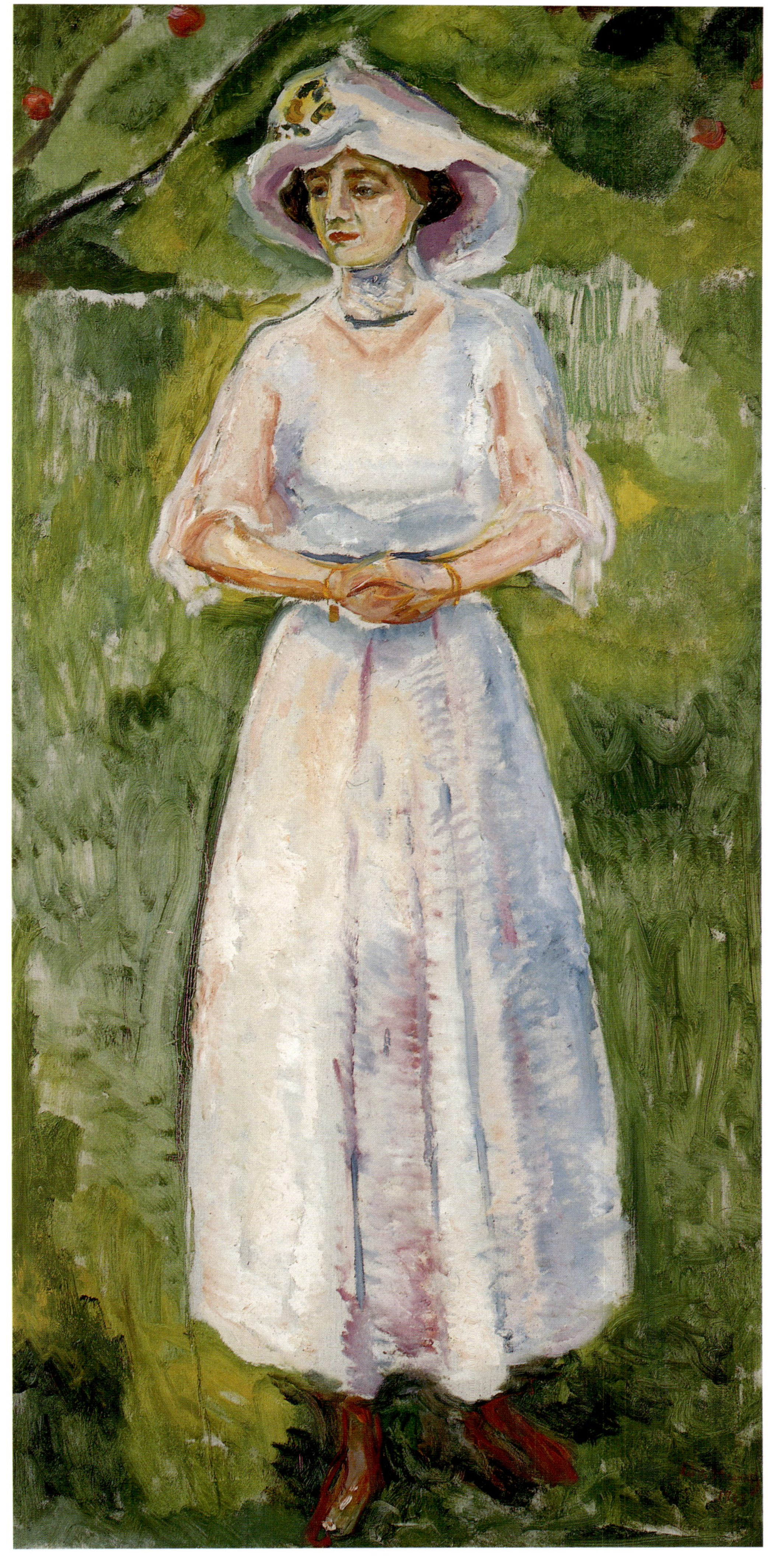

41. Ludwig Meidner (Germany, 1884–1966)

Selbstbildnis (Self Portrait), 1912

Oil on canvas, 31⅝ x 23⅝"

Gift of Mr & Mrs. Sydney M. Shoenberg, Jr., 1963

Self Portrait (1912) is an important work by one of Germany's major Expressionist artists. Though still today without the international reputation of Max Beckmann, Ludwig Kirchner or Emile Nolde, Ludwig Meidner became their equal, especially as a portraitist, as early as 1912, the year *Self Portrait* was painted.[1] In that year he made his public debut with a group calling itself the *Pathetiker*—advocates of intensely emotional and personal feeling through art. 1912 also inaugurated the decade during which he made his best art works based on three themes: Berlin street scenes, apocalyptic visions, and portraits of German avant-garde personalities. Especially when viewed as a series these works go beyond private pathos—what Meidner called "letting myself stream out"—to memorialize the tragic era which culminated in World War I.

An important part of his portraiture of these avant-garde figures were his self-portraits, of which the Washington University painting is a prime example. These portraits, in a variety of media, are Meidner's most richly varied and consistently forceful images, which reveal a self-regard that was anxiety-ridden, self-critical, and anything but flattering. Many of his self-portraits were done before a mirror late at night when the artist felt himself to be most completely alone. *Self Portrait* was probably done under such circumstances. Since he painted with his right hand, the palette he holds in *Self Portrait* must be understood as held in his left hand, a left hand turned into its opposite by the mirror. Thus, in a purely literal sense, what we see here is the artist looking at himself, not at us.

Meidner's self-portraits not only place him in the vanguard of twentieth-century Expressionist masters, but also put him in the company of the old masters of self-portraiture, Rembrandt and Van Gogh. Aesthetic rank, however, was less important to Meidner than the assurance that his self-portraits gave him of a self joining a community of other selves who aspired heroically and passionately to "higher things" in art and literature. Meidner was a self-conscious artist for whom a wide context, a "being in the world" politically and spiritually, was vital. With image and word he celebrated kindred spirits, especially those whose "higher things" had to do with revolutionary changes of self and society. Meidner singled out Vincent Van Gogh and Walt Whitman as the two most important influences, but he also identified with biblical prophets and Nietzsche's Zarathustra. Admittedly, such comrades were suitable less for a political activist than a poet-intellectual. Indeed, putting himself in their company sometimes pushed his self-regard close to megalomania. However, it may also have nourished that self-centeredness induced by dread and guilt which Existentialist philosophers declare shatters self-satisfaction and energizes conscience. Be that as it may, Meidner's self-portraits visualize a self-regard that is as much derisive as assertive.

As for this *Self Portrait,* at first glance it could be taken for a caricature, a burlesque of subject and style, a parody of self-esteem cast in the then-fashionable bravura manner of such older Berlin modernists as Max Liebermann, Max Slevogt and Lovis Corinth. With almost "teutonic frenzy" (to use Corinth's terminology), bold sweeping strokes, excited scribbling and abrupt slashes conjure a Meidner who seems to be ogling himself, a model, or a viewer, with manic glee.

However, a more careful look suggests that *Self Portrait* is more complex than a mere comic exaggeration. What one sees is a shifty—or, more precisely, shifting—Meidner: now leering goblin, now winsome, Chaplinesque bohemian; now grim artist/worker, now bourgeois poseur play-acting before a baroque cascade of red drapery. Although at work, he is dressed in his Sunday best: dark blue suit, white collar, flowing cravat and hat. There is something touching about this outfit. The suit is rumpled, the shirt ill-fitting, the hat several sizes too large. One should note how the hat frames Meidner's face in something like a black halo, not an inappropriate effect for features which are malevolent rather than merely mischievous. On the other hand the artist positively flaunts the tools of his trade, a palette and no less than seven brushes! The portrait equivocates between pride and insolence, and between bravado and affirmation. It is an equivocation that is deliberate and passionate and no different from the equivocation or self-contradiction celebrated in Meidner's Whitmanesque poetry. In Meidner's *Hymn to Myself* he calls himself an "owl eyed Puss In Boots . . . soaring to seventh heaven . . . (with) fly specked cheeks," as well as "a tough guy and gang leader . . . sometimes praying devoutly—sometimes nihilistically whining."[2]

Meidner's voice, though, differs significantly from Whitman's. In *Song of Myself* when Whitman declaims: "Do I contradict myself? Very well then, I contradict myself. (I am large. I contain multitudes)," he does so without anguish. In sharp contrast, Meidner's self-contradiction both in his paintings and his poems is agonized, despairing and ironic. About his painting of self-portraits done in 1912 he wrote:

> *I shall never be able to forget that summer. Befouled over and over again by scabies, misery and madness it made me old, the plans of my youth were blasted and my courage crumbled. Arrayed in a smock so plastered with dried paint that it was stiff like armor, girded with a ravenous palette and brushes bared like teeth, so stood I steadfast the whole night through and painted myself in the leering mirror. . . . Within me crackled far-off spaces and the trumpet blasts of catastrophes yet to come. . . . Oh savage bloated bell, jagged arms and legs, oh face split with diabolical laughter—and then the laughter turned rancid.*[3]

Excepting the reference to his wearing an artist's smock, this passage reads like a rhapsodic evocation of *Self Portrait.*

Victor H. Miesel

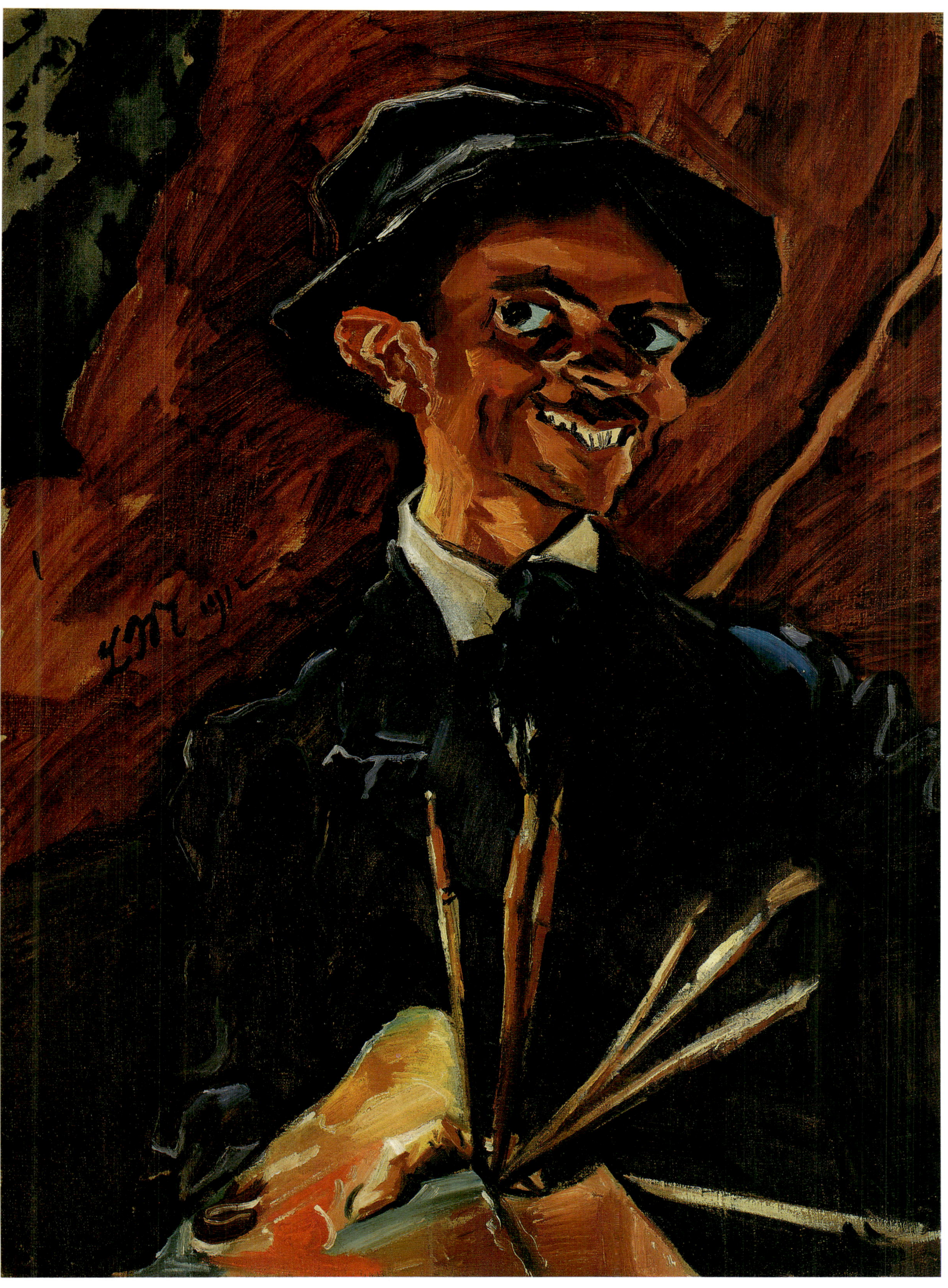

42. Paul Klee (Switzerland, 1879–1940)
Überbrückung (Transition), 1935

Oil on canvas, 17 x 25⅝"
University purchase, Kende Sale Fund, 1945

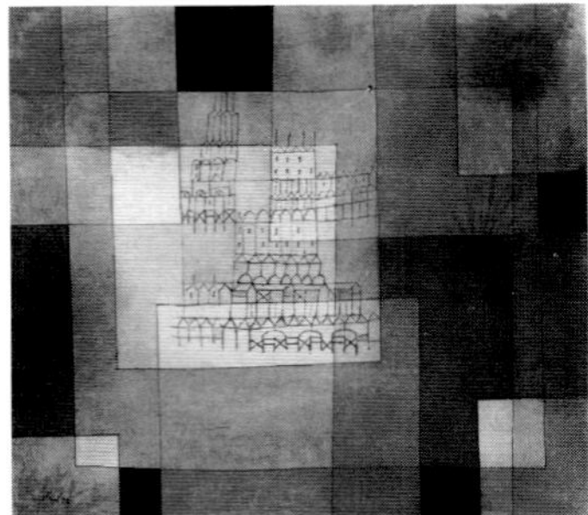

Paul Klee
Polyphonic Architecture, 1930
Oil on canvas, 16½ x 18¼"
The Saint Louis Art Museum
Purchase

To his students at the Bauhaus Klee offered the following pronouncement:

> *There is polyphony in music. In itself the attempt to transpose it into art would offer no special interest. But to gather insights into music through the special character of polyphonic works, to penetrate deep into this cosmic sphere, to issue forth a transformed beholder of art, and then to lurk in waiting for these things in the picture, that is something more. For the simultaneity of several independent themes is something that is possible not only in music; typical things in general do not belong just in one place, but have their roots and organic anchor everywhere and anywhere.*[1]

It would be difficult to overemphasize the centrality of the concept of polyphony in Klee's thinking about art.[2] For him, the idea of "the simultaneity of independent themes" was a key not only to all higher aesthetics, but also to all organic life and to the structure of the universe. A substantial proportion of his work as artist, theorist and teacher was dedicated to investigations in this realm. Klee also postulated the notion of a "higher polyphony." This idea referred in one sense to the supreme musical achievements of the late eighteenth century—above all to the achievements of Mozart, Klee's main divinity—but it also implied for Klee a kind of visionary, utopian synthesis in art.

Überbrückung is a late example of Klee's signature work in the field of color polyphony. Between 1920 and 1932, Klee worked with a great variety of pictorial formats and pedagogical illustrations which he considered "polyphonic" in one sense or another.[3] One of the most prominent of these formats involved the use of overlapping, interpenetrating planes of color and transparent layers of paint to create pictorial depth, modulate the interactions of color and achieve a simultaneous interaction and perception of color themes in a single painting. The overlapping, transparent plane method also represented for Klee a modern, twentieth-century approach to creating, quantifying and teaching about pictorial space. It served, therefore, as a substitute for the eminently logical and teachable, but "dead," metaphor of Renaissance perspective. It was also a method of spatial construction which conformed to the rationalistic, geometric, constructivist thinking prevalent among Klee's colleagues at the Bauhaus.

More specifically, *Überbrückung* demonstrates one of Klee's principal variations upon his overlapping plane technique, a variation involving "depicted" or implied, rather that actual, transparency. That is, where linear planes intersected and appear to overlap in the painting, Klee indicated the zone of intersection with a completely new color. In actual color transparency, he would overlay one thinned wash on top of another and so create the third, transitional color by a combination of the other two. Another outstanding example of this technique of "depicted" polyphony is Klee's *Polyphonic Architecture* (1930) in The Saint Louis Art Museum.[4] The titles of Klee's compositions occasionally refer to autobiographical emotions and circumstances. 1935 was indeed for him a year of transition in a period of extreme transition. In 1932 he had been dismissed from his teaching position at the Düsseldorf Academy, as a result of the Nazi's campaign to "restore the indigenous character" of German art instruction. After being, in effect, hounded out of Germany, he was obliged in 1933 to seek refuge in Switzerland, where, although a native, he was not a citizen. (His application for Swiss citizenship was not approved in his lifetime.) He was therefore, in a sense, a man without a country. In 1935 his difficulties were immeasurably compounded when he learned that he had contracted scleroderma, a progressive skin disease which caused his death five years later. Thus the years from 1933 to 1936 formed a period of great professional as well as personal hardships. Formerly so prolific and inventive, Klee found it hard to maintain his creative impetus. His output declined as he groped unsuccessfully for new directions, and he felt compelled at times to return for sustenance to earlier ideas.

Thus *Überbrückung* is a retrospective painting, looking back to a style that had occupied Klee some years before, and belonging to an interim period in his career. The title also clearly refers, in a formal sense, to the transitional color zone which forms a boundary separating and joining the lighter values (earth-tones and neutrals) in the lower part of the work and the dark blues above. We know too from the titles of many other works that the artist was at this time given to pondering his own mortality, both in humor and in earnest. It is therefore likely that, given his love of punning and multi-dimensional meaning, he was also thinking in this title of the mortal transition between below and above, between earth and heaven, or, in the more purely landscape sense, between land and sky.

Although Klee's polyphonic formats tend to emphasize the constructive and the rational, they are often distinguished, as is *Überbrückung,* by his uniquely whimsical and playful sensibilities. Here these sensibilities are expressed in the animated irregularity of the forms, particularly the strongly highlighted peach-toned forms, and their lively rhythmic dispersion as they dance across the surface. This improvisatory, "contrapuntal" type of drawing is found in Klee's work from about 1915 on. It was originally inspired by his friendship with and exposure to the work of Wassily Kandinsky, and became integrated with Klee's own native tendency toward doodling and free linear improvisation. The lines have an identity of their own, not dependent on images from nature, and they flow along like melodic lines in musical composition. They are executed in the narrow-line technique of his early drawings, soon to be supplanted by the heavier brush-drawn lines of his late style, which came into full flower in 1937 and enabled his production to recover impressively during his remaining years.

Andrew Kagan

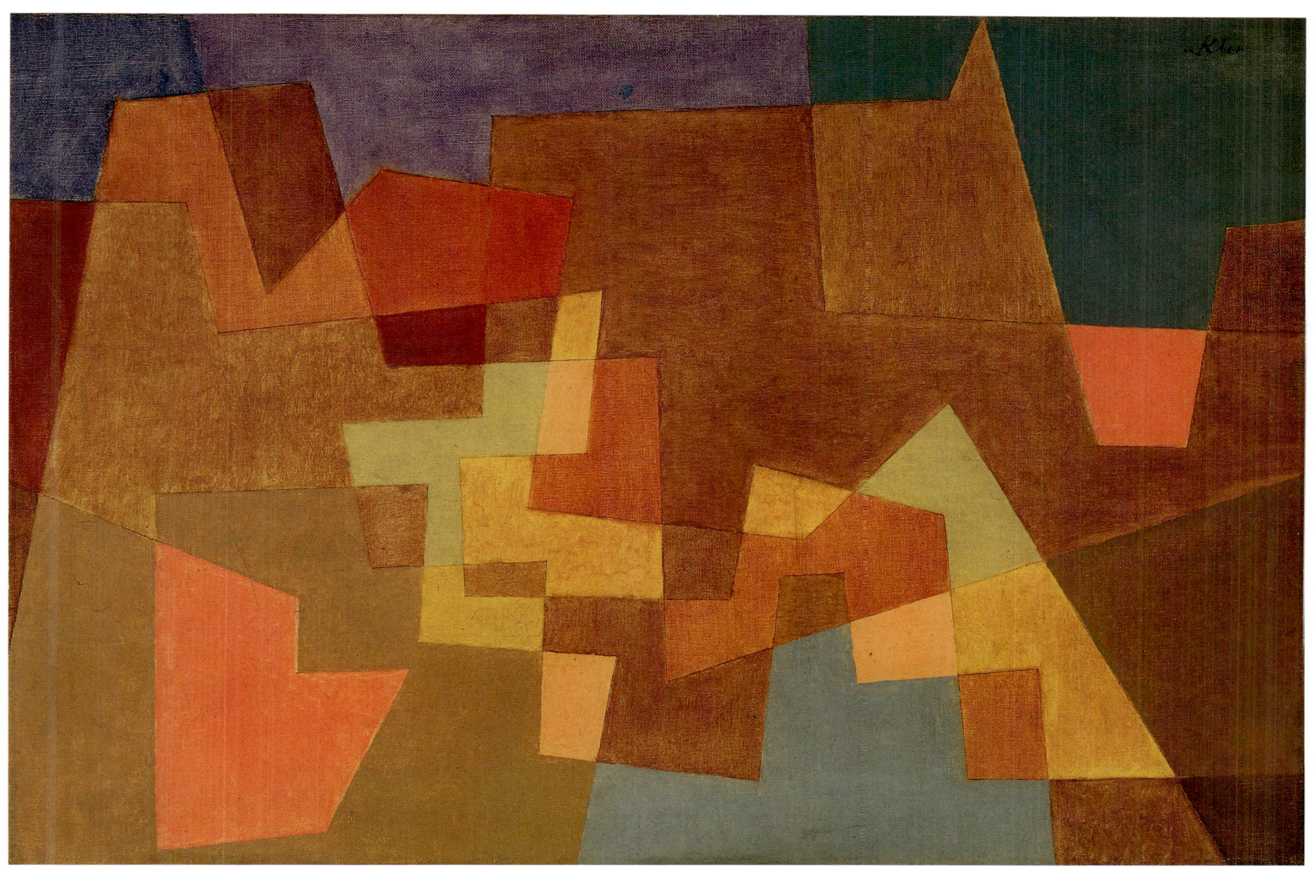

43. Max Beckmann (Germany, 1884–1950)
Les Artistes mit Gemüse (Artists with Vegetable), or *Four Men Around a Table,* 1943

Oil on canvas, 59 x 45⅜"
University purchase, Kende Sale Fund, 1946

Max Beckmann is widely regarded as the greatest native-born German painter of his generation, yet his achievement is often distorted. Commonly labeled an Expressionist, he found the designation abhorrent. Indeed, during the 1920s most critics regarded Beckmann's art as anti-Expressionist—as an antidote to murky utopianism and emotional and stylistic excesses. His painting was seen as essentially Realist, tracing the curve of Germany's spiritual course through the vicissitudes of the Weimar Republic. Accordingly, in this spirit he is today generally grouped with the German "neue Sachlichkeit" (New Objectivity) artists of the 1920s, such as Dix and Grosz. But this view, too, constitutes a reductive distortion of Beckmann's artistic achievement.

In an essay of 1927, "The Artist in the State," Beckmann presented a conception of his artistic project that set him apart from his German contemporaries. "The artist in the new sense," he wrote, "is the conscious shaper of the transcendent idea. . . . The work of art becomes a symbol and source of power for the partly still dormant power in the responsible human being. Art is the mirror of the God that humanity is."[1] This conception, which contains elements of Schopenhauer and gnosticism, casts a different light on Beckmann's ostensibly Realist art of the 1920s, and can serve to orient us to the openly allegorical subject matter that predominated after 1933, a change coinciding with the seizure of power by the National Socialists. Fired from his teaching position in Frankfurt, his art banned from exhibition, Beckmann embarked upon an "inner immigration;" in 1937 he fled to Amsterdam, where he remained, except for a half-year's sojourn in Paris, until 1947, when he assumed a visiting professorship at Washington University in St. Louis.

In Amsterdam, Beckmann painted in isolation, cut off from the art world; he worked under these conditions for a decade. Before 1933 he had considered the artist a public figure, exercising a constructive social role; in exile he adopted a different view. There are, he explained in his London lecture of 1938, "two worlds: the world of spiritual life and the world of political reality. Both are manifestations of life which may sometimes coincide but are very different in principle. I must leave it to you to decide which is the more important."[2]

This dualistic conception seems to have influenced *Les Artistes mit Gemüse* (as it is titled in the artist's own handlist), on which Beckmann worked intermittently between April 1942 and January 1943.[3] Shown seated in candlelight around a table are Beckmann himself and three fellow German artists, all wartime exiles in Amsterdam. Beckmann is seen in the lower right, the abstract painter Friedrich Vordemberge-Gildewart to his left; wearing the fur hat is the painter Herbert Fiedler; beside him sits the poet Wolfgang Frommel. On the wall behind Frommel is an enframed area—variously interpreted as a mirror or picture, but which could plausibly be a window as well. Whatever its identity, it appears to reveal a raging inferno.

Previous commentators have noted the strange, quasi-ritualistic air of this image: there is no psychological interaction between the figures; each is shown in a kind of frozen self-absorption, holding an object that takes on the character of an attribute. Three of the "attributes" are easily recognized: Beckmann holds a mirror, which reflects not his own face but the white face of a clown; Vordemberge-Gildewart holds a carrot or turnip, the vegetable from which the painting derives its title; Fiedler grasps a fish. Frommel's object, however, is not so easily identifiable. Among previous commentators, Jedlicka simply ignores it; Clark reads it as a crystal ball; the Göpels believe it to be "probably a head of cabbage (or bread?)"; Schulz-Hoffmann assumes it is bread.[4] The opacity and apparent thinness of the object, suggested by the position of Frommel's hands, argue against a crystal ball; Beckmann's title for the painting, with "Gemüse" in the singular form, would seem to exclude cauliflower; and the blue-green color is incompatible with the appearance of all but moldy bread. In any case, it seems plausible that the respective attributes relate to each artist's self-understanding of his artistic project, or to Beckmann's own characterization of it.

Whatever the meaning of the individual objects, two things are certain and surely significant for any interpretation: all of the figures were exiles in wartime Amsterdam, and all were artists, to whom Beckmann accorded a privileged status as mediators of a "dormant power" of transcendent origin. The general theme of the work has an interesting relationship to gnosticism[5]: the notion of alien life in a hostile world was a central concept of gnosticism, and it is tempting to read the status of these four German refugees in Holland as a metaphor for their alien status as representatives of "spiritual life", as heralds of "the God that humanity is" in the then hostile, oppressively dark world of "political reality." The juxtaposition of the light of the candle with the raging flames can also be related to gnostic imagery: light in gnosticism is identified with the transmundane deity; it, too, is an alien presence in a world engulfed and controlled by darkness, a faint sign of transcendent reality. Fire, on the other hand, is identified with matter, death, and corruption.[6]

One should not approach Beckmann as an illustrator of gnostic myths; rather, gnosticism offered him a compelling system of metaphors for interpreting his experience and forging his highly original mythic images. Put in less esoteric terms, what is depicted here, in Margot Clark's apt characterization, is "intellect and . . . spirit, holding out against brutish power."[7]

Charles W. Haxthausen

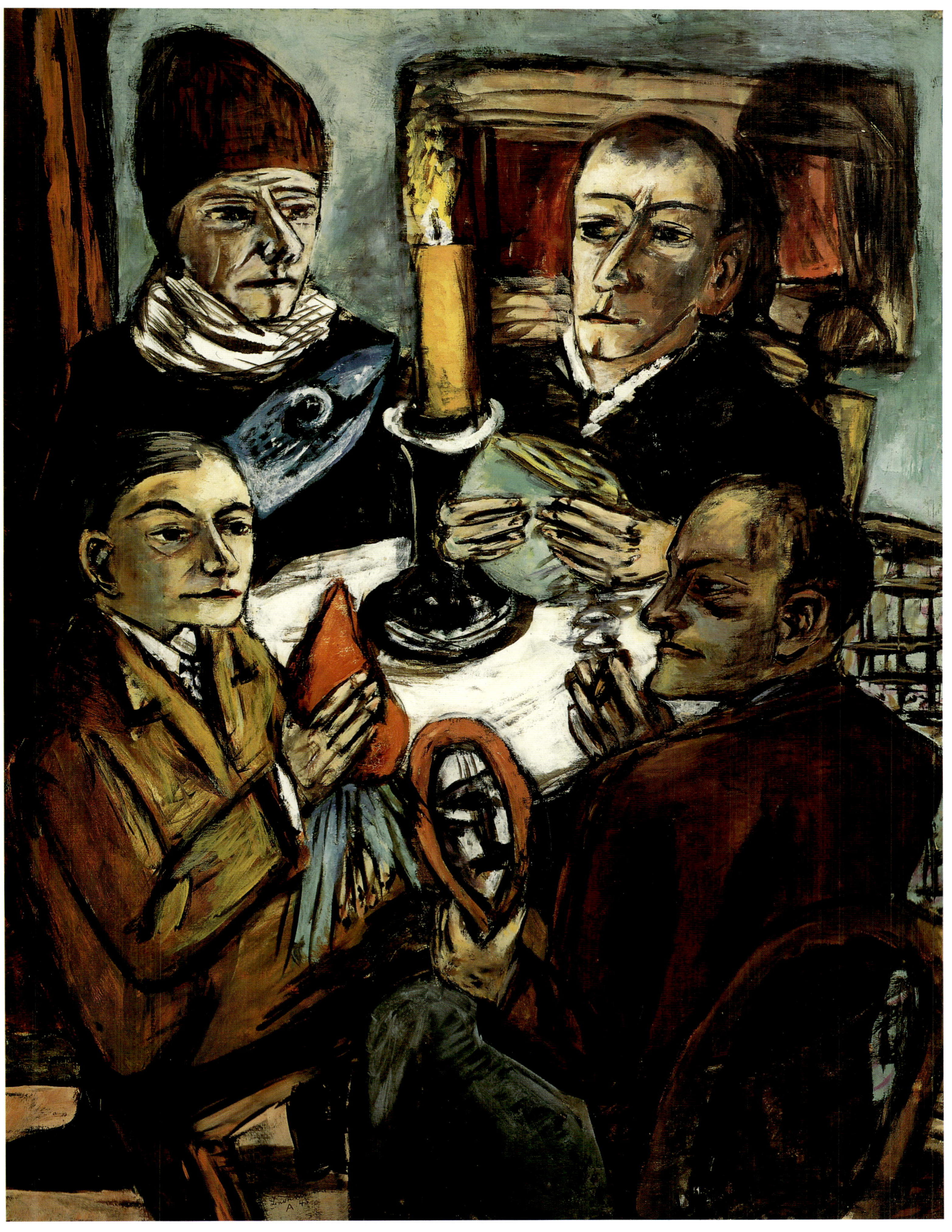

44. Theo van Doesburg
(Holland, 1883–1931)
Composition VII: The Three Graces, 1917

Oil on canvas, 33½ x 33½"
University purchase, Yeatman Fund, 1947

Theo van Doesburg is best known for the central role he played in animating the group of primarily Dutch painters and architects who became associated with *De Stijl,* the journal van Doesburg founded in Leiden in 1917, and for whose publication there and in several other European cities he was responsible until his death in 1931. A man of extraordinarily diverse interests matched by prodigious energy, van Doesburg was active not only as a painter and an architect but also as a sculptor, graphic designer, urban planner, poet and critic; in addition, he produced numerous applied designs for stained glass windows, floor tiles and furniture. Although his reputation as a vanguard artist of international stature is inextricably linked with his leadership of what has come to be known as the De Stijl movement, it is worth noting that van Doesburg also helped shape the direction of the Bauhaus at a crucial stage of its evolution during the early 1920s, while at the same time he was becoming actively involved in the Dada movement.

Just as van Doesburg's career as a whole cannot be circumscribed within the limits of De Stijl, so his development as a painter cannot be measured solely by comparison with the superficially similar, Neoplastic style of Piet Mondrian. While Mondrian's paintings and aesthetic philosophy had an unmistakable influence on van Doesburg's development, the work of several other artists was equally important in helping him forge his distinctive artistic identity during the 1910s. *The Three Graces,* which van Doesburg painted in the first half of 1917, provides an excellent example of his debts to other artists as well as his original contributions to the abstract art of De Stijl.

Born in Utrecht in 1883, van Doesburg briefly studied acting in Amsterdam, but as a painter he was apparently largely self-taught. His first paintings were in a traditional, figurative style that he later described as his "brown period." The beginning of World War I in August 1914 brought a temporary halt to van Doesburg's art-related activities, but military service in neutral Holland did not prevent him from making contact with vanguard Dutch artists who later joined in founding *De Stijl.* In November 1915, he published his first, extremely positive response to Mondrian's recent, abstract work which, he wrote, aroused a "purely spiritual" feeling. The following February, van Doesburg visited Mondrian in the artists' colony at Laren, where he met Bart van der Leck as well; around the same time he also encountered the painter Vilmos Huszar, who was pursuing abstraction in both painting and stained glass. While Mondrian's abstract art integrating figure and ground was characterized by a simplified, grid-like composition developed from his experimentation with Cubism, van der Leck's and Huszar's practice, like van Doesburg's, was more closely tied to natural motifs, flattened, simplified, and eventually rendered in rectangular planes of bright color. Indeed, the salient features of van Doesburg's *The Three Graces*—its black ground as well as its suspended red, yellow and blue rectangular planes—are directly indebted to the lateral wings of van der Leck's *Composition 1916, no. 4 (Mine Triptych)* (Dienst Verspreide Rijkskollekties, on loan to Gemeentemuseum, The Hague), which van Doesburg saw at the end of December 1916. The black ground common to *Mine Triptych* and *The Three Graces* is an unusual feature found in only one other work by van Doesburg (*Composition VI,* also of 1917), but the planes of primary color that appear to float on the surface are reminiscent of several applied art projects van Doesburg executed in 1917, including stained glass windows as well as a wall painting for a townhouse in Alkmaar.

Although no preliminary sketches for van Doesburg's painting have been identified, the image was probably achieved through the same gradual process of simplification from a naturalistic motif that characterized his other paintings of the period as well as his work in the medium of stained glass. It has been suggested that van Doesburg may have worked from a photograph of J. B. Carpeaux's sculpture, *The Three Graces,* a reproduction of which appears in his 1919 publication of three earlier lectures, *Drie Voordrachten over de nieuwe beeldende kunst.*[1]

Composition VII: The Three Graces, which was signed with van Doesburg's monogram and dated on the verso (the inscription was covered when the canvas was re-lined in 1959), was exhibited in the summer of 1917 as *Composition 5; Motif: The Three Graces.*[2] Why the numbering subsequently changed from 5 to VII is not known; the present designation appears on a list of works prepared by van Doesburg himself, probably in 1927.[3]

Until shortly after van Doesburg's death, when, in preparation for a retrospective exhibition in Paris, his widow, Nelly, had most of his paintings reframed, *The Three Graces* was displayed in a frame designed by the artist. Composed of thin strips of wood painted white and mounted on similarly thin surrounding wood strips painted black, the device was comparable to those used at the time by van Doesburg as well as Huszar.[4] Mondrian also investigated various frame configurations in an effort to clarify the relationship of the painted canvas to the surrounding space.

In 1936, *The Three Graces* was included in the Museum of Modern Art's ground-breaking exhibition, Cubism and Abstract Art. Eleven years later, the painting was brought back to New York for inclusion in a retrospective exhibition arranged by Nelly van Doesburg at Peggy Guggenheim's Art of This Century Gallery. Anxious to acquire an example of "the style of architectural abstraction [that] has had the most profound influence on a variety of branches of contemporary art, especially architecture and typography," on April 15, 1947 the Committee on Art Collections at Washington University urged the chancellor to approve acquisition of *The Three Graces* from the exhibition at Art of This Century Gallery.[5]

Nancy J. Troy

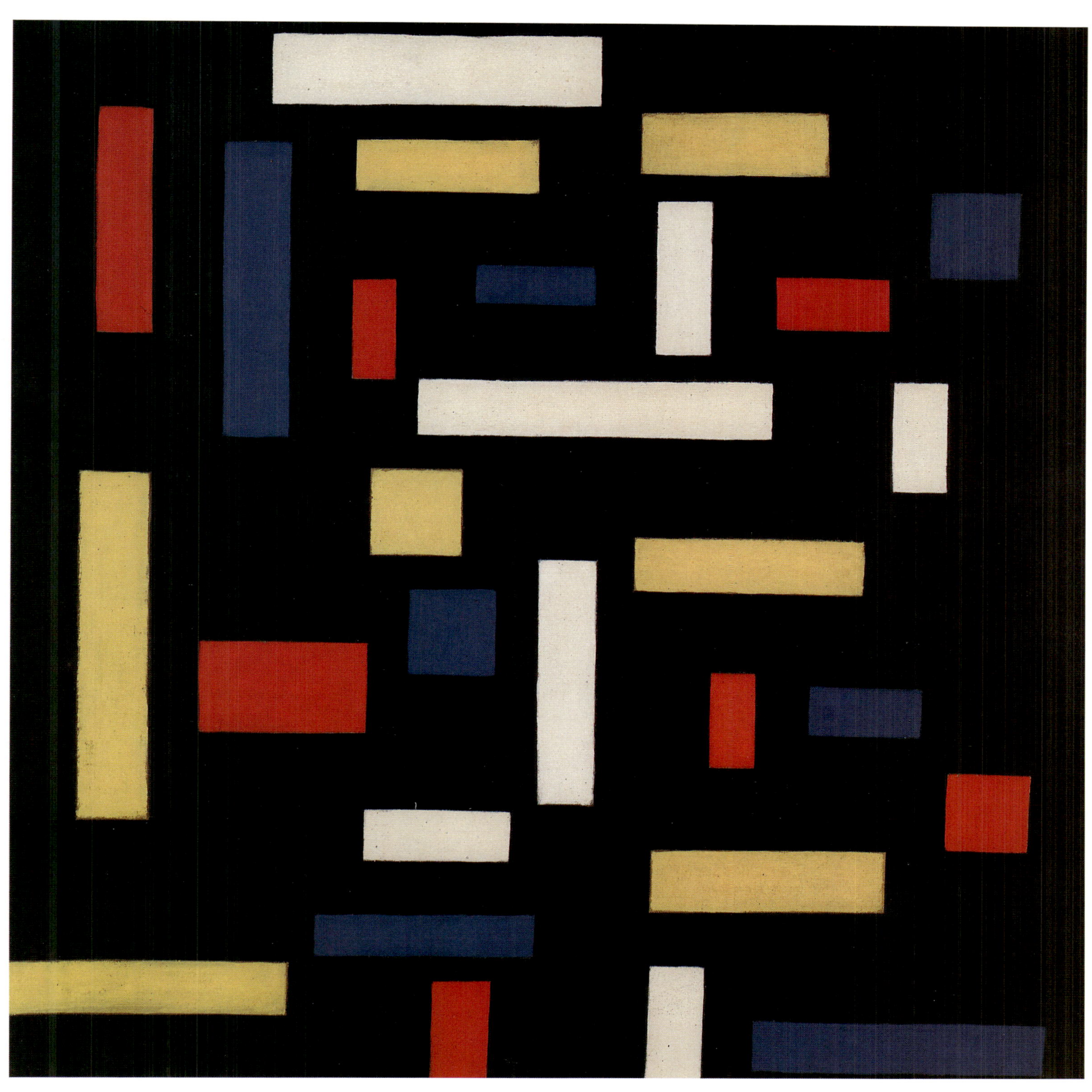

45. Antoine Pevsner
(France, b. Russia, 1884–1962)
Bas Relief en Creux (Sunken Bas Relief), 1926–27

Relief in brass and bronze, 23¾ x 24⅝ x 12¼"
University purchase, McMillan Fund, 1946

Antoine Pevsner was born in Orel, Russia in 1884. In 1922, he left Russia, following his brother Naum Gabo and Wassily Kandinsky, before he went to Paris in 1923, where he died in 1962. He wrote the *Realist Manifesto* with his brother in 1920, and since then he has been considered as one of the fathers of constructivism—though he called himself a "realiste constructeur."[1]

Pevsner's early work explores the dynamic relations between circles and ellipses, focusing on a central motif of crossing axes. The artist's early drawings studied the relationships between these shapes, which the artist highlighted by dynamic contrasts of light and the use of asymmetrical axes. In the early 1920s, the artist began to break away from two-dimensional surfaces but continued his experiments with the spacial interplay of shapes and lines. He first introduced a three-dimensional use of the crossed axes in *Construction dans l'espace (Construction in Space)* (1923–25, Musée National d'Art Moderne, Centre Georges Pompidou, Paris), and slightly later created a variation of this shape in *Projection dans l'espace (Projection in Space)* (1924–27, Baltimore Museum of Art). At this time he also began to create masks, heads, and bas reliefs—one of the most famous being the *Portrait of Marcel Duchamp* (1926, Yale University Art Gallery, New Haven, Connecticut). These experiments resulted in Pevsner's *Bas Relief*, the artist's first and only sunken bas relief. A unique work in his oeuvre that incorporates his fundamental form of the crossing axes, the bas relief is one of Pevsner's important early works and represents his early artistic development.

Pevsner constructed *Bas Relief* with overlapping patterns in three dimensions that echo and contrast with one another, thus creating dynamic rhythms within the work. The curves in the *Bas Relief* echo throughout the piece, creating a mirror effect that suggests infinite space. These varied echoes based on curves are often stopped short or broken by vertical lines. Such forms revive dynamic tensions within the work.

In this bas relief, the central shape is more complex than the other forms, as it is composed of curved as well as straight lines. The four elements in the central shape are slightly asymmetrical and slightly off-center. Such asymmetrical elements sustain dynamic rhythms which are enlivened by shapes either hollowed or full. All these elements lead to the slightly off-centered main form: an arrow. This arrow-like shape gathers the essential rhythms suggested and created in this work, but its forward thrust becomes all the more forceful as its pool of dynamic rhythms is emphasized as well as dramatized by an interplay of contrasted hollowed and full shapes.

In *Bas Relief en Creux* the crossing axes are more complex in comparison with those found in *Bas Relief* (1932, private collection). This work is constructed after variations upon the basic shape of the crossing axes whose shadow, cast in depth, is very close to the central shape found in *Bas Relief en Creux*. Moreover, another variation upon the form of the crossing axes appears in the three-dimensional construction, *Construction dans l'espace (Construction in Space)* (1929, Kunstmuseum, Basel). Here, only the basic shape of the oblique crossing axes is kept, and its dynamism is reinforced with its contrasted hollowed and full forms as well as with the arrow-like base.

The title of the drawing *Pour la Rencontre des Planètes (For the Meeting of Planets)* (1924, Wilhelm Lehmbruck Museum, Duisburg) implies the significance of the crossed axes to the artist's world view:

> *They enable us to reveal the hidden forces found within nature; with them the new rhythms of the great axes of construction and other orbits can be pre-established within time and space. The masterly work of art creates by itself a whole cosmogonic system. . . .*[2]

The artist considered that such invented, yet revealing, forms could be verified either in nature or by science, thus proving that the artist's intuition was correct.

Aube Lardera

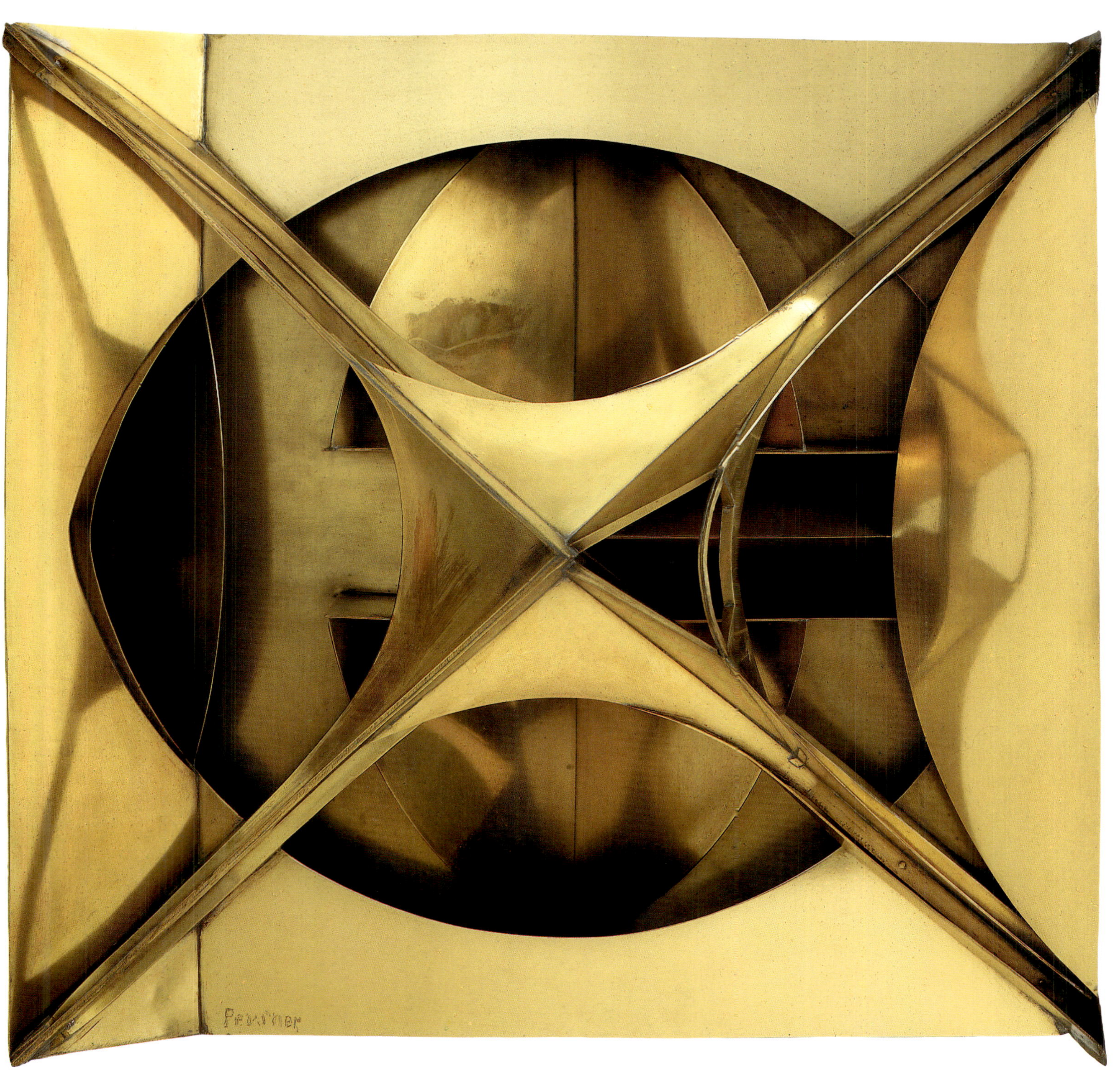
Pevsner

46. Naum Gabo
(United States, b. Russia, 1890–1977)
Linear Construction in Space No. 1 (Variation), 1942–43 (c. 1959)

Plexiglass with nylon monofilament, 24⅛ x 24¼ x 10"
Gift of Mr. Joseph Pulitzer, Jr., 1965

Naum Gabo is one of the pioneers of modernism most closely identified with efforts to link science and art in a new language of technologically-oriented sculpture.[1] Born in Russia the son of a metals factory manager and brother of Antoine Pevsner, Gabo was educated at the University of Munich where he studied medicine and the natural sciences. He gradually shifted his professional ambitions to sculpture, however, with the aim of capturing scientific principles and insights in three-dimensional constructed form. Mathematical models were an important early influence on his work, as were the cubist sculptures of Pablo Picasso and Alexander Archipenko.

With the outbreak of World War I, Gabo fled from Germany to Oslo, Norway. He worked there until his return to Revolutionary Russia in 1917, precociously developing a method he termed stereometric assemblage, which opened up solid mass to a dynamic interplay of space and light through a system of honeycombed, interpenetrating planes. Gabo's efforts to reform traditional sculpture led to the introduction of new materials—sheet metal, plywood, glass, and plastic—with non-artistic, industrial connotations. Modeling and carving were replaced by construction, and all traces of representation soon gave way to uncompromising abstraction. In his famous *Realistic Manifesto* published in Moscow in 1920, he stated that art should be made as "the engineer constructs his bridges, as the mathematician his formula of the orbits."[2] He also declared time, space, light, and movement to be the only true sculptural materials and proclaimed his belief in the "constructive" power of twentieth-century artists to reshape the world.

One of the themes central to Gabo's work throughout his career was the dematerialization of solid form. His first steps in this quest involved the use of thinner and thinner membranes in his honeycombed structures to make them lighter. The introduction of clear plastic and glass produced new light-transmitting properties, and the stringing techniques he developed further decomposed the solidity of surfaces. As Gabo's peripatetic career shifted from Russia to Germany and then France and (with the onset of World War II) England, his work in general became increasingly refined and purified, partly due to the availability of better, more easily workable plastics. Two of the sculptures that best exemplify these developments are his well-known *Linear Construction in Space No. 1* of about 1942 and the closely related *Linear Construction in Space No. 1 (Variation),* as represented in Washington University's collection.[3]

The dates of these key works and their different versions are difficult to establish conclusively. Gabo may have made a first small model for the *Linear Construction in Space No. 1* as early as 1938, but this work has disappeared. Another larger model appears to date from c. 1941–42, and one fully realized example is inscribed 1942. The earliest known version of *Linear Construction in Space No. 1 (Variation)* is documented by Gabo as made in 1942–43. This variation, a distinct and repeated type, differs from the original version only in the addition of notches or steps to the end pieces, creating a more animated silhouette. The *Linear Construction* sculptures are among Gabo's most famous series, and he made numerous versions of both types over the years, generally on commission or order, often varying the size, number of strings, and thickness of the plastic. The version in the Washington University collections was made about 1959 and is one of only five in this particularly large scale. Its attributed date is based on the fact that it was sold by Gabo to Fine Art Associates in New York in December 1959, from whom it passed to Louise and Joseph Pulitzer, Jr., and thence to Washington University.

The works in the *Linear Construction* series are the first in which Gabo employed stringing, a device that became one of his signature stylistic elements. Other artists, most notably Henry Moore and Barbara Hepworth, began using strings in their sculptures at about the same time, and it is debatable as to who had the idea first.[4] Moore purportedly borrowed the device from mathematical models at the Science Museum in London, of a type that Gabo had known since his early years in Germany. It is clear that Gabo drew heavily on certain specific types of models for sculptural forms earlier in the 1930s, and that he appreciated their airiness and delicacy and the way they projected mathematical or topological formulae into space. From them came his idea of incising onto the plastic surfaces of his sculptures a pattern of thin lines for a sense of radiation and expansion. Soon he converted the incised lines to actual strings.

In *Linear Construction in Space No. 1* and its *Variation,* the underlying structure of the sculpture is formed by a frame of plexiglass which is notched around its edges to hold the strings, and which supports at its center a plexiglass plane with an oval hole on the diagonal. The strings are actually nylon filament tightly wound around the frame. They stretch inward at steadily increasing angles, forming radiant lines that intersect into sensuous, interfolding curves. As the viewer moves around the sculpture, light plays off the strings, energizing the patterns of weaving lines and forms. The transparency of the plastic and the "virtual" surfaces described by the strings are totally open to space and light, and a sense of time is expressed through the evolving visual rhythms. The sculpture becomes an instrument of light, alive with reflections, captivating in its extreme purity and delicacy, and liberated from the weight of physical mass. It is one of the most effective embodiments of some of the scientific ideas that Gabo was intent on communicating, such as spatial curvature and the penetration of all bodies by space. Its immediate impact, however, comes from the potent visual, physical, and even emotional effects it evokes. Few works reveal better the subjectivism of experience that merges with technology at the heart of Gabo's constructivist idiom.

Steven A. Nash

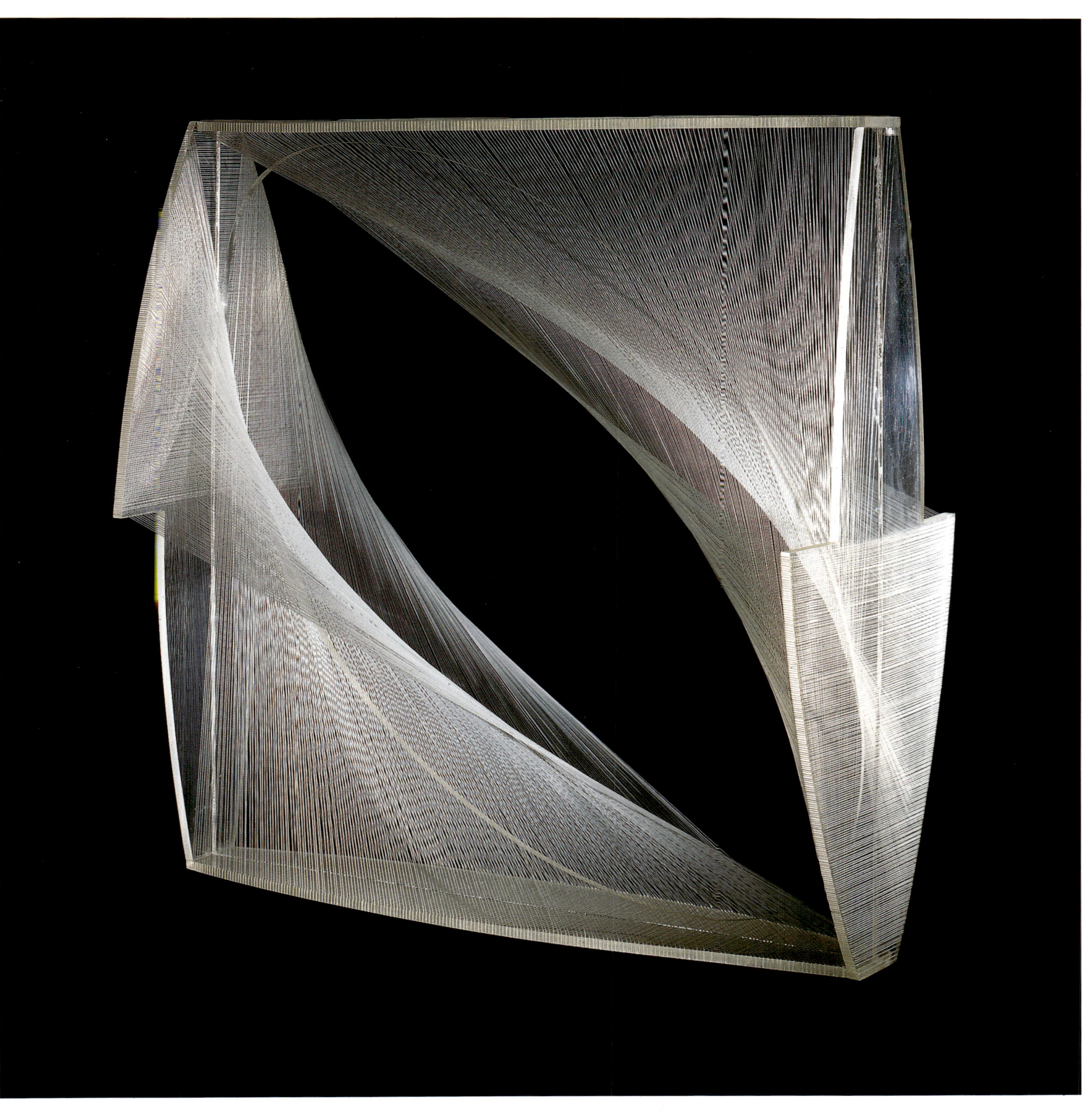

47. Fernand Léger (France, 1881–1955)

Les Grands Plongeurs (The Divers), 1941
Ink wash and charcoal, 75 x 42"
University purchase, Kende Sale Fund, 1946

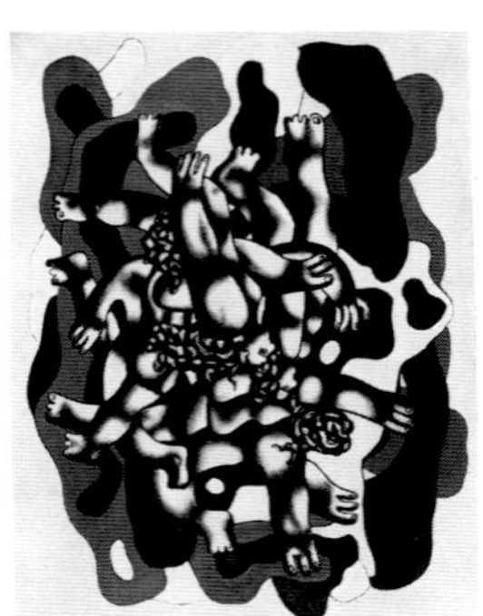

Fernand Léger
Divers II, 1941–42
Oil on canvas, 90 x 68"
The Museum of Modern Art, New York

Though clearly one of the masters of twentieth-century art, Léger is often recognized more for his contribution to Cubism during the years 1910–14 or for his post-Cubist works inspired by the city and the machine that he produced after World War I, than for his late figurative works. However, recent exhibitions and publications have cast Léger's monumental figurative cycles of the 1940s in a new light.[1] *Les Grands Plongeurs, Les Belles Cyclistes,* the *Constructors* and the various works leading up to *The Great Parade* (1954, Guggenheim Museum), Léger's last major painting, have now become icons of mid-twentieth-century art.

As early as 1909–10, in his pivotal work, *Nudes in the Forest* (Kröller-Müller Museum, Otterlo), Léger incorporated figures as tubular, abstract shapes in an overall Cubist structure. In such classic masterworks as *Le Grand Déjeuner (Three Women)* (1921, Museum of Modern Art) massive rounded figures dominate the composition. Léger's *Les Grands Plongeurs* images, recalling his drawings and paintings of acrobats during the late 1930s, are more linear clusters of figures in an ambiguous space. Compositionally, they derive from such abstract paintings as *La Racine Noir (The Black Root)* (1941, Collection Adrien Maeght, Paris) which convey a similar impression of mass suspended in space.[2]

Léger's actual source for *Les Grands Plongeurs* was seeing diving figures on the beach and on the docks at Marseilles, the port from which he embarked for the United States in 1940. He was working on a composition of five or six divers at that time. After setting up his studio in New York, Léger visited a public swimming pool, which he described as follows:

> *It was no longer five or six divers, it was two hundred at once. It was impossible to tell whose this head, this leg and that arm were. One could no longer distinguish. So then I mixed the limbs in my picture together and understood that in this way I was much closer to the truth than Michelangelo when he occupied himself with every individual muscle.*[3]

Even in the few figures and compressed space in the Washington University *Les Grands Plongeurs,* Léger conveyed the illusion of many figures plunging and surfacing underwater. In this and other works in the *Plongeurs* series, the reference to Michelangelo is inescapable, the most obvious comparison being the falling figures of the damned in Michelangelo's *Last Judgment* (Sistine Chapel). However, Léger clearly wished to distinguish his own efforts from those of the earlier master, even to surpass him, as indicated in the above statement. Léger indeed "mixed the limbs" in his *Plongeurs* so that each composition became a complex mass of interlocking arms, legs and heads. Yet often the figures appear to be floating freely rather than falling or plunging.

The sense of weightless mass in Léger's figures, *Les Grands Plongeurs* in particular, is characteristic of his late work. Even in the later *Plongeurs* paintings, in which figures become flatter, more linear and interspersed with planes of color, there remains the impression of solid, stocky bodies that inhabit these abstract spaces. The other notable characteristic in *Les Grands Plongeurs* is the illusion of motion which is lacking in the other series. In the classic period of the 1920s and in such late works as the *Cyclists* and *The Great Parade,* there is a sense of frozen, arrested movement. But even in the most abstract of the *Plongeurs* compositions, Léger conveyed vertical, horizontal or elliptical motion through line, shape and overlapping. He achieved this effect in both vertical and horizontal formats.

Léger acknowledged the importance of movement in the *Plongeurs* series, which occupied his attention primarily in his first few years in New York, though the theme appears in his work as late as 1946, after his return to France.

The energy in these works may also have been attributable to his life in this country. He wrote:

> *I was struck by the intensity of contrasts of movement. It's what I've tried to express in painting. . . . In America I painted in a much more realistic manner than before. I tried to translate the character of the human body evolving in space without any point of contact with the ground. I achieved it by studying the movements of swimmers diving into the water from very high.*[4]

In his essay on Léger's *Plongeurs,* Siegfried Giedion noted that the problem that intrigued the artist was "the representation of movement in a mass." He suggested that the "divers" might have been based upon bathers stretched out on the sand, which Léger then reconfigured in space on a vertical plane.[5]

The Washington University drawing, though identified in contemporary publications as "Etude pour les Plongeurs,"[6] does not, in fact, appear to be a study for a specific painting in the *Plongeurs* cycle. Its near life size (75" high) suggests more a full-scale cartoon for a mural, of which Léger did several during the late 1930s and early 1940s, including one of *Plongeurs,* c. 1942, for the home of architect Wallace K. Harrison.[7] The composition and *grisaille* rendering of the St. Louis drawing are related to the central section of *Divers on a Yellow Background* (1941, Art Institute of Chicago) as well as to *Divers II* (1941–42, Museum of Modern Art). In both, the composition of figures is tightly woven in vertical movement through space. In the drawing, a female figure at right swims upward as an adjacent figure plunges downward. As well as these clearly identifiable figures, other limbs, a large hand and a third head fill the void. Linear definition, while present in this work, is secondary to the dramatic chiaroscuro modelling of form, which is characteristic of Léger's 1941 drawings and paintings. Léger's divers inhabit a shallow Cubist space, and their sculptural form resembles a relief, not unlike Matisse's "Backs" series.

The Washington University example represents Léger's drawing style at its strongest. Whatever its relationship to a finished painting, it stands on its own as a signal example of the artist's work in America.

Robert M. Murdock

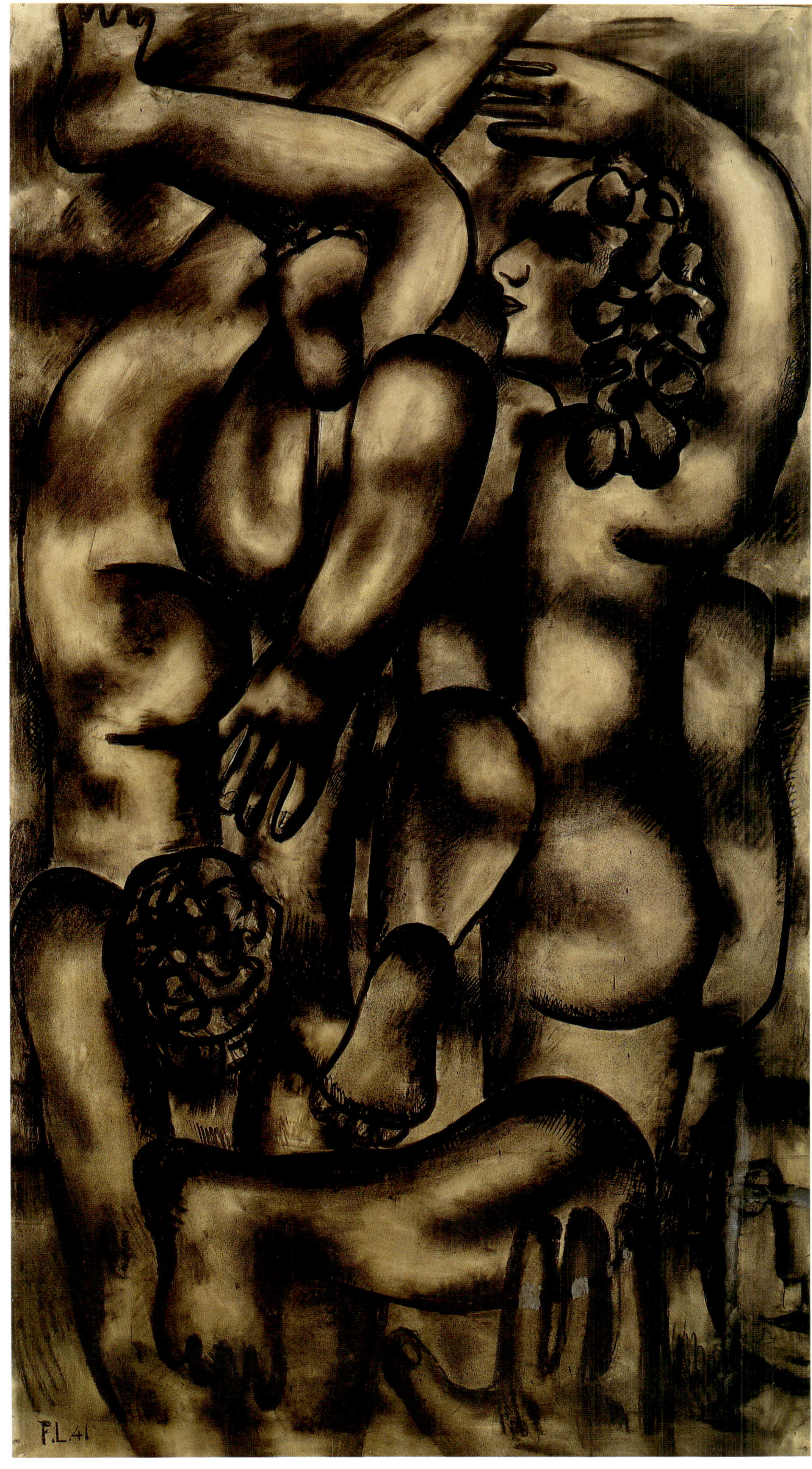
F.L.41

48. Fernand Léger (France, 1881–1955)

Les Belles Cyclistes (The Women Cyclists), 1944
Oil on canvas, 29 x 36"
Gift of Mr. Charles H. Yalem, 1963

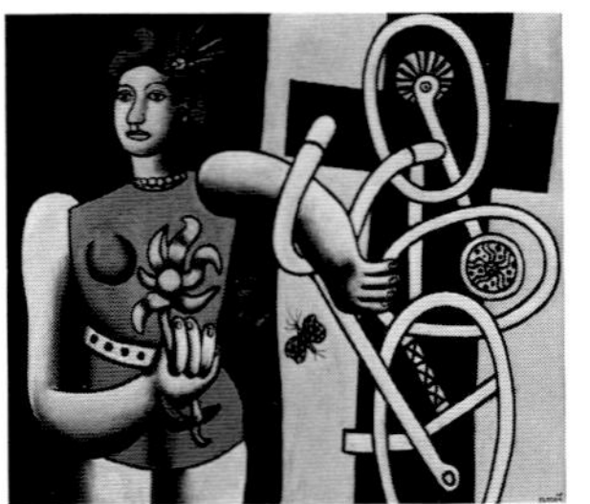

Fernand Léger
Big Julie (La Grand Julie), 1945
Oil on canvas, 44 x 50⅛"
The Museum of Modern Art, New York
Acquired through the Lillie P. Bliss Bequest

If Léger's *Plongeurs* recall Michelangelo and Rubens, his *Cyclistes* series continues the grand tradition of nineteenth- and twentieth-century French figure painting, including Renoir, Seurat, Picasso and Henri Rousseau—scenes of holidays and recreation on an epic scale. As in Rousseau's paintings, which Léger admired, figures stare out at the viewer, immediate and direct, yet curiously detached. The spirit of this subject—a rest stop on a cycling tour—is one of playful relaxation and athletic vigor rather than lassitude. The women are poised, ready to set off again. But in contrast to the rhythmic motion in Léger's *Les Grands Plongeurs, Les Belles Cyclistes* appear static, as if posing for a photograph.

In a frequently quoted statement about the figure in his art, Léger noted that for him a bunch of keys or a bicycle was of equal importance to the figure, in terms of its plastic value. He also acknowledged that in his work since 1905, he had purposely made his figures inexpressive.[1] In *Les Belles Cyclistes* and in related works, Léger does seem to give equal weight to figures, bicycles and abstract elements. Playing upon its inherent structure of curves and straight lines, Léger used the bicycle as a visual device, to unite and anchor the figures in the composition.

Léger began *Les Belles Cyclistes* while he was still working on *Les Grands Plongeurs* and living in New York, where he moved in 1940 and remained until 1946. He had been in the United States on three previous trips, and had responded enthusiastically to American cities, life and culture. What appealed to him was not "high art," but rather folk art and popular culture. In his populist attitude and his desire to create an idealized art for the people, he favored the garish side of American life. In a contemporary statement for the Museum of Modern Art he described his impressions:

> *For me the contrast in the United States between the mechanical and the natural is one of great anti-melodic intensity. But bad taste is also one of the valuable raw materials for the country. Bad taste, strong colors—it is all here for the painter to organize and get the full use of its power. Girls in sweaters with brilliant colored skin; girls in shorts dressed more like acrobats in a circus than one would ever come across on a Paris street. If I had seen only girls dressed in "good taste" here I would have never painted my "Cyclist" series, of which "La Grande Julie" in the Museum [1945] was the culmination.*[2]

Because of gas rationing during the war, cycling had become popular in the United States at that time. Léger's *Cyclistes* undoubtedly arose from observation, as had his *Plongeurs* from seeing swimmers on the docks and on the beach at Marseilles. Léger was obviously captivated by young American women in their colorful shorts and jerseys, which he translated both literally and abstractly in this series.

Cyclistes share formal and physical characteristics with the *Plongeurs,* with massive bodies, intertwined arms, legs and feet, and bold definition of contours. Also present in both series are the seemingly random bands of primary and secondary color. While Léger had used abstract color areas as early as 1912, this complex integration of color shapes with a figure composition was characteristic of his 1940s paintings made in this country.

Léger's swaths of color may have been inspired by New York at night, with neon signs bathing people and surroundings in colored light, which he evoked in this statement:

> *You are in the middle of speaking to someone and suddenly the person you are talking to becomes blue. Then there is a change of color. The blue changes and the person in front of you is red, yellow. This projected color floats free in space. I wanted to achieve the same effect in my pictures.*[3]

Léger's color bars create rhythmic patterns and strong axes, highlighting figures and defining their spatial relationships to each other and to the whole. Perhaps because *Les Belles Cyclistes* are more static, and the modelling more generalized, the color areas seem more assertive than in *Les Grands Plongeurs.*

In the Washington University painting the dominant element is a cross of red and blue, with secondary areas of yellow and green. Above the central figure is a cloud or tree form that seems to disappear behind the red bar and pass in front of the blue one; it serves to lock together the arms of the cross. Relative to the severe geometry of the basic composition, which resembles that of a Constructivist painting, the bicycles, the drapery over the handlebars and the plant in the hand of the seated figure at right, add a more lyrical note. A plant, branch or, in *La Grande Julie,* a flower, is a regular motif in these works. In this and several other related paintings and drawings, the composition consists of four women, as opposed to the *belle equipe* (fine team) subjects which combine male and female figures and bicycles.

Here women stand with their arms on each other's shoulders, and the standing figure at right playfully rests her hand on the head of the seated figure below. The wheels and frames of the bicycles are tightly interlocked with the figures. In the initial state, the composition is identical to that of the Washington University painting, but lacks the superimposed bands of color. In another version from 1944, color bands are curved rather than cruciform, and envelop the figures—two standing and two reclining. In *Les quatre cyclistes (Four Women Cyclists)* (1943–1948, Musée National Fernand Léger, Biot), Léger used the same arrangement of figures as in the St. Louis painting, but freely adapted the color bands. However, in its larger scale, additional detail and more precise delineation, this later work suggests the renewed classicism that occurred in Léger's art after his return to France.[4]

Washington University's work typifies the colorful exuberance of Léger's American period as well as his delight in both physical and popular culture. Yet, it also retains the classical restraint and monumentality that characterize his figure compositions throughout his career.

Robert M. Murdock

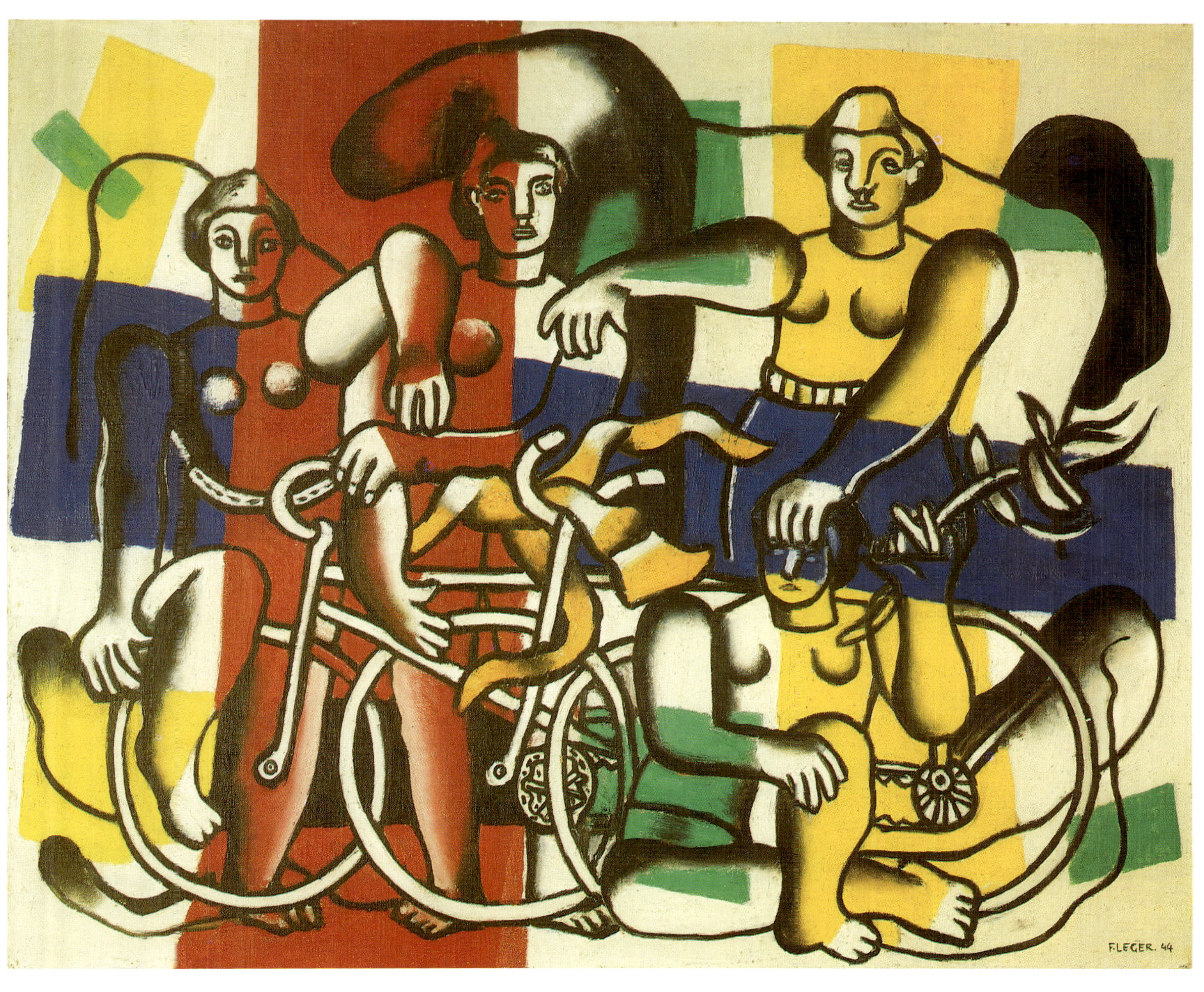
F. LEGER. 44

49. Joan Miró (Spain, 1893–1983)

Joie, 1925

Oil on linen, 39⅝ x 29"
Gift of Mr. and Mrs. Richard K. Weil, 1963

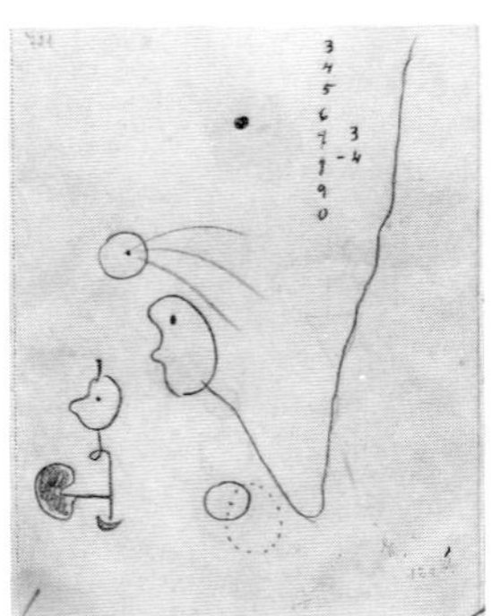

Joan Miró
Preparatory collage for *Joie*
(F.J.M. 721, quadern F.J.M. 697–743)
Fundacio Joan Miró, Barcelona
ARS, New York/ADAGP, Paris

From 1925 to 1927, Miró executed a series of 115 paintings that are distinguished by their washy, monochromatic grounds, oneiric atmospheres, and reduction of the pictorial structure to a few notational elements of line, shape and color.[1] Described by Jacques Dupin as "dream paintings" and by Rosalind Krauss and Margit Rowell as "magnetic fields," this series includes *Joie.*

With an extreme economy of pictorial means, *Joie* challenges the structure of western illusionistic painting. The ground is sized with glue, upon which Miró applied a diluted wash of oil paint which he allowed to seep into the linen support in irregular patterns. The richly variegated surface suggests a boundless and undifferentiated space from which Miró's weightless line and delicate figuration seem to emerge. Stretched across this space like a tightrope, Miró's line defines the minimal contours of a mustachioed bourgeois gentleman wearing a top hat. At the apex of the inverted triangle that establishes the axis of the figure's body is a small circle from which a coiling red form seems to emerge: a sign for the figure's sex or entrails.

The biomorphic form may also have scatological associations. It is related to a sign for excrement in *The Hunter/Catalan Landscape* of 1923–24 (The Museum of Modern Art, New York), ironically calling into question the propriety of the bourgeois gentleman. To the left of the figure is a dotted line—Miró's sign for movement—and a word fragment that relates Miró's investigation of language to the extended verbal puns of Cubist painting. The letters may alternatively be read as adumbrations of "JOIE" (that is to say, joy, thus providing the title of the painting), "JOU" from "JOUER" (to play) or "JOURNAL" (the gentleman's newspaper), and "JOUIR" (to enjoy, but also in sexual argot, to come). Miró's characteristic ambiguity opens a fissure in interpretation, as the viewer negotiates through alternating themes of bourgeois domesticity, scatology, and sexual fulfillment.

Beginning in 1923–24, Miró abandoned the anecdotalism and detailed description that characterized his early work and began to explore an increasingly cryptic language of pictorial signs. In a letter of August 10, 1924, Miró explained to Michel Leiris:

> *I am moving away from all pictorial conventions (that poison). In spreading out my canvases, I have noticed that the ones that have been painted touch the spirit less directly than the ones that are simply drawn (or that use a minimum of color); the intromission of exciting materials (colors), however stripped of pictorial meaning, "shakes up" your blood and the exhalted sensation that "claws" at the soul is ruined. . . . This is hardly painting, but I don't give a damn.*[2]

The formal structure of *Joie* is complex. Freed from its traditional function as descriptive contour, Miró's line is simultaneously spatial marker, sign, surface structure, and writing (the artist's signature may be a later addition). Combining the resources of painting and poetry, Miró defined his work as a form of *écriture* (writing). Sources for the artist's conception of *peinture-poésie* (painting/poetry) have been proposed in the work of Paul Klee (with which Miró was acquainted by 1924); the dual verbal/visual structures of the calligramme, which Apollinaire had reinvented for the twentieth century; and in Symbolist poetry, particularly the works of Rimbaud, Lautréamont, Jarry, and Mallarmé. A more immediate source for Miró's poetic conception of painting as a form of writing is suggested by his friendships with the poets and painters of the *Rue Blomet* group in Paris—André Masson, Michel Leiris, Robert Desnos, Antonin Artaud, and Jacques Prévert—and his involvement with the nascent Surrealist movement.

Miró's artistic relationship with Surrealism is, however, problematic. A member of the movement almost from its inception, Miró adopted the technique of automatism—the unmediated transcription of internal sensations and psychic responses in a process of verbal and/or visual free association—more as a radical method of pictorial construction than as a form of psychic research. In an interview with James Johnson Sweeney in 1948, Miró explained:

> *Forms take reality for me as I work. In other words, rather than setting out to paint something, I begin painting and as I paint the picture begins to assert itself, or suggest itself under my brush. The form becomes a sign for a woman or a bird as I work. Even a few casual wipes of my brush in cleaning it may suggest the beginning of a picture. . . . The first stage is free, unconscious; but after that the picture is controlled throughout. . . .*[3]

Nevertheless, this two-stage process corresponds only in part to the manner in which the "dream paintings" of 1925–27, including *Joie,* were executed. A drawing in Miró's notebook (F. J. M. 721, Fundació Joan Miró, Barcelona) that has been identified as a preparatory sketch for *Joie* belies the artist's later description of his spontaneous process of image formation; the exact composition of the drawing—with the exception of the richly variegated ground—is replicated in the painting.

Robert S. Lubar

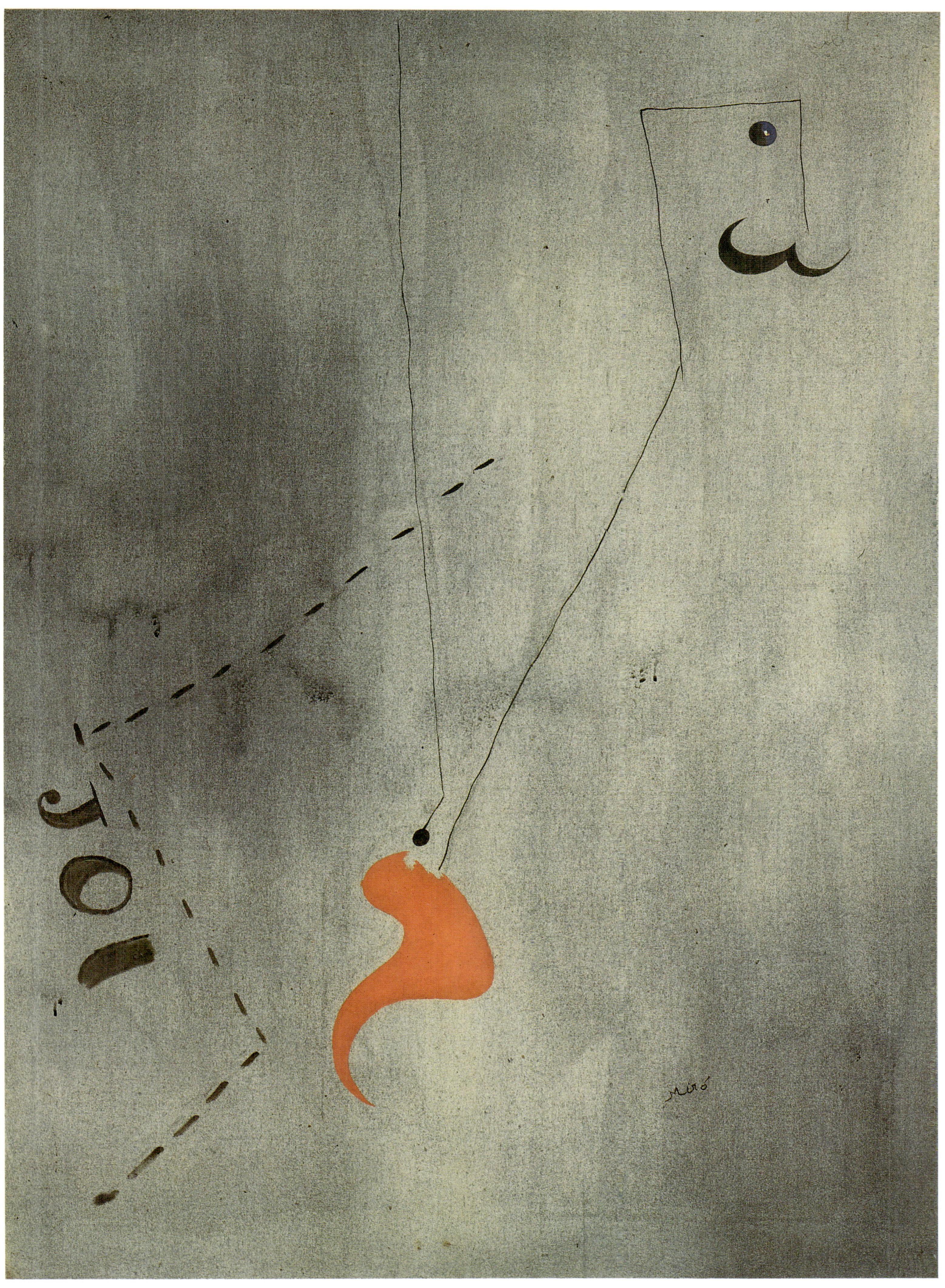
Miró

50. Joan Miró
(Spain, 1893–1983)
Peinture (Painting), 1933

Oil on canvas, 51⅞ x 77¾"
University purchase, Kende Sale Fund, 1945

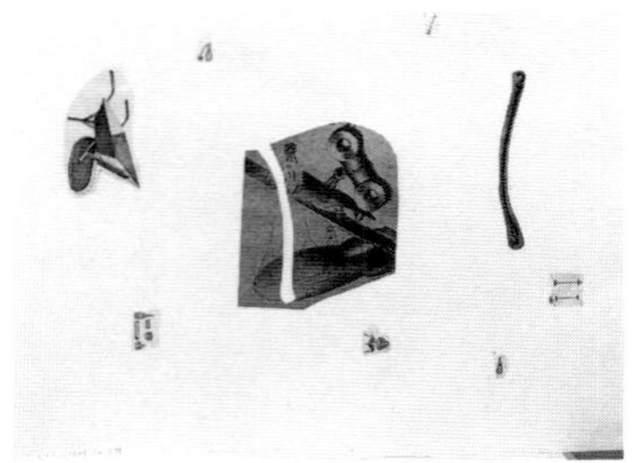

Joan Miró
Preparatory collage for *Peinture*
3 July, 1933 (F.J.M. 1301)
Fundacio Joan Miró, Barcelona
ARS, New York/ADAGP, Paris

This majestic canvas belongs to a group of eighteen paintings, called *Peinture,* that Miró executed between March and June 1933 in the attic of his parents' apartment in Barcelona. Formerly known as *Composition,* Miró disdained such titles for his paintings as he clarified in a letter from 12 October 1934 to his dealer Pierre Matisse: "I give you permission to choose titles based on the real things my works might suggest to you, provided these titles do not evoke some tendency or other, something I want to avoid completely: 'Composition,' for example (which evokes the abstraction-création group), or literary titles in the Surrealist manner."[1] The *Peinture* series is the work of a mature artist in full possession of his skills as a draughtsman and colorist. Compared with the "dream paintings" of 1925–27 and the "Dutch interiors" of 1928, a greater monumentality now enters Miró's art: forms are simplified and arranged in rhythmic compositions of interlocking shapes in constant metamorphosis, and color is flattened and applied in large blocks. The *Peinture* series is stylistically related to a group of paintings on wood from the summer of 1932 in which the artist explored a specifically feminine morphology using large, organic forms and pure, intense hues. Methodologically, the series is also related to the object/sculptures of 1932 and a suite of drawing/collages composed of photographs and postcards from the summer and autumn of 1933.

All the paintings in the series are based on preparatory collages composed of advertisements from sales catalogs for industrial machinery, tools, domestic appliances, and silverware. Seventeen of the collages, including the collage for *Peinture,* are housed in the Fundació Joan Miró in Barcelona (F.J.M. 1301). The entire series of eighteen collages was produced before Miró began work on the individual paintings. In *Peinture,* the biomorph in the upper left, with two semicircular forms protruding like horns, is based on an advertisement for a wheelbarrow. To its right, the white organic form was suggested by a perfume bottle and atomizer. It also recalls the organic concretions of the sculptor Jean Arp, with whom Miró was in close contact. Miró arranged the objects in the preparatory collages without any apparent concern for consistency of size, scale, object type, or classification. Affixed to the walls of his studio, the collages provided the artist with a point of departure for his spontaneous process of image formation.

Collage as an end in itself entered Miró's work in 1928 in a series of Spanish dancers noted for their unorthodox materials (including feathers, asphalt, and sandpaper) and decidedly anti-pictorial spirit. Several of these collages were discussed by Louis Aragon in his essay "La Peinture au défi" ("Challenge to Painting"), published in the catalog of the first major exhibition of collage in Europe at the Galerie Goemans, Paris, 1930. On this occasion, Aragon identified the collages of Miró, Max Ernst, Marcel Duchamp, Pablo Picasso, Francis Picabia, and Salvador Dalí, among others, as mechanisms of disruption that challenged conventional aesthetic norms, and which ushered painting into the uncharted realm of poetic and psychic investigation.

Unlike the collages of 1928, however, Miró transforms his raw materials in *Peinture* into a universe of highly aestheticized, organic, proliferating forms with multiple associations. A tension is maintained between the large fields of diluted color that carve out a deep, recessional space in the painting, and the carefully delineated, solid forms that appear to hover on its surface. As forms collide in this weightless universe, contours merge and areas of color are altered or exchanged. The constant mutability of Miró's figuration is analogized with the process of spontaneous association that initially gave rise to the signs.

Although Miró gave full reign to the suggestive play of forms in *Peinture,* he remained opposed to the notion of abstraction as an end in itself. "For me a form is never something abstract," Miró commented to James Johnson Sweeney. "It is always a sign of something. It is always a man, a bird, or something else. For me painting is never form for form's sake."[2] Nevertheless, just as a specific object may occasionally assert itself in *Peinture*—an ideogram for a figure or an animal—it also seems to dissolve before its identity can be firmly fixed. To this end, the theme of the eighteen paintings that constitute the series *Peinture* is genesis and metamorphosis. Miró's subject has been likened to the primitive conception of a dynamic, non-causal universe in constant flux, a space without boundaries in which objects and images circulate freely.

Robert S. Lubar

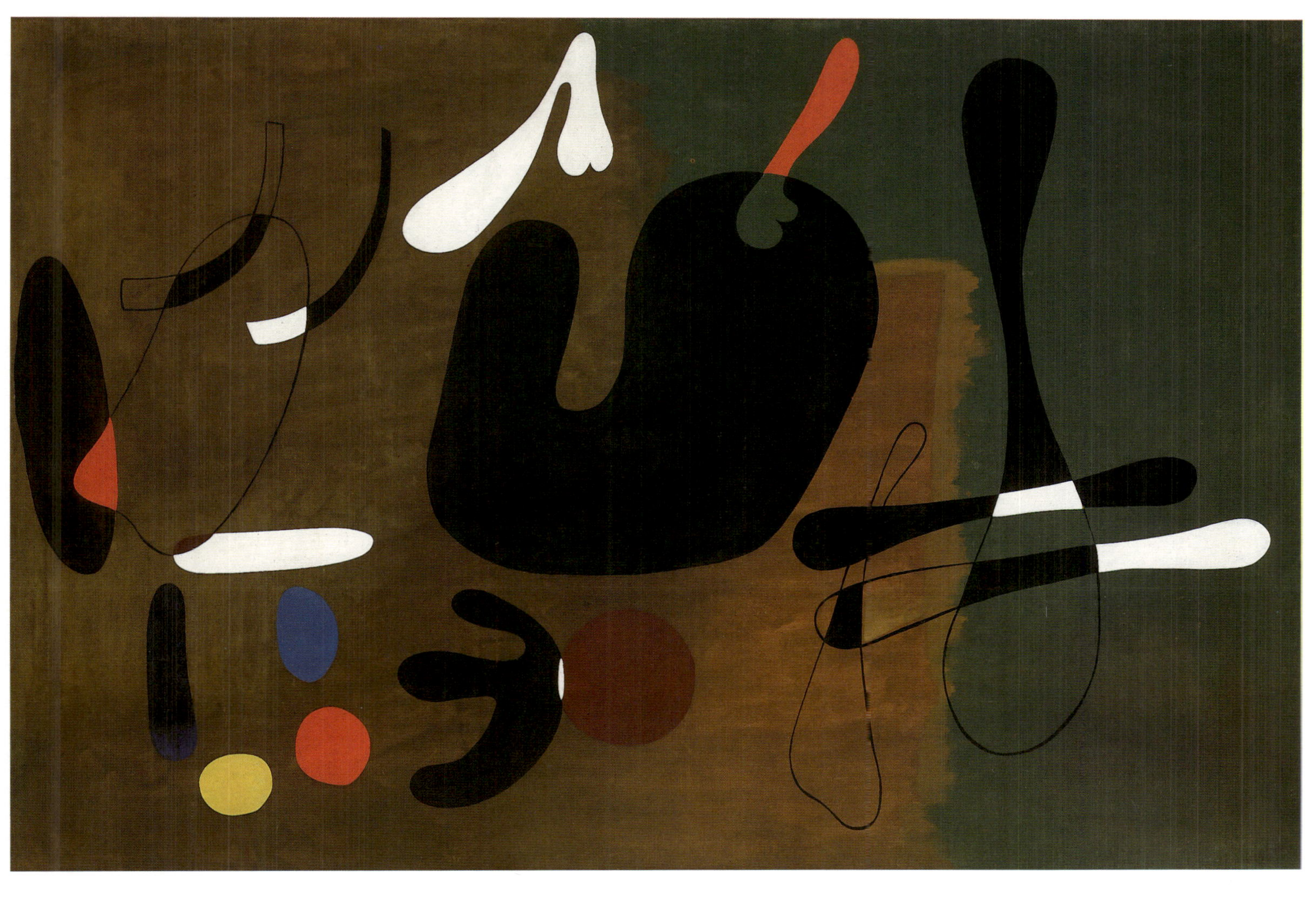

51. Max Ernst
(Germany, 1891–1976)
The Eye of Silence, 1943–44

Oil on canvas, 42½ x 55½"
University purchase, Kende Sale Fund, 1946

One of Horst W. Janson's most significant purchases in 1946 was Max Ernst's *The Eye of Silence,* acquired from the artist's friend and New York dealer Julian Levy. Ernst had been an active member of the European avant-garde since the appearance of his early Dada collages and paintings made just after World War I through his important role in the development of Surrealism in Paris during the 1920s, 1930s and beyond. *The Eye of Silence* is one of the most highly-regarded paintings in a series of animated landscapes begun in the late 1930s, and it is a powerful restatement of the major symbolic themes of the individual, myth, and nature that recurred throughout the artist's work.[1] The painting presents a view of a lone woman reclining by the shore of a lake surrounded by fantastic formations of plants, faces, animals, columns and towers overgrown by a plant-like web of indeterminate character that binds the forms into a frozen mass.

Max Ernst was a self-taught artist and perhaps this lack of formal training allowed him the freedom to explore new and unconventional techniques to accomplish his artistic ends. Ernst manipulated images to produce visual shocks and dislocations that evoked the mystery and psychic power of dreams and stimulated the mind and emotions of his viewers. He explored technical processes that used the element of pure chance to liberate the same powers in the artist.[2] In *The Eye of Silence* Ernst used a technique known as décalcomania, which was developed in 1935 by his Surrealist colleague, Oscar Dominguez. In the décalcomania process, a thin layer of paint is applied to a smooth surface, such as a piece of glass, which is then pressed onto the surface of the painting. As the artist shifts the piece of glass and then removes it, the paint is smeared into an elaborate series of chance patterns that add a compelling element of visual texture and depth. Peering into the designs, Ernst discovered the nascent forms of animals, plants, and architectural elements that make up the phantasmagoric landscape of a living jungle.[3]

Ernst's powerful inner vision is based on a shifting sense of identity that reflects the inter-connectedness of the world. The artist consciously pursued this goal as his images were defined and re-defined in a process of deliberate ambiguity.[4] The ambiguity of the images in *The Eye of Silence* is reflected in the title, a mixed metaphor of sight and sound. In fact, the ambiguities of the entire composition are enhanced by the dramatic contrast between the foreground, an unfamiliar world of dreams, and the backdrop of a realistically rendered sky with dark storm clouds.

The visual ambiguities within *The Eye of Silence* are expressed in the forms that rise from the shore of the lake. On the right edge of the painting a statuesque form strongly resembling a tree at first glance seems to rise from a trunk-like column with branches and foliage. However, the two arched side supports, obscured by décalcomania patterns in green and yellow, also suggest the ruins of an ancient stone aqueduct. The green-yellow wall that occupies the mid-ground presents an even more complex assortment of forms. The center of the wall is dominated by a half-formed face with a spiral nose, a small, smiling mouth and a dull red eye framed by a curved cheekbone and heavy eyebrow. The left edge of the wall is formed by the profile view of a giant bull's head complete with curving horns, massive brow and opaque, sightless eye. The bull's head is a reference to the mythical Minotaure, a bull-headed, human-bodied monster that guarded the labyrinth.[5] Along the left edge of the painting another series of walls and formations rises precipitously. The darker sections on the left show elements of masonry and arches that recall ancient, overgrown ruins. The entire formation, including the rocky foreground connected to it, is enriched by lacy décalcomania patterns and dull, round red and blue spheres that dot the landscape with ever-vigilant yet sightless eyes.

A red-skirted woman wearing a mantle of leaves reclines on the lower right shore of a still, cold mountain lake whose unknown depths are hinted at by the reflections of the central wall that climbs vertically from its rear shore. The woman tilts her head and looks down, quietly waiting, both a witness to and an element of the larger ambiance of ambiguity and mystery. Ernst pursued the theme of the individual in nature through the 1920s and 1930s in such well-known works as *Nature at Dawn* (1938, Dorothea Tanning) and the *Nymph Echo* (1937, private collection, Paris) that depicted haunting forest environments populated with anthropomorphic figures and birds.[6] The theme had great emotional significance for the artist that was based on traumatic childhood experiences involving his family which he later expressed in autobiographical essays.[7] In the 1940s the theme of the interconnectedness of nature was expressed in a long series of works that relied on an increasingly dominant use of the décalcomania technique. Such important works as *Fascinating Cypress* (1940, private collection), *Europe After the Rain* (1940–42, Wadsworth Atheneum), and *Totem and Taboo* (1941, private collection, New York) continued the artist's preoccupation with this theme.

These paintings of the early 1940s and *The Eye of Silence* are documents of the artist's personal traumas during World War II. Ernst was arrested in September of 1939 as a German alien living in France and was interned in three prisons and detention camps before escaping to the United States with the help of Peggy Guggenheim and other friends.[8] Unlike most of the artistic political refugees who stayed in New York, Ernst explored the United States and so added to his experience of this country and especially its landscape and native peoples. In the summer of 1943 he and his new wife, American painter Dorothea Tanning, summered in Arizona where they returned to live three years later. Ernst began *The Eye of Silence* on that trip and finished it in 1944 when they stayed with their friend and dealer Julian Levy at his house on Long Island.

The Eye of Silence is one of the last of the brooding and menacing scenes that marked the end of the dislocations and horrors of the war. In the years to follow Max Ernst again restated the central themes of these works but with a new vision of lightness and hope.

Evan M. Maurer

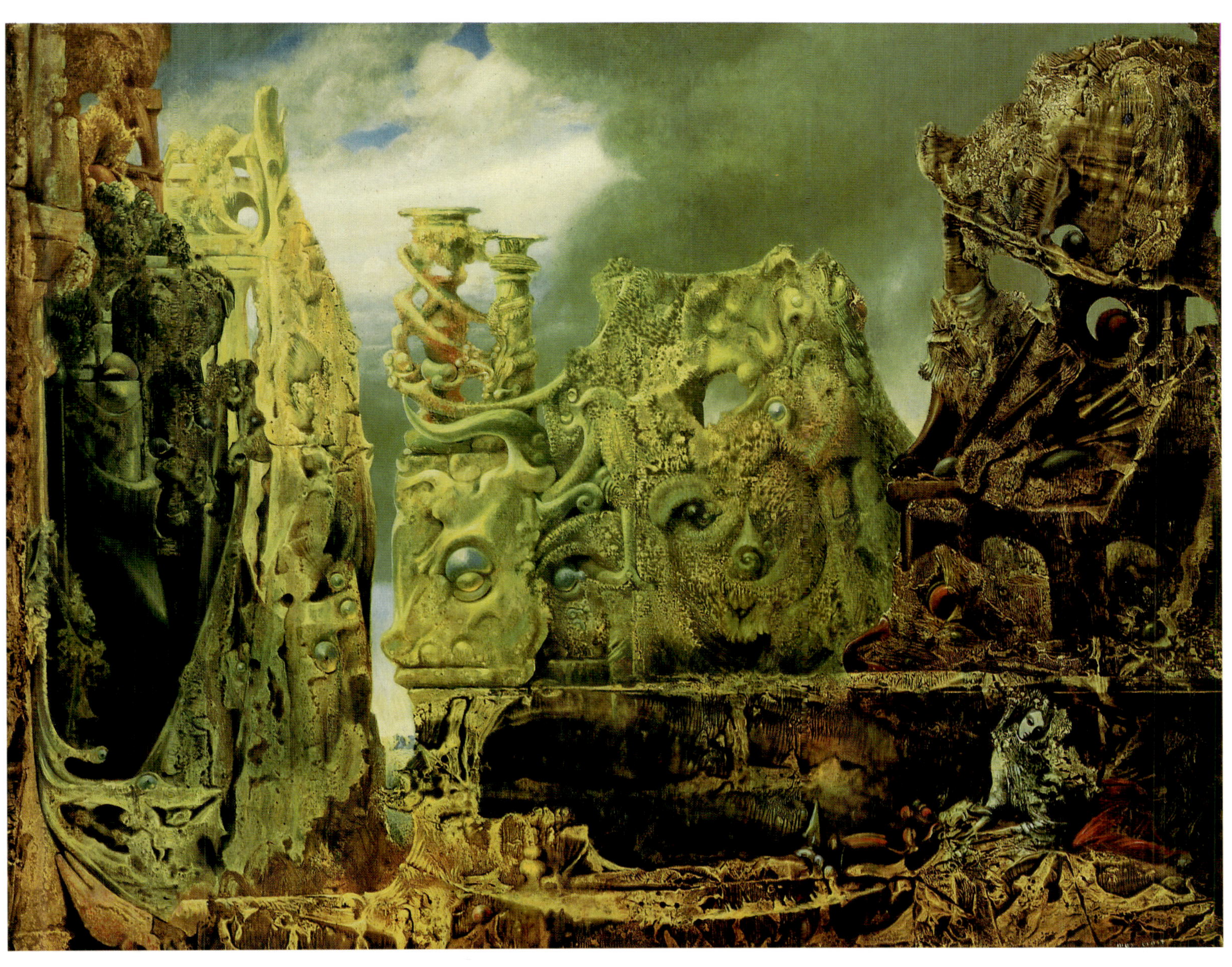

52. Yves Tanguy
(United States, b. France, 1900–1955)
La Tour marine (Tower of the Sea), 1944

Oil on canvas, 36 x 13¾"
University purchase, Kende Sale Fund, 1946

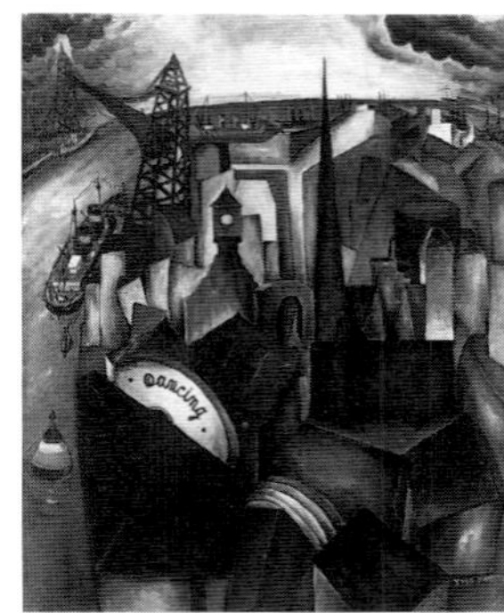

Yves Tanguy
Untitled (Dancing), c. 1925
Oil on canvas, 24 x 19½"
Private collection
Photograph courtesy Pierre Matisse Foundation, New York
ARS, New York/ADAGP, Paris

Yves Tanguy, a self-taught painter, joined the Surrealist movement in 1925 and remained one of its most loyal members until the mid 1940s. He was encouraged to use automatic techniques to explore his subconscious by Surrealism's founder, André Breton. By the late 1920s, Tanguy's paintings had evolved into extra-terrestrial landscapes, where strange bone-rock forms ritually interact in luminous, translucent spaces suggesting an amalgam of earth, air, and sea.

In *La Tour marine*, the viewer stands below, accenting the confrontational sharp angularity of the mechano-morphic figure which is compressed and brought forward by its narrow vertical framework. Only a hint of Tanguy's earlier intense chemical colors remain, in the cinnamon red stone shape anchored between two triangles at the back of the figure and repeated in the smaller ovoid forms in the foreground, reminiscent of the object-toys in de Chirico's paintings.[1] Otherwise, the greyish-white translucency of Tanguy's palette has transformed the figure-tower into a cold, metallic cloth-like substance consistent with the menacing, icicle sharp triangular forms of the upper portion. Formal echoes of the recent past are present in comparison to *Vers le nord lentement (Slowly toward the North)* (1942, The Museum of Modern Art, New York), and in *Le Palais aux rochers de fenêtres (The Palace of Windowed Rocks)* (1942, Musée National d'Art Moderne, Paris). However, *La Tour marine*, completed in July 1944, is the first known Tanguy painting where the cool palette and sharp angularity prefigure his work of the late 1940s and early 1950s.

La Tour marine dates from Tanguy's early American years. Arriving in New York in December of 1939, Tanguy and his wife, artist Kay Sage, spent two years in Greenwich Village, which Tanguy described as "the most infernal city in the world."[2] In 1941 they moved to Woodbury, Connecticut where they were neighbors of Calder, Masson, and Gorky. Throughout Tanguy's American period, his work was commissioned and exhibited by his childhood friend Pierre Matisse. *La Tour marine* was shown at the Matisse Gallery in 1944.

Evidence suggests that Tanguy's state of mind during his American period was one of increasing loneliness and isolation from his roots in Brittany and Paris. In the early 1940s he wrote to André Breton of his terrible feelings of separation and alienation from American life. In September 1944, three months after completing *La Tour marine*, Tanguy wrote to Breton of being demoralized by the inability to publish a series of drawings he had been working on for a year. In July of 1946, he wrote to artist Jacques Hérold: "I do not live in an ivory tower but almost on a desert isle, go to New York as little as possible, work just what I have to maybe a little less."[3]

The theme of a tower connected to the sea in *La Tour marine* is a theme that is repeated throughout the work of this poet-painter.[4] In an untitled painting of circa 1925 (Pierre Matisse collection, New York), a circle of dark blue sea and a series of boats surround a jutting conglomerate of building forms where tower images predominate. To the left is the sharp conical shape that remains an insistent image throughout Tanguy's lifetime. Beside it is a smaller church tower, reminiscent of the fifteenth-century one that still dominates Tanguy's seaside home of Locronan in Brittany. At the edge of Tanguy's imaginary peninsula is a precariously leaning Eiffel Tower-like form that serves as a bridge connecting land to water. Similar tower forms are found in such paintings as *La Fille aux cheveux rouges (The Girl with Red Hair)* (1926, Pierre Matisse, New York), *Le Phare (The Lighthouse)* (1926, private collection, France), and *Genèse (Genesis)* (1926, private collection, France). In *Genèse* a female figure walks a tightrope past such Surrealist symbols as a hand holding a match stick emerging from behind a cloud-like grassy hillock to her destination at the pinnacle of a phallic-like tower.[5]

A major source for the interior universe created by Tanguy is the ancient Celtic traditions of Brittany. From his home in Locronan, an ancient druidical center in the isolated western tip of Brittany, Tanguy could look out over the wide expanse of the Bay of Douarneznez where crystalline light from the endless horizon merges sand, sea and sky. As a child Tanguy would have heard the famous Celtic myth of the mysterious city of "Y's," which, according to legend, sunk beneath the bay of Douarneznez. Fishermen were said to sometimes catch glimpses of its ramparts, palaces, and churches. He would have seen the giant, phallic-shaped menhirs, relics of the Bronze Age, such as the 150-ton menhir of Kerloas at Plouarzel which looms like a tower in a copse of low bushes. It is believed that the ancient menhirs of Brittany were part of a druidical tradition, a tradition where the distinction between matter and non-matter, between life and death is different from western Christian beliefs. These beliefs were passed down through the centuries to Tanguy's generation in the Legends of the Dead. Like the being-objects in Tanguy's paintings, the Celtic gods are not understood in human form because of the continuous flow of life into a non-material Otherworld that is as real as life on earth.[6]

More than any other surrealist artist, Tanguy used the automatist techniques which allow the unconscious mind to direct the hand in a state of free association. He drew the figures directly on the canvas with no previous underdrawing and he often deliberately painted his canvases upside down to expel any intrusion of external reality.[7] His long, thin brush created forms of microscopic precision. He rendered the figures with a supra-real intensity, an intensity simultaneously denied by their non-reality in any recognizable living form. This intense visual contradiction produces the effect the Surrealists call "the marvelous." André Breton described Tanguy's paintings as "the words of a language we have not yet heard, but a language we shall soon read and speak." And in the words of poet John Ashbery, "he was perhaps the Poussin of the same inner landscape of which Pollock was the Turner."[8]

Susan Nessen

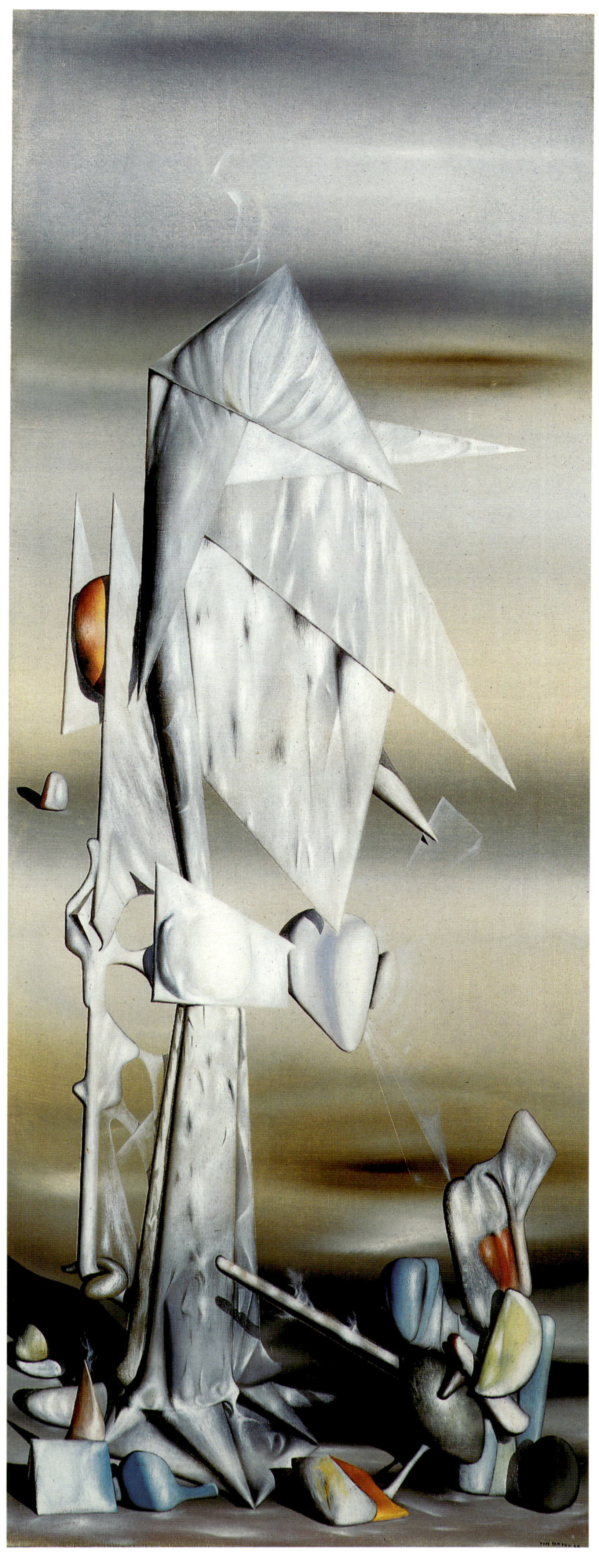

53. Roberto Sebastián Antonio Echaurren Matta (France, b. Chile, 1912)

Glimmer of Violence, 1958

Oil on canvas, 57¾ x 44⅞"
Gift of Mr. Joseph Pulitzer, Jr., 1962

A characteristic example of his mature style, *Glimmer of Violence* summarizes Matta's artistic and intellectual interests of the preceding two decades. Born to a prestigious Chilean family of European background, Matta had initially studied architecture in Santiago. In 1935 he emigrated to Paris, where he worked under Le Corbusier for two years. Profoundly influenced by the evocative writings of Federico García Lorca, Pablo Neruda, and Gabriela Mistral in 1936, Matta soon abandoned architecture for art. Joining the Surrealists in 1937, he espoused their emphasis on the subconscious and use of automatist method. He quickly developed a biomorphic, at times visceral, imagery intended to express the turbulent power of the psyche. Sometimes entitled *Psychological Morphologies,* his early paintings were intended as abstract equivalents for mental and emotional states, often in the process of chaotic evolution.[1]

Like his colleagues Yves Tanguy and Max Ernst, Matta fled the war to the United States, where he remained from late 1939 until 1948. Settling in New York, he created a series of paintings that suggest primal forces of cosmic creation and destruction; during the early 1940s they often resembled a volcanic landscape with land erupting and sky melting. Interested in both scientific and esoteric fields of knowledge, he studied physics, chemistry, non-Euclidean space, the tarot, and the mystical writings of Eliphas Levi, among others. Matta's paintings were created as metaphors for a limitless, unspecific mental or spiritual space, usually suffused with astral light (which Matta expressed in colors ranging from translucent silver-gray to high-keyed hues of yellow, orange, pink, blue, and green).

Matta's presence in New York during the 1940s provided a crucial catalyst for the development of Abstract Expressionist painting. As the youngest expatriate Surrealist and the most fluent in English, he enthusiastically shared with American artists his automatist techniques and fascination with constantly evolving processes. His spontaneous gesturalism and belief in the evocative power of abstraction directly affected the art of Arshile Gorky, Robert Motherwell, William Baziotes, Jackson Pollock, Peter Busa, and others.

Around 1945–48, affected by the horrors of the war, Matta began to populate his vast voids with androgynous, anonymous, quasi-robotic figures, huddled together or separated by labyrinthine partitions. Vaguely resembling the victims of nuclear holocaust or the androids of science fiction, these disturbing figures were partly inspired by other works of art in Matta's personal collection, including Native American hybrid-creature carvings and Alberto Giacometti's sculpture *Hands Holding the Void* (1934–35, Yale University Art Gallery). In *Glimmer of Violence* the figures cluster as if in consultation or confrontation; their transparent or stripped flesh partially exposes their skeletons (ribs in one figure, pelvis in another). The composition suggests a sense of alienation and tension, of past or potential violence, of external forces beyond the figures' control (suggested by the surging blade-like form in vivid yellow and the slashing strokes of paint in the peripheral areas). These effects reflect the artist's conviction that art serves as a kind of "internal warfare," and he described his paintings of this period in terms of their personal and social implications:

> *I was attempting to use a social morphology, not a personal psycho-morphology: to move away from the intimate, imaginary forms of the vertebrates, unknown animals and rare flowers which expressed my feelings, toward the cultural, totemic expressions of civilizations. Whilst remaining in the laws of morphology, this was no longer a matter of the formation of an organism symbolizing myself, rather the formation of cultures in confrontation with social landscapes: battlefields where feelings and ideas were pitted against each other. Everything ended up in a whirlwind where the ego and the world engaged in conflict on an almost cosmic level.*[2]

Despite growing success with exhibitions at the Pierre Matisse Gallery, Matta returned to Europe in 1948. Breaking away from the Surrealists, he rejected limiting definitions of his art—henceforth he had no single nationality and his art officially belonged to no group or movement. An expatriate for more than fifty-five years, Matta has divided his time between Italy and France, with regular visits to England, Spain and Latin America.

In addition to painting prolifically, often on a monumental scale, he also made sculptures and prints during the 1950s–70s. During the 1980s his paintings gained a fresh vitality, as Matta moved away from figurative subjects to more cosmic allusions.

Valerie J. Fletcher

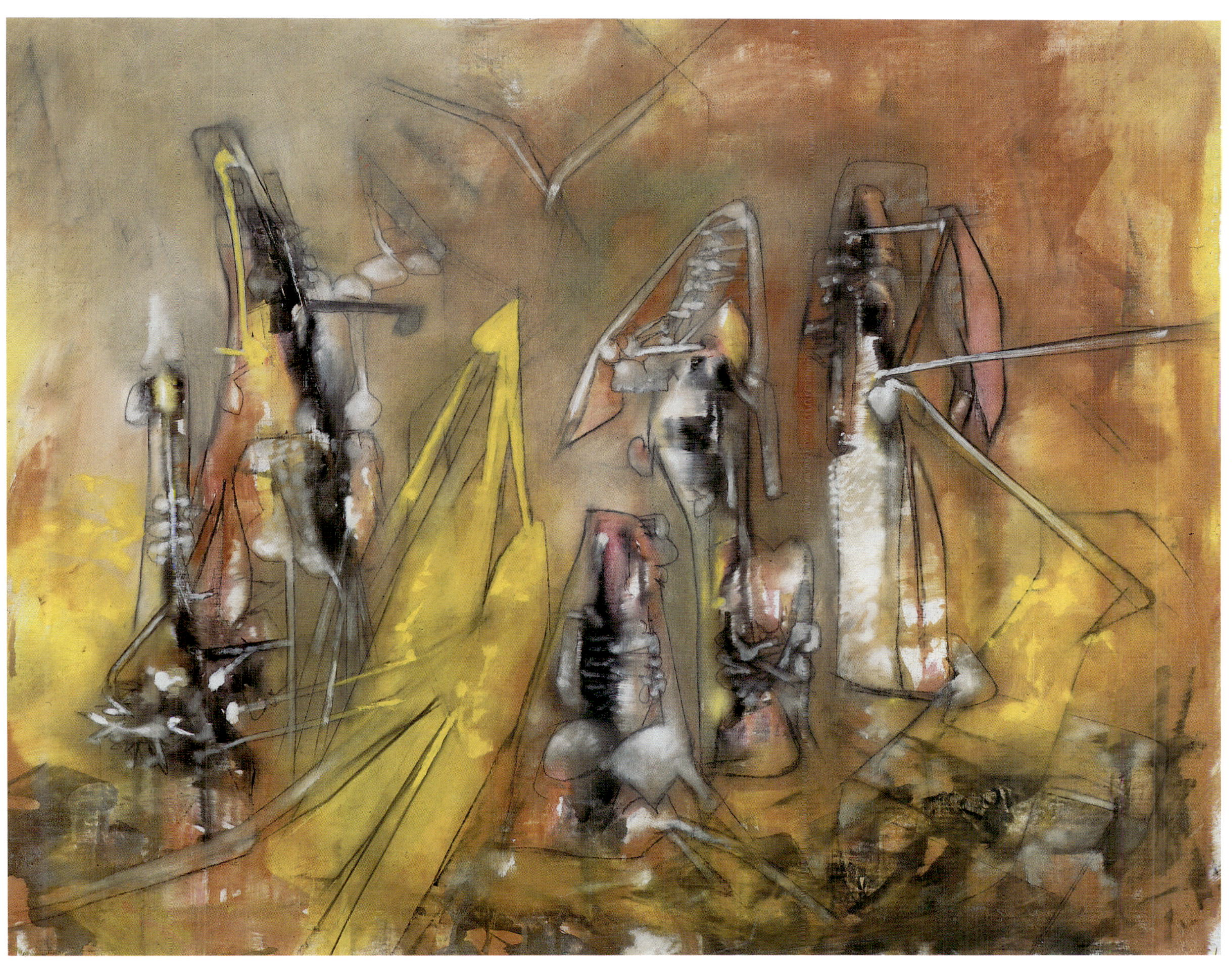

54. Henry Moore
(United Kingdom, 1898–1986)
Reclining Figure, 1933

Reinforced carved concrete, 20¼ x 31½ x 12¼"
University purchase, Kende Sale Fund, 1946

During his student years at the Royal College of Art in London in the early 1920s, Henry Moore rejected the approved curriculum founded on canons of beauty rooted in the Italian Renaissance. Stimulated by the writings of such champions of avant-garde art in England as Roger Fry and Ezra Pound, the young Moore discovered for himself principles of form, design, and composition in the rich and varied traditions of ancient, non-western, and so-called primitive cultures. All were accessible to him through the encyclopedic collections of the British Museum, and his sketch notebooks from the period document his fascination with these unfamiliar, exotic, and for Moore, formally and aesthetically liberating objects. Whereas the non-western sculptural traditions were fundamental to the artist's own sculptural development in the late 1920s, between 1931 and 1934 he responded to new sources in French Surrealist art, above all in the works of Hans (Jean) Arp and Alberto Giacommetti.

Moore included *Reclining Figure* (1933) in the first major manifestation of Surrealism in England, the *International Surrealist Exhibition,* held in June 1936 at the New Burlington Galleries, London, comprising 390 works by sixty-eight exhibitors from fourteen countries.[1] Although a member of the organizing committee, Moore was participating in other group exhibitions at the time, such as *Unit One* in 1934 and *7 x 5* in 1935, devoted to constructive and geometric abstract tendencies in modern British art.[2] The sculptor himself never felt entirely absorbed into either modernist direction, as he wrote in 1937: "The violent quarrel between the abstractionists and the surrealists seems to me quite unnecessary. All good art has contained both abstract and surrealist elements, just as it has contained both classical and romantic elements—order and surprise, intellect and imagination, conscious and unconscious. Both sides of the artist play their part. . . ."[3]

The theme of the reclining figure (with one exception) first appeared in the artist's drawings and sculpture in 1924, and remained a privileged motif through more than sixty years of sculptural activity, one that Moore has termed "an absolute obsession."[4] Washington University's sculpture represents a turning away from the artist's previous conception of the body as a solid, unitary form where the mass of the carved stone matrix dominated the final configuration. By the early 1930s, Moore was no longer representing the figure at rest so much as experimenting with variations on the theme, rich in metaphoric possibilities. Through simplification, reduction, distortion, and displacement of human body parts and their inventive reconstruction, he played with the idea of the reclining figure rather than simply the motif itself. Here the underlying premise of a supine female is retained, but the degree of abstraction has disassociated the figure from the natural world to establish a fantastic view of Woman.

The basic composition of Washington University's sculpture recalls the slightly earlier *Reclining Figure* (1930, National Gallery of Canada, Ottawa), notably in the upturned, exaggerated breasts and the splayed, raised knees, as well as the rooting of the body on a solid plinth. But where the earlier piece retains the familiar enclosed contour and block-like solidity found in his other sculptures of the period, the latter piece exhibits a more open form and assymetrical pose through the prevalent use of holes that detach arms and legs from the core of the body. The resulting anatomically untenable figure is further deconstructed by the reduction of head, hands, and feet to organic protuberances, as well as by the addition of three strut-like extensions that link torso and thighs. Technically, these modifications—the breakdown of the solidity of the core of the piece—were made possible by the choice of reinforced concrete over natural stone. Adhering to his principals of "truth to material" and "significant form," Moore wrote of the present sculpture: "It was done after doing several other pieces in concrete which did not satisfy me as being quite right for their material. But this figure I think does make a 'form' use of the unique possibilities of reinforced concrete—that is, it's a mixture of thinner and pointed and tubular composition (which metal reinforcement allows) with the hard stone-like finish of carving (for concrete is an artificial stone and so can have the qualities of stone finish)."[5]

The influence of French Surrealism is particularly evident in the biomorphic body where volumes have become more fluid, establishing a contrapostal articulation of compressed and stretched elements, tensed and relaxed masses, and the modulation of space as a three-dimensional agent. Recalling the amorphous sculpture of Arp or ameboid shapes in Joan Miró's paintings of the early 1930s, the smooth, highly reduced, curvilinear forms suggest the organic flow of elusive microscopic or cosmic life forces. The bundle of rods that connect torso and legs in *Reclining Figure* repeats a similar motif found in Giacommetti's 1929 plaster *Reclining Woman Who Dreams* (Hirshhorn Museum and Sculpture Garden, Washington, D.C.). Although there is a formal kinship, Moore may have arrived at his organic formulations independently in his "transformation" drawings of 1932, in which he began by sketching the natural forms of shell, pebble, or bone and then proceded to alter the organic shapes into human forms through a process of free association.

Rooted in the classical Mediterranean tradition of the recumbent river gods, personifications of nature's flowing energy, and filtered through Moore's encounters in the mid-1920s with Renaissance statuary and Toltec-Mayan sculptures, the subject of the reclining figure was transformed in the early 1930s into a metaphor for landscape, in which the reclining female body assumes the contours and rhythms of a mountain range. The free-flowing, allusive shapes and open, receptive pose of *Reclining Figure* furthermore suggest the fecundity of Woman as a life-giving natural force. In essence, Moore arrived at a machine-age equivalent of the paleolithic "Venus" fertility cult figurines he saw as part of a universal world language of sculpture.[6]

Richard A. Born

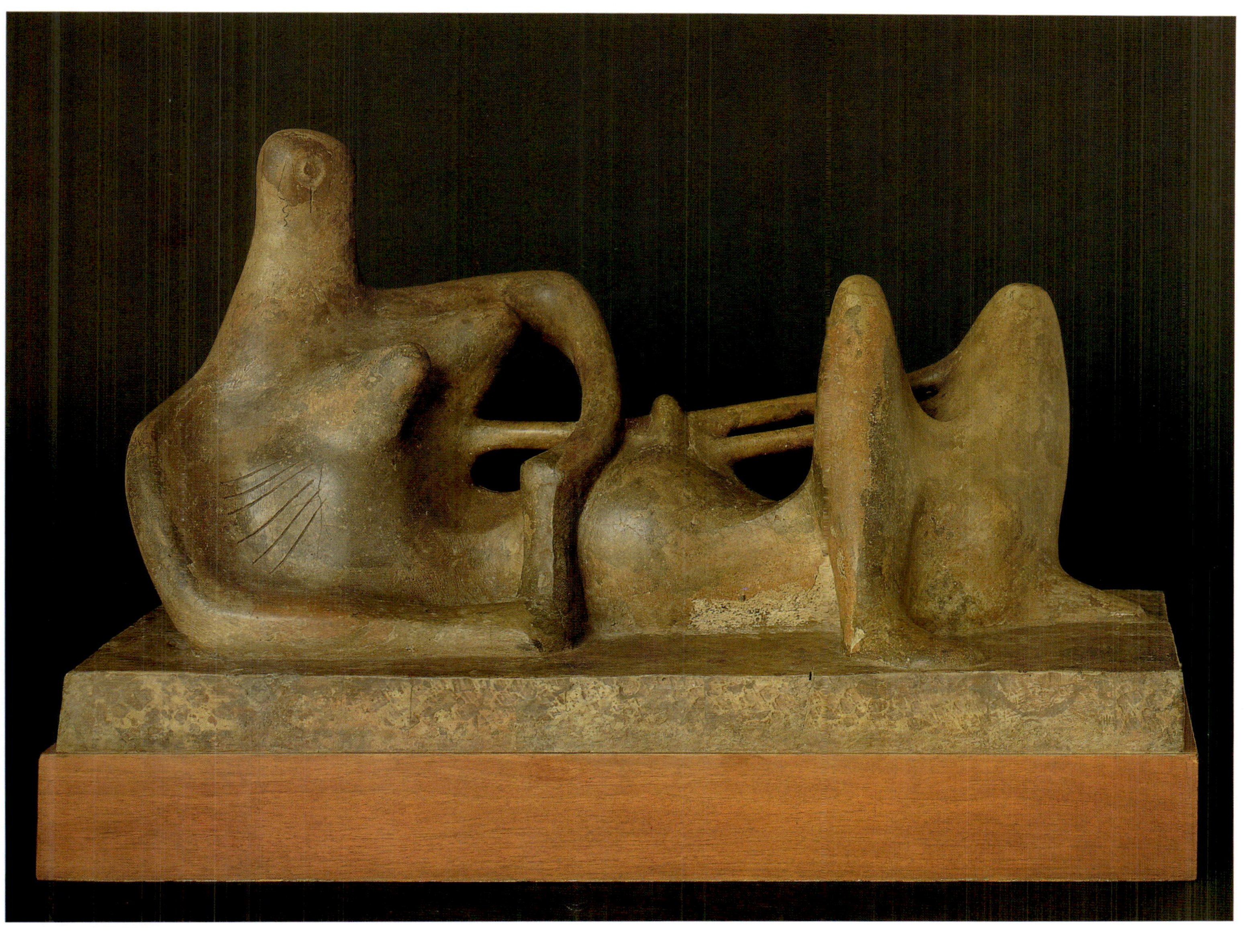

55. Nicolas de Staël (France, b. Russia, 1914–1955)

Composition, 1946

Oil on canvas, 61 x 32"
Gift of Mr. & Mrs. Richard K. Weil, 1966

Though Russian by birth, Nicolas de Staël was brought up in Brussels and in 1938 made his principal home in Paris.[1] Having been forced by the Revolution to flee St. Petersburg with his family in 1919, he subsequently lost both his parents by the age of seven. De Staël's short life was fraught with extremes of tragedy and good fortune, circumstances which buffeted his passionate and sensitive nature sufficiently to cause him to take his own life at the age of forty-one. Always independent in his life and his art, he charted a complex course in his mature work, compressing a prolific career into little more than a decade.

Both de Staël's personal struggle as an artist as well as the tension and uncertainty of immediately post-war Paris are reflected in the artist's work of the mid-1940s. Although he pointedly denied any subject matter in the paintings of this period and the majority bear the generic title "Composition," the works are nevertheless intensely expressive.[2] 1946 represented a turning point for de Staël, away from personal tragedy and deprivation toward greater security and good fortune. With the death in February 1946 of Jeannine Guillou, his constant companion of more than eight years who had born his first child only four years before, de Staël not only married Françoise Chapouton in May of that year but also began to receive his first financial encouragement from dealer Louis Carré, with whom he made an informal contract, and Jacques Dubourg (later his principal dealer), who bought his first painting by de Staël that year.

During 1946 de Staël worked slowly, producing approximately 26 to 27 paintings.[3] In general his work from the mid to late 1940s is thickly painted and sombre in hue, in marked contrast to his work of the 1950s, which is more often brilliant in color and increasingly thinly painted. *Composition* (1946), while characteristically built up in layers of paint, reveals a relatively large portion of light tonalities. Although the artist favored the brush over the palette knife until 1949, here the work's highly textured surface, especially in the upper portion of the composition (the brown and black passages), is probably due to dragging partially dried medium across the surface of the canvas, in some cases across areas of paint not yet fully dry, endowing the painting with a physical presence further developed by de Staël's later use of the palette knife.[4] Bright color emerges from underlayers of paint, deliberately allowed to show along the edges of subsequent layers in a manner typical of the work of this period. Because the bright passages tend to advance visually, the entire composition locks together, creating a dichotomy between the physical depth of the painted surface and the shallowness of the pictorial space. The artist has built up the layers of paint in between in subtle relations of tertiary hues, ranging from greys to putty green, pale rose, and beige—a palette confirming his admiration at this time for the work of his friend and mentor Georges Braque, as well as for Corot, Velasquez and early Dutch masters.

De Staël's compositions of the mid-1940s tend to be dynamic and characterized by conflicting forces, reflecting the artist's dominant concern with pictorial structure as well as his state of mind at the time. Later in the 1940s, as greater stability entered his life, de Staël's work simultaneously reflected an unprecedented calm. In the case of Washington University's painting, the whole composition is unified by a spare surface calligraphy—black strokes sweeping diagonally across the canvas, reinforcing some of the existing rhythms in the paint surface and offering a counterpoint to others. One unusual aspect of this painting lies in the passages of solid uninterrupted paint surface in the lower corners of the composition, particularly in the lower left where a warm grey hue overlies red passages which lend a rosy glow to the surface. This setting off of the dense network of de Staël's central composition lends the image a figural aspect enhanced by the overplay of long diagonals. In this regard the work suggests comparison with *De la danse* (1946, Musée National d'Art Moderne, Paris), which in its size and composition implies a relationship on a human scale, engaging the viewer physically. Inasmuch as *Composition* (1946) and de Staël's work of the mid-1940s in general represent a conscious move away from pure abstraction, both the artist's struggle for existence as well as the surge of optimism that he felt at this time come through in this painting.

The optimism that de Staël felt in 1946 might in large part be attributed not only to his new marriage and improved financial circumstances but also to his friendship of two years with Braque and Jean Bauret, a businessman who collected de Staël's work and once owned this painting. For de Staël, Braque, thirty-two years his senior, was "le plus grand des peintres vivants de çe monde" (the greatest living painter in the world) and the younger artist benefited greatly from his move in 1947 into a studio around the corner from Braque.[5] Clearly Braque encouraged in de Staël the use of a rich palette and a painterly surface as well perhaps as a growing response to the visible world in his work. Both Braque and Bauret continued to play critical roles in de Staël's life, offering inspiration, support and encouragement. During the war years, when materials were hard to obtain, Bauret provided de Staël with canvas in exchange for paintings. When the artist moved away from his abstract mode of the 1940s into landscape, still life and the figure in the 1950s, causing some artists and dealers to change their view of de Staël, Bauret continued to admire and collect his work. Critical support of this kind was more essential to de Staël than the sudden and tremendous success of his work, both in the United States as well as in France and England, in the 1950s.

As one of the most famous French painters of his generation, de Staël became extremely well-represented in American private collections. In spite of the direct relationship of the artist's late work to the visible world, the enduring structure and monumentality of the paintings of the 1950s is indebted to de Staël's work of the 1940s, which some critics still consider his best.

Eliza Rathbone

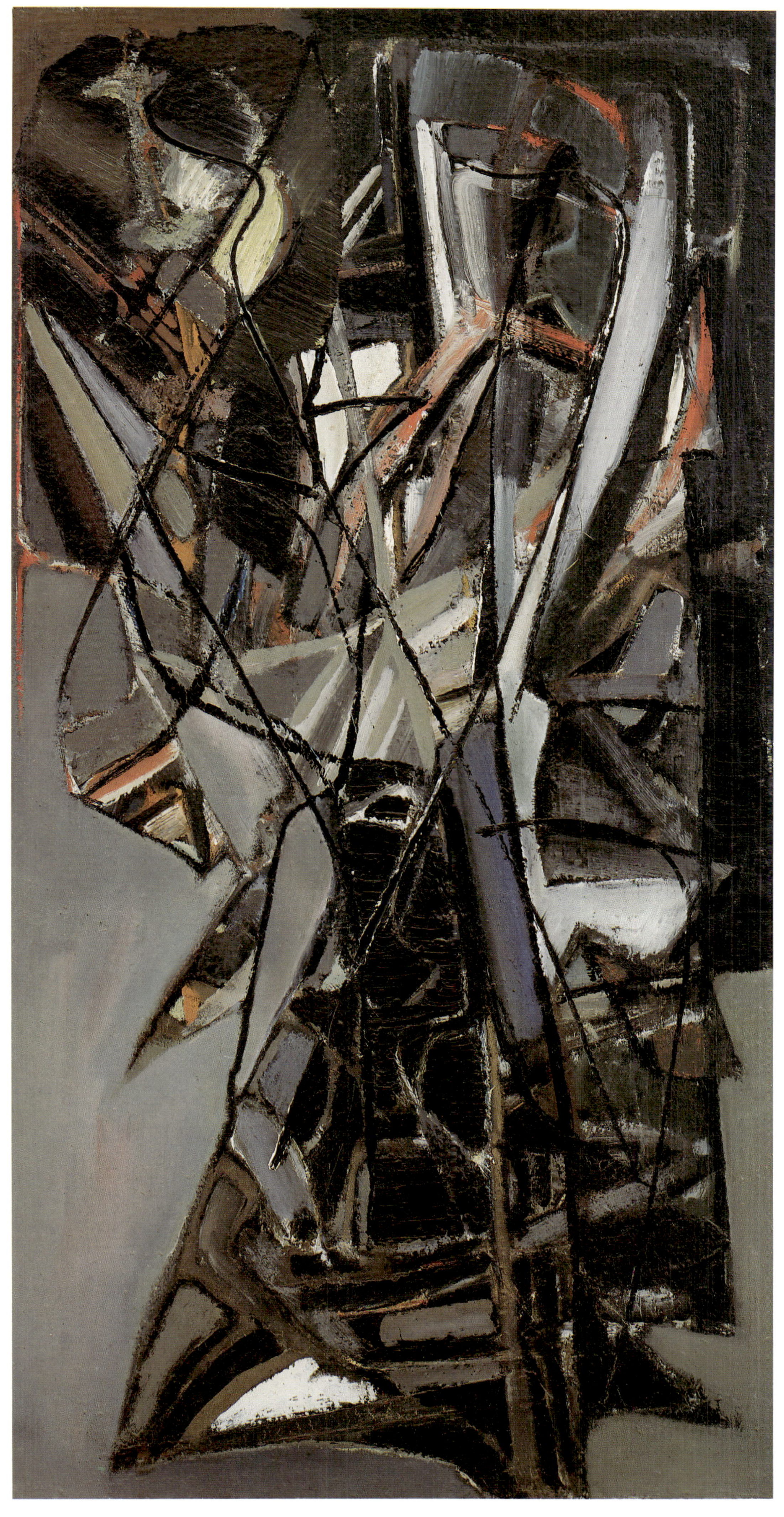

56. Jean Dubuffet (France, 1901–1985)

Poches aux Yeux (Bags under the Eyes), 1959
Paper maché, 16¾ x 6 x 4¼"
Gift of Florence S. Weil, 1982

Jean Dubuffet was first and foremost a painter.[1] Filled with insatiable curiosity and driven by the urge to form, he moved in his long and creative life from the graphic and pictorial media into sculpture and, beyond it, to sculptural architecture, dance, and musical composition. But while works on paper as well as paintings on various supports occupied the first decade of his artistic effort—1943 to 1953—his initial achievement in three dimensions (if one leaves aside some early works and a few *papier maché* masks of the 1930s) is traceable to a group of sculptures started in March of 1954 under the title *Petites statues de la vie precaire (little statues of a precarious life).*

In these, the artist pursued objectives that were to be articulated a year later in a catalogue statement for *The New Decade*, an exhibition including the artist's work at the Museum of Modern Art. Dubuffet writes as follows:

> *The merit which we Occidental nations attribute to art and the attention lavished on it tend to substitute a specious product which is the counterfeit of art. Too highly honored, art is rarely nowadays a free celebration (to which one would rush even if it were forbidden and probably rush even faster because it is forbidden). It has become, instead, a game of ceremonies which leads it far into alien terrain. Its true and only terrain is rapture and delirium; it is extra-curricular and doesn't belong in the school schedule. To help art regain its place, it should, I believe, be stripped of all the tinsel, laurels and buskins in which it has been decked, and be seen naked with all the creases of its belly. Once disencumbered, it will doubtless begin again to function—to dance and yell like a madman, which is its function, and stop putting on pretentious airs from its professor's chair.*[2]

In keeping with such emphasis upon the ecstatic, dionysian function of art and consonant also with previously articulated anti-cultural positions, Dubuffet's *les petites statues* dance into the world with whimsical abandon, gesticulating and grimacing to their hearts' content. The materials deployed for the purpose are as ephemeral as the moods and states of minds bestowed upon these heads and figurines. Through various ordinary materials, the artist conveys delight and rapture, mocking disrespect, irony and sheer joy in the condition of living. Despite their fragility, almost all of the statues have been preserved even though they merely seem to be holding out as if at the verge of extinction, perhaps to stress by their own threatened state the precariousness of existence as a whole.

The first sequence of *petites statues* covers a span of little more than one half of 1954 and originally contained forty-one sculptures. Both of the Dubuffet works in the Washington University collections, *Tête Barbue* and *Poches aux Yeux*, are part of a group of thirty-two statues completed between October 1959 and November 1960.

Poches aux Yeux, translatable as *Bags under the Eyes*, is one of twenty *papier maché* heads, shaped in the malleable, fragile lightweight material that Dubuffet used most frequently during the second phase. A monogram under the painted wooden base, that is certainly not authentic, reads "JD-54." In the artist's handwritten *Journal des Travaux*, in the volume marked *A Partir du 4 May 1959 et Jusq'au 15 May 1961* (Foundation Jean Dubuffet, Paris), the work is number 16 and dated, together with four comparable works, November 27, 1959. Its height is given as 44 cm and the medium described as "pâte de papier teintée de gris." Facial features are embedded in a radically flattened surface where they assume the appearance of Dubuffet's high impasto paintings of the same period, suggestive of a relief more than of a sculpture in the round. Descriptive detail, although explicitly rendered, emerges clearly only after the viewer has adjusted to the nuances that set off the particulars against the summary treatment of the surface. Deep crevices in the grey monotone separate areas in which a large, diagonally tilted mouth, a conspicuously flattened and mercilessly bent nose, and a sagging chin constitute a plausible physiognomy. Under a pair of eyes that are almost but not quite lined up, one cannot miss the heavy bags referred to in the title. The head of the imaginary subject rests on a neck that does double duty as a base. An upward aiming crop of hair provides a diagonal elongation on the top. The wrinkled *papier maché* material transmits its surface quality to the subject to render a crackled face eroded by time and care.

Poches aux Yeux is a sculpture conceived as frontal relief. It nevertheless is clearly delineated against the surrounding space through a rugged, irregular contour. The distinct outline of the head and neck shape retains some pertinence for the backside of the sculpture, as if the reverse were meant to echo the portrait in more generalized, abstracted form. The work is indicative of the artist's tendency to transcend the artificial border between figurative and abstract art and between the opposing connotations of material and form. It is within an essentially abstract framework that the features of a vital human presence provide an enriching dimension and it is within Dubuffet's unfailing sense of form that the language of his materials reaches its full potency.

Thomas M. Messer

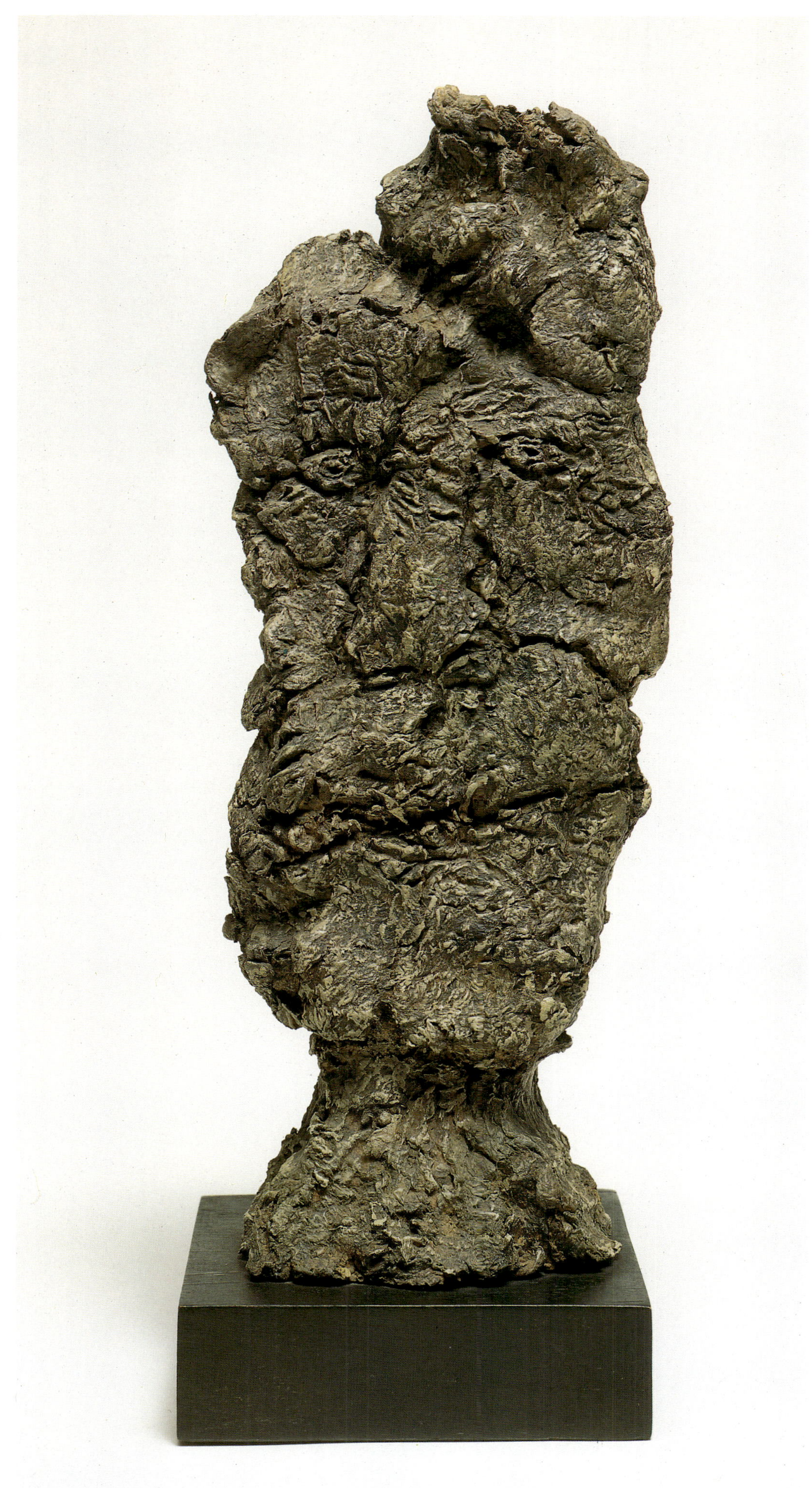

57. Jean Dubuffet (France, 1901–1985)
Tête Barbue (Bearded Head), 1959

Driftwood, 11 x 8½"
Gift of Florence S. Weil, 1982

Tête Barbue or *Bearded Head* is a piece of reworked driftwood. "J.D. 59" is burned into the material by the artist. A printed inscription in another hand on the bottom of the wooden base identifies the work by its title. The *Journal des Travaux* (Dubuffet Foundation, Paris) lists the object as number 21 with a height of 29 cm, the medium as "bois de la plage" (driftwood), and dates it on December 5, 1959, simply titling it "tête."

The sculpted head is, essentially, an *object trouvé* (found object). Although only minimally reworked, the artist has succeeded admirably in imparting to the inert material human attributes and a sense of radiating life. The blond and brittle driftwood shape, covered with rounded, abscess-like barnacles, is in itself strongly suggestive of a head shape and only its downward elongation into a neck base would appear to have been extensively reworked. Prominent protrusions are peripheral to a smooth inner core, defining the latter much as dense hair growth and a bushy beard may ring the cheeks of a human face. The facial structure and the round head, set off against each other, function as two concentric circles which, reinforced by the globular shapes of the barnacles, lend the entire composition a distinctly rounded, spherical character.

In *Tête Barbue*, Dubuffet, like the cloud-watching Leonardo before him, appears merely to be noting a human semblance in the amorphous but suggestive forms of nature. The low threshold between the depiction of organic and human life is crossed here primarily through an act of visual reorientation. The discreet, minimal intervention caused by the artist's hand merely awakens features that already slumber in the inert matter. By burning a few lines and dotting the wood in the same manner, already existing semblances of human features emerge comprehensibly. A pair of deeply set eyes, a bulky nose and other barely insinuated details emerge explicitly. The manual, as opposed to the mental, transformation is very slight and even so, remains conjectural and subject to individual interpretation. The back of the sculpture in the round recedes into raw material which, in its natural state, invites comparison with the evocations of the featured front.

Although both sculptures, *Poches aux Yeux* and *Tête Barbue*, belong to the family of *Petite statues de la vie precaire*, they are markedly different in their respective concepts and execution, thereby defining the wide range that exists within the assigned category. Both take as their subject matter heads resting on necks that serve as a base and elaborate distinct physiognomies. But where *Poches aux Yeux* is modelled in the artificial substance of *papier maché*, *Tête Barbue* relies upon ordinary driftwood for its expressive effects. In the first instance the artist uses his material much as he would a canvas and the resulting sculpture therefore is held in low relief not unlike his materiological paintings. By contrast, the shape of the wooden material distinctly defines a sculpture in the round while incidentally evoking the artist's concurrent obsession with paintings of bearded personages. The resulting expressions are rather somber in the case of the eroded face with the bags under the eyes while a buoyant vitality characterizes the personality that smiles through the blond wood.

Both works imply Dubuffet's disdain for "serious" art, his rejection of hierarchies in the choice of materials, and a related preference for the humble and "ignoble."

Thomas M. Messer

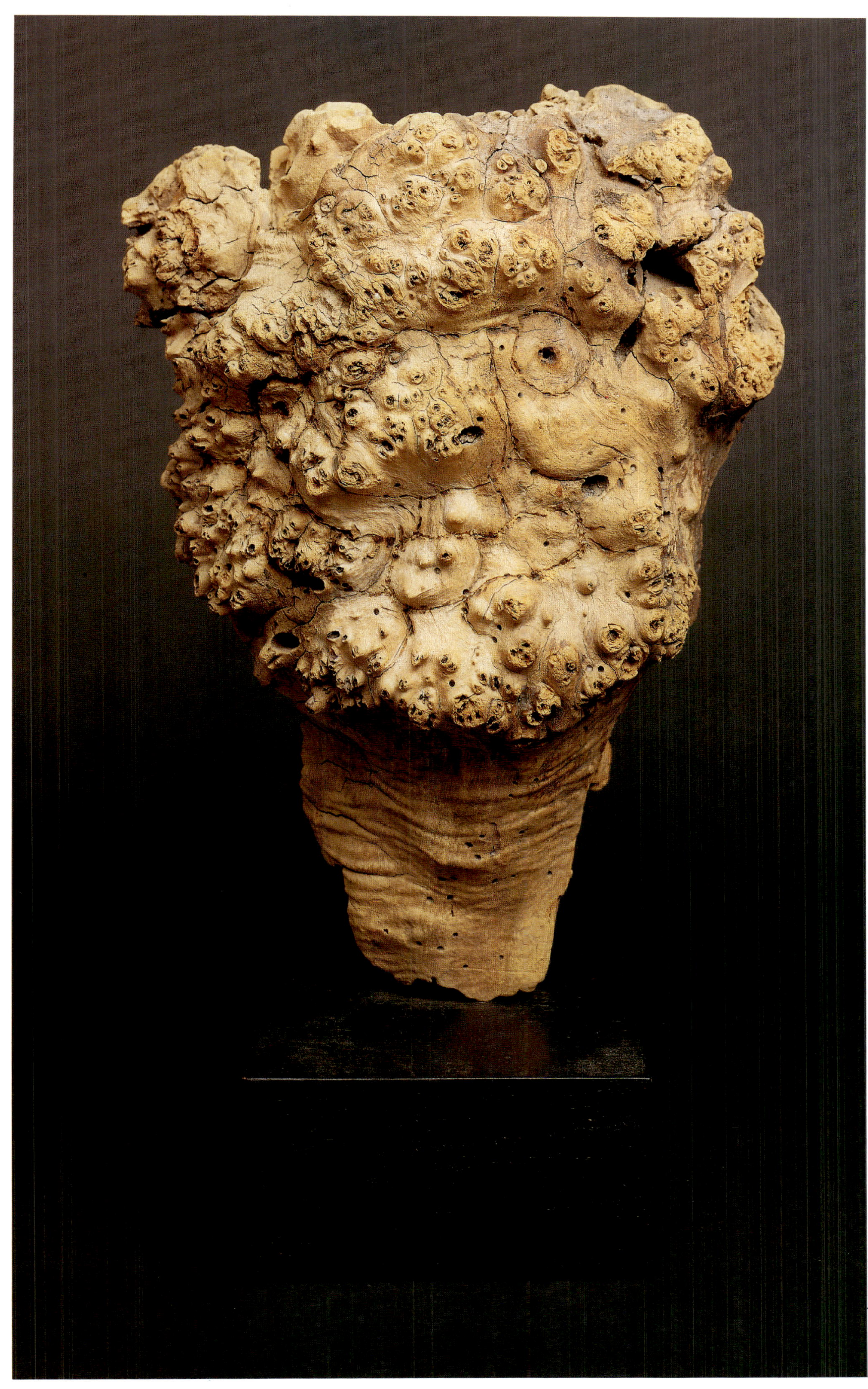

58. Pierre Soulages (France, b. 1919)
Peinture 200 x 265 cm, 20 Mai 1959 (Twentieth of May 1959), 1959

Oil on canvas, 78¾ x 104½"
Gift of Mr. and Mrs. Richard K. Weil, 1961

Pierre Soulages is the most important French painter alive today.[1] Born on December 24, 1919 in Rodez, in southwest France, Soulages started painting very early, moved by his fascination for the contrast created by black shapes on a white page. In 1938, he briefly attended the Ecole des Beaux-Arts in Paris but, disappointed by its academic rigidity, he soon dropped out and decided to work on his own. During World War II, he was a farm laborer and could not devote himself to painting until 1946 when he moved to Paris. Soulages' first exhibition, in 1947, during the *Salon des Surindépendants*, received immediate notice from critics and painters as different as Francis Picabia and Hans Hartung. His large dark pieces stood out against the polychromatic works of other painters. In 1948, he participated in the exhibition *Französische Abstrakte Malerei* (French abstract painters) that travelled throughout Germany and won him great respect among German painters. In 1949, he had his first solo exhibition in Paris, and in 1952 he joined the Galerie Louis Carré, which carried the works of other important French artists including Fernand Léger, Raoul Dufy, and Jacques Villon.

But Soulages' consecration came from the United States, where the response of professionals and collectors was the most favorable. James Johnson Sweeney, curator of the Museum of Modern Art in New York, visited his studio as early as 1948, purchasing a painting on behalf of the Museum in 1952. Soulages first exhibited in New York, at the Betty Parsons Gallery in 1949 and at the Sidney Janis Gallery in 1950, and he participated in the landmark *Younger European Painters* exhibition presented at the Solomon Guggenheim Museum in 1953. Thereafter his reputation in the United States was solidified and many of the major American museums showed his work. From 1954 to 1968, he had solo exhibitions almost every year in New York, first at the Sam Kootz Gallery (until 1966) and then at the Knoedler Gallery. During his many travels to the United States, Soulages established lasting friendships with great American painters, notably Mark Rothko. In 1964, he received the Carnegie Award and in 1966 the Museum of Fine Arts in Houston, Texas organized the first retrospective exhibition of his work.

In France, Soulages switched to the Galerie de France in Paris, in 1956, where his work has been exhibited regularly since. In 1967, the Musée National d'Art Moderne de Paris organized a retrospective exhibition, initiating a series of such exhibitions in a number of museums worldwide. Soulages work is represented in museum collections throughout the world, with 146 pieces, 45 of which are part of diverse collections in the United States. The international art world recognized Soulages' career of accomplishment, awarding him the Prix National de Peinture in France in 1987 and the Proemium Imperiale for Painting in Japan in 1992.

Pierre Soulages' abstract style corresponds to the European and American postwar movement, but it does not relate to any "school;" indeed, its singularity is striking. His canvases have no illustrative titles, not even that of "composition"—they are designated by the uniform term "painting," followed by the dimensions of the canvas and the date of their completion. Soulages thus indicates that his paintings are objects presented to the viewer's gaze, objects inviting the viewer to construct or deconstruct his or her own meaning. But these objects are neither image nor language: they represent nothing exterior to themselves and have no significance assigned by the painter. Rather, they aim to provoke by allowing the viewer a share of their emotions in the encounter.

Frequently, before 1979, Soulages based his painting on the contrast between regions of black neighbouring other dark colors and white or other light colors. His painting is characterized by the strength of its assertions, modeled by wide black touches and by the power that emerges from the rhythm of black on white. From 1979 on, his black tones invade the surface of the whole canvas, which is generally of large dimensions and often assembled in polyptichs. The entire composition escapes, however, a simple monochromatic effect as the black paint is worked in streaks and in flat tints in order to reflect the light. It offers the viewer a luminous and colorful image which is continually renewed.

Washington University's *Twentieth of May 1959*, like other works of the late 1950s, combines an immobility of shapes with a striking dynamism and clearly belongs to this second style particularly used since 1956. It is a piece characterized by its rhythm and the dynamic beat of its shapes in space. Wide streaks of black rise in a burst to meet the diagonal at a right angle. The play of light in *Twentieth of May 1959*, which is one of the last pieces of this style and one of the most successful, foreshadows Soulages' achievements since 1979. It can be compared to *Eighteenth of April 1959*, which was purchased by the Sonja Henie-Niels Onstad Kunstscenter and which is now in the Musée d'Art Moderne de Saint-Etienne. It also bears similarities with *Twenty-Second of May 1959*, a piece painted in a static style of the same period, which belongs to the Museu de Arte Contemporanea da Universidad de Sao Paulo.

Pierre Encrevé
translated by Miren Lacassagne

59. Karel Appel (Holland, b. 1921)

Heads in Space (Abstraction), 1958

Oil on canvas, 54 x 78"
Gift of Mr. Richard K. Weil, 1963

By 1958, when Karel Appel painted *Heads in Space*, he had already achieved international fame as one of the principal organizers of Cobra, an international group dedicated to the free expression of artistic ideas. Coined by the Belgian poet Christian Dotrement, Cobra was an acronym formed from the cities COpenhagen, BRussels, and Amsterdam, from which many of the artists came. Their goal was to make art in response to their own creative instincts, as opposed to formulas taught in academies, enshrined in museums, and praised by scholars. They were moved by art created by children, the insane, and primitive cultures—people free from such corrupting influences as formal artistic training and "accepted" prewar art. The Cobra group found inspiration in folk tales and myths, because these sources had roots in the fundamental human experience.[1]

As a Cobra artist Appel had earned notoriety for his mural *Questioning Children* (1949), commissioned for Amsterdam's City Hall, which had created such an uproar that the City Council ordered it whitewashed. Soon afterward the Dutch artist received more favorable popular and critical responses to his work with his first important one-man show at the Palais des Beaux Art, Brussels (1953), followed by exhibits in Paris and New York (1954), and by winning the UNESCO prize at the 27th International Biennale, Venice (1954) and the international graphics prize at the Ljubljana Biennale, Yugoslavia (1957). Two years after he painted *Heads in Space*, Appel won first prize for Dutch artists from the Netherlands Committee for the Guggenheim International Award, and subsequently became the youngest artist ever to win the Guggenheim International first prize for his painting *Vrouw met Struisvogel (Woman with Ostrich)* (1957, Stedelijk Museum, Amsterdam). In 1968 Appel was knighted by Queen Juliana of the Netherlands.

Heads in Space, thus, is the work of a mature artist, secure in his place as an internationally respected image-maker, full of exuberance and confidence. The work is a wonderful example of Appel's post-Cobra style, in which he de-emphasized his reliance on imagery drawn from children's art and, while retaining a predilection for the bright primary colors that marked his Cobra paintings, moved in the direction of greater abstraction. Canvases from this period are in some ways similar to the work of American Abstract Expressionists. Yet, unlike many of his American counterparts, Appel seldom completely rejected figurative elements.

> *I am not at all an abstract painter and I am not a fashionable painter. Abstract painting is a fashion, a style. I always use forms that are based on existing forms. You must not look at the details but at the thing as a whole. To me it is the totality that matters. I consider myself as a figurative painter and I paint in an expressionistic way. Standing in front of my canvas, I don't try to make a painting. What comes out is a cry or a child or a tiger behind its bars.*[2]

Hence in his Guggenheim-winning *Woman with Ostrich*, the magnificent *Birds and Animals* (1958) in the UNESCO building in Paris, or Washington University's *Heads in Space*, we see the artist combining the furious energy and spontaneity of the action painter with a Cobra palette of primary colors and figurative imagery that can be deciphered at a glance.

"My paint tube," Appel once exclaimed "is like a rocket which describes its own space. . . . Painting, like passion, is an emotion full of truth and rings a living sound—like the roar coming from the lion's breast."[3] Appel's declaration makes perfect sense in the context of *Heads in Space*. The artist's words characterize both the way he painted the canvas and the sense of furious energy it conveys—huge streams of heavy, tube-squeezed paint hang on the surface, and bold brush or palette knife strokes whip the paint into a thick impasto. Two figures (with perhaps a third, outlined in green at the top center of the canvas), bodies united (in an act of passion?) in a sea of blue at the bottom, pull apart, or twist around one another across the canvas against a background of yellow and red. Such characteristics established Appel's fame as an individual working in a style wholly his own, as opposed to the attention he earned as one of the founding and most effective Cobra artists.

If *Heads in Space* owes a debt to Cobra, or is linked to the Cobra movement in any way, it is in the sense of exuberant freedom it conveys and the degree to which the creative process itself is emphasized. To the extent that those aspects of *Heads in Space* strike the observer as paramount, one might argue that there is much of Cobra in the canvas. Still, Appel here has moved away from the obviously figurative images of people and animals, of fields of color bounded by clearly defined borders, all depicted in a style linked directly to the art of children, that marked so many of his (and other Cobra artists') Cobra-era works.

In the early 1960s Appel's work became increasingly figurative as he moved away from the wildly abstract, highly energized nature of such paintings as *Heads in Space*. At the end of the 1970s Appel demonstrated that his stylistic evolution was still in progress. In a dramatic break with his prior approach to painting, he began to emphasize the individual brushstrokes themselves, creating images in which broad bands of color were applied to the canvas in single slashes. By the early 1980s he was exhibiting works that, while abstract, had both a figurative and a narrative component—works that struck some observers as pessimistic, frightening, sometimes magical—paintings that included images of gray cities dominated by dark cloud-like forms, or huge figures that had an ominous aspect. In the late 1980s Appel returned to the Cobra imagery of animals and humans, depicted in bright colors and painted in a manner that emphasizes the energetic quality of the creative process itself. For in these new works Appel, as he did in *Heads in Space*, makes no effort to hide the impact of his brush on the paint itself—his brushstrokes dominate the surface of the painting as they shape and intermingle colors applied thickly to the canvas. The images are instantly identifiable as Appel's, as is the style he uses to create them.

Aaron M. Shatzman

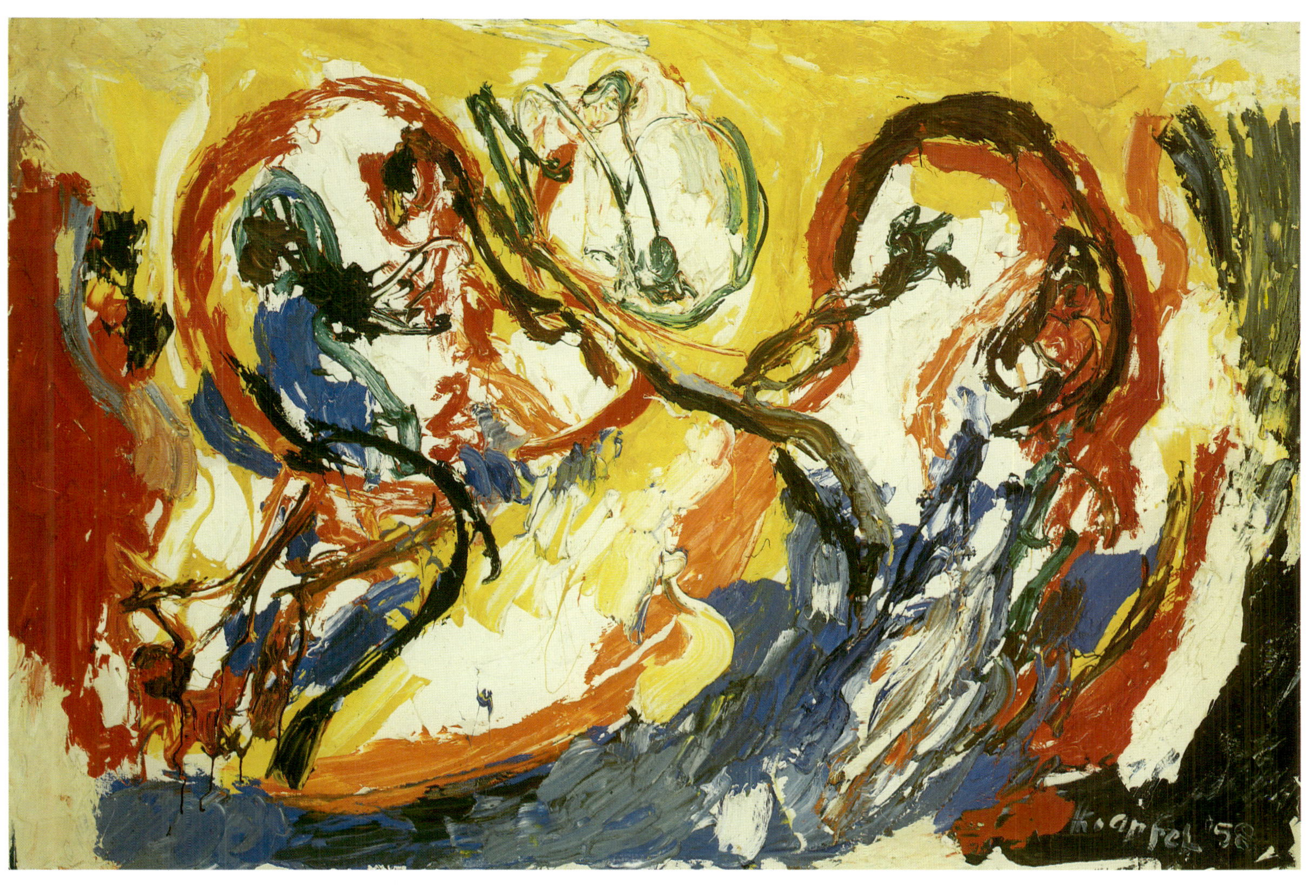

60. Lucebert (Lubertus J. Swaanswijk) (Holland, b. 1924)

The Menaced House, 1962

Oil on canvas, 51½ x 79½"

Bequest of Mrs. Harry (Ruth) Franc, 1989

"My grandfather," Lucebert once remarked, "was Bosch, my father is Ensor and my father-confessor is Paul Klee."[1] Certainly the figures swirling around the house-like form (complete with carefully delineated rooms) in the center of *The Menaced House* set against a dark void background suggest a dream-vision, perhaps even a nightmare. But there is a child-like playfulness to these monsters. One wonders if the goblins mean to frighten or to entertain. Do these demonic figures want us to turn away in fear, to hide; or do they want to make us laugh?

Well before his first one-man exhibition of paintings in 1958 at Galerie Espace in Haarlem, Lucebert had achieved recognition as a writer. The author of many books of poetry, he received Amsterdam's Lyricist Prize in 1956 and the great Holland Prize for literature in 1968. Even after success as a painter came to him, he continued to write poems and plays, to illustrate books, and to help make films.

Early in his career as a painter, some were skeptical that a successful writer could, in fact, switch to painting. In the Netherlands, where his fame as a poet had been established in the 1950s,[2] critics acknowledged his talent as a painter later than they did in other countries, where observers were not predisposed to evaluate the artist as a poet who also happened to paint a bit. Lucebert has responded to such attitudes among his countrymen by noting that his earliest significant artistic creation was a boyhood work, *The Adventures of Gussie & Linkie, and of Micodemus Watjekou (Slap in the Face) & Don Sebastian de la Gorilla*, which he wrote and drew. This was, he has said, "my masterpiece that got lost . . . and all that came after it, and all that will come after it, wants to look like it."[3] Therefore, he always has been, he asserts, *both* painter and writer. Throughout his career, his canvases have enjoyed highly literate and provocative titles.

The son of a house painter, Lucebert (born Lubertus J. Swaanswijk) grew up in Amsterdam. After a three-year course in basic education, he joined the family house-painting business. Then, in storybook fashion, an art lover chanced to walk past a house on whose siding Lucebert had displayed his talent as an image-maker. The work made a favorable impression, and the young house painter received an invitation to submit a drawing for a scholarship (which he won) to the Arts and Crafts School, directed by the architect Mart Stam. Pressured by his family to work rather than to study, Lucebert stayed less than a year.

Most students of art history know Lucebert through his association with the Cobra group—young artists mostly from Copenhagen, Brussels, and Amsterdam (hence CoBrA) who banded together from 1948–51, wrote manifestos, cooperated in the creation of joint works, experimented with film-making, published a magazine, and organized a number of exhibitions (Brussels and Amsterdam 1949, Liege 1951). In the Netherlands Cobra had been preceded in 1948 by another experimental group, Reflex, whose organizing members—Constant, Corneille, Appel, Rooskens, Wolvecamp and Brands—all became members of Cobra. The group published two issues of *Reflex*: the second contained a two-page poem by Lucebert, who went on to join his countrymen as a member of Cobra.

It is ironic that Lucebert's participation in Cobra activities came primarily as a poet, since of the thirty or so artists affiliated with that group, none has painted in a style more clearly identified as "typically Cobra" than has Lucebert, and none has remained, over the years, truer to its animating ideals or imagery. Indeed, Lucebert can be seen as the quintessential Cobra image-maker, and Washington University's *The Menaced House* can be described, and perhaps best understood, as a Cobra painting, produced from an unadulterated human creative impulse with a universal appeal.

In *The Menaced House*, we see Lucebert focusing on typical Cobra themes, using basic Cobra images. The house can be any house, any shelter in any culture. The dark void background is universal. The creatures relate to no specific culture or continent or era. Are these figures animals or humans? Are they reptiles or mammals, fish or birds, monsters or children's toys? The questions will be the same no matter the viewer's gender, age, race, or nationality. Do not all humans find safety in their homes? Do not all of us sometimes fear the dark that lies outside the security of our rooms? Does not everyone at some time wonder what lurks in the woods at night, or feel that the world outside his or her home is chaotic, threatening, menacing? Has not every culture created folk-tales that suggest the imagery Lucebert paints here? Is it not possible that the dream is more real than our experiences while awake?

The Menaced House is one of a series of large oils Lucebert exhibited at the New London Gallery in December 1962, a year after signing a six-year contract with Marlborough. His energy, and what a critic of that exhibition identified as "primitive force, sometimes menacing, but often, and in the best sense child-like in its insistence,"[4] typify both Cobra and Lucebert's mature style. He has never forsaken that approach to painting. Through the 1960s and '70s Lucebert continued to create works full of caricatures of human or animal figures engaged in furious activity. Commonly his colors have been brighter—more typically Cobra—than the dark tones he used in the early 1960s (and in *The Menaced House*), but he has not strayed from the themes that marked Cobra, nor from imagery that reveals a childlike impetuosity.

Aaron M. Shatzman

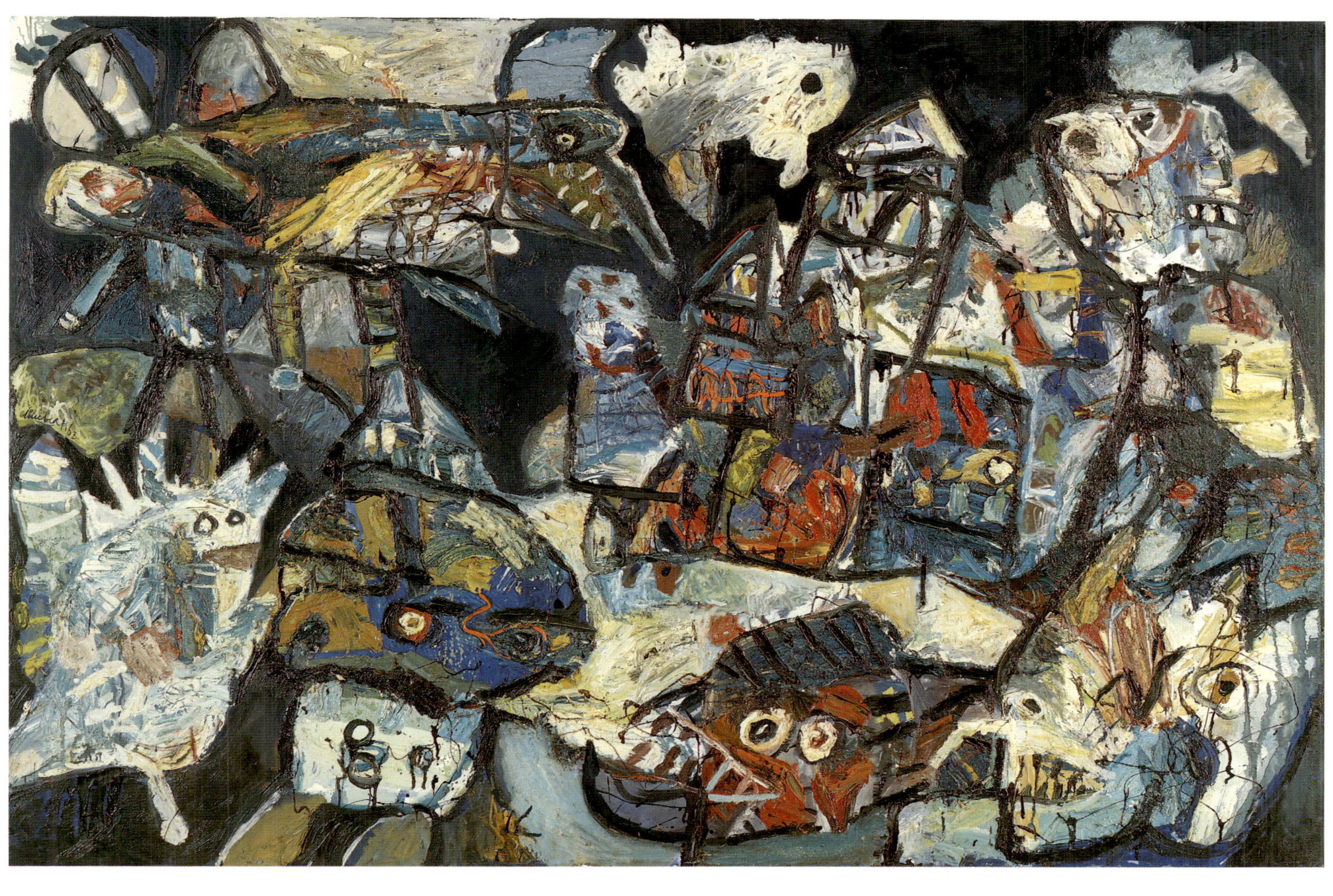

61. Alberto Burri (Italy, b. 1915)

Gran Ferro M3, 1959

Welded cast iron, paint, 78¼ x 75¼"
Gift of Richard K. Weil, 1963

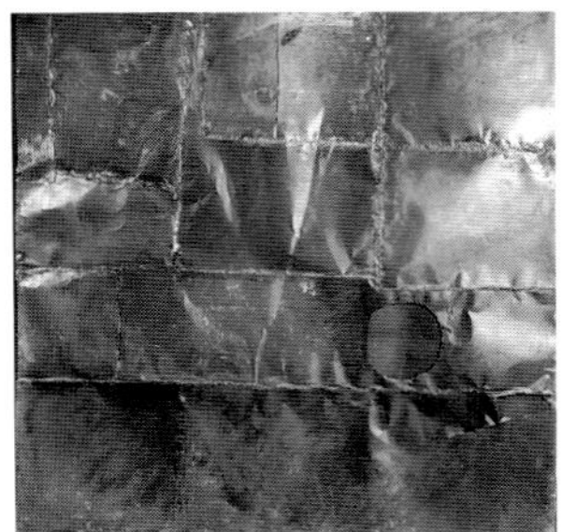

Alberto Burri
Gran Ferro M1 (Great Iron), 1958
Sheet iron assemblage, 75 x 79½"
Washington University Gallery of Art, St. Louis
Gift of Mr. Joseph Pulitzer, Jr., 1963

Alberto Burri is one of the most important and influential Italian artists to have emerged since 1945. He made his way to art by a path through the University, to the Medical School at Perugia where he specialized in African tropical diseases, to service with the Italian Army in the African campaign (1942–43). Captured by the English, he provided medical care for Italian soldiers for eighteen additional months, until the Americans moved him to a prison camp in Texas. He turned to recreational painting during his confinement—a pastime he hadn't enjoyed since his student days. His subjects were drawn from landscape and realized in oil on used burlap sacks, stretched over improvised wooden stretchers.

The war, his extended service as a physician, and his imprisonment in Texas affected Burri's decision to quit medicine for art. His family was disappointed, lamenting the waste of so many years of study and the uncertainty of a life in art.

Self-taught, Burri explored landscape, still-life, figure painting, and non-objective compositions in 1946–50, often using such "non-art" materials as tar, pumice, and internal braces designed to misalign the canvas into a "hunchbacked" shape (*gobbo*). During these years Burri took a studio in Rome, where he sampled the exhibitions, followed the trends of aesthetic discussions, and used his skills in observation to grasp the innovations of Cubism, Constructivism, Dada and Surrealism. He recognized the innovations of early modernism, but felt impelled to establish a new direction in response to the war and the degradation of his people.

In 1949 he stumbled upon worn and patched burlap sacks discarded by the flour miller of his home town, Citta di Castello, Umbria. Knowing of Cubist collage and the work of Kurt Schwitters, Burri began to paint with sacks, bits of rag, and pigment by 1950–51, in a series of works he called *sacchi* (sacks). *Object trouvé* (found object) is a related technique, in which manufactured objects are "identified" by an artist as works of art—e.g., Duchamp's *Fountain*, or *Bottle Rack*. Burri can be said to have identified his imagery in the raw material of repaired and discarded jute sackings, which he stretched and cropped with additions (or deletions) as needed in order to be presented as paintings.

Seven years into the *sacchi*, Burri began a series of collage paintings using thin sheets of wood which he blasted and charred with fire. After two years with the burned wood, Burri found sheets of iron in a factory which he recognized as offering a new opening for his art. He later moved to plate and sheet plastics in new burnings, combining plastic and paint, carved and painted cellotex, and earth and glue painted cracquelures. "If I don't have one material, I use another. It is all the same."[1]

The *Ferri*, made from 1957 to 1961, are not *object trouvé*, but are composed of newly-made, thin cast-iron sheets, cut and recomposed into rectangular plates related in form to the *sacchi*. They emphasize constructivist order, vertical and horizontal lines, and the relation of elements to framing edges. The *Ferri* deal with the properties of iron—the warping and buckling from welding and the subtleties of color, weight, and light reflection that can be drawn from unlikely materials. The surface records the process of making the *Gran Ferro* with its scrapes, dimples and rustings, in opposition to painted or varnished sections.

Gran Ferro M3 (1959)—a prime example of the iron-genre—has been invited to a number of retrospective exhibitions and is often reproduced. *Gran Ferro M3* was acquired from Galleria Odyssia, Rome, shortly after it was created, and given to Washington University in 1963. It shows a weathered and enduring surface, marked with eye-engaging scars, abrasions, bumps, and discolorations. The surface reveals a hand-crafted aspect through warping and the subtleties of color; the paint application reinforces the sense of age and wear. *Gran Ferro M3* reflects the organic side of the *Ferri*, in contrast to the constructivist side typified by the Washington University Gallery of Art's other Burri, *Grand Ferro M1*. *Gran Ferro M3* is vitally open, with every form irregular. It sides with dynamism and movement rather than with symmetry and closure.

Because of the material from which they are crafted, the *Ferri* are sometimes defined as sculpture. However, like the *sacchi*, *legno*, and other invented media, Burri conceived them as paintings, concerned with the reductive nature of modernist art—flatness, verticality and horizontality, and its delimitations. The material speaks for itself: Burri can be seen as the earliest spokesman of *art povera* (literally, poor art), in which discarded or overlooked materials are utilized to create works of art. All of Burri's early work was greeted as scandalous, provocative and offensive. His common materials were deemed shocking, and an insult to tradition. One may recall that Marcel Duchamp said, "A painting that doesn't shock isn't worth painting."[2]

Burri's picture-making knows no limits of technique or material, but stops only at his artistic goal of expressing—through rhythm and proportion, order and organization—new harmonies. He astonishes the observer with his materials, but time absorbs the shock, anger, and fancied vulgarity, leaving visible his refined proportions, clarity of mind, and exquisitely-felt asymmetries of line, color and texture. Burri's work has influenced a generation of artists which includes Lucio Fontana, Yves Klein, Otto Peine, Raymond Hains, Mimmo Rotella, Corrado Marca Relli, Robert Rauschenberg and the major figures of a later generation from Germany—Joseph Beuys and Anselm Kiefer.[3]

Gerald Nordland

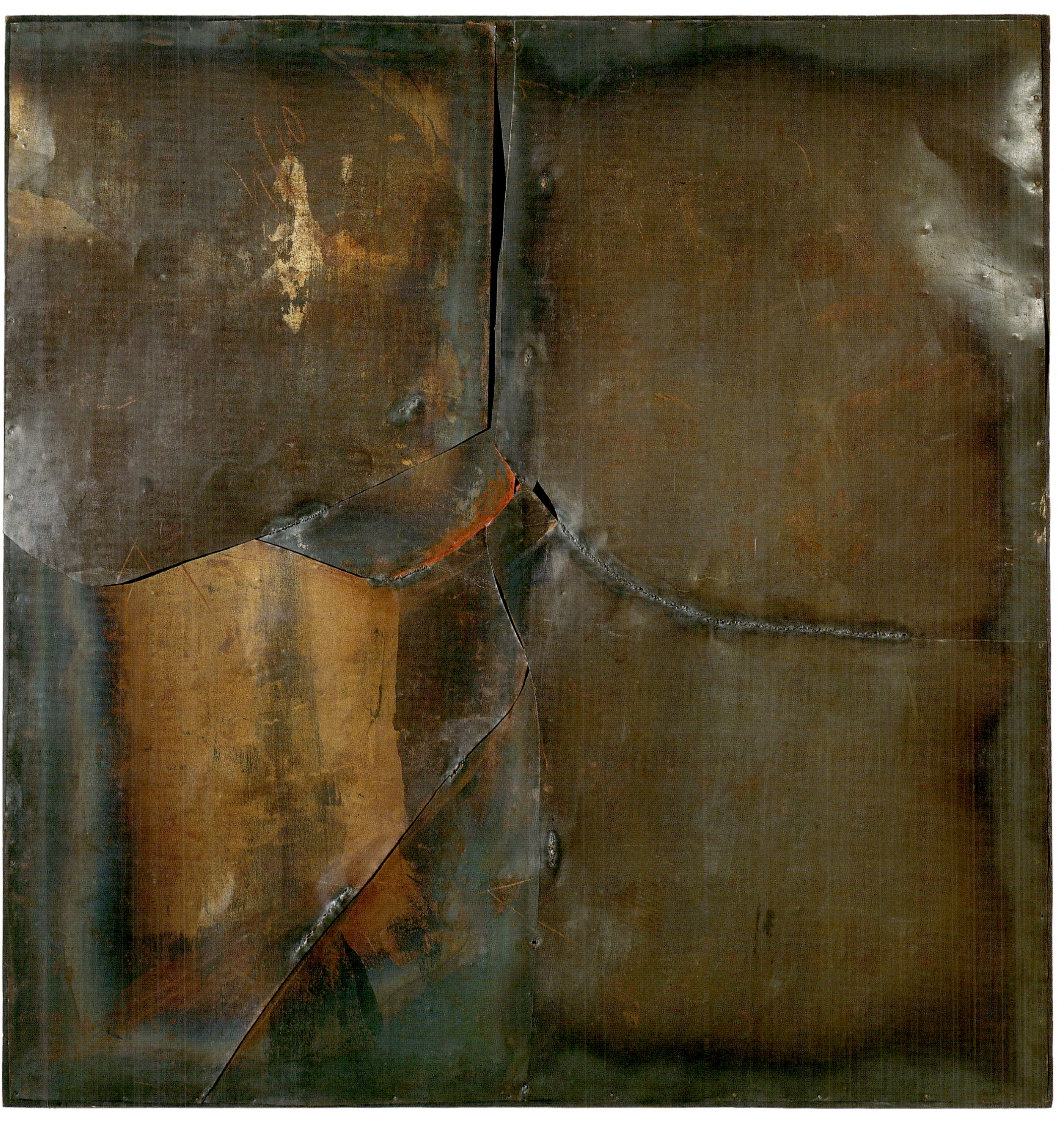

62. Antoni Puig Tàpies (Spain, b. 1923)

Porta Marró (The Spanish Door), 1959

Mixed media, sand, on canvas, 76¾ x 51"
Gift of Mr. and Mrs. Richard K. Weil, 1962

Significantly, the title that Catalonian artist Antoni Tàpies[1] originally gave to the 1959 painting was *Porta Marró (Brown Door)* rather than *The Spanish Door*, the name by which it has been widely known. Included in a number of expositions in the United States in the early sixties, the painting was given the title *The Spanish Door* by Martha Jackson, Tàpies' first American agent. Although seemingly incidental, this anecdote from the history of the work reveals the way this painter's art has been perceived and the many clichés which surround it.

That one should have spoken of *The Spanish Door* emphasized the specifically regional or national characteristics of his art, which was seen by some critics as an alternative to the more or less international style into which *art informel* (Informalism) had evolved in the second half of the 1950s. Nevertheless, while allusions to his country's culture are found in Tàpies' work, which naturally refer to Catalonia more than Spain, they were never descriptive.

It is important to keep in mind that the "Spanish-ization" of *The Spanish Door* was directly related to contemporary political situations and to the use that not only the American administration but the Spanish government made of their respective artistic vanguards during the 1950s and early 1960s. It also helps explain the polarized reception that Tàpies' work received in the United States: whereas critics at the time, including Harold Rosenberg, Clement Greenberg, and Thomas Hess, showed little or no interest, such institutions as the Guggenheim Museum of New York included Tàpies in important group shows and devoted a retrospective exhibition to his work in 1962.

The Spanish Door is representative of those works referred to as Tàpies' matter paintings—works which are characterized visually by densely textured surfaces and painted within a limited color range, in which ochers, grays and browns predominate, giving the overall appearance of a wall. The wall-like nature of these matter paintings allows a plurality of readings: the wall as the partition that denies access or prevents our seeing through it, the wall that reflects the passage of time, or the surface on which to inscribe graffiti. Above all, the wall represents the alter ego of the artist (Tàpies means "walls" in Catalonian), through which Tàpies expresses his desire to meld with the material in a formless continuum and break with the dualism characteristic of our society.

The plastic aspects derived from the textural qualities or subtleties of color in these "walls" are not fundamental. Neither the object represented nor the scribbled graphics are important in themselves. The intentional elements that the artist attributes to the matter, the configurations that it acquires, are the essential aspect. When referring to the images in his paintings, Tàpies does not usually speak so much of an "arm," a "bed," or a "door," for example, but of material "in the shape of an arm," "in the shape of a bed," or "in the shape of a door."

In the matter paintings, the first of which date from 1954, Tàpies developed certain aesthetic concepts and artistic elements which he had already touched on in early works. Not to underestimate the influence of hallucinatory experiences in the painter's sickly youth, the determined exposure of material or deceitful aspects of existence in matter paintings, they remind us of the ideas and work of some Surrealist artists. These would include especially Joan Miró, Max Ernst and Brassaï, who were quite important for Tàpies after 1948. The synthesis of the organic-natural and the rational-artificial, so significant in modernist architecture (mainly Antoni Gaudí and Josep Maria Jujol), and the philosophy of such medieval Catalonian mystics as Ramon Llull, in which mystic experience cannot be disassociated from the material world, were also proverbial in the development of matter painting. Tàpies has always been attracted by the world of magicians and illusionists. Equally important is his interest in mysticism and the thinking of medieval alchemists. In the same way that the wizard seeks ambiguity, playing with the real and the unreal, or as the alchemist sought the philosophical stone through which he could achieve the mutation of substances, Tàpies envisions creation as the artist acting upon matter so as to submerge himself in it and transform it, giving shape to a part of his internal flow.

Nevertheless, the condition inherent in matter is *becoming*, the resistance to being made to conform or be compartmentalized according to a preestablished code of thought. In spite of Tàpies' attempt to imprint his own order into matter, the shapes and images of his paintings seem to extend beyond their limits. The closed square of *The Spanish Door* makes us think that the image is not contained within the painting and that it encounters its borders suddenly, as though by surprise. The three rectangular appendices which elongate the door at each side confirm such a perception. At the same time, a continuous series of points and incisions at the bottom of the work suggest their indefinite extension far beyond it.

Given the architectural nature which the image of a door possesses by definition, it is not surprising to find that material in the shape of arches, windows and doors have also made up Tàpies' iconographical repertory since its inception. Of course, these windows and arches are covered and the doors are closed; they do not allow us to see through them or permit access to the adjoining room. His paintings represent ambiguity and paradox, showing Tàpies' opposition to western rationalism that tends to consider the signifier as something exterior to the signified, distrusting the former as an obstacle to achievement of the supposed interior purity of ideas. In a way that cannot but remind us of concepts central to Zen Buddhism, Tàpies seeks to express in paintings like *The Spanish Door* the intimate relationship between the exterior and the interior, affirming in this way the coexistence of opposites and the simultaneous duality and unity of all things.

Manuel J. Borja-Villel
translated by Gail Swick

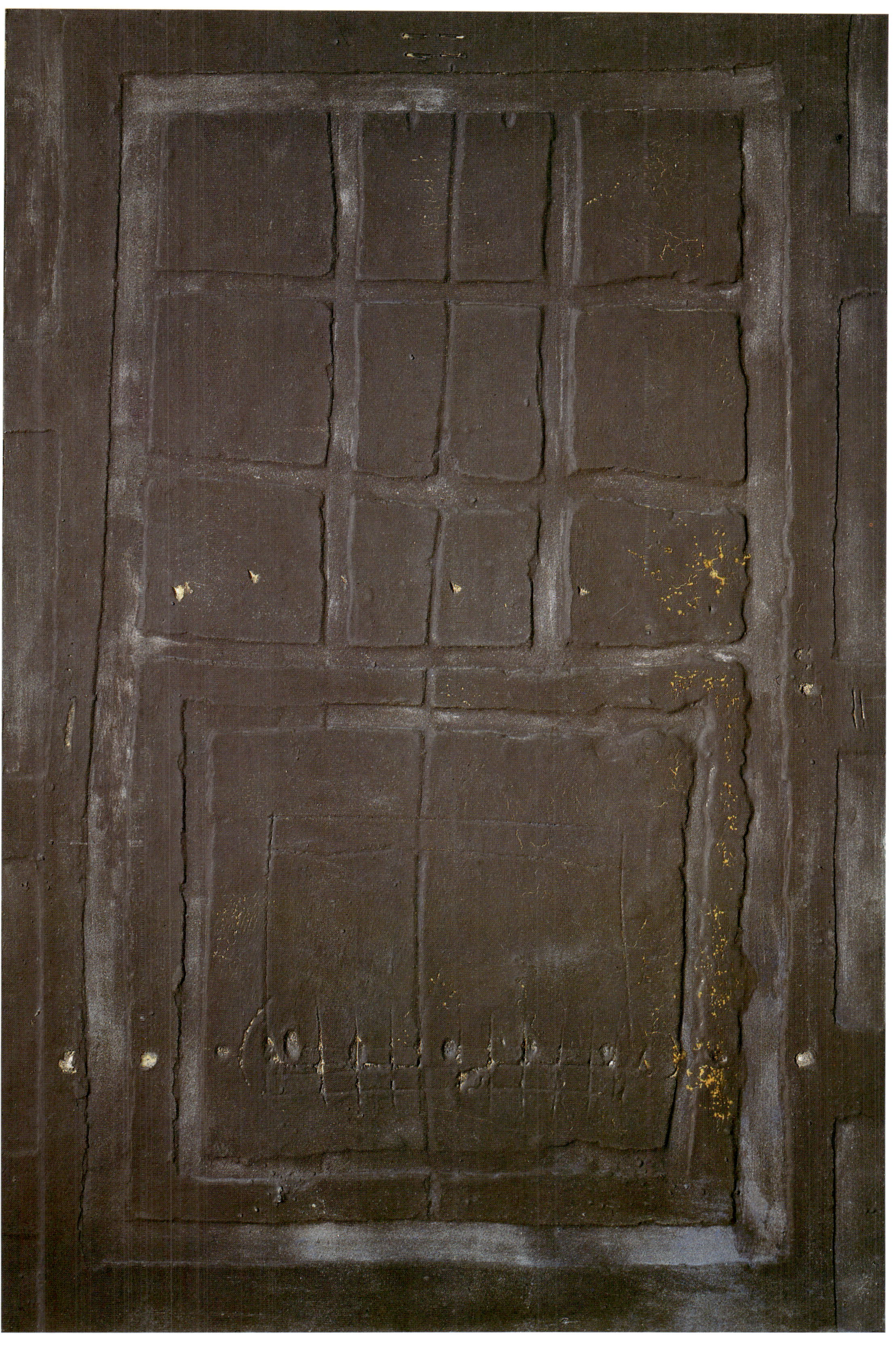

63. Lucio Fontana
(Italy, b. Argentina, 1899–1968)
Spatial Concept, New York 22, 1962

Incised and perforated sheet brass, 52 x 25¼ x ¾"
Gift of Mr. Joseph Pulitzer, Jr., 1967

If the history of Italian art in the twentieth century were to be compressed, *Futurismo* and *Spazialismo* would characterize the first half of the century, *arte povera* and *transavanguardia* the second half. In his 1946 *White Manifest,* Lucio Fontana defined the transition from an art of motion and violent overturn that had foundered on the shoals of fascism, to an art of media reconciliation and spatial harmony in which painting, sculpture and architecture promised to merge. The vitalistic energy of the Futurist Movement was his principal source of inspiration. Intuitively he understood, and in his work he anticipated, the miracles of electronic communication and the conquest of space.

Making space, light and motion an integral part of his Spatialist concept of art, Fontana traded illusion for reality. What had remained excessively ambitious in Futurist manifestos was now brought into sharper focus. For Fontana, space no longer functioned, as it had for the Futurists, in the context of the figure—the flow of space around or through sculpture, the trompe l'oeil space of painting—but it became the physical arena in which this artist subdued the recalcitrant forces of form, light and motion. Hence *Spazialismo* and *Concetto Spaziale,* denotations of Fontana's revolutionary departure from past media definitions.

The Futurists boasted that their formal innovations were more dynamic than those of the Cubists whose style, they imputed, lacked their own superior visual fragmentation. Fontana may have gone the Futurists one better with his cuts and tears, more radical alternatives, for sure, to the Cubist collages. "If any of my discoveries is important," Fontana has said, "the hole is. . . . I did not make holes in order to wreck the picture. On the contrary, I made holes in order to find something else."[1] The Cubist paste-on was a means of obviating the necessity of dealing with illusory perspective in a picture. Fontana's perforations of the canvas or metal surface do not add a secondary illusion (wax cloth with the imprint of chair caning, newsprint) but substitute real for pictorial space.

In the fall of 1961, Fontana visited New York for the first time, accompanied by the critic Michel Tapié who had just published a monograph on the artist.[2] The Martha Jackson Gallery featured his lacerated, impastoed and bejeweled canvases, dedicated to Venice, which had made a big splash that summer in *Arte e Contemplazione* at the Palazzo Grassi. "For sheer megalomanic tastelessness this show has no equal," Sidney Tillim wrote,[3] voicing the universal rejection that befell Fontana's work in this country. A generation of younger artists was feeling its oats and, chauvinistically, had no use for this highly touted European competitor. Yves Klein's blue monochromes met with the same fate at Leo Castelli's half a year before.

Fontana was hurt that his enthusiasm for America and things American remained unreciprocated. "È magnifico, il Pop," I still hear him exclaim to me in 1964. He realized, though, that he was being attacked, not for his theoretical positions (the critics were unaware he had any), but for his luxurious surfaces, a painterly analogue to Fellini's *La Dolce Vita,* then recently released. These pictures were irreconcilable with the Greenbergian puritanism in which American art criticism was steeped.

As such across-the-board rejection never had been his lot in Europe, Fontana's confidence in the fairness of American judgment was shaken for years to come. Ultimately, it kept him from attending the opening of a large-scale exhibition—*ambienti spaziali* and all—which the Walker Art Center in Minneapolis accorded him in 1966. Nonetheless, it did not temper his enthusiasm for New York's burgeoning art scene, nor did it diminish his delight in the Manhattan skyline. He left the city with the most vivid impressions of the sledgehammer boldness of its buildings during daylight and their luminous dissolution at night.

Fontana resolved to devote a series of paintings to New York as he had to Venice before. Back in his studio he decided on sheet metal as the more appropriate material—one he had not used in his work—and on gold, his favorite color. One should bear in mind that for Fontana there existed no hierarchy of media, nor did this utopian searcher for art's fourth dimension draw a strict line between second and third dimensions. His perforations and incisions act as unifying devices to whatever they support, reducing if not obliterating the materials' specificity.

At the Galleria dell' Ariete the following June, Fontana expressed his admiration for the steely erectness of New York's skyscrapers, their mirrorlike daytime exteriors and the sparkle of their transformation at night, in a series of vertical, steel and brass, slashed and punctured panels. *New York 22* records the deliberateness of the artist's touch as well as the hardness of his tools. Five holes, made with a blunt instrument, inside a hand-drawn oval, the artist's metaphor for the universe, run down the center of a space that is twice as high as it is wide.

The vertical punctures, incisions and indentations lend this brass sheet an embattled, wounded appearance, reminiscent of a building pockmarked by renovation and worn down by time. However, properly illuminated we observe but the gilded shimmer of its surface—a surface with the consistency of rippling silk or windswept water—in which we encounter our own distorted picture. Fontana understood New York better than New York understood Fontana. He would not see the city again but left us a memorable impression.

Jan van der Marck

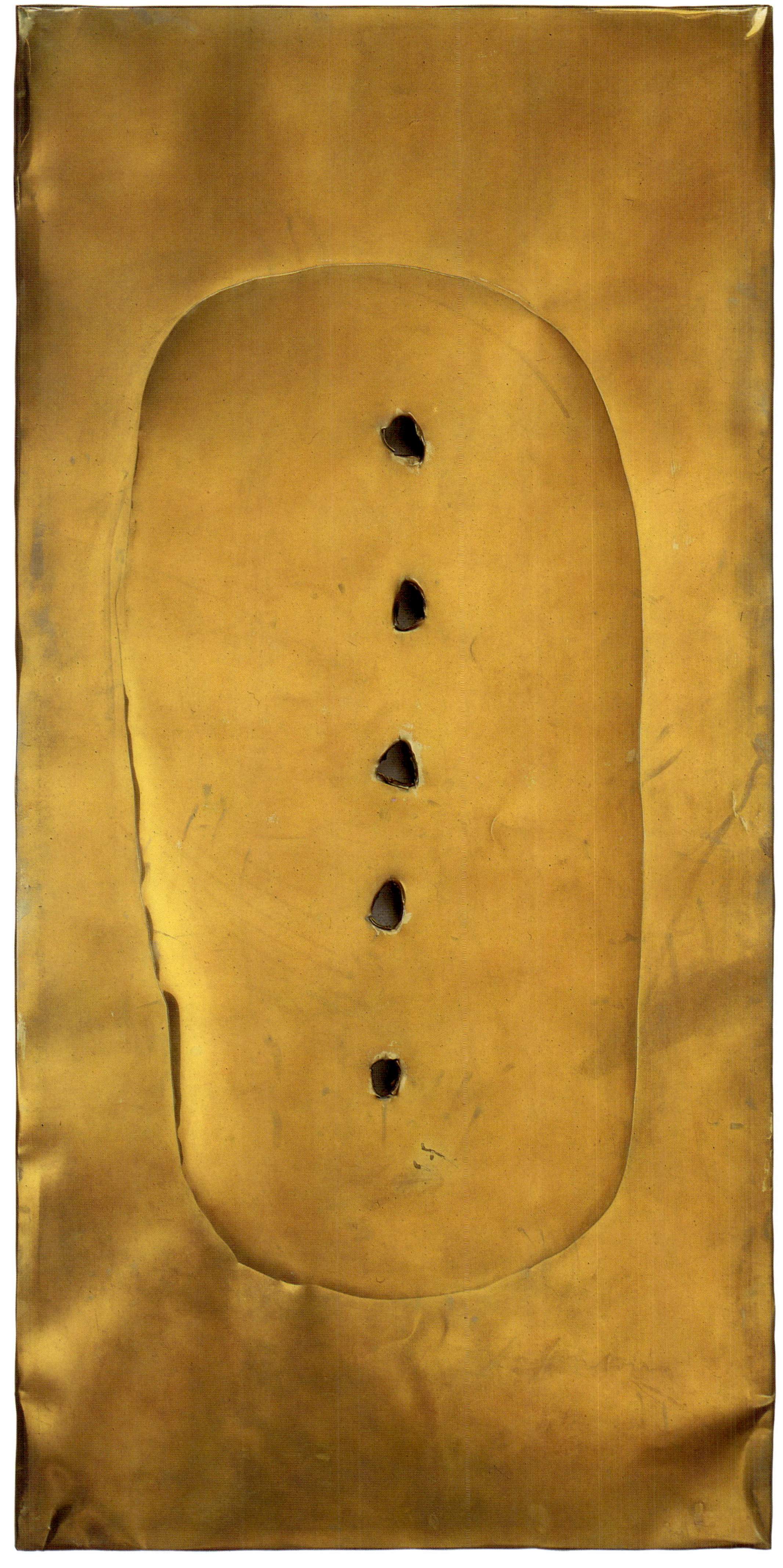

64. Eduardo Chillida (Spain, b. 1924)

Rumor de Limites #4 (Rumor of Limits), 1960

Forged iron, 40½ x 37 x 30"

Gift of Mr. and Mrs. Richard K. Weil, 1962

Eduardo Chillida stands as a major sculptor during the second half of the twentieth century.[1] Raised in the Spanish tradition of iron sculptors and trained as an architect, Chillida's work grapples with the concepts of form and space, growth and decay, surface and volume. *Rumor de Limites* is one of a series of seven sculptures that aggressively attack the nature of sculpture's conceptual and physical limits.

In *Rumor de Limites* Chillida wrestles with space. With every piece, with every step of his work, he conquers space. Only for short stretches do the elements maintain their directions; then they bend, twist, take turns, and are bisected, notched, and interrupted again and again in their course. There is no continuous organic flow; every so often a new decision is made for a new attack of the space. This emanates from where the sculpture touches the ground. It seems not so much to rest on it but to take off from it, to rise and to unfold due to its inherent powers. The sculpture then confronts invisible opposing powers which force it in this or that direction: a drama that is carried out between the power of the material and the power of the space.

The material is iron. Forged iron. It is almost the only material used by the artist in his early years. To forge iron means to work with hammer and tongs in a blazing fire. It requires enormous physical strength; it also requires mental strength to force upon the elements one's own will, which allows the material to speak and yet defeats it at the same time. The result is not just a heap of iron but a creation of free imagination—a dramatic but also lyrical creation that does not exist in nature: a work of art, fashioned by the hand of man, incomparable with anything else.

Rumor de Limites is incomparable also with other sculpture of the period, even though wrought-iron as an artistic material was discovered before Chillida. He stands in a European—especially Spanish—tradition. The great Catalonean architect Antoni Gaudi was also a forger of iron, as his buildings in Barcelona with their Art Nouveau grates and balustrades demonstrate. Likewise, sculptor Julio Gonzalez, with his magnificent wrought-iron sculptures, realized that one had to destroy the profiles of iron in order to gain new powers from it. Chillida does the same thing, however, in a completely different manner: he destroys sheets of industrially-made iron. Destruction did indeed constitute an important aesthetic principle in this century, no matter whether one destroyed existing materials or used previously destroyed materials like scrap metal (as did Chillida's contemporary, Jean Tinguely, who "refined" old iron into his plastic humoresques).

Over the years Chillida's art became less dramatic, less linear, more spacious and monumental, yet it continued to define space. In *Rumor de Limites*, one can speak of free gestures in space, not too far from what was, after the middle of the century, called "action painting" in painting. It is "informal" art, as far as sculpture can be informal, since the working process itself takes too long to allow the same spontaneity, for example, as Jackson Pollock's art. Nevertheless, its "lines," too, are dynamic and in motion. It never comes to a stop and seems to be in full action, as it were, suddenly solidified in the midst of action.

In spite of this dynamism there is a great amount of static calm in Chillida's plastic oeuvre. His entire art is based in this polarity of static and dynamic. Even *Rumor de Limites* possesses a strong sense of grounding, in spite of its abruptness of motion and the fact that it seems to take off from the ground. The sculpture is not very big but its message is monumental; it seems fitting that Chillida soon afterwards received orders for monumental sculptures from all over the world. Since 1989 one of the finest has stood in the United States, in Dallas, in front of I.M. Pei's concert hall. The sculptor has created monumental works in many countries of the world, from Europe to Japan, and, of course, particularly in Spain. In 1977 he fulfilled a lifelong dream. He created a group of wrought-iron sculptures—*Wind Combs* (San Sebastian, Spain) as he called them—some of which cling to rocks in the ocean and others to the opposite rocks on the shore: a marvellous dialogue amidst a tremendous scenery. In this powerful work some aspects are felt which were introduced in the early 1950s and which also constitute the character of *Rumor de Limites*: the power of the plastic gesture and the free expansion into space. Some decades later the nervous restlessness noticeable in the early work has given way to a majestic calm; nevertheless, in it Chillida's mental restlessness, his "inquiétude," remains.

Werner Schmalenbach
translated by Eva Strohm

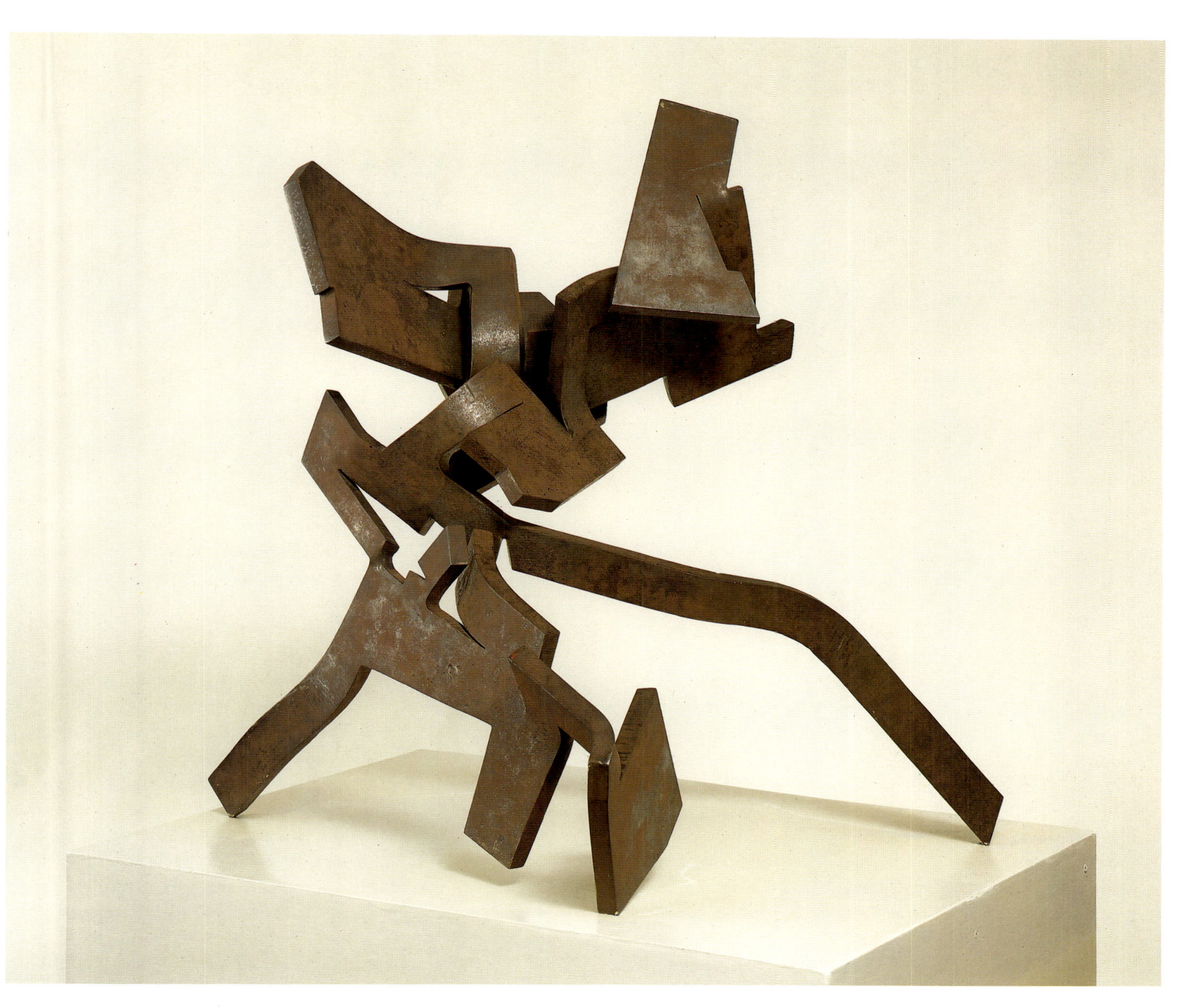

65. Pietro Consagra (Italy, b. 1920)
Racconto di Marinaio (A Mariner's Tale), 1961

Bronze, 51½ x 48 x 4"
Gift of Mrs. Mark C. Steinberg, 1964

Pietro Consagra, one of the most innovative Italian artists of the last forty years, has contributed significantly to restoring the prestige of Italian art on an international level.[1] His bronze sculpture, *Racconto di Marinaio* (1961), belongs to the series titled *Dialogues* and is representative of his art of the 1950s, his most creative period, that earned him the Gran Premio della Scultura (Grand Prize of Sculpture) at the Venice Biennale in 1960.

Born in Sicily in 1920, Consagra arrived in Rome in 1944 and was among the founders of *Forma*, an artistic movement created in 1947 to assert the importance of pure abstract form and creative freedom. This position was in direct opposition to the naturalistic Realism supported by the Italian Communist Party. In 1947 he visited Paris where he met such important European artistic vanguards as Hans Arp, Constantin Brancusi, Henri Laurens, Fernand Léger, and Antoine Pevsner. However, Consagra's acknowledged artistic influence was primarily Futurism, especially the dynamism of Umberto Boccioni. In addition, he was particularly attracted to Pablo Picasso's "monuments to the tragedy of human condition" and the *Mobiles* by Alexander Calder because of their "renewed plastic awareness towards a form of art more functional and less intimate."[2]

Consagra's first works, created between 1947 and 1952, were slender, vertical, pointed iron sculptures called *Totems*, which were derived from his experience with Constructivism and inspired by dramatic episodes of contemporary Italian history, such as the liberation from fascism and the people's struggles against the mafia in Sicily.

In 1954 Consagra initiated a new stylistic phase of his art with his series of *Dialogues* (1954–61), consisting of sculptures that represent an evolution of forms toward flat, quadrangular patterns, easily accessible at a glance. These sculptures, viewed against a wall, were created on a human scale with a definite frontal orientation to emphasize their two-dimensional patterns. As the artist explained in his writings, he wanted to abolish the traditional "ideology of the power" of three-dimensional objects situated like monuments in the middle of a square.[3] The goal of the artist was to create sculpture that performed both a social and aesthetic role as an integral feature of its surrounding area. To Consagra the *Dialogues* confronted the viewer with their directness, and stimulated an aesthetic conversation between the viewer and the bronze or wood surfaces which were engraved with deep gouges resembling wounds. In the *Dialogues*, especially those made between 1956 and 1960, the dramatic chiaroscuro effects of the surfaces are reminiscent of *Art Informel*. But, unlike *Art Informel*, Consagra left nothing to chance or to uncontrolled passions. His forms were developed in a Constructivist manner, and while the series evolved through different stages, the basic form of the maquettes never changed. *Dialogues* also refer to Consagra's use of both geometric and anthropomorphic forms, in dialectical opposition, that are linked together in a dynamic tension. In the first *Dialogues*, such as *Figures* of 1954 (Yale University Art Gallery) and *Colloquy* of 1955 (Museo de Arte Contemporanea de Universitade, Sao Paulo, Brazil), the forms appear slightly human or anthropomorphic, but they are built up with rectangles that are geometrically organized to form jutting corners and rigid forms to create a tense, dynamic surface design.

Beginning in 1957, in such works as *Dialogue In Front of A Mirror* (Museum of Modern Art, New York), Consagra created his sculptures with overlapping forms pressed into a low relief in order to obtain a more dense surface. This stylistic transformation finds its greatest expression in *Racconto di Marinaio* and the comparable *Free Dialogue* of the same year (Galleria Nazionale d'Arte Moderna, Rome). In these sculptures the contrast between surface and depth, solid and space is minimal; the forms are engraved into the bronze, creating a panel of abstract signs. The black areas, tarnished with the mat patina, are contrasted to, and are in perfect balance with, the bright, shiny planes which reflect light and become animated and colored. Through these means Consagra shapes an abstract screen, full of great suggestive effect and lyrical expression.

The themes of human scale and contrast of forms and surfaces in the *Dialogues* are further developed in Consagra's art after 1963, up to his most recent achievements. In a series of sculptures and a book entitled *Frontal City* (1968), the sculptor used the forms and shapes of his former frontal works for an architectural project in which the buildings for a town plan are designed to unify art and life on an urban scale. Thus the work of art can represent a utopian way of living with the suggestion of freedom and imagination. Many of the more recent works, such as *Frame* (1972), *Plastico in Ferro* (*Iron's Plastic*, 1977), *Bifrontale in Ferro* (*Bifrontal Figure in Iron*, 1977), and *Planets* (1987, Roma, Galleria dei Banchi Nuovi), appear increasingly more colorful and joyful, while such earlier works as *Dialogues* represent a phase of solitary meditation and deep concentration.

Consagra's concept of a sculptural design combining abstract form with a human scale and expression found their greatest realization in the *Dialogues* series of which *Racconto di Marinaio* and its companion piece, *Free Dialogue*, are the last and highest evolution of these aesthetic ideas.

Anna Imponente

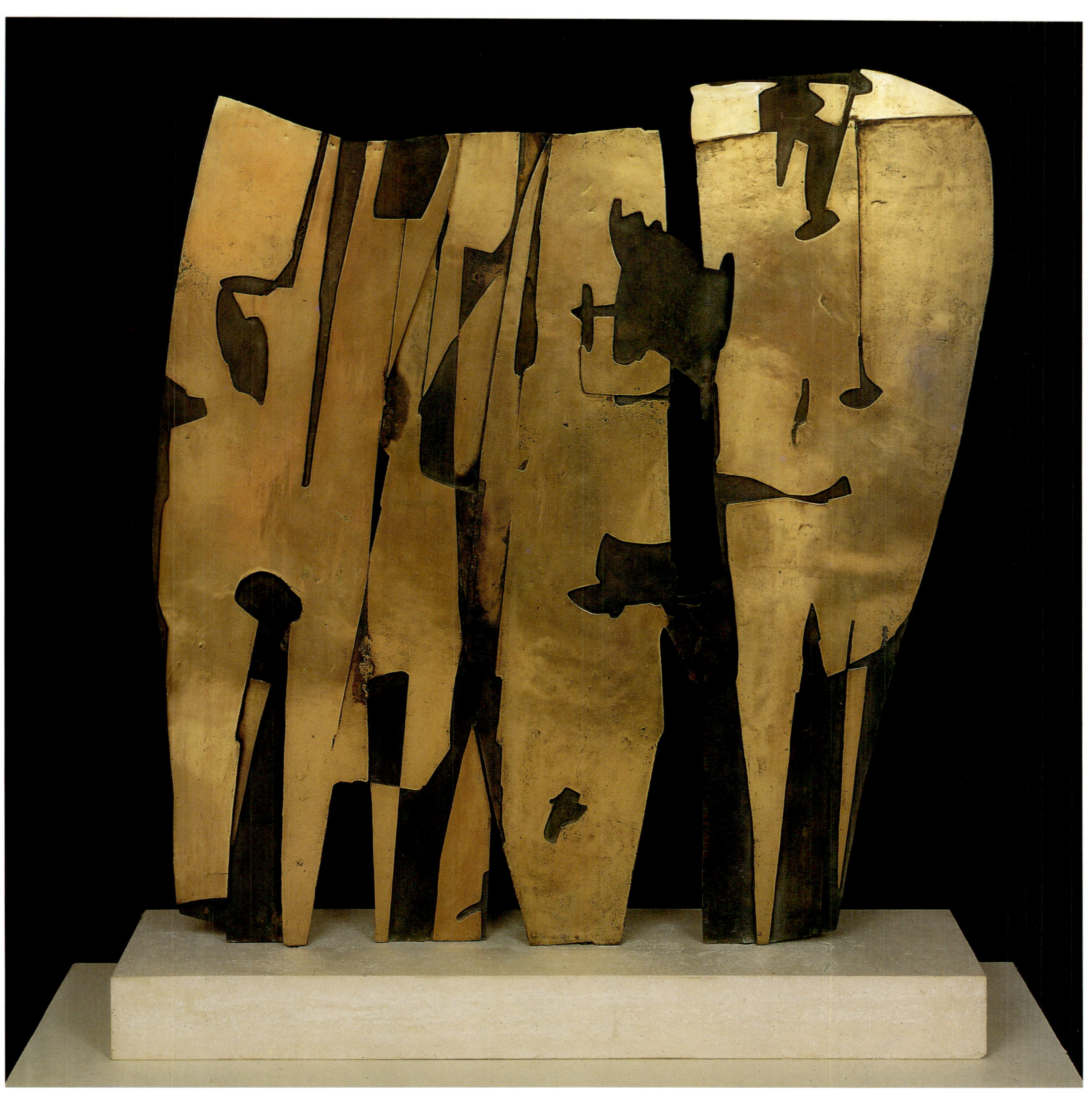

66. George Bellows (United States, 1882–1925) *Portrait of Geraldine Lee, No. 1*, 1914

Oil on panel, 22 x 18"
University purchase, Bixby Fund, 1966

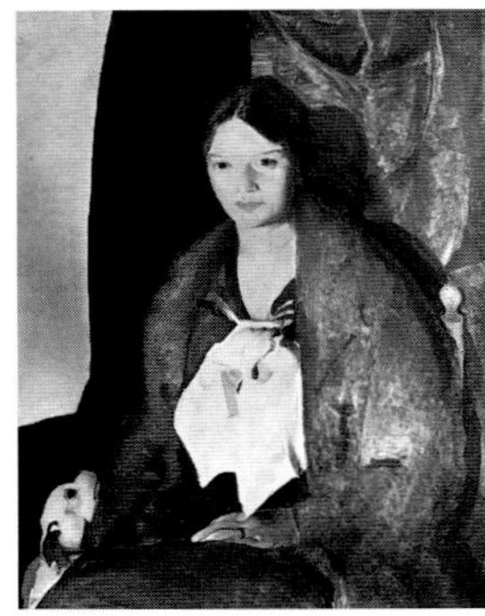

George Bellows
Portrait of Geraldine Lee, No. 1, 1914
Uncut appearance of the portrait
Photograph courtesy the Smithsonian Institution

Born and raised in Columbus, Ohio, George Bellows in 1904 went to New York to study art.[1] Studying under Robert Henri, the dynamic leader of The Eight who became his mentor and life-long friend, Bellows first made his reputation with dramatically lighted, grittily realistic urban genre subjects as well as urban landscapes. Beginning in 1911, when he first summered on the island of Monhegan, Maine, Bellows began to paint with a lighter palette and then stronger colors. After 1916 he developed a second career as a lithographer. During the 1920s, when he was associated with the artists' colony of Woodstock, New York, Bellows attempted increasingly monumental pieces. Early in 1925, complications of a ruptured appendix cut short his further artistic development.

Throughout Bellows' career, portraiture was a strong, if intermittent, theme, which included some of his most important works. Like other students of Robert Henri, who was primarily a portraitist, Bellows produced strong, Caravagesque portraits among his earliest paintings, some of them quick studies, but many others quite formal portraits of fellow artists and what appear to have been street urchins. He achieved early success with his urban scenes but did not receive significant portrait commissions until a visit to his home town, late in 1912, resulted in formal portraits of art patrons and members of the faculty of his alma mater, Ohio State University. This group of often sensitive but mainly conservatively formatted portraits, still against a dark background, was followed by a burst of concentrated portrait activity in a strikingly different manner during the summer of 1914, when Bellows painted more than fifteen[2] fairly large-scale portraits. The picturesque island of Monhegan is the place where Bellows had discovered the charms and expressive potential of the wild landscape.[3] On his first visit, in 1911, and again through the summer and fall of 1913, he had been carried away by a love of landscape painting, finding new subjects and inspiration everywhere on the island. It is surprising, therefore, that during the summer of 1914 he turned his back on the motifs that so recently had enchanted him, producing only two landscape paintings during the entire season.

The same reasons that caused Bellows to devote that summer to portraiture also shaped the appearance of those portraits. Like Robert Henri, Bellows throughout most of his career was intensely interested in aesthetic theory and systems of color and composition. Early in 1914 he immersed himself in the writings of the aesthetician Denman Ross, who advocated for the artist a much more controlled approach.[4] Ross wrote about line, texture, balance, and other aesthetic factors, but his most fully-developed and influential discussion was of a system for what he called set palettes. Before beginning his painting, the artist should analyze his subject and organize the palette it required, premixing both the blended secondary colors and the stepped admixtures of white or black that made those colors lighter or darker (the quality known by the technical term, "value"). Such palettes typically were limited in the number of colors; they also were organized in terms of discrete steps of value. One immediate effect of Bellows' adoption of Ross' system was that Bellows began to think in terms of values and, what is more, in terms of a wider range of values than he had been using. Portraits in a studio setting, where he had complete control over lighting, lent themselves to this new way of thinking, as landscapes largely did not. As Bellows wrote to Henri: "I have been painting people all summer in a house with three sides open to the sun, which I open and close on [choice]. Every portrait is in a new light."[5] His portrait of *Geraldine Lee, No. 1,* especially as it originally appeared, is typical of his other portraits painted that summer, in the wide range of values, from nearly black to nearly white, and in the very strong, directed light effect, which blanches color in the face, for instance, allowing Bellows to use the very high values of his set palette.[6]

Another system of formal control, which Bellows used apparently in all of his work that summer, was to organize his compositions according to a system of proportions based upon golden-section divisions of the sides of the painting's rectangle. In *Geraldine Lee, No. 1,* for instance, the strong vertical line of the proper left side of the coat is aligned with a golden-section division of the painting's width; the face is contained within two such divisions. Even such details as the slanting line of the hair on the proper left side of the forehead and the slanting line of the lowest part of the bow are aligned with diagonals from the center of the right edge to golden-section divisions of the painting's top and bottom edges. Numerous other alignments give the portraits of 1914 a formal, sometimes quite conspicuously geometric character.

When *Geraldine Lee, No. 1* was cut down, using a power saw, from the standard size for that summer, 38 x 30 inches, to its present dimensions, 22 x 18 inches, is not known. It was signed, in its present form, by the artist's widow. Because Bellows is known to have at different times cut down or even destroyed his paintings, and because several others from this time were cut down to the same size,[7] it seems probable that the artist cut down *Geraldine Lee, No. 1,* presumably because his taste had changed and his allegiance to his method that summer had waned. The cropping had the effect of undoing some of the more obvious effects of his method by eliminating the extreme contrast on the left side, by undoing most of the geometry, and by changing an originally somewhat stiff portrait into a compellingly intimate one. The strong light effect, which had been sufficient to breathe life into the large portraits of 1914, gives a powerful impact to the sense of personality in the close-up. Due to its strong presence, it is hard to fully credit Bellows' very modernist statement that he painted Geraldine Lee Nott, daughter of a local fisherman, simply because she provided a "motif."[8]

Michael A. Quick

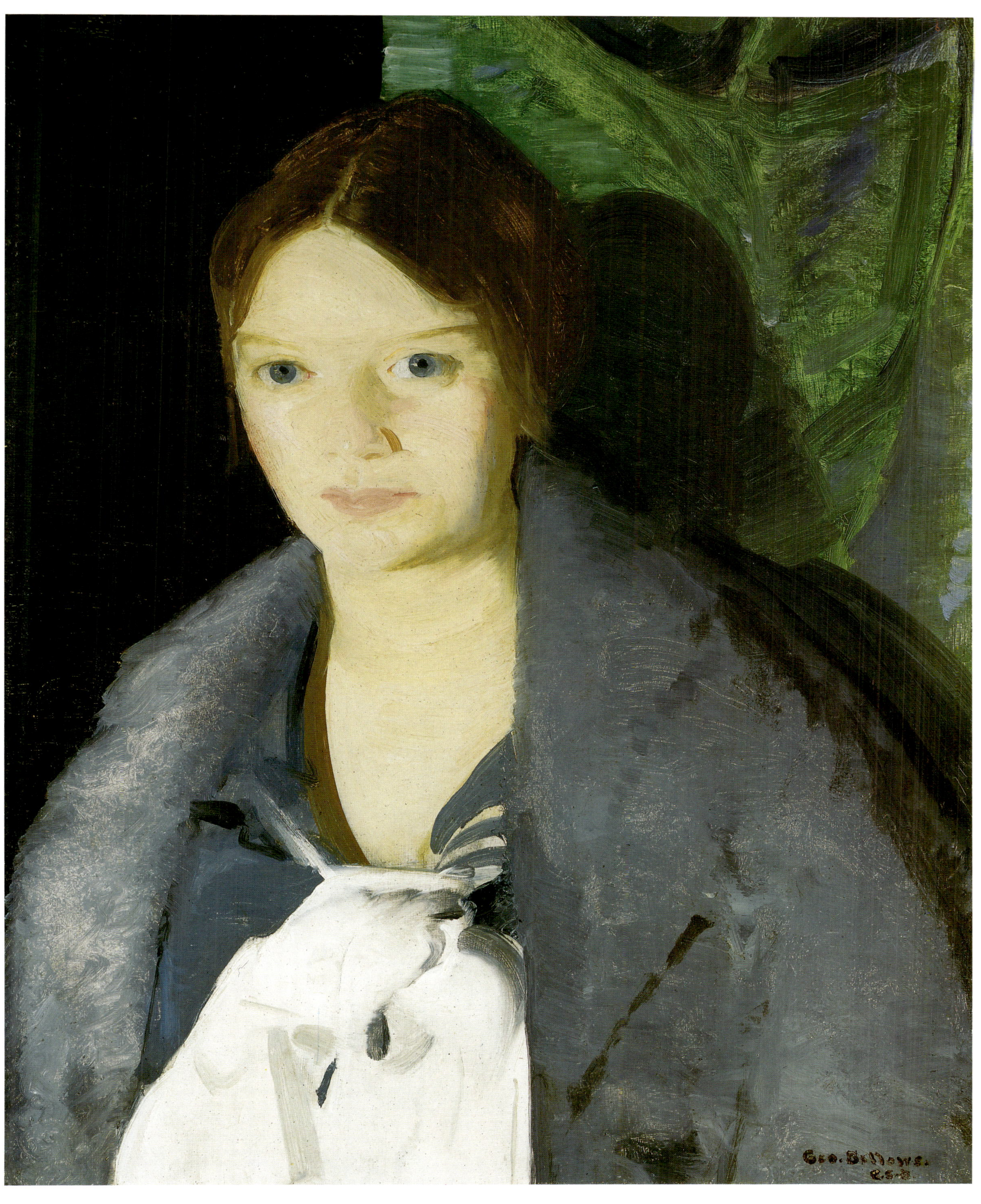
Geo. Bellows.
E.S.B.

67. Lyonel Feininger (United States, 1871–1956)
Bridge I, 1913

Oil on canvas, 31½ x 39½"
University purchase, Bixby Fund, 1950

The summer of 1913 proved a particularly happy and productive period in Feininger's life. From April to September he lived in Weimar, a city which he dearly loved and to which he would return in 1919 as one of the first instructors at the Bauhaus under Walter Gropius. An American by birth, Feininger had lived in Germany since 1887, where, at the age of 17, he went to study music. After switching to art, he established an international reputation as a cartoonist and caricaturist, creating such popular comic strips as *The Kin-der-kids* and *Wee Willie Winkie's World.* His introduction to Cubism in Paris in 1911 revolutionized his art, and two years later he was invited by Franz Marc to exhibit with other European modernists at the First German Autumn Salon in Berlin. During his summer in Weimar, Feininger completed the five works shown in that exhibition.

In a letter to his wife, Julia, Feininger described that summer in Weimar as "decisive in many respects, . . . a period of intuitive creative work."[1] He went sketching daily on his bike, making hundreds of drawings of the city and the neighboring villages.

> *Sketching out-of-doors these last days I got into a sort of ecstasy. At the end of an afternoon my whole being was functioning instinctively, my capabilities were increased to the utmost. I stood on one and the same spot drawing the same motif three or four times until I got it according to my vision. That goes beyond mere observation and recording by far. It is a magnetic coordinating, liberating from all restrictions.*[2]

The arched stone bridge over the Ilm river in Ober-Weimar and the gentle landscape around it proved one of Feininger's favorite subjects. On 21 August he wrote to his wife of being "spellbound" by "this little river Ilm." "I cannot get away from the loveliness of the greens," which he described standing

> *on the bridge for a long while looking down into the water, which is very high now; a few inches more and the meadows in front of the castle would be flooded. The river is so beautiful now, this muddy grayish brown-green; like a veiled mirror it reflects the trees and the sky, which also is of a misty greenish hue.*[3]

Bridge I is one of a half dozen paintings Feininger made of this tranquil river setting over a seven-year period. Only the first painting (*Bridge 0*, 1912, location unknown), rendered more naturalistically and completed the previous year, included people. *Bridge I* and the remaining works in the series explore the correspondence between the architectonic structure of the bridge, the simple geometry of the houses beyond and the organic forms of nature. The four arches which comprise the bridge's distinctive silhouette focus the viewer's attention across the surface of the painting and provide the structure which underlies the painting's Cubist geometry.

In 1917 critic Paul Westheim described this painting as "joyful, somewhat elastic and springy." He likened the repeating arches to "ribs of a Gothic vault," and found "the same swing" in the crystalline reflections in the water. "The whole," he wrote, "is gently animated by the wavelike motion of the forms."[4] Westheim's reading of the painting as a combination of vaulted forms and wavelike motions underscores the painting's connection, formally, thematically and symbolically, with two other categories of paintings that form an important part of Feininger's oeuvre and to which he devoted substantial effort that same summer—marine paintings and churches.

From childhood Feininger had dreamed of being a marine painter and in 1913 painted his first true marine painting. Executed on the same size canvas as *Bridge I*, it showed two multi-masted vessels tossed by the jagged green waves of a stormy, churning, Cubist sea (*Side-Wheeler [Mail Steamer]*, 1913, private collection). For the artist the regularly repeating rhythms of the sea gave physical evidence of the clarity and order underlying nature's forms. Even more important than the sea, however, were the picturesque village churches in the Thuringian forest around Weimar. During the summer of 1913, Feininger made numerous sketches and completed three canvases of his favorite church at Gelmeroda, whose distinctive spire and low Gothic nave he had sketched seven years before. On 15 June Feininger wrote to his friend, artist Alfred Kubin, that the church steeples in Weimar and the neighboring villages were "among the most mystical achievements of so-called civilized man." He described standing in front of them "for hours, stealing up on the secret of their form."[5]

In *Bridge I* Feininger's transformation of the rounded arches of the bridge into pointed Gothic arches and the proliferation of that motif across the surface of the painting invest this tranquil scene with a throbbing spiritual presence. In the upward thrust of their gently sloping forms, the arches unite the natural and the man-made in a manner calculated to evoke a sense of order and harmony—calculated, that is, to visualize the invisible. The subtle and rather narrow range of greens, yellows and gray-browns with which Feininger rendered the scene correspond closely with his verbal description of the area and serve to reinforce the sense of unity contained in the forms. As he explained to Kubin, Feininger considered

> *expression, monumentality . . . [and] concentration . . . the highest value in a work of art. . . . Form and color, both not naturalistically rendered but carried to a new formal relationship—this always was, and surely will continue to be, art, not a short-lived matter of fashion, a pastime—but eternity.*[6]

Bridge I seems the physical realization of these goals.

Ruth L. Bohan

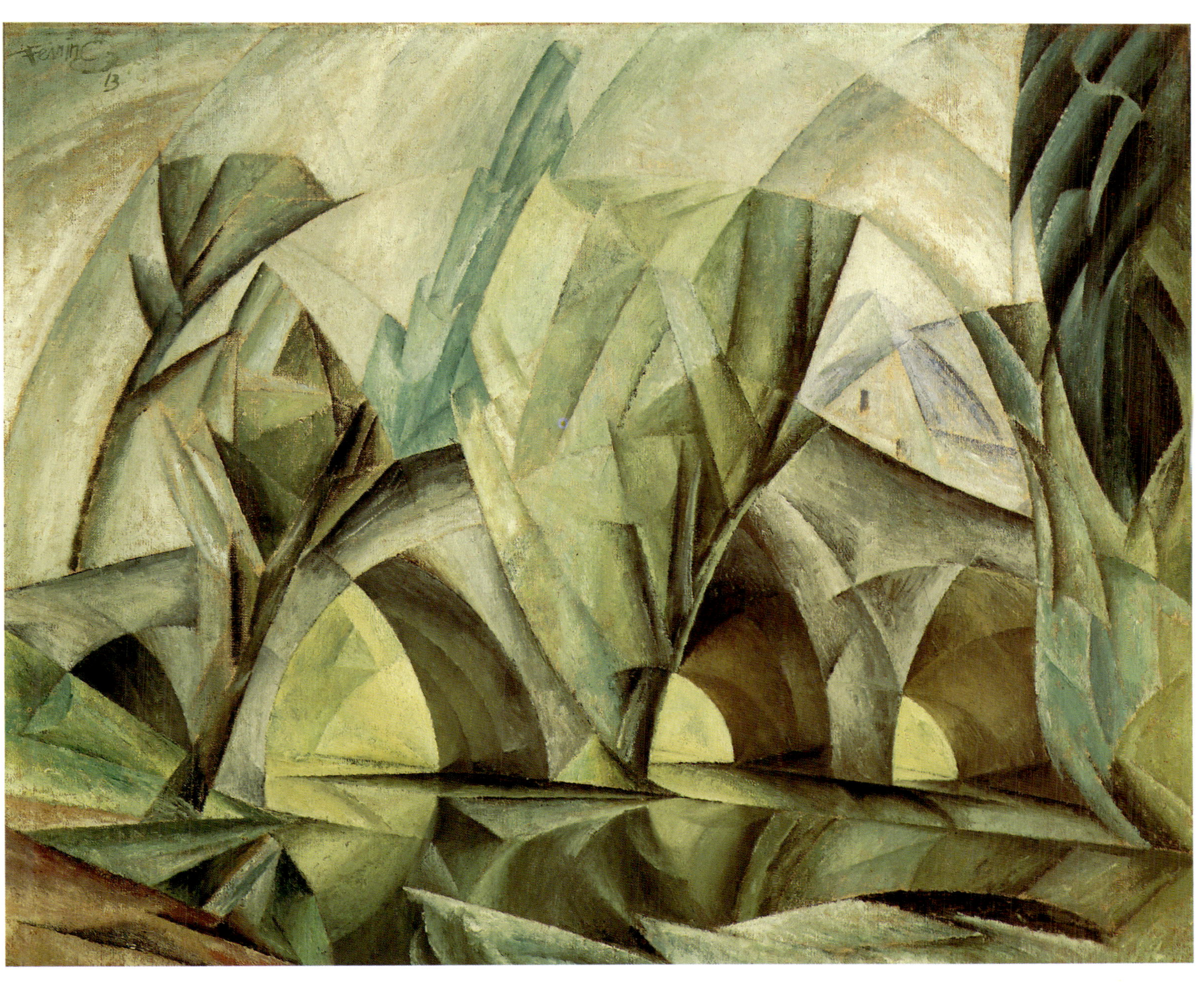

68. Marsden Hartley (United States, 1877–1943) *The Iron Cross,* 1915

Oil on canvas, 47¼ x 47¼"
University purchase, Bixby Fund, 1952

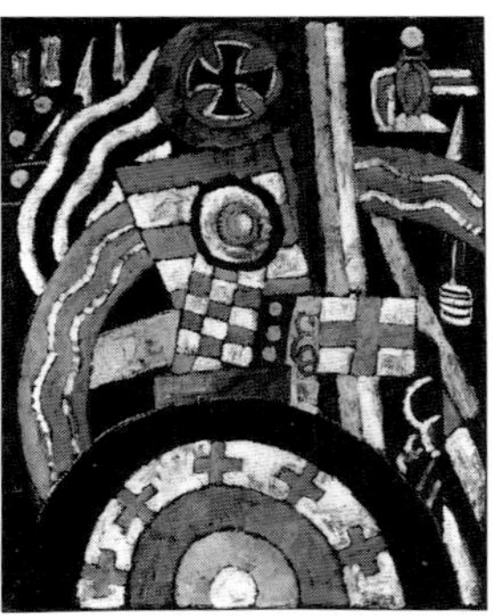

Marsden Hartley
Abstraction: Military Symbols, 1914
Oil on canvas, 40 x 32"
The Toledo Museum of Art, Ohio
Gift of Edward Drummond Libbey

From November 1914 through the fall of 1915 Hartley painted more than a dozen powerfully emblematic paintings which he called his War Motifs. Also known as the German Officer paintings, the fourteen extant works in this series pay tribute to the idea of comradeship and in particular to two of Hartley's dearest German friends, the young Prussian military officer, Karl Von Freyburg, and his cousin, the sculptor, Arnold Rönnebeck. Hartley met both men in Paris in 1912, visited them briefly in Berlin in early 1913 and in April of that year moved to Berlin where he lived for nearly two years. On October 7, 1914, barely two months after the outbreak of World War I, Von Freyburg was killed in battle in France. A few months later, Rönnebeck was seriously wounded. Hartley was devastated by the news of Von Freyburg's death and stopped painting for a month. When he resumed painting in November, the German Officer series was born.[1]

The paintings in this series are among the most private and enigmatic in Hartley's long and distinguished career. Painted by an American on German soil in wartime and replete with various nationalist and military symbols, they constitute a brilliant personal synthesis of two of the leading avant-garde tendencies of the war years—Cubism and Expressionism. When first exhibited in the United States in 1916, the paintings were severely criticized for what were perceived to be their pro-German sentiments, a characterization which Hartley vehemently denied. In a statement issued with the exhibition, Hartley claimed:

> *The forms are only those which I have observed casually from day to day. There is no hidden symbolism whatsoever in them; there is no slight intention of that anywhere. . . . They are merely consultations of the eye . . . my notion of the purely pictural.*[2]

It was only after Hartley's death in 1943 that the personal nature of the symbolism became more fully understood.

In a letter to Washington dealer Duncan Phillips, Rönnebeck explained that the paintings symbolized himself and Von Freyburg, both of whom had received the Iron Cross for bravery. The red "4" on the blue ground of a uniform epaulet stands for the 4th regiment of the Kaiser's guards in which Von Freyburg fought. The curvaceous "E" refers to Rönnebeck's regiment of the grand-grenadiers, for which Queen Elisabeth of Greece served as patroness. The black and white checkerboard, present along the lower border of the Washington University painting, pays tribute to Von Freyburg's love of chess. Other identifiable symbols are the blue and white diamond pattern of the Bavarian flag and the distinctive Iron Cross, centered along the upper margin of the painting.

Rönnebeck recalled that as he lay recuperating in a Berlin hospital during the war Hartley had asked permission to place the Iron Cross by his easel in remembrance of the fallen Von Freyburg. The medal, a simple cast iron Maltese Cross edged in silver, had been designed in 1813 at the instigation of Frederick William II during the German war for liberation. In *The Iron Cross* the black and white cross is placed on a red ground and inscribed in a green circle. In other paintings in the series the red-green coloring is reversed or replaced by a red-gold cross on a green ground near the center of the composition. The circular bands of black and white, which vary in width and surround the red cross, create a bold bull's eye effect.

Hartley was well aware of the multiple meanings associated with the figure of the cross and employed these to great advantage in his War Motif paintings. He once contemplated a vocation in the priesthood. In *The Iron Cross,* his placement of the iron cross along the painting's upper edge, with bands of color extending diagonally down from it, recalls the traditional depiction of the Christian cross suspended in the heavens with rays of colored light emanating from it. Equally familiar, particularly during wartime, would have been the simple red cross symbolizing the relief efforts of the International Red Cross. Echoes of such a cross seem strongly inscribed in the red cross and white circular surround emboldened by small amounts of green near the painting's midpoint. With its overlapping associations with religious, military and humanitarian causes, the image of the cross typifies the layering and ambiguity evident throughout the series.

The large scale, brilliantly patterned surfaces and symbolic content of the German Officer paintings give brilliant expression to Hartley's love of the pomp and pageantry of the German war effort at the same time that they provide a somber reminder of the war's enormous cost in human life. Hartley wrote to his friend Rockwell Kent that the many parades and formal military displays which he saw in the German capital stimulated his "child's love for the public spectacle." Hartley greatly preferred the "ruggedness and vitality" of the German people to what he judged the "utterly feminine" characteristics of the French,[3] and was impressed as well with the tradition of German mysticism in which he was well read. He wrote to Alfred Stieglitz that:

> *The German is most essentially a symbolist and there is every evidence that mysticism has had its home here. . . . I am mystic too but what I want to express is not national but universal.*[4]

A similar spirit of universalism, couched now in the symbols of internationalism, seems evident in *The Iron Cross* as in other paintings in the series. The emphasis on Germanic symbols and insignia characteristic of the earlier works in the series has now given way to more abstract military allusions. Many of the flags and military insignia in *The Iron Cross* incorporate the colors and the designs associated with a number of countries involved in the war effort, giving the painting less of a partisan and more of an international spirit. Hartley's creative fusion of Cubist (French) and Expressionist (German) stylistic tendencies might also be thought of in broadly international terms. Even as peace continued to elude the combatants in the trenches, Hartley achieved a creative and compelling union in his art.

Ruth L. Bohan

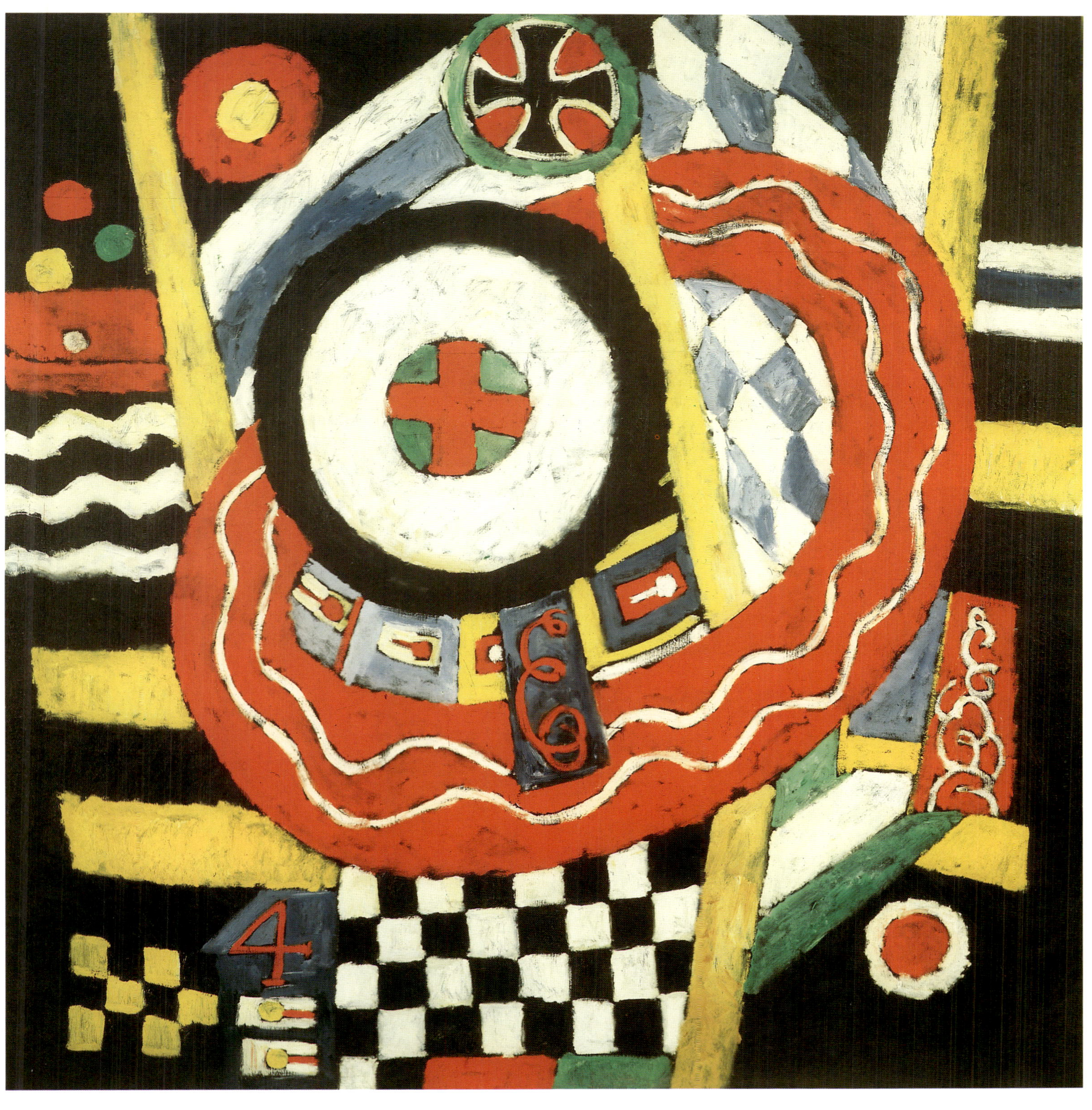
4

69. Joseph Stella
(United States, 1880–1946)
Man in Elevated (Train), 1918
Oil, wire and collage on glass, 14¼ x 14¾"
University purchase, Kende Sale Fund, 1946

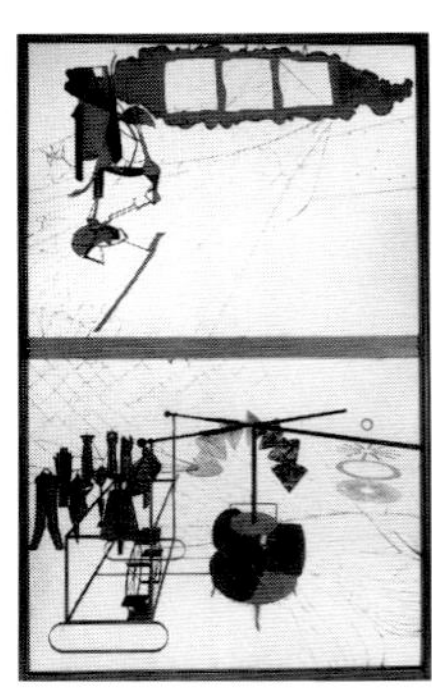

Marcel Duchamp
The Large Glass, The Bride Stripped Bare by Her Bachelors, Even, c. 1915
Oil and lead wire on glass, 109¼ x 69⅛"
Philadelphia Museum of Art
Bequest of Katherine S. Dreier

Joseph Stella's *Man in Elevated (Train)* is at once a witty tribute to the personal and professional ties he shared with his friend, artist Marcel Duchamp, and a record of the widespread impulse toward experimentation and greater self-expression which characterized the American modernist community in the aftermath of the Armory Show. Born in Italy and initially intent on a career in medicine, Stella quickly switched to art following his arrival in New York in 1896. He studied briefly at the Art Students League and during the first decade of this century produced a number of drawings of miners and immigrants which display his skills as a draftsman and his attachment to the art of the old Italian masters. It was not until a trip to Paris in 1911–12 introduced him to the burgeoning art of the Cubists and Futurists that Stella switched his allegiance to the more radical art of his day. Throughout the remainder of the 1910s and continuing into the early 1920s, Stella produced his most boldly experimental work, much of it concerned with what he termed the "comedy" and "tragedy" of the urban industrial world.[1]

Man in Elevated (Train) was completed in 1918, the year Stella began his master work, *Brooklyn Bridge* (1918–20, Yale University Art Gallery). Both works record Stella's fascination with the steely surfaces and machine-tooled forms of New York's intra-city transportation systems. But where the *Brooklyn Bridge* elevates the experience to one of religious transcendence, *Man in Elevated (Train)* couches it in the ironic detachment of Dada. The work portrays a man seen in profile through the rectangular window of an urban commuter train. His face is obscured by reflections on the surface of the window. To the right a portion of his large-brimmed black hat, starched white collar, navy blue suit, firm jaw and neatly trimmed brown hair overlap the vertical supports of the car in which he rides. The man's head is tilted slightly downward and to the left, where the page from a contemporary journal absorbs his attention. In contrast to the nuanced naturalism evident in a charcoal study for this work (*Man Reading A Newspaper,* 1918, Gertrude Stein Gallery, New York), in the completed glass painting, the man, even more than his machine-made environment, seems controlled by the smooth surfaces, regular contours and crisp regularity of the machine.

Technically, conceptually and thematically the work acknowledges two well-known works by Duchamp: *The Bride Stripped Bare by Her Bachelors, Even* (1915–23, Philadelphia Museum of Art) and *Sad Young Man on a Train* (1911, The Peggy Guggenheim Foundation). Stella owned three preliminary studies for Duchamp's glass painting, and during the years Duchamp labored on the *Large Glass,* Stella produced more than a dozen of his own reverse paintings on glass. Of these, *Man in Elevated (Train)* exhibits the greatest technical and intellectual daring. Like Duchamp Stella outlined his principal forms with wire (Stella also used heavy string), and in one of his earliest attempts at collage, used fragments from a contemporary journal and a piece of wallpaper to suggest the open page and decorated cover of the reading material that occupies the man's downturned gaze. In lieu of the varnished dust particles and foil covered pigment with which Duchamp transformed the clear surface of his glass panel, Stella filled in the areas bounded by the wire with the more familiar medium of oil. Unlike Duchamp, Stella remained firmly committed to his role as a painter, and seems to have considered his glass paintings largely experimental, for they were rarely exhibited during his lifetime.

If the *Large Glass* encouraged Stella to experiment with new methods of construction, *Sad Young Man on a Train* suggested the setting and personal context for the work. Stella first saw *Sad Young Man on a Train* at the Armory Show. Both works show a man alone in a train, and both are autobiographical. Where Duchamp included his pipe for identification, Stella provided his hat, which he wore in several other profile self-portraits. For Duchamp the train was an inter-city train traveling between Paris and Rouen; for Stella it was the commuter train that carried him regularly between his home in Brooklyn and Duchamp's studio and the art galleries in Manhattan. Both works suggest the movement of the train by the repetition of forms, and both display a fondness for the mechanistic world of machines.

Man in Elevated (Train) draws additional connections between the artists' bachelor-like lives and the bride-bachelor relationship of the *Large Glass.* Where Duchamp's bachelor thinks about his elusive bride, isolated from him in the upper panel of the *Large Glass,* Stella, a self-styled Don Juan, contemplates an unknown woman, perhaps his own bride, while riding alone on a commuter train. His thoughts are reflected on the surface of the train window, where one of the forms, a fan-like shape visible in triplicate in the center of the composition, closely resembles a similarly-shaped element in the upper portion of the *pendu femelle.* Just as the elusive form of Duchamp's bride achieves concrete reality on the surface of the *Large Glass,* so the bride in Stella's mind assumes concrete form on the reflective surface of the rectangular train window. Stella thus restates the bride-bachelor relationship of the *Large Glass* in more realistic terms and with himself in the role of Duchamp's anonymous bachelor machine.

A deftly shielded eroticism and allusions to the fourth dimension provide additional ties to Duchamp and the *Large Glass.* Stella appears thoroughly knowledgeable of Duchamp's cryptic notes on the subject of the fourth dimension, and, like Duchamp, conceived of his bride as a three-dimensional reflection of a four-dimensional object.

Although Stella chose not to continue to work in this highly experimental and thoroughly Duchampian vein, the experience of working on glass, of visualizing the invisible, and of exploring themes of transparency and opacity would continue to feed his creative imagination for years to come.

Ruth L. Bohan

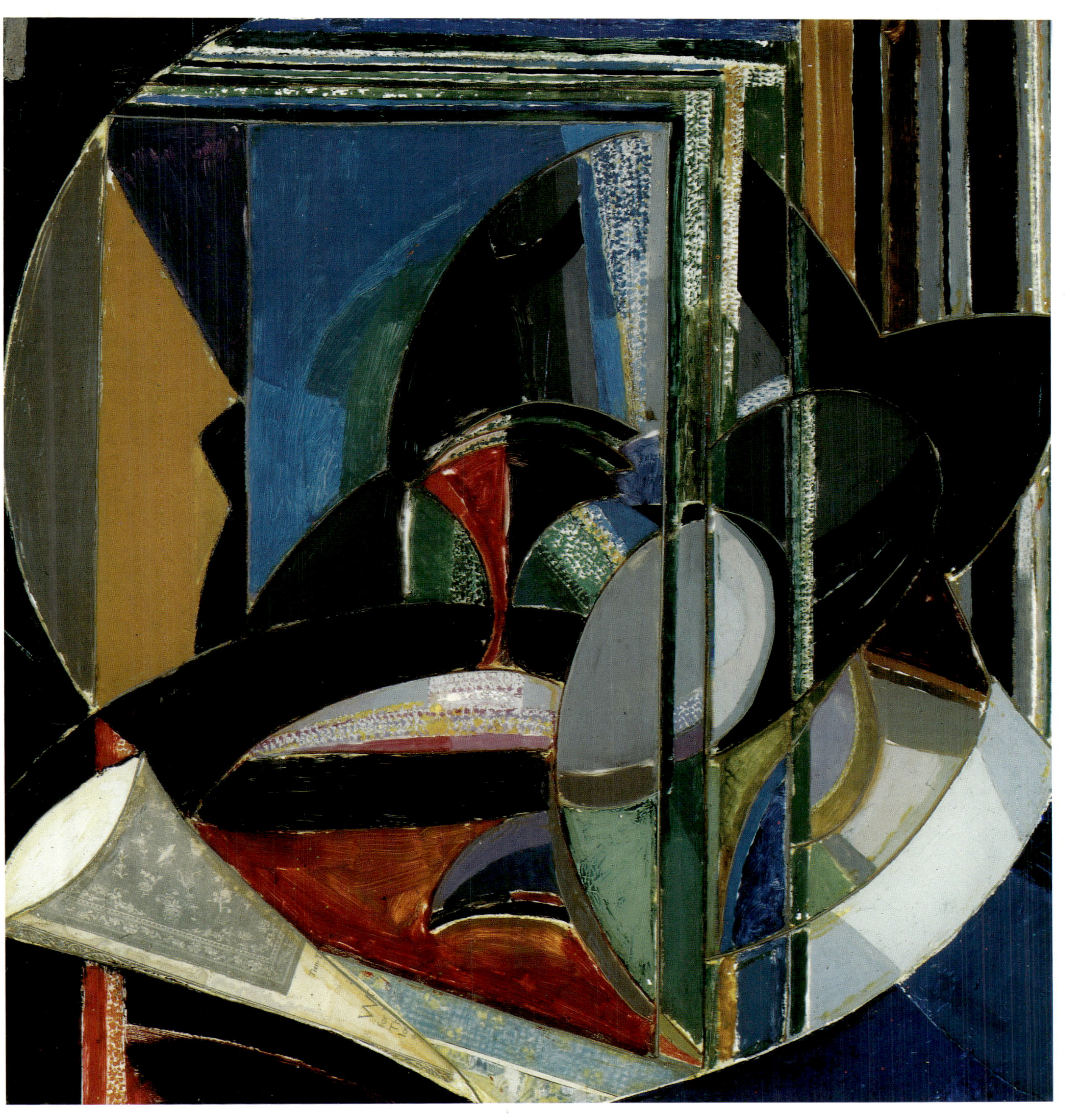

70. Arthur Dove (United States, 1880–1946) *Sand and Sea,* 1943

Oil and sand on canvas, 27 x 36"
University purchase, Bixby Fund, 1952

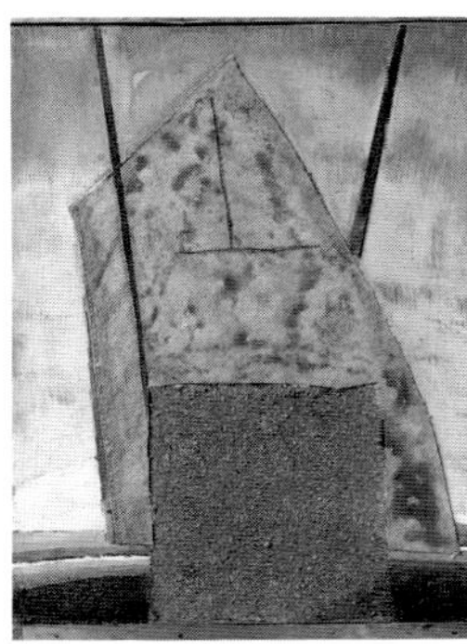

Arthur Dove
Huntington Harbor, 1926
Collage on metal plate, 12 x 9½"
The Phillips Collection, Washington, D.C.

Arthur Dove has long been recognized as a pioneer of modern art in the United States. By 1912, Dove had established in his *Nature Symbolized* series the roots of his characteristic motifs based on organic and expansive forms which paralleled the processes of growth and movement he found in the natural world around him. Throughout the 1920s and '30s, Dove developed a rich and fertile art that was one of the finest achievements of modernism in the United States. However, although it is not as well known, Dove's late work was equally important.

Sand and Sea, one of Dove's best late paintings, was done during October and November 1943. In his journal for October 25, 1943 Dove noted that he had "put sand on 27 x 36 again and paint;" other references to it appeared in the journal until November 12. Dove recorded the painting in his journal as *Sand and Sea* in a list he compiled in his journal at the end of 1944. It was exhibited in Dove's one-man show which opened March 21, 1944 at Alfred Stieglitz's gallery, An American Place, in New York.[1]

Graduating from Cornell University Dove supported himself as an illustrator for many years. In 1908–09, he spent eighteen months abroad, traveling to Paris and the south of France. By 1912, Dove had developed what was among the most advanced work done by any American artist. However, he did not immediately follow up on his stylistic breakthroughs, and worked only sporadically until 1920. Dove often lost valuable time from his painting because he insisted on maintaining his independence, away from the city and close to the land and water. In 1910 he bought a chicken farm near Westport, Connecticut; in 1923 he bought a yawl on Long Island Sound in which he lived with his second wife, Helen Torr; in 1934 he moved to the old family farm in Geneva in an attempt to save it. Each enterprise demanded long hours of backbreaking, ill-rewarded labor, which finally took a terrible physical toll. After moving back to Long Island in 1938, to an old post office in Center Port, Dove suffered a heart attack, which was followed by a complicating disease that kept him a semi-invalid for the remainder of his life.[2] It is a terrible irony that only then, forced by illness, could he give full concentration to his art and find the independence he had so long sought.

After 1939, he was at last settled and able to work with a renewed sureness and confidence, almost without interruption. This brought a new harmony and stability to his art, which reflected the new serenity that he had found, despite or probably because of his infirmity. As a result, his art underwent significant modifications. The shapes in his paintings became larger and broader, with an expanded scale of the internal parts that matched the now larger size of his canvases. There were fewer shapes than in the earlier work, and each was now described clearly and distinctly, with no overlapping of forms. There was now less gradation and modulation of paint and color within the forms. These developments, and in *Sand and Sea* the extensive application of sand to the surface, accounted for the sheer power and the physical impact that were new to Dove's art. They both reflected and contributed to the new scale and physical presence that marked American art after 1945. Dove sought a new rigor in his paintings, and he moved toward what he termed "pure painting," in which "reality and abstraction meet."[3]

In *Sand and Sea,* reality and abstraction indeed converged. Dove retained references to the subject, although they were now highly abstracted. The sand is literally evident, and we glimpse the sea (and perhaps the sky) in the four distinct and separate areas of various gradations of blue. It is as if we were looking straight down from an airplane, at an aerial view of the beach and ocean. Dove, as were such other artists as Arshile Gorky and Stuart Davis, was intrigued at this time with the new, more abstract vision of the world afforded by the airplane. Dove made this vision literal in at least one painting, titled *Flight* (1943, Phillips Collection, Washington, D.C.). This would account in part for the new flatness of shapes which were here apparent. However, if the forms were flatter, Dove consciously retained a sense of dimension through his use of real sand, the emphatic drawing that generated the rhythms and movements, and the newly deepened and enriched color. He thereby created an expansive space with a real dimension, but without the literal, substantial bulk that we associate with older European art.

For all the new elements in *Sand and Sea,* it nevertheless had unmistakable sources in Dove's earlier work. Since Dove loved the water and lived on or near it for much of his life, the painting retained the distinct autobiographic tenor that marked much of his early work, which was permeated by themes of water and ocean. The motif was used specifically in the 1940 painting *Beach* (collection unknown); the literal use of sand appeared in his collage *Huntington Harbor* (1926, Phillips Collection, Washington, D.C.). That *Sand and Sea* properly relates to Dove's collages of the 1920s indicates the new degree of physicality he sought after 1940.

The forms in *Sand and Sea* combined the organic, biomorphic shapes that recall Dove's earlier work and the 1930s work of Picasso, Klee, Arp and Miro, with some geometric configurations that showed an awareness of aspects of structuralist painting of the 1930s. In addition, Dove's late art had more connections with the art of a younger generation than has generally been recognized. For example, the biomorphic thumb shapes at center parallel those found in certain surrealizing paintings by Arshile Gorky, or by Mark Rothko in such works as *Ritual* (1944, Walker Art Center, Minneapolis). The use of sand also appeared in paintings by Jackson Pollock, and in Robert Motherwell's *In Beige with Sand* (1945, The Saint Louis Art Museum).

William C. Agee

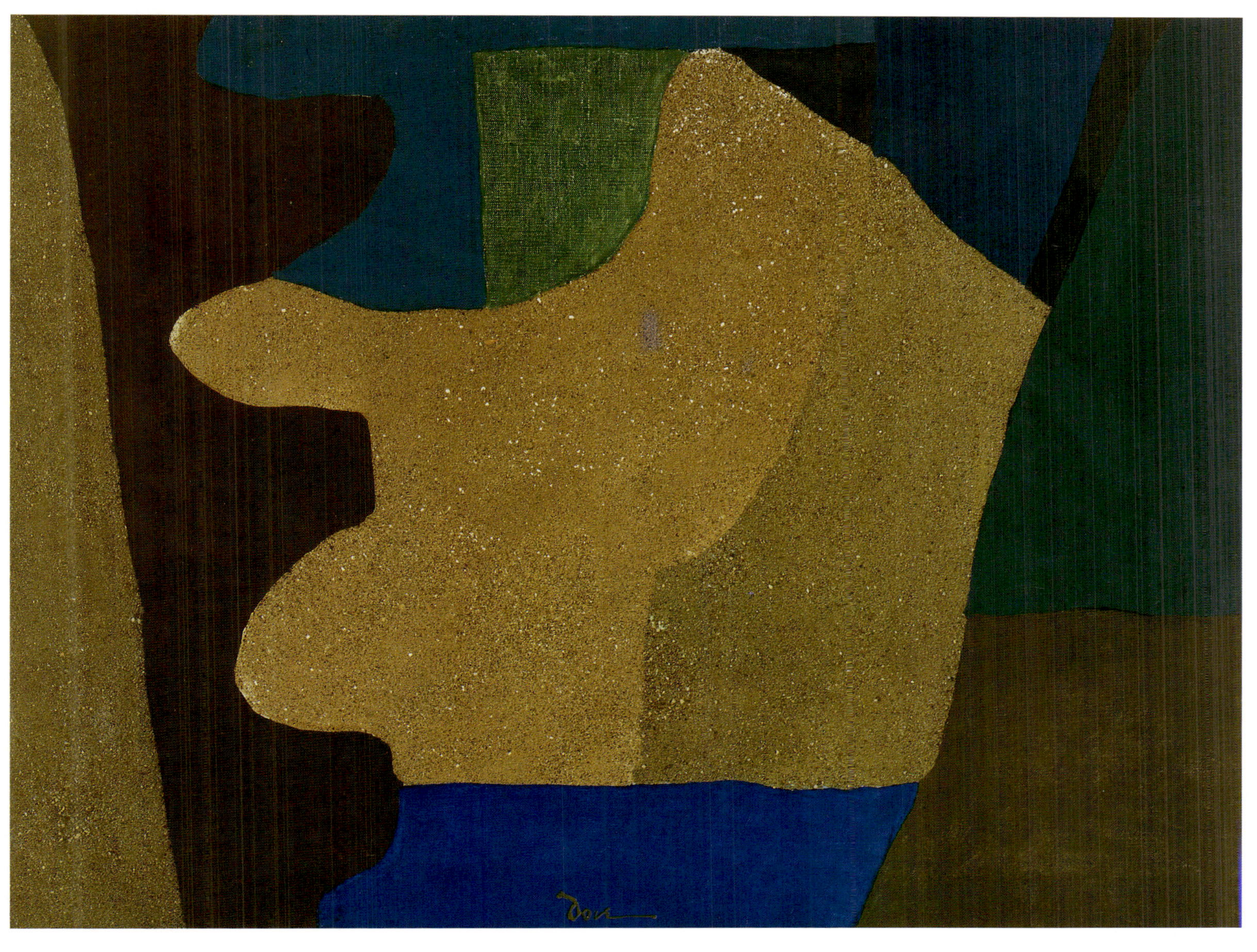

71. Stuart Davis
(United States, 1892–1964)
Max No. 2, 1949

Oil on canvas, 12 x 16"
University purchase, Bixby Fund, 1952

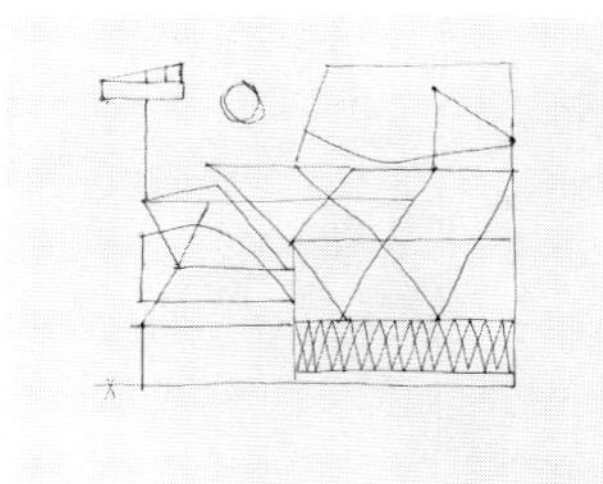

Stuart Davis
Study for Max No. 2, 1932
Ink on paper, 8 x 10"
Washington University Gallery of Art, St. Louis
Purchase, Nathan Cummings Fund
Photo courtesy Salander-O'Reilly Gallery, New York

Stuart Davis was one of America's most important artists. He affected American art for six decades, and from 1920 until 1940 he was arguably America's most important modernist.[1] After 1945, with the emergence of Abstract Expressionism, Davis' Cubist-based art seemed out of date to many. And, due to ill health, his production during the 1940s slowed almost to a halt. *Max No. 2,* of 1949, marked the beginning of a remarkable resurgence that lasted until his death in 1964 and had a significant impact on American art of the 1950s and '60s.

His parents were both artists and they encouraged Davis to decide on his course at an early age. From 1909 until 1913, he studied with Robert Henri, the great teacher who instilled a passionate belief in the spirit and power of art. Henri taught that the power of art derived from the vitality of modern life, especially the life of the streets, a spirit that stayed with Davis all his life. By 1913, however, Davis had begun to question Henri's reliance on subject matter. At the Armory Show he was exposed to Post-Impressionism, Cubism and Matisse, which showed him the possibilities of a more "objective" structure and color. From 1913 until 1921, Davis patiently absorbed lessons on Van Gogh, Seurat and Matisse.

In 1921 he began a close study of Cubism, and by 1924 he had established the hallmarks of his personal style: a flat, linear, geometric Cubism, wedded with a bright, high-keyed color. His art took as its subject the uniquely American world of common objects and scenes of New York and Gloucester. In these years he did some of the most famous modern American paintings: the *Egg Beater* series (1927–28, Whitney Museum of American Art, New York; Mr. and Mrs. James A. Fisher; William H. Lane collection; The Phillips Collection, Washington, D.C.); *House and Street* (1931, Whitney Museum of American Art, New York); *Swing Landscape* (1938, Indiana University Art Museum, Bloomington); *Report From Rockport* (1940, Mr. and Mrs. Milton Lowenthal); and *The Mellow Pad* (1945–51, Mr. and Mrs. Milton Lowenthal). These last works were composed of myriad shapes covering the entirety of the painting surface. Through his work and through his prolific writing and speaking Davis was a crucial force in furthering modern art in America during the 1930s.

After 1945, Davis and his art became less visible and he was in a less central position. He had long been plagued by alcoholism, and by 1948 he had virtually stopped painting. He was so ill that he was hospitalized in critical condition. Davis recovered to the extent that in 1949 he resumed painting with a renewed intensity, and his late work is one of the glories of modern American art.

In *Max No. 2* Davis first established the defining elements of his late style: fewer, larger and broader shapes were distilled with a new clarity and were intensified by an ever more brilliant palette, set within a Cubist-based grid-frame. The color showed a new engagement with Matisse, the master who had inspired Davis since 1913. It strongly suggests an awareness of Matisse's cutouts, especially *Jazz* (1947, Museum of Modern Art), as well as the high-keyed paintings of 1948.

Max No. 2 demonstrated that Davis was more closely related to the developments of Abstract Expressionism than is generally supposed. Although he rejected the spontaneous gestural style of Jackson Pollock—a "Belch from the Unconscious" was how he termed it—Davis was drawn to the new size and scale, as well the new broadness and power of such artists as Rothko and Baziotes and later of de Kooning and Kline. In fact, Davis did a drawing (Fogg Art Museum) which included a sketch of *Max No. 2* set side-by-side with a Rothko and a Baziotes. The stability and clarity which Davis introduced in *Max No. 2* were the characteristics which appealed to a younger generation of artists emerging in the late 1950s, such as Donald Judd, who were seeking alternatives to painterly expressionism. His late style aimed for maximum power and impact; thus, we may speculate, came the painting's title.

After 1940, Davis usually based his compositions on earlier drawings or paintings. He felt that if the motif had been a good idea before, it would remain so twenty years later. In this way an idea or a form retained a distinct reality in time. The motif only had to be reworked in terms of his present style for it to take on a new life. He termed this the "Amazing Continuity." *Max No. 2* is based on an ink drawing in a 1932 sketchbook. This drawing in turn was a distillation of other sketches of Gloucester, Massachusetts, where Davis spent every summer from 1915 until 1935. Although distilled and highly abstracted, the drawing has a basis in observed reality. In *Max No. 2,* and in its source drawing, the streets, the docks, and the iron work at the lower right have all been rendered in flat, linear, Cubist-based patterns. In the painting, each shape is accentuated by luminous, pearlescent hues. It is the painting that announced a late flowering of Cubism, and, more importantly, the re-emergence of a great American artist.

William C. Agee

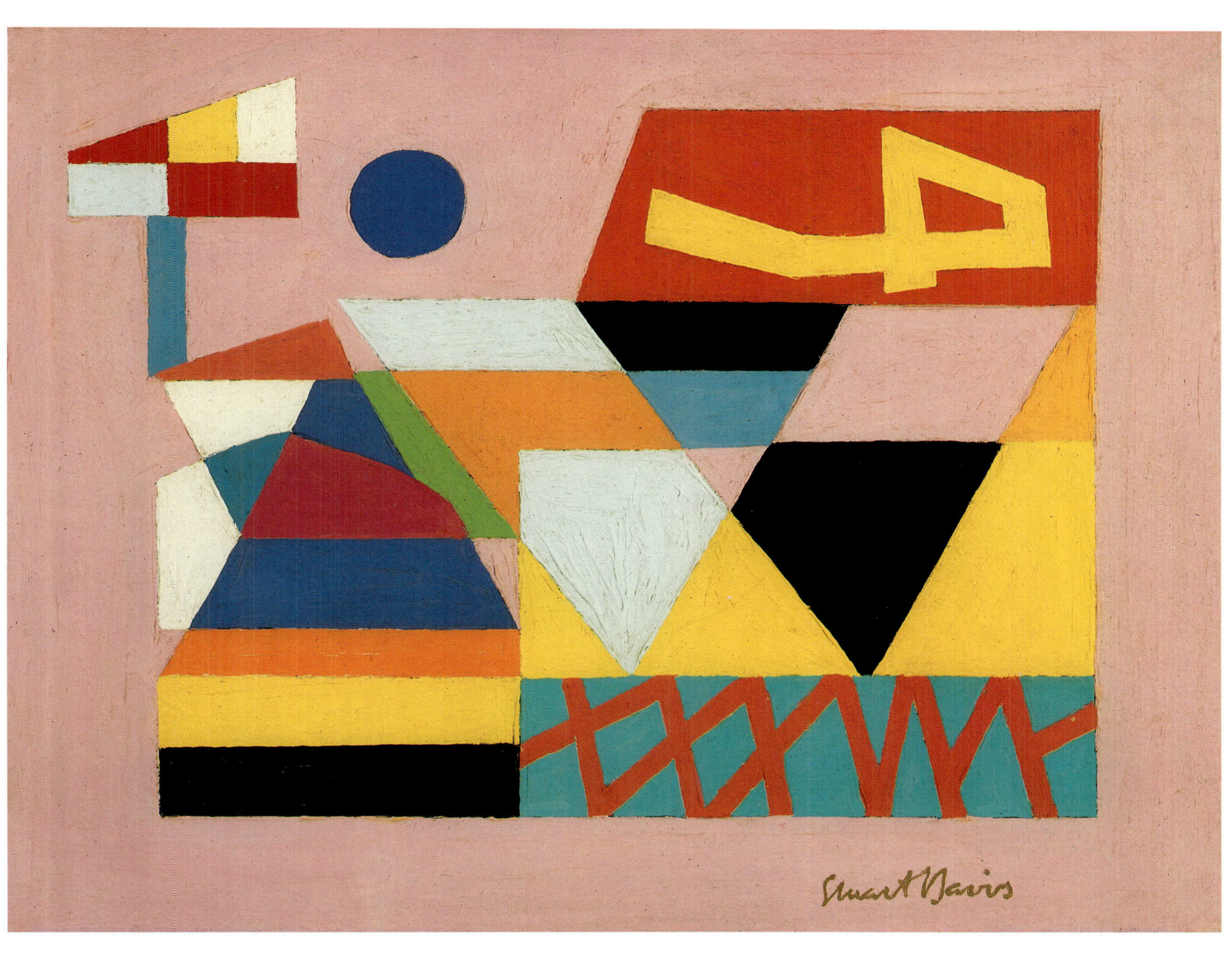
Stuart Davis

72. Josef Albers
(United States, b. Germany, 1888–1976)
Homage to the Square: Aurora, 1951–55

Oil on Masonite, 40 x 40"
University purchase, Bixby Fund, 1966

The *Homage to the Square* series was the magnificently obsessive conclusion to Josef Albers' life and art.[1] The former Bauhaus master and renowned art teacher at the progressive Black Mountain College in North Carolina began them in 1950, when he was sixty-two years old, and worked on them for the quarter of a century that remained in his life. Restricting himself to four closely related formats, Albers painted over a thousand of these *Homages* and created hundreds of print images. These arrangements of solid-colored squares nested within squares became synonymous with his name. His diligent (to some), maniacal (to others) repetition became sufficiently well-known to enter popular culture: *Life Magazine, Realités, Vogue,* a public television special, cartoons in *New Yorker.* The *Homages* became clichés of the best sort. They entered the everyday vocabulary of modern living.

Like Albers' other abstractions, *Homage to the Square* achieves its success because it gives both calm and diversion, focus and ambiguity. Like all of Albers' *Homages,* it puts pure, unadulterated color on a new level. Here colors refer to nothing but themselves: not to a subject, mood, or era. They have no connotations unless we have chosen to read associations into them. And, due to the precision of the arrangements, the interaction of color—the mysterious effect by which one color appears, deceptively, to penetrate its neighbor—occurs in full force. On one level, the *Homages* are an art stripped bare, pared down to the minimal essentials. On another, they are enormously complex, betraying considerable forethought and suggesting vast visual and philosophical possibilities. It is an enduringly potent combination, this simultaneous mix of being and nothingness.

The *Homages* bear the trademark of much great late work: a grappling with ultimate essentials, a powerful spirituality. Grounded solidly in their craft, they search for the sublime. In the *Homages to the Square,* Albers also had a key point to make about the mutability of color perception. In *Homage to the Square: Aurora,* as with other paintings in the series, he listed all his colors, with their manufacturers' names, on the reverse side of the panel. By turning to those codes, one learns how brilliant he was at making the same colors look different and different colors appear the same.

Albers craved light in both his working situation and the finished product. He was so desperate for it that, rather than subject himself to the hazards of the natural world (which would have forced him into the situation of someone like Bonnard, who simply would not paint on dark days), he painted inside a studio where he was assured of an ideal brightness. He invariably did all of the *Homages to the Square* under fluorescent lights. The paintings lay flat on simple work tables—four-by-eight-foot plywood panels on sawhorses. Over one table the fluorescent bulbs were arranged warm, cold, warm, cold; over the other they were warm, warm, cold, cold. He wanted to see each painting under different conditions, but, in both cases, highly luminous ones. Although his paintings in fact look best in natural daylight, he would in no way be victim to its vicissitudes in his working method.

The luminous character of Albers' paintings spiritualizes them. It removes them from human reality and puts them on the celestial plane. They have a godlike, other-worldly aspect. In a century when many artistic movements and trends in thought have stressed a probing of the self, Albers' work is geared toward transcendence. *Homage to the Square: Aurora*—as suggested by the title Albers gave the work once it was completed—is a prime example of an *Homage* that achieved an unexpected, ethereal, heavenly glow.

In this painting, irreconcilable motions occur precisely as the artist intended. You feel stretched across the picture plane, your arms pulled taut, and at the same time you jump upwards. You are looking at a flat, two-dimensional object, its single plane carefully sub-divided and decorated, yet suddenly you find yourself on a complicated course through a proscenium stage. You go inward and outward at the same time, and then you move simultaneously to left and right.

A coincidence of divergent elements and the sense of progression in time are apparent in the way that the overall composition of *Homage to the Square: Aurora* appears both grounded and ascendant. The painting deliberately eschews earthly forces in deference to the heavenly. Through the 1:2:3 system on which it is based, it has its feet on the earth and its head in the cosmos. The central, or "first" square, is like a seed: the heart of the matter, the core from which everything emanates. The intervals underneath that first square, created by either two or three larger outlying squares, are doubled to the left and right of it and tripled above it. In the four-square format, for example, which is ten units wide and high, from left to right each of the outer squares is one unit wide, the middle square four units. Underneath the middle square, each of those outer squares is half a unit high. Above, each is one and a half units high.

Rudolf Arnheim, in *The Power of the Center,* explores the effects of this ratio, the way in which it shifts the normal equality of earthly (horizontal) and heavenly (vertical) elements of a single square in favor of the heavenly. "This asymmetry produces the dynamics of the theme, a squeezing below, an expansion above. It promotes a depth effect, which would be counteracted if all the squares were grouped symmetrically around the same center."[2] The asymmetry is subtle—the squares are *almost* centered—so consequently the upward thrust is gradual rather than pronounced. Thus the spiritual element is achieved with a soft voice rather than a loud shout. Like all true spiritualism, Albers' is achieved in poignant, muted tones, rather than with evangelical ardor. Herein lies the magic of *Homage to the Square.*

Nicholas Fox Weber

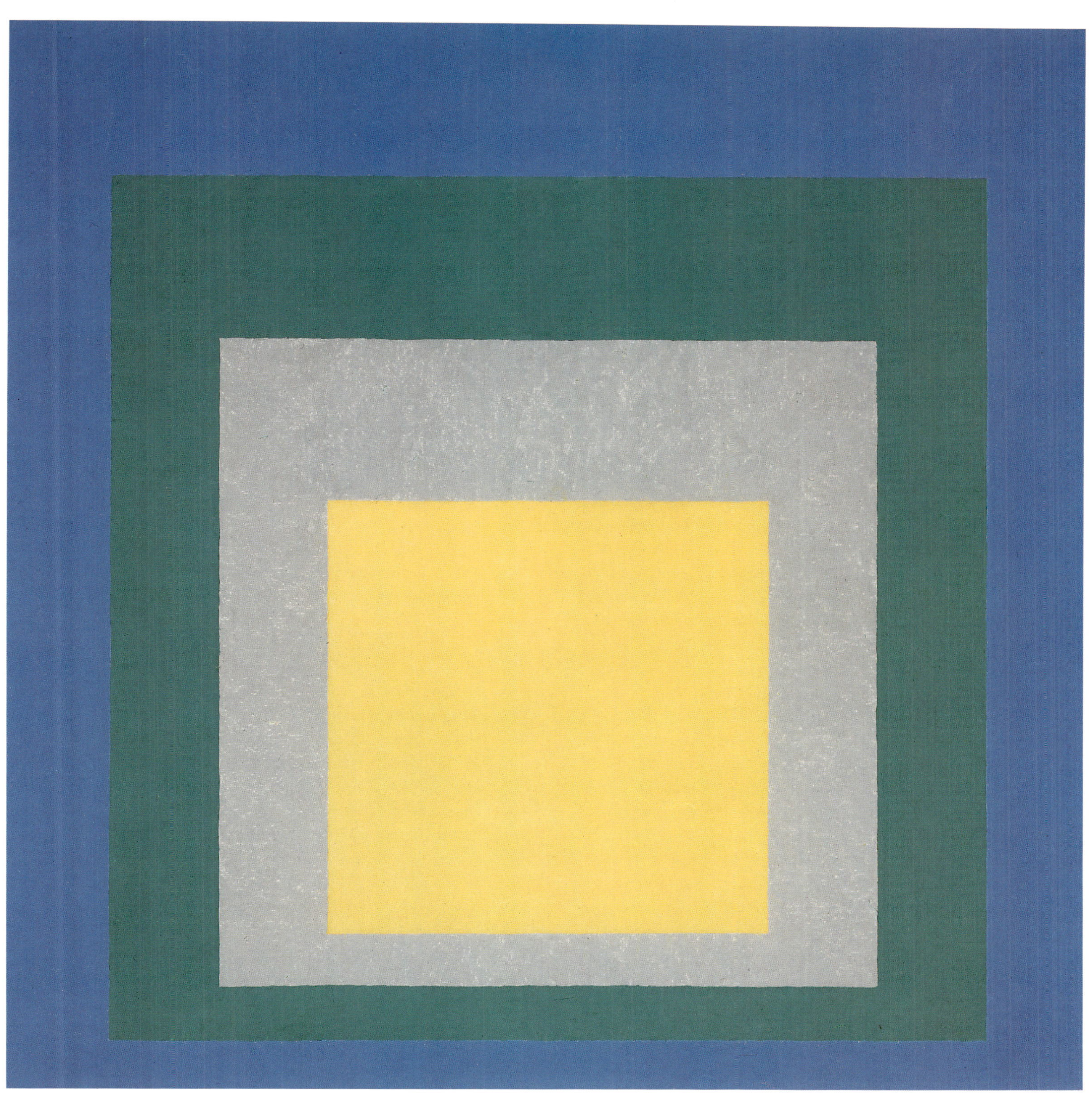

73. Alexander Calder
(United States, 1898–1976)
Bayonets Menacing a Flower, 1945

Painted sheet metal and wire, 45 x 58¼ x 19"
University purchase, McMillan Fund, 1946

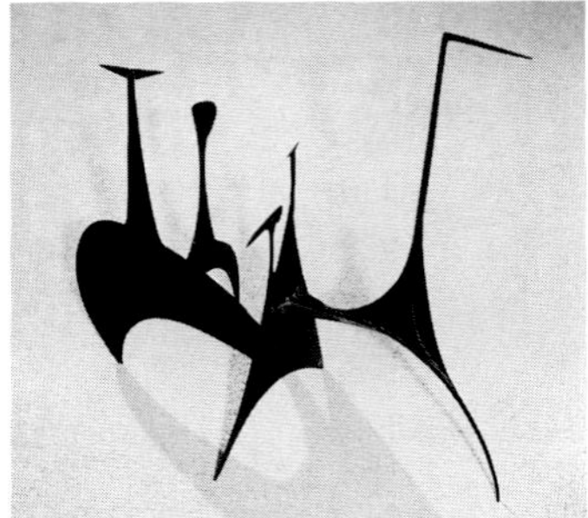

Alexander Calder
Spiny, 1942
Sheet aluminum, painted, 26 x 30 x 14⅜"
The Museum of Modern Art, New York
Nelson A. Rockefeller Bequest

Bayonets Menacing a Flower, created in 1945, is a consummate example of the standing mobile as Alexander Calder refined this genre in the middle years of his artistic career.[1] Calder, the artist who invented the mobile and the stabile, succeeded in developing a compelling hybrid of the two, and created a work of great visual interest and physical presence. In this construction the sculptor fused the grandeur and monumentality of his stabiles with the delicacy and lyricism of his wind-driven mobiles.

Calder first developed his kinetic sculpture in 1932, after making the animals and figures in open-wire constructions for the previous six years that gave the artist his initial critical attention on both sides of the Atlantic. His experiments with motion were based on his training as a mechanical engineer and his interest in astronomical models. Calder's early mobiles were geometric abstractions presented in the primary colors espoused by Mondrian and the neo-plasticists, whom he had met in 1930. He created motorized devices initially, but soon tired of the mechanical problems. Calder attempted to demonstrate various kinds of motion, different speeds and amplitudes.

Wind-driven mobiles, which also appeared in 1932, included painted biomorphic elements reminiscent of the abstract surrealist imagery of Joan Miró and the painted reliefs of Jean Arp, both of whom were friends of Calder. By the mid-1930s, Calder had also developed his stabiles—architectonic constructions from cut-out metal sheets that were bolted together (the artist remained opposed to welding and soldering). With *Gothic Constructions from Scraps* (1936, estate of the artist), the sculptural vocabulary that Calder would use for decades was fully developed. The interpretation of interior and exterior spaces, the buoyancy of the stabiles as they rest lightly on the ground, and the use of dynamic surfaces in monumental stabiles are prefigured in this example. In the late 1930s, Calder found the standing mobile a practical solution to the limitations of suspended devices. His inventive works were often intended to suggest grazing animals or insects with spindly legs in motion. For the most part, these works were made of medium gauge wire, and appeared delicate but lively. Only in the 1940s did Calder move decidedly to combine the previously architectural stabiles with the more organic character of the wind-driven devices.

By the early 1940s Calder had successfully joined stabile with mobile, and *Bayonets Menacing a Flower* is a tour-de-force as he incorporated new visual effects as well as meaningful content. In this decade Calder became the most celebrated American sculptor of his generation, and had a well-received solo exhibition at The Museum of Modern Art in 1942. With such examples as *Spiny* (1942, The Museum of Modern Art), Calder created more organically-based stabiles than his architectonic constructions of the previous decade. *Spiny* features attenuated appendages that suggest fantastic beasts or large birds. Increasing the scale somewhat in *Bayonets Menacing a Flower,* Calder achieved a more dynamic composition by piercing the metal sheets and thereby incorporating "negatives" of his characteristic biomorphs. The shapes formed by openings in the metal are echoed in the petal-like forms attached below. Perfected in this work is the masterful counterbalancing of elements that are suspended within the stabile. These moving elements are not attached, but only balanced on long wires. "Flowers" that are the terminus of the mobile are joined to a long "stem" and hung within an opening in the stabile. The heavy wire that forms the curving stem is free to pivot within the construction, while separately attached petals can oscillate freely. Often Calder's titles are given after the completion of the sculpture, and this is undoubtedly the case here: several spiky protrusions appear to confront the gaily twirling flowers. The stabile itself, with curving necks and sharp points, is menacing in appearance.

Calder's art has traditionally been viewed in formalist terms, and has appeared unrelated to historical events at the time of its creation. Yet, *Bayonets Menacing a Flower,* constructed in 1945, seems to suggest the threatening circumstances occasioned by World War II. Throughout the war Calder had experienced the effects of the conflict despite the fact that he was not drafted into the Army. In his mid-forties, with two small children during these years, he contributed to the war effort by doing occupational therapy in veterans hospitals. In 1942 he participated in the *Artists for Victory* exhibition at the Metropolitan Museum of Art, New York. Several of these constructions incorporated menacing effects: *Spiny's* jagged protuberances give it a monster-like appearance, and Calder described *Morning Star* (1943, The Museum of Modern Art) as a "medieval weapon thrown from a horse—sort of a lance with a round head and little spikes."[2] *Man-Eater with Pennants* (1945, The Museum of Modern Art) is even more threatening because of its overall scale and intricate moving parts. This standing mobile, which measures fourteen feet by thirty feet, features giant lances that pivot from supporting rods—engulfing the visitor within moving projectiles.

Bayonets Menacing a Flower is smaller and less aggressive, but the title is a disturbing one, and suggests that Calder was concerned with violence and the destruction of nature. In the post-war years Calder designed the sets and costumes for *Nucléa,* a play by French author Henri Pichette, which was intended to dramatize the horror of atomic warfare. Calder's set included tower-like stabiles with spiky projections not unlike *Bayonets Menacing a Flower.*

By combining his lyrical plant forms with attenuated, spiky projectiles, by joining kinetic and static elements, black and white, large scale and small, Calder constructed one of the finest examples from his early artistic maturity. In the following two decades he continued to develop variations on the standing mobile, increasing the overall scale of his constructions, and finding other solutions to the joining of whimsical elements suggestive of flowers or clouds, with more grandiose conceptions of craggy mountains or sleek city forms.

Joan M. Marter

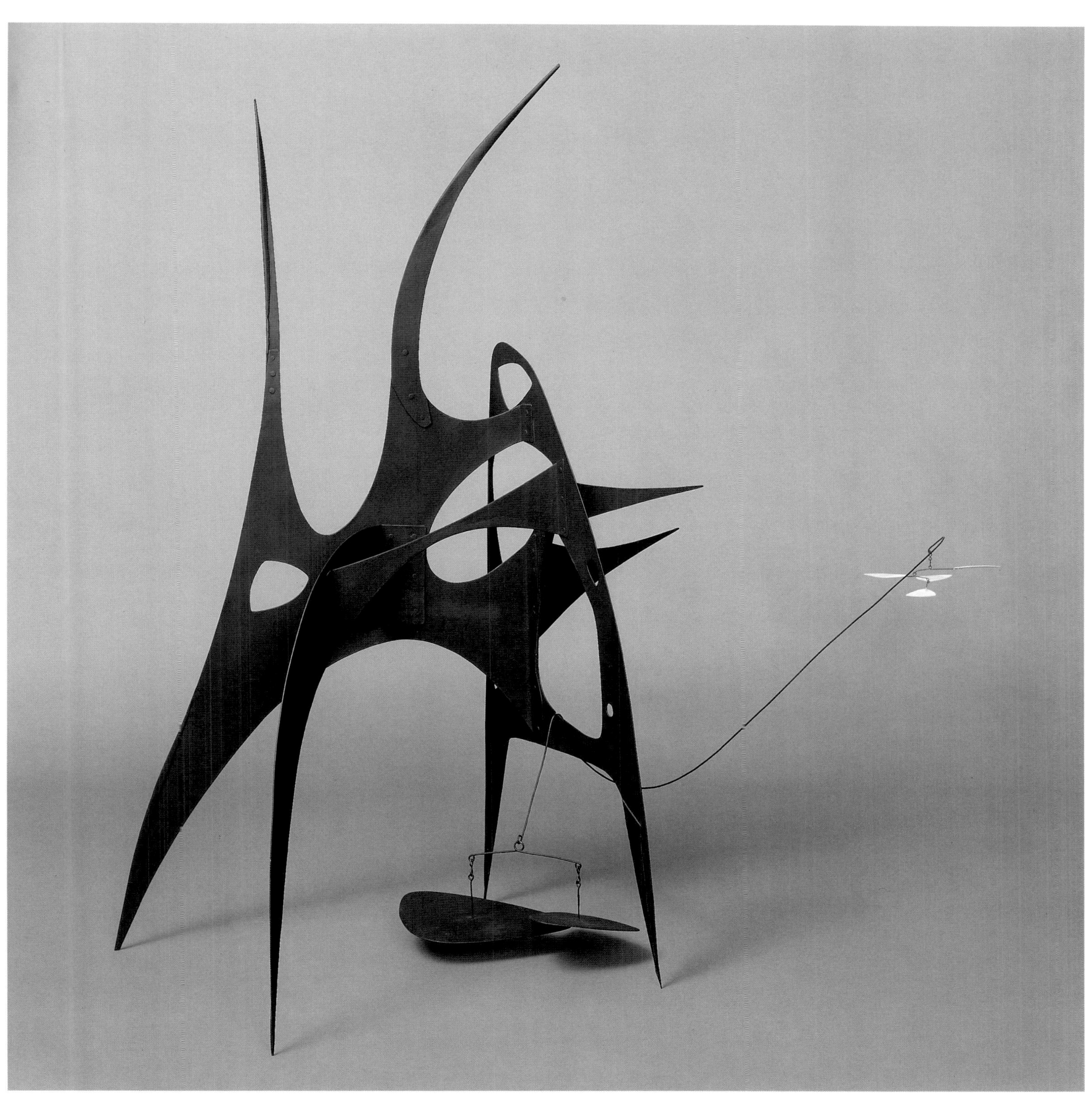

74. Alexander Calder (United States, 1898–1976) *Five Rudders,* 1964

Painted sheet metal and rods, 154"
Gift of Mrs. Mark C. Steinberg, 1964

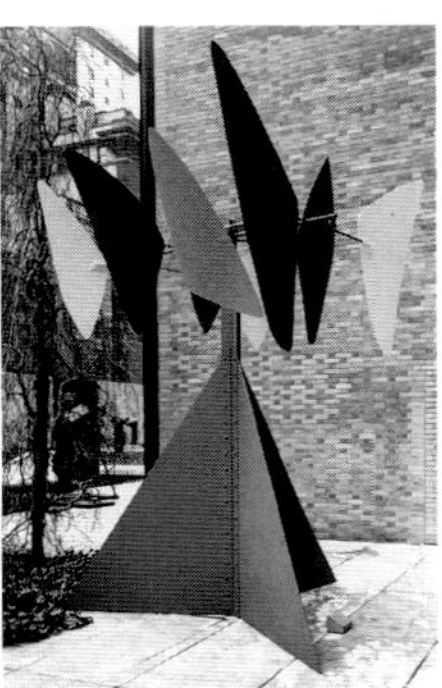

Alexander Calder
Sandy's Butterfly, 1964
Sheet steel and iron rods, 12'8" x 9'2" x 8'7"
The Museum of Modern Art, New York
Gift of the artist, 1966

Five Rudders of 1964, because of its size and overall compositional arrangement, was probably always intended for an outdoor setting. Here Calder successfully enlarged the basic format for a standing mobile that first appeared in his art some thirty years earlier. In this lively and energetic realization of his conception, the black rudders assume great visual prominence in the composition: they cut through space, and rotate on structural supports of iron rods. The spectator finds this work engaging as it is activated by currents of air, and moves in varying directions, and at different velocities. *Five Rudders* is also a sturdy work with a base similar in construction to the bolted sheets of steel found in Calder's large stabiles. The tripod format successfully supports the large biomorphs attached to rods. These planar elements can spin or oscillate as they are activated by the wind.

Standing mobiles first appeared in Calder's *oeuvre* in the mid-1930s. For example, in 1935 a collector who resided in Rochester, New York commissioned him to design a large mobile for her garden. The untitled standing mobile (now in the Memorial Art Gallery, Rochester, New York) measured over eight feet high. The piece featured an open pyramidal base made of iron rods supporting a series of iron discs that could move freely. This construction became an important prototype for standing mobiles of succeeding decades.

Calder's works increased dramatically in scale in the post-war years. At the height of his popularity during the 1950s and 1960s, Calder made many giant stabiles, and found new variations for his mobiles. This free-standing device is one of his most successful examples, particularly as a safe, compact outdoor work for a public collection. *Sandy's Butterfly* (1964, The Museum of Modern Art) is a closely related standing mobile, which is almost identical in height to *Five Rudders.* However, the construction is more varied in hue, with mobile elements painted white, black and yellow. In *Five Rudders* all of the "rudders" are black, and the base is red. Both works suggest that Calder took seriously his own goals to make compositions of motions as well as colors and shapes.

Calder's achievements were recognized both in the United States and abroad. He received commissions for public buildings, and had increased the scale of his stabiles to accommodate his creation of constructions for public sites. His sculptures became something of a status symbol—indicating by their presence in cities or corporate headquarters the substantial commitment of their patrons to public art. But Calder actually struggled to retain the whimsical qualities of his wind-driven devices, while searching for a practical approach for an outdoor location. Standing mobiles abound in Calder's production of the 1950s and early 1960s. By attaching his mobiles to the base, the artist provided a practical solution to the problem of finding a method for "suspending" a kinetic device. Such works as *Spirale* (1958, UNESCO, Paris) represents a new interest in greater monumentality for his standing mobiles. As in examples dating back to the 1930s, Calder chose a tripod based to balance a sequence of bars and plates.

Five Rudders gives evidence of Calder's enduring fascination with ships and shipbuilding. In 1922, Calder found a position as a fireman on a passenger ship traveling from New York to San Francisco via the Panama Canal. In addition to his many trips on trans-Atlantic passenger vessels, Calder took a new interest in the methods of shipbuilding when he increased the scale of his stabiles. His first giant stabile, *Teodelapio* (1962, Spoleto, Italy) was fabricated by Italsider, an Italian shipbuilding firm, which developed the construction from Calder's maquettes. In the early stages of preparation of his works, Calder had developed a technique of working with paper templates that could be assembled—similar to those used in shipbuilding. In addition, the bolting techniques that he used to join the steel forms was similar to those found in ocean liners and other seagoing vessels. The frankly visible bolts in *Five Rudders,* as well as the large paddle-like shapes of the moving forms, can easily be connected to marine craft. One could argue that the motion of the broad metal sheets that are hinged vertically to connecting rods and oscillate to the left and right is similar to the action of a rudder.

Many would find this large standing work to be among the most appealing of its genre, for the construction is larger than human scale, but not so monumental that the mobile elements are too heavy to move. Subsequent to this period, Calder would continue to experiment with wind-driven mobiles as public commissions. Unfortunately, as the scale increased, so did the overall weight of the metal elements. The random motions and lively character of his earlier standing and suspended mobiles was lost in the ambitions for a monumental work. *Five Rudders* remains an important outdoor sculpture from Calder's artistic maturity.

Joan M. Marter

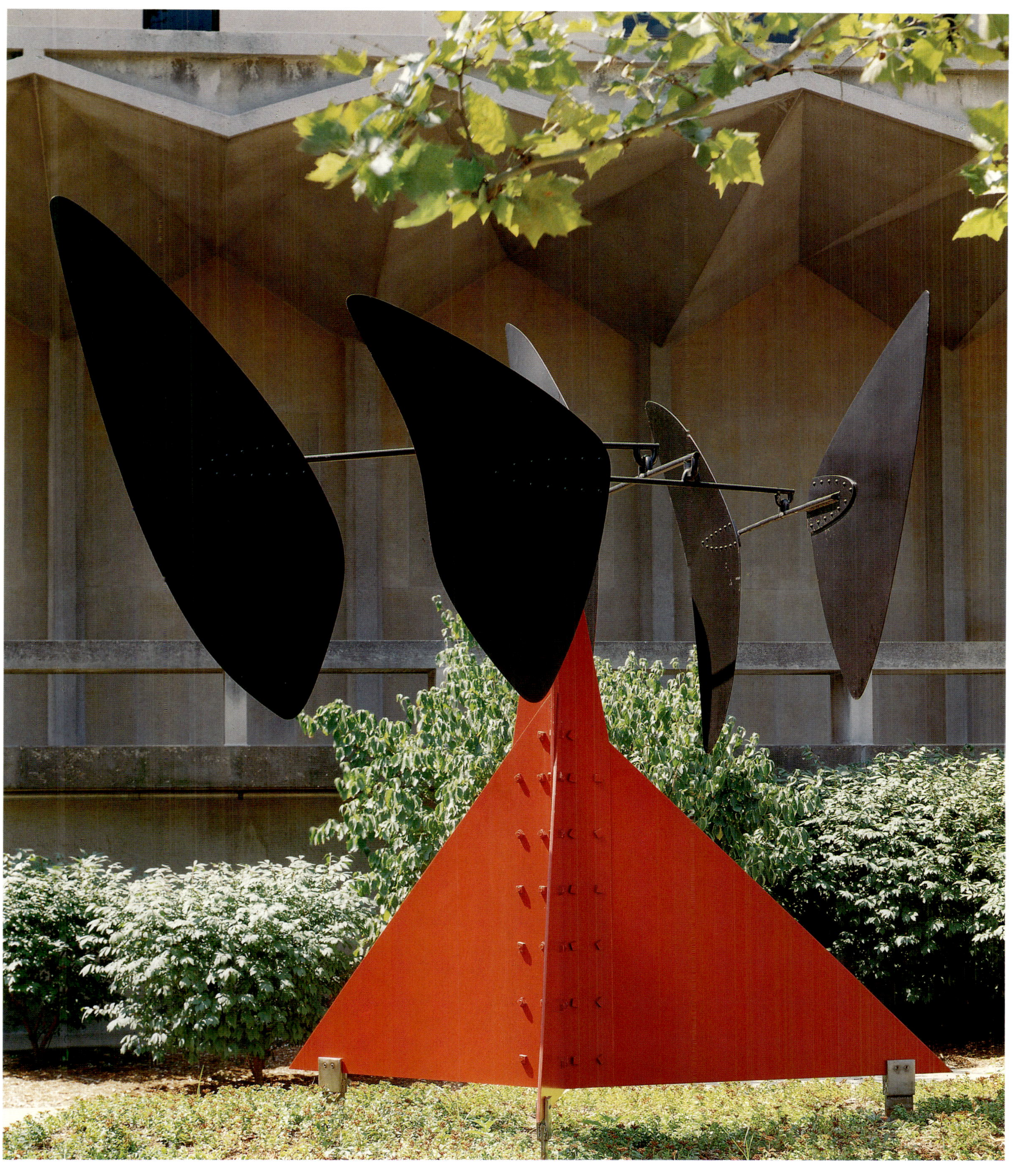

75. Philip Guston
(United States, 1912–1980)
If This Be Not I, 1945

Oil on canvas, 42⅜ x 55¼"
University purchase, Kende Sale Fund, 1945

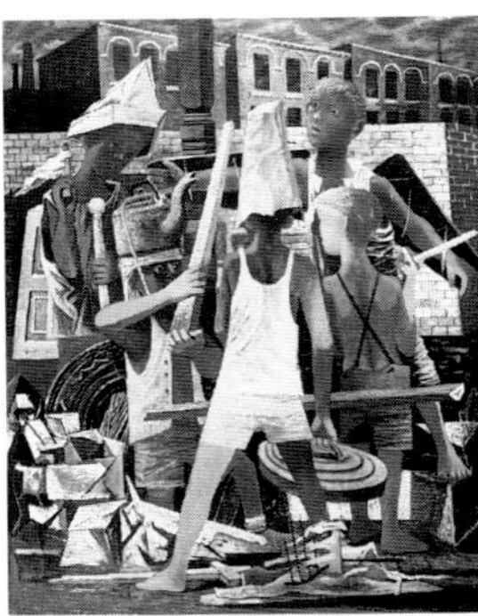

Philip Guston
Martial Memory, 1941
Oil on canvas, 40⅛ x 32¼"
The Saint Louis Art Museum
Purchase, Eliza McMillan Fund

If This Be Not I (1945) is a summation and turning point in Guston's early career. Throughout the 1930s he worked in a realist style, painting social justice themes; especially prevalent were Ku Klux Klansmen and children engaged in mock battles. These were action-filled narratives or were imbued with a sense of past or impending violence. After taking up residence in Iowa City to teach at the University of Iowa in 1941, Guston's painted moods changed and became more melancholy, culminating in *If This Be Not I.*

Within a distressed worm-wood frame made to Guston's specifications is a scene of apparent devastation.[1] A group of barefoot children wearing improvised, militaristic costumes and masks are shown amidst a welter of litter. They have paused in their play; the faces that are visible are resigned and self-absorbed. The porch space is tightly constricted, with all of the figures enclosed between the columns at the front and back. The brick buildings and tall windows identify the street scene with Iowa. Notwithstanding the grim, seemingly war-torn setting, a pretty dappled light plays over the whole.

The picture is replete with art historical echoes, of which Guston is known to have been familiar. Most emphatically, the image is a bittersweet mockery of Commedia dell'Arte representations of blithe actors. Likewise, Pablo Picasso, during his so-called Rose Period, juxtaposed the costumed lives of performers with their actual, threadbare, dejected existence. Guston's thematic strategy follows that example as well as the one set by Max Beckmann, in whose work one finds elaborately costumed groups enacting perplexing events that have an implied air of violence. Too, both Picasso and Beckmann often depicted children thrust into elder roles, their innocence betrayed by events in the adult world. Guston modifies this situation by excluding adults altogether, adding to the impression of an orphaned band of children whose parents might have been killed at war.[2] Guston's enclosed stage space is reminiscent of Italian Renaissance art—for example, the *Annunciation* by Piero della Francesca, and there, too, a pair of columns defines the space.[3] The battle scenes of Paolo Ucello had long been an influence on Guston,[4] and may be detected once more in the massing of diagonal and vertical linear elements above the figure's heads. Giorgio De Chirico's mysterious, empty cityscapes, often described with arcaded streets and portentous clocks, are echoed in Guston's image as well.[5] Amidst this wealth of sources, Guston has placed the image of his recently born daughter Musa, right of center.[6]

Not only is the painting a synthesis of numerous sources, its meaning is equally multivalent. Most prominent are the Christian iconographic referents. For instance, the nearly nude back of a young male next to the column resonates with associations of a flagellation such as was painted by Piero. The coincidentally-crossed rope and wire, taken together with the "Son" seen on the wall signage at the upper left, suggest that the young, innocent, crowned child (Musa) is meant to recall the young King of Kings who will later be murdered. That kind of crucifixion, with a rope, had often been shown by Guston in his earlier Klan subjects.[7] The appearance of the rope is unfortunately imbued with a macabre, personal association too: as a child Guston found the body of his father who had hung himself.[8]

The title of the painting is known to have been suggested by Guston's wife, also named Musa. She took it from a Mother Goose nursery rhyme entitled "The Old Woman and the Peddler," in which an elderly woman awakens from sleep but is not able to recognize herself.[9] For Guston, a new father, the words—If this be not I—may apply to his feelings for his young child and her lineage.

Guston is known to have worked on *If This Be Not I* for about a year before sending it to New York for his first one-person exhibition at the Midtown Gallery.[10] It immediately became a rather well-known representation of the newly successful young artist, being reproduced nine times between 1945 and 1947, in magazines as diverse as *Art News* and *Life*. Even as it summarized the profoundly-pondered themes and thoroughly-digested sources of admiration of his early career, the painting spelled an end, too, to Guston's representational concerns. Soon after, in a development that would recur in his career, Guston changed stylistic direction even in the face of considerable success.[11] He began a series in which the cross is particularly prominent, but the figures are far more abstracted; soon after, he turned to complete abstraction.

Mark Rosenthal

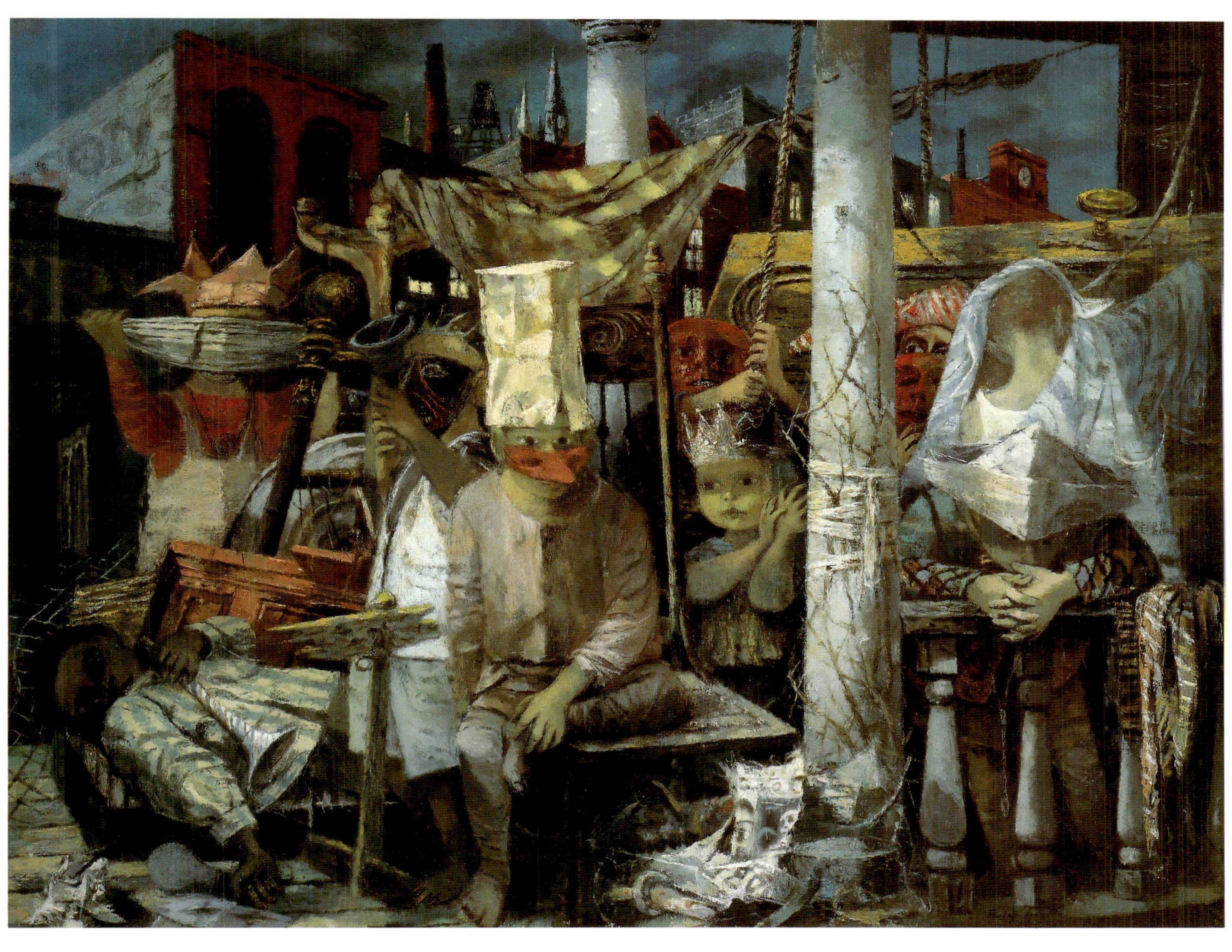

76. Philip Guston
(United States, 1912–1980)
Fable I, 1956–57

Oil on canvas, 65 x 75"
University purchase, Bixby Fund, 1957

During the second half of the 1950s, while Philip Guston was a leading participant in the New York School, he shifted his palette and gestural style away from his oft-characterized Abstract Impressionist approach of the first part of the decade to a new phase in his development, of which *Fable I* is among the early examples.[1] He added blacks, blues, and greens to the predominantly red tonalities of his immediately preceding works. Always vibrant, though at times somber, this less ingratiating coloristic atmosphere is joined with an altogether more energetic brush stroke. The colored lines still drip and seem to rain down, but without any of the precious delicacy of before. Although Guston still massed and suspended pictorial events in the center of a composition, these are now more strident and even competitive amongst themselves. He characterized the new style with the term "corporeality," by which he meant that even the slashing lines have a physicality similar to the patches of color. The background for this dramatic interplay of forms is an ethereal blue, perhaps daylight, realm that recalls Guston's exclamation about Watteau: "those powder blues!"[2]

Many writers have noted the start of an anthropomorphic sensibility to Guston's organic abstraction of the later 1950s. For instance, Dore Ashton referred to *Fable I* as a "drama, with its cast of characters,"[3] and H.H. Arneson, describing a similar painting, spoke of a "crowd of figures circling in depth in a dance that is a battle."[4] These observations are abetted by the fact that Guston turned from the neutral titles of the preceding years toward more poetic and theatrical designations reflecting his voracious reading habits. If *Fable I* does, indeed, have a literary source, it may have lead to the bird-like form in the upper center. Nevertheless, at this time Guston's canvases were still, primarily, the terrain whereon his painted gestures operated independent of reference.[5]

As the work of the later 1950s evolved, however, a new mood became evident. Guston's now-brooding palette consisted solely of greys and blacks, and the anthropomorphic associations of the large, blocky shapes became impossible to ignore. In his typically restless fashion, Guston had become dissatisfied with abstraction just after achieving some of his most exciting works in this mode.[6]

Mark Rosenthal

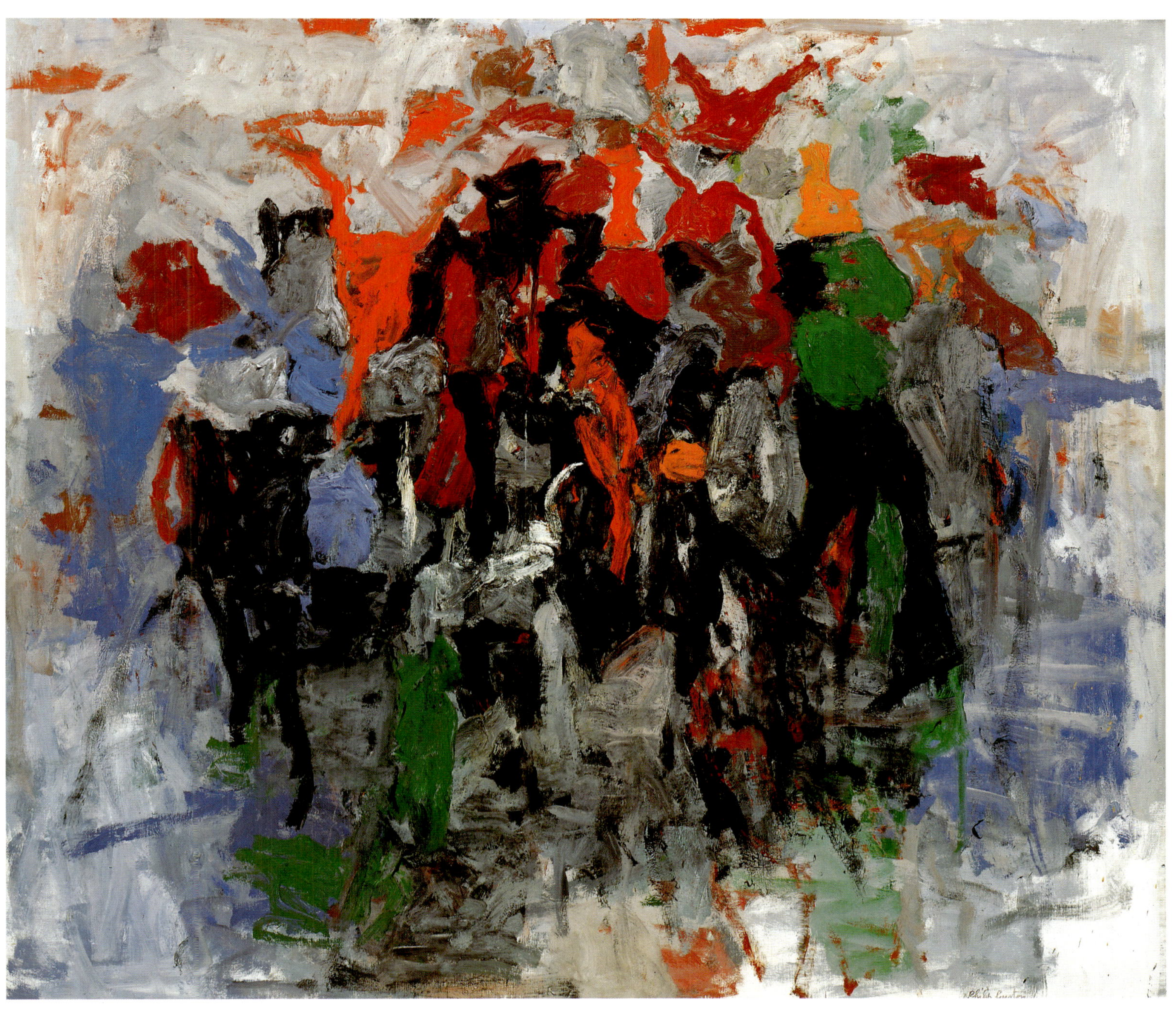

77. William A. Baziotes (United States, 1912–1964) *Night Form,* 1947

Oil on canvas, 48 x 36"
Gift of Frederic Olsen Foundation, 1954

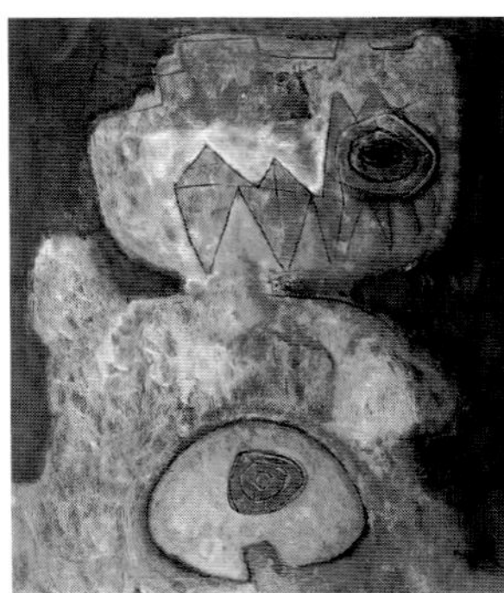

William A. Baziotes
Dwarf, 1947
Oil on canvas, 42 x 36⅛"
The Museum of Modern Art, New York
A. Conger Goodyear Fund

In 1947 William Baziotes completed a group of powerful canvases, each featuring a large central organic shape laden with meaning. As Baziotes was deeply influenced by the instinctual process of the Surrealists, such complex images as *Night Form, Cyclops* (1947, The Art Institute of Chicago) and *Dwarf* (1947, The Museum of Modern Art, New York) articulate the multiple and often disparate ideas that surfaced as he painted. Seemingly toylike, the works hint at primordial and macabre myths and suggest the darker forces of their era. The subjects, Baziotes maintained, revealed themselves while he worked or when the painting was finished.

Night Form, like *Dwarf* and *Cyclops,* rivets the viewer to a large staring eye comprised of concentric circles. Its muted, scumbled colors heighten the transfixing effect of the creature's gaze and the figure, which was painted slowly and deliberately, appears trapped in a viscous matrix. Baziotes wanted his art to take effect slowly, to haunt and to obsess. This attitude characterized his version of Abstract Expressionism and his life-long immersion in the evocative power and mood of the poetry of Baudelaire and the Symbolist poets. As early as 1935 he wrote of his goal to translate the Verlaine/Rimbaud/Mallarmé "soul states" into art.[1] The aura of silence that marks so much of his work reflects his contemplative state of mind as well as his kinship with the Symbolist painters and poets who in their work evoked a world of silence consistent with their themes of darkness and the night. *Night Form* is one of Baziotes' many paintings of the night which carry such titles as *Mirror at Midnight* (1942, private collection, New York) and *Night Mirror* (1947, Vassar College Art Gallery).

Baziotes' favorite poem by Baudelaire, "Favors of the Moon," conjures up a nighttime of evil and madness, of "savage and voluptuous beasts," of "the poisonous nurse of all the moonstruck of the world." For Baziotes, too, night could be a time of beauty that reveals unexpectedly an element of morbidity or terror. Nighttime could be strange or fearsome, evocative of chilling moments, or linked to the macabre and the primeval. Significantly, Baziotes specifically described *Night Forms* (probably referring to the Washington University work) as "primeval, as if the teeth and skulls of ancient people have been found in a cave."[2] The association of the macabre with the primeval was intensified by Baziotes' study of fossils, such as those referred to as the Asphalt Group in the American Museum of Natural History in New York City. In this group the remains of animals which had been trapped and buried alive in a tar pit are not displayed clinically but suggestively, conveying a feeling of terror at the moment of death.

In a 1949 letter to Alfred H. Barr, Jr., about his painting *Dwarf,* Baziotes placed the staring eye, prominent also in *Night Form,* in this context. The "eye" in *Dwarf,* comprised of concentric circles as in *Night Form,* was inspired by "having looked at lizards and prehistoric animals. They have for me a particular fasination of their own, passive and yet so deadly. . . ."[3] He stressed also the painting's mixture of horror and humor. *Cyclops* too, with its prominent eye, was for Baziotes cute, toylike, but chilling; this is as well an apt description for *Night Form.*

The associations Baziotes attributes to teeth, skulls and deadly primeval eyes must be seen in the context of his own time—in the late 1940s, in a world still reeling from the effects of World War II. That the artist thought of war in relation to *Dwarf* is clear in his 1949 letter to Barr, where he likens the painting's truncated form to photos of maimed World War I victims. Adolph Gottlieb and Mark Rothko also spoke of the relevance to their era of the terror and fear in "primitive expression." Indeed, the mythic and primordial art of the 1940s with its specters, Molochs, dwarfs, cyclopses and night forms is a fitting response to the historical moment. As noted historian Paul Fussell writes, "That such a myth-ridden world could take shape in the midst of a war representing a triumph of modern industrialism, materialism and mechanism is an anomaly worth considering."[4] *Night Form,* a silent, muted work with somber colors and a staring eye, is a haunting image, evoking a mood that corresponds to its unsettled times.

Mona Hadler

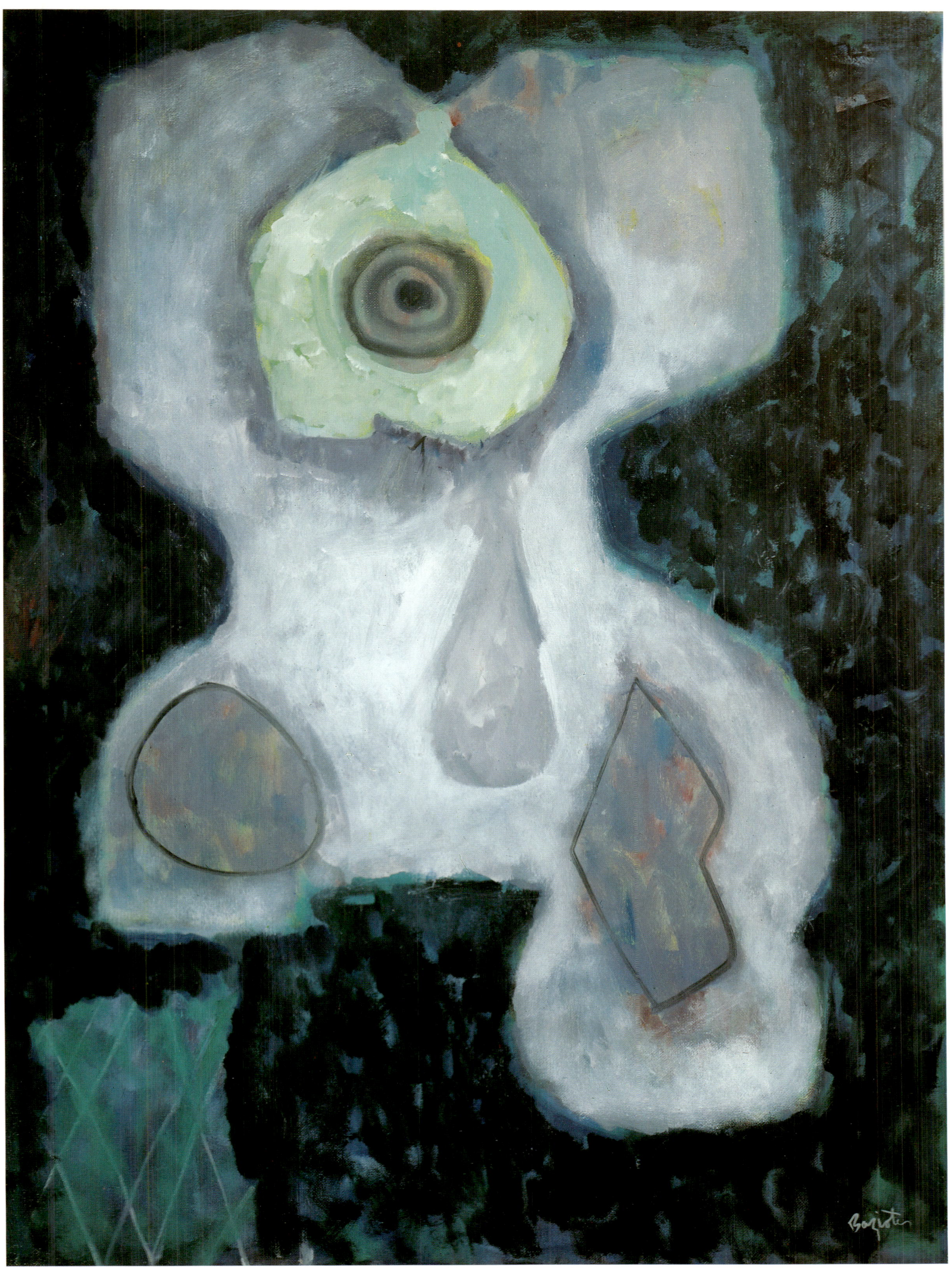

78. Arshile Gorky
(United States, b. Armenia, 1904–1948)
Golden Brown, 1943–44

Oil on canvas, 43⅝ x 55⅝"
University purchase, Bixby Fund, 1953

Despite his celebrity as one of the founders of the New York School, initially few museums acted with Washington University's prescience to acquire a major painting by Arshile Gorky. Following the artist's death, Gorky was unevenly represented in important public collections, a situation that gradually remediated as the painter's posthumous reputation skyrocketed.[1] *Golden Brown* was purchased from the Sidney Janis Gallery, New York, in January 1953 by Frederick Hartt, then curator of the Washington University art collections. Gorky did not title, sign, or date *Golden Brown,* and there is at least some question as to whether or not Gorky would have considered the painting finished.[2] The Sidney Janis Gallery titled the piece and assigned the date, 1943. Another version of the *Golden Brown* painting exists, *Housatonic Falls,* 1943–44 (private collection). Gorky's cataloguer, Jim Jordan, believes that this painting "appears to be slightly less finished than the closely related *Golden Brown.*"[3] The two works seem to have actually been developed more or less simultaneously. *Housatonic Falls'* imagery is not as legible, which might suggest it followed *Golden Brown* or that the works were executed as pendants.

Golden Brown is typical of the manner in which Gorky worked and displays his usual means of constructing a painting. The painting feels rich, full of incidents. A sign-painter's linear brush (the use of which Gorky learned from de Kooning) sweeps a long black network of drawing lines that highlight the borders of certain shapes and supply definite edges. Layered colors are dry-brushed above an underpainting that contains a fairly detailed drawing. The stages through which he passed as he created a painting can help us to ascertain the date of his works.[4] Because of the relationship between *Golden Brown* and *Housatonic Falls* and the *Waterfalls and Landscapes* series, this dating has not been contested.

The *Waterfalls and Landscapes* series that Gorky was executing in the early to mid-1940s is generally conceded to mark the arrival of his mature style.[5] Thematically related, these works form a cycle depicting the topography surrounding his home.[6] The paintings survey the landscape in western Connecticut, and—as do all of Gorky's mature paintings—they contain complex programs.[7] Rarely was Gorky a purely "realist" (let alone Realist) artist. He wove into a myth of his lost Armenia the particularities of whatever current sight he beheld. He peopled these already conflated images with current or past loves, representations of himself or his family.

Golden Brown depicts the countryside near where Gorky lived in the last years of his life in Sherman, Connecticut. The landscape, which is the most legible part of the work, has already been described in the literature. The great solar disk along the right edge floats tangential to a mountain. This peak rises from the river (probably the Housatonic) that flows along the painting's lower half and in the lower center breaks into a waterfall (the Housatonic Falls). The picture's lower left depicts the river's gorge and remnants of mill buildings that had utilized the Falls' waterpower. The imagery Gorky developed in the pictures of which the *Golden Brown* is the most significant was subsequently recited in *The Calendars* series.

In addition to the landscape that dominates the painting's lower right half, there are ample hints of figuration throughout the piece.[8] The major figurative theme which dominates the upper half of *Golden Brown* has never been explicated. In the upper left, sitting cross-legged and wearing a persimmon-colored robe (or caftan) and a tall inverted conical hat (a Kalpak), is a bearded man beside a torch. The burning torch is visible as a black "Y"—a spot of fire issuing from its dark top. The torch rises from a platform that may be a throne or a great bed. This platform's upper surface is indicated by trapezoidal lines and the raised front edge contains some regular architectural modeling. The seated man gazes into the center of the picture.

Egg-shaped and self-contained, in the upper center of the painting is a neatly bordered, high-valued cartouche. Within this ovoid, at the same scale as the man in the upper right, is a woman dancing. She wears a black dress, closely fitted at the waist; perhaps to indicate another fabric, the bodice is blue. Her arms (or a second set of breasts) are thrown upward as she bends back toward the right; her hair descends from her head in three darkly tinged shapes (two of these may be arms).

The entire outline of the dancing woman is magnified and recapitulated as the center of *Golden Brown.*[9] Almost symphonically—like a musical theme that is first softly stated, then becomes the dominant melody—this dancer's shape organizes the whole of the picture. It blends into the landscape, permeating it. This can be seen if the light-colored cartouche is incorporated as the rib section of the larger figure. At the top of the work, what would seem to be a mountain with horizontal black lines crossing it is the dancer's left upraised arm. The dancer's waist is drawn in black and the full skirt flares out to touch the water flowing at the bottom of the picture. Gorky's second wife, Agnes Magruder, had been a dancer.[10]

The ensemble of the man gazing at the woman bent backward before him iterates the central figures of Eugène Delacroix's *The Death of Sardanapalus* (1828, Musée du Louvre). Augmented with players from Gorky's life and set in a landscape different from Delacroix's, Gorky's painting features the same cast of characters and relative positions. If this spatially rhyming organizational arrangement were unique in Gorky's career it might be suspect, but the echoed figures in *Golden Brown* are not Gorky's only such exposition of this compositional technique.

Gorky used this echoing—a smaller and a larger version of the same figure within one work—in his very last painting, *The Black Monk* (1848, Baron Thyssen Bornemisza Collection). In that painting the Monk appears twice, once tiny (in the foreground), and once huge (on the horizon). Thus, a technique that we first witness in *Golden Brown* appeared several years later in the last climactic moment of the artist's life.

Harry Rand

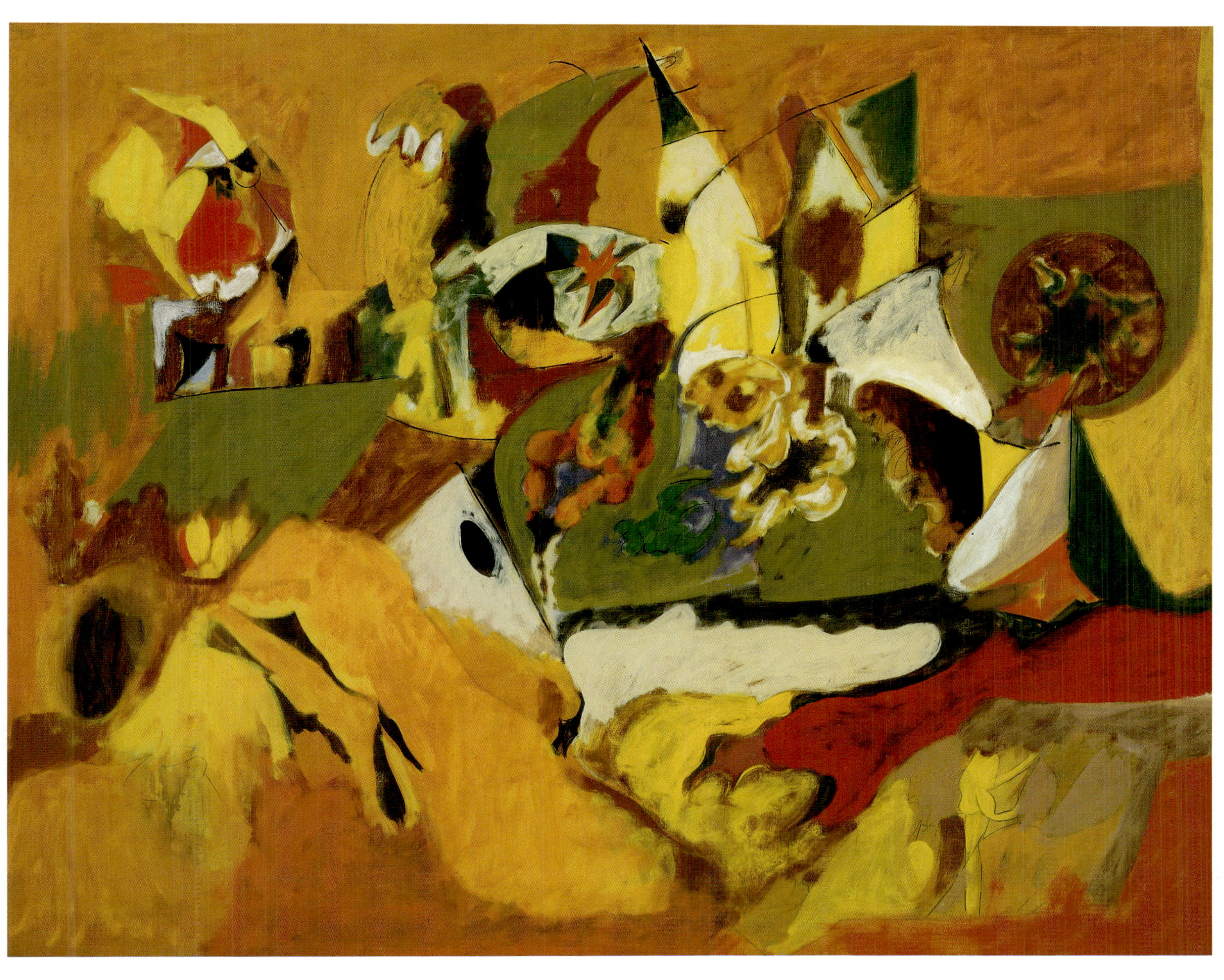

79. Jackson Pollock
(United States, 1912–1956)
Sleeping Effort Number 3, 1953

Oil on canvas, 49⅞ x 76"
University purchase, Bixby Fund, 1954

In 1947, Pollock arrived at the epochal innovations of his signature "drip" style of painting. This idiosyncratic, idiomatic form of absolute art served not only to establish Pollock's identity and reputation as a major artist, but also, and even more significantly, to lead American artists out of the backwaters of provincialism and into the mainstream continuum of international high art.[1] By devising a style of painting that grew directly out of a highly original process of painting—pouring enamels onto canvas laid on a floor, dispensing with the entire traditional apparatus of brushes, oil paint, sizing, and easels—Pollock was able to defeat all tendencies toward conservative regionalism and sterile self-allusion, and to place himself and his work at the very edge of the new.

One problem with existing on the edge of the avant-garde is that it is not generally possible to survive there for long. Pollock was able to sustain his drip method for about five years. At that point, his impetus began to wane and his sense of what he was doing clouded, as must inevitably occur in such a rarified and challenging situation. One can only dwell among the utterly unfamiliar for so long before one's sense of pure invention begins to fail, and worse, one succumbs to a threatening sense of alienation and even disorientation. That is one explanation why Picasso, after the radical phases of his so-called "analytic" and "synthetic" Cubist periods, reverted in 1917 to the most reactionary style of neoclassical portrait studies, which look back a century to the fluent drawing manner of Ingres. Picasso clearly needed to restore his flagging powers by "returning to his roots."

Similarly, Pollock began to return in 1951 to his own roots, reintroducing to his work the elements of figurative abstraction that had characterized his psychologically and mythologically expressive drawings and paintings of the early 1940s. In *Sleeping Effort Number 3* we find again the type of violently distorted human figure that marked the extremely powerful, but not yet fully mature, work of Pollock's apprentice years. The "recumbent" format of the figurative elements in *Sleeping Effort Number 3* seems to recall that of Eduard Manet's famous *Olympia* of 1863 (itself based on Titian's *Venus of Urbino* of 1538). It is not at all unusual for an artist to borrow an historic image to serve as an armature around which to structure a new work, which suggests Pollock's need to consult prior formal sources for sustenance and regeneration.

In *Sleeping Effort Number 3* Pollock returned also to a more traditional brushwork and oil medium, having for the time being exhausted the power of the drip medium per se to satisfy further his creative instinct. The oil paint permitted Pollock to build up a heavily brushed impasto on the surface in the tradition of figurative expressionism to which his early work belongs. Interestingly, Pollock has here attempted to synthesize his older oil technique with his more recent enamel technique, or, more precisely, to underpin the new with the old, as he painted the glossy Duco directly over the thick, more matte tube oils. The physical properties of enamel paints were essential to Pollock's innovative drip style, because oil paint when thinned to a pouring consistency will not hold together in the way that Duco enamel does. Pollock therefore could not have poured oil in the continuous, opaque skeins which constitute the drip paintings.

The raw, acid colors and halting, abrupt contrasts in *Sleeping Effort Number 3* bespeak Pollock's renewedly turbulent sensibility. The forms and paintwork here are not harmonious, fluid and rhythmic, as are even some of the most powerful and dramatic of the drip paintings. Pollock's emotional problems have been examined and analyzed frequently, and require little rehearsal here. After tormenting bouts with alcoholism in the early and mid-1940s, he had for a while stopped drinking, and he had enjoyed a period of relative calm, stability and satisfaction, coinciding roughly with the pinnacle of his creativity, between 1947 and 1951. Subsequently, his personality began once again to disintegrate. The crisis in his art was accompanied by a crisis in his personal life. His marriage to Lee Krasner grew increasingly troubled, and he succumbed once again to alcohol and to episodes of physical violence. Disturbing, fragmented figures began to reappear in his art, as they had in the early 1940s. His difficulties, in part perhaps a problem in coping with success, inaugurated the personal decline which culminated with his death in a suicidal auto wreck at the age of 44.

Andrew Kagan

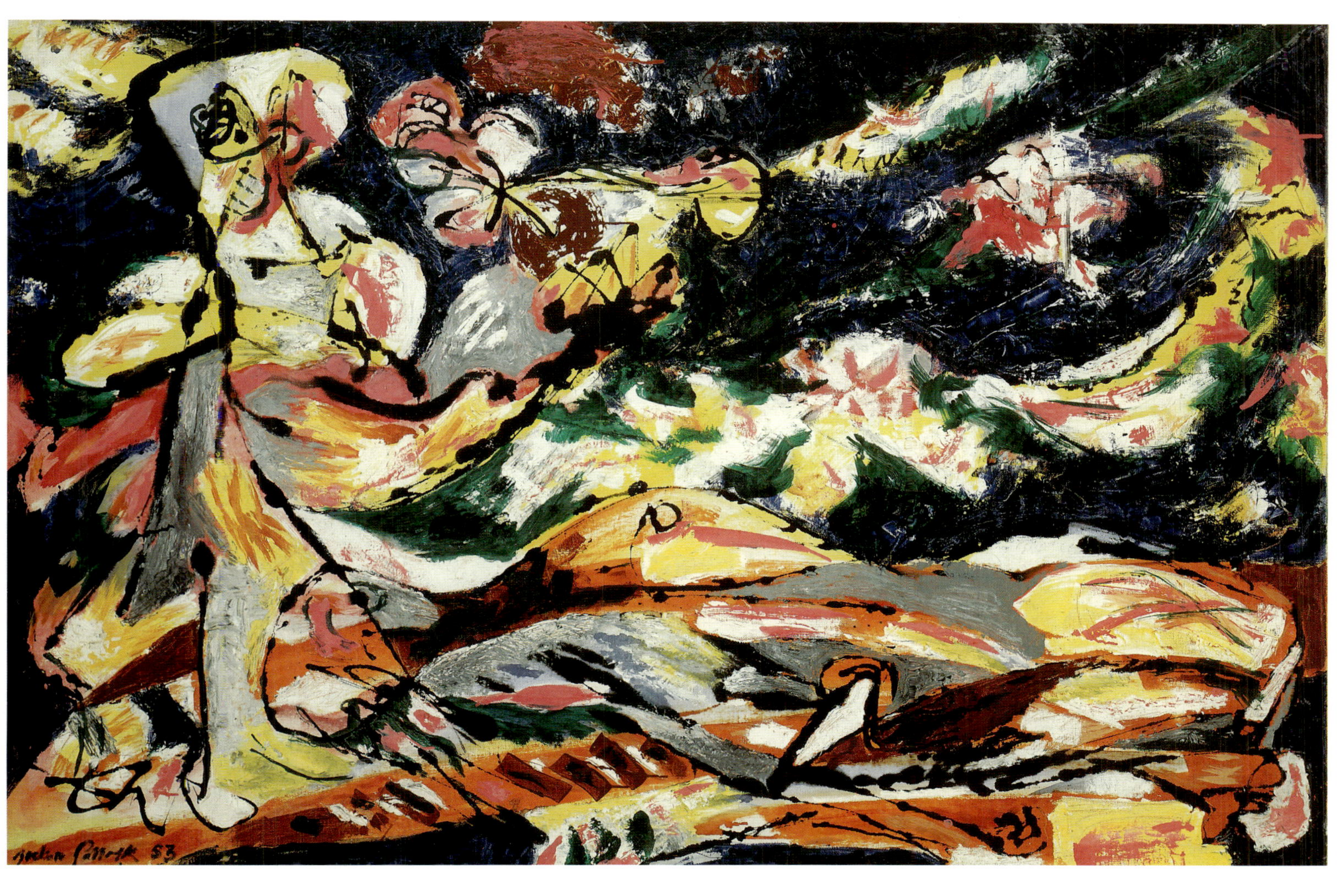
Jackson Pollock 53

80. Willem de Kooning (United States, b. Holland, 1904)
Saturday Night, 1956

Oil on canvas, 68¾ x 79"
University purchase, Bixby Fund, 1956

One of the giants of the New York School, an artist and personality who bridges the gap between Gorky's Apollonian reserve, Kline's naturalist grandeur, and Pollock's Dionysian abandon, Willem de Kooning painted on into old age, like a solitary Montaigne in his tower, extending the chronicle of Abstract Expressionism into the last decade of this century. Perhaps he suffers Camille Pissarro's fate: not as generally celebrated in the popular press as the work of some of his colleagues, de Kooning's art nevertheless spanned the range of modernity's central style, as Pissarro's spanned Impressionism.

Saturday Night perches at a crucial moment in de Kooning's development.[1] It conveys, in a wholly abstact vocabulary, the lessons of history painting's multi-figure compositions, a tradition of pastoral landscape studies, and a newer artistic dialect of urbanism. It recalls and summarizes his earlier paintings by suggesting the possibility of the figure, and hints at the broadly expressive and full-blown Abstract Expressionist gestural painting that was to follow. De Kooning's early work had been figurative: in 1938 he began a series of "Women" which he developed through the mid-1940s. Thereafter references to the figure resurface in de Kooning's work regularly throughout his career. In the early 1950s de Kooning's painting reconsidered the female figure.[2] A close examination reveals that *Saturday Night* may have begun as a single-figure painting—with the head at what is now the right edge—but evolved into something else entirely. *Saturday Night's* forms are not the verticals of a figure painting, but arise from horizontal registers and provide a grand outdoors scale that predicts his abstract landscapes of the early 1960s.[3] At that time his work shifted to suggest landscapes from East Hampton, Long Island, which became his home in 1963 when he moved from Manhattan to The Springs to escape the New York art world.[4] Full of rich incident and color, *Saturday Night* reveals itself not only as a gorgeous painting, but a crucial work in de Kooning's development.

De Kooning's technique, brushwork, and use of color in *Saturday Night* is remarkable, yet he never applied his wealth of academic technical knowledge to display traditional virtuosity. He used thin, translucent colors as vibrant glazes against thick opaque impastos for a rich surface which recalls the luxuriousness of baroque painterliness. The painting was approached from at least three sides. Dripped paint indicates these changes of direction, but brush strokes show that as well, as do inversions of the "horizon" and the change in scale between the uppermost painting surface and the lower levels. *Saturday Night* seems to have been worked on in two campaigns. The earlier attempt is thinly painted, and the handling is diffident and hesitant. The canvas was probably turned at least once after this layer dried and de Kooning reconsidered the composition. In the second painting campaign—probably several months later—paint is applied in more intensely saturated hues and in a far more exuberant and assured manner. There are passages where the paint is applied wet on wet, and areas of *scrafitto* where the paintbrush's blunt wooden end drew through areas of wet paint. Other areas are wiped with a stiff cardboard edge to produce shapes with sharp borders on one side and trailing edges of dragged paint on the other. In one passage in the upper center, the regular corrugation of the cardboard's reverse ribbing ridged the paint in parallels. Such shapes seem midway between surface movement of the brush and forms. We see an artist completely familiar with all the tools of his craft, academically trained, and something of a virtuoso. This gestural abstract style was heavily indebted to Gorky, recently deceased, whose massive influence de Kooning has graciously and repeatedly acknowledged over the years.

The title of *Saturday Night* might refer to the moment of completion, and not to some iconographical element in the picture or to a supposed expressive intent. If so, the title does not necessarily identify the work's subject, but may be part of the documentary information, part of the content, like the artist's signature. Intention, the artist's willful regard to the work, should not be allowed to insinuate (auto)biographical implications where none are needed.[5]

De Kooning's balancing of the dispersed surface incidents throughout *Saturday Night* does not evidence modernism's "overall" painting; this is a muffled recitation of classical composition. Compositionally, *Saturday Night* is closer to Poussin than to Pollock. Like Franz Kline—whom de Kooning met in 1940 and who, thereafter, became his best friend—de Kooning's approach cannot be considered "academic." De Kooning divides the surface into increasingly finer forms balancing their weight; colors are repeated throughout the work. These echoes pass over the painting's surface, and colors are repeated in depth from layer to layer, from the innermost levels to the uppermost surface. The whole is regularized throughout in a way that is quite classical.

Saturday Night's anatomical references are variously recorded. Gestural movement of the paint suggests lines and forms derived from the figure. The influence of Gorky's last work is also evident—especially in the linear treatment of black. Black appears within the painting's intricacies and as lineation on the surface.[6] Surface areas contain such typical de Kooning forms as the oval, which derives from his early schooling in figure drawing, his discussions with John Graham about figuration, and his own anatomical studies in New York. The oval—drawn freehand with a brush as two intersecting curves—seems to be the ultimate reductionist depiction of anatomical form as a concave lens: flesh projected forward by underlying muscle and molded by restraining skin.

A ravishing painting rich with incident and color, *Saturday Night* looks backward to de Kooning's earlier works, looks forward to his abstractions of the 1960s, and stands at a pivotal point in his development as a significant contributor to twentieth-century art.

Harry Rand

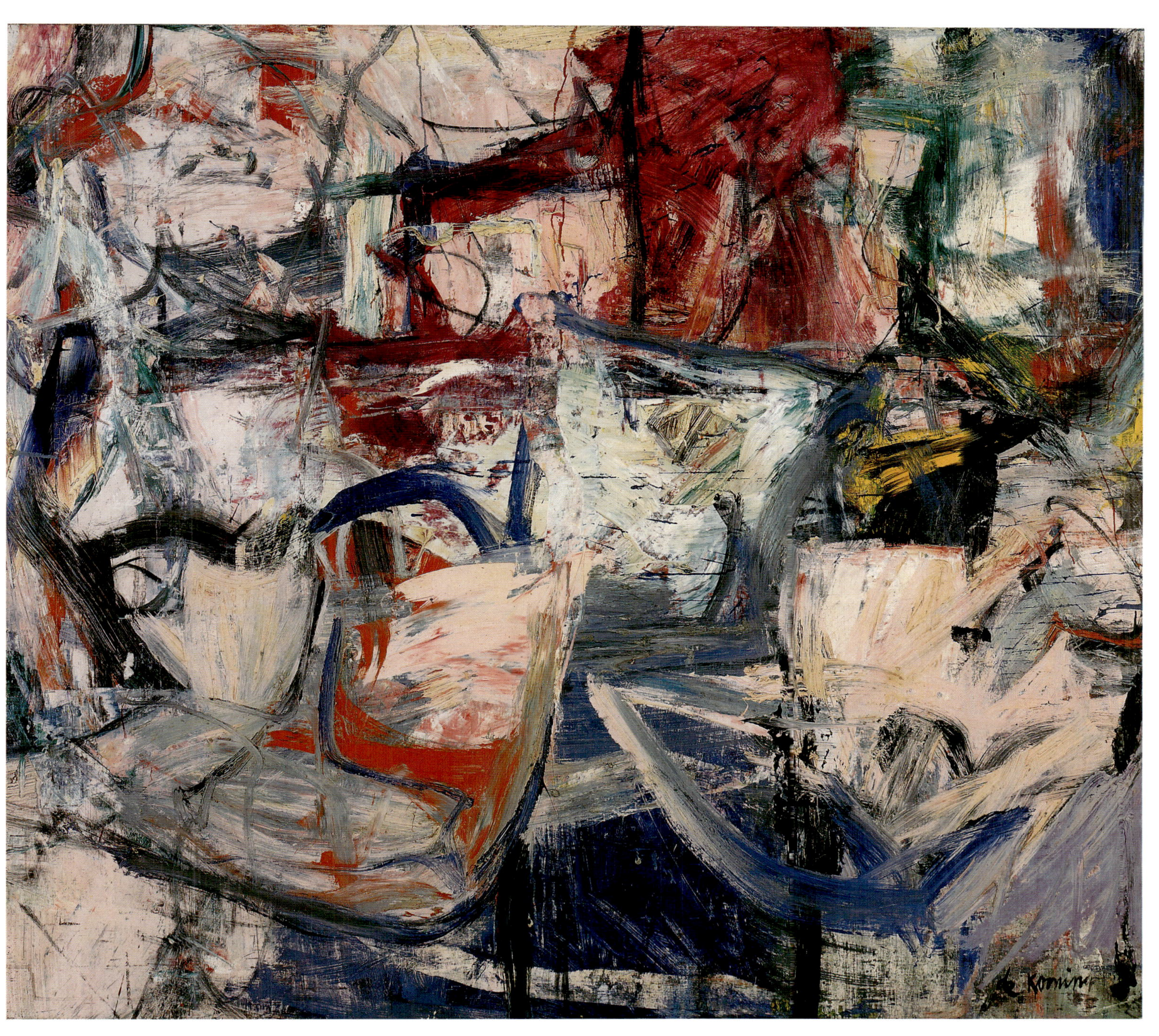

81. Sam Francis (United States, b. 1923)

Arcueil, 1956

Oil on canvas, 82 x 72½"

Gift of Mr. and Mrs. Richard K. Weil, 1962

After graduating from the University of California–Berkeley in 1950 Sam Francis decided to leave his native California and move to Paris because he felt an attraction to the French pictorial sensibility—to Cezanne, Bonnard, Matisse and, above all, Monet. His Berkeley paintings had been amazingly avant-garde and secured him an important place among the first generation Abstract Expressionists, but his work underwent a fundamental change in the diffused light of Paris. He and Canadian artist Jean-Paul Riopelle were the first North American artists to convey what was known as the "New American Painting" to Paris. Sam Francis helped foster an awareness of Abstract Expressionism and forge a vital exchange between it and Tachism. In 1956 when Michel Tapié organized the pivotal *Art Informel* exhibition in Paris, Francis was the sole American artist represented in the show, which included the work of Karel Appel, Jean Fautrier, Jean Dubuffet, Lucio Fontana and Georges Mathieu. At the same time Francis' paintings were included in the New York Museum of Modern Art's exhibition *Twelve Americans,* which also certified Philip Guston and Franz Kline.[1]

It was during that same year that Francis painted *Arcueil* (the artist had just rented a studio in the Arcueil district of Paris). By this time Francis' painting had developed from the cellular, large monochromes of intense color of the early 1950s which had originally established his reputation. In *Arcueil* and other works done in Paris in the '50s he retains the all-over aspect of the earlier work. Clusters of orange petals predominate, but now they are relieved by other colors. Here complementary blue and yellow shapes float in the upper part of the painting. In a push-pull action they can also be seen as piercing the orange web. The pigment seems to have been applied in layered stains over a white primer, giving the painting an opulent richness. Although the all-over application of color relates Francis' work to that of Clyfford Still and Mark Rothko, the cellular forms were certainly his own invention and may possibly be traced to his microscopic studies of organic forms during his undergraduate medical training. *Arcueil* is characterized by a soft fluidity of expanding colors, moving ceaselessly through space. Francis is, above all, a colorist and the colors are placed spontaneously onto the canvas. In fact, they appear to have placed themselves on their own volition upon the white surface. "Color is the real substance for me, the really underlying thing, which drawing and line are not."[2] Or, in different form, Francis wrote:

Color is the pattern
that plays across
the membrane of
the mind.[3]

Color does this by creating the sense of flickering light as well as forming space in the luminous atmospheric paintings which Sam Francis made in the mid-1950s.

Peter Selz

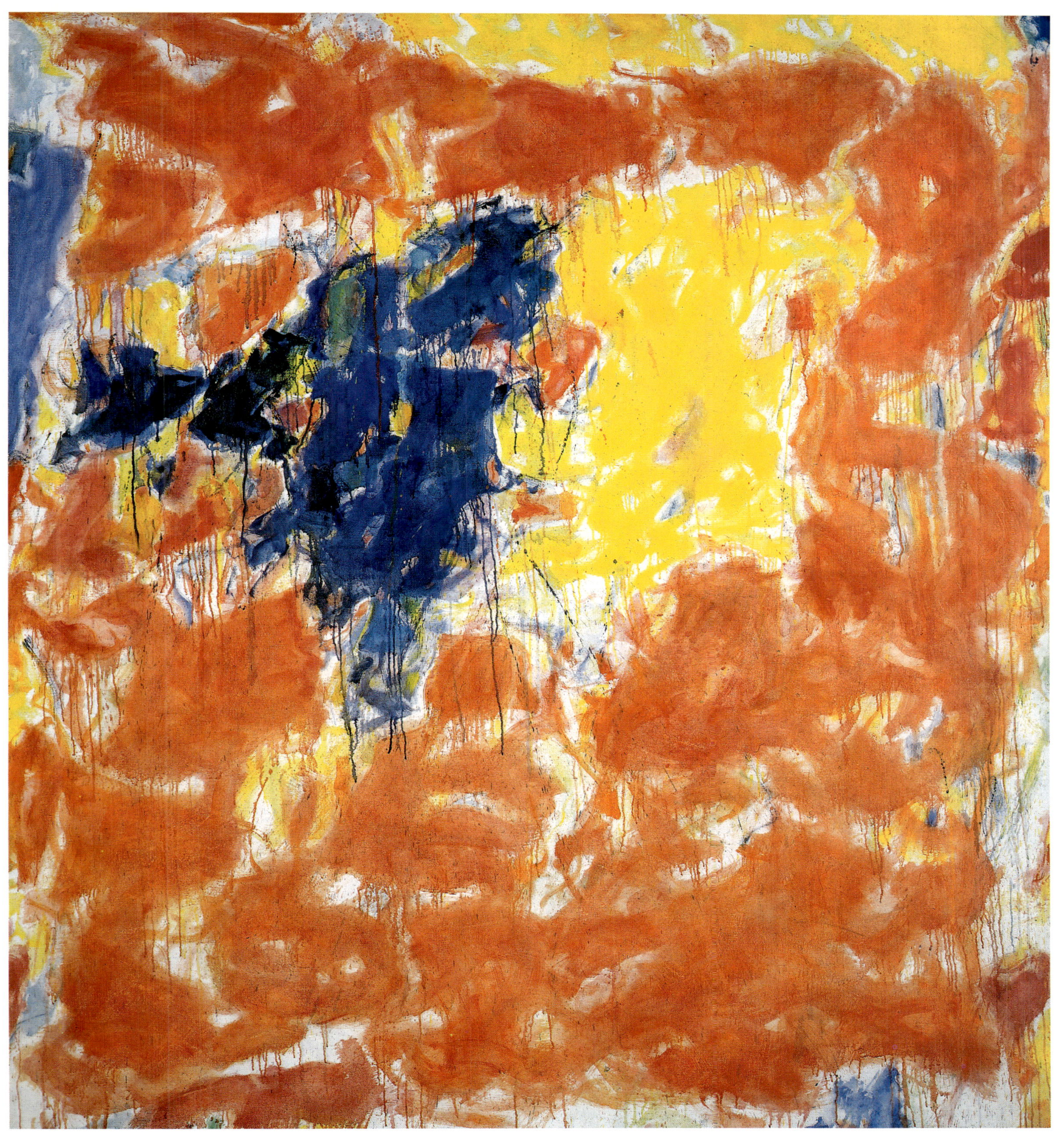

82. Sam Francis (United States, b. 1923) *Floating Blue,* 1959

Oil on canvas, 48¼ x 54"
Gift of Mr. and Mrs. Richard K. Weil, 1972

In 1957 Sam Francis took his first of many trips to Japan. He had been invited to Tokyo to execute a mural commission for a theater in the Sogetsu School of Sofu Teshigahara, a famous master of flower arrangement and a sculptor, in a building designed by Kenzo Tange. Having been a student of Zen, Francis was somewhat prepared for this pivotal journey. He recalls: "The very first impression of the Orient was one of *deja vu*—of having been there before. The minute I got off the airplane I knew what was going to happen for the next few hours—and it did. . . . It was like . . . returning to some place . . . specifically warm and exhilarating, dark and shot through with light!"[1]

A symbiotic relationship exists between Francis' paintings and the Japanese tradition which considers art, above all, as a meditative experience. Although he shares the importance of painting-as-process as well as the largeness of scale with his Abstract Expressionist colleagues, his painting, evoking light and space, is closely attuned to the Japanese sense of aesthetics and forms a parallel to the "intentionless intention" in haiku poetry. Certainly, the white spaces which invade his work from this time forward are related to the tradition of Chinese and Japanese painting and the primacy of the void. In *Floating Blue,* for example, the white is by no means a mere background to the blue figuration. The painting is, rather, a dialogue between white and other colors in which blue predominates.

Sam Francis was drawn to blue from early in his career. A small untitled watercolor of the Berkeley hills (private collection), done in 1948 during his student days, consists almost entirely of different hues of blue. In works from his Paris period swirling clusters of dark blue petals, painted with interlocking brushstrokes, spread an all-over tissue vertically down the surfaces of his canvases. In *Saturated Blue* (1953, Collection Franz Heyer, Zurich) he used the color with a full, intense richness. Then, when he initiated his cellular structures, as in *In Lovely Blueness* (1955–57, Musée National d'Art Moderne, Centre Georges Pompidou, Paris), delicacy and grace took over from the dense character of the previous work. A few years later, during the "Blue Balls" series which occupied him from 1960 to 1963 in Paris, Bern, Tokyo, Santa Barbara and Santa Monica, he immersed himself totally in a world of blueness.

In *Floating Blue* a maze of brightly colored splintered forms is assembled in a cross-like configuration. This painting evokes a gaily decorated Japanese dragon or one of Francis' very personal images to which he has referred as "demonic tricksters" or "dappled demons." Many associations and interpretations are possible and the potency of the image cannot be reduced to specific meanings. There is never any sense of persuasion in the work of Sam Francis, who writes: "My painting is anything anybody wants to see in it."[2] Although a work such as *Floating Blue* is abstract, figurative images can be deduced. At this time in his career we can detect a relationship to organic Surrealism. From the beginning of his development as an artist Sam Francis was familiar with the work of Joan Miró and he continued to share with the Spanish painter an understanding that the artist can direct chance to charter the imagination.

In 1958 Francis had taken a trip around the world. Then he settled down briefly in New York and Paris before taking his second trip to Japan, returning at the end of the year to New York where he lived and worked in the Chelsea Hotel. He remained there for most of 1959 and worked on a large mural for Chase Manhattan Bank. It was probably during this period that he painted *Floating Blue.* It is related to one of his major paintings, *Moby Dick* (1958, Bartos collection, New York), a picture in which a fierce burst of color juts from a central matrix of kaleidoscopic color and discharges vehement energies, dispersing them into tinted white fields. In these paintings Francis created dynamic images, derived from the unconscious and structured by physical modes; a painting such as *Floating Blue* presents a fine example of his exploration of space and light by means of joyous radiance of color.

Peter Selz

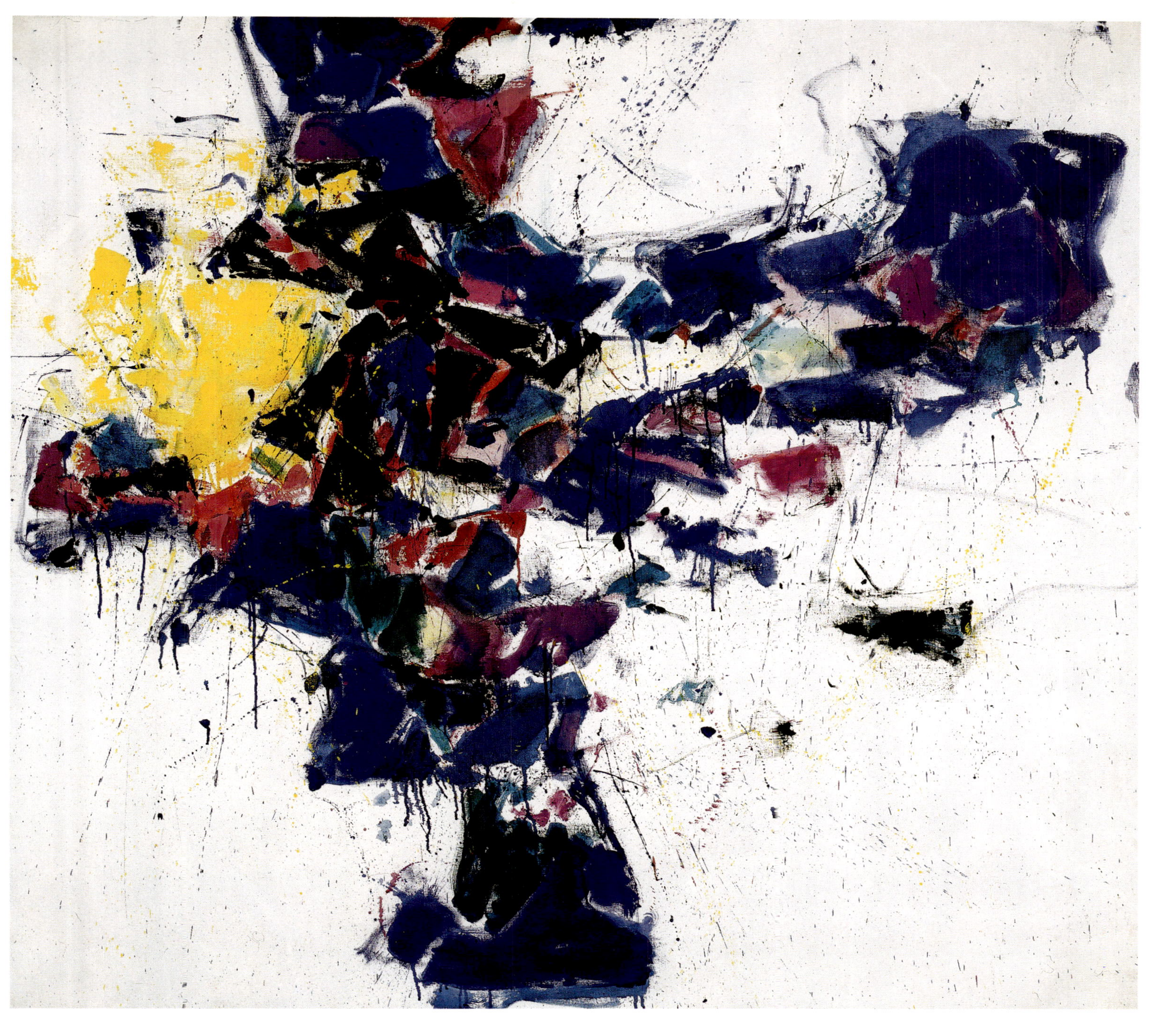

83. Robert Rauschenberg (United States, b. 1925)

Choke, 1964

Oil and silkscreen on canvas, 60 x 48"
Gift of Mr. and Mrs. Richard K. Weil, 1972

Choke belongs to Rauschenberg's second series of silkscreen paintings—the color silkscreens—executed between August 1963 and June 1964. Rauschenberg had begun working with the silkscreen process in 1962 in an extended series of black and white paintings. The silkscreens represented a significant departure from Rauschenberg's combines, the works with which he had been preoccupied since the mid-1950s. In the combines, a vast array of found objects and materials were intermingled with expressionistically painted passages. In *Monogram* (1955–59, Moderna Museet, Stockholm), for example, one of the most famous combines, a stuffed Angora goat, its face clotted with paint and its middle encircled by an automobile tire, was set out to pasture on a horizontal platform collaged with a street barricade, a tennis ball, the heel of a shoe, and assorted printed matter. It was through such works that, by the early 1960s, Rauschenberg came to be recognized as a father figure of assemblage and as a major transition figure between Abstract Expressionism and Pop Art.[1]

In October 1962, Rauschenberg began to use commercially prepared screens to transfer to canvas images derived from newspapers, magazines, and his own photographs; on canvas, he joined them with other silk-screened images and painted passages. Although Rauschenberg's silkscreens share with Pop Art a sense of flatness, the use (or imitation) of commercial printing processes, and a focus on mass-media imagery, they remain expressionistic, painterly, and diverse in their representations. Rauschenberg exploited diversity in order to reveal how we receive and process information in the urban industrial world.

While much of Rauschenberg's work offers demonstrations of how one can find order, patterns, interrelationships, and even a kind of solace in an apparently haphazard world, *Choke* seems to take as its subject the anxieties generated by upheavals in American political and social life. The form, content, and screening techniques used to produce the work all convey a sense of urgency.

In this relatively late color silkscreen, Rauschenberg made no attempt to utilize the time-consuming, four-color separation process that is part of conventional silkscreening and that he used in his earliest works in this medium. Rather than transferring the images to canvas in the colors in which they appeared in the original source illustrations, he used the shorthand technique of reproducing them in a single color—generally red, black, or blue. Whereas the photographic images found in earlier silkscreen paintings were often reproduced in their entirety, those in *Choke* are fragments of images known from previous works. The legibility of some of the images is further complicated by their ghostly transfer, an effect produced by the deliberate use of insufficient amounts of ink and by the vigorous painterly activity, which often overlaps and obscures the screened images.

Clearly seen at the top of the canvas, however, is a vertically disposed "ONE WAY" sign, which splits the painting down its center and seems to shatter its imagery. Transferred in hot red and yellow hues and leaving a fiery trail of drips, the sign suggests a rocket "blasting off," an image frequently seen in Rauschenberg's silkscreens. The upward-thrusting arrow seems to signal the need for release or escape, presumably from the other images and from the general congestion on the canvas. Other "ONE WAY" signs appear on a streetpost positioned upside down near the bottom edge of the canvas; the arrows indicate conflicting directions and hence seem to signal disorder. In addition to "ONE WAY," other verbal cues in the painting include "ARMY" (on a helicopter), "[TOM]ORROWS WEATHER" (on a temperature indicator), and "PUBLIC SHELTER" (on the streetpost). Close observation reveals that to the right of center is a seemingly random cluster of letters and punctuation marks stencilled backwards in black. These marks and letters, which are unique to *Choke* in the silkscreen series, suggest a garbled message, a strangled communication. Among the other images and image fragments are the head and upper body of the Statue of Liberty, the open sea, a flagwaving boyscout parade, the army helicopter, a man carrying bundles walking through a demolition sight, and a man standing before the billboard-scale temperature indicator.

In *Made in the U.S.A.,* Sidra Stich suggested that Rauschenberg's images reflect the frenzied state of American cities in the early 1960s: from revised traffic patterns and urban demolition and renewal to ghetto riots and civil rights demonstrations.[2] Although Stich maintains that Rauschenberg withholds personal commentary and judgment, the work's title, together with the imagery and manner of execution, seems to reveal the artist's feelings of frustration with aspects of American political and social life. It is known that both as an artist and a man Rauschenberg protested against blind patriotism (as represented by the flagwaving boyscout parade), against the war in Vietnam (as signalled by the army helicopter), and against the questionable state of freedom in America (as symbolized by the Statue of Liberty). The urgent need for release expressed by the upward-thrusting "ONE WAY" sign was his very human response to certain contemporary realities.

Roni Feinstein

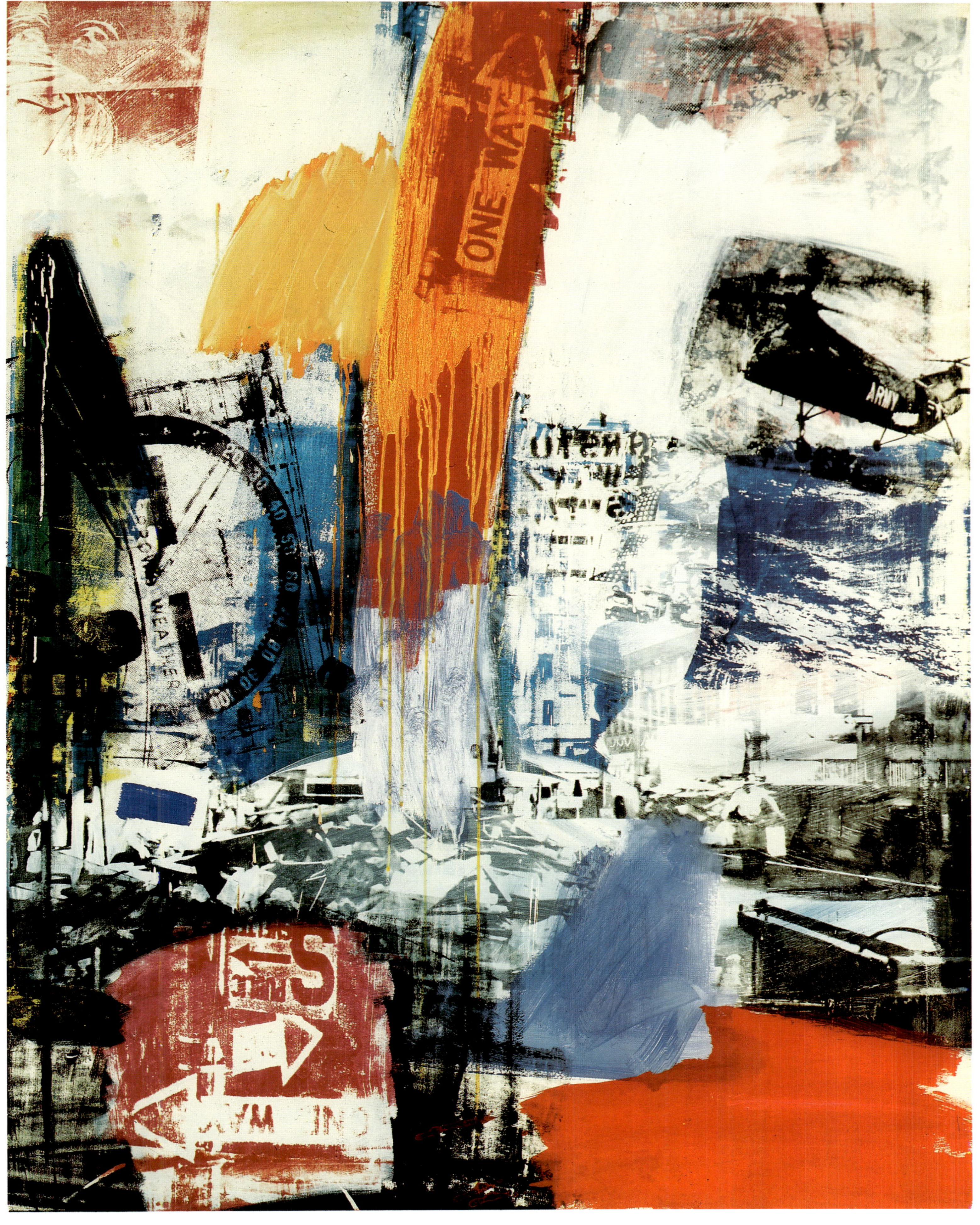
ONE WAY
ARMY
WEATHER

84. Gene Davis
(United States, 1920–1985)
Equinox, 1965

Acrylic on canvas, 90½ x 92⅞"
University purchase, Bixby Fund, 1969

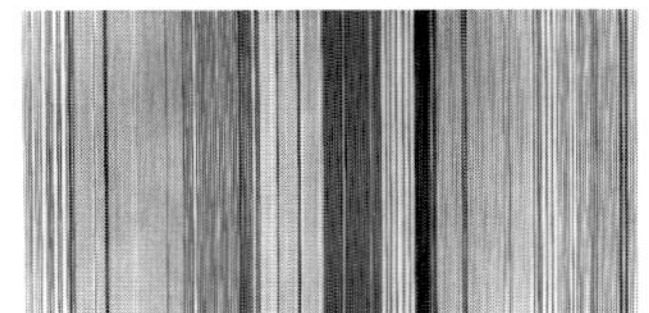

Gene Davis
Raspberry Icicle, 1967
Synthetic polymer acrylic on canvas, 116 x 219⅝"
National Museum of American Art, Smithsonian Institution, Washington, D.C.
Museum Purchase

Gene Davis achieved his principal renown as a painter of vertical stripes, a colorist of remarkable range, and a leader of the Washington Color School, perhaps one of the most famous schools of American painting to develop outside New York in the mid-twentieth century.

Davis came to art relatively late in life, after a successful career as a writer and journalist, including a stint as a radio correspondent at the White House during the Roosevelt and Truman administrations. His artistic "training" consisted of a series of conversations with the Washington artist and teacher Jacob Kainen, several sojourns to the Washington Workshop Center of the Arts, and a few studio visits exchanged with Kenneth Noland. The paintings that influenced Davis the most at the beginning of his career were those of Paul Klee at the Phillips Collection, the primary showcase for modern art in the nation's capital at the time; of Arshile Gorky in the collection of Washingtonian Alfred Auerbach; and of Barnett Newman, which he saw on regular trips to New York to look at vanguard American painting.

Although Davis' first painting was a biomorphic hard-edge abstraction, based loosely on the work of Jean Arp, he was soon encouraged by his conversations with Kainen and a meeting with Willem de Kooning to turn his talents to Abstract Expressionism. "My Abstract Expressionist works were my leaping-in place," he said later. "I learned art by immersing myself in the prevailing tastes." Over the next three years (1958–61), he produced a series of relatively small canvases demonstrating both a sophisticated color sense and what the artist called a "boldness of attack and rawness of spirit."[1]

In 1958, in a conscious effort to bring new creative energy to his work by denying the conventions of Abstract Expressionism, Davis painted *Peach Glow* (estate of the artist), a small work of pale vertical edge-to-edge pink stripes. Drawing his inspiration from Barnett Newman's "zips," Jasper John's flags and targets, and Paul Klee's geometric patterns, Davis soon fixed on the stripe as his signature image and developed it with remarkable energy and inventiveness. He began to vary radically the color of his stripes and to arrange stripes and clusters of stripes in complicated orchestrations of color and interval. One canvas might be dense with bands of edge-to-edge stripes while another might open up with passages of empty canvas; one might be constructed from wide bands, another from narrow pinstripes; one canvas might be characterized by dark moody colors, another by brilliant colors, even Dayglo paints. Almost all of the variants on stripe painting were developed over a short time. "During the period between 1958 and 1960," Davis later said, "I staked out almost all the different types of stripe paintings. . . . Then, ten years later, I came back and picked up on loose threads."[2]

From 1962 to 1968, however, Davis concentrated on one type of painting in particular—complex, hard-edge, uniform-width stripes—and he did so with such consistency and to such memorable effect that these seven years became known as his classic stripe period. In one group of paintings from this period Davis imposed a larger order by dividing the canvas and painting each half in a dramatically different range of colors. An untitled work of 1964 in the collection of the National Museum of American Art, with its reds on the left and blues on the right, falls into this category. So does *Boudoir Painting* (1965, location unknown), with pinks, olive greens, and browns on the left, and blues, violets, yellows, and reds on the right. *Equinox,* also from 1965, pits predominantly cool colors on the left two-fifths of the canvas against predominantly warm ones on the remaining three-fifths.

In 1959, Davis had begun to experiment with magna paints stained into raw canvas. The technique had been introduced into the community of artists in Washington by Kenneth Noland and Morris Louis, who had seen it used by Helen Frankenthaler during their famous visit to her studio in 1952. In the early 1960s, all three men seemed to be forsaking Abstract Expressionism at the same time; all three began to favor bold, flat images in bright colors over complicated compositions and exaggerated brushwork, as well as acrylics stained into canvas over oils brushed across primed canvas. This set of shared formal preferences eventually brought these artists, and several others, together into a group that became known as the Washington Color School.

Almost immediately, Davis, a fiercely independent man, began to distinguish his work from that of his fellow Washington artists. The lucidity of his first fully-realized stripe paintings, such as *Peach Glow,* yielded to stripe paintings of remarkable complexity. Having tried to "avoid any complex adventures for the eye,"[3] he began to offer the viewer a "feast for the eyes."[4] Instead of developing the stripe as a format for color, he began to use color "as a means of defining interval."[5] All of these strayings from the formalist fold eventually drove a wedge between Davis and Clement Greenberg, the preeminent critic of the formalist movement. Greenberg was annoyed that Davis rejected his efforts to dictate the kinds of works Davis should paint and exhibit, and for years Greenberg's disfavor handicapped the artist in achieving the level of recognition he deserved.

Because Davis had learned the stain technique from Louis and Noland, some observers mistakenly assumed that he derived his subject matter from the two men as well. In fact, when Davis finally settled on the stripe as the primary vehicle for his art in 1958, he anticipated Louis' 1961 pillar paintings by three years and Noland's horizontal-band series by eight years.

Throughout his career, Davis worked to maintain his radical edge by experimenting with emerging movements—from earthworks to conceptual art to "bad" painting. Except perhaps for the artist's whimsical micro-paintings, these works rarely achieved much importance. But his willingness to experiment, even at the risk of failure, infused the dry geometry of his best-known image with unflagging vigor and freshness.

Steven W. Naifeh and Gregory White Smith

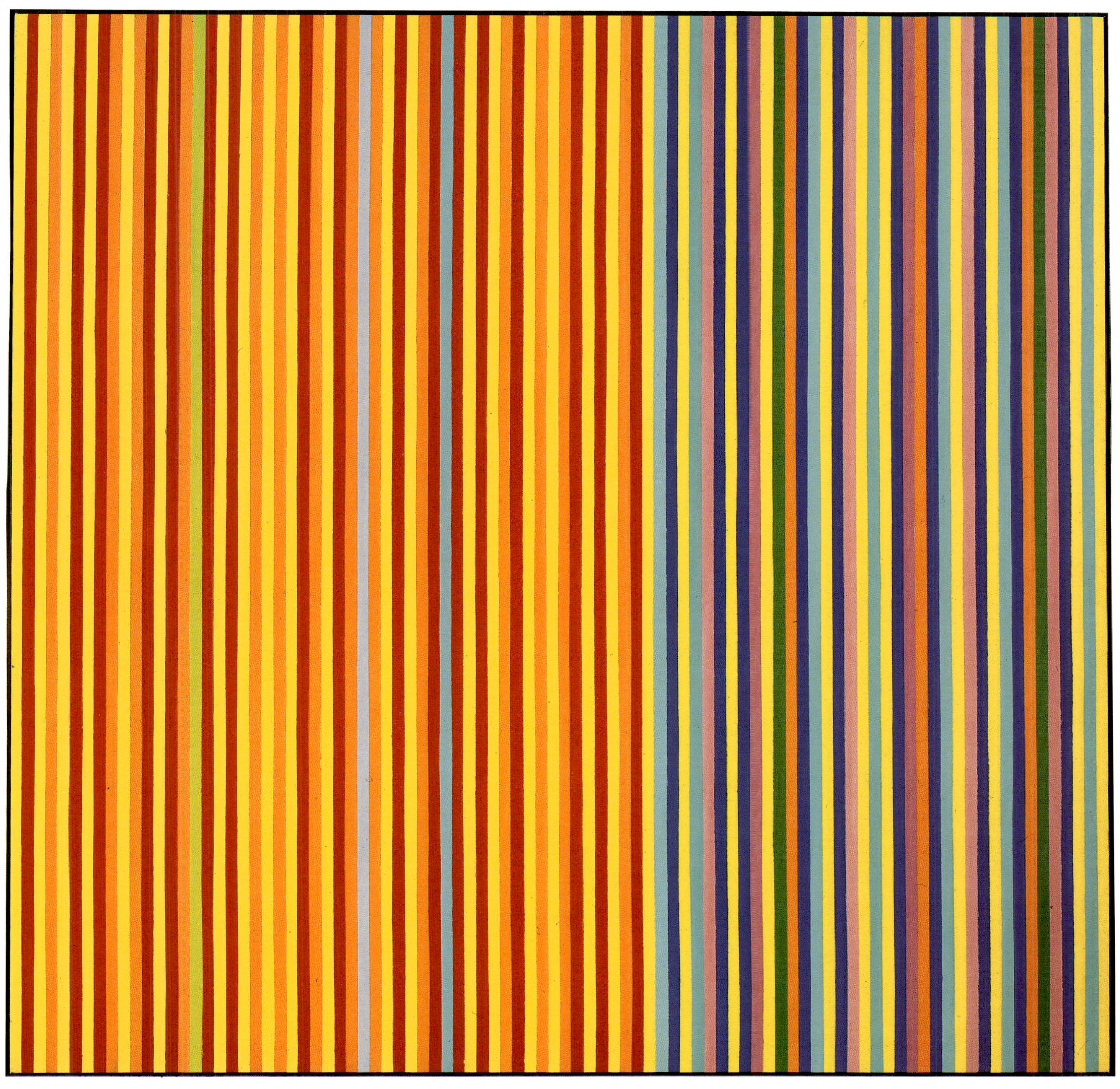

85. Tom Wesselmann (United States, b. 1931)

Bedroom Painting #2, 1968

Oil on canvas, 43½ x 83½"

University purchase, Bixby Fund, 1968

In order to comment on my painting, *Bedroom Painting #2,* I have to start at the beginning.[1] In art school I was oriented to be a painter—to work in two dimensions. So, for some time, I resisted using three dimensional elements in my work. But since graduation in 1959, I had been accumulating found objects that I felt I would have to use. When I broke this restriction of two dimensionalism in 1961 and started using assemblage elements, it sparked a long term interest in finding formal ways to make my work as intense as possible. For the next few years I experimented heavily with form changes—including the introduction of light, sound, movement, tv and the painting continuing onto the floor with rugs and standing objects. It wasn't until 1964 that I broke the two dimensional geometric restriction on the shape of the painting. Up to that point my paintings had been in conventional shapes—rectangles, circles and diamonds—shapes that were not germane to the image, but were an externally imposed restriction, or challenge. With *Landscape #1* (1964, location unknown) I let the car protrude beyond the edges of the painting. This intensified the subject matter and reinforced my interest in spatial intensity as the car became more "forward." *Landscape #1* was soon followed by my first fully-shaped work, a nude torso, *Great American Nude #61* (1965, location unknown).

By 1967, I had done most of the form changes I was going to do in that era of my work, and I began to focus increasingly on the shape of the canvas. I conceived what I called "drop-outs." The first ones were based on a rectangle with one side dropped away in the form of a breast. Also in 1967, I extended this idea to full "drop-outs," where the whole painting became a negative shape. The painting represents only what is seen through the interstices of the nude—usually the hole formed between the body and an arm, as in *Seascape #23* (1967, Sidney Janis Gallery, New York). I tried the one side "drop-out" with a nude and still life composition, in *Great American Nude #96* (1967, location unknown). In this case, the table drops out, emphasizing the still life elements suspended against the white wall. I felt only marginally satisfied with the result. While my eyes liked the somewhat eccentric shapes of the "drop-outs," my brain said "too contrived," so I stopped doing them. (Although I did change my mind in the early 1970s and explored that area further.)

Late in 1967, I began my *Bedroom Painting* series, which marked a crucial change in my work. In these paintings the scale of the elements changed dramatically, as my vantage point moved in closer and focused on body parts, rather than the whole nude. The corresponding still life elements increased in size and importance. The resultant image was more graphic, blunt and exciting. In Washington University's *Bedroom Painting #2,* I applied the "drop-out" table form, trying to make it work more to my satisfaction. When I set out to write this essay, I intended to state it was the first time I had used this device, but it just seemed that way because I felt it was so successful. In fact, I think this is the last time this particular form appears in my work. *Bedroom Painting #2,* finished in early 1968, was a crucially important work to me. It was the first time I had dealt with the nude and a small amount of related elements in a larger focus—elements that previously would have been small parts of a large composition. Now, the nipple, cigarette and ash tray, orange, mouth and rose become strong and compelling presences. (I had actually done this once or twice, previously, especially in *Great American Nude #53* [1964, collection of the artist], but I didn't perceive the problem and solution in quite the same terms.)

Bedroom Painting #2 was the first time I tackled what seemed like a painting in two parts, in that the smoke tended to break the image in half. The problem was intensified by the fact that the right side was much stronger visually than the left side. Making the left side more empty in relation to the right side was part of the solution. It gave more impact to the nipple, which is emphasized by its pale surroundings and the cigarette butt. Perhaps the basic compositional problem doesn't sound so difficult, but I spent one of the longest periods ever, for me, trying to resolve the painting. I did probably more preliminary oil studies for this than for any work before or since. The final result was all the more satisfying, and made me want to keep the painting for its overall importance to me. However, when Washington University wanted to buy it, my dealer, Sidney Janis, prevailed on me to sell it. While I'm glad it is in a museum, I still miss it after all these years and it remains one of my most favorite works.

Tom Wesselmann

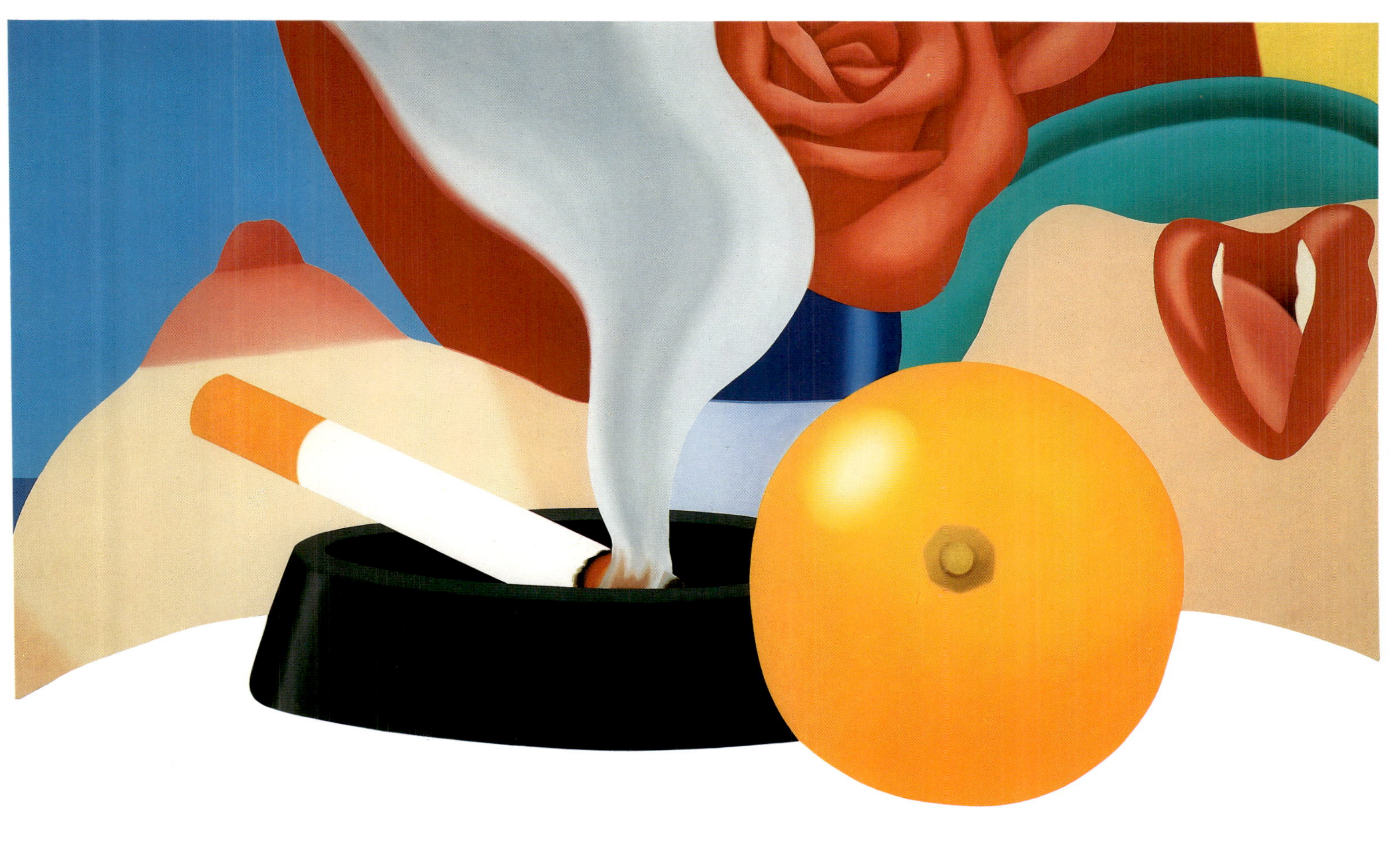

Notes

"A Gallery of Modern Art"

1. "Dr. Compton Admits He Can't Understand Modern Paintings," *St. Louis Post-Dispatch,* 15 April 1946, p. 1; Reed Hynds, "W. U. Collection of Contemporary Art to Go on Exhibition Monday in Givens Hall," *St. Louis Star-Times,* 13 April 1946, p. 1; and Horst W. Janson, *Modern Art in the Washington University Collection* (St. Louis: Washington University, 1946), p. 4. The new gallery was a converted classroom in Givens Hall, the School of Architecture at Washington University.

2. Janson, *Modern Art in the Washington University Collection,* p. 4.

3. Cornelia Carr, ed., *Harriet Hosmer: Letters and Memories* (New York: Moffat, Yard & Col, 1912), pp. 25-26. See also Joni L. Kinsey, entry 20, on Hosmer's *Oenone.*

4. See Joni L. Kinsey, entry 21, on Ball's *Freedom's Memorial.*

5. "Twas His, Tis Ours: The Crow Museum Delivered to St. Louis," *The Missouri Republican,* 11 May 1881, p. 1; J. Thomas Scharf, *History of Saint Louis City and County* (Philadelphia: Louis H. Everts & Co., 1883), p. 1622; "St. Louis Museum of Fine Arts," *Harper's Weekly* (June 25, 1881); *American Architecture and Building News* X, no. 297 (September 3, 1881): n.p.; "An Art Gift to St. Louis," *New York Times,* 12 May 1881, p. 1; William R. Hodges, "The St. Louis School and Museum of Fine Arts," *Magazine of Art* (London) VIII (1885): 85-88.

6. "Twas His, Tis Ours," p. 1.

7. Scharf, *History of Saint Louis,* p. 1619. See Gabriel P. Weisberg, entry 3, on Brion's *Invasion,* and J. Gray Sweeney, entry 13, on Church's *Twilight.*

8. *Palette Scrapings,* the Washington University art students' newsletter, reported the purchase of Dupré's *Haying Scene* on May 27, 1882, describing it as a "strikingly beautiful picture" (vol. 1, no. 3, p. 52). An engraving of the painting later appeared as the logo for the paper. In addition, the *Spectator* (St. Louis) regarded the painting as "the sweetest and most winsome picture in the room" (92 [June 17, 1882]: 726). See Gabriel P. Weisberg, entry 6, on Dupré's *In Pasture,* and Joni L. Kinsey, entry 22, on Chase's *Courtyard of a Dutch Orphan Asylum.*

9. Minutes of the Board of Control, St. Louis School and Museum of Fine Arts, 9 February 1894, note that Ives had persuaded local arts patron Charles Nagel to purchase Sorolla's painting for the Museum (The Saint Louis Art Museum archives). See also Priscilla Muller, entry 9, on Sorolla's *¡Otra Margarita!.*

10. Edward Strahan, *Art Treasures of America* (Philadelphia: n.publ., 1879). For additional information on Charles Parsons see Graham Beal, *Charles Parsons Collection of Paintings* (St. Louis: Washington University Gallery of Art, 1976). See also Elizabeth C. Childs, entry 1, on Daumier's *Le Dessinateur;* Gabriel P. Weisberg, entry 2, on Breton's *Wine Shop-Monday;* Fronia E. Wissman, entry 5, on Corot's *Le Chemin des Vieux;* and J. Gray Sweeney, entry 14, on Church's *Sierra Nevada.*

11. "Twas His, Tis Ours," p. 1; *Advancing Saint Louis in Art—Value of Art in Developing the City,* series D, no. 1 (St. Louis: Saint Louis Museum of Fine Arts, January 1906), n.p. See also Mary Hamel-Schwulst, entry 7, on Lhermitte's *La Moisson;* Aimée Brown Price, entry 10, on Puvis' *Charité;* Joyce K. Schiller, entry 25, on Dewing's *Brocart de Venise;* and Joni L. Kinsey, entries 24, 26, and 28, on Inness' *Storm on the Delaware,* Tryon's *Before Sunrise,* and Hassam's *Diamond Cove.*

12. *The St. Louis School and Museum of Fine Arts, 1906–1907, Schedule of Lecture Courses, Special Exhibitions* (pamphlet, The Saint Louis Art Museum archives), n.p.; *Advancing Saint Louis in Art* (1906), n.p. Much of the information surrounding the early history of the St. Louis School and Museum of Fine Arts, including its dissolution and the formation of the City Art Museum, was researched by Gerald D. Bolas, Gallery director from 1977 to 1988, and published on the occasion of the Gallery's centennial celebration in his essay "One Hundred Years of the Washington University Art Collection," in *Illustrated Checklist of the Collection: Paintings, Sculpture and Works on Paper* (St. Louis: Washington University Gallery of Art, 1981), pp. 6–11.

13. See Joni L. Kinsey, entries 23 and 27, on Eakins' *Portrait of Professor W.D. Marks* and Twachtman's *House in Landscape.*

14. "A Washington University Art Center," *The Washingtonian* VI, no. 7 (April 1929): 1–4, 16–17; Janson, "The New Art Collection at Washington University," p. 200.

15. Quoted from an unpublished typescript of Horst W. Janson's lecture, 15 May 1981, in celebration of the centennial of the art museum at the Washington University Gallery of Art (Washington University Gallery of Art archives); Janson, "The New Art Collection at Washington University," p. 200; Janson, quoted by Reed Hynds, "W.U. Collection of Contemporary Art," p. 1.

16. Janson, "The New Art Collection at Washington University," p. 201; Hynds, "Yielding Place to New," *Artnews* XLV, no. 4 (June 1946): 33.

17. Janson, centennial lecture (1981). See Jean Sutherland Boggs, entry 30, on Picasso's *Glass and Bottle of Suze,* and Mark Rosenthal, entry 34, on Gris' *Still Life with Playing Cards.*

18. See Ruth L. Bohan, entry 69, on Stella's *Man in an Elevated (Train),* and Mark Rosenthal, entry 75, on Guston's *If This Be Not I.*

19. Howard Derrickson, "Dream of Campus Art Gallery: The University's Collections of Art as Tools for Teaching," *Washington University Magazine* (October 1956): 12; Derrickson, "Art and Artists: Controversial Works of Pollock," *St. Louis Post-Dispatch,* 25 January 1953; and "Washington U. Buys de Kooning Paintings," *St. Louis Post-Dispatch,* 16 May 1956. See also Ruth L. Bohan, entries 67 and 68, on Feininger's *Bridge I* and Hartley's *Iron Cross;* William C. Agee, entry 70, on Dove's *Sand and Sea;* Harry Rand, entries 78 and 80, on Gorky's *Golden Brown* and de Kooning's *Saturday Night;* Andrew Kagan, entry 79, on Pollock's *Sleeping Effort;* and Mark Rosenthal, entry 76, on Guston's *Fable.*

20. Derrickson, "Dream of Campus Art Gallery," pp. 9, 13; George McCue, "Music and the Arts—Exploratory Spirit at Steinberg Hall: New Associates Group to Support Expanded Art Activities," *St. Louis Post-Dispatch,* 17 November 1968.

21. Margaret Brink, "Interview with William N. Eisendrath, Jr. Curator at Steinberg Hall," *St. Louis Globe-Democrat,* 1962.

22. "Collections: Taste on Campus," *Time* Magazine (July 21, 1967). See Joan Marter, entry 74, on Calder's *Five Rudders;* Jean Sutherland Boggs, entry 31, on Picasso's *Les Femmes d'Alger;* Jack Flam, entry 29, on Matisse's *Still Life with Oranges;* Dennis Adrian, entry 39, on Ensor's *Le Christ Tourmente;* Mark Rosenthal, entry 35, on Gris' *Still Life: Table with Red Cloth;* Jan van der Marck, entry 63, on Fontana's *Spatial Concept;* Stephen Nash, entry 46, on Gabo's *Linear Construction in Space;* Robert Murdock, entry 48, on Leger's *Les Belles Cyclistes;* Valerie Fletcher, entry 53, on Matta's *Glimmer of Violence;* Victor H. Miesel, entry 41, on Meidner's *Selbstbildnis;* and Patricia Berman, entry 40, on Munch's *Portrait of Irmgard Steinbart.*

23. McCue, "Exploratory Spirit at Steinberg Hall"; Beth Ann Boundy, "The Best Informed on Modern, Modern Art," *St. Louis Globe-Democrat,* 21–22 December 1968. See William C. Agee, entry 71, on Stuart Davis' *Max #2;* Stephen W. Naifeh and Gregory White Smith, entry 84, on Gene Davis' *Equinox;* and Tom Wesselmann, entry 85, on his *Bedroom Painting #2.*

24. See Eliza Rathbone, entry 55, on de Stael's *Composition;* Thomas M. Messer, entries 57 and 58, on Dubuffet's *Poches aux Yeux* and *Tête Barbue;* Pierre Encrevé, entry 58, on Soulages' *Peinture;* Aaron M. Shatzman, entry 59, on Appel's *Heads in Space;* Gerald Nordland, entry 61, on Burri's *Gran Ferro M3;* Manuel J. Borja-Villel, entry 62, on Tàpies' *Porta Marró;* Werner Schmalenbach, entry 64, on Chillida's *Rumor de Limites #4;* Anna Imponente, entry 65, on Consagra's *Racconto de Marinaio;* Peter Selz, entries 81 and 82, on Francis' *Arcueil* and *Floating Blue;* and Roni Feinstein, entry 83, on Rauschenberg's *Choke.*

25. For the history of museums in the United States see Edward P. Alexander, *Museums in Motion: An Introduction to the History and Functions of Museums* (Nashville: American Association for State and Local History, 1979).

26. "Twas His, Tis Ours", p. 1.

1 Daumier, *Le Dessinateur*

1. Daumier's first contribution to a Salon was in 1849 with *The Miller, His Son and the Ass* (Burrell Collection, Glasgow), a canvas based on a literary theme drawn from the fables of La Fontaine; he followed it with two paintings and one drawing in the Salon of 1850. Thereafter, with the exception of one painting shown in the Salon of 1861, he ceased to exhibit in the Salon. On his ambitions as a painter during the Second Republic, see T. J. Clark, *The Absolute Bourgeois: Artists and Politics in France, 1848–1851* (London: Thames and Hudson, 1973), chap. 4 and Bruce Laughton, *The Drawings of Daumier and Millet* (New Haven: Yale University Press, 1991), chap. 5

2. For a complete listing of the numerous works by Daumier in all media on the subject of artists, amateurs, collecting, exhibitions, and critics, see Louis Provost, *Honoré Daumier: A Thematic Guide to the Oeuvre,* ed.

Elizabeth Childs (New York and London: Garland, 1989), pp. 78–79. Several drawings and watercolors related to the present panel have been identified by K. E. Maison in *Honoré Daumier: Catalogue Raisonné of the Paintings, Watercolours and Drawings,* vol. 2 (Greenwich: New York Graphic Society, 1968), nos. 371, 374–376.

3. See Baudelaire's essay on Daumier, "Quelques caricaturistes français" (1857), reprinted in *Curiositiés esthétiques/L'Art romantique* (Paris: Garnier Frères, 1962), n.p.

4. Examples of Second Empire Salon paintings celebrating the lives of famous Renaissance artists include works by Jean-Ernest Aubert (Salon 1852), Alexandre Colin (Salon 1855), Joseph Robert-Fleury (Salon 1855), and Jules-Jean-Baptiste Trayer (Salon 1852), to name a few.

5. An example of the popular "dix-huitièmiste" genre by Meissonier is *Un peintre montrant des dessins* (Wallace Collection, London), in which an elegant artist shows his work to an amateur in a sumptuous atelier setting.

6. Examples of salon paintings of modern studio interiors or scenes featuring artists and amateurs include works by Jules Holzafel (Salon 1852), Henri Baron (Salon 1853), Antoine-Emile Plassan (Salon 1853), Florent Willems (Salon 1853), Victor Chavel (Salon 1855), Simon Horsin-Déon (Salon 1855), and Horace Vernet (Salon 1855). It should be noted, however, that these are hardly dominant themes in the exhibitions, as there are only a handful of these pictures in Salons where typically well over a thousand pictures were shown. Therefore, Daumier's choice of the artist/amateur theme should not be interpreted as part of a salon strategy.

2. Breton, *Wine Shop—Monday*

1. For reference to this work see Hollister Sturges et al., *Jules Breton and the French Rural Tradition* (Omaha, Nebr.: Joslyn Art Museum, 1982), p. 71. The author of the catalog entry on this painting, Candace Clements, correctly identified this work relative to the 1859 Paris Salon.

2. Over the past ten years I have been shown at least ten versions of *Recall of the Gleaners,* either in part or in whole, for authentication as works by Jules Breton. In almost each case the work was a weak copy, completed by an unknown artist from the original or even from a photograph of the work; in a few instances there existed the possiblity that Breton could have had some hand in a study. These works attest to the broad interest in Jules Breton's imagery, especially with works that were visible in public exhibition.

3. For reference to Gambart and this painting see Jules Breton's letter to Charles Parsons, October 10, 1904, Washington University Gallery of Art Archives, St. Louis. Breton noted, in an attempt to work out the early provenance of the work, that "I sold this canvas which you own, *Monday,* to Mr. Gambart, the well-known dealer. . . ." Gambart was well established in England where he was a primary sponsor of modern art.

4. All the figures and the models who served Breton are identified in the letter from Breton to Parsons, October 10, 1904.

5. Castagnary, as quoted by Clements in Sturges, *Jules Breton,* p. 71.

6. See Gabriel P. Weisberg, *The Realist Tradition, French Painting and Drawing, 1830–1900* (Cleveland: The Cleveland Museum of Art, 1980), p. 13, for a discussion of early Breton imagery.

3. Brion, *The Invasion*

1. See Gabriel P. Weisberg, *The Realist Tradition, French Painting and Drawing 1830–1900* (Cleveland: The Cleveland Museum of Art, 1980), p. 136, for additional discussion of this painting.

2. The category of genre painting in the nineteenth century needs considerable investigation, as painters and writers were using this type of work to comment on contemporary themes and personalities in a more significant way than has been thought.

4. Diaz, *Wood Interior*

1. For additional information on Diaz see Phillipe Burty, "N. Diaz," in *Maîtres et Petits Maîtres* (Paris: G. Charpentier, 1877); Théophile Silvestre, "N. Diaz," in *Les Artistes Français* (Paris: G. Charpentier, 1878); Robert L. Herbert, *Barbizon Revisted,* exh. cat. (Boston: Museum of Fine Arts, 1962); Jean Bouret, *L'École de Barbizon* (Neuchâtel: Ides et Calandes, 1972); and Kermit S. Champa, *The Rise of Landscape Painting in France: Corot to Manet,* exh. cat. (Manchester, N.H.: Currier Gallery of Art, 1991).

5. Corot, *Le Chemin des Vieux*

1. See Alfred Robaut, *L'Oeuvre de Corot, par Alfred Robaut, catalogue raisonné et illustré, précédé par l'histoire de Corot et des ses oeuvres par Etienne Moreau-Nélaton,* 4 vols. (Paris: H. Floury, 1905). Robaut details Corot's career with first-hand reports, documents, photographs, and images of known and now-lost paintings; this remains the most important source for any study of the artist and his work.

2. In the exhibition catalogue *Exposition de l'oeuvre de Corot* (Paris: Ecole des Beaux-Arts, 1875) the variant is listed as no. 65 with the dimensions of 40 x 33 cm and was lent by the dealer Léon Marcotte.

3. See Etienne Moreau-Nélaton, *Histoire de Corot et de ses oeuvres par Etienne Moreau-Nélaton d'après les documents recueillis par Alfred Robaut* (Paris: H. Floury, 1905), fig. 229 and pp. 293–96, for details of Corot's painting campaign in August 1872. See also Robaut, *L'Oeuvre de Corot,* no. 2063.

4. See William R. Johnson, *The Nineteenth-Century Paintings in the Walters Art Gallery* (Baltimore: The Trustees of the Walters Art Gallery, 1982), pp. 13–28, and for collectors in the Boston area with similar tastes see Alexandra R. Murphy, "French Paintings in Boston: 1800–1900," in *Corot to Braque: French Paintings from the Museum of Fine Arts, Boston,* exh. cat. (Boston: Museum of Fine Arts, 1979), pp. xvii–xlvi.

5. Jules-Antoine Castagnary, as translated in Maurice Hermel, *Corot and His Work,* vol. 1 (Glasgow: James Maclehose & Sons, 1905), p. 30.

6. Corot, as quoted in Théophile Silvestre, *Histoire des artistes vivants: Français et étrangers* (Paris: E. Blanchard, 1856), p. 95, and translated in Hermel, *Corot,* p. 31. See also Hermel, *Corot,* vol. 2, pl. 68, for an etching of the Washington University picture.

6. Dupré, *In Pasture*

1. See Karl Cartier, "Silhouettes d'artistes, Julien Dupré, peintre," *Journal des Arts* (May 9, 1903), n.p., and his "Julien Dupré," in *Figures contemporaines,* vol. 6 (Paris: H. Floury, 1896–1903), n.p. See also Gabriel P. Weisberg, *The Realist Tradition, French Painting and Drawing* (Cleveland: The Cleveland Museum of Art, 1980), p. 287.

2. This painting has not been the subject of detailed investigation in the Huntington collection. The figure is more mannered and elongated than the more mature girls from the 1880s. For further reference see the Huntington Art Museum Archives, Huntington, West Virginia.

3. Cartier, "Silhouettes d'artistes," n.p.

4. Washington University Gallery of Art Archives, St. Louis, Missouri. The variant at the University of Kentucky Art Museum measures 53 x 78 inches. There are also differences in background vegetation. For further information see *Beginnings: A University Art Museum Collects,* exh. cat. (Lexington: University of Kentucky Art Museum, 1979), p. 24 n. 8.

7. Lhermitte, *La Moisson*

1. *La Moisson* was shown at the 1883 Salon of the Société des artistes Français as no. 1518, and also at the Exposition Nationale de 1883 as no. 466. Lhermitte recalled the exhibits, as well as the Paris World's Fair of 1889 where *La Moisson* earned a medal of honor, in a letter from Paris written to express his pleasure that the oil had been acquired by the St. Louis Museum (28 February 1912, Washington University Gallery of Art Archives). On the widespread revival of scholarly interest in French nineteenth-century Realism and Naturalism, see Gabriel P. Weisberg, *The European Realist Tradition* (Bloomington: Indiana University Press, 1982), pp. vii–ix. Of the many European painters who succeeded Courbet, Millet, and Breton as painters of rustic subjects, Lhermitte was certainly the best-known—especially after 1884 and the death of Jules Bastien-Lepage. For the "grand manner" series, see Mary Michele Hamel, "A French Artist: Léon Lhermitte (1844–1925)" (Ph.D. diss., Washington University, St. Louis, 1974), p. 37ff, and Hamel, *Léon Lhermitte,* exh. cat. (Oshkosh, Wisc.: Paine Art Center and Arboretum, 1974), pp. 17–18, 23. See also the valuable new archival publication by Monique Le Pelley Fonteny, *Léon Lhermitte (1844–1925): Catalogue Raisonné,* preface by Jacques Thuiller (Paris: Cercle d'Art, 1991), which includes Lhermitte's personal notes, family and studio photographs, and many unknown sketches, among other materials. *La Moisson* of 1883 and related works are treated pp. 36, 100–101; 174, 392–93; 449, 504–5. See also Fonteny, ed., *Léon Lhermitte et le pays des moissonneurs,* vol. 44 of *Les dossiers du musée d'Orsay* (Paris: Réunion des Musées Nationaux, 1991), pp. 13–15, 45.

2. See Hamel, *A French Artist,* pp. 37–38, 49–50 n. 7, and Fonteny, *Le pays,* pp. 11–16.

3. See Hamel, *A French Artist,* p. 78ff, and Hamel, *Lhermitte,* pp. 17–24.

4. See *Charles Gleyre: ou les illusions perdues* (Winterthur: Kunstmuseum, 1974), entry 94.

5. See Hamel, *A French Artist,* pp. 42, 51 n. 19. See also Robert Rosenblum and H. W. Janson, *19th-Century Art* (New York: Abrams, 1984), p. 477.

8. Bonnat, *Peasant Girl*

1. For a monographic survey of Bonnat's life, career, and oeuvre, see Alisa Luxenberg, "Léon Bonnat (1833–1922)" (Ph.D. diss., New York University, 1991).

2. To invigorate what was perceived as an artistic community in decline, the French government signed into law various reforms of the art institutions, including the Ecole des beaux-arts and the Salon. See Albert Boime, *The Academy and French Painting in the Nineteenth Century* (London and New York: Phaidon, 1971).

3. The Luxembourg's purchase of the *Portrait of Cardinal Lavigerie* (1888, Musée Historique, Versailles) in 1892 was instigated by the financially-strapped sitter's offer to sell. A famous national and religious figure, Lavigerie recognized that his portrait functioned as patrimony and, in consequence, levied great pressure on the State to secure it for a French collection.

4. See illustrated costume books, such as *Zur Geschichte der Kostüme* (Munich: Braun and Schneider, n.d. [c. 1880–1910]), pl. 866.

5. See J. Moncla, *Le Courier de Bayonne* 10, no. 1282 (5 juillet 1861): 3, and William Bürger (pseud. for Théophile Thoré), "Salon de 1861," *L'Indépendance* (1861), reprinted in *Salons de W. Bürger 1861 à 1868,* vol. 1 (Paris: Vve. Jules Renouard, 1870), p. 40. For various reviews of Manet's *Spanish Singer,* see George Heard Hamilton, *Manet and His Critics* (New Haven: Yale University Press, 1954), pp. 24–32.

6. This development in the reception of the sketch is discussed by Boime in his *The Academy and French Painting.*

7. In 1884, Bonnat gave an unfinished canvas, *Italienne,* to a benefit auction for the children of the late artist Ulysse Butin, with the promise to complete it. Knoedler Gallery bought it for 18,000 francs. See *Chronique des arts et de la curiosité* (31 mai 1883): 173.

8. The increasing numbers and prices of nineteenth-century genre subjects reflected contemporary tastes, and Bonnat's Italian subjects fetched handsome prices. For example, he received 3,700 francs in 1873 for *Pasqua Maria,* 15,000 francs in 1877 (as much as a history painting) for *Danseurs italiens,* and a whopping 44,500 francs in 1879 for *Scherzo* ("Vente Collection Théophile Gautier," *Chronique des arts et de la curiosité* [18 janvier 1873]: 18; "Vente Galerie Oppenheim," *Chronique* [31 mars 1877]: 131; "Vente Collection Garfunkel," *Chronique* [13 décembre 1879]: 310).

9. Other American collectors of and sitters to Bonnat included John Wolfe, Charles Gibson, T. R. Butler, John T. Johnston, A. H. Stewart, Leland Stanford, William T. Walters, George Schuyler, John Jacob Astor IV, and Marshall Field.

9. Sorolla y Bastida, *¡Otra Margarita!*

1. *Christian Advocate* (14 January 1909), n.p.

2. See Bernardino de Pantorba, *La vida y la obra de Joaquín Sorolla* (Madrid: Editoiral Mayfe, 1953), p. 55; Leonard D. Abbott, "Two Spanish Painters of Genius," *The Chautauquan* LV (1909), p. 480.

3. Priscilla E. Muller, "Sorolla and America," in Edmund Peel, ed., *The Painter Joaquín Sorolla* (London: Philip Wilson Publishers Ltd., 1989), pp. 55, 61, 64, 65–68.

4. Rodolfo Gil, *Joaquín Sorolla* (Madrid: Saenz de Jubera Hermanos, 1913), pp. 27–29.

5. Pedro de Madrazo, review article in *La Ilustración española y americana,* Año XXXVIII-núm. XXI (June 8, 1894): 346.

6. Madrazo, review article in *La Ilustración española y americana,* Año XXXVI-núm. XLIII (November 22, 1892): 350–51.

7. A. Garciá Llansó, "Joaquín Agrasot y la escuela pictoricó moderna," *La Ilustratión Artística,* Año XI-núm. 549 (July 4, 1892): 418–21.

8. See *La Ilustración Artística,* Año XII-núm. 582 (February 20, 1893): 128, 130. Subsequent to *¡Otra Margarita!,* Sorolla's conception of art reiterated the ideals expressed by Y. Yxart, a Catalan critic whose reviews of Barcelona's Fine Arts Exhibition began to appear in May 1891 (see *La Ilustración Artística,* Año X-núm. 490 [May 18, 1891]: 306). Maintaining that modern art should externalize an inner vision of the life, dreams and realities of its time and transmit through its lens each generation's world view, Yxart believed that objective realism should surrender to a projection of personal visions and emotions which would impart a sincere impression of a fleeting moment. The artist should capture the fleeting moment of a figure's gestures with a single stroke. With tone, color and a sense of atmosphere, the artist would achieve a palpable, evocative reality.

9. See Pantorba, *Joaquín Sorolla,* pp. 39–40.

10. See *La Ilustración española y americana,* Año XXIX-núm. VIII (February 28, 1885): 115. "Pobra Margarita" is inscribed on Sorolla's study for *¡Otra Margarita!* in the Museo Sorolla, Madrid (cat. no. 312).

11. Trinidad Simó considers *¡Otra Margarita!* to be related to the subject of prostitution (see his *J. Sorolla* [Valencia: V. Garcia, 1980], p. 97).

10. Puvis de Chavannes, *La Charité*

1. For additional information on Puvis de Chavannes see Louise d' Argencourt, Jacques Foucart, et al., *Puvis de Chavannes,* exh. cat. (Paris and Ottowa: Grand Palais and National Gallery of Canada, 1976–77), and Richard Wattenmaker, *Puvis de Chavannes and the Modern Tradition* (Toronto: Art Gallery of Ontario, 1975).

2. See Maxime Du Camp, *Paris, ses organes, ses fonctions et sa vie dans la seconde moitié du XIXe siècle,* 5th ed., vol. 4 (Paris: Hachette, 1875), p. 129. See also Du Camp, *La Charité privée à Paris* (Paris: Hachette, 1885); and Du Camp, *Paris bienfaisant* (Paris: Hachette, 1888). During the previous regime, government had been leery of charity carried out by religious institutions; see Pierre de la Gorce, *Histoire du Second Empire,* vol. II (Paris: Plon-Nourrit, 1894), p. 180.

11. Cole, *Aqueduct Near Rome*

1. See the account of the "discovery" of Thomas Cole by William Dunlap in his *History of the Rise and Progress of the Arts of Design in the United States,* vol. 3 (New York: G. P. Scott, 1834), pp. 359–60. For additional information on Cole see Howard Merritt, *Thomas Cole* (Rochester: University of Rochester Memorial Art Gallery, 1969); Louis L. Noble, *The Course of Empire, Voyage of Life and Other Pictures of Thomas Cole, N.A., with Selections from his Letters and Miscellaneous Writings, Illustrative of his Life, Character, and Genius* (Cambridge: Belknap Press of Harvard University, 1853); and Ellwood C. Parry III, *The Art of Thomas Cole: Ambition and Imagination* (Newark, London and Toronto: University of Delaware Press and Associated University Presses, 1988).

2. William Cullen Bryant, "To Cole, The Painter, Departing for Europe" (1829), in *The Poetical Works of William Cullen Bryant,* vol. 1, ed. Parke Godwin (New York: D. Appleton and Company, 1883), p. 219.

3. For more detailed information on the identification and history of this chain of aqueducts see Thomas Ashby, *The Aqueducts of Ancient Rome* (London: Oxford University Press, 1935), pp. 136, 190, 228, 232.

4. The sketches are preliminary studies for the following paintings: UR=*Aqueducts Near Rome;* LR=*Landscape Composition, Italian Scenery* (1832, Memorial Art Gallery, University of Rochester); LL=*Sunset on the Arno* (1832, private collection); UL=*The Vesper Hymn* (1833, Yale University Art Gallery).

5. Cole to Daniel Wadsworth, 13 July 1832, in *The Correspondence of Thomas Cole and Daniel Wadsworth,* ed. J. Bard McNulty (Hartford, Conn.: Connecticut Historical Society, 1983), p. 57.

6. Nathalia Wright, ed., *Letters of Horatio Greenough, American Sculptor* (Madison, Wisc.: University of Wisconsin Press, 1972), p. 143.

7. Dunlap, *Arts of Design,* pp. 154–55.

8. Noble, *The Course of Empire,* p. 165.

9. Thomas Cole, "Sicilian Scenery," *Knickerbocker* XXIII (February 1844): 244.

10. Nathaniel Parker Willis, *Pencilings by the Way,* vol. 1 (Philadelphia: Carey, Lea, and Blanchard, 1836), p. 107.

12. Durand, *A New England Landscape*

1. John Durand, *The Life and Times of A. B. Durand* (New York: Charles Scribner, 1894), p. 198.

2. See Asher B. Durand, "Letters on Landscape Painting," *The Crayon* I (1855): 1. Durand's "Letters" appeared frequently in subsequent issues of *The Crayon.*

3. *The [New York] Evening Post,* 3 January 1870, Fine Arts section.

4. Sarah Burns, *Pastoral Inventions: Rural Life in Nineteenth-Century American Art and Culture* (Philadelphia: Temple University Press, 1989).

5. Thomas Cole, "Lecture on American Scenery: Delivered before the Catskill Lyceum, April 1, 1841," *Northern Light* (May 1, 1841): 25–26, reprinted in Marshall Tymn, ed., *Thomas Cole: The Collected Essays and Prose Sketches* (St. Paul, Minn.: John Colet Press, 1980), p. 199.

6. Durand, "Letters on Landscape Painting," *The Crayon* I (1855): 97.

13. Church, *Twilight*

1. William M. Bryant, "Turner's Sunrise and Church's Sunset at the Loan Exhibition," *The Spectator* 37 (May 28, 1881): 527; also reprinted in "The Loan Exhibition at the Crow Museum," *The Western* (1881): 419.

2. "The National Academy of Design: Fourth Notice," *The Albion,* 3 June 1865, Fine Arts section.

3. See J. Gray Sweeney, "'The Nude of Landscape Painting': Emblematic Personification in the Art of the Hudson River School," *Smithsonian Studies in American Art* 3, no. 4 (Fall 1989): 43–66. For Church's use of this type of symbolism see pp. 53–59.

4. The confusion between Church's "great picture" of 1860, *Twilight in the Wilderness,* and *Twilight: Mount Desert Island, Maine,* painted five years later in a greatly altered social and personal context, has overshadowed the later work, much to its disadvantage. The confusion was already a problem in the nineteenth century, and has retarded appreciation of the 1865 picture even today. Modern scholars have been negative or confused in their commentaries on the picture. For example, Franklin Kelly asserted that *Mount Desert Island, Maine,* "despite certain merits is ultimately an unconvincing recapitulation of a theme Church had treated so many times before. The sky is marked by turgid formlessness, as opposed to the turbulent, but carefully structured sky of *Twilight in the Wilderness*" (*Frederic Edwin Church and the National Landscape* [Washington, D. C.: Smithsonian Institution Press, 1988], p. 126). Even the late David C. Huntington mistakenly assumed that the picture represented Church's optimistic response to the end of the war—a pendant of closure with the painting of 1860 (*The Landscapes of Frederic Edwin Church: Vision of an American Era* [New York: George Braziller, 1966], p. 62).

5. Church to William H. Osborn, 7 July 1864, Olana Historic Site Archives, Hudson, New York.

6. Letters in the Olana Historic Site Archives. I would like to thank Gerald L. Carr for bringing these documents to my attention, and James Ryan for making copies available.

7. The Jenkins Collection was auctioned on May 2 and 3, 1876, and according to Gerald L. Carr the buyer for *Twilight* was listed as "Putnam" (no description, date or dimensions were recorded in the catalogue). Carr speculates that Putnam and Parsons may have been the same person, but he has not been able to definitively establish the identity of Putnam. In any event, by 1880 Parsons owned the picture.

14. Church, *Sierra Nevada*

1. Parsons to Church, 24 November 1880, Olana Historic Site Archives, Hudson, New York. For information on Charles Parsons see Graham W. J. Beal, *Charles Parsons Collection of Paintings,* exh. cat. (St. Louis, Mo.: Washington University Gallery of Art, 1977).

2. Church to Charles DeWolf Brownell, 16 May 1895, Olana Historic Site Archives.

3. See Katherine Manthorne, *Creation and Renewal* (Washington, D.C.: Smithsonian Institution Press, 1985), and her *Tropical Renaissance: North American Artists Exploring Latin America, 1839–1879* (Washington, D.C.: Smithsonian Institution Press, 1989). For information about the aesthetic sensibilities in Church's work see Joseph D. Ketner and Michael J. Tammenga, *The Beautiful, the Sublime, and the Picturesque: British Influences on American Landscape Painting,* exh. cat. (St. Louis, Mo.: Washington University Gallery of Art, 1984).

4. Church to Parsons, 11 April 1883, Parsons Papers, Missouri Historical Society, St. Louis, Missouri.

5. Ibid.

6. Church to Parsons, 3 June 1883.

7. Church to Parsons, 11 April 1883.

8. Church to Parsons, 14 April 1883.

9. Church to Parsons, 28 April 1883.

10. Ibid.

15. Gifford, *The White Mountains*

1. Henry T. Tuckerman, *Book of the Artists: American Artist Life* (New York: G. P. Putnam & Son, 1867), p. 524.

2. Ibid., p. 525.

3. "Fine Arts: Gifford's Pictures," *The Home Journal,* 24 March 1860, p. 2.

4. John F. Weir, "Sanford R. Gifford: His Life and Character as Artist and Man," in *Gifford Memorial Meeting of the Century* (New York: Century Rooms, 1880), p. 20.

5. Ibid., p. 21, 22.

6. *The Crayon* 5 (1858): 57, 147.

7. William McHenry Bryant, "The Loan Exhibition at the Crow Museum," *The Western* (1881): 413.

8. Weir, "Sanford R. Gifford," p. 12.

16. Gifford, *Rheinstein*

1. "Reception at the Tenth Street Studio Building," *The [New York] Evening Post,* 28 March 1873, p. 2.

2. See Bartlett Cowdrey, *National Academy of Design Exhibition Record: 1826–1860* (New York: The New York Historical Society, 1943), p. 183.

3. See Ila Weis, *Poetic Landscape: The Art and Experience of Sanford R. Gifford* (Newark, Del.: University of Delaware Press, 1987), p. 294.

4. Ibid., p. 294.

5. Interestingly the very height of the rock itself had insured the essential preservation of the castle, as it was difficult to access, and therefore was not reduced for building materials as were many other medieval structures in the seventeenth and eighteenth centuries. I am indebted to Alfred Michler for this information.

6. See J. Gray Sweeney, "The Nude of Landscape Painting: Emblematic Personification in the Art of the Hudson River School," *Smithsonian Studies in American Art* 3, no. 4 (Fall 1989): 42–65. See also Stewart Elliott Guthrie, *Faces in the Clouds: A New Theory of Religion* (New York: Oxford University Press, 1993), *passim.*

7. S. G. W. Benjamin, "Our American Artists: V. Sanford R. Gifford," *Wide Awake* VIII, no. 5 (May 1879): 306.

8. J. F. W. [John Ferguson Weir], "A Visit to the Studio of Mr. Sanford R. Gifford," *The [New York] Evening Post,* 18 March 1875, p. 1.

17. Bingham, *Daniel Boone*

1. For the most recent revisionist reading of Bingham see Nancy Rash, *The Painting and Politics of George Caleb Bingham* (New Haven, Conn.: Yale University Press, 1991). See also Elizabeth Johns, "The 'Missouri Artist' as Artist," in *George Caleb Bingham,* ed. Michael E. Shapiro (St. Louis, Mo.: St. Louis Art Museum, and New York: Harry N. Abrams, 1990), pp. 133–39.

2. See J. Gray Sweeney, "An American Moses: George Caleb Bingham's *Daniel Boone Escorting Settlers through the Cumberland Gap,*" in *The Columbus of the Woods: Daniel Boone and the Typology of Manifest Destiny* (St. Louis, Mo.: Washington University Gallery of Art, 1992), pp. 41–51.

3. See Chester Harding, *My Egotistigraphy* (Cambridge, Mass: John Wilson and Son, 1866), pp. 35–36; Leah Lipton, "Chester Harding and the Life Portraits of Daniel Boone," *American Art Journal* 16, no. 3 (Summer 1984): 4–19; and Lipton, "George Caleb Bingham in the Studio of Chester Harding, Franklin, Mo., 1820," *American Art Journal* 16, no. 3 (Summer 1984): 90–92.

4. Bingham to James S. Rollins, March 30, 1851, quoted in "Letters of George C. Bingham to James S. Rollins," ed. C. B. Rollins, *Missouri Historical Review* 23 (October 1937–July 1938): 13–14.

5. Ibid., p. 21. Bingham's claim that the subject of Daniel Boone was "one which has never yet been painted" is puzzling in light of the fact that William Ranney had exhibited a painting entitled *Daniel Boone's First View of Kentucky* at the American Art-Union's annual exhibition in the fall of 1850, and it must have been seen by Bingham. Furthermore, the Art-Union *Bulletin* for May 1850 contained an engraving after Ranney's painting. Bingham's statement may have been disingenuous, and perhaps a crude attempt to manipulate the managers of the Art-Union. It is clear that Bingham felt he was in competition with Ranney in painting western subjects. See Sweeney, *Columbus of the Woods,* p. 59 n. 115.

6. See Sweeney, "An American Moses," pp. 48–49.

7. Bingham's image of Boone represents a fundamentally conservative political view of western expansion, although it can be said to embody a progressive nationalist perspective that typified Whig ideology in the early 1850s. Perhaps the best indication in the picture of this progressive tendency is the perspective or viewpoint Bingham establishes. He places his figures advancing directly toward the spectator from the east. This implies that the unfolding of national history was to be viewed from the vantage point of the western territories. Dawn Glanz was the first scholar to point this out. See her *How the West Was Drawn* (Ann Arbor, Mich.: UMI Research Press, 1982), p. 23.

18. Wimar, *The Abduction*

1. Biographical material and additional information on the artist's early years and artistic development can be found in Joseph D. Ketner, "The Indian Painter in Düsseldorf," in *Carl Wimar: Chronicler of the Missouri River Frontier* (Ft. Worth, Tex.: Amon Carter Museum, 1991), pp. 30–75.

2. Martha Levy Luft, "Charles Wimar's *The Abduction of Daniel Boone's Daughter by the Indians,* 1853 and 1855: Evolving Myths," *Prospects* 7 (1982): 311–12.

19. Wimar, *The Buffalo Hunt*

1. Carl F. Wimar, letter to his parents, 20 February 1855, Carl Wimar Papers, Missouri Historical Society, St. Louis.

2. For a detailed account of Wimar's Missouri River expeditions see Rick Stewart, "An Artist on the Great Missouri," in *Carl Wimar: Chronicler of the Missouri River Frontier* (Ft. Worth, Tex.: Amon Carter Museum, 1991), pp. 77–186.

3. John C. Ewers, Ethnologist Emeritus at the Smithsonian Institution, remarked on these and other traits in *The Buffalo Hunt* that are indicative of its accurate portrayal of the plains Indians' hunting techniques in his "Fact and Fiction in the Documentary Art of the West," in *The Frontier Re-Examined,* ed. John F. McDermott (Urbana, Ill.: University of Illinois Press, 1967), p. 84.

4. George Catlin, in his foreword to *Letters and Notes on the Manners, Customs, and Conditions of North American Indians* (London: n. publ., 1844), n.p.

5. Rena Coen first noted this detail in her pioneering article "The Last of the Buffalo," *American Art Journal* 5 (November 1973): 83–94.

20. Hosmer, *Oenone*

1. The most comprehensive work on Hosmer's life and career is Dolly Sherwood, *Harriet Hosmer: American Sculptor, 1830–1908* (Columbia, Mo.: University of Missouri Press, 1991).

2. For more on Hosmer's relationship with Crow see Cornelia [Crow] Carr, ed., *Harriet Hosmer: Letters and Memories* (New York: Moffat, Yard & Col, 1912).

3. Hosmer's female colleague at the school was Jane Peck, who studied chemistry at the same time Hosmer studied anatomy. See Dolly Sherwood, "Harriet Hosmer's Sojourn in St. Louis," *Gateway Heritage* 5 (Winter 1984–85): 43. A number of Hosmer's anatomical drawings are reproduced in the article.

4. For many years this bust was also considered to be an *Oenone,* but was recognized as *Daphne* in the late 1960s, primarily due to the foliage drapery at the bustline. See Hosmer's letter to Wayman Crow, 10 April 1853, in Carr, *Harriet Hosmer,* pp. 25–26. In this letter Hosmer also thanks Crow for commissioning her first full-scale sculpture (*Oenone*). The closeness of Hosmer to the Crows is further evidenced by Hosmer's many affectionate letters (in which she addressed Mr. Crow as "Pater"), and by the fact that in later years Hosmer called Cornelia Crow her "best friend." See Carr, *Harriet Hosmer,* and Hosmer's papers in the Watertown Public Library and in the Schlesinger Library, Radcliffe College, Boston.

5. Hosmer to Crow, 15 February 1857, in Carr, *Harriet Hosmer,* p. 79. Other local collectors agreed with Hosmer's assessment of *Oenone.* Author Theodore Winthrop wrote to his friend Frederic E. Church during a visit to St. Louis, "A work of Miss Hosmer's has recently arrived to one of her patron friends here—a statue of enone [sic]—it has some good things but is rather flaccid, mannerish and uncalled for, nor is it quite as sensitively chaste as a marble should be—I am inclined to doubt if the work of a mannish woman can ever compare in purity of sentiment with the work of a man of that feminine delicacy of thought and ideal, necessary for sculpture" (Winthrop to Church, 25 April 1857, Frederic Church Papers, Olana State Historic Site, Hudson, New York).

6. See Theodore Finkelston, "'Old Bullion' Bronzed: Business's Monument to Western Opportunity," *Gateway Heritage* 11 (Fall 1990): 48–57. Hosmer was the sculptor of choice for the Western Sanitary Commission's *Freedom Memorial* in 1873, but the St. Louis committee resorted to Thomas Ball after learning what she would charge. See entry 21 on Ball's *Freedom's Memorial.*

7. James Hall, *Dictionary of Sources and Symbols in Art,* rev. ed. (New York: Harper and Row, 1979), pp. 180–81, 234.

8. Contemporary reviews suggested that Oenone is grieving over Paris' death. See *A Guide to the Sculpture, Paintings, Coins, and Other Objects of Art in the Halls of the St. Louis Mercantile Library Association* (St. Louis: Missouri Democrat Books, 1862), p. 6. *The London Art Journal* reiterated the idea: "This statue portrays Oenone in deep and speechless grief at the death of Paris" (as cited in Carr, *Harriet Hosmer,* p. 42). Hosmer herself wrote that "The figure represents Oenone abandoned by Paris, and all I can say is, that I wish it were a thousand times better than it is and the best excuse I have for its shortcomings is that it is the first one I ever made" (Hosmer to Wayman Crow, September 1856, in Carr, *Harriet Hosmer,* p. 72).

9. See *A Guide to the Sculpture,* p. 6.

10. Alfred Lord Tennyson, "Oenone," in Christopher Ricks, ed, *The Poems of Tennyson* 2nd ed., vol. 3 (London: Longman Group, 1987), pp. 1, 419–33. See also Tennyson's "The Death of Oenone" (publ. 1892), in ibid., pp. 220–24.

11. For more on this subject see Alicia Faxon, "Images of Women in the Sculpture of Harriet Hosmer," *Woman's Art Journal* 2 (Spring/Summer 1981): 25–34.

12. Hosmer to Crow, August 1854, in Carr, *Harriet Hosmer,* p. 35.

13. As quoted in Dorothy Brockhoff, "Harriet Hosmer: Nineteenth-Century Free Spirit," *Washington University Magazine* (Fall 1976): 38.

14. Unidentified letter from Hosmer, in Carr, *Harriet Hosmer,* p. 172.

15. After having shipped *Oenone* to the Crows she wrote to her friend Cornelia, "Somewhere on the ocean, my daughter Oenone is now probably very seasick. If you do not experience the same sensation when you see her, I shall be content. Sooner or later she will appear to you in St. Louis, and I can only say I wish she were more worthy of those who are to adopt her . . ." (Hosmer to Crow, 30 June 1856, in Carr, *Harriet Hosmer,* p. 71).

16. See also Susan Waller's discussion of Hosmer's *Zenobia* (1859, Wadsworth Atheneum, Hartford) in which the work is interpreted as a direct reflection of Hosmer's understanding of women's roles and her own difficulties as an artist. Susan Waller, "The Artist, the Writer and the Queen: Hosmer, Jameson, and *Zenobia,*" *Woman's Art Journal* 4 (Spring/Summer 1983): 21–28. Additional readings of Hosmer's work from a feminist perspective may be found in a variety of sources. See for example Joseph Leach, "Harriet Hosmer: Feminist in Bronze and Marble," *The Feminist Art Journal* (Summer 1976): 9–13, 44–45, and Faxon, "Images of Women."

21. Ball, *Freedom's Memorial*

1. Ball to Stille, January 18, 1867, Stille Papers, Historical Society of Pennsylvania. Cited in Wayne Craven, "Thomas Ball and the Emancipation Group," *Elvehjem Art Center Bulletin* (Madison: University of Wisconsin, 1976–1977): 47.

2. The story is recounted in several sources: *Inaugural Ceremonies of the Freedmen's Memorial Monument to Abraham Lincoln* (St. Louis: Levison & Blyth, 1876), pp. 6–9 (Eliot Papers, record group 100/00/3/7, folder 6, Washington University Archives, St. Louis); William G. Eliot, *The Story of Archer Alexander: From Slavery to Freedom, March 30, 1863* (Boston: Cupples, Upham, and Co., 1885), pp. 11–15; *St. Louis Daily Globe,* July 4, 1873; *The Daily Democrat,* July 4, 1873; and Eliot Papers, record group 100/00/3/1, notebooks 8, 83, 85, 94. The Lincoln Park sculpture was dedicated on April 14, 1876, the 11th anniversary of the president's assassination, with President Grant and Frederick Douglass in attendance. Eliot was to have introduced the sculpture and provided an overview of its history, but he was unable to attend and Yeatman presided.

3. For Hosmer's *Thomas Hart Benton* see Theodore Finkelston, "'Old Bullion' Bronzed: Business's Monument to Western Opportunity," *Gateway Heritage* 11 (Fall 1990): 48–57.

4. See *Inaugural Ceremonies,* p. 8, and Thomas Ball, *My Threescore Years and Ten, An Autobiography* (Boston: Roberts Brothers, 1891), pp. 281–82. Eliot traveled in Europe in late 1869 and early 1870. See Eliot Papers, notebooks 7, 90.

5. Eliot reported that when he first saw the plaster original in Ball's studio he discussed the Sanitary Commission's project with him and that the sculptor offered to produce the work at cost (Eliot, *Archer Alexander*, p. 13). For details on the Philadelphia project see Craven, "Ball and the Emancipation Group," pp. 45–47.

6. *Inaugural Ceremonies*, p. 9. Eliot's own response to the memorial is recorded in a letter introducing his son, Rev. Thomas Eliot, to Ball. He informs Ball that on his visit to Florence his son "will enjoy seeing whatever works you may have on hand." He concludes the letter by saying, "The Memorial Monument is a perfect success and is thus far the only satisfactory work done in honor of the great Emancipator and of his still greater achievements" (Eliot to Ball, May 24, 1876, Eliot Papers, record group 100/00/3/2).

7. James Hall, *Dictionary of Subjects and Symbols in Art*, rev. ed. (New York: Harper and Row, 1979), p. 119.

8. For more on Ball's iconography and its sources see Vivien G. Fryd, "Sculpture as History: Themes of Liberty, Unity and Manifest Destiny in American Sculpture, 1825–1865" (Ph.D. diss., University of Wisconsin, Madison, 1984), pp. 225–27.

9. Ball, *My Threescore Years*, p. 253.

10. Eliot, *Archer Alexander*. For an overview of Alexander's history see also Candace O'Connor, "The Image of Freedom," *The St. Louis Post Dispatch*, 23 February 1989, sec. E.

11. At the unveiling of the Lincoln Park bronze James Yeatman noted that the St. Louis version was not the altered design: "An exact copy of the original group as first designed by Mr. Ball has been executed by him in pure white Italian marble for the Western Sanitary Commission, and will be permanently placed, as "Freedom's Memorial," in some public building of St. Louis" (*Inaugural Ceremonies*, p. 9).

22. Chase, *Dutch Orphan Asylum*

1. See Ronald Pisano, *A Leading Spirit in American Art: William Merritt Chase, 1849–1916* (Seattle: Henry Art Gallery, 1983), pp. 62–63.

2. The businessmen included Samuel A. Coale, Captain W. R. Hodges, Samuel Dodd, and Charles Parsons (Pisano, *William Merritt Chase* [New York: Watson-Guptill Publications, 1979], p. 12).

3. Charles Henry Miller, as quoted in Katharine Metcalf Roof, *The Life and Art of William Merritt Chase* (New York: Charles Scribner's Sons, 1917), p. 56. Also cited by Pisano, *William Merritt Chase*, p. 13.

4. Pisano, *William Merritt Chase*, pp. 15–16.

5. Ibid., p. 4.

6. Keith L. Bryant, Jr., *William Merritt Chase: A Genteel Bohemian* (Columbia, Mo. and London: University of Missouri Press, 1991), p. 94.

23. Eakins, *Professor W.D. Marks*

1. Elizabeth Johns, *Thomas Eakins: The Heroism of Modern Life* (Princeton: Princeton University Press, 1983), p. 3.

2. Marks had also worked in industry and at Lehigh University before being invited in 1877 to join the University of Pennsylvania as the Asa Whitney Professor of Dynamic Engineering, a department he founded. See "Philadelphia's Contributions to Urban Engineering," *FAS Reports* (Faculty of Arts and Sciences Reports), February 1983, p. 6.

3. While maintaining his professorship, Marks designed the power plant (the first in the United States built expressly for such a purpose), the building's equipment and engines, and the company's organizational structure.

4. Marks overcame many obstacles to build and run the plant. For an overview see "Philadelphia's Contributions to Urban Engineering," p. 6.

5. See Gordon Hendricks, *The Photographs of Thomas Eakins* (New York: Grossman Publishers, 1972), pp. 6–8, and Lloyd Goodrich, *Thomas Eakins* (Cambridge, Mass.: Harvard University Press for the National Gallery of Art, 1982), pp. 268–77. Marks' own report on the experiments, which mentions Eakins, is W. D. Marks et al., *Animal Locomotion: The Muybridge Work at the University of Pennsylvania, The Methods and the Results* (Philadelphia: J. B. Lippencott & Co., 1888), see especially pp. 9–13.

6. See William Dennis Marks, "The Mechanism of Instantaneous Photography," in Marks et al., *Animal Locomotion*, p. 13. For a more recent description of the machine see the letter from Prof. Robert Lagemann, Department of Physics and Astronomy, Vanderbilt University, 21 September 1981, Washington University Gallery of Art Archives, St. Louis, Missouri.

7. See Marks, "The Mechanism of Instantaneous Photography," p. 27.

8. The provenance of the Washington University painting includes Marks' family (Washington University Gallery of Art Archives).

9. Photographic portraits of Marks compare favorably to Eakins' depiction. See "Philadelphia's Contributions to Engineering," p. 6 and Washington University Gallery of Art Archives.

24. Inness, *Storm on the Delaware*

1. As with his purchases of Dwight Tryon's work, William Bixby's correspondence with Charles Lang Freer about Inness' art may have contributed to the purchase of this painting. See Linda Merrill, *An Ideal Country: Paintings by Dwight William Tryon in the Freer Gallery of Art* (Washington, D.C.: Freer Gallery of Art, 1990), p. 62.

2. See Marjorie Dakin Arkelian and George W. Neubert, *George Inness Landscapes: His Signature Years, 1884–1894* (Oakland, Cal.: Oakland Museum of Art, 1978).

3. Inness, "A Painter on Painting," *Harper's New Monthly Magazine* 57 (February 1878): 458.

4. The pioneering study of Tonalism is Wanda Corn, *The Color of Mood: American Tonalism, 1880–1910* (San Francisco: De Young Memorial Museum of Art, 1972). See also William Gerdts, Diana Dimodica Sweet, and Robert R. Preato, *Tonalism: An American Experience* (New York: Grand Central Art Galleries, 1982). Although Inness is the best known of these painters, both presently and in his own day, a critic as astute as Charles Lang Freer wrote to a friend in 1893 that he believed "poor Inness is sure to be forgotten while Tryon will live forever" (Freer to Wilson Eyre, 2 October 1893, Freer Papers, Washington, D.C., cited in Merrill, *An Ideal Country*, p. 61).

5. For more on this problem see William Gerdts, "American Tonalism: An Artistic Overview," in Gerdts et al., *Tonalism*, pp. 17–28.

6. Arthur Hoeber, "By Way of Preface," in *An Exhibition of 18 Pictures by the American Master of Landscape Painting, the Late George Inness, N.A.* (Chicago: Henry Reinhardt's Galleries, 1911), cited in Nicolai Cikofsky, Jr. and Michael Quick, *George Inness* (Los Angeles: Los Angeles County Museum of Art, 1985), p. 64.

7. Cikofsky and Quick, *George Inness*, p. 96.

25. Dewing, *Brocart de Venise*

1. For additional information on Dewing see Susan Hobbs, "Thomas Wilmer Dewing: The Early Years, 1851–1855," *The American Art Journal* 13, no. 2 (Spring 1981): 4–35; Hobbs, "Thomas Dewing in Cornish, 1885–1905," *The American Art Journal* 17, no. 2 (Spring 1985): 2–32; Patricia Jobe Pierce, *The Ten* (Hingham, Mass.: Patricia Jobe Pierce, 1976); Joyce Karen Schiller, "Frame Design by Stanford White," *The Bulletin of the Detroit Institute of Arts* 64, no. 1 (Summer 1988): 20–31; and Schiller, "Thomas Wilmer Dewing" (M.A. thesis, Wayne State University, Detroit, 1975).

2. In England the books were called "Yellow Backs" and were sold in train stations. They were also sold in the United States but not as extensively.

3. Royal Cortissoz, "Art Buffalo II," *New York Herald Tribune*, 13 July 1901.

4. According to Wanda Corn, "the word 'tonalist' was occasionally used in the first decade of the twentieth century to describe painters such as Charles M. Dewey, Robert Minor, George Bogart . . ." (*The Color of Mood: American Tonalism 1880–1910* [San Francisco: DeYoung Memorial Museum of Art, 1972], p. 22). One could surmise that the usage of such a term was popularized by Corn.

5. Charles C. Baldwin, *Stanford White* (1931; reprint, New York: Da Capo Press, 1976), p. 374.

26. Tryon, *Before Sunrise*

1. Since Wanda Corn's groundbreaking exhibition which formally titled the movement, there have been a number of studies of American Tonalism, as well as an increasing number of monographs on individual artists. See Wanda Corn, *The Color of Mood: American Tonalism, 1880–1910* (San Francisco: De Young Memorial Museum of Art, 1972), and William Gerdts, Diana Dimodica Sweet, and Robert R. Preato, *Tonalism: An American Experience* (New York: Grand Central Art Galleries, 1982).

2. Most of the Tryon paintings were deaccessioned from Washington University's collection in the 1940s.

3. Bixby also collected Asian art. See for example the letter from City Art Museum, St. Louis, Director Samuel Sherer to Bixby with which he returned nine Tryons and eleven Chinese paintings to him (Sherer to Bixby, 14 December 1922, Bixby papers, Missouri Historical Society, St. Louis).

4. Freer had started collecting Tryon's work in the early 1890s and Bixby bought his first, *Clearing After Showers* (1900, location unknown) shortly after the work's completion. Freer bid for several paintings, including a Tryon, on Bixby's behalf at auction that year, but eventually arranged for Bixby to purchase *Clearing* directly from the artist. Tryon mentioned Freer's involvement in the transaction in his first letter to Bixby (Tryon to Bixby, 6 February 1900, Bixby papers). The relationship among the three men is also discussed in Linda Merrill, *An Ideal Country: Paintings by Dwight William Tryon in the Freer Gallery of Art* (Washington, D.C.: Freer Gallery of Art, 1990), pp. 76–77, passim.

5. Tryon's letters to Bixby are filled with commentary not only on painting, but also on fishing, which was his second passion. In 1904 Tryon made a fly rod for Bixby (Tryon to Bixby, 20 October 1903 and 16 June 1904, Bixby papers). In later years it seems that Bixby made a few purchases for Freer; the 1914 purchase of a Whistler letter in London is one example. See Freer's letters to Bixby, Bixby papers, Missouri Historical Society.

6. "I am entirely willing that the "Before Sunrise" go to the St. Louis Fine Art Gallery. . . . It is really a museum picture and I am very glad to have it go to your museum. Now that you have decided on it I want to say that I feel it is one of my most important works. There are several eastern museums after it but they are so slow in their decisions that they lose their chance when they have it. Thoughtful ones who know most about art are aware that the best American work being produced now is going well west of N.Y. State. The west and the middle west are destined I think eventually to get the cream of the art of America" (Tryon to Bixby, 15 April 1907, Bixby papers). After the 1904 World's Fair in St. Louis the majority of the school's collection was housed in the new City Art Museum and at least until the 1920s Bixby's Tryon collection was displayed in a separate room of its own. See letters from Samuel L. Sherer, Director, City Art Museum to Bixby, 11 December 1922, Bixby papers.

7. Tryon to Bixby, 25 March 1907, Bixby papers.

8. Tryon to Bixby, 5 April 1907, Bixby papers.

9. Tryon to Bixby, 20 February 1900, Bixby papers.

10. Tryon to Bixby, 20 January 1906, Bixby papers.

11. Tryon to Bixby, 13 April 1906, Bixby papers. Such comments are repeated a number of times. In January 1907, shortly before Bixby purchased *Before Sunrise,* Tryon wrote: "You have such an important group of my pictures that I am always glad to have my best work go to you and Mr. Freer, and as you do not have a chance to watch my work as it progresses I have to hold it and send it to you when completed. Do not think that I am in any way trying to force your inclination as I know how important that one loves the pictures they possess" (Tryon to Bixby, 29 January 1907, Bixby papers).

12. Tryon frequently advised Bixby in the early years that his paintings took time to appreciate: "Do not be disappointed if you do not see it all at first. The best art is subtle and does not reveal itself without an effort on the part of the spectator. All my work is based on the supposition of alert intelligence and sympathy of the beholder. Work which one sees quickly through is soon tiresome and has no further mission" (Tryon to Bixby, 20 February 1900, Bixby papers).

27. Twachtman, *House in Landscape*

1. See Richard J. Boyle, *John Twachtman* (New York: Watson-Guptill Publications, 1979), p. 10.

2. Ibid., p. 13.

3. See Lisa N. Peters, "Twachtman's Greenwich Paintings: Context and Chronology," in Deborah Chotner, Lisa N. Peters, and Kathleen A. Pyne, *John Twachtman: Connecticut Landscapes* (Washington D.C. and New York: National Gallery of Art and Harry N. Abrams, 1989), pp. 13–21.

4. The other members of the group, known as "Ten American Painters" from the title of their first exhibition in 1898 at the Durand-Ruel Galleries in New York, included Frank W. Benson, Joseph DeCamp, Willard Metcalf, and Edmund Tarbell. When Twachtman died in 1902 his place was taken by William Merritt Chase. See William H. Gerdts et al., *Ten American Painters* (New York: Spanierman Gallery, 1990), pp. 9–11.

5. Newspaper accounts reported The Ten as saying they "no longer felt the atmosphere of [The Society of American Artists] congenial to their views and purposes of art," but they were careful to add that it was "not the intention of these gentlemen to organize a rival society" ("Eleven Painters Secede," *New York Times,* 9 January 1898, p. 13, cited in Gerdts et al., *Ten American Painters,* p. 12).

6. See Chotner, Peters, and Pyne, *John Twachtman,* p. 5, passim.

7. See for example *Snowbound* (early 1890s, Montclair Art Museum, Montclair, New Jersey) or *Last Touch of Sun* (c. 1893, Manoogian Collection, Detroit).

8. In many ways Twachtman's late style contains elements of both American Impressionism and American Tonalism. For an introduction to the latter see Wanda Corn, *The Color of Mood: American Tonalism 1880–1910* (San Francisco: DeYoung Memorial Museum of Art, 1972).

9. See Florence N. Levy, ed., *American Art Annual* 3 (Boston: Noyes, Platt & Co., 1900–01), p. 76.

28. Hassam, *Isles of Shoals*

1. See David Park Curry, *Childe Hassam: An Island Garden Visited* (New York: The Denver Art Museum and W. W. Norton, 1990). Hassam met Thaxter in Boston about 1883 when he served as her watercolor instructor and began illustrating her publications soon afterwards.

2. Curry, *Childe Hassam,* p. 31.

3. Ibid., pp. 21, 25.

4. For more on the resorts see Marie L. Ahearn, "Health Restoring Resorts on the New England Coast," in *Essays from a Victorian Society Autumn Symposium,* ed. Richard Guy Wilson, vol. 8 of *Nineteenth Century* (Philadelphia: Victorian Society in America, 1982). Hassam had a studio in a cottage near the Appledore Hotel, probably built in 1888 (see Curry, *Childe Hassam,* p. 38).

5. For a listing of additional guests, see Curry, *Childe Hassam,* pp. 25–26. William Morris Hunt died at Appledore, drowning off the rocky coast.

6. See for example Celia Thaxter, *Among the Isle of Shoals* (Boston: J. R. Osgood, 1873).

7. See Curry, *Childe Hassam,* pp. 13–14, and Celia Thaxter, *An Island Garden* (Boston: Houghton Mifflin, 1894).

8. See Kathleen M. Burnside, "Childe Hassam," in William Gerdts et al., *Ten American Painters* (New York: Spanierman Gallery, 1990), pp. 103–107.

9. See Curry, *Childe Hassam,* pp. 14, 94. For more on the "Aesthetic Movement" see Doreen Bolger, et al, *In Pursuit of Beauty: Americans and the Aesthetic Movement* (New York: Metropolitan Museum of Art, 1986).

10. As a related issue, Hassam had a high regard for Whistler, so much so that he once visited Charles Lang Freer to see his collection. The original patron of *Diamond Cove,* William K. Bixby relied greatly on Freer's advice on collecting and the connection may have contributed to Bixby's knowledge of Hassam. For more on this relationship see entry 26 on Dwight Tryon.

29. Matisse, *Still Life with Oranges*

1. See *Paintings, Sculpture and Drawings in the Cone Collection* (Baltimore: Baltimore Museum of Art, 1967), p. 31, fig. 36, and Alfred H. Barr, Jr., *Matisse: His Art and His Public* (New York: The Museum of Modern Art, 1951), p. 67.

2. Lawrence Gowing writes: "Both pictures seem to have been derived from *Buffet et table* rather than directly from the still-life group; these are perhaps the first works by Matisse that we have which were not painted entirely from the subject" (Gowing, *Matisse* [New York and Toronto: Oxford University Press, 1979], p. 24). John Elderfield implies such a procedure by raising the possibility that the picture was painted in Paris, in distinction to *Sideboard and Table,* which was painted in Toulouse (Elderfield, *Henri Matisse: A Retrospective* [New York: The Museum of Modern Art, 1992] p. 103). According to Barr, Matisse remembered that *Sideboard and Table* and the Baltimore picture were painted in Toulouse in 1899, but no mention is made of where the Washington University picture was painted (Barr, *Matisse,* p. 48 nn. 4, 5, p. 531).

3. Nicholas Watkins remarks that the Washington University painting "may have been a bold study blocking in the main color areas of the left-hand half of *Sideboard and Table...*" (Watkins, *Matisse* [New York: Oxford University Press, 1985], p. 38). Barr says the two smaller paintings "are probably studies for the left-hand side of the *Sideboard and Table* but may possibly be postscripts to it" (Barr, *Matisse,* p. 48).

4. "Cette peinture est la troisième toile travaillée sur nature d'après un même sujet, mais toutes trois traitées de façon differente" (Marguerite G. Duthuit to Robert Buck, 12 January 1968, Washington University Gallery of Art archives, St. Louis).

5. See for example Barr: "This picture may be a study which Matisse intended to carry further but stopped when he found that he had obtained what he wanted" (Barr, *Matisse*, p. 48 n. 5, p. 531).

6. Gowing, *Matisse*, p. 26.

7. See for example Douglas Mannering, *The Art of Matisse* (New York: Excalibur Books, 1982), p. 14, where the painting is dated c. 1902.

8. Gowing, *Matisse*, p. 27.

30. Picasso, *Bottle of Suze*

1. Interestingly one of the first to write about *papiers collés* and the use of newsprint was the Dadaist poet Tristan Tzara, but not for another nineteen years. See Tristan Tzara, "Le papier collé ou le proverbe en peinture," *Cahiers d'art* VI, no. 2 (1931): 61–73.

2. See Robert Rosenblum, "Picasso and the Art of Eroticism," in *Studies in Sex and Society*, vol. 3, ed. Theodore Robert Bowie and Cornelia V. Christienson, of *Studies in Erotic Art* (New York: Basic Books, 1970), pp. 337–50; see also Rosenblum, "Picasso and the Typography of Cubism," in *Picasso 1881–1973* (London: Paul Elek, 1973), pp. 49–75.

3. See Pierre Daix and Jean Rosselet, *Picasso, the Cubist Years, 1907–1916: A Catalogue Raisonné of the Paintings and Related Works*, trans. Dorothy S. Blair (Boston: New York Graphic Society, 1979), p. 188 n. 129, and entry 523.

4. See Patricia Leighten, *Reorganizing the Universe: Picasso and Anarchism, 1897–1914* (Princeton: Princeton University Press, 1989), and Leighton, "Picasso's Collages and the Threat of War, 1912-13," *Art Bulletin* LXVII, no. 4 (December 1985): 653–72.

5. Quoted in Françoise Gilot and Carlton Lake, *Life with Picasso* (New York: McGraw-Hill, 1964), p. 77.

31. Picasso, *Les Femmes d'Alger*

1. For the paintings see Christian Zervos, *Pablo Picasso* (Paris: Cahiers d'art, 1942), nos. 342(A), 343(B), 345(C), 346(D), 347(E), 348(F), 349(G), 352(L), 353(I), 354(K), 355(J), 356(H), 357(M), 359(N), 360(O); for the lithographs see Fernand Mourlot, *Picasso Lithographs*, trans. by Jean Didry (Paris: Boston Book and Art Publisher, 1970), nos. 265 (20 January 1955) and 266 (5 February 1955); and for the drawings see Michèle Richet, *Musée Picasso Catalogue of the Collections II: Drawings, Watercolours, Gouaches, Pastels*, trans. by Augusta Audubert (London: Thames & Hudson, 1988), pp. 414–15, nos. 1322 (21 December 1954) to 1391 (7 February 1955).

2. Roland Penrose, *Picasso: His Life and Work* (New York: Harper, 1959), p. 350. See also Hélène Parmelin, *Picasso Plain: An Intimate Portrait*, trans. by Humphrey Hare (London: Seckler and Warburg, 1963), pp. 77–79, and Françoise Gilot and Carlton Lake, *Life with Picasso* (New York: McGraw-Hill, 1964), p. 203. For drawings in Picasso's notebooks see Arnold and Marc Glimcher and Matthew Marks, eds., *Je suis le cahier: The Sketchbooks of Picasso, catalogue raisonné* (Boston and New York: Atlantic Monthly Press, 1986). Parmelin also confirms that Picasso "would in no circumstances even look at a reproduction of Delacroix's *Les Femmes d'Alger*, and carried them everywhere in his head" (Parmelin, *Picasso Plain*, p. 77). We do not know whether Picasso ever went to the museum in Montpellier but on frequent trips by car from Vallauris to Perpignan in 1953 and 1954, it would have been a convenient stop, not quite halfway along the 800-kilometer drive.

3. "To behave like *Les Femmes d'Algers* meant . . . if possible doing nothing" (Parmelin, *Picasso Plain*, p. 79).

4. Penrose, *Picasso*, p. 351.

5. This statement seems difficult to apply to Washington University's relatively tranquil painting but it is more comprehensible with some of the earlier transformations in the series, like version C of 18 December 1954 in which the crouching figure of the woman at the left appears evil and obscene. See Françoise Gilot, *Matisse and Picasso* (New York: Doubleday, 1990), p. 317.

6. Penrose, *Picasso*, pp. 351–52.

7. See Maurice Jardot, *Picasso: Peintures 1900–1955* (Paris: Musée des Arts Décoratifs, 1955), no. 127.

8. Parmelin, *Picasso Plain*, p. 79.

9. Penrose, *Picasso*, p. 351.

10. Ibid.

32. Braque, *Still Life with Glass*

1. For additional information on Braque see Douglas Cooper, *Georges Braque* (Edinburgh: International Festival, 1956); Maurice Gieure, *Georges Braque* (Paris: Editions P. Tisne, 1956); Jean Leymarie, *Braque* (Lausanne: Skira, 1961); John Golding, *Braque, Still Lifes and Interiors* (London: London South Bank, 1990); and N. Manguin, ed., *Catalogue de l'Oeuvre de Georges Braque*, 7 vols. (Paris: Maeght, 1962ff).

33. Braque, *Still Life with Oysters*

1. The unrevised entries in the catalogue raisonné for the two Washington University pictures are incomplete in terms of provenance. The dimensions ascribed to them are also inaccurate.

2. *Peintres decorateurs*, traditional French artisan decorators, were renowned for their skill in producing those effects of illusion—false marble, imitation woodgraining, simulated moldings and so forth—so dear to the French middle classes.

34. Gris, *Still Life with Playing Cards*

1. Juan Gris, "Des possibilités de la peinture," in Daniel-Henry Kahnweiler, *Juan Gris: His Life and Work*, trans. Douglas Cooper (New York: H. N. Abrams, 1969), p. 141.

2. See Gris, *Letters of Juan Gris, 1913–1927*, trans. Douglas Cooper (London: privately printed, 1956).

3. For more on Gris' interest in the subject of the senses, see Mark Rosenthal, *Juan Gris* (New York: Abbeville Press, 1983), pp. 53, 106, 113, 131.

35. Gris, *Still Life: Table with Red Cloth*

1. Douglas Cooper dates the painting to November or December, 1926 (*Juan Gris: Catalogue Raisonné de l'oeuvre peint établi avec la collaboration de Margaret Potter*, vol. II [Paris: Berggruen, 1977], p. 408); however, a photograph said to be of Gris' studio in Boulogne-en-Seine, where he lived from April to November in that year, shows the painting on an easel (Ministerio de Cultura, *Juan Gris*, ed. Gary Tinterow [Madrid: Ministerio de Cultura, Banco de Bilbao, 1985], p. 443). The painting is signed LL: "Juan Gris 26."

2. Gris, *Letters of Juan Gris, 1913–1927*, trans. Douglas Cooper (London: privately printed, 1956), entries CCXII, CCXLII.

3. For a discussion of Gris' exploration of the open window theme, see Mark Rosenthal, "Juan Gris, en la ventana abierta," in Ministerio de Cultura, *Juan Gris*, pp. 53–63.

4. Cited in René de Costa, "Juan Gris and Poetry: From Illustration to Creation," *Art Bulletin* LXXI (December 1989): 687.

36. Duchamp-Villon, *Le Cheval*

1. "La puissance de la machine s'impose et nous ne concevons plus guère les vivants sans elle . . ." (Duchamp-Villon to Walter Pach, 16 January 1913, published in Walter Pach, *Raymond Duchamp-Villon, Sculpteur, 1876–1918* [Paris: Jacques Povolozky, 1924], p. 19, author's translation).

2. Albert Elsen, "The Sculpture of Duchamp-Villon," *Artforum* 6 (October 1967): 22.

3. William C. Agee, "Notes on the Sculpture," in George Heard Hamilton and William C. Agee, *Raymond Duchamp-Villon, 1876–1918* (New York: Walker and Company, 1967), pp. 93–94.

4. Judith Zilczer, "Raymond Duchamp-Villon, Pioneer of Modern Sculpture," Philadelphia Museum of Art *Bulletin* 76, no. 330 (Fall 1980): 15–16, fig. 21.

5. Henri Matisse, as cited in Pach, *Raymond Duchamp-Villon*, p. 15, and in Pach, *Queer Thing, Painting* (New York: Harper, 1938), p. 145.

6. Marcel Duchamp, "Raymond Duchamp-Villon," in *Collection of the Societe Anonyme*, ed. George Heard Hamilton (New Haven: Yale University Art Gallery, 1950), p. 3.

37. Lipchitz, *Pierrot with Clarinet*

1. See Alan G. Wilkinson, *Jacques Lipchitz: A Life in Sculpture* (Toronto: Art Gallery of Ontario, 1989). For additional information on Lipchitz see A. M. Hammacher, *Jacques Lipchitz* (New York: Harry N. Abrams, 1975), and Deborah A. Sttot, *Jacques Lipchitz and Cubism* (New York and London: Garland Publishing, 1978).

2. Jacques Lipchitz and H. H. Arnason, *My Life in Sculpture* (New York: Viking Press, 1978), p. 18.

3. Ibid., p. 37.

4. Ibid., p. 58.

38. Lipchitz, *Mother and Child*

1. Jacques Lipchitz and H. H. Arnason, *My Life in Sculpture* (New York: Viking Press, 1978), pp. 16, 109.

2. Quoted in Henry R. Hope, *The Sculpture of Jacques Lipchitz* (New York: The Museum of Modern Art, 1954), pp. 17–18.

3. Lipchitz and Arnason, *My Life in Sculpture*, p. 183.

39. Ensor, *Le Christ Tourmente*

1. For additional information on Ensor see Libby Tannenbaum, *James Ensor* (New York: The Museum of Modern Art, 1951); Paul Haesaerts, *James Ensor* (New York: Abrams, 1959); Roger Van Gindertael, *Ensor* (Boston: New York Graphic Society, 1975); and Diane Lesko, *James Ensor: The Creative Years* (New Jersey: Princeton Press, 1985).

40. Munch, *Portrait of Irmgard Steinbart*

1. See for example *Expressionisten*, exh. cat. (Basel: Galerie Beyeler, 1955), p. 41, and *Illustrated Checklist of the Collection: Paintings, Sculpture, and Works on Paper* (St. Louis: Washington University Gallery of Art, 1981), p. 60.

2. Munch to Schiefler, November-December 1913, reprinted in Arne Eggum et al., eds., *Edvard Munch/Gustav Schiefler Briefwechsel*, vol. 1 (Hamburg: Verlag Verein für Hamburgische Geschichte, 1987), p. 467, letter 618.

3. For additional information on Munch see Eggum, *Edvard Munch: Paintings, Sketches and Studies*, trans. Ragnar Christophersen (Oslo: J. M. Stenersens Forlag, 1984), and Reinhold Heller, *Edvard Munch: His Life and Work* (Chicago and London: University of Chicago Press and John Murray Publishers, 1984).

4. Heller, *Edvard Munch*, p. 176.

5. Neither Irmgard Steinbart's father's first name nor either of their birth or death dates are known, according to Eggum et al., *Munch/Schiefler Briefwechsel*.

6. Hugo Perls, "Erindringer om Edvard Munch," *Kunst og Kultur* (1962): 45–46.

7. Sissel Biørnstad (research librarian, Munch Museum, Oslo), personal communication, 14 April 1993. By 1917, when *Portrait of Irmgard Steinbart* was exhibited in Stockholm, the canvas had entered the collection of V. Torkildsen, a Norwegian ship owner.

8. Munch, quoted in Eric Büttner, "Der leibhaftige Munch," in Jens Thiis, *Edvard Munch* (Berlin: Rembrandt-Verlag, 1934), p. 92.

41. Meidner, *Selbstbildnis*

1. *Self Portrait* is initialled "L. M." in Old German script and dated "1912," center left. The painting is listed in an inventory Meidner made in 1916 when he was inducted into the Army. It was dated there 1912 (Meidner, *Dichter, Maler und Cafes* [Zurich: Verlag Die Arche, 1973], p. 48). It was first reproduced, incorrectly dated 1916, in the first monograph dedicated to the artist (Lothar Brieger, *Ludwig Meidner* [Leipzig: Klinkhardt and Biermann, 1919]). See Victor Miesel, *Ludwig Meidner* (Ann Arbor: University of Michigan Museum of Art, 1978) for the most comprehensive study of this artist's life and work in English.

2. Meidner, *Septemberschrei: Hymnen/Gebete/Lasterunge* (Berlin: P. Cassirer, 1920), p. 75.

3. Meidner, *Septemberschrei*, pp. 6-7.

42. Klee, *Überbrückung*

1. *The Thinking Eye: The Notebooks of Paul Klee*, vol. I, ed. Jurg Spiller, trans. R. Manheim (New York: Wittenborn, 1964), p. 269.

2. See Andrew Kagan, *Paul Klee/Art & Music* (Ithaca, N.Y.: Cornell University Press, 1983), esp. chap. 1, pp. 40–93.

3. Ibid., pp. 40-93, 112-21. See also Christian Geelhaar, *Paul Klee and the Bauhaus* (Cologne: n.publ., 1972), pp. 129–63.

4. Kagan, *Paul Klee/Art & Music*, pp. 117–21.

43. Beckmann, *Les Artistes mit Gemüse*

1. Max Beckmann, "Der Künstler im Staat," in *Max Beckmann: Frankfurt, 1915–33*, exh. cat., ed. Klaus Gallwitz (Frankfurt: Städtische Galerie im Städelschen Kunstinstitut, 1983), pp. 17ff.

2. Printed in Beckmann, *On My Painting* (New York: Hanuman Books, 1988), pp. 11–12.

3. For Beckmann's diary references to his work on the painting, see Erhard and Barbara Göpel, *Max Beckmann: Katalog der Gemälde*, vol. I (Berne: Verlag Kornfeld, 1976), p. 377.

4. See Gotthard Jedlicka, "Max Beckmann in seinen Selbst-bildnissen," in *Blick auf Beckmann: Dokumente und Vorträge*, ed. Hans Martin Frhr. von Erffa and Erhard Göpel (Munich: R. Piper, 1962), pp. 111–31; Margot Clark, "Max Beckmann: Sources of Imagery in the Hermetic Tradition" (Ph.D. diss., Washington University, St. Louis, 1975), pp. 54–77; Erhard and Barbara Göpel, *Max Beckmann*, vol. 1, pp. 377–78; and Carla Schulz-Hoffmann and Judith C. Weiss, *Max Beckmann Retrospective*, exh. cat. (St. Louis and Munich: The Saint Louis Art Museum and Prestel Verlag), p. 286, entry 99.

5. See Clark, "Sources of Imagery," and Friedhelm Fischer, *Max Beckmann: Symbol und Weltbild* (Munich: Prestel Verlag, 1972).

6. See Hans Jonas, *The Gnostic Religion: The Message of the Alien God and the Beginnings of Christianity*, 2nd ed. (Boston: Beacon Press, 1963), pp. 49–51, 57, 197–99.

7. Clark, "Sources of Imagery," p. 58.

44. van Doesburg, *The Three Graces*

1. Robert P. Welsh, "Theo van Doesburg and Geometric Abstraction," in *Nijhoff, Van Ostaijen, "De Stijl": Modernism in the Netherlands and Belgium in the First Quarter of the 20th Century*, ed. Francis Bulhof (The Hague: Martinus Nijhoff, 1976), p. 84 n. 33. Noting the absence of preliminary sketches, Welsh further suggests that "the title might well represent little more than a metaphor for the use of the three primary colors."

2. Ibid., n. 32.

3. Evert van Straaten, ed., *Theo van Doesburg 1883–1931: Een Documentaire op basis van materiaal uit de Schenking van Moorsel* ('s-Gravenhage: Staatsuitgeverij, 1983), p. 185.

4. The painting in its original frame is visible in a photograph of Nelly van Doesburg dating from 1931 or 1932 and reproduced in van Straaten, *Theo van Doesburg*, p. 178.

5. Lawrence Hill to Arthur H. Compton, 15 April 1947, Washington University Gallery of Art archives, St. Louis, Missouri.

45. Pevsner, *Bas Relief*

1. For additional information on Pevsner see B. Dorival, *Le Dessin dans l'oeuvre d'Antoine Pevsner* (Paris: Prisme, 1965); R. Massat, *Antoine Pevsner et le constructivisme* (Paris: Caractères, 1956); and P. Peissi, et al., *Antoine Pevsner* (Neuchâtel: du Griffon, 1961).

2. "L'autre—contruction d'art—nous donne la possibilité de mettre à pré-établir les rythmes nouveaux des grands axes de construction et d'autres orbites dans le carré de temps et d'espace. L'oeuvre d'art géniale crée par elle-même un système cosmogonique . . ." (Pevsner, *Abstraction-Création, Art Non-Figuratif* 2 [1933]: 35).

46. Gabo, *Linear Construction*

1. The main sources on Gabo's life and art are Herbert Read and Leslie Martin, *Gabo* (London: Lund Humphries, 1957), and Steven Nash and Jörn Merkert, *Naum Gabo: Sixty Years of Constructivism* (Munich: Prestel-Verlag, 1985).

2. A translation by Gabo of the *Realistic Manifesto* from Russian to English is found in Read and Martin, *Gabo*, pp. 151–52.

3. Full listings and catalog entries on the known versions of these two sculptures are found in Colin C. Sanderson and Christina Lodder, "Catalogue Raisonné of the Constructions and Sculptures of Naum Gabo," in Nash and Merkert, *Naum Gabo*, pp. 229–31, 233–34, cat. nos. 48.1–17 and 53.1–11, respectively. The version of *Linear Construction in Space No. 1 (Variation)* in the Washington University collection is cat. no. 53.9. It is one of a total of eleven versions of this sculpture. The bibliography specific to this version includes Rosamond Bernier, "Une collection du Middle West," *L'Oeil* 156 (December 1967): 33; *A Galaxy of Treasures from St. Louis Collections*, exh. cat. (St.

Louis: St. Louis City Art Museum, 1961), fig. x; *Works of Art of the Nineteenth and Twentieth Centuries: Collected by Louise and Joseph Pulitzer, Jr.*, exh. cat. (St. Louis: St. Louis City Art Museum, 1968), no. 94; and *Modern Painting, Drawing and Sculpture: Collected by Louise and Joseph Pulitzer, Jr.*, exh. cat. (Cambridge, Mass.: Fogg Art Museum, 1971–72), no. 173.

4. On the history of stringing in modern sculpture and the issue of precedents, see Steven Nash, "Naum Gabo: Sculptures of Purity and Possibility," in Nash and Merkert, *Naum Gabo*, pp. 35, 37.

47. Léger, *Les Grands Plongeurs*

1. For example, see *Fernand Léger: The Later Years*, exh. cat. (London: Whitechapel Art Gallery, 1987-88). The first exhibition to feature the late work was at the Solomon R. Guggenheim Museum in 1962 (see *Fernand Léger: Five Themes and Variations*, exh. cat. [New York: Solomon R. Guggenheim Museum, 1962]).

2. Peter de Francia, *Fernand Léger* (New Haven, Conn.: Yale University Press, 1983), p. 134. See also Guggenheim Museum, exh. cat., p. 19.

3. Quoted in Charlotta Kotik, "Léger and America," in *Fernand Léger* (Buffalo and New York: Albright-Knox Art Gallery and Abbeville Press, 1982), p. 50.

4. Quoted in Katherine Kuh, *Léger* (Urbana: University of Illinois Press, 1953), p. 55.

5. Siegfried Giedion, "Les Plongeurs ou Mouvement dans l'Espace," in *Fernand Léger: La Forme Humaine dans L'Espace* (Montreal: Les Editions de l'Arbre, 1945), p. 51. See also François Hertel, "Léger, Disciple de Michel-Ange," in ibid., including illustrations of drawings by Michelangelo and by Léger.

6. Ibid. Washington University's drawing is illustrated as "Etude pour les Plongeurs" (1941), no. 12. The drawing is listed as "Study for *The Divers*, 1941" but is not illustrated in Monroe Wheeler, *Modern Drawings* (New York: Museum of Modern Art, 1944), p. 93. An "Etude pour Les Plongeurs (en noir)" is listed in *Fernand Léger: "Les Plongeurs,"* exh. cat. (New York: Jacques Seligmann & Co., Inc., 1943), entry no. 8.

7. Susan Willmoth, "Léger and America," in Whitechapel, exh. cat., p. 49.

48. Léger, *Les Belles Cyclistes*

1. Fernand Léger, "Comment je conçois la figure,' in *La Figure dans l'oeuvre de Léger* (Paris: Louis Carré, 1952), pp. 29–33. The essay is translated in Fernand Léger, *Functions of Painting*, Edward F. Fry, ed. (New York: Viking Press, 1973).

2. Quoted in James Johnson Sweeney, "Eleven Europeans in America," *The Museum of Modern Art Bulletin* XIII, nos. 4–5 (1946): 15. Washington University's version of *Les Belles Cyclistes* is illustrated on the same page.

3. Quoted in Peter de Francia, *Fernand Léger* (New Haven, Conn.: Yale University Press, 1983), p. 132.

4. The first painting, identified as *Les Belles Cyclistes (1er état)*, 1944 (private collection, courtesy of Barbara Divver Fine Art), is reproduced in Frank Elgar, *Léger: Peintures 1911–1948* (Paris: Editions du Chêne, 1948), pl. XI. The variation with two reclining figures is now in the collection of Stefan Edlis, Chicago, and is illustrated in *Fernand Léger: The Later Years*, exh. cat. (London: Whitechapel Art Gallery, 1987–88), no. 61. It was also exhibited and reproduced in *Fernand Léger* (New York: Acquavella Galleries, 1987), no. 43. *Les Quatre cyclistes*, 1943–1948, now in the collection of the Musée National Fernand Léger, Biot, is reproduced in Werner Schmalenbach, *Fernand Léger* (New York: Abrams, 1976), p. 41. It was exhibited in the 1956 Léger retrospective at the Musée des Arts Décoratifs, Paris. The brochure for the exhibition at Valentine Gallery (*Léger: New Paintings* [New York: Valentine Gallery, 1945]), lists *Les Belles Cyclistes*, nos. I and II. It is possible that Washington University's version was no. II.

49. Miró, *Joie*

1. For additional information on Miró see Jacques Dupin, *Joan Miró: Life and Work* (New York: H. N. Abrams, 1961); Fundació Joan Miró, *Obra de Joan Miró* (Barcelona: Centre d'Estudis d'Art Contemporani, 1988); William Rubin, *Miró in the Collection of the Museum of Modern Art* (New York: Museum of Modern Art, 1973); Sidra Stich, *Joan Miró: The Development of a Sign Language* (St. Louis: Washington University Gallery of Art, 1980); and Carolyn Lanchner, *Joan Miró* (New York: Museum of Modern Art, 1993).

2. Miró to Leiris, 10 August 1924, translated and printed in Margit Rowell, ed., *Joan Miró: Selected Writings and Interviews* (Boston: G. K. Hall, 1986), pp. 86–87.

3. Quoted in James Johnson Sweeney, "Joan Miró: Comment and Interview," *Partisan Review* 15, no. 2 (February 1948): 206–12; reprinted in Rowell, *Selected Writings*, pp. 207–11.

50. Miró, *Peinture*

1. Reprinted in Margit Rowell, ed., *Joan Miró: Selected Writings and Interviews* (Boston: G. K. Hall, 1986), p. 124.

2. James Johnson Sweeney, "Joan Miró: Comment and Interview," *Partisan Review* 15, no. 2 (February 1948): 206–12; reprinted in Rowell, *Selected Writings*, pp. 207–11.

51. Ernst, *The Eye of Silence*

1. Most studies on Ernst and the artist's own writings acknowledge the importance of ancient myth and modern psychology as key factors in his work. See John Russell, *Max Ernst: Life and Work* (New York: Harry N. Abrams, 1967); Max Ernst, *Ecritures* (Paris: Editions Gallimard, 1970); Evan Maurer, "Images of Dream and Desire: The Prints and Collage Novels of Max Ernst," in *Max Ernst: Beyond Surrealism* (New York: The New York Public Library, 1986); Maurer, "Dada and Surrealism," in *Primitivism in 20th Century Art* (New York: The Museum of Modern Art, 1984).

2. See Russell, *Max Ernst*, pp. 157–58, and Max Ernst, *Max Ernst, Beyond Painting* (New York: Wittenborn, Scholtz, 1948), pp. 4–7.

3. In the 1920s Ernst began using the techniques of collage and frottage to create his images. In collage, printed and photographic images were cut out and rearranged to explore a re-definition of identity. Frottage is a technique of transferring the outline and texture of an object by placing it under paper or canvas and rubbing the surface with pencil, chalk or paint. The resulting chance designs are used as stimuli to the artist's imagination from which the image emerges. See Ernst, *Max Ernst*, pp. 7–9, 12–18.

4. As Max Ernst wrote in 1932, "Just as the poet has to write down what is being thought-voiced inside of him, so the painter has to limn and give objective form to *what is visible inside him*" (as quoted in Russell, *Max Ernst*, p. 142).

5. The Minotaure was a favorite mythological theme of Surrealist artists and poets who used the name as the title of one of their most successful art magazines published with Max Ernst's involvement from 1933–39. See Herbert S. Gershman, *A Bibliography of the Surrealist Revolution in France* (Ann Arbor: University of Michigan Press, 1969), p. 51.

6. Uwe M. Schneede, *Max Ernst* (New York: Praeger, 1972), pp. 108–9, 116.

7. Ernst, *Beyond Painting*, pp. 26–29. In his autobiographical essay, "Some Data on the Youth of M. E.," Ernst described the traumatic conjunction of the death of his pet bird with the birth of a sister that established the close psychological tie between birds and humans often expressed in his art.

8. Russell, *Max Ernst*, pp. 125–30.

52. Tanguy, *La Tour marine*

1. In 1923 Tanguy saw a painting by de Chirico in the window of an art gallery that so moved him by its poetic, revelatory powers that it confirmed his resolve to become a painter. See Marcel Jean, *The History of Surrealism* (New York: Grove Press, 1960), p. 162.

2. Tanguy, letter to Jacques Hérold, July 1946, private collection. Quoted through the courtesy of Mme. Jacques Hérold.

3. Tanguy to Hérold, September 1944, private collection. Letters from Tanguy to André Breton (March and April 1940) quoted through the courtesy of the Bibliothèque Littéraire Jacques Doucet, Paris.

4. The theme can be traced to the seafaring tradition and Celtic mythology of his native Brittany. His father and paternal ancestors had been naval officers and Tanguy served as an apprentice officer in the merchant marines for a year and a half from the age of eighteen.

5. The tower has been interpreted as a symbol of civilization. See Uwe Schneede, *Malerei des Surrealismus* (Cologne: Du Mont-Schauberg, 1973), pp. 72–73. For an iconographical interpretation of *Genèse* see Susan Nessen, "Surrealism in Exile: The Early New York Years, 1940–42" (Ph.D. diss., University of Michigan, Ann Arbor, 1986), pp 144–48.

6. For an analysis of the influence of the Celtic drudicial tradition in Brittany on Tanguy, see Nessen, "Yves Tanguy's Otherworld: Reflections on a Celtic Past and a Surrealist Sensibility," *Arts Magazine* (January 1988): 22–29.

7. Information on Tanguy's painting technique courtesy of friends who watched him paint: conversation with Marcel Jean, 17 January 1989; conversation with Gordon Onslow-Ford, 8 July 1991; conversation with Anne Alpert (Matta's first wife), 14 December 1988.

8. John Ashbury, "Yves Tanguy, Geometer of Dreams," *Art in America* (15 November 1974): 71–74.

53. Matta, *Glimmer of Violence*

1. For additional information on Matta see Valerie Fletcher, *Crosscurrents of Modernism: Four Latin American Pioneers* (Washington, D.C.: Smithsonian Institution, 1992).

2. Matta, "12th Street: October 1941–July 1942," in Germana Ferrari Matta, ed., *Matta: Entretiens Morphologiques, Notebook No. 1, 1936–1944* (London: Sistan, 1987), p. 229.

54. Moore, *Reclining Figure*

1. For a concise discussion of Surrealism in England in the 1930s and the 1936 International Surrealist Exhibition see Anna Gruetzner, "Some Early Activities of the Surrealist Group in England," *Artscribe* 10 (1978): 22–25. A photograph of *Reclining Figure* in the galleries of the 1936 London exhibition is reproduced in Gruetzner, "The Surrealist Object and Surrealist Sculpture," in Sandy Nairne and Nicholas Serota, eds., *British Sculpture in the Twentieth Century,* exh. cat. (London: Whitechapel Art Gallery, 1981), p. 21.

2. Moore's activity within the English Surrealist movement is intensively examined in Christa Lichtenstein, "Henry Moore and Surrealism," *The Burlington Magazine* 123, no. 944 (November 1981) 645–58. On Moore's relationship to constructive, abstract art in England in the 1930s see Herbert Read, "British Art 1930–1940" and "A Nest of Gentle Artists," in *Art in Britain 1930–1940 Centred Around Axis, Circle, Unit One,* exh. cat. (London: Marlborough Fine Art Ltd. and Marlborough New London Gallery, 1965), pp. 5–8.

3. Henry Moore, "The Sculptor Speaks," *The Listener* 18, no. 449 (18 August 1937): 338–40, reprinted in Jeremy Lewison, ed., *Circle: Constructive Art in Britain, 1934–1940,* exh. cat. (Cambridge, England: Kettle's Yard Gallery, 1982), p. 68.

4. Moore, quoted in Philip James, ed., *Henry Moore on Sculpture* (London: MacDonald and Co., 1966), p. 265.

5. Moore, undated letter, Washington University Gallery of Art archives, St. Louis.

6. On Moore's admiration for such stone-age figurines see his statement of 1935, reprinted in James, ed., *Moore on Sculpture,* pp. 164–65. The notation "fecundity" occurs no less than eight times in the artist's sketch notebooks from 1921 to 1926. Related references on the pages of these books include "Eve," "Venus" and "Mother and Child."

55. de Staël, *Composition*

1. For biographical details as well as specific documentation of de Staël's work see *Nicolas de Staël,* introduction by André Chastel, letters annotated by Germain Viatte, and catalogue raisonné by Françoise de Staël and Jacques Dubourg (Paris: Les Editions du Temps, 1968). For additional information on de Staël see Douglas Cooper, *Nicolas de Staël* (London and New York: Weidenfeld and Nicholson, and W. W. Norton, 1961); Guy Dumur, *Nicolas de Staël* (Paris: Editions Flammarion, 1975), trans. Finton O'Connell (New York: Crown Books, 1976); and Eliza E. Rathbone, Nicholas Fox Weber, and John Richardson, *Nicolas de Staël in America* (Washington, D.C.: The Phillips Collection, 1990).

2. In a statement made by de Staël for the Museum of Modern Art in 1947 regarding the painting they had recently acquired, he declared, "Il n'y a pas de sujet" (there is no subject) (The Museum of Modern Art, Dept. of Painting and Sculpture, Nicolas de Staël, *Painting* (1947), collection file [artist's questionaire]). Two years later he wrote to Pierre Lecuire, "All painting has a subject whether one wishes it or not" (de Staël to Lecuire, 3 December 1949, reprinted in *Lettres de Nicolas de Staël à Pierre Lecuire* [Paris: privately published, 1966], n.p.).

3. See Dubourg and de Staël, catalogue raisonné, in *Nicolas de Staël.*

4. This observation is partially based on a conversation (1990) between the author and Elizabeth Steele, paintings conservator.

5. De Staël to Mme. Guillou (mother of Jeannine Guillou), March 1946, quoted in Chastel, introduction to *Nicolas de Staël,* p. 76.

56. Dubuffet, *Poches aux Yeux*

1. For additional information on Dubuffet see *Jean Dubuffet: Forty Years of his Art* (Chicago: University of Chicago and David and Alfred Smart Gallery, 1984); James T. Demetrion et al., *Jean Dubuffet 1943–1963: Paintings, Sculptures, Assemblages* (Washington, D.C.: Smithsonian Institution, 1993); Richard L. Feigen, ed., *Dubuffet and the Anticulture* (New York: Richard L. Feigen & Co., 1969); Andreas Franzke, *Jean Dubuffet,* trans. Robert Erich Wolf (New York: Harry N. Abrams, 1981); Franzke, *Jean Dubuffet: Petites statues de la vie precaire* (Bern and Berlin: Verlag Gachnang and Springer, 1988); Max Loreaux, *Catalogue des travaux de Jean Dubuffet,* 27 vols. (Paris and Lausanne: Jean-Jacques Pauvert, 1966–1979); and Thomas Messer, *Jean Dubuffet: A Retrospective* (New York: Solomon R. Guggenheim Museum, 1973).

2. Dubuffet, as quoted in *The New Decade,* exh. cat., ed. Andrew Carnduff Ritchie (New York: The Museum of Modern Art, 1955), p. 17.

57. Dubuffet, *Tête Barbue*

For bibliographical information on Dubuffet see notes to entry 56.

58. Soulages, *Twentieth of May 1959*

1. For additional information on *Soulages* see Bernard Ceysson, *Soulages* (New York: Crown Publishers, 1980); Pierre Daix and James Johnson Sweeney, *Soulages* (Neuchâtel: Ides et Calendes, 1991); Pierre Encrevé, *Soulages, l'oeuvre complet sur toile, catalogue raisonné* (Paris: Editions du Seuil, 1994); Herbert Juin, *Soulages* (New York: Evergreen Gallery Books, 1959); and James Johnson Sweeney, *Soulages* (Greenwich, Conn.: New York Graphic Society, 1973).

59. Appel, *Heads in Space*

1. See Bert Schierbeek, *The Experimental Artists* (Amsterdam: J. M. Meulenhoff, n.d.), and Willemijn Stokvis, *Cobra* (New York: Rizzoli, 1988).

2. Quoted in Ed Wingen's introduction to Appel, *Het gezicht van Appel/The Face of Appel* (Venlo, Holland: Van Spijk, 1977). His *pasage humain* (human landscape) paintings and such works as *Feast in Lapland* (1958, Stedelijk Van Abbemuseum) or *From the Beginning* (1961) move as close to pure abstract expression, or non-figurative "action painting," as Appel would come.

3. Quoted in Hugo Claus, *Karel Appel, Painter* (New York: Harry N. Abrams, 1962), pp. 5–6. See also Alfred Frankenstein, *Karel Appel* (New York: H. N. Abrams, 1980), pp. 52, 161, and *Appel's Appels,* exh. cat. (Toronto: Rothmans of Pall Mall Canada, 1962), p. 36.

60. Lucebert, *The Menaced House*

1. Quoted in K. Roberts, "Show at the New London Gallery," *Burlington Magazine* 105 (December 1963): 577.

2. Post-war experimental poets in the Netherlands established a group they called the "Vijftigers" (Fifty-ers). In 1953 a Dutch critic labelled Lucebert "the Emperor of the fifty-ers" (J. Eijkelbloom, *Lucebert* [Amsterdam: J. M. Meulenhoff, 1964], p. 5). See also Willemijn Stokvis, *Cobra* (New York: Rizzoli, 1988), pp. 24–25.

3. Quoted in Eijkelbloom, *Lucebert,* pp. 6, 9, 13.

4. Roberts, "New London Gallery," p. 577.

61. Burri, *Gran Ferro M3*

1. Alberto Burri, conversation with Gerald Nordland, Citta di Castello, October 1976. See also Nordland, *Alberto Burri* (Los Angeles: University of California Press, 1976).

2. Pierre Cabanne, *Dialogue with Marcel Duchamp* (N.Y.: Viking Press, 1971), p. 69.

3. James Johnson Sweeney was among the first to recognize Burri, calling his sense of materials "carnal." See his *Burri* (Rome: L'Obelisco, 1955). Sir Herbert Read extolled the work as "an alchemical process in which rubbish is

redeemed in the alembic of the artist's sensibility, to become the 'perfect body' of a work of art" (*Alberto Burri* [London: Hanover Gallery, 1961], n.p.). Thus far, Burri has enjoyed more than 100 solo exhibitions in eight European nations and the U.S.

62. Tàpies, *Porta Marró*

1. For additional information on Tàpies see Anna Agustí, *Tàpies, Obra Completa* (Barcelona: Fundació Antoni Tàpies and Edicions Polígrafa, 1988); *Antoni Tàpies: Thirty-three Years of his Work* (Buffalo, New York: Albright-Knox, 1977); Manuel J. Borja-Villel, "Tàpies i la crítica", in *Tàpies: els anys 80* (Barcelona: Ajuntament de Barcelona, 1988), pp. 56–77; Manuel J. Borja-Villel, *Antoni Tàpies: The Matter Paintings* (Ann Arbor, Mich.: University Microfilm, 1989); Roland Penrose, *Tàpies* (Barcelona: Edicions Polígrafa, 1977); and Michael Tapié, *Antonio Tàpies et l'oeuvre complète* (Barcelona: Dau al Set, 1956).

63. Fontana, *New York 22*

1. Quoted in "The Last Interview Given by Fontana," *Studio International* (November 1972): 184. For additional information on Fontana and the United States see Jan van der Marck, "Fontana Then and Now," in *Lucio Fontana: Conquest of Space* (New York: Marisa del Rey Gallery, 1986), pp. 4–7. See also Enrico Crispolti, *Fontana Catalogo Generale* (Milan: Electra, 1986), vol. 2, p. 415.

2. Michael Tapié, *Devenir de Fontana* (Torino: Edizioni d'arte Fratelli Pozzo, 1961).

3. Sidney Tillim, *Arts* (January 1962): 36.

64. Chillida, *Rumor de Limites*

1. For additional information on Chillida see Claude Esteban, *Chillida* (Paris: Maeght Editeur, 1971); *Eduardo Chillida*, exh. cat. (Houston: Houston Museum of Fine Arts, 1966); and Peter Howard Selz, *Chillida* (New York: Harry N. Abrams, 1986).

65. Consagra, *Racconto di Marinaio*

1. For additional information on Consagra see Anna Imponente and Rosella Siligato, *Pietro Consagra* (Rome: Galleria Nazionale d'Arte Moderna, 1989).

2. Pietro Consagra, *Necessita' della scultura* (Rome: Lentini, 1956), n.p.

3. Consagra, *La citta' frontale* (Bari: De Donato, 1969), n.p.

66. Bellows, *Geraldine Lee*

1. For a biography of Bellows, see Charles Hill Morgan, *George Bellows, Painter of America* (New York: Reynal, 1965). For additional information on Bellows see Margaret Christman, *Portraits by George Bellows* (Washington, D.C.: Smithsonian Institution, 1981); Marianne Doezema, *George Bellows and Urban America* (New Haven, Conn.: Yale University Press, 1992); and Michael Quick et al., *The Paintings of George Bellows* (New York: Harry N. Abrams, 1992).

2. Bellows' record books (collection of the family) list sixteen portraits, a family group, and two seascapes as the result of the summer's work. In a letter to Robert Henri, Bellows wrote, "I will have about twenty things when I leave" (21 August 1914, Robert Henri Papers, Beineke Library, Yale University).

3. Bellows' first campaign of painting rural landscape had been during January 1909, on a visit to Zion, New Jersey. During the summer of 1910, while visiting an estate in the Catskills, he had painted a modest series of landscape sketches. In addition, some of his river landscapes on the undeveloped fringes of Manhattan have some quality of raw nature, but it was on Monhegan in 1911 and 1913 that Bellows truly discovered the wild landscape for himself.

4. See Denman Ross, *A Theory of Pure Design: Harmony, Balance, Rhythm* (Boston: Houghton Mifflin, 1907), and Ross, *On Drawing and Painting* (London: Constable, 1912). Bellows' interest in the theories of Ross parallels that of Robert Henri.

5. Bellows to Henri, 21 August 1914, Robert Henri Papers.

6. The entry for *Geraldine Lee, No. 1* in the artist's record book indicates that Bellows set the following palette for this painting: R[ed] ⅔, Y[ellow] ⅓, G[reen], B[lue], P[urple], B[lac]k (Book A, p. 325, collection of the family). The pairs of numbers apparently refer to steps in value. Bellows wrote in his letter of 21 August 1914 to Robert Henri, "I have been using what seems the most useable palette I have ever found. My base is R ⅔ Y ⅓ Blue pure. I find almost any color will fit in with these when occasion demands" (Robert Henri Papers). The paints he used were those prepared by Hardesty Maratta and sold in tubes labelled for the hue. The record book entry for the quite differently colored portrait, *Geraldine Lee, No. 2* (Butler Institute of American Art, Youngstown, Ohio), indicates that Bellows painted it with the following palette: RP, RO ⅔, Y ⅓, BG, BR.

7. According to the record books, the following paintings from 1914–15 were cut down to 22 x 18 inches: *Portrait of Emma in a Night Light* (1914, location unknown); *Girl in Blue Green* (1915, location unknown); and *Lucie* (1915, Collection of Everett D. Reese).

8. In a letter dated February 7, 1917 to Mary Witherspoon, who had seen *Geraldine Lee, No. 1* in an exhibition in Fort Worth, Bellows responded to her questions by writing: "To tell you why I painted Geraldine Lee would necessitate an essay on my philosophy of life and of art. The reasons for painting her were not different than the reasons for painting anything else. She offered me a subject or a 'point of departure' as we say, or a 'motif' or let's just say some ideas for the play of my creative fancy" (collection of Mary Witherspoon, cited in Jane Myers, "'The Most Searching Place in the World': Bellows's Portraiture," in Quick, *The Paintings of George Bellows*, p. 197, photocopy in author's possession).

67. Feininger, *Bridge*

1. Quoted in June L. Ness, ed., *Lyonel Feininger* (New York and Washington: Praeger, 1974), p. 73.

2. Ibid., p. 72.

3. Ibid., pp. 72-73.

4. Paul Westheim, "Lyonel Feininger," *Das Kunstblatt* I (1917), as quoted in Ulrich Luckhardt, *Lyonel Feininger*, trans. Eileen Martin (Munich: Prestel-Verlag, 1989), p. 80.

5. Quoted in Ness, *Lyonel Feininger*, p. 40.

6. Ibid., p. 45.

68. Hartley, *The Iron Cross*

1. For additional information on Hartley see Roxana Barry, "The Age of Blood and Iron: Marsden Hartley in Berlin," *Arts Magazine* 54 (October 1979): 166–71; Marsden Hartley, *On Art*, ed. Gail R. Scott (New York: Horizon, 1982); Barbara Haskell, *Marsden Hartley* (New York: Whitney Museum of American Art, 1980); Gail Levin, "Hidden Symbolism in Marsden Hartley's Military Pictures," *Arts Magazine* 54 (October 1979): 154–58; Townsend Ludington, *Marsden Hartley: The Biography of an American Artist* (Boston: Little, Brown, 1992); Gail R. Scott, *Marsden Hartley* (New York: Abbeville Press, 1988); and William H. Robinson, "Marsden Hartley's 'Military'," *Bulletin of the Cleveland Museum of Art* 76, no. 1 (January 1989): 2–26.

2. Hartley, printed in *Camera Work* 48 (October 1916): 12; reprinted in Hartley, *On Art*, p. 67.

3. Quoted in Levin, "Hidden Symbolism," p. 157.

4. Ibid.

69. Stella, *Man in Elevated*

1. For additional information on Stella see John I. H. Baur, *Joseph Stella* (New York: Praeger, 1971); Ruth L. Bohan, "Joseph Stella's *Man in Elevated (Train)*," in *Dada/Dimensions*, ed. Stephen C. Foster (Ann Arbor: UMI Research Press, 1985), pp. 187–219; Irma Jaffe, *Joseph Stella* (Cambridge: Harvard University Press, 1970); Joann Moser, *Visual Poetry: The Drawings of Joseph Stella* (Washington, D.C. and London: Smithsonian Institution, 1990); and Judith Zilczer, *Joseph Stella: The Hirshhorn Museum and Sculpture Garden Collection* (Washington, D.C.: Smithsonian Institution, 1983).

70. Dove, *Sand and Sea*

1. Arthur Dove Journals and correspondence with Alfred Stieglitz, Archives of American Art, Smithsonian Institution, Washington, D.C. and New York.

2. For additional information on Dove see Ann Lee Morgan, *Arthur Dove: Life and Work, with a Catalogue Raisonné* (Newark: University of Delaware Press, 1984); Sherrye Baker Cohn, "The Dialectical Vision of Arthur Dove: The Impact of Science and Occultism on his Modern American Art" (Ph.D. diss., University of Michigan, 1982); Morgan, "Toward the Definition of Early Modernism in America: A Study of Arthur Dove" (Ph.D. diss., University of Iowa, 1973); and William H. Lane Foundation, *Paintings and Water Colors by Arthur G. Dove* (Worcester: Commonwealth Press, 1961).

3. Arthur Dove Journals, 17 December 1942 and 20 August 1942.

71. Stuart Davis, *Max No. 2*

1. For additional information on Davis see Lowery Stokes Sims, *Stuart Davis: American Painter* (New York: Metropolitan Museum of Art, 1991); Karen Wilkin, *Stuart Davis* (New York: Abbeville Press, 1987); John R. Lane, *Stuart Davis: Art and Art Theory* (New York: Brooklyn Art Museum, 1977); James Johnson Sweeney, *Stuart Davis* (New York: Museum of Modern Art, 1945); and the Stuart Davis Papers, Fogg Art Museum Archives, Harvard University.

72. Albers, *Homage to the Square*

1. For additional information on Albers see Eugen Gomringer, *Josef Albers: His Work as Contribution to Visual Articulation in the Twentieth Century* (New York: G. Wittenborn, 1968); *Josef Albers: Homage to the Square,* exh. cat. (New York: Museum of Modern Art, 1964); and Nicholas Fox Weber, *The Drawings of Josef Albers* (New Haven, Conn.: Yale University Press, 1984).

2. Rudolph Arnheim, *The Power of the Center* (Berkeley, Los Angeles, and London: University of California Press, 1988), p. 146.

73. Calder, *Bayonets Menacing a Flower*

1. For additional information on Calder see Margaret Calder Hayes, *Three Alexander Calders: A Family Memoir* (Middlebury, Vt.: Eriksson, 1977); Jean Lipman, *Calder's Universe* (New York: Viking Press and Whitney Museum of American Art, 1976); Joan Marter, *Alexander Calder* (New York: Cambridge University Press, 1991); and James Johnson Sweeney, *Alexander Calder,* exh. cat. (New York: Museum of Modern Art, 1943), 2nd ed. printed with bibliography in 1951.

2. Quoted in Bernice Rose, *A Salute to Alexander Calder,* exh. cat. (New York: Museum of Modern Art, 1969), p. 14.

74. Calder, *Five Rudders*

For bibliographical information on Calder see notes to entry 73.

75. Guston, *If This Be Not I*

1. On the verso LR of the frame is inscribed, "Frame made for Philip Guston by Carl Sandelin Framemaker 851 Lex. Av."

2. Regarding the context of World War II for the picture, Ross Feld proposes that the figure at the lower left wears the striped garb of a concentration camp survivor (*Philip Guston,* exh. cat. [San Francisco: San Francisco Museum of Modern Art, 1979], p. 17)

3. Dore Ashton suggests that Guston was also influenced by Piero's *Baptism,* specifically that the figure seen from behind on the right is a homage to Piero. She further suggests that the figure at the lower left is a Renaissance fallen angel, and the child with the bandage before its eyes is meant to recall Renaissance allegorical figures of Justice (Ashton, *Philip Guston* [New York: Grove Press, 1960], p. 66).

4. See for example Guston's *Work and Play,* a mural of the Queensbridge Housing Project, New York, 1940.

5. Musa Mayer notes her father's interest in de Chirico and cites a letter in which he describes a similar atmosphere existing in Midwestern towns (Mayer, *Night Studio* [New York: Penguin Books, 1988], pp. 36–37).

6. Ibid., p. 8 (Mayer was born in 1943).

7. For example, *Conspirators* (1932, estate of the artist).

8. Mayer, *Night Studio,* pp. 10–11.

9. Alison de Lima Greene, "The Artist as Performer," *Arts* 63 (November 1988): 55.

10. Ashton first reported that Guston worked on the painting for about a year (Ashton, *Philip Guston,* p. 65). Although she further states that it was the centerpiece of the Midtown exhibition, Greene reports that the painting was not, in fact, listed in the gallery's catalog (Ibid., p. 61 n. 24).

11. Among other events of 1945, beside his first solo show in New York, Guston won the Carnegie Prize that year.

76. Guston, *Fable I*

1. *Fable I* less resembles *Fable II* (1957) than *Painter's City* (1956–57). *Fable II* is illustrated in Robert Storr, *Philip Guston* (New York: Abbeville, 1986), p. 36; *Painter's City* is illustrated in Dore Ashton, *Philip Guston* (New York: Grove Press, 1960), p. 79.

2. Quoted in Ashton, *Philip Guston,* p. 80.

3. Ibid, p. 110.

4. *Philip Guston,* exh. cat. (New York: Solomon R. Guggenheim Museum, 1962), p. 29.

5. In 1965 Guston wrote: "What is called the picture is what remains—an evidence" (quoted in *Philip Guston* [San Francisco: San Francisco Museum of Modern Art, 1979], p. 40).

6. In the later 1950s Guston began to achieve his greatest success, including solo exhibitions at the Sidney Janis Gallery, New York (1956, 1958), representing the United States in the 1959 São Paulo Bienal, and inclusion in major survey exhibitions at the Whitney Museum (1955, 1956, 1957, 1958, 1959), Carnegie Institute (1955, 1958), Museum of Modern Art (1956), and exhibitions abroad, as well as considerable critical attention. (See exhibition history and bibliography in *Philip Guston,* San Francisco, pp. 133–47).

77. Baziotes, *Night Form*

1. Baziotes to Byron Vazakas, 29 March 1935, Collection Bruno Palmer-Poroner, New York. For a discussion of Baziotes and poetry see Mona Hadler, "William Baziotes: A Contemporary Poet-Painter," *Arts Magazine* LI, no. 10 (June 1977): 102–10.

2. Baziotes, interview by Donald Paneth, 1952, "William Baziotes, A Literary Portrait," p. 9, Baziotes File, Archives of American Art, Smithsonian Institution, Washington, D.C..

3. Baziotes to Alfred H. Barr, Jr., 26 April 1949, Baziotes File, Archives of The Museum of Modern Art, New York. The letter is printed and discussed in Mona Hadler, "William Baziotes: Four Sources of Inspiration," in *William Baziotes: A Retrospective Exhibition,* exh. cat. (Newport Beach, Calif.: Newport Harbor Art Museum, 1978), pp. 84–89. Barbara Cavaliere writes about *Night Form* in this catalogue and relates it to *Dwarf* (pp. 45–46).

4. Paul Fussell, *The Great War and Modern Memory* (New York: Oxford University Press, 1975), p. 115. Stephen Polcari in his *Abstract Expressionism and the Modern Experience* (New York: Cambridge University Press, 1991) has written insightfully about the impact of World War II on Abstract Expressionism. See his chapter on Baziotes, pp. 213–32.

78. Gorky, *Golden Brown*

1. For further discussion on the art and biography of *Arshile Gorky* see Ethel K. Schwabacher, *Arshile Gorky* (New York: MacMillan Co., 1957); Jim M. Jordan, *The Paintings of Arshile Gorky* (New York: New York University Press, 1982); Harry Rand, *Arshile Gorky: The Implications of Symbols* (Berkeley: University of California Press, 1991).

2. A similar palette, color scheme, partially finished surface, and uncharacteristically uneven resolution of forms can be found in *Dialogue of the Edge* (Michener Collection, University of Texas, Austin, n.d.)—a work which is almost certainly unfinished.

3. Jordan, *The Paintings of Arshile Gorky,* p. 415. *Golden Brown* is the following entry in this catalog, #267, which he also dates to 1943–44.

4. Even with such autographic evidence we are often at a loss to assign a Gorky work to a particular period, as he revised older works and post-dated pictures to skew the appearance of his artistic evolution.

5. One version of *Waterfall* (1942–43, The Tate Gallery) is resplendently colored in rich and diverse hues which, upon inspection, prove to be mainly accurate naturalistic transcriptions. Another version of *Waterfall* (1943, The Hirshhorn Museum and Sculpture Garden) is a pale linear revision of the Tate painting. They seemed to have been worked in dialogue, so that placing them in sequence is difficult. The richest and most colorful of all these works, *Water of the Flowery Mill* (1944, The Metropolitan Museum of Art), drips thinned paint down the canvas.

6. These works were begun in the early 1940s; the central period of their composition seems to be about 1943, the year with which *Golden Brown* has been dated. Gorky would normally have titled the work with something descriptive or suggestive of his narrative intentions. His titles usually refer to identifiable specifics of a work, or some ironic play on the component imagery. He would not have described the appearance of a work.

7. For a complete description of Gorky's subjects and an analysis of how these images reside in his art, see Rand, *Arshile Gorky.*

8. For example, in the lower right, anticipating similar figures by de Kooning, a reedy yellow figure cavorts on what would be the near bank. But this personage is hardly the legible figure so typical of Gorky's mature work; it may be a partially evolved form, or a cipher for something intended for this passage but not executed. Unlike the putative imagery frequently insinuated into his work by well-meaning admirers, once Gorky's actual figuration becomes evident it is indisputable.

9. Reciting a shape more than once within a painting is akin to "rhyme" in poetry in which the same sound is woven through a work, repeating, and sometimes even utilizing exact repetition of a word or phrase.

10. His first wife, Marny George, had been a model and ice-show skater; accordingly, there may be some elision of the poses of a dancer and an ice skater doing a "layback."

79. Pollock, *Sleeping Effort*

1. For a more complete exposition of my views on Pollock's career, see my "Improvisations: Notes on Pollock and Jazz," *Arts Magazine* 53, no. 7 (March 1979): 96–99, and "The Morality of Absolute Art: Individualism as Ideal in the Painting of Jackson Pollock and Morris Louis," *Arts Magazine* 61, no. 9 (May 1987): 54–60. Both essays are to be reprinted in the forthcoming *Absolute Art.* For additional information on Pollock see B. H. Friedman, *Jackson Pollock: Energy Made Visible* (New York: Düsseldorf and London: McGraw-Hill, 1972); Steven Naifeh, *Jackson Pollock: An American Saga* (London: Pimlico, 1992); Francis Valentine O'Connor and Eugene Victor Thaw, *Jackson Pollock: A Catalogue Raisonné of Paintings, Drawings, and Other Works,* 4 vols. (New Haven, Conn. and London: Yale University Press, 1978); and Deborah Solomon, *Jackson Pollock: A Biography* (New York: Simon and Schuster, 1980).

80. de Kooning, *Saturday Night*

1. The primary resources on de Kooning's art and life are Paul Cummings, *Willem de Kooning: Drawings, Paintings, Sculpture* (New York, Berlin, and Munich: Prestel-Verlag and Whitney Museum of American Art, 1983), and Diane Waldman, *Willem de Kooning* (New York: Abrams, 1987).

2. De Kooning started *Woman I* in 1950 and completed the work in 1952. It was purchased by the Museum of Modern Art, New York, in 1953. Compared to his abstractions these voluptuously figurative works were sensual contemporary portrayals.

3. In 1956 de Kooning had an exhibition at Sidney Janis on urban and suburban landscapes, and was invited to show at the 1956 Venice Biennale whose theme was "American Artists Paint the City."

4. In 1953 he moved to The Springs, and the change seemed to have a demonstrable effect: he soon began to paint abstract landscapes (for example, *Palisade,* 1957) which he continued through 1963. He first showed these works at an exhibition at the Sidney Janis Gallery in May 1959.

5. A strongly contrary view of de Kooning is contributed, with massive documentation, by Kirsten Hoving Powell's "Resurrecting Content in de Kooning's *Easter Monday,*" *Smithsonian Studies in American Art* 4 (Summer/Fall 1990): 87–101. Unfortunately, the conclusion reached by this author is that de Kooning's supposed manipulations of ink transferred from newspaper clipping to his canvasses allowed him "to parody the seriousness of the Abstract Expressionists search for the spiritual through the personal gesture, while placing him in the vanguard of such 'neo-Dada' artists as Jasper Johns and Robert Rauschenburg" (p.99). I find this position untenable.

6. *Saturday Night's* luminous rich colors are generally high-values, with some dark blue and black that contribute structural elements. *Saturday Night's* dark blue is applied thickly to the painting's commercially primed canvas. This dark paint was wiped, and has cracked in small places where, thinly applied, it shows cleavage. Small bubbles in *Saturday Night's* paint and the overall richness of the medium suggest that by this time de Kooning was experimenting with his "Mayonnaise" paint emulsion; he could never get his paint rich enough, nor did he like commercial mixtures that dried too quickly and did not allow time for successive revision.

81. Francis, *Arcueil*

1. For additional information on Francis see *Sam Francis: The Fifties* (Washington, D.C.: The Phillips Collection, 1980), and Peter Selz, *Sam Francis* (New York: H. N. Abrams, 1975).

2. Sam Francis, conversation with the author.

3. Francis, poem, privately printed.

82. Francis, *Floating Blue*

1. Sam Francis, quoted in Jan Butterfield, "The Other Side of Wonder," in *Sam Francis* (Boston: Institute of Contemporary Art, 1980), n.p.

2. Francis, conversation with the author.

83. Rauschenberg, *Choke*

1. For additional information on Rauschenberg see Lawrence Alloway, *Robert Rauschenberg* (Washington, D.C.: National Collection of Fine Arts, 1976); Roni Feinstein, *Robert Rauschenberg: The Silkscreen Paintings, 1962–1964* (New York: Whitney Museum of American Art, 1990); and Mary Lynn Kotz, *Rauschenberg: Art and Life* (New York: Harry N. Abrams, 1990).

2. Sidra Stich, *Made in the U.S.A.: An Americanization in Modern Art, the 50s and 60s,* exh. cat. (Berkeley: University of California Art Museum, 1987), pp. 52–54.

84. Gene Davis, *Equinox*

1. Gene Davis, quoted in Steven W. Naifeh, *Gene Davis* (New York: Arts Publisher, 1982), pp. 37, 27. For additional information on Davis see Jacquelyn Serwer, *Gene Davis: A Memorial Exhibition* (Washington, D.C.: Smithsonian Institution, 1987), and Donald Wall, ed., *Gene Davis* (New York: Praeger Publishers, 1975).

2. Naifeh, *Gene Davis,* p. 55.

3. Leslie Judd Ahlander, "An Artist Speaks: Gene Davis," *Washington Post,* August 26, 1962, sec. G, p. 7.

4. Mary Swift, "An Interview with Gene Davis," *Washington Review* 4, no. 4 (December 1978–January 1979): 7.

5. Marcia Tucker, *The Structure of Color* (New York: Whitney Museum of American Art, 1971), p. 16.

85. Wesselmann, *Bedroom Painting*

1. For additional information on Wesselmann see *An Exhibition of New Work by Tom Wesselmann: February 6–March 2, 1968* (New York: Sidney Janis Gallery, 1968), and Tom Wesselmann, *Tom Wesselmann* (New York: Abbeville Press, 1980).

Contributing Authors

Dennis Adrian
William C. Agee
Patricia Berman
Jean Sutherland Boggs
Ruth L. Bohan
Manuel J. Borja-Villel
Richard A. Born
Elizabeth C. Childs
Pierre Encrevé
Roni Feinstein
Jack Flam
Valerie J. Fletcher
John Golding
Mona Hadler
Mary Hamel-Schwulst
Charles W. Haxthausen
Anna Imponente
Andrew Kagan
Joseph D. Ketner
Joni L. Kinsey
Aube Lardera
Robert S. Lubar
Alisa Luxenberg
Jan van der Marck
Joan M. Marter
Evan M. Maurer
Thomas M. Messer
Victor H. Miesel
Priscilla E. Muller
Robert M. Murdock
Alexandra R. Murphy
Steven W. Naifeh
Steven A. Nash
Susan Nessen
Gerald Nordland
Aimée Brown Price
Michael A. Quick
Harry Rand
Eliza Rathbone
Mark Rosenthal
Joyce K. Schiller
Werner Schmalenbach
Peter Selz
Aaron M. Shatzman
Gregory White Smith
J. Gray Sweeney
Nancy J. Troy
Nicholas Fox Weber
Gabriel P. Weisberg
Tom Wesselmann
Alan G. Wilkinson
Fronia E. Wissman
Judith Zilczer

Index of Artworks

by page number

Donors

Mrs. Harold Ackert
Gerald B. Allen
Alumni of School of Fine Arts
The American Academy and Institute of Arts & Letters
Anonymous Donors
Philip M. Arnold
Mr. and Dr. Adam Aronson
Mrs. R. Kirk Askew
Joseph R. Atkin
Mr. and Mrs. Howard Baer
Marvin Bank
Walter Barker
Wesley J. Barta
Mrs. William S. Bedal
Bonni Benrubi and Dennis Powers
Betty Cornell Benton
Betty Parsons
Mr. and Mrs. Jessie Bishop
William K. Bixby
Mr. and Mrs. Harold G. Blatt
Dr. Harold Blumenfeld
Mr. and Mrs. Edward Boccia
Gerald D. Bolas
Mr. and Mrs. Stewart Borchard
Mrs. Ingram F. Boyd
Philip Bragar
Mr. and Mrs. Robert S. Brookings
Mrs. Erwin Bry
Bryan, Cave, McPheeters, and McRoberts
Stephen Bunyard and Cheryl Griffin
Paul Burlin
Burns Society of St. Louis
August A. Busch I
Letterio Calapai
Estate of Fern Madole Calhoun
Mary and Clarkson Carpenter III
Anne V. Champ
Mr. and Mrs. Norman B. Champ, Jr.
Joseph Gilbert Chapman
Mrs. S. Chauvenet
Adelaide Cherbonnier
Joseph H. Clarke
Dr. Malvern B. Clopton
Mr. and Mrs. Sidney S. Cohen
Mr. and Mrs. Thomas Comegys
Contingency Fund for Asian Art
Robert Creeley
Wayman Crow, Sr.
Mr. and Mrs. Nathan Cummings
Thomas S. Currier
Mr. and Mrs. Irvin Dagen
J. Lionberger Davis
John T. Davis
John T. Davis, Jr.
Ruth Grand Decker
Doris Dix
Bernard Drewes
Harald Drewes
Werner Drewes
Wolfram Drewes
Leo Drey
Richard Duhme
The Heirs of Mrs. Frederick Eiseman
Mr. and Mrs. William N. Eisendrath
H. Louis Eisenstein
Reverend Dr. William Greenleaf Eliot
Mrs. Hugo Emmerich
Lady Kathleen Epstein
Famous-Barr Company
Leicester Faust and Audrey Faust Wallace
Ron and Frayda Feldman
Mrs. Hugh Ferriss
William Fett
Robert Fisher
Milton Fischmann
Eleanor M. and C. Harry Foster
Mrs. Harry L. Franc
Mr. and Mrs. Robert L. Freedman
Mrs. R.A. Frevert
Galerie Chalette
Jack Garden
Dr. Mark S. Gold
Mrs. Max A. Goldstein
Mr. and Mrs. Herbert Gralnick
Estate of Evalyne S. Grand
Paul R. Grand
Mr. and Mrs. Ronald Greenberg
Ronald, Lawrence, and Robert Greenberg
Mr. and Mrs. Edward Greensfelder
Mr. and Mrs. Gerald Greenwald
Griesedieck Family
Mr. and Mrs. Leslie Grodsky
Mr. and Mrs. Joseph H. Groud
Frederic R. Gruger, Jr.
Musa Guston
Alvin Haimes
Michael Hall
Professor and Mrs. Thomas Hall
Mr. and Mrs. Gilbert Harris
Mr. and Mrs. Joseph Helman
Edward R. Hoyt
Gwen Mills Hudson
Rabbi and Mrs. Ferdinand M. Isserman
Halsey C. Ives
Donald M. Jacobsen
Dr. and Mrs. Sidney S. Jick
Carol Jones
Robert Jordan
Dr. and Mrs. Harold Joseph
Dr. and Mrs. Lawrence Kahn
Kappa Alpha Theta
Patricia John Keightley
Martha V. W. Keller
Gyorgy Kepes
David Keppel
Stephen Kliternick
William R. Kohn
Robert Kolbrener
Samuel Kootz Gallery
Aimee Lamb
Ronald Allen Leax
Mrs. John S. Lehmann
George E. Leighton
Mr. and Mrs. W. J. Lemp
John Frank Lesser
Mr. and Mrs. Sam J. Levin
Mr. and Mrs. Alan Lewin
Monte Lopata

Robert Maki

Mrs. William McChesney Martin, Jr.

Marquis de Mattei Estate

Dr. and Mrs. Edward Massie

Mr. and Mrs. Morton D. May

Morton J. May

James McGarrell

Eliza McMillan

William N. McMillan

Mr. and Mrs. Don Meyer

Signora La Contessa Beatrice Monte della Corte

Thomas Corsan Morton

Mortarboard Society

Mr. and Mrs. Morris Moscowitz

Shiko Munakata

Museum of Finnish Architecture

Music Hall and Exposition Association

Charles Nagel, Sr.

Helen and Jack Nash

Alvin S. Novack

Daniel C. Nugent

Frederic Olsen

Robert H. Orchard

Reese and Marilyn Arnold Palley

Charles Parsons

Joseph Pennell

Raymond and Debra Petke

J. Harold Pettus

Nathaniel Phillips

Phyllis Plattner

Edythe Polster

Dr. and Mrs. Arthur L. Prensky

Mr. and Mrs. Joseph Pulitzer, Jr.

William F. Quinn

Dr. and Mrs. Bruce Redler

Melissa Henyan Redler

Mr. and Mrs. Charles Reger

Mr. and Mrs. Marcus Rice

Dr. and Mrs. Thomas Roberts

Jean Reed Roberts

Mr. J.D. Robinson

Mr. and Mrs. Richard S. Rosenthal

Judith Grand Rubenstein

Michael Rubin

Mr. and Mrs. Bernard Ruderman

The Saint Louis Printmarket Fund

Heirs of Charles F. von Saltza

Elaine and Julian Samuels

Mr. and Mrs. Donald Samuels

Philip Samuels

Richard J. Schaap

Barry Schactman

Schaeffer Gallery

Steven Schapiro

Aurelia Schlapp

Carl Schurz Memorial Foundation

Mrs. J.L. Schwab

Dr. Alfred S. Schwartz

Arnold Shanklin

Mr. and Mrs. Ethan A. Shepley

Mr. and Mrs. John Shoenberg

Mr. and Mrs. Robert Shoenberg

Mr. and Mrs. Sydney M. Shoenberg, Jr.

Mr. and Mrs. John Simon

Jerome Singer

Mr. and Mrs. James W. Singer

Odyssia A. Skouras

Mr. and Mrs. Walter Skrainka

Dr. Abigail Eliot Smith

Wallace H. Smith

Family of William Eliot Smith

Robert Bruce Snow

Harvey R. Soule

David and Jane Soyer

Dr. Eugene Spector

Dr. Isaias Spilberg

St. Louis University

Steinberg Art Gallery Associates

Mrs. Mark C. Steinberg

Mrs. Ernest W. Stix

Mrs. Henry S. Stix

Mr. and Mrs. Stan Strembicki

Dr. Benjamin Strong

Students of Belle Cramer

Mr. W. H. Stuyvesant

Robert Sutner

Stanley Tasker

Wanda and Tom Taylor

Steven and Marilyn Teitelbaum

Berenice and Harry Tenenbaum

Mr. and Mrs. Joseph L. Tucker

Nicholas Vahlkamp

Eric Verhalle

Susan S. Vesper

Paul Waldman

Mrs. George W. Wales

Mrs. Mahlon B. Wallace, Jr.

Washington University Alumni Association

Washington University Archaeological Society and Friends

Washington University Art and Architecture Library

Washington University Board of Directors

Washington University Department of Art and Archaeology

Washington University School of Fine Arts

Washington University School of Fine Arts Collaborative Print Shop

Washington University, Special Collections, Olin Library

Mrs. Horton Watkins

Mr. and Mrs. Mark S. Weil

Mr. and Mrs. Richard K. Weil

Charles J. Weinraub

Ann and Shelley B. Weinstein

Benjamin Weiss

Clayton and Ann Wilhite

Eugene F. Williams, Jr.

Armond G. Winfield

Constance Wittcoff

J. Max Wulfing

Charles H. Yalem

James E. Yeatman

Edward H. Young

Howard Youngstein

Dr. William van Zandt

Anders Leonard Zorn

A Gallery of Modern Art
was set in a modern version
of Garamond and printed
in four-color process
with scanned halftones
by Amilcare Pizzi, S.p.A.,
of Milan, Italy.

It was designed
by Nathan Garland
of New Haven.